The Rise of Fiscal States

From the Netherlands to the Ottoman Empire, to Japan and India, this groundbreaking volume confronts the complex and diverse problem of the formation of fiscal states in Eurasia between 1500 and 1914. This series of country case studies from leading economic historians reveals that distinctive features of the fiscal state appeared across the region at different moments in time as a result of multiple independent but often interacting stimuli such as internal competition over resources, European expansion, international trade, globalization and war. The essays offer a comparative framework for re-examining the causes of economic development across this period and show, for instance, the central role that the more effective fiscal systems of Europe during the seventeenth and eighteenth centuries played in the divergence of East and West as well as the very different paths to modernization taken across the world.

BARTOLOMÉ YUN-CASALILLA is Professor of Early Modern History at the Universidad Pablo de Olavide in Seville, Spain, and Head of the Department of History and Civilisation at the European University Institute in Florence, Italy.

PATRICK K. O'BRIEN is Professor of Global Economic History at the London School of Economics and Political Sciences, and Convenor of a European Research Council programme on 'Regimes for the Production and Diffusion of Useful and Reliable Knowledge in the East and the West' (URKEW).

FRANCISCO COMÍN COMÍN is Professor of Economic History at the Universidad de Alcalá.

The Rise of Fiscal States: A Global History 1500–1914

Edited by

Bartolomé Yun-Casalilla

Patrick K. O'Brien

with

Franciso Comín Comín

CAMBRIDGE
UNIVERSITY PRESS

CAMBRIDGE UNIVERSITY PRESS
Cambridge, New York, Melbourne, Madrid, Cape Town,
Singapore, São Paulo, Delhi, Mexico City

Cambridge University Press
The Edinburgh Building, Cambridge CB2 8RU, UK

Published in the United States of America by Cambridge University Press,
New York

www.cambridge.org
Information on this title: www.cambridge.org/9781107013513

First published 2012

Printed in the United Kingdom at the University Press, Cambridge

A catalogue record for this publication is available from the British Library

Library of Congress Cataloguing in Publication data
The rise of fiscal states : a global history, 1500–1914 / edited by
Bartolomé Yun-Casalilla, Patrick O'Brien.
p.   cm.
Includes index.
ISBN 978-1-107-01351-3 (hardback)
1. Fiscal policy–History.   I. Yun Casalilla, Bartolomé.
II. O'Brien, Patrick Karl.
HJ192.5.R567 2012
332′.0420903–dc23
2011049969

ISBN 978-1-107-01351-3 Hardback

For Larry Epstein
In memoriam

Contents

Figures

Tables

xiv   List of tables

Contributors

REVD PROFESSOR RICHARD BONNEY is Professorial Research Fellow (South Asia Security) at RUSI, Whitehall, London. He was Professor of Modern History at the University of Leicester from 1984 to 2006 and is now Emeritus Professor there. He is the author of *Jihad: From Qur'an to Bin Laden* (2004) and *False Prophets: The 'Clash of Civilizations' and the Global War on Terror* (2008). He has eleven articles, including just war and holy war, forthcoming in the *Encyclopedia of War* (2011). His latest book, co-edited with Tridivesh Singh Maini and Tahir Malik, is an important collection of interviews entitled *Warriors after War: Indian and Pakistani Retired Military Leaders Reflect on Relations Between the Two Countries, Past, Present and Future* (2011).

FRANCISCO COMÍN COMÍN is Professor of Economic History at the Universidad de Alcalá (Madrid, Spain) and received the National History Award in 1990. His recent publications include the books *Tabacalera y el Estanco del Tabaco, 150 años de historia de los ferrocarriles en España, La Empresa Pública en Europa, Historia de la Hacienda pública, Privatisation in the European Union: Public Enterprises and Integration, Transforming Public Enterprise in Europe and North America, Historia de la cooperación entre las Cajas de Ahorros* and *Economía y economistas españoles en la guerra civil*.

MARTIN DAUNTON is Professor of Economic History at the University of Cambridge and Master of Trinity Hall. He was formerly the President of the Royal Historical Society. He has published two books on the politics of British taxation since 1799, and two volumes on the economic and social history of Britain between 1700 and 1950. He is currently writing a book on the economic governance of the world since the Second World War.

KENT G. DENG, an economic historian of China, is Reader in Economic History at the London School of Economics. He is also

Fellow of the Royal Historical Society. His research covers both premier and modern times over the very long run. He has published five monographs and a number of articles, ranging from knowledge formation, technological diffusion, maritime development, demography, commerce, the peasantry and the state.

WANTJE FRITSCHY is senior lecturer in the History Department of VU University Amsterdam. Since 2004 she has had a personal professorship in the history of early modern public finance. In collaboration with the Institute of Dutch History in the Hague and six colleagues, she created an electronically accessible database on provincial public finance in the Dutch Republic, accompanied by seven printed volumes (www.inghist.nl/Onderzoek/Projecten/GewestelijkeFinancien/en). She has published numerous articles on the subject and currently (2010/11) enjoys a fellowship in the Netherlands Institute of Advanced Studies to write a book on the public finance of the Dutch Republic in a comparative perspective.

PETER GATRELL teaches at the University of Manchester where he is Professor of Economic History and a member of the Humanitarian and Conflict Research Institute. He has written extensively on Russian economic history and the history of war and population displacement in the twentieth century. His books include *A Whole Empire Walking: Refugees in Russia during World War 1* (1999), *Warlands: Population Resettlement and State Reconstruction in the Soviet–East European Borderlands, 1945–1950* (2009), and most recently, *Free World? The Campaign to Save the World's Refugees, 1956–1963* (2011). He is currently completing a book entitled *The Making of the Modern Refugee*.

MARJOLEIN 'T HART is Associate Professor in Economic and Social History at the University of Amsterdam. She has published widely on the history of early modern Netherlands, in particular on the Dutch Revolt and financial institutions. Her major publications include *The Making of a Bourgeois State. War, Politics and Finance during the Dutch Revolt* (1993) and *A Financial History of the Netherlands* (1997, with Jan Luiten van Zanden and Joost Jonker), and recently *Globalization, Environmental Change, and Social History* (2010, with Peter Boomgaard).

EDWIN HORLINGS is a senior researcher in the Science System Assessment Department of the Rathenau Institute, an institute of the Royal Netherlands Academy of Arts and Sciences. He has a PhD in economic history and has more than twenty years' experience in quantitative analysis. His current work focuses on the organizational and behavioural dynamics of science, aimed specifically at contributing to science policy.

PAUL JANSSENS is visiting professor at Ghent University. In his capacity as Research Director of the Centre for Fiscal History (University of Brussels), he published, amongst other titles, *Drie eeuwen Belgische belastingen* (1990) and *Fiscaal recht geboekstaafd* (1995). He is also President of the Council of the Belgian Nobility and published various contributions in peer-reviewed journals and books on the Belgian nobility. His monograph *L'évolution de la noblesse belge depuis la fin du moyen âge* (1998) was honoured with the triennial History Award of the Dexia Bank. Recently, he supervised and (co-)edited the two-volume *La Belgique espagnole et la principauté de Liège, 1585–1715* (2006) as well as *Vivre noblement. The Changing Lifestyle of the Belgian Nobility, 15th–21st Centuries* (2011).

MARIA EUGÉNIA MATA is Associate Professor of Economic History at the Universidade Nova de Lisboa and ex-President of the Portuguese Economic History Association. Her recent publications include 'Environmental Challenge in the Canning Industry (The Portuguese Case-study of the Early Twentieth Century)' (2010), 'Large Portuguese Firms from the Marshall Plan to EFTA: Early Stirrings of Managerial Capitalism?' (2010), 'As Small Events May Have Large Long-run Effects on Business Perspectives (Portugal, 1940s)' (2010) and 'Managerial Strategies in Canning Industries: The Portuguese Case-study of the Early Twentieth Century' (2009).

MASAKI NAKABAYASHI is Associate Professor at the Institute of Social Science, the University of Tokyo. He specializes in Japanese economic history, focusing on economic institutions and organizations. His publications include 'Flexibility and Diversity: The Putting-out System in the Silk Fabric Industry of Kiryu, Japan' (2007) and 'The Rise of a Factory Industry: Silk Reeling in Suwa District' (2006).

MICHAEL NORTH is Professor and Chair of Modern History at the University of Greifswald. He specializes in the economic, social and cultural history of modern Germany within a wider European context and leads a multi-country research group that focuses on the history and culture of the Baltic borderlands. Among other works, he has authored *Deutsche Wirtschaftsgeschichte*, 2nd edn (2005), 'Material Delight and the Joy of Living' (2008) and *The Expansion of Europe* (2011).

PATRICK K. O'BRIEN, Fellow of the British Academy, is Professor of Global Economic History at the London School of Economics, where he convenes a large-scale European Research Council funded project on the Formation, Development and Diffusion of Useful and Reliable Knowledge in the West and the East from the Accession of the Ming to the First Industrial Revolution. He has published several books and over one hundred articles in the broad field of British, European and global economic history.

ŞEVKET PAMUK is professor at the London School of Economics and Political Science. He is the author of *The Ottoman Empire and European Capitalism, 1820–1913* and *A Monetary History of the Ottoman Empire*, both published by Cambridge University Press. He has also authored many articles in the *Journal of Economic History* and other economic history journals. In recent years, he has been working on institutions in the Ottoman Empire and more generally the Middle East from a political economy perspective.

LUCIANO PEZZOLO is Associate Professor of Early Modern History in the Department of Humanities at the University Ca' Foscari of Venice. He has published extensively on the economic history of Venice and the military and financial history of late medieval and early modern Italy.

RENATE PIEPER is Professor of Economic History at the University of Graz in Austria and a member of the European Academy. She has published extensively on Spanish and Austrian state finances and, more recently, the transmission of information and goods from the Americas to Europe. In 2005 she co-edited a volume of essays in honour of Horst Pietschmann, *Latin America and the Atlantic World (1500–1850)*.

FAUSTO PIOLA CASELLI is Professor of Economic History at the LUMSA University of Rome. He has researched the papal financial network in the late Middle Ages, with particular attention to state balance sheets and to the development of public accounting. He has also dealt with public finances in the early modern period, focusing on the creation of national public debts and the development of tax systems in a comparative perspective, and organizing sessions at several IEHA congresses on these topics. He edited *Government Debts and Financial Markets in Europe* (2008) and co-edited *Guilds, Markets and Work Regulations in Italy, 16th–19th Centuries* (1998).

JOHN F. RICHARDS, Professor of History at Duke University, specialized in the Mughal empire, early modern world trade and the British colonial state. His books include *The Unending Frontier. An Environmental History of the Early Modern World* (2003), *Kingship and Authority in South Asia* (1998) and *The Mughal Empire* (1993). He died in Durham, North Carolina in 2007.

Director of the Asia Institute and Professor of History at UCLA, R. BIN WONG has written or co-authored more than sixty articles published in Chinese, English, French, German and Japanese. His research has examined Chinese patterns of political, economic and social change, especially since the eighteenth century, both within Asian regional contexts and compared with European patterns. Among his books, *China Transformed: Historical Change and the Limits of European Experience* also appears in Chinese. His latest book, co-authored with Jean-Laurent Rosenthal, *Before and Beyond Divergence: The Politics of Economic Change in China and Europe*, will also appear in Chinese and French.

BARTOLOMÉ YUN-CASALILLA is Head of the Department of History and Civilization at the European University Institute in Florence and Professor of Early Modern History at the Universidad Pablo de Olavide (UPO) in Seville, Spain. He has dedicated various monographs to the history of consumption as well as social networks and the history of European aristocracies. He is a practitioner and theorist of transnational, global and comparative history, as well as the history of the Spanish Empire, as reflected in *Marte contra Minerva. El precio del imperio español, c. 1492–1600*. He is the founder and co-director of the graduate programme 'Historia de Europa, El Mundo Mediterráneo y su Difusión Atlántica, 1492–2000' at the UPO, where he also directs a research project on the circulation, reception and appropriation of new goods in the Atlantic World.

Acknowledgements

This volume is the outcome of a very long story and long stories are only possible with the help and perseverance of many people and institutions. We would like to thank Francisco Comín Comín (University of Alcalá de Henares) and Fausto Piola Caselli (University of Cassino), who organized together with the two editors a section in the thirteenth International Economic History Congress (Buenos Aires, 2002) at which most of these essays were presented. Paco Comín was also the organizer of a previous and preparatory workshop in Madrid. We would like to thank him as well as the *Instituto de Estudios Fiscales* of Madrid, which financed that seminal meeting.

We also would like to show our gratitude for the endurance, encouragement and work of Michael Watson, crucial as always at Cambridge University Press. The authors of the different essays, tolerantly accepting our comments and requests over several years, have also earned our gratitude. We hope we are able to compensate them with the final product. This work has been possible thanks to the financial support of the Leverhulme Foundation in London and the European University Institute in Florence. At the University Pablo de Olavide (UPO) in Seville we have drawn upon the resources of the research group PO9-HUM 5330, financed by the *Junta de Andalucía* with support from FEDER. Three people have been essential in the administrative work as well as in the process of mailing, translating, correcting and editing the chapters. At the London School of Economics we counted on the help of Miatta Fahbulled. Dr Niall Whelehan revised the first version of all chapters at the EUI, and Dr Bethany Aram undertook their revision and correction at the UPO. Her contribution to the editing process was really decisive. While two anonymous referees helped increase the quality and consistency of the volume, the editors are especially indebted to one of them, who ingeniously proposed a central idea for the title.

At an early stage, Larry Epstein took care of this project at the LSE and discussed some central ideas of the volume with Patrick O'Brien. Larry's passing sadly curtailed a contribution that we all considered central to this volume. To him the book is dedicated.

B. Yun-Casalilla and P. K. O'Brien

Florence and Oxford, 26 December 2010

1   Introduction: the rise of the fiscal state in Eurasia from a global, comparative and transnational perspective

Bartolomé Yun-Casalilla

Introduction

This volume confronts the problem of the formation of fiscal states in Eurasia. Its chapters deal with a variety of phases in the formation of fiscal units deploying different approaches and methodologies. A variety of chronologies and a plurality of political boundaries qualifies notions of European exceptionalism and unity.[1] Europe appears as a diversified space where some polities look more similar to Asian cases than they do to their neighbours. Together, the essays collected here serve to degrade simplified modernization theories that contend that societies pass through the same stages to reach similar outcomes.

Although societies responded to the same stimuli in concrete but often comparable ways, this volume essentially supports the thesis that the formation of fiscal regimes can only be understood in terms of a heterogeneous historicity, varying in space and time. Eurasian history provides us with a set of case studies that undermines any simplistic views of Western primacy, demolishes the overly teleological Schumpeterian perspective on the formation of fiscal states and displays distinctions between fiscal regimes and 'fiscal states'. The latter term is reserved to describe nations and democratic states as they emerged over the nineteenth century.

I wish to thank Patrick O'Brien for his help, comments and encouragement when writing this chapter. I am responsible, however, for all the remaining shortcomings.

[1] Some chapters take as a reference the current nation-state framework rather than more heterogeneous political entities, for example Austria and not the Habsburg Empire. Others, however, aim to analyse the set of polities that preceded the nation-state: i.e. the group of Italian republics and kingdoms (and Papal States) prior to Italian unification. Some authors opt for a mix and sequential approach: Castile and then Spain, or even the different and changing territories that we today call China over a period of more than two thousand years. In many cases, such as France, Portugal, Belgium, the Netherlands and Japan, political stability over the centuries makes current borders a plausible way to define the geopolitical analytical framework. In other cases, authors have decided to look at imperial units and their processes of expansion, change and decline: the Ottoman Empire, the Mughal and East India Company and Russia.

Schumpeter's seminal essay constituted an attempt to understand
the problems of Austria and its post-First World War crisis in terms
of its fiscal history. For Schumpeter, the crucial step in the formation
of fiscal states consisted in the shift from a system based on resources
derived from the king's domain (a *domain state*) to another system where
the kingdom became involved in providing the prince with funds (*tax
state*).[2] Taxes became the backbone of the 'modern state' and something
impersonal, 'a machine manner [sic] only by serving, not by dominat-
ing spirits'. For the Austrian economist, who assumed that the (fiscal)
state works for the common good by creating the conditions for economic growth, the fiscal state is a product of Western history linked to
the rise of the nation-state and democracy, and distinct from the private
and public spheres.[3]

Almost fifty years after Schumpeter published these ideas, D. North
opened a new debate on the subject. For North the key to economic
growth was not fiscality, but rather the formation of a state that defended
property rights, that led to economic change. Yet this state obviously
attained a monopoly over violence as well as the capacity to obtain private resources in order to use them to defend the social order and well-
defined individual property rights, with the consequent reduction of
transaction costs. Thus, North's fiscal state was one that exchanged
services of protection and order for fiscal resources as efficiently as possible to facilitate economic growth. According to North, such conditions appeared precociously in late-seventeenth-century England.[4]

[2] This shift flowed from the exhaustion of the royal domain and the increasing needs of
the state. Thus the fiscal state implied the rise of a public sphere that differed fundamentally from the private sphere of the prince and that already anticipated the rise of
democratic fiscal states. Several stages can be distinguished in the process identified
by Schumpeter. First, the king had to tax the wealth and incomes of those who controlled the kingdom's resources. Second, taxes were assessed and collected by kings
who came to represent states: 'l'état c'est moi!'. This implied the dissolution of feudal communities and the emergence of individuals as key nodes in the relationship
between state and society. The final step, democracy, placed control of fiscal systems
with the people. Schumpeter's (and Goldscheid's) fiscal sociology represented the fiscal system as a reflection of the nature of a society, of its political structure as well
as its spirit, and the 'fiscal history of a people is above all an essential part of its general history'. J. A. Schumpeter, 'The crisis of the tax state', in R. Swedberg (ed.), *J.
Schumpeter, the economics and sociology of capitalism* (Princeton University Press, 1991),
pp. 99–140.
[3] Ibid., p. 111. The term 'fiscal state' is used by authors in this volume in a general
way not always associated with the ideas of Schumpeter. Instead of relying upon
Schumpeter, I will try to maintain a distinction between fiscal regimes and fiscal systems not necessarily linked to the nation-state and tax states. See R. A. Musgrave,
'Schumpeter crisis of the tax state: an essay in fiscal sociology', *Journal of Evolutionary
Economics* 2 (1992), 89–113.
[4] See mainly, D. North, *Structure and change in economic history* (New York: Norton,
1981).

This introductory chapter attempts to offer an overview of the inter-actions between different fiscal regimes, and the global, comparative and transnational perspectives essential for understanding processes of divergence and convergence as a background to the ways in which fiscal states evolved during the nineteenth and twentieth centuries.[5] It will also propose a cross-reading of the different chapters, aiming to place them within the context of Schumpeter's and North's theories on the rise of fiscal states and the modern nation-state's political economy.

War and international trade as forces in fiscal history: a global and long-run perspective

Today historians recognize the importance of war and international com-merce as forces that have promoted the development of fiscal systems and states to change. Schumpeter and North themselves emphasized both phenomena. Nevertheless, with the exception of certain recent work, the application of such reasoning to only European cases has facilitated some misconceptions.[6] Let me, however, undertake a series of reflec-tions, even at the risk of repeating ideas familiar to specialists.

★★★

From Marco Polo until *c*. 1713 important changes took place in the interlinking of different fiscal systems.

In the fifteenth century Eurasian trade and commerce across the Mediterranean not only increased rivalries among republics, such as Genoa and Venice, that aimed to control trade routes, but also provided them with the necessary resources for the taxation of international com-merce.[7] Inserted in that trade, the Ottoman Empire is a good example of how combinations of war and trade affected fiscal development in the fifteenth century.[8] Military expansion under the rule of Mehmed II and

---

[5] J. L. Cardoso and P. Lains (eds.), *Paying for the liberal state: the rise of public finance in nineteenth-century Europe* (Cambridge University Press, 2010).

[6] An excellent exception that, nevertheless, does not exhaust the subject of how the interaction of different fiscal systems through war affected each of them, is R. Findlay and K. O'Rourke, *Power and plenty. Trade, war, and the world economy in the second mil-lennium* (Princeton University Press, 2007).

[7] See Pezzolo, Chapter 11 in this volume. For the Venetian case and the wars with Genoa and then with the Turks, which had a crucial impact on expansion to the main-land and the formation of the fiscal state, see F. C. Lane, *Venice. A maritime republic* (Baltimore and London: The Johns Hopkins University Press, 1973), pp. 189–201, 225–39 and 324–7; and S. R. Epstein, *Freedom and growth. The rise of states and markets in Europe, 1300–1750* (London: Routledge, 2000), pp. 149–51.

[8] For a general perspective, F. Braudel, *The Mediterranean and the Mediterranean world in the age of Philip II* (London: Collins, 1972) Vol. II, chapter 2, remains useful. See also different works by Pamuk and particularly Chapter 13 in this volume.

his successors was a way of controlling resources by the state, while the stability of the whole imperial system was based on long-distance trade networks.[9] The essays on the Italian states (Pezzolo, Chapter 11) and the Ottoman Empire (Pamuk, Chapter 13) also highlight the key role of competition between states to capture international commerce in order to favour merchants' property rights, which constituted a powerful agent of change in fiscal systems. These developments, as predicted by North's general theory but contrary to his historical analysis, occurred not only in Europe, but in other areas as well.

European expansion overseas stimulated political competition, increased globalization and effected the development of fiscal regimes in different ways depending on local circumstances.

Denis O. Flynn has related European Atlantic expansion to the need for precious metals generated by the development in China of tax payments in coin from the fifteenth century.[10] Although the idea may require certain nuances, it will certainly be decisive to a better understanding of fiscal systems from a global perspective in the future. Whatever the answer to this question might be, oceanic expansion is certainly important to the history of fiscality in Eurasia (and not just Europe). Until about 1580, Portugal enjoyed an exceptional situation derived from its status as a pioneer in voyages of discovery. This initial advantage may have enabled Portugal to confront important changes in relative prices without the need for a profound fiscal reform. Under Portuguese law, the monopoly on overseas trade was automatically recognized as a regal right, which placed huge resources in the king's hands.[11] But this situation also meant that the fiscal regime did not imply any deep societal or parliamentary involvement in the kingdom's fiscal system. Portugal remained a sort of *domain state*, like England, Denmark, the German states (M. North, Chapter 6) and many other polities in Europe during the same epoch, where the king's domains constituted the main sources of crown income.[12] Furthermore, Portugal was also a *rentier state* in

[9] I. Wallerstein, H. Decdeli and R. Kasaba, 'The incorporation of the Ottoman Empire into the world-economy' in H. Islamoglu-Inan (ed.), *The Ottoman Empire and the world-economy* (Cambridge University Press, 1990), pp. 88–97.
[10] D. O. Flynn and A. Giráldez, 'China and the Manila Galleon', in D. O. Flynn (ed.), *World silver and monetary history in the 16th and 17th centuries* (Aldershot and Brookfield: Ashgate, 1996), pp. 71–7.
[11] An excellent and brief analysis of the Portuguese empire and its impact on the Portuguese economy is J. M. Pedreira, '"To have or not to have". The economic consequences of Empire: Portugal (1415–1822)', in P. K. O'Brien and L. Prados de la Escosura (eds.), *The cost and benefits of European imperialism from the conquest of Ceuta, 1415, to the Treaty of Lusaka, 1974. Revista de Historia Económica* 1 (1998), 93–122.
[12] L. E. Petersen 'From domain state to tax state (synthesis and interpretations)', *Scandinavian Economic History Review* 23 (1975), 116–42.

that a high proportion of its revenues did not come from the kingdom's economy, but from other territories. Mata's essay (Chapter 9) shows that the royal fiscal system hardly penetrated Portuguese society until the eighteenth century, though very clear symptoms were already present by 1630–50.[13]

The Castilian case looks different. Atlantic expansion also augmented royal income from overseas, which allowed the crown considerable autonomy. At the same time, the Treaty of Tordesillas (1494) avoided whatever type of overlap with Portugal that would lead to competition between the two states in order to guarantee the general property rights of each of their mercantile classes. The American empire created, moreover, significant differences between the king of Castile and other princes whose capacity for gathering tax revenues was strongly constricted by their parliaments.[14] Castile did not, however, evolve into a *rentier state* because its fiscal system penetrated deeply into Castilian society and economy. On the other hand, and in contrast to Portugal, the fact that Castile's society numbered among Europe's most urbanized and dynamic favoured the formation of a relatively efficient fiscal regime capable of responding to international credit and supporting a fiscal system largely dependent upon Genoese and German bankers with tax revenues paid to the crown.

The global scope of these Iberian fiscal regimes, particularly the Castilian tax regime around which the Habsburg dynasty built an international composite monarchy, brought radical changes to American societies where tribal polities and two empires – the Inca and Aztec – were much weaker in military and fiscal terms and were easily taken over by the military–fiscal might of Castile. Differences appear immediately between the relationship of Castile to America and that of Portugal to Asia. In Asia, Portuguese power faced problems derived from the opposition of stronger fiscal and military enemies. Spaniards in America interacted with weaker states and pre-Colombian fiscal systems. At the same time, the fiscal regime of Spain's composite monarchy was marked by enormous asymmetries across its territories. Castile's capacity to mobilize resources from a dynamic domestic economy and its colonies in the Americas created conditions for a political stalemate that retarded the need for reforms in the kingdoms of Aragon, Valencia, Catalonia, Navarre, Sicily, Sardinia and Naples.[15] In this respect, the

---

[13] Pedreira, "'To have or not to have'".
[14] B. Yun-Casalilla, *Marte contra Minerva. El precio del Imperio español, c. 1450–1600* (Barcelona: Crítica, 2004), chapters 5 and 6.
[15] M. Rodríguez Salgado, *The changing face of the Empire. Charles V, Philip II and Habsburg authority, 1551–1559* (Cambridge University Press, 1998).

fact that the Hispanic monarchy, with Portugal added to it in 1580, was a dynastic and 'multinational' composite monarchy would also be decisive. The monarchs of Castile were much more active than is usually thought in guaranteeing their subjects positive conditions for commerce and property rights.[16] Yet it is no less certain that, de facto, these advantages (and certain problems derived from them) were guaranteed to political and financial allies, like Genoa, or to the subjects of the monarchy's other territories, such as the Catholic Low Countries.

Clashes on the battlefields between the Castilian and other fiscal systems became a crucial factor in European history. The Ottoman Empire had created a relatively efficient fiscal system, but it became necessary to develop it further to confront the Habsburgs' power in the sixteenth century (Pamuk, Chapter 13). Confrontation with Castile from the end of the fifteenth century led to reforms in an archaic French system (Bonney, Chapter 4). In Italy, the involvement of the different polities in the wars between Spain and France led to changes in the fiscal regimes of Milan, Venice and the Duchy of Tuscany. The changes in the Austrian system were related to wars in Central Europe, but also to more global confrontations with the Ottoman Empire (Pieper, Chapter 7).

During the seventeenth century, wars, the expansion of oceanic trade and colonization continued to be decisive for the evolution of fiscal regimes throughout Eurasia. Glete has characterized the period 1560–1660 as a second phase in the formation of European fiscal–military states.[17] The war against the Spanish Habsburgs and the need to expand a colonial system were decisive for the formation of a relatively efficient fiscal system in Holland, where a combination of medieval parliamentarianism and republicanism led to a financial revolution and facilitated the development of international banking and the foundation of the Bank of Amsterdam in 1609. During the early modern period 'war remained the major driving force in Dutch state formation' (Fritschy, 't Hart and Horlings, Chapter 2). Thanks to the reforms of Richelieu, which were also closely connected to the wars with Spain, the Thirty Years War and Louis XIV's wars with England and Holland, the fiscal regime also changed in France. Sweden, deeply involved in warfare, also combined components of archaism and a modern fiscal system.[18] In Central Europe, where colonial expansion had little

---

[16] Yun-Casalillla, *Marte contra Minerva*, pp. 161–5.
[17] J. Glete, *War and the state in early modern Europe. Spain, the Dutch Republic and Sweden as fiscal-military states, 1500–1600* (London and New York: Routledge, 2002), pp. 22ff.
[18] Ibid., passim.

impact, war played a key role. The threat from a 'Swedish military state was the direct cause of the development of Denmark–Norway and Brandenburg–Prussia into similar states'.[19] In the latter the fiscal reforms that began in 1647 were directly related to warfare in the region (M. North, Chapter 6). For Austria and some of the territories federated into the Holy Roman Empire, these were also key years for fiscal reforms (M. North and Pieper, Chapters 6 and 7). In the Catholic Low Countries, whose status as a political frontier had prevented the Habsburgs from making burdensome fiscal demands, Janssens notes (Chapter 3) that the *benevolences* increased during the seventeenth century. Similarly, in the Papal States, 'Papal finances developed under the influence of political and military emergencies' (Piola Caselli, Chapter 12). The same could be observed for Milan, Naples and other Italian states within the Spanish Habsburg system, where the crown's fiscal pressure increased during the seventeenth century as never before, as the system moved towards the formation of a tax state.[20] A crucial step towards the formation of the western European tax state was taken in England in 1688, when a fiscal revolution took place there that combined parliamentary control of taxes and the accumulation of debt with the formation of a central bank to support public credit. The outcome was a system in which a political and social consensus among the elites became the basis for the reduction of risk associated with monarchical taxation and borrowing.[21]

Yet a European perspective on these phenomena is not sufficient. The essays brought together here demonstrate that the leap towards globalization led by Portugal, Castile and then Holland and England, also became important for the workings of Asian fiscal systems. It is better known that Castilian monetary stability was only maintained until 1609 thanks to the remissions of American silver that made it possible to avoid debasement measures especially negative for Castilian society. It is also possible that American silver may have helped attain monetary

---

[19] Ibid., p. 28.
[20] Apart from chapters 11 and 12 in this volume, see A. Calabria, *The cost of Empire. The finances of the kingdom of Naples in the time of Spanish rule* (Cambridge University Press, 1991); G. Muto, *Le finanze publiche napolitane tra riforma e ristaurazione (1520–1634)* (Naples: Edizioni Scientifiche Italiane, 1980); A. Bulgarelli Lukacs, '"Domain state" e "Tax state" Nel regno di Napoli (secoli XII–XIX)', *Società e storia* 106 (2004),781–812; L. Pezzolo and E. Stumpo, 'L'imposta diretta in Italia dal medioevo alla fine dell'ancien regime', *Nota di Lavoro. Dipartimento di Scienze Economiche* 12 (2007) (accessed 6 December 2010 at www.dse.unive.it/fileadmin/templates/dse/wp/Note_di_lavoro_2007/NL_DSE_pezzolo_stumpo_12_07.pdf).
[21] J. Brewer, *The sinews of power. War, money and the English state, 1688–1783* (Harvard University Press, 1990); and Daunton, chapter 5 in this volume.

stability from 1481 to 1585 in the Ottoman Empire, where debasement had been habitual in the fifteenth century. To what extent might this have been behind the relative efficiency of the sixteenth-century Turkish bureaucratic and fiscal system? Figures offered by deVries suggest that a very high the proportion of American silver travelled east to Asia even in 1600, and the studies of Pamuk demonstrate considerable monetary circulation in the Ottoman Empire.[22] American silver also oiled the fiscal system of the Mughal empire, which was based on a strongly monetized economy (Richards, Chapter 17). It is also clear that Chinese commerce with Europe, whether through the Pacific or the Indian Oceans, had a positive effect on the workings of the fiscal systems of the countries involved by providing them with the supplies of silver necessary to make them more liquid and to render the payment of part of the Chinese taxes in coin more frequent.[23] Tilly observed that, in the development of fiscal systems, the degree of urbanization and circulation of money played a fundamental role.[24] It is very probable that American silver, although not the sole cause of their development, was one of the factors that *helped* societies not very urbanized but where markets were energetic to build up more sophisticated financial–fiscal systems.

The worldwide circulation of American silver was not the only effect of the incipient globalization that impacted the different fiscal systems. It also coincided with what we might call the globalization of military techniques. The growth of military expenditures and international connections among fiscal regimes also became evident in the Eurasian empires, from Turkey to China, the Mughal empire

---

[22] J. deVries, 'Connecting Europe and Asia: a quantitative analysis of the Cape-route trade, 1497–1795' and S. Pamuk, 'Crisis and recovery: the Ottoman monetary system in the early modern era, 1550–1769', both in D. O. Flynn, A. Giráldez and R. von Glahn (eds.), *Global connections and monetary history, 1470–1800* (London: Ashgate, 2003), pp. 35–106 and 133–48.

[23] Of course one should admit qualifications. The circulation of silver did not make a similar quantity available to pay taxes. An important part of the silver was retained from Seville itself to the coasts of the Indian and Pacific Oceans. It is evident, moreover, that the capacity to pay taxes in coin depended upon the degree of mercantile development and not the amount of metal available. On the other hand, the largest share of the taxes in all of these countries was not paid in silver but rather in coins of worse quality. It is no less certain, however, that the abundance of silver encouraged international commerce and displaced a good part of the money of lesser value into more modest circuits that nourished taxes, and provided security for the systems of loans between the great financiers and the fiscal systems. These ideas have been developed in different essays by D. O. Flynn and A. Giráldez. See, for example, 'China and the Manila Galleon'.

[24] C. Tilly, *Coercion, capital, and European states, AD 990–1990* (Cambridge, MA: Blackwell, 1990).

and Japan, where the effects were even more contradictory than in Europe.

New techniques of warfare developed during the military revolution in the West were imported into China via Islamic networks, Portuguese, German and Dutch soldiers, and even through the movements of Jesuit missionaries in different parts of Asia.[25] By 1640, the Ming dynasty's fiscal-cum-military weaknesses were exposed by Manchu invaders who had managed to acquire European technologies for warfare.[26] Unsurprisingly, shortly after the Qing dynasty was established the state began to develop a fiscal apparatus designed to be prepared for warfare. Extra funds came partly from the imperial domain (5 per cent of cultivated land and property), but mainly from the extension of the tax base across the whole empire. The Chinese fiscal regime continued to be more benevolent than its European counterparts, but it too made demands for more taxation.[27] In India the continued expansion of the Mughal empire fed the insatiable 'appetite for resources' of a 'Leviathan' and warfare became the main force leading to an increasing penetration of the fiscal system into local societies and economies (Richards, Chapter 17).[28] In Japan, the reforms of the 1590s led to a fiscal system based on taxes collected in rice, which could add up to 40–50 per cent of its gross output (Nakabayashi, Chapter 16). This was so in spite of the Japanese fiscal regime being a prototype *domain state*.

★★★

The period *c.* 1713–1815 continued to witness fiscal changes derived from the combination of warfare and global trade. This history, well known for European states, acquires greater meaning when placed in the framework of Asian states and the relationships between them and European polities. In Europe, colonial conflicts and maritime wars led to huge efforts to fund armed forces, particularly navies. But in almost all countries warfare and mercantilist policies promoted attempts to rationalize and homogenize the tax systems to fund rising naval and military expenditures.

---

[25] See N. Di Cosmo, 'Did guns matter? Firearms and the Qing formation', in L. A. Struve (ed.), *The Qing formation in world-historical time* (Cambridge, MA: Harvard University Press, 2004) pp. 121–65.

[26] Di Cosmo, 'Did guns matter?'.

[27] E. S. Rawski, 'Was the early Qing "early modern"?' in Struve, *The Qing formation*, pp. 213–18.

[28] Quoted in T. Raychaudhuri, 'The Mughal empire', in T. Raychaudhuri and I. Habib (eds.), *The Cambridge economic history of India*, Vol I: *c.* 1200–*c.* 1750 (Cambridge University Press, 1982), p. 173. See also chapter 17 in this volume by J. F. Richards, and 'Mughal state finance and the premodern world economy' in J. F. Richards, *Power, administration and finance in Mughal India* (London: Ashgate, 1993), chapter 5.

At the same time, an expanding world economy led to massive flows of new products into Europe, which paved the way for significant changes in tax structures. This process had already begun in the fifteenth century when Asian commerce, especially products like spices, became crucial for the functioning of the fiscal systems of mercantile Italian republics. Customs duties on imports of raw materials and exotic products (tea, tobacco, cocoa and even coffee) became increasingly important in comparison with traditional levies on land (paid mostly by the third estate) and customary indirect taxes on the consumption of such basic foodstuffs as wine, beer, meat and oil. Many states established monopolies for the distribution of imported commodities from which additional revenue was obtained.

All this had two effects. On the one hand, until these exotic products became widely consumed, it shifted the burdens towards the middle classes and privileged elites (nobility and clergy) who consumed these imports. On the other hand, such taxes were easier to collect because per capita incomes of the middle classes were rising. From the theoretical perspective of D. North, it could be said that different European states attempted to take advantage of the displacement of relative prices in order to adapt their systems of resource extraction to changes in the structure of international commerce and consumption. The political effects were also crucial in the sense that the theory predicts. The expansion of colonial and global trade reinforced agreements between princes and merchant groups in the international arena. The mercantilist state exploited external opportunities for its own internal articulation by offering defence for external and domestic markets. At the same time, in Europe, states found themselves obliged to compete to guarantee and defend the property rights of the mercantile classes. Very meaningfully, the resort to debasements, a negative policy for traders that strained relations between them and their princes, became rarer. Again, the case studies presented here are very significant in this respect. Debasements became inconceivable in countries with strong parliaments such as England or the Netherlands, but still took place in Russia. They were also less frequent in absolutist systems such as Spain or Brandenburg–Prussia – a fact less emphasized by historians and absent from D. North's narrative. Trade led to the fiscal regimes' greater independence from aristocracies and corporate towns, which smoothed their relations with princes. Quite logically, but also paradoxically if we consider the common narrative on this matter, new opportunities for taxation prolonged traditional alliances between old elites and the state because they reduced the latter's need to instigate fundamental changes in social and institutional systems, at least during the first half of the eighteenth century.

Even those countries where these developments were not readily evident can be considered illustrative of the importance of this phenomenon. For example, in France, the limited shift on the incidence of taxes to trade – compared with Spain – explains in part the fiscal discontent that became a crucial cause of the French Revolution. In Genoa and Venice, declining gains from international trade led to weaker fiscal systems based less on customs duties and, as a consequence, also to political failures. Something similar happened in the Ottoman Empire, where the political economy based on a system of 'provisioning' and limited taxes on trade also weakened the Empire.

The trajectories of the Asian countries described in this volume gain meaning in this context while further highlighting what happened in Europe. Partly due to its fiscal rigidity (based on the taxation of agrarian output), the Mughal empire experienced similar difficulties until its takeover by the English East India Company in 1757 (Richards, Chapter 17). Even so, the company retained the Mughal tax system and an impressive growth in revenues mainly resulted from military expansion, plunder and the exploitation of monopolies such as the salt trade. In the Manchu empire, a fiscal regime largely based on land taxes and a salt monopoly provided the basis for funding an army that failed to keep internal order or repel external aggression until customs became more important as a source of public revenue (Wong, Chapter 15). In Japan the situation was similar. Tax farming continued to be the overwhelming source of revenue both for the Shogun and local lords (Daimyo) and foreign trade provided only a fraction of fiscal revenues before the late nineteenth century (Nakabayashi, Chapter 16).

In general, variations in opportunities to shift the composition of revenues towards trade represent an important difference between states and distinguish the most efficient fiscal regimes both in Europe and Asia.[29] One should also consider, moreover, that by that time the bases of European fiscal states had changed decisively. In most cases they were no longer composite monarchies in which negotiation incurred the obligation of respecting privileges, but proto-nation-states advancing towards homogenous jurisdictional systems and a more concrete

---

[29] Cf. K. Pomeranz, *The great divergence. Europe, China and the making of the modern world economy* (Princeton University Press, 2000), pp. 194–206; K. N. Chaubdury, *Trade and civilization in the Indian Ocean: an economic history from the rise of Islam to 1750* (Cambridge University Press, 1985).

definition of the forms and rights of individual property. It may be in the eighteenth century when European countries appear most clearly to be taking the path to the formation of developed fiscal states much more quickly than those of Asia.

★★★

In the nineteenth century, globalization and war remained important for the formation of fiscal states in Eurasia, although differentially according to the region, for peace became more frequent than war in Europe.

In many European countries public debts skyrocketed during the Napoleonic Wars and kept growing for decades thereafter. The crisis of the Old Regime and the rise of liberal society emerged hand-in-hand with fiscal crises. By 1815 war had accelerated the crisis of the old political systems and, along with them, the fiscal systems of the Old Regime. European fiscal systems, with the exception of Great Britain, had demonstrated their incapacity to withstand the conflict. The outcome was the emergence of reformed systems, which represents the final stage in the formation of tax states: that is, fiscal states in which central governments monopolized taxation, privileges ended and individuals and not corporations became the basis for tax collection. In many postrevolution countries, parliaments began to take control of budgets and to manage national debts. The way of confronting this problem varied greatly from one country to another, notwithstanding one general fact: in most cases, the reforms were carried out in a context of peace and commercial competition. In some cases, such as those of Italy and Germany, the process ended in national unification and the formation of centralized fiscal states.[30]

Yet from the mid nineteenth century, various European nations concentrated the enormous military potential that they had accumulated since the eighteenth century over the European periphery and Asia, requiring decisive reforms in these areas.[31] The Romanovs began to change their fiscal system following defeat by the French and English in the Crimea and continued with them after their defeat by Japan. In China, the Opium War against England exposed the deficiencies of the old system and led to a feeling of humiliation that provoked reform. The principles of good government as identified with low taxes went through a crisis that ended in a system in which customs duties became

[30] For a detailed analysis that also complements the case studies in this volume, see J. L. Cardoso and P. Lains (eds.), *Paying for the liberal state.*
[31] C. Bayly, *The birth of the modern world, 1780–1914. Global connections and comparisons* (Blackwell: Oxford, 2004), pp. 265–71.

the backbone of Chinese public revenues, as had been the case in several western areas of Eurasia in the eighteenth century. Globalization and war also changed the Japanese regime when the Meiji revolution and the rise of a new fiscal system and tax state was pushed onwards by political confrontations with the US and China (Deng, Wong and Nakabayashi, Chapters 14–16).

The significance of early reforms can be assessed by considering the history of those territories, such as those of the Ottoman Empire, where changes were slower, more limited and smoother. The Empire failed to suppress nationalistic movements in Greece and Egypt, while external aggressions exposed the weakness of the whole system. Although Pamuk stresses its flexibility (Chapter 13), it is also clear that the maintenance of long-established internal political balances of power led to the Empire's diminished efficiency as a military–fiscal state and hence to its progressive decline and eventual break-up.

These studies also suggest that fiscal reforms introduced not only in Europe but, more importantly, in Asian countries, created adequate conditions for foreign investments. Such was the case of Russia as well as of many states of Central, South and East Asia that entered international markets for capital. The rule of the East Indian Company in India depended on English financial markets (Richards, Chapter 17). In China, nineteenth-century fiscal reforms paved the way for the entry of international finance into China's public debt (Wong, Chapter 15). In Japan, the wars against China and Russia, as well as the aftermath of the Meiji revolution, made the country's national finances accessible to British capital (Nakabayashi, Chapter 16).

It has been said for Europe that 'no European model dominated or was exported from one nation to the other',[32] which reinforces the central argument of this volume. It does so, moreover, without negating the transfer of formulas of imposition and debt, or even of management of the fiscal state. Nevertheless, when we broaden the scale to a Eurasian dimension (and probably also if we include an American perspective), the conclusion could be different. In this case, we perceive that the internationalization of economic relations and war in the second half of the century in Asia accelerated the reforms leading to the formation of the fiscal state – even often at the cost of authentic changes in the political structure.

---

[32] J. L. Cardoso and P. Lains, 'Introduction. Paying for the liberal state', in Cardoso and Lains (eds.), *Paying for the liberal state*, p. 21.

Some suggestions on the formation of the fiscal state from a comparative perspective

Historians have recently tried to bring comparative methods to bear on the formation of fiscal states. Bonney and Daunton (Chapters 4 and 5) provide comparisons between France and Britain. Comín and Yun (Chapter 10) analyse the Castilian–Spanish tax regimes by comparing them to the French and English cases. Pezzolo's comparisons between Italian republics and princely states (Chapter 11) explain how the state and investors built financial trust in public debt in different ways. Something similar could be said about Wong's essay on China (Chapter 15), which is a fine example of asymmetric comparison. Marjolein 't Hart's recent study compares early modern financial revolutions in England and the Netherlands and O'Brien has just placed the fiscal histories of the Ottoman and the Mughal empires side by side. In previous essays, Bonney compared England and France and Glete offered analytical depictions of Spain, the Dutch Republic and Sweden.[33]

Such advances have occurred without a typology or theory for the purpose. Basically this volume contributes case studies to this research programme. Yet, some middle-range comparisons are possible because similar situations, processes and outcomes occurred everywhere in the formation of fiscal states. Let me propose only some of these possibilities as examples of the many ways in which this volume can contribute to more general debates.

(1) *Centralization, negotiation and trust in the functioning of fiscal systems*. The essays in this volume demonstrate that centralization accompanies the formation of fiscal states. Indeed, it appears to be a sine qua non of the very concept of a fiscal state. Historians of Europe have long emphasized the importance of centralization in relation to absolutist states, such as France, Russia or Prussia in the eighteenth century. But the process was also present in political systems with 'republican' components, such as the Netherlands and Great Britain, and in city-states like Venice or Genoa. Furthermore, there seems to be no major contrast over the long run between Eastern and Western parts of Eurasia. From Japan to the Ottoman Empire we find the same processes at work.

---

[33] R. Bonney, 'Towards the comparative fiscal history of Britain and France during the "long" eighteenth century', in L. Prados de la Escosura (ed.), *Exceptionalism and industrialisation: Britain and its European rivals, 1688–1815* (New York: Cambridge University Press, 2004); P. O'Brien, 'Fiscal and financial preconditions for the formation of states in the West and the East', presentation to panel 110 organized by W. Fritschy at the 123rd Meeting of the American Historical Association, New York, 9–11 January 2009; Glete, *War and the state*.

There was, however, no centralization without negotiation, and it is myopic to think that those polities that did not fit English and Dutch models were simply arbitrary, autocratic and predatory, as Acemoglou, Johnson and Robinson propose in several articles that return to the theory of D. North.[34] The current focus on the fiscal limits of Western absolutism has shown that negotiation, although usually conflictive, was also very present in absolutist regimes.[35] This volume clearly corroborates that idea, especially in the cases of France (Bonney, Chapter 4) and Castile (Comín and Yun, Chapter 10). These essays, moreover, extend this revisionism of the big paradigms to the Asian cases, which have been associated with images of despotism since the Enlightenment. In China, bargaining took place between the imperial centre and a society of taxpayers based on a widespread idea of good government, a concept which included centralized economic regulation at low fiscal cost (Wong, Chapter 15). The emergence of a proto-Weberian civil service provided some sort of basis for politics as long as its professionalism and openness to talent prevented its systematic control by local elites. For the Ottoman Empire, negotiations between the Sultan and the elites of Istanbul and the provinces were essential for the functioning of the Empire, where institutions like *malikane* and the provisioning system became cornerstones of the political economy of the Ottoman dominions and constituted a commitment to negotiations and understandings between state and society (Pamuk, Chapter 13).

By putting the accent on the presence of conflictive negotiation in absolutist systems another narrative can be developed. The fiscal and financial advantages of states such as the Netherlands and Great Britain that experienced precocious fiscal and financial revolutions based on agreements between the king and the parliament has been documented and analysed.[36] Both states possessed fiscal systems with high degrees of stability, because, as Daunton underlines (Chapter 5),

---

[34] See, among other works, D. North, 'The rise of Europe: Atlantic trade, institutional change and economic growth', *American Economic Review* 95 (2005), pp. 546–79.

[35] R. Bonney, *Political change in France under Richelieu and Mazarin, 1624–1661* (New York: Oxford University Press, 1978); and J. B. Collins, *Fiscal limits of absolutism. Direct taxation in early seventeenth-century France* (Berkeley: University of California Press, 1988); W. Beik, *Absolutism and society in seventeenth-century France: state power and provincial aristocracy in Languedoc* (New York: Cambridge University Press, 1988); A. M. Hespanha, *As vésperas do Leviathan: instituições e poder político: Portugal, séc. XVII* (Coimbra: Livraria Almedina, 1994). See a general overview in J. F. Schaub, 'La Peninsola Iberica nei secoli XVI e XVII: la questione dello stato', *Studi Storici* 1 (1995), 9–49.

[36] P. O'Brien, 'Contentions of the purse between England and its European rivals from Henry V to George IV: a conversation with Michael Mann', *Journal of Historical Sociology* 19:4 (2006), 341–63, at 347.

both parliamentary sovereignty and accepted fiscal and financial institutions led to a greater social consensus and stability in the collection
of taxes and in the management of public debts.[37] But these essays
also reveal that other ways to create trust between central powers
and elites, including merchant elites, worked out on many occasions.
Thanks to that, states such as France, Spain, Brandenburg–Prussia
and even Sweden could mobilize considerable resources for warfare
in early modern Europe. The growth of Spanish fiscal income during
the sixteenth century, though very much linked to American treasure, was also related to a conflictive pact between king and kingdom
without which the whole system could not work. In most eighteenth-
century European states, the trust in a powerful king, who invested
important sums on prestige but who also defended a mercantilist policy, must also have been one of the reasons for controlling the public
debt rates. Though the differences seem to be positive for republics, a comparison between them and princely states in Renaissance
Italy also proves the existence of informal agreements leading to the
construction of trust without parliamentary control of the budget
(Pezzolo, Chapter 11). The low interests of the Papal States' debts
can only be explained in terms of the trust that good management
and ideological (religious) affinity created (Piola Caselli, Chapter
12). In brief, the vicinity of merchant and financial classes to power
facilitated, not always easy, agreements between them and the functioning of fiscal regimes.

(2) *War and its effects in Europe and Asia.* One of the most frequent
comparisons between Asia and Europe identifies the supposed greater
intensity of wars in the West as key to the precocious development of
the fiscal state in Europe.[38] As indicated already, the essays collected
in this volume clearly ratify this view by revealing conflicts between
states as one of the fundamental challenges confronted by different fiscal regimes. At the same time, they caution against over-simplification
in this respect.

On the one hand, in the long run, wars were evidently very present in
Asia, where they also produced important changes. China, often cited
as an example to the contrary, offers a different impression here. Deng
(Chapter 14) demonstrates that a unified China, with a general fiscal
regime for the whole country, emerged from wars among pre-existing

---

[37] P. O'Brien, 'The nature and historical evolution of an exceptional fiscal state and its
possible significance for the precocious commercialization and industrialization of the
British economy from Cromwell to Nelson', *Economic History Review* 64 (2011), 408–
46. I thank P. O'Brien for his permission to use this article before its publication.

[38] For a general discussion of this point, see Pomeranz, *The great divergence*, pp. 195–7.

political units and under the threat of nomads in the north. Until 1800, 'both the legitimacy of the fiscal state and the rationale for the Chinese empire were determined by demands for external security'. Internal wars in Japan led to a concentration of fiscal competencies and a reform carried out in the 1590s. Under both the Mughal empire and the East India Company, wars provided a reason to reinforce the fiscal system (Richards, Chapter 17). The same could be said for the Ottoman Empire (Pamuk, Chapter 13). Hence war does not appear to have been a vital difference between Europe and Asia when considering the history of both continents in the very long run.

It is also to be noted, on the other hand, that a correlation between war and development in the Schumpeterian fiscal state or between war and the creation of a political economy supporting economic growth is not uniform. War was not always a necessary condition for these developments, nor did all wars produce them. The example of the Spanish empire may be the most illustrative. From the fifteenth century it comprised a political unit in continual conflict, whose wars led to tense pacts with the immediate effect of crystallizing institutions and forms of mobilizing resources unpropitious to economic growth.[39] The specific conditions in which bellicose conflicts affected different political units and even the geopolitics surrounding them could be just as positive. Janssens (Chapter 3) demonstrates that the war-torn Habsburg Low Countries tended more to a moderate fiscal burden than to the contrary. The Catholic United Provinces became a *rentier state* from the end of the sixteenth century. Although these provinces suffered many negative effects from the conflict with Holland, it appears just as true that the Hispanic monarchy paid most of the costs of protection in the area.

Finally, and as indicated above, the great advances towards the formation of fiscal states registered in nineteenth-century Europe took place during prolonged periods of peace. The fiscal state and the political economy generated around it at that time appear to have been much more connected to the need to guarantee internal order and the defence of property rights in themselves than to conflicts among countries.

(3) *Different paths to the fiscal state.* A comparison of the studies presented here on various levels also belies the myth of a common model of evolution towards the fiscal state. Contrary to what Schumpeter would have preached, the phases appear very diverse and differ according to the regions. The passage from a *domain state* to a *fiscal state* depended a lot on the legal constitution of each area, and no type of *path dependency*

---

[39] This is the central thesis of Yun-Casalilla, *Marte contra Minerva*.

marks models for the transition between them. It also appears clear that
the trends towards centralization and more democratic forms of negotiation over revenues were not linear. In some places, such as Spain and
the Mughal and Ottoman Empires, the devolution of functions or periods of decentralization resulted from bargaining between central and
local power structures. The rise of fiscal states cannot be considered
as a teleological process, but as the outcome of very varied historical
circumstances, some of which became more general in the nineteenth
and twentieth centuries.

(4) *The problem of information.* The collective and comparative consideration of the cases presented here create heuristic possibilities deriving
from the existence of common traits sometimes overlooked in research.
One of the most evident and least emphasized today is the importance
of factors such as the difficulties, costs and benefits of obtaining information within the different fiscal regimes. All of the cases studied here
show that the possession of information about different territories, their
populations and economic resources, their institutional systems, their
social composition and their local tax schemes were prerequisites for
both centralization and efficient negotiation. In Japan, for example, the
need to know levels of land productivity was crucial for the distribution and collection of taxes (Nakabayashi, Chapter 16). In the Mughal
empire, information about harvests was the basis for tax distribution.[40]
In Castile, data for volumes of trade and personal income were the
bases for taxation.

Information was never free but emerged from a process of bargaining
with local social groups in the context of political relationships. The
impossibility of producing and applying a cadastre such as the *Catastro
de Ensenada* in Spain is a good example (Comín and Yun, Chapter 10).
For the cadastres to work not only had social resistance to be overcome,
but central rulers needed to negotiate with local authorities that usually sold this information for economic, social or political advantages.
Furthermore, as the example of the *Catastro de Ensenada* shows, bargaining for information could end up frustrating the policies of central
authorities. This was also the case in Austria, in spite of a long tradition
of direct taxes on land. For vast empires where distance and diversity, be it ecological, economic, social or even institutional, were readily
apparent, the dependence of central rulers on local elites for information was an essential prerequisite for taxation. Russia is an excellent
example.

---

[40] Richards, 'Mughal state finance', pp. 298–9.

Fiscal states in a transnational and geopolitical perspective: some paths for research

As it is very well known, the formation and functioning of fiscal states was everywhere strongly linked to transnational forces, and international financial systems also became steadily more important. Fiscal systems were basically 'national' in character, but often depended upon international financial networks. National frameworks, including parliaments, political representation, territoriality and sovereignty, are considered deeply in these essays. Furthermore, some authors, like Pezzolo (Chapter 11), suggest that the sense of belonging to a common community created conditions for a social consensus that led to compliance with demands for taxes. Trust was many times enhanced by a sense of community, as the British case in the nineteenth century demonstrates (Daunton, Chapter 5), and it has been historically the case that most consolidated sovereign debts remained in the hands of the sovereign's subjects.

Nevertheless, these essays also show that transnational financial networks were also called upon to fund states. This was clearly the case for the Habsburg dominions under the Spanish monarchy, which famously interacted with German, Flemish and Genoese international firms.[41] The seventeenth-century Portuguese tax system was inextricably associated with Jewish international networks stretching from Lisbon and the Low Countries to Brazil and Southeast Asia.[42] French kings depended for most of the early modern period on Tuscan bankers and Swiss Huguenots, while Dutch capital was very important for English public finances.[43] In the Ottoman Empire, Jewish, Greek and Armenian bankers were extremely active in the seventeenth and eighteenth centuries (Pamuk, Chapter 13). On many occasions war created urgent requirements for funds that could only be provided by big international bankers. War reinforced the intertwining of international financial networks with international trade because the transfer of funds and bills of exchange depended heavily on trade and the movements of commodities. At the same time, the increasing and unaffordable needs of states

---

[41] H. Kellenbenz, *Die Fugger in Spanien und Portugal bis 1560* (Munich: E. Voegel, 1990); F. Ruiz Martin, *Pequeño capitalismo, gran capitalismo: Simón Ruiz y sus negocios en Florencia* (Barcelona: Crítica, 1990).

[42] J. Boyajian, *Portuguese bankers at the court of Spain, 1626–1650* (New Brunswick, NJ: Rutgers University Press, 1983).

[43] For a synthesis regarding the French, Dutch and English cases, see H. Van der Wee (*et al.*), *La banque en Occident* (Anvers: Fonds Mercator, 1991) pp. 180–265; L. Neal, *The rise of financial capitalism: international capital markets in the age of reason* (Cambridge University Press, 1990).

were a factor in the growing importance of what Felipe Ruiz Martín has called 'cosmopolitan capital'. Only this form of capital, due to its international dimensions and sophisticated techniques, was able to match their requirements.[44]

Though very well known, this situation creates some interesting questions. To what extent did the cosmopolitan character of financial capital and its autonomy beyond the control of the states influence the way that states behaved? When historians consider absolutism and its depredatory character they seem to forget the capacity these international financiers had to recompose their own networks, thus limiting the monarch's capacity of manoeuvre. For example, there is no doubt that the Spanish Habsburgs' bankruptcies hurt Genoese bankers. But what were the real consequences? We know that they were negotiated bankruptcies in which the state did not have an entirely free hand to dictate the situation because of the capacity of the Genoese to reorient their own financial networks in other directions.[45] The Austrian monarchy paid for default on its debts to Oppenheimer by practical exclusion from the European credit market (Pieper, Chapter 7). Some nineteenth-century fiscal states still repudiated parts of their debts, but these measures became less and less effective and more and more dangerous to confidence in the international financial markets on which they were heavily dependent (Mata, Chapter 9, and Comín and Yun, Chapter 10). Today, the study of fiscal states and, in particular, the study of public debt, must consider transnational dimensions and the tensions between politically well-defined 'national' territories and wide, flexible transnational financial networks. The current economic and financial crisis and the clear tension between the global character of financial circuits and the sovereignty of the nation-state obviously make this question even more important.

The impression when reading the essays presented here is, however, that this interaction between states and international capital was less important in Asia before the nineteenth century. Russian dependence on international bankers only became important from the eighteenth century onwards. The same can be said about China, the Mughal empire and Japan, which for centuries remained dependent on local capital networks. The less-developed debt system in the Eastern area of Eurasia made it possible to avoid a dependence on international capital and, consequently, this type of limit on political unity is apparently less

[44] Ruiz Martín, *Pequeño capitalismo, gran capitalismo*, passim.
[45] F. Ruiz Martín, 'Las finanzas españolas en tiempos de Felipe II', *Cuadernos de Historia. Anexos de la Revista Hispania* 2 (1968), 109–73.

present, even in spite of the diffusion there of the military revolution, which was one of the reasons for it in Europe.

States were not closed laboratories for the development of fiscal systems. They were inserted in a transnational system of knowledge in which transfers of experience, successes, failures and emulation were important.[46] Their fiscal systems were perhaps the central component of state-building. National banks, as introduced in the Netherlands and which spread to England, began as Italian public banks and were imitated in Spain and Austria. Failures like Law's experiment in Bourbon France seem to have delayed the introduction of similar models of finance in Europe in general, and could explain the reluctance of Bourbon Spain to establish a central bank.

The diffusion of fiscal techniques moved around Eurasia for a gamut of reasons and with different consequences. The Spanish Habsburgs provoked a rebellion in the Low Countries when Alba tried to introduce the *alcabala* there. Something similar happened in Portugal in the seventeenth century. Austria imitated the Castilian fiscal system in the sixteenth century (Pieper, Chapter 7) and in the eighteenth century almost all countries in Europe tried to obtain information and to produce cadastres for the introduction of *l'impot unique* (Pieper, Chapter 7, and Comín and Yun, Chapter 10). In the same century, Austria copied some experiences from Milan. Some states in nineteenth-century Asia imitated systems and formed customs already common in Europe. The history of taxes and therefore the history of the formation of fiscal states is a history of diffusion, of receiving, adapting and reacting to policies tried elsewhere. Why taxes were adopted, adapted or rejected helps historians understand the making of fiscal states and the fiscal sociology of each state. Fiscal alliances and financial organizations are transnational, not national.

Geopolitics has been always present in fiscal history and, though not considered much explicitly in the present volume, it emerges implicitly in many of the examples. For centuries, the Italian mercantile republics and the Ottoman Empire benefited from trade with China to build their fiscal regimes (Pezzolo, Chapter 11, and Pamuk, Chapter 13). The Levantine trade did not disappear in the late sixteenth and seventeenth centuries. Yet the rise of alternative routes to Asia via the Cape of Good Hope and the Indian Ocean or via the Pacific through New Spain and Spanish links to America reduced the comparative advantage of the Italian republics and their capacity to tax long-distance trade, as is

---

[46] T. Ertman, *Birth of the Leviathan: building states and regimes in medieval and early modern Europe* (New York: Cambridge University Press, 1997).

obvious in their return to taxes on the agrarian sector and domestic consumption. The shift to warfare and big international conflicts from the Mediterranean to the Atlantic in the seventeenth and eighteenth centuries favoured the survival of the Ottoman Empire in spite of the comparative inefficiency of its fiscal regime, and allowed for a pact between centre and periphery, which also implies a devolution of functions very similar to that which was taking place in Castile and the Spanish monarchy[47]. Dutch, French and English intromissions in American trade and the extroversion of the Spanish empire provoked by the union with Portugal are some of the reasons for the decreasing volume of silver arriving in Seville and the crisis of the Castilian fiscal system. These developments even enhanced the tendency to increase taxation in the rest of the Spanish empire, particularly in the Italian territories. The development of new proto-national mercantilist fiscal systems in Spain, France, England and the Netherlands during the eighteenth century was strongly linked to tensions in the Atlantic. Increasing pressure from the USA and European countries in Asia was decisive, as we have seen from the dramatic changes in their fiscal systems.

Within empires and multinational composite monarchies, states reallocated resources across different areas in very asymmetric ways, mainly for military reasons and territorial imbalances in the development of bureaucracy. The effect of such processes is interesting not only from the fiscal and financial perspective, but also from the economic one. Mercantilist empires, for instance, were based on the creation of infrastructures useful for promoting trade with colonies and sometimes for extracting their resources. But these empires also involved high expenditures in overseas territories due to high protection costs, which are basic to any consideration of the fiscal state and its formation. R. Grafe and A. Irigoin have shown that the fiscal revenue remaining in Spanish America during the eighteenth century not only increased but also was unequally distributed there.[48] Due to geo-strategic reasons, areas like Cuba were financed by using fiscal resources from other regions, thus creating excellent conditions for the development of industries sometimes linked to naval and warfare sectors. The case of the states of Milan and Sicily in the sixteenth century or even that of the Low Countries in the seventeenth century (Janssens, Chapter 3), reveals a sort of *rentier*

[47] I. A. A. Thompson, *War and government in Habsburg Spain, 1560–1620* (London: Athlone Press, 1976).

[48] R. Grafe and A. Irigoin, 'Nuevos enfoques sobre la economía política española en sus colonias americanas durante el siglo XVIII', in F. Ramos and B. Yun (eds.), *Economía Política desde Estambul a Potosí. Ciudades, estados, imperios y mercados en el Mediterráneo y en el Atlántico ibérico, c. 1200–1800* (Valencia: Universidad de Valencia, forthcoming).

state based on the need to preserve political order and fidelity by easing fiscal pressure. In other words, taxation and expenditures by states and empires had economic and social consequences because some regions made net gains from the process and others suffered net losses.

Net transfers can also be detected across states. Swedish campaigns in the war against Spain were supported by Richelieu using French funds, some of which were spent in the Central European and German areas, and affected their economies.[49] Cash flows from Spain to the Catholic Low Countries benefited the Protestant provinces of the Netherlands, and Austria took advantage of money remittances from other countries during different moments of its history (Pieper, Chapter 7).

One could expect that the optimum size for the efficiency of fiscal states responds to an inverted 'U'. Small political units have impediments to raising enough funds in order to be competitive in the defence of their subjects' property rights and markets. Big polities suffer diseconomies of scale, problems of information and the very high costs of negotiating with distant local elites. The transfer of funds and their security over long distances could produce very high financial costs. The category of small political units applies to the Italian republics. As big polities, the Spanish, Chinese, Ottoman, Mughal and Russian empires fit the second case. Yet there is not a rule in this sense.

In the long run many different technological, political and economic factors could change the theoretical optimum. This happened to the Italian city-states and small principalities, which became politically and fiscally weaker when bigger national monarchies start developing in Spain, France and Britain.

Apart from that, the exceptions to the theoretical rule are to be noted. A very small country like the Netherlands was able to construct a very efficient empire and fiscal system thanks to international trade and finances. Some advantages may have also ensued from the possibilities of creating trust based on personal knowledge, political affinities, reputation, etc., in this case. Another small to medium sized country, like Britain in the eighteenth century, was able to build a whole empire and become the leading power in the world. This also has to do with geopolitics. The British empire pivoted on a proto-national state, which comprised a very coherent political and economic unit. The empire helped to develop the domestic economy and its economic specialization, which was also positive in fiscal terms. This proto-national core made a difference with respect to some previous experiences like the Spanish one. Until the eighteenth century the Spanish empire was grounded on a composite, extended and disperse 'pluri-national' polity in which the

---

[49] Glete, *War and the state.*

potential benefits of the fiscal system did not invigorate the Castilian economy, with other members of the empire, like the Low Countries, or allies, like Genoa, profiting most in financial and commercial terms. This situation ensued in spite of the royal monopoly, which, as Oliva Melgar has shown, was, in fact, an 'international monopoly' of which other countries such as the Netherlands, France, Genoa and even Great Britain took advantage.[50]

Size, territorial dispersion and institutional diversity, relative position in global and international networks, capability to import fiscal techniques and financial advances, and the different degrees of independence in regard to movements of international capital are, therefore, relevant factors in the efficiency of fiscal systems and in their final transition to the fiscal state.

New ideas and old paradigms: D. North and J. Schumpeter in Eurasian perspective

The essays presented in this volume pay attention to taxation systems and the problem of debt, both inextricable from the formation of fiscal states. They emphasize, above all, the first of these aspects and overlook, on the other hand, the study of fiscal regimes. Some of them go beyond fiscal matters to deal with the wider aspects of political economies. Their thematic ordering by areas responds to diverse regional criteria.

When seen from the perspective of 1914, it seems obvious that cases of precocious success accumulate in *North Atlantic Europe*.

Fritschy, 't Hart and Horlings sketch a precise overview of the formation of the fiscal state in the Netherlands (Chapter 2). During the sixteenth century, an accord between parliament and the monarch took place there, which Tracy has classified as a financial revolution. Yet, at the same time, the fiscal system remained strongly decentralized, heavily weighted towards provincial and local estates, and the distribution of quotas among the different states began to show stiffness, since it did not adapt to different rhythms of economic and demographic growth. One of its great successes resided in the capacity to respond efficiently to the needs of war and to growing indebtedness through an excise system in which tax farming had great importance. Nevertheless, during the eighteenth century, competition with England, where economic

---

[50] J. M. Oliva, *El Monopolio de Indias en el siglo XVII y la economía andaluza. La oportunidad que nunca existió* (Huelva: Servicio de Publicaciones de la Universidad de Huelva, 2004).

growth permitted an expansion of fiscal revenues, revealed the international weakness of the Dutch system. The fiscal regime was based on 'the relative importance of progressive taxes relative to regressive taxes' from 1590 to 1913, 'the low degree of taxation on [the] most remunerative sector' (the international merchants), and the predominance of domestic investors in the public debt' (pages 59–62).

Janssens (Chapter 3) explains how the fiscal system of the Habsburg Low Countries mainly revolved around an accord between the ruling classes and local elites, on the one hand, and the sovereigns, on the other. During the Spanish period, this pact explains that warfare in the area was largely paid for by Spain. The agreement between the Habsburgs and the oligarchies maintained itself during the eighteenth century, in spite of the emperor's increasing demands. The balance of power remained evident in the distribution of taxes as well as in their reduced volume and characteristics, among which taxes on consumption stand out, especially burdening the poorest classes. The fiscal burden was far from light also because low *per capita* agrarian productivity drastically reduced the population's resources. The introduction of the French system in nineteenth-century Belgium was apparently obstructed by difficulties in obtaining information. The proportion of taxes derived from wealth grew over the century, but so did that derived from earnings and impositions on consumption. 'Overall the tax system became more regressive between 1840 and 1912' and taxes on personal earnings were not introduced until 1916.

Bonney opens his essay on France (Chapter 4) with an affirmation valid for other states: 'absolutist pretensions had perforce to grant privileges that had the effect, over time, of limiting the exercise of power ... in fiscal matters' (see page 93). Bonney reveals the limits of absolutism, the importance of venality and the role of reforms like those of Sully, and then Law. He considers the second's failure as a sharp break in the process of reform of the fiscal state that, nevertheless, had two positive effects: 'currency stability' between 1726 and 1785 and 'decline, in real terms, of the state's total debt' (page 101). Likewise, Bonney explains the social implications of diverse types of taxes, direct and indirect, and contextualizes them according to the political arguments of the time in order to explain the fiscal reasoning which led to the French Revolution. Political instability, the increase of debt and rising expenses were the principal problems of the nineteenth-century French fiscal state, according to Bonney.

Daunton (Chapter 5) considers how trust was constructed in Great Britain around the fiscal system during the eighteenth and nineteenth centuries. He does so, moreover, in comparative perspective with France. The force of the English system in the eighteenth century resided in parliamentary representation and in the possibilities for control of the fisc by representatives and creditors. The obligation to discuss the annual budget required transparency and administrative efficiency in a system based on income from the land, but in which customs and excise taxes progressively acquired greater weight. Compared to the French case, the other great advantage of the British system was the efficiency of its system of indebtedness due to low interest rates and the common aim of land-owners and traders in avoiding financial default. After the Napoleonic Wars, the great challenge of the British tax state, according to Daunton, was to re-establish confidence. This goal was obtained progressively through a reduction of public spending and, above all, due to the conception of the state 'as a neutral arbitrator between interests', which 'articulated a language of public trust'. Important improvements in the administration and control of taxes and the introduction of an 'income tax' finally provoked a change 'from deep suspicion to widespread acceptance' towards the end of the nineteenth century (see pages 133 and 142).

The German territories, Austria and Russia are the case studies for *Central and Eastern Europe.*

M. North (Chapter 6) analyses the fiscality of medieval German cities, secular ecclesiastical princely territories and imperial finances. His study provides evidence of the progressive crisis of the *domain state* and the emergence of the *tax state* in these areas, largely due to war. The result was the appearance of a system based on negotiation with different social groups and administrative centralization, as well as a growing importance of indirect taxes. North's analysis of Brandenburg–Prussia after 1640 describes reforms that would lead during the eighteenth century to an absolutist fiscal state, which broadened the fiscal base through taxes on the land and indirect taxes on consumption, customs or monopolies. Yet 'the royal domain continued to be a major source of revenue'. Per capita fiscal exactions still remained far from those of England or France. Fiscal unification, debt internationalization and the adoption of income tax would all take place during the nineteenth century.

The fiscal history of Austria, analysed by Pieper (Chapter 7), is not very different. Pieper likewise describes the crisis of the *domain state*, the advance of the fiscality the emperor imposed upon his territories (Austria, Bohemia and Hungary), the interregional (im)balance of income among them, and the social limits to the expansion of central taxation. The problem of fiscal information between centre and periphery in the application of policies that attempted to annul group privileges is especially relevant in this case. Austrian fiscality demonstrated a high degree of flexibility and capacity for expansion between 1750 and 1850, and combined with a certain equilibrium the use of direct taxes (*contributionale*) and indirect taxes on commerce and consumption. An expansion and liberalization of the public debt accompanied the passage from a system of tax farming to one of direct administration in the eighteenth century.

Russia presents a very diverse case. If war was also important, the country's enormous extension and continual growth under the Romanovs is key to understanding the Russian fiscal system, according to Gatrell (Chapter 8). Presided over by highly autonomous regional powers, this system was marked by problems of information and even the army's direct seizure of resources. From the eighteenth century, the advance of the fiscal state is especially evident, alongside the growing importance of indirect taxes on consumption, import duties and protective tariffs, and the expansion of debt underwritten by international bankers as well as, in the nineteenth century, taxes on industrial activity.

South Atlantic Europe and the Mediterranean area is represented by the cases of Portugal, Spain, the Italian republics and principalities, the Papal States and the Ottoman Empire.

Regarding Portugal, Mata (Chapter 9) emphasizes the different phases in the formation of a fiscal state whose debility was still evident at the end of the nineteenth century. The precocious mercantile empire constructed in the fifteenth century provided the king with important resources, but retarded the formation of a system that could involve the kingdom in royal taxation. In the context of a second world system characterized by greater international competition, seventeenth-century wars gave way to the creation of new taxes. A new cycle of Brazilian gold did not prevent this process from continuing, especially after 1750, and culminating in the development of the liberal fiscal state in the nineteenth century. This state would prove very weak, due to an inability to convert its debt (especially its foreign debt) into economic growth, and thereby into growing fiscal returns. The bankruptcy of 1892, the last in a long series, and the great importance of customs tariffs in total state revenues, could be considered proof of the debility of the system compared to other European cases.

Castile (and Spain from *c.* 1714) constitutes a different model (Comín and Yun, Chapter 10). In this case as well, the income derived from empire marked a difference with respect to other European countries until 1700. Yet the need to back up credits provoked by war demanded the development of a fiscal system in the sixteenth century and even attempts to reform it in the seventeenth century. Inserted in an imperial conglomerate, the Castilian composite monarchy found itself obliged to finance the protection costs of the empire, thus creating enormous asymmetries among its different polities. The loss of the Spanish Habsburg's European dominions in the eighteenth century and the formation of a proto-nation-state under Bourbon domination would change the rules of the game. If we consider the capacity to make state income expand, the eighteenth-century Bourbon administration may be considered a success. Nevertheless, expanding revenues cannot conceal the debility of a system unable to confront growing debts at the end of the eighteenth century and resting upon a society of orders with a limited capacity for generating economic growth. The bourgeois liberal revolution would bring reforms in the taxation system and institutional framework but, in a context of insecurity and internal wars, these were not enough to create an efficient fiscal state propitious for economic growth at the rate of countries like France, Prussia (Germany) or Britain during the nineteenth century. Neither declarations of bankruptcy nor recourse to the monetization of debt could be avoided.

Pezzolo (Chapter 11) undertakes the difficult task of analysing the Italian mosaic between the fifteenth and eighteenth centuries. As indicated previously, one of the most interesting aspects of his comparison between republics and principalities concerns the way trust affects the public debt's interest rates. These fiscal systems, already highly developed in the fifteenth century, derived a good share of their income from commerce and artisan production. Nevertheless, passage to a secondary position in the international commerce of the sixteenth and seventeenth centuries explains the growing importance of indirect taxes on consumption and direct taxation. Considering the formation of a nation-state on an international scale, fragmentation and political weakness would be the keys to Italian fiscal history. Pezzolo's figures, nevertheless, demonstrate a clear tendency towards the reduction of interest on the debt, which apparently corroborates a growing 'efficiency of the institutional framework'. If this tendency appears more evident in the case of the republics, it is also clear in the principalities, which demonstrates that one of the most important factors was 'the identification of interests between creditors and ruling elites' (see pages 279–80).

The problem of debt is also very present in Piola Caselli's study of the Papal States (Chapter 12). In this case as well, the identification between the central government of the Vatican and the creditors – with a strong religious component – appears key to the low interest rates during the early modern period. Yet, according to Piola Caselli, it was also due to healthy fiscal management. As in other states in Italy and southern Europe, in the seventeenth century a good share of taxes fell upon consumption, and the practice of tax farming was very common. In the eighteenth century 'customs at the town gates represented the main element of the fiscal structure', though 'Roman consumption was still the backbone of taxation' (see pages 298–9).

More than the fiscal system itself, Pamuk's study (Chapter 13) centres on the political economy and the institutional framework of the Ottoman Empire. In contrast to previous accounts, Pamuk demonstrates the system's great flexibility in the long run, as well as the importance of negotiation and pragmatism in its functioning. The period 1450–1580 would be marked by a process of centralization (that included the emergence of a bureaucracy controlled from Istanbul), military expansion, growing income and monetary stability. The ideology of 'provisioning', which obliged the state to guarantee imports of food to supply the great cities, favoured ambiguous policies toward commerce, thus impeding mercantilist policies. The fiscal regime, based on 'agrarian taxes' and 'tax farming', evolved towards a process of decentralization and the long-term cession of taxes to the elites (the *malikane* system), which was key to a balance of power that would survive until the nineteenth century. The period 1780–1914 was characterized by attempts at fiscal centralization, expansion of the debt (especially the external debt) and 'Western-style' reforms, all in the midst of war and attempts to prevent the Empire's disintegration. The moratorium on the payment of public debt in 1875–76 and the creation of the Ottoman Public Debt Administration in 1881 'to exercise European control over parts of the Ottoman finances' clearly demonstrate the limited effects of the reforms (see page 329).

Asia is represented by China, Japan and Mughal and British India. Although the inclusion of Southeast Asia could have provided a richer perspective on the continent, the editors consider the cases selected sufficient to advance some preliminary considerations.

Deng and Wong analyse the case of China from different perspectives. Beyond the history of fiscality, their analyses focus on the political economy of the Chinese empire.

From a very long-run perspective, Deng shows how the Chinese fiscal system formed as a result of internal wars and external pressures before the common era. During this period '[n]egotiations between rulers and farmers led to the recognition for the first time in Chinese history of private landholding rights including private land ownership' (see page 337). These negotiations ran parallel to the formation of an efficient bureaucracy and the establishment of bases for a direct relationship between the state and farmers that would last two millennia. Such developments, while based on the need to resist nomadic invasions and low fiscal pressure (sustained, moreover, by the Confucian principle of *ren*, or benevolence), would nevertheless lead to very high incomes in comparison with those of neighbours, as well as the state promotion of agricultural development and the common good. The state revenues, proceeding preferably from agricultural taxes (long charged in coin) would be 'permanently frozen' in 1712. Deng nevertheless devotes special attention to the study of two moments (960–1279 and 1840–1911) when military needs shifted a good part of the fiscal burden onto commerce.

Concentrating on a shorter period (1500–1914), Wong (Chapter 15) develops some ideas introduced by Deng. He emphasizes the centrality of the concept of 'good government', very possibly part of the accord between the state and farmers, for understanding the workings of the fiscal state. Wong explains how the Qing maintained the preceding system and perfected the bureaucracy after 1644. The Chinese tax regime remained based on agrarian taxes (with the exception of commerce in salt), but a larger share of them were redirected towards poor or frontier regions or to the central government. This essay also establishes two great differences with Europe: the importance of non-military reasons for the adoption of campaigns of fiscal intensification (irrigation and improvements in the system of granaries) and a crucial difference in the relationship between the bureaucracy and local elites: 'while distinctions similar to "private" and "public" were drawn in some instances, these did not become part of larger negotiations demarcating well-bounded spheres of autonomy and activity for elites' (see page 367). When, 'in the second half of the nineteenth century the state could no longer limit itself to low levels of taxation' the reason, once again, was war, whose effects are analysed in detail (pages 372–7).

According to the picture of Nakabayashi (Chapter 16), Japan appears to have been for centuries a *domain state* with all of its characteristics. The reforms of the 1590s, however, entailed a step towards greater penetration of the fisc in the social fabric as well as a delegation of fiscal functions to the lords by the emperor, ultimate proprietor of the land. The system, based on taxes on the land often paid in kind, reached its limit in the difficulties of increasing agrarian production. As stated, the main changes took place in the nineteenth century and, above all, after the Meiji rebellion. It was also then that the state 'recovered' the seignorial rights to charge taxes, freed the land market by ceding the property to the farmers in exchange for a fee in coin according to its price, and the public debt expanded. Wars before 1914 would provoke the last reforms: some degree of parliamentary control over budgets, the creation of a national bank, entry into the gold standard, and the expansion of the international public debt.

In India the domination of the East India Company in the eighteenth century accelerated the passage to the formation of a fiscal state. As Richards (Chapter 17) suggests, there are notable parallels between the Mughal empire and that of the Company. In both cases, a very expansive monetary economy sustained military fiscal regimes. Also, in both cases, the most important income derived from taxes on the land and there existed a component of negotiation with local princes who retained part of the taxes. Nevertheless, the English period entailed a reduction in the relative weight of taxes derived from the land and an increase of income from commerce and customs. A scheme was created to guarantee military expenses and a greater proportion of funds directed toward the centre of the empire, while investments in economic improvements, patronage, charitable institutions, etc., became negligible. This more centralized system, in which a smaller proportion of expenses were undertaken 'in situ', accompanied in the nineteenth century an increase in the deficit that required an expansion of debt and led to growing demands for information from the British parliament.

Although readers may draw their own conclusions, I will, nevertheless, underline certain ideas.

The essays compiled here demonstrate that the modern fiscal state in which violence is only institutional and used in defence of citizens' rights is not only an archetype generally speaking, but, more importantly, it entails a recent development in history.

For centuries, the state's tax collectors competed frequently among themselves and with private agents acting for states. The 'devolution of functions' studied by Thompson for Castile, and the importance of military entrepreneurs, like Oxentierna or Wallenstein in Central Europe, reveal the weakness of the state's monopoly on fiscal coercion.[51] In France, military officers were delegated by the government to maintain the troops and the *fermier generales* retained high degrees of autonomy in many different senses. Fiscal crises often paved the way for revolutions that were symptoms of weak fiscal regimes. Sales of offices and jurisdictions in many areas of Europe reveal states that had to resort to decentralization to deal with problems derived from war and public expenditures. In many countries, soldiers continued to collect taxes in the eighteenth century and the concept of a centralized budget did not exist until the nineteenth century in the overwhelming majority of

---

[51] Thompson, *War and government.*

nation-states.[52] Nor did most European countries experience a clear separation of public and private spheres until the nineteenth century. Instead we see an enormous degree of private patrimonialization and the enhancement of clientelism in the distribution of public offices and in the management of fiscal resources.[53] Several countries practised default as recently as one hundred years ago.

Even the apparently neutral English state of the eighteenth and nineteenth centuries destroyed property rights in order to redistribute them to the benefit of the more powerful classes through *enclosures,* thus revealing something far from novel: rather than the fruit of justice, economic growth appears as a collateral effect of the struggle of individual interests that shape institutional structures.

Economic historians today, attracted by the English and Dutch models, place the accent on the need for similar systems to induce economic growth. In some ways, it is a lesson derived from recent history. It may be a fair lesson, although we might also ask if the fiscal state and the political economy articulated around it created the conditions for growth or, on the contrary, if growth made it possible to articulate a more efficient fiscal system. The fiscal income of England certainly grew more quickly than that of either Spain or France even before the reform of 1688. We may be facing one of those vicious circles so dear to historians. When viewing history form a global perspective, which broadens the scale of analysis spatially and temporally, nuances become necessary. Some years ago Epstein emphasized the possibilities for growth in medieval Italy, where the political economy was very different from that predicted in D. North's model.[54] This volume ratifies that idea and goes beyond it. Observation of the growing indices of urbanization in Europe or in China before the industrial revolution could lead to the conclusion that the fiscal organization of the state conceived of by North has not been a sine qua non condition for growth.

Since it is the product of an abstraction, D. North's notion of a state which favours economic growth might be considered impeccable. For the historian, however, it appears clear that it has not been indispensable always and everywhere for economic expansion. This fact is important, for it takes us back to the need to nuance the protagonism of political and, above all fiscal, structures in economic growth in all times and societies. This agrees with the current view, according to which the weight

---

[52] See, for example, the different essays by Comín and Yun and Pieper, and Glete in *War and the state.*
[53] Ertman, *Birth of the Leviathan.*
[54] Epstein, *Freedom and growth,* passim.

of the fiscal state in pre-industrial societies could be very reduced, and its capacity to interfere in economic activities very indirect (which does not mean that it was not notable). Nevertheless, the greater or lesser capacity of different fiscal states to mobilize resources in defence of their citizens' property rights became continually more decisive, beginning in the eighteenth century. In this respect the English case, otherwise exceptional, as demonstrated in these studies, may reveal the need for an efficient fiscal state in the historical conjuncture into which the world entered after 1750.

The fragility of nineteenth-century fiscal states is also clear. In spite of this weakness, and although more slowly than England, many of them were capable of rapid growth. The short life of the Schumpeterian fiscal state, barely identifiable in Europe until the end of the nineteenth century, appears equally clear. This impression becomes even greater when Asia enters the analysis and we confirm that the changes undergone in some European countries since the seventeenth century were not incorporated until the period after 1880. A delay, on the other hand, not exclusive to Asia.

The study of the formation of fiscal states paves the way for a critique of the universality of the Schumpeterian stage theory as a tool for historical analysis. Ormrod and Bonney rightly considered it too teleological, and our essays reinforce this critique.[55] For the histories of China and India, the concept of *domain states* is irrelevant and Schumpeter's sequence of stages and transitions are not heuristic. Effective tax systems emerged as responses to very diverse pressures and contexts. From antiquity, different imperial states such as Rome or China had been able to generate tax resources much higher than the personal revenues from the property of their emperors and rulers.

In the long run, the Schumpeterian fiscal state is a prerequisite for democracy and for the making of the 'Weberian' state. But the ways in which the different areas of the world have reached that point are multiple and varied. The Schumpeterian concept of the tax state, taken literally, has explanatory limits. Nevertheless, Schumpeterian perspectives seem useful. They push us to enquire into when and why different fiscal systems penetrated societies and therefore ascertain whether princes' revenues were personal or emerged by way of collective cooperation. Research into the extent to which intermediate social bodies and corporations mediated relations between individuals (taxpayers) and the state helps us understand the political context in which states operated.

---

[55] R. Bonney and D. Ormrod, *The rise of the fiscal state in Europe, c. 1200–1815* (New York: Oxford University Press, 1999).

Schumpeter was right to stress the significance of fiscal sociology that analyses how different forms of negotiation depended on institutional and sociological frameworks. Furthermore, bargaining between different social groups is not understandable without considering the social situations of the agents involved. The same is true for the reproduction of the social order, the privileges of the different social groups or the political institutions that emerged out of the dynamics of fiscal systems. Fiscal sociology also analyses the reproduction of the different fiscal systems and their effects on economic development and, consequently, by loops of interconnections, on the fiscal outcome and performance.[56]

Current fiscal history, which emphasizes ideas of consensus and social order as a basis for fiscal extraction, also shows the need to study what we could call the moral economy on which social consensus is grounded. Again the idea of good government in China, which is close to some early modern European conceptions, is telling (Wong, Chapter 15). The same importance could be given to the idea of *provisioning* in the Ottoman Empire (Pamuk, Chapter 13).[57] Both ideas – along with the negotiations to which they were attached – provided bases for the functioning of whole fiscal systems. For the same reason, the idea of 'distributive justice' appeared prevalent and crucial in Castile. By 'distributive justice' one understood that the king treated people not according to their needs, but according to their status, which obviously gave preference to the privileged orders.[58] Such preference did not mean that there were not mechanisms for balancing wealth or alleviating poverty, although a ruler or fiscal system that neglected privilege would surely face opposition from the elites. Such considerations prove the historicity of what Montesquieu called the 'spirit of the laws' and prevents us from mechanically transposing our own moral principles when trying to explain the formation of consensus and negotiation over taxation.

★★★

---

[56] On the seminal character of the concept of fiscal sociology and the way it can enhance the analysis of the state see, among others, J. Backhaus, 'Fiscal sociology: What for?', *American Journal of Economics and Sociology* 61:1 (2002), 55–77.

[57] The literature on the 'provisioning' system in the Ottoman Empire is becoming very large. See, among others in English, E. Özveren, 'Black Sea and the grain provisioning of Istanbul in the Longue Durée', in B. Marin and C. Virlouvet (eds.), *Nourrir les Cités de Méditerranée: Antiquité – Temps Modernes* (Paris : Maisonneuve et Larose, 2003); O. Yıldırım, 'Bread and empire: the workings of grain provisioning in Istanbul during the eighteenth century', *Economic Research Center, Working Papers in Economics* 01/04 (2002); R. Shechter, 'Market welfare in the early-modern Ottoman economy – a historiographic overview with many questions', *Journal of Economic and Social History of the Orient* 48:2 (2005), 253–76.

[58] On distributive justice, see B. Cárceles Gea, *Fraude y administración fiscal en Castilla: La Comisión de Millones (1632–1658): Poder fiscal y privilegio jurídico-político* (Madrid: Servicio de Estudios del Banco de España, 1994).

The formation of a tax state is thus part of the formation of the state. In this sense, the basis for the tax state as an integral political concept seems to be the nation-state. Likewise, the modern concept of a tax state evokes the idea of a direct relationship between individuals, *citizens* and state. It implies that tax revenues are produced by nations and should be used for their benefit. It evokes the notion of a democratic political system in which states are supposed to protect property rights and to create the conditions for economic growth, external security and internal order.

Yet historically, the formation of fiscal states in Eurasia was a very diverse and complex process. Distinctive features of the fiscal state have appeared in each country at different moments in time and as reactions to heterogeneous stimuli. Among these stimuli, war and trade have had a special importance, though the correlation between them was not predictable or universal. Though war and international trade created the base for the development of the fiscal state, it was only in the nineteenth century that they had any general impact in that sense across Eurasia. In the seventeenth and eighteenth centuries, fiscal systems emerged in Europe that look more effective when compared with those of Asian empires. This disparity created an economic and geopolitical divergence that would only be reduced in the twentieth century. In any case, the differences within these great areas were very large. Overall, what emerges from these studies is that similar features, blended in different proportions, have been present across Eurasia in the long run. In many particular aspects the differences were greater among polities than between Europe and Asia. Only a typological study of the different cases could permit us to go beyond this generalization. That is the task for the future.

Part I

North Atlantic Europe

2   Long-term trends in the fiscal history of the Netherlands, 1515–1913

Wantje Fritschy, Marjolein 't Hart and Edwin Horlings

Introduction

For over four hundred years the Netherlands was one of the wealthiest and most stable regions in the world. According to deVries and Van der Woude, the Dutch Republic was the first modern economy. Already during the Dutch Golden Age (*c.* 1580–1670) the degree of urbanization was unparalleled; markets were relatively free and monetized; and, above all, the Republic had 'a well-ordered government long capable of protecting the security of its citizens, nurturing the economic interests of its merchants and fishermen, establishing vigorous institutions to advance its colonial ambitions, and maintaining domestic tranquillity'.[1] A key feature of the Dutch state was its fiscal system, which was able 'to tap a broad tax base with an almost progressive set of levies' and 'to support a public debt in which the population invested with confidence'.[2]

In the nineteenth century the Netherlands was still among the richest nations. Even in 1820, when the British Industrial Revolution was well under way, per capita income in the Netherlands was still somewhat higher than in Britain. However, from a geopolitical perspective, the Netherlands had become a shadow of its glorious past. The country also failed to follow the example of its immediate neighbours on the path of industrialization. DeVries stated that the Netherlands was not backward but simply obsolete: 'Its population is skilled, but with the wrong skills; its capital stock is large, but unproductive; its economic and legal institutions are stable and highly developed, but irrelevant to modern

---

[1] J. deVries and A. van der Woude, *The first modern economy. Success, failure, and perseverance of the Dutch economy, 1500–1815* (Cambridge University Press, 1997), p. 714; A. Maddison, *Dynamic forces in capitalist development* (Oxford University Press, 1991), p. 30, also attributes the advanced nature of the Dutch economy to the modernity of its institutions.

[2] DeVries and van der Woude, *The first modern economy*, pp. 714–15.

needs.'[3] Apparently, the very features that made the country modern in the Golden Age delayed its transition into the age of nationalism and industrialization.

Thus, Dutch fiscal institutions that once coincided with a buoyant economy in the seventeenth century seemed less efficient in the nineteenth century. Yet how far did the financial system of the state change over time? What was the possible impact of the fiscal system on the economy, and to what degree did the economy foster the state in the long run? This chapter focuses on long-term trends in the level and structure of government finances from *c.* 1515 until 1913. We are particularly interested in continuities in Dutch financial history, to the extent that Republican structures and solutions survived into the nineteenth century, and to the extent that they were efficient.

The efficiency of government can only be examined properly on the basis of a definition. On one level an efficient government is able (i) to raise sufficient funds, (ii) with which to safeguard its territory from foreign incursions and (iii) to perform the functions that secure sustained economic growth, promote social stability, protect property rights, enhance the quality of life, et cetera, (iv) while placing a minimal burden on economy and society. Therefore, our contribution starts with an overview of the interrelations between war and state formation. Second, this chapter examines the efficiency of fiscal institutions in the early modern period. The third part offers a long-term view of the role of public debt. The fourth part will analyse developments in the tax burden, the tax base and the structure of the tax system. The last part analyses the effects of the fiscal system of the Netherlands in the long run. While in many respects the Dutch fiscal state was comparable to other European states, the conclusion will emphasize that the Republic displayed a remarkable 'efficiency', especially in the seventeenth century.

War and state formation in the Netherlands: six periods

For centuries, war (and preparation for war) was the main dynamic driving state formation in Europe.[4] High degrees of differentiation and

---

[3] J. deVries, *Barges and capitalism. Passenger transportation in the Dutch economy (1632–1839)* (Utrecht: HES Publishers, 1981), pp. 215–18.

[4] G. Ardant, 'Financial policy and economic infrastructure of modern states and nations', in C. Tilly (ed.), *The formation of national states in Western Europe* (Princeton University Press, 1975), pp. 164–142; C. Tilly, *Coercion, capital and European states, AD 990–1990* (Cambridge, MA: Blackwell, 1990); T. Ertman, *Birth of the Leviathan. Building states and regimes in medieval and early modern Europe* (Cambridge University Press, 1997).

commercialization, in numerous towns as well as in the countryside, drove state formation in the Netherlands in the direction of the constitutional type of government, with strong representative assemblies. In the fifteenth and sixteenth centuries, when the Low Countries were first added to the heritage of the Dukes of Burgundy and then became part of the Habsburg Empire, the overlords had to grant significant bargaining powers to the regional representative assemblies (the Provincial States) in order to find the necessary funds for warfare.[5] For the Dutch, geopolitical competition became particularly strong in the late sixteenth century with the start of the Dutch revolt against Spain. The independent federation of the northern Netherlands, established in the period 1572–81 with the purpose of mutual support in the war, enhanced the power of the regional assemblies. The provinces became the sovereign constituents, sending delegates to the States General, the meeting of the United Provinces that decided on war and peace and other matters that pertained to the Union. Each province, in turn, was made up from various delegates from the towns and rural quarters.[6]

Thereafter, war remained the major driving force in Dutch state formation. Foreign threats and the desire to influence the international balance of power forced the provinces to continue their cooperation in the Union during the time of the Dutch Republic (1572–1795). The Batavian–French interlude (1795–1813) was determined by revolutionary and Napoleonic Wars. Even though the period c. 1813–1913 was relatively quiet, the War of Belgian Secession (1830s) caused a severe constitutional crisis and a restructuring of government finances.

Throughout the seventeenth century, the United Netherlands still found a place among the great European powers.[7] However, in the eighteenth century the Dutch failed to keep up with the pace of development of some major competing nation-states. In 1795, the republican structure collapsed. In 1798 the first national budget was presented to an elected parliament in the new, centralized northern Netherlands. The semi-absolutist reign of King William I of Orange that was established in 1813–15 was to include the territory of the southern Netherlands up to 1830. In this century, state formation became less dominated by military expenditure, and internal political considerations came to the

---

[5] H. van der Wee, *The Low Countries in the early modern world* (Aldershot: Variorium, 1993), p. 16.

[6] J. I. Israel, *The Dutch Republic. Its rise, greatness, and fall, 1477–1806* (Oxford: Clarendon Press, 1995), pp. 179–95.

[7] Cf. the comparable expenses of several European states: M. Körner, 'Expenditure', in R. Bonney (ed.), *Economic systems and state finance* (Oxford University Press, 1995), p. 400.

fore. A major factor in this process was public expenditure on the urban level, which was financed not only by subsidies from the central state, but after about 1870 increasingly by autonomous urban loans.

The shifts in Dutch types of government may be summarized as follows, each period with a distinctive set of characteristics:

(1) *1515–72*: central foreign rule, direct taxes and urban credit based on excises
(2) *1572–c. 1700*: provincial indirect taxes and credit in a rising federal republic
(3) *c. 1700–95*: provincial direct taxes and credit in a declining federal republic
(4) *1795–1813*: establishment of central fiscal system during a revolutionary period
(5) *1813–48*: semi-absolutist monarchy, ending in a near state bankruptcy
(6) *1848–1913*: constitutional monarchy, new direct taxes, shift to local public finance.

The fiscal institutions of the early modern Netherlands

By tradition, the Burgundian and Habsburg overlords had repartitioned the sums necessary for their wars over the separate regions of the Netherlands. Within each region cities and countryside districts had to be assessed. In tax collection, the towns strived for autonomy. In exchange for immediate financial support in emergencies, individual cities had been granted many of the 'regalia' or domanial rights originally belonging to their overlord. The year 1514 witnessed a step towards greater efficiency with the *Informacie*, a new assessment for the county of Holland, not based on area, but on the relative income and wealth of cities and villages. A significant corollary was that this put an end to the ruthless exploitation of the countryside by a powerful city like Dordrecht.[8]

From the start of his reign (1515) Charles V contested the right of cities to introduce new taxes or to raise rates without his consent. Along with the *Informacie*, these policies strengthened central bureaucratic and

---

[8] Cf. in northern Italy, urban exploitation of the countryside remained much stronger: S. R. Epstein, *Freedom and growth. The rise of states and markets in Europe, 1300–1750* (London: Routledge, 2000), p. 146. As for the economic conditions under the *Informacie* itself, see Jan Luiten van Zanden, 'Taking the measure of the early modern economy: historical national accounts for Holland in 1510/14', *European Review of Economic History* 6 (2002), 131–63.

foreign rule. Yet many of the advantages of the *Informacie* were undone as the assessment ledgers were not renewed during the sixteenth century. Instead, the distributional *quotas* were fixed, new privileges were granted, and within the rapidly changing economy the burden of direct taxes became quite uneven again.

In the following centuries, despite the change to a new (republican) government, many of these deficiencies in the collection of direct taxes persisted. Local authorities remained responsible for the amount they had to pay, and for the actual implementation of the assessment at the local level. Only in 1584, 1632 and 1732 were repartitions renewed in the province of Holland. The fixed proportions prevented automatic tax increases along with population or economic growth. The inequalities grew more burdensome in the eighteenth century, when many localities (other than Amsterdam, Rotterdam and The Hague) experienced massive de-urbanization. Even in 1835 the payable amounts in some cadastral districts were only 5 per cent of the registered value, in others as much as 13 per cent.[9] The first renewal of the registry was realized as late as 1875.

Fixed repartitions also hindered fiscal development at the Union level during the time of the Republic. The distribution of Union expenses occurred in permanent *quotas*, the provinces remaining fiscally autonomous in finding the necessary means. Holland continued to pay about 60 per cent of the total expenditures of the Dutch Republic, even though in the eighteenth century its population and economy relatively declined. The rates of the other provinces remained between 3 and 12 per cent, despite economic and population growth in the inland areas. Moreover, the inland provinces often paid less than they had promised, in particular for the navy. The inefficient distribution of *quotas* was finally abolished when centralized taxes were imposed in 1806.

The bulk of the *quotas* was spent on land warfare. Before the revolt, the protection of commerce by convoy at sea had been organized by the merchants themselves, or by their city governments, which levied duties on their own account. Attempts at the centralization of the navy by Burgundian and Habsburg rulers failed.[10] During the Republic, five separate admiralties were installed; they were made responsible for the collection of the duties. Although the sums fell officially under the responsibility of the States General and the rates were decided upon

---

[9] F. N. Sickenga, *Geschiedenis der Nederlandsche belastingen sedert het jaar 1810* (Utrecht, 1883) Vol. I, p. 36.
[10] L. Sicking, 'Hollands voorsprong ter zee', *Holland* 31(1999), 244–51, at 245.

centrally, evasions and frauds were difficult to control.[11] As the customs revenues were supposed to be employed directly for the upkeep of the local navy establishment, the members of the Admiralty Boards were able to divert a lot of the funds to their own profit. Moreover, Dutch customs rates hardly increased at all over the centuries, whereas the British government managed to increase these duties (under more strict central control) considerably, in particular during the eighteenth century.[12]

The necessary additional sums for the Dutch navy had to be provided by the provincial *quotas* too. Yet the funds promised by the inland provinces often came in late and incomplete. A consequence was that the finances of the navy languished.[13] Nevertheless, between 1775 and 1790 the Dutch navy was reinforced, this time supported by the inland provinces too. By then, their local textile industries had become dependent on the safety of transatlantic cotton imports. The number of ships in the line was increased from twenty-six to forty-eight. Yet in competition with the British navy this was no longer sufficient.

As for loans and debt service, the institutions of the Netherlands were quite efficient. All provinces used loans to partially finance war efforts. The strongest public credit was found in the province of Holland. There, the tradition of a safe public debt stemmed from the early sixteenth century. In 1515 five of the six major cities in Holland agreed to unite to find buyers for a capital sum of 22,400 Dutch pounds with interest and capital to be paid out of future terms of the *aide* (or the *ordinaris bede*, a levy based on property taxes). This institutional novelty was the first step on the road to Holland's provincial credit.[14] An important characteristic of this loan was that it was raised in the form of heritable annuities at the low interest rate of 6.25 per cent instead of the high rate on life annuities of 16.67 per cent.[15]

The next important step in fiscal development has been labelled by James Tracy as a 'financial revolution', in line with the term used for British progress in the 1690s.[16] In the 1540s, the States of Holland were

---

[11] J. deVries, *De economische achteruitgang der republiek in de achttiende eeuw* (Leiden: H. E. Stenfert Kroese, 1968), p. 20; J. Hovy, *Het voorstel van 1751 tot instelling van een beperkt vrijhavenstelsel in de Republiek* (Groningen: Wolters, 1966), pp. 96–118.

[12] J. Brewer, *The sinews of power. War, money and the English state* (London: Unwin Hyman, 1989), p. 211.

[13] J. R. Bruijn, *The Dutch navy of the seventeenth and eighteenth centuries* (Columbia: University of South Carolina Press, 1993), p. 155.

[14] J. D. Tracy, *A financial revolution in the Habsburg Netherlands* (Berkeley: University of California Press, 1985) pp. 58, 73.

[15] At that time, Spain was blessed with quite low interest rates too: around 5–7%; see Comín and Yun-Casallila, chapter 10 in this volume.

[16] Tracy, *A financial revolution*, p. 3.

persuaded not only to sell annuities on the credit of the six great cities together, for the war of Charles V against France, but also to levy collective excises to secure the debt service on these loans, instead of funding them through the receipt of the *aides*. No exemptions were allowed to clergy or nobility. The emperor had to make the concession that the excise revenue would proceed to the coffers of the provincial receiver, and that the debt service would be administrated by the province itself.

These new institutional arrangements implied an important reinforcement of the provincial level of the fiscal state, which led to the emergence of a free market of provincial annuities. However, the outbreak of the 1572 revolt caused a severe crisis in the provincial credit system, lasting up to the 1590s. Although urban credit regained strength in the 1580s, provincial loans remained virtually impossible for three decades.[17] In the early seventeenth century, loan financing was still a shaky option for the government. Only after 1621 did public debt become prominent again in Dutch fiscal institutions.

However, the revolt did spur the development of the excise system. Up to 1572, provincial excises had existed only in the towns. Rural localities had to pay their part by way of a land tax. In the 1570s truly 'provincial' means were introduced in the form of excises as well as direct taxes on cattle, sown lands, servants, etc. The sheer number of the different excises, and their high rates, became the cornerstone of the seventeenth century Republic.[18] Total revenues of the excises soon became more than four times that of the tax on land and houses (real-estate tax). The collection of most of these 'common means' was farmed out. Tax farming was not necessarily 'inefficient' in the early modern setting and it ensured the provision of tax funds at specified times, whereas the collection of funds by state employees could be subject to severe arrears. The auctions of farms in each town were supervised by representatives of the other towns in order to avoid local arrangements. Moreover, in contrast to France, the farms in the Netherlands were relatively small and restricted to terms of six months or one or two years, which prevented the formation of powerful monopolies.[19]

---

[17] J. Tracy, 'Keeping the wheels of war turning. Revenues of the province of Holland, 1572–1619', in G. Darby (ed.), *The origins and development of the Dutch revolt* (London: Routledge, 2001), p. 144; M. van der Burg and M. 't Hart, '*Renteniers* and the recovery of Amsterdam's credit (1578–1605)', in K. Davids, M. Boone and P. Janssens (eds.), *Urban public debts, urban governments and the market for annuities in Western Europe, 14th–18th centuries* (Turnhout: Brepols, 2003).

[18] W. Fritschy, 'A "financial revolution" reconsidered: public finance in Holland during the Dutch Revolt, 1568–1648', *Economic History Review* 56 (2003), 57–89.

[19] M. 't Hart, *The making of a bourgeois state. War, politics and finance during the Dutch Revolt* (Manchester University Press, 1993), p. 193.

Tax farmers were subject to occasional popular discontent, as in most other countries. In combination with widespread political unrest, tax revolts in 1748 eventually resulted in the abolishment of most tax farms in Holland. From then on, almost all taxes were collected. Costs remained relatively low: they remained at 9 per cent, much lower than the rate of 17 per cent introduced after the centralization of the provincial tax systems in the United Kingdom of the Netherlands in the nineteenth century.[20]

The raising of loans was also decentralized in the province of Holland. The necessary sums were divided across the receivers of Holland's sixteen (later eighteen) tax districts, which paid interest out of their share of the provincial means. For their mediation, they received a brokerage sum (first 1 per cent, later 0.33 per cent). This method proved to be an efficient solution for raising funds: the tax receiver was always a man of substantial means and was trusted by the local financial elite. Furthermore, receivers in Holland and the Union acted as back institutions in the credit system.

In the army, payments to the companies were mediated by groups of middlemen: the *solliciteurs-militair*. As the *quotas* promised by the provinces often came in too late, the *solliciteurs-militair* took care of prompt payments to the soldiers. At the beginning of the seventeenth century, these semi-public army bankers were able to charge high interest rates for their services (even as high as 12 per cent in the pressing war situation of the 1620s). However, the States of Holland managed to obtain better control by restricting these interest rates to a maximum of 7 per cent in 1676, which was further reduced to 5.2 per cent in 1681. At the end of the eighteenth century these levels were not allowed to exceed 3.48 per cent.[21] Although this kind of mediation implied additional costs, an enormous advantage was that the *solliciteurs-militair* prevented the outbreak of mutinies, which were quite devastating in many other European states of the time.

The burden of debt

Since 1515, public borrowing had been a structural element in the public finances of the Dutch Republic, which was interrupted only in the last decades of the sixteenth century. Throughout the seventeenth century,

[20] J. Fritschy, *De patriotten en de financiën van de Bataafse Republiek. Hollands krediet en de smalle marges voor een nieuw beleid* (The Hague: Stichting Hollandse Historische Reeks, 1988), p. 151.
[21] H. L. Zwitzer, *De militie van den staat. Het leger van de Republiek der Verenigde Nederlanden* (Amsterdam: Van Soeren & Co, 1991), pp. 91–8.

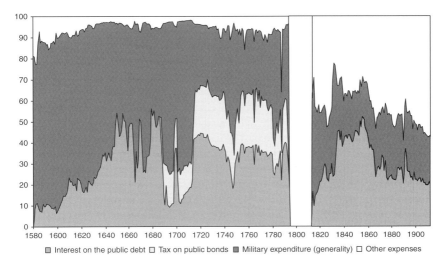

Figure 2.1 The composition of public expenditure in Holland
(1581–1792) and the Netherlands (1814–1913) (%)
Note: The tax on interest payments concerns expenses that would
have been made if there had not been a special levy on the value
of public bonds, by which interest payments were reduced. It was
included to show the effect of this particular tax.

the interest burden constituted about one-third of the budget, as seen
in Figure 2.1. After the War of the Spanish Succession (1702–13), however, interest payments required on average about two-thirds of public expenditure, whereas war expenditure came to comprise about
one-third.[22] By 1795 the entire Republic – including the West India
Company, the East India Company, and the admiralties – was indebted
to the extent of 766 million guilders. In 1807 the total debt stood at
about 2.5 times the Dutch Gross National Product.[23]

How had Holland been able to sustain the increase in its debt? The
most obvious answer was the introduction of new excises to increase
the tax yield. Yet limits were reached after the expansion of the tax base
came to a halt after 1675. A traditional, but insufficient, alternative to

[22] Cf. the debt burden in the papal state, where debt charges amounted to 50–60% of
the expenses too, although this amount tended to decline during the eighteenth century; see Fausto Piola Caselli, chapter 12 in this volume.
[23] T. Pfeil, *'Tot redding van het vaderland'. Het primaat van de Nederlandse overheidsfinanciën in de Bataafs-Franse Tijd 1795–1810* (Amsterdam: Van Soeren & Co., 1998),
p. 351.

borrowing was the personal assessment lists (*personele quohieren*) that registered all movable and immovable possessions of those with more than the minimum amount of property. However, in the final quarter of the seventeenth century, personal assessments were gradually abandoned in favour of taxes on real estate and on the value of stocks and bonds, which effectively lowered the rate of interest by 25 to 75 per cent.[24] Alongside heavy cuts in military expenditure, these measures allowed Holland to cope with a rising interest burden. Other provinces chose the much simpler solution of a voluntary conversion of the interest from 4 to 3 per cent, as soon as the capital market allowed it.

During most of the seventeenth and eighteenth centuries, the steady accumulation of debt was counterbalanced by a decrease in interest rates. In the early years of the Republic the scarce supply of capital and the uncertain future of the new federation had raised interest rates to 12 per cent. By 1640 it had fallen to 5 per cent, which can be attributed to the increased demand for investment opportunities. During the eighteenth century the return (after taxation) on government bonds in peacetime was 2.5 per cent in Holland, and 3 per cent in the other provinces (still much lower than in most other European countries at that time).[25]

After 1754 a vigorous redemption policy was pursued. For instance, in Holland the debt was reduced from about 360 million guilders in 1753 to about 320 million in 1780. Still, interest payments continued to comprise roughly 40–50 per cent of the total expenditure in Holland.[26] On the level of the Union, where debts were also contracted, severe financial difficulties arose after the War of the Spanish Succession. Even a temporary stop on interest payments was necessary. Thereafter, an interest reduction from 4 to 3 per cent was imposed, and the long-term debt of the Union was reduced from about 59 million in 1746 to about 18 million in 1796.[27]

[24] L. van der Ent, W. Fritschy, E. Horlings and R. Liesker, 'Public finance in the United Provinces of the Netherlands in the seventeenth and eighteenth centuries', in M. Ormrod, M. Bonney and R. Bonney (eds.), *Crises, revolutions and self-sustained growth. Essays in European fiscal history, 1130–1830* (Stamford: Shaun Tyas, 1999), pp. 249–93, at 266. The database used for this publication has been largely expanded after the completion of the text of this chapter and has been made electronically available and partly translated: see www.inghist.nl/Onderzoek/Projecten/GewestelijkeFinancien/Verzamelposten/translations.

[25] Ibid., pp. 264–70.

[26] E. H. M. Dormans, *Het tekort. Staatsschuld in de tijd der Republiek* (Amsterdam: NEHA, 1991), p. 101; Van der Ent *et al.*, 'Public finance', p. 268: Overijssel from *c.* 50% around 1720 to less than 20% by the end of the century; Groningen from 30% around 1720 to just over 10% by the end of the century.

[27] Dormans, *Het tekort*, pp. 156, 165.

When the Dutch Republic was turned into a unified (nation) state, all public debts were merged into one single national debt. In order to service the outstanding 766 million guilders, the tax system had to be reformed. In 1806 the Patriot regime introduced a single national system of taxation, devised by one of its leading financial experts, I. J. A. Gogel. The reform basically extended the tax system of Holland to the rest of the country, which resulted in a substantial increase in revenues. However, the gains of increased financial efficiency were cancelled out by high defence expenditure and the 'reparations' demanded by the French. As a result expenditure glaringly exceeded revenue by an enormous margin.[28] As capital grew scarce, interest rates shot up. Forced loans were needed to finance the deficit. After the Netherlands were incorporated into the French Empire in 1810, Napoleon simply decided to cease interest payments on two-thirds of the debt, the so-called *tiërcering*.

William I of Orange, the new king of the independent Netherlands in 1813, prioritized the restoration of a good relationship with the capital market. Already in 1814, a law had been pushed through parliament that provided for the gradual reduction of the French *tiërcering* in order to win over investors in new state bonds.[29] Despite the obvious reluctance of parliament, William I could not do without loans for his aspirations to modernize the economy of the Netherlands, which involved large infrastructural investments and industrial subsidies. In this century, the amounts spent on war (and on the service of war-related debts) decreased proportionally, as the emphasis in public expenditure shifted in the direction of more 'societal' functions (see Figure 2.1). This was in line with developments in most other European states.[30]

The dependency on loans in the first decades of the nineteenth century was not particular to the Dutch fiscal state. In Britain and France, loans rather than taxes were the decisive factor in public revenue.[31] For

---

[28] In 1798–1810 average expenditure was 102% higher than average revenue. See Tom Pfeil, 'Het Nederlands bezuinigingsbeleid in de Bataafs-Franse tijd (1795–1810): illusie en werkelijkheid', in W. Fritschy, J. K. T. Postma and J. Roelevink (eds.), *Doel en middel. Aspecten van financieel overheidsbeleid in de Nederlanden van de zestiende eeuw tot heden* (Amsterdam: NEHA, 1995), pp. 133–50.

[29] W. Fritschy, 'Staatsvorming en financieel beleid onder Willem I', in C. A. Tamse and E. Witte (eds.), *Staats- en Natievorming in Willem I's Koninkrijk (1815–1830)* (Brussels: Vubpress, 1992), pp. 215–37, at 220.

[30] P. Flora *et al.*, *State, economy, and society in Western Europe 1815–1975: the growth of mass democracies and welfare states* (Frankfurt: Campus Verlag, 1983), Vol. I, pp. 355ff.

[31] D. E. Schremmer, 'Taxation and public finance: Britain, France and Germany', in P. Mathias and S. Pollard (eds.), *Cambridge economic history of Europe, Volume VIII,*

almost all Western European states the relationship of government to the bourse was at least as important as its relationship with parliament. Ministers of finance had to be bourse specialists. In the Netherlands, however, these loans reached extreme proportions. Whereas occasionally France and Britain experienced a budget surplus, caused by economic growth, the Netherlands suffered from continuous deficits as government was unable to tap the sources of wealth efficiently, due to tensions between north and south (see below). Parliament grew more and more discontented with the absolutist financial strategies of the king, on which it could exert hardly any influence. Budgets were voted for ten-year periods and loans were raised continually without parliamentary consent. The War of Belgian Secession in the 1830s finally sealed the fate of the economic and political ambitions of William I, and in 1840 he abdicated. From the new budget, it appeared that 88 per cent of tax revenues would be spent on interest payments, which pointed towards state bankruptcy.[32] The reorganization of debt was begun in 1844/45 by the minister of finance, Van Hall, who brought about a long-term decline in the interest burden again. The share of interest payments dropped from a level of about 6 per cent of GDP in 1844 to below 2 per cent after 1870.[33]

By then, the Netherlands had become quite hesitant to service debts centrally, due to the fiscal crisis of the 1830s and 1840s, and hence a shift occurred towards local budgets. Local public expenditure as a percentage of total public expenditure increased from about 25–30 per cent in 1870 to about 45–50 per cent in 1913. A socialist-inspired welfare state ideology (which had been gaining ground since the 1890s) enhanced the local expenses. Similar shifts from 'central' to 'local' were noticed in Britain and Germany.[34] Much of the additional expenditure on infrastructure, education, poor relief, hygiene, health care and others, was financed by way of urban loans. Whereas the national debt remained level during the period 1900–14 (1,100 million guilders), the debt of the local authorities doubled from 256 million to 521 million.[35]

the industrial economies: the development of economic and social policies (Cambridge University Press, 1989), p. 318.

[32] W. Fritschy and R. van der Voort, 'From fragmentation to unification: public finance, 1700–1914', in M. 't Hart, J. Jonker and J. L. van Zanden (eds.), *A financial history of the Netherlands* (Cambridge University Press, 1997), pp. 64–94, at 77.

[33] J. P. Smits, E. Horlings and J. L. van Zanden, *Dutch GNP and its components 1800–1913* (Groningen: Groningen Growth and Development Centre, 2000).

[34] R. H. van der Voort, *Overheidsbeleid en overheidsfinanciën in Nederland 1850–1913* (Amsterdam: NEHA, 1994), p. 184, graph 6.2.

[35] Centraal Bureau Voor de Statistiek, *Zeventig Jaren Statistiek in Tijdreeksen* (The Hague: Staatsuitgeverij, 1970), pp. 128–30, table R.

Table 2.1. *Population growth in Britain and the Netherlands,*
1500–1913 (%)

	Britain	Netherlands
1500–1550		0.6
1550–1600	0.6	0.4
1600–1650	0.5	0.4
1650–1700	−0.1	0.0
1700–1750	0.3	0.0
1750–1800	0.8	0.2
1800–1850	1.4	0.8
1850–1913	1.2	1.1
Size (1700)	5 million	1.9 million

Sources: E. A.Wrigley and R. S. Schofield, *The population history of England, 1541–1871:*
a reconstruction (London: Edward Arnold for the Cambridge Group for the History of
Population and Social Structure, 1981); H. Nusteling, 'Periods and caesurae in the
demographic and economic history of the Netherlands, 1600–1900', *Economic and social*
history of the Netherlands 1 (1989), 87–117.

Tax burden, tax base and tax structure

Unsurprisingly, debt had to be financed by way of taxation. The fiscal
potential of an economy always depends on three factors, namely the
number of inhabitants, their average annual income (which also serves
as a proxy for consumption and property or wealth), and the development of population and incomes through time. In the seventeenth
century, the possible 'deficiencies' in the Dutch fiscal system were offset by the astounding wealth of its small population. In the eighteenth
century, though, increasing fiscal efficiency could not undo the effects
of the small size of its population (see Table 2.1).

Table 2.1 offers a comparison of population size and population
growth in the Netherlands and Britain. After 1815, the unification of the
northern and southern Netherlands seemed a solution to a stagnating
economy. Not only did it double the population size, but the new kingdom also combined the wealthy agro-commercial economy of the north
with the newly industrializing south, and with the reinstituted East
Indian colonies. However, apart from the religious tensions between
the Protestant north and the Catholic south of the new kingdom, the
fiscal integration of both parts became a source of discontent, as an
important share of the huge increase of the tax burden in the south had
to be used for interest payments to debt holders in the north. Figure 2.2

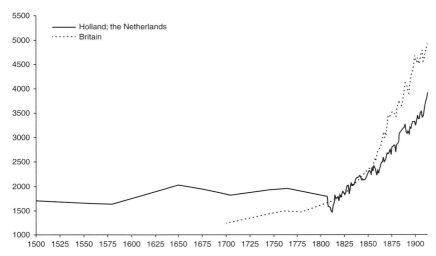

Figure 2.2 Real per capita gross domestic product in Holland
(1500–1800), the Netherlands (1800–1913) and Britain (1700–1913)
at constant prices (1990 dollars)
Sources: J. P. Smits, E. Horlings and J. L. van Zanden, *Dutch GNP
and its components 1800–1913* (Groningen: Groningen Growth and
Development Centre, 2000), pp. 228–30; J. L. van Zanden, 'The
Dutch economy in the very long run', in E. Szirmai *et al.* (eds.)
Explaining economic growth (Amsterdam: NorthHolland, 1993), pp.
267–83; J. L. van Zanden, 'Economic growth in the Golden Age.
The development of the economy of Holland', *Economic and Social
History of the Netherlands* 4 (1993), 270; A. Maddison, *Monitoring
the world economy, 1820–1992* (Paris: OECD Publications and
Information Centre, 1995).

offers a comparison of the size and the development of incomes in both
countries. Until about 1800 per capita income in Holland fluctuated
around a fairly stable level. The development of Holland corresponds
with the general pattern of early modern European growth, which was
characterized by long-term stagnation. The Golden Age (*c.* 1580–1670)
was the only period of observable growth and even then the economy
grew at a mere 0.3 per cent per year.[36] Only after 1800 did the Dutch
economy achieve a sustained increase in per capita income.

[36] L. Noordegraaf and J. L. van Zanden, 'Early modern economic growth and the
standard of living. Did labour benefit from Holland's Golden Age', in K. Davids
and J. Lucassen (eds.), *A miracle mirrored: the Dutch Republic in European perspective*
(Cambridge University Press, 1995), p. 76.

Britain seems to have achieved sustained growth by the eighteenth century. After 1750 its demographic and economic experience fits in with Kuznets's definition of modern economic growth: a sustained increase in per capita income combined with considerable population growth.[37] In short, whereas the Dutch tax base did not increase at all until 1800, Britain realized an explosive increase in its fiscal potential after 1700. The ability of the Dutch Republic to compete in the international arena was consequently gradually undermined in the eighteenth century.

Despite the break around 1810 (see Figure 2.2), there was more continuity in the economic development of the Netherlands than the data suggest. Although the economy grew at unprecedented rates, the fundamentals of growth did not immediately change. The increase in per capita GDP between 1815 and 1850 was based mainly on a revival of policies and industries from the Old Regime within the context of the centralized state of the United Kingdom of the Netherlands. In addition, higher average incomes did not translate into greater well-being for the entire population. The period was characterized by an increase in income inequality, de-urbanization, wage rigidity and high mortality. It was not until after 1850 that there began a process of modern economic growth, based on structural productivity growth, an increase in consumer demand, and general improvements in the standard of living. Then, also, market integration increased, as provincial boundaries disappeared and new railways were constructed.[38]

Looking, then, at the aggregate tax burden over time, Tables 2.2 and 2.3 present estimates relative to the population and national income of the northern Netherlands. They show a surprising continuity from the early eighteenth until the late nineteenth century. With the exception of 1820, when part of the burden was borne by the southern Netherlands, real revenues remained virtually constant at about 24 guilders per capita. Only after 1870 did per capita revenues increase rapidly.

A more detailed analysis for the Republic reveals considerable differences among the provinces. Whereas Holland experienced a 40 per

---

[37] S. W. Kuznets, *Modern economic growth. Rate, structure and spread* (New Haven: Yale University Press, 1966).

[38] H. Knippenberg and B. de Pater, *De eenwording van Nederland. Schaalvergroting en integratie sinds 1800* (Nijmegen: Sun, 1988), p. 48; J. P. Smits, *Economische groei en structuurveranderingen in de Nederlandse dienstensector, 1850–1913. De bijdrage van handel en transport aan het proces van 'moderne economische groei'* (Amsterdam: Vrije Universiteit, 1995), pp. 183–94.

Table 2.2. *Nominal and real tax revenues per capita in the Dutch Republic and the Kingdom of the Netherlands in comparison with the development of real wages and real per capita gross domestic product, 1670s–1913 (real tax revenues at prices of 1800 using a consumer price index)*

	Real wage	Real p.c. GDP	Netherlands		Holland		Overijssel		Drenthe	
	1820=100	1820=100	Nominal	Real	Nominal	Real	Nominal	Real	Nominal	Real
			ƒ	1800ƒ	ƒ	1800ƒ	ƒ	1800ƒ	ƒ	1800ƒ
1670s	126	107			19.4	28.7	10.3	14.9	7.5	11.3
1716	124	102	16.3	23.7						
1740s	127	106	18.6	24.3	26.0	38.7	8.1	12.1	5.5	9.4
1790s	102	101	16.3	18.6	30.8	40.0	6.6	6.5	5.5	5.5
1820	100	100	18.3	24.3						
1850	121	129		24.5						
1870	127	149	20.8							
1913	228	221	32.2	38.2						

Notes: Overijssel: 1672, 1740/45 and 1795; Drenthe: 1672, 1740/45 and 1795; Holland: 1672, 1754 and 1795; Holland in 1672/75, 1740/45 and 1788/92; real per capita GDP: until the 1790s Holland in 1672/75, 1716, 1740/45 and 1795; 1820–1913 the Netherlands; the data for 1820 refer only to the northern Netherlands; SOURCES: J. deVries and A. van der Woude, *The first modern economy. Success, failure, and perseverance of the Dutch economy, 1500–1815* (Cambridge University Press, 1997), pp. 54–5, 97; J. P. Smits, E. Horlings and J. L. van Zanden, *Dutch GNP and its components 1800–1913* (Groningen: Groningen Growth and Development Centre, 2000), pp. 228–30; J. L. van Zanden, 'The Dutch economy in the very long run', in E. Szirmai *et al.* (eds.), *Explaining economic growth* (Amsterdam: NorthHolland, 1993); J. L. van Zanden, 'Economic growth in the Golden Age. The development of the economy of Holland', *Economic and social history of the Netherlands* 4 (1993), p. 270; van Zanden, 'The prices'.

Table 2.3. *Aggregate burden of state taxation in Holland and the Netherlands, 1575–1913 (total tax revenues as a percentage of regional and national GDP at current prices; average of five years around each benchmark year)*

	1575	1600	1650	1700	1750	1790	1820	1850	1870	1913
Holland	1.9	5.2	5.4	9.7	13.5	12.3	9.5[a]	11.5[b]		
Overijssel					(9.3)[c]		6.4[a]	9.4[b]		
Drenthe					(9.6)[c]		5.1[a]	9.1[b]		
Netherlands							8.2	9.8	8.0	8.5

Notes: [a] 1827; [b] 1849; [c] calculated by combining data on total tax revenues in 1742, the population size in 1742 (Drenthe) and 1748 (Overijssel), average per capita income in the inland provinces in 1742, and the level of per capita income relative to the other inland provinces in 1820. Since the income estimates of 1742 were based on tax data, they were probably underestimated, which means that the tax burden is overstated; the data for 1820 refer only to the northern Netherlands; SOURCES: see Table 2.1; J. deVries and A. van der Woude, *The first modern economy. Success, failure, and perseverance of the Dutch economy, 1500–1815* (Cambridge University Press, 1997), p. 702.

cent increase in real per capita taxes between the 1670s and 1790s, the per capita revenue in two other inland provinces (Drenthe and Overijssel) was more than halved. This was the result of the fixed *quotas* system. The eighteenth century was a period of stagnation in Holland, whereas the economic circumstances in the agricultural inland economies improved due to a rise in agrarian prices. Still, even the sums paid by the inhabitants of an inland province such as Overijssel should not be underestimated. Around 1700, they paid twice the per capita amount that was paid in Britain.[39]

The estimates in Table 2.3 show that the increase in per capita revenues in Holland corresponded to a rise in the tax burden relative to total provincial GDP. The share of taxes on income almost tripled in the final quarter of the sixteenth century, it almost doubled between 1650 and 1700, and then rose to an unprecedented 13.5 per cent around 1750. Remarkably, the level of Holland's taxation was higher in the eighteenth century than in the nineteenth century. The figures for Overijssel and Drenthe suggest a similar drop between 1750 and 1820. Thereafter, the provincial tax burden seems to have converged to some extent: the

[39] W. Fritschy, 'Taxation in Britain, France and the Netherlands in the eighteenth century', *Economic and Social History in the Netherlands* 2 (1990), 57–79, at 64.

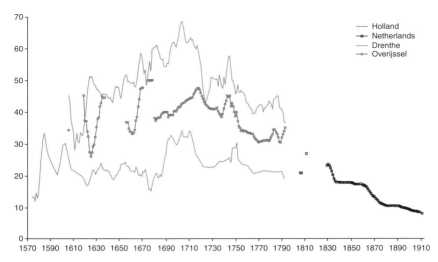

Figure 2.3a The share of taxes on real estate in total tax revenues in three provinces of the Republic and in nineteenth-century Netherlands, 1570–1913 (%)

levels of taxation in Drenthe and Overijssel were comparable with the national average.

The impact of taxation on economic development, however, depends more on the nature than on the level of the taxes that were levied. We have classified the taxes of the three provinces of the Republic and of nineteenth-century Netherlands into four categories: (i) real estate, (ii) other direct taxes on property, income and wealth, (iii) transaction duties (including the excises on domestic trade [*waag, rondemaat* and *grove waren*]), and (iv) excises.[40] Figures 2.3a–d make it possible to compare the importance of each type of taxation in Holland, Overijssel, Drenthe and the entire Netherlands as well as to examine continuities and discontinuities in the long-term development of the fiscal structure.

The first observation that can be made with regard to the four figures is that there was a high degree of similarity in annual fluctuations and the general direction of change in the structure of provincial taxes

---

[40] The main obstacle to an accurate comparison is that the common means [*gemene middelen*] contain different types of tax: excises, transaction duties, direct taxes on land and property, and so forth. For Holland we could distinguish the different types from 1650 onwards. For the preceding period (1572–1649) we have applied the average share of each category in 1650–55.

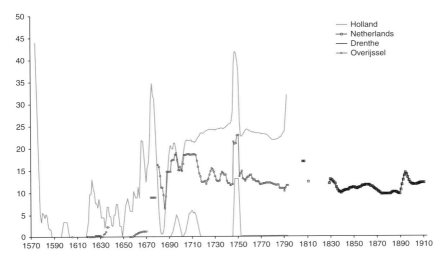

Figure 2.3b The share of taxes on property, income and wealth in total tax revenues in three provinces of the Republic and in nineteenth-century Netherlands, 1570–1913 (%)

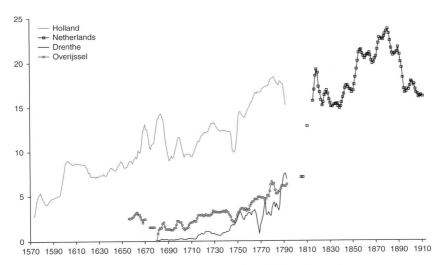

Figure 2.3c The share of transactions duties in total tax revenues in three provinces of the Republic and in nineteenth-century Netherlands, 1570–1913 (%)
Note: Inheritance tax, mortgage rights, stamps and so forth.

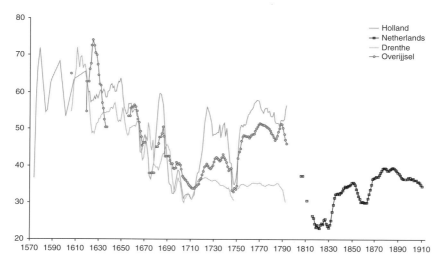

Figure 2.3d The share of excises in total tax revenues in three provinces of the Republic and in nineteenth-century Netherlands, 1570–1913 (%)

between 1570 and 1800. Rural Drenthe and Overijssel relied more on real-estate taxes, whereas Holland – the rich and highly urbanized centre of world trade – had a larger proportion of transaction duties. After 1700 the relative importance of real-estate taxes declined, particularly in the inland provinces, which was compensated for by an increase in the share of excises. In Holland, the lessening role of direct taxes was taken over by transaction duties and taxes on property, income and wealth.

The long-term development of the composition of tax revenues shows a remarkable degree of continuity, in particular between the tax structures of Holland (until 1795) and the Netherlands (starting in 1806, and continuing to 1850 at least). This seems obvious given that the national tax system of 1806 was based on the fiscal system of Holland, which guaranteed the highest possible yield in a period of dire financial need.

Another continuous trend was the low rate of customs. Apart from the early decades of the Revolt, duties on imports were always extremely low, much lower than in neighbouring countries. Whereas Dutch rates stood generally at around 3 per cent, occasionally raised to 5 per cent, Britain and France levied 20 per cent or more on the value of their imports.[41] The nineteenth century showed a continuation of

[41] 't Hart, *The making of a bourgeois state*, pp. 102–3.

this trend. Customs revenues in the Netherlands varied between 3.2 and 3.9 per cent during 1816/1830, between 2.2 and 2.9 per cent in 1831/1855, and fell below 1.7 per cent between 1856 and 1913. By comparison, Belgium's rates were at least twice as high up to 1870 (and were still substantially higher than the Dutch rates thereafter). Between 1821 and 1850, the French imposed duties that were five to seven times higher than the Dutch, whereas the British rates were a staggering ten to fourteen times as high as the Dutch.[42] Only later in the nineteenth century did these rates converge to some degree, although the Dutch rates were always lower than those in Great Britain, Italy, Germany, Spain, Portugal or France.[43]

The effects of fiscal policy

The effect of taxation on the distribution of income and wealth can be deduced from the composition of revenues outlined above. Following deVries and van der Woude the taxes of Holland and the Netherlands were classified as (i) progressive taxes that lowered income inequality, (ii) regressive taxes that raised inequality, and (iii) indeterminate taxes.[44] Most direct taxes and transaction duties were progressive, because they mainly weighed on households with an income above average (e.g. duties on mortgages, inheritance tax, levies on the number of servants, etc.). Excises on luxury commodities (e.g. wine or sugar) were progressive, but most other excises were regressive. For the nineteenth century the licence tax (*patentbelasting*) was classified as a regressive tax because it disproportionately taxed smaller entrepreneurs. A couple of taxes had to remain indeterminate, the most important being customs duties and shipping rights, and the real-estate tax (*verponding*), since it also burdened poor property owners.

Figure 2.4 shows the relative importance of progressive taxes relative to regressive taxes. The indeterminate taxes, of which the distributional effect cannot be specified, were left out of consideration.[45] The data clearly display a long-term trend towards more progressive taxation from *c.* 1590 to 1913. Two discontinuities can be discerned: (i) the second half of the seventeenth century and (ii) the 1850s and 1860s.

---

[42] E. Horlings, *The economic development of the Dutch service sector, 1800–1850. Trade and transport in a premodern economy* (Amsterdam: NEHA, 1995), p. 136.

[43] See also M. E. Mata, chapter 9 in this volume.

[44] DeVries and van der Woude, *The first modern economy*, p. 112.

[45] The indeterminate taxes had a stable share in Holland's revenues of *c.* 23%. The level was higher in the Netherlands immediately after the Napoleonic Wars when they had a share of about 40% (1814–30). After 1830 this share declined rapidly to less than a quarter in 1880 and it stabilized at about 30% in the early twentieth century.

Figure 2.4 The share of progressive taxes in the combined revenue of progressive and regressive taxes in Holland and the Netherlands, 1572–1913 (%)
Source: The definition of progressive and regressive taxes was taken from J. deVries and A. van der Woude, *The first modern economy. Success, failure, and perseverance of the Dutch economy, 1500–1815* (Cambridge University Press, 1997), p. 112. Indeterminate taxes were excluded from the calculations.

In these periods shifts in taxation accelerated the move towards a more progressive fiscal system.

The progressive shift of the seventeenth century was the result of a levelling off of regressive excise revenues after the 1640s and the introduction of new forms of taxation on property, income and wealth in the 1680s. In the period 1600–50 the more progressive 'common means' contributed an average of 7 per cent to total tax income, but between 1650 and 1700 their share increased to 20 per cent.

The second half of the nineteenth century was altogether a special period in Dutch fiscal history. The year 1850 saw sea changes in the development of taxation. The enormous amounts of money made available by colonial exploitation (see below) and the reorganization of the public debt were used to reform the fiscal system. Between 1850 and 1865 the national excises on mutton and pork (1852), grain milling (1855) and fuel (1863) were abolished.[46] The loss of revenue was offset

---

[46] Van der Voort, *Overheidsbeleid*, pp. 110–20, 185; 'De hervorming onzer plaatselijke belastingen', *Economist* (1864), 131–60.

by higher excise rates for luxury articles like sugar, brandy and wine. Municipal finances were restructured as well: after 1865 all local excises were eliminated. The state levied additional percentages on a number of direct taxes (e.g. the personal wealth tax) and transferred their yield in subsidies to the local governments.

The tax reforms of the 1850s and 1860s had a tremendous impact on consumer demand. The share of taxes in consumer expenditure on excised goods fell from c. 9 per cent in 1850 to c. 4.5 per cent in 1860 and less than 2 per cent in 1870. Lower taxes implied lower consumer prices and consequently greater opportunities in the household budget. The development of household expenditure after 1850 reflects the effects of tax reform: (i) the consumption volume of excised goods actually increased by more than the price effect of the excise abolitions, (ii) food consumption shifted from low-grade to high-grade goods (from potatoes and rye bread to wheat bread, from mutton and pork to beef and veal), (iii) and in the long run – after 1865 when the increase in real wages reinforced the demand effects of tax reform – expenditure shifted towards industrial products and services.[47]

As for the effects of the low custom rates, this policy may have been conducive to the development of Amsterdam's staple and financial markets. For Dutch international merchants, the low degree of taxation on this most remunerative sector of the economy actually implied a significant subsidy for their commercial enterprises, the more so as merchants from neighbouring countries had to deal with much higher domestic tax rates. Yet the effect on overall economic development remains to be seen. The British policy of placing a significant burden of taxation on the international sector of the economy probably alleviated the tax burden on home consumption and may have increased the tax base in the long run.

A distributional effect of the continuously high level of Dutch debt may be mentioned here as well. As public debt was not contracted from foreign investors, the part of tax income spent on interest payments was received again by the domestic capital owners.[48] During the eighteenth century, approximately 8 per cent of GDP was paid out in interest on public bonds. Lack of other investment opportunities and the reliability of Dutch bonds rendered Holland's obligations attractive, despite

---

[47] E. Horlings and J. P. Smits, 'Private consumer expenditure in the Netherlands, 1800–1913', *Economic and Social History in the Netherlands* 7 (1995), 15–40.

[48] In the early modern period virtually all bonds were held by numerous Dutch creditors. In this respect, the Dutch Republic resembles Venice, whose debt was likewise held by a large number of domestic investors. Milan, on the other hand, was much more dependent upon a small group of creditors, many of them from outside the state; see L. Pezzolo, chapter 11 in this volume.

an extremely low real interest rate. In the early nineteenth century, debt servicing even accounted for 14 per cent of GDP.[49] Although by 1840 about one-quarter of the bonds were contracted by foreign creditors, and although part of the bonds had been bought by charitable institutions,[50] in the allocation of funds the Dutch budgets tended to increase income inequalities.

The allotment of interest payments was increasingly skewed in a geographical sense during the time of the union with Belgium. The southern provinces contributed almost half of the kingdom's tax revenues, whereas the finances of the kingdom were heavily biased in favour of the northern provinces. The greater part of the public debt was of Dutch origin (*c*. 98 per cent, from which Holland creditors profited enormously), investments in infrastructure were placed mainly in the north, and about three-quarters of the subsidies for trade and transport went to northern entrepreneurs. As a result, between 1816 and 1830 the Belgian provinces contributed an average of 46 per cent to total state income and received only 19 per cent of total expenditure. The Union was thus undermined by sizeable, albeit invisible, transfers of public funds to the north, which amounted to an average of 5.3 percent of Dutch GDP or 3.8 per cent of Belgian GDP.[51] The extension of Dutch taxes to the south confronted Belgians with a 26 per cent rise in per capita taxes between 1817 and 1828; excises were raised by as much as 257 per cent.[52] In the northern provinces total per capita tax payments remained more or less the same, while excises increased by only about one-third.

Inequalities in the fiscal system of the United Netherlands may well have been among the main reasons for Belgium's secession from the Union. The loss of Belgian tax revenues (after the Secession in 1831) had a devastating effect on Dutch state finances. Tax revenues were almost halved, whereas expenditure fell by only 20 per cent. The state had to find alternative and preferably large sources of income.

---

[49] J. L. van Zanden and A. van Riel, *Nederland 1780–1914. Staat, instituties en economische ontwikkeling* (Amsterdam: Balans, 2000), p. 36; deVries and van der Woude, *The first modern economy*, p. 149.

[50] In the seventeenth century approximately one-fifth of the bonds was held by institutional investors (such as orphanages); M. 't Hart, 'Public loans and moneylenders in the seventeenth century Netherlands', *Economic and Social History in the Netherlands* 1 (1989), 129. Figures for the nineteenth century are unfortunately not available.

[51] E. Horlings, 'Miracle cure for an economy in crisis? Colonial exploitation as a source of growth in the Netherlands 1815–1870', in B. Moore and H. van Nierop (eds.), *Colonial empires compared: Britain and the Netherlands, 1750–1850* (Aldershot: Ashgate, 2003).

[52] On the low level of Belgian taxes in the eighteenth century see P. Janssens, chapter 3 in this volume.

Table 2.4. *The share of regular taxes, net transfers of tax revenues from the Southern Netherlands (1816–1830) and colonial remittances (1832–1877) in total state revenues, 1816–1877 (%)*

	1816/ 1822	1823/ 1830	1832/ 1839	1840/ 1849	1850/ 1859	1860/ 1869	1870/ 1877
Regular taxes	61	52	63	60	59	60	76
Belgian transfers	29	39					
Colonial remittances			33	36	37	34	13
Total	*90*	*91*	*96*	*96*	*96*	*94*	*89*

Source: E. Horlings, 'Miracle cure for an economy in crisis? Colonial exploitation as a source of growth in the Netherlands 1815–1870', in B. Moore and H. van Nierop (eds.), *Colonial empires compared: Britain and the Netherlands, 1750–1850* (Aldershot: Ashgate, 2003).

The reintroduction of excises on grain, coal, peat and soap added 5 to 6 million guilders to total revenue. Yet this was insufficient to alleviate financial distress, and (correctly) regarded as economically and socially harmful. The definitive solution was found in the introduction of a system of intensive colonial exploitation in the Dutch East Indies (the *Cultuurstelsel* [Cultivation System] of 1832). Soon after it had been launched, the *Cultuurstelsel* began to produce enormous profits and it provided the government with the income it needed to compensate for the loss of Belgian revenues (Table 2.4).

The enormous yields of the *Cultuurstelsel* (c. 1,250 million guilders between 1832 and 1869) were used to repay the debt, to reform the tax system and to create a national system of railways and waterways.

Conclusion

From 1500 onwards, the Netherlands generally had stable and rational governments. The administrations were generally efficient and displayed a high degree of ingenuity in finding alternative ways to match revenues and expenditures. Defence forces were generally adequate, new forms of taxation were developed along with new financial instruments for public borrowing and, after 1830, the Dutch state did not hesitate to integrate the exploitation of the East Indies into its financial programme. Even though excises placed a considerable burden on consumer demand, Holland's tax policies gradually became more progressive.

Until 1800, the Netherlands did not experience sustained economic growth. Yet the absence of sustained growth was natural to most pre-industrial economies as was witnessed by the experience of other European countries.[53] The apparent inefficiency of federal institutions in the later eighteenth century (cf. the time of the Fourth English Naval War, 1780–84), was actually caused less by the poor performance of its fiscal institutions, or by insufficient expansion of the tax base, than by the increasing economic and military powers of competing nation-states with much larger populations and economies. By comparison, in the seventeenth century it had been the Republic which had been blessed with population growth and expanding economic opportun-ities, whereas many of the competing nations were experiencing eco-nomic crises and were plunged into (civil) wars.

Yet, during some periods the Dutch fiscal system could be labelled inefficient. Of the six periods of its history, the first decades of the Kingdom of the Netherlands (1813–50), when the tax base was roughly double its former size, seem to have been the least efficient of all. In these years, budgets were not balanced, the Belgian population was confronted with unfair financial burdens, tax policies aimed at the restriction of regressive excises failed, the overall effects of the king's absolutist policies on economic growth were doubtful, and upon his abduction he left the Dutch state nearly bankrupt. Thus, despite the centralization and modernization of the Dutch state after 1795, the state functioned in a highly inefficient manner in these decades.

Still, we have charted changes in the level and structure of public finance between the sixteenth and the nineteenth centuries and found a surprising degree of continuity. Clearly there are breaks in the devel-opment of revenues and expenditures, but similarities seem to prevail. The main source of long-term continuity was the debt. Public credit, sustained as it was by an overall reliable tax system, was a prominent feature throughout Dutch history, supported both by the wealth of the tax base and by careful debt management. On the whole, the relation-ship between the state and the capital market was excellent.

In retrospect, a comparison with Britain is most revealing. Both countries stood out, at least in the early modern period, by incorp-orating a 'financial revolution' in their fiscal structures, allowing sig-nificant extensions to the public debt, based on a relatively flexible tax base.[54] Yet the timing of these novelties in institutional spheres was

---

[53] Noordegraaf and van Zanden, 'Early modern economic growth', p. 76.

[54] P. O'Brien, 'Fiscal exceptionalism: Great Britain and its European rivals. From civil war to triumph at Trafalgar and Waterloo', *London School of Economics Working Paper* (2001), p. 17.

Republic of the Seven United Netherlands

Figure 2.5 Republic of the Seven United Netherlands
NB: An electronic database with financial data also for most of the
other provinces has become available, partly in English translation,
after the completion of this chapter; see www.inghist.nl/Onderzoek/
Projecten/GewestelijkeFinancien/Verzamelposten/translations.

Table 2.5. *The growth of state finance in seventeenth-century Holland compared to eighteenth-century Britain*

	Holland 1572–1713	Britain 1688–1815
Increase in real tax revenues	c. 18 times [a]	c. 15 times
Increase in the share of taxes in national income	c. 11 times [b]	c. 5 times
Average amount of war expenditure per year in 1694–97 (£)	4.2 million	4.5 million
Population c. 1700	1.9 million	5.0 million

Notes: [a] Based on average tax revenues in 1572–81 and 1704–13; [b] average tax revenues for 1572–81 and 1704–13 adjusted for population growth and the increase in real wages.

somewhat different. Table 2.5 allows a comparison of a couple of the key features.

Since the establishment of the independent Republic (*c.* 1572), Dutch state formation was characterized by increasing efficiency over some 120 years. Its main competitor, Great Britain, only achieved a similar level of efficiency a century later. In this perspective, the Dutch fiscal achievements of the seventeenth century stand out as quite remarkable indeed.

3   Taxation in the Habsburg Low Countries and Belgium, 1579–1914

Paul Janssens

Political autonomy under Spanish and Austrian imperial rule (seventeenth–eighteenth centuries)

Fiscal autonomy

In 1781, shortly after acceding to the throne, Joseph II visited the Austrian Netherlands and expressed his disappointment with its political regime, which in his opinion was not monarchical, but aristocratic in character. This was a telling characterization of the balance of power between the monarch and ruling elites that had taken shape upon the restoration of Spanish authority at the end of the sixteenth century, but had hardly changed when Maria Theresa died in 1780.[1]

In the historiography, the meetings of estates are represented as counterbalancing the powers of the ruler in traditional monarchies. In many parts of Europe, monarchs were financially dependent on the estates, which approved taxes. Elsewhere – e.g. in some French provinces – the monarchy had succeeded in abolishing their fiscal authority. This may have been Philip II's objective in the Netherlands. Alba's fiscal reforms (1569) certainly point in that direction, but the rebellion thwarted these plans. The archdukes Albrecht and Isabella took a similar step in 1600 when they succeeded in collecting ordinary taxes on an annual basis.

By that time, the royal *aides* ('assistance', or taxation solemnly requested by the monarch) changed in nature. From a tax comprising a changeable sum, requested at irregular intervals, it evolved into a tax with a fixed sum presented to the estates for approval at the same time

---

[1] P. Janssens, 'The Spanish and Austrian Netherlands, 1579–1780', in J. C. H. Blom and E. Lamberts (eds.), *History of the Low Countries*, new edition, (New York & Oxford: Berghahn Books, 2006) pp. 221–73, 497–99. See also P. Janssens (ed.), *La Belgique espagnole et la principauté de Liège, 1585–1715*, 2 vols. (Brussels: La Renaissance du Livre, 2006); H. Hasquin (ed.), *La Belgique autrichienne, 1713–1794: Les Pays-Bas méridionaux sous les Habsbourg d'Autriche* (Brussels: Crédit Communal, 1987); and J. Stengers, *Histoire du sentiment national en Belgique des origines à 1918. Vol. 1 : Les racines de la Belgique jusqu'à la révolution de 1830* (Brussels: Racine, 2000).

every year. The reason for this change was the accumulation of a provincial burden of debt. In order to be able to pay the high and frequent
aides requested in times of war, estates were forced to raise public loans.
Thus the approval of annual *aides* became inevitable in order to pay
off contracted debts. Indeed, the estates themselves were in favour of
permanent taxes in order to safeguard the interests of those who had
subscribed to government loans. By 1600, this evolution was complete
in the Habsburg Netherlands. The archdukes demanded an annual *aide*
of 3.6 million guilders, a sum that far surpassed the amount required
to repay debt. The extra money covered the running costs of the state
and war expenses.

Warfare in the seventeenth century increased the need for money.
This is why, in addition to annual *aides*, estates also granted additional
taxes, but called them *subsides* (grants) in order to emphasize their
exceptional nature. Even in peacetime, the modernization of warfare,
the building of fortifications and the increase in the number of troops
swallowed up more money. By the eighteenth century, the *subsides* also
become a regular feature of tax revenues. In 1725, the provincial estates
accepted for the last time a permanent increase in taxation (for the
maintenance of the Brussels court). After that, the level of ordinary
taxation remained stable while increased prosperity and the expanding
population actually reduced average burdens of taxation. For example,
customs income almost doubled during the Austrian period (without
any notable increase in tariffs). By contrast, *aides* and *subsides* were not
tied to the incomes of taxable households. Year after year, the demand
was for fixed sums paid by the entire population.

In principle, the amount of the *aides* and *subsides* was determined by
the monarch's financial needs. The central government had no solid
information on tax revenues collected by local authorities and provincial estates. During years of rebellion in the sixteenth century, monarchs had to relinquish their hold on the gathering of taxes. In Brabant,
the auditor's office lost all control over the levying of taxes and local tax
revenues were simply passed on from estates' collectors. After 1748, the
Viennese court made attempts at reform to ease the parlous financial
situation of many towns and provinces. But at the end of the eighteenth century, when the financial situation had improved, the government still allowed for annual reductions of 10 per cent on the *aides* and
subsides.

Meanwhile, the central authorities endeavoured to gain information
on provincial and local bookkeeping in order to monitor the financial
management of subsidiary authorities. They appointed government
commissioners to investigate taxable capacity but the unwillingness of

the estates to cooperate meant that during the regime of Maria Theresa, the commissioners made little progress.

The government then planned to impose uniform bookkeeping on all local authorities and set up a special committee in 1764 to oversee *aides* and to draw up overall accounts of local and provincial finances. This was no easy task. There were 557 villages in the Duchy of Brabant alone. In each village there were several separate sets of books, so that more than 2,000 individual Brabant accounts qualified for survey. The total number of authorities in the Austrian Netherlands obliged to render accounts can be estimated at 5,000. The task dragged on for years and only speeded up in 1784, when Joseph II told the officials of the Vienna audit office to complete financial surveys of most provinces of the Austrian Netherlands.

Any refusal to approve the annual *aides* and *subsides* was, however, tantamount to a declaration of conflict. No province could legally refuse 'consent' to pay the ordinary taxes. Thus, the declaration made by the estates of Flanders in 1754 not to accord formal approval to the annual *aides* and *subsides* unless the cities gained extra representation, must be put in perspective. Like all the other provinces of the Austrian Netherlands, the County of Flanders retained its authority to withhold consent to extraordinary taxes. Nevertheless, the refusal to grant the *aides* and *subsides* was not without significance. The imperial government recognized that negotiations with the estates were occasions to satisfy their wishes. Botta Adorno, Maria Theresa's representative in the Austrian Netherlands in the mid eighteenth century, called this *persuader à la flamande* [Flemish-style persuasion], over the delaying tactics applied by the estates of Brabant whenever they were dissatisfied with imperial policy.

Thus, the approval of ordinary or permanent taxation did not provide the estates with a really effective means of exerting pressure on imperial policy. But things were very different in relation to demands for varying amounts of extraordinary taxation requested by the monarch at irregular intervals. These taxes were given the name of *don gratuit* and were levied when *aides* and *subsides* could not cover increasing royal expenditures in times of war. While peace was maintained in the Austrian Netherlands throughout most of the eighteenth century, Austria itself was repeatedly involved in military conflicts in Central Europe. Peaks in extraordinary taxation coincided with wars: against the Bourbons in Italy in 1734–35; the War of the Austrian Succession (1740–48), which led to French occupation of the Netherlands; the Seven Years War (1756–63); and the War of the Bavarian Succession (1778–79) against Prussia. During these years the estates could attach conditions to their approval of extraordinary taxation and the balance of power between the monarch and the estates became largely dependent on geopolitical conditions which prompted emperors to try to control the composition of the estates.[2]

Political representation

During the seventeenth and eighteenth centuries, broad coalitions were formed between the clergy, the aristocracy and urban patricians. They all owned similar assets and drew income from ownership of land, houses and government bonds, while the guildmasters obtained income primarily from moveable investments in their own enterprises. In Brussels and Antwerp, the imperial government could reform the estates because men of wealth turned a blind eye to the disenfranchisement of the guilds and the lower-middle classes.

This aristocratization of the estates offered Spanish and Austrian Habsburgs an attractive alternative to direct confrontation with the ruling elite and worked to exclude two social groups from power: the higher aristocracy and the guilds. The great lords lost their power base in the Councils of State because they demanded a say in foreign policy and defence. They continued to occupy command positions in the army and were sometimes charged with prestigious diplomatic missions. Some even obtained appointments to the court in Madrid or Vienna, but their political role in the central government became a thing of the past. Even their influence as provincial governors was continually whittled away. The guilds really wanted a say in economic policy where their interests too often clashed with other social groups and with the government, who did not wish to pursue economic policies subject to the demands of local lobbies.

The imperial government reached a *modus vivendi* with a broad category of wealthy people of private means. Unlike the great aristocratic dynasties and the guilds, these 'notables' did not make claims to participation in imperial government policy. They were content with the exercise of power in the towns and the countryside, and a crucial foundation for this political consensus was the arrangement over costs of defence. Before 1659, these costs were largely passed on to the American colonies and the taxpayers of Castile, because the Netherlands were

---

[2] P. Janssens, 'De achttiende eeuw. Een lage, maar zware belastingdruk', in P. Janssens, H. Verboven and A. Tiberghien, *Drie eeuwen Belgische belastingen* (Brussels: Fiscale Hogeschool, 1990), pp. 44–8. See also H. Coppens, *De financiën van de centrale regering van de Zuidelijke Nederlanden aan het einde van het Spaanse en onder het Oostenrijks bewind, ca. 1680–1788* (Brussels: Koninklijke Academie, 1992).

an indispensable cornerstone of the imperial policy of the Spanish Habsburgs. During the wars against Louis XIV, the contribution of the Spanish Netherlands went up, but Spain and the empire overseas continued to carry the lion's share. The Spanish Netherlands were able to play on their strategic position as the bulwark against French hegemony in Europe, and passed on a large part of the cost of warfare. Under the Austrian regime defence expenditure decreased in times of peace but shipments of money from the Austrian Netherlands provided major support for the Habsburgs when they were involved in wars in Central Europe. For the Habsburg Netherlands, independence from either the Spanish or Austrian monarchy would undoubtedly have increased involvement in warfare. Meanwhile, they retained their religious identity and a fair measure of self-government that guaranteed lower levels of taxation.[3]

Fiscal revenues: the data

In the specialized literature there is often some confusion concerning the scale of total revenue from taxation in the Austrian Netherlands as well as the sovereign's share. Harsin is one of the few authors to offer a clear statement: 'To summarize, in Flanders or Brabant, provincial and communal taxes exceeded impositions of the central power by two or three times.'[4] To reach this conclusion, Harsin drew on the statistical summary for the year 1782. However, his mistake was to separate the taxes by towns, village communities and estates. He conflates collection with allocation and thus overestimates the fiscal share of the towns and villages.

The statistical summary for the year 1782 was produced during the reign of Joseph II. It was the imperial government's first systematic examination of the total tax on the Austrian Netherlands. To this end all the accounts from villages, towns and estates were amalgamated by the government by province.[5] This laborious task was carried out for all regions, except for Luxembourg, Hainault and Namur. In the case of these three provinces, only the accounts of the estates were collected;

---

[3] Janssens, 'De achttiende eeuw', pp. 48–52.
[4] P. Harsin. 'Les finances publiques belges sous l'Ancien Régime', *Histoire des finances publiques en Belgique* (Brussels: Bruylant, 1950), Vol. I, p. 14.
[5] Y. Coutiez, 'A propos des réformes de Joseph II: le bilan des finances locales pour 1782', *Revue trimestrielle du Crédit Communal de Belgique* 156 (1986), 3–23; and P. Lenders, 'De Junta der Besturen en Beden (1764–1787) en haar werking in de Oostenrijkse Nederlanden', *Bijdragen en mededelingen betreffende de geschiedenis der Nederlanden* 92 (1977), 17–36.

local accounts are missing, meaning that the sovereign's share in total revenues from taxation in the Austrian Netherlands can be calculated with certainty only for seven of the ten principalities. For the remaining three provinces this can, however, be done by extrapolation (using data for 1778). Total tax revenues cannot be calculated accurately from the 1782 figures, but again, it is possible to make a rough estimate based on extrapolation.

I will examine the available data for the year 1778, which as Bigwood rightly points out relate to net income, after deductions for collection charges and the exemptions granted to insolvent municipalities.[6] These data cannot be used to assess total tax revenue, but they can be used to work out the division between the sovereign and the local authorities.

The figures for 1778 show that more than one-third of the fiscal income ended up in the hands of the sovereign. Just over a quarter was used by the local authorities for their own purposes. That leaves just under 40 per cent, which went to redeem and service debt. Loans were often raised by the provincial estates to finance extraordinary royal taxes. The share for the sovereign was thus significantly higher than his direct share might lead us to suppose, and can be estimated as two-thirds of the total tax revenue. Nevertheless, we must observe that the provincial loans to finance extraordinary taxes for the sovereign were undoubtedly more substantial than the local loans. For local expenditures, the precise division remains unknown.

Fortunately, Zelck's research into the estates of Brabant enables us to measure the respective shares of the local authorities, the provincial estates and the sovereign in Brabant taxation.[7] Zelck estimated the expenditures of the estates and compared them to the figures for total revenues from Brabant for 1782. He shows that 36 per cent of the tax revenue was reserved for the sovereign; the estates spent 24.5 per cent discharging debts and paying interest. As provincial loans were basically raised to finance extraordinary royal taxes, the sovereign's share of Brabant taxes came to well over half (60.5 per cent). The remainder is divided into two very unequal parts: 35.7 per cent of the total taxes funded local level administrative expenditures and the repayment

---

[6] G. Bigwood, *Les impôts généraux dans les Pays-Bas autrichiens* (Louvain: Librarie française et internationale, 1900), 'annexe L'. See also P. Moureaux, 'Les finances centrales des Pays-Bas autrichiens', *Finances publiques d'Ancien Régime. Finances publiques contemporaines en Belgique de 1740 à 1860. Processus de mutation. Continuités et ruptures. Colloque international (Spa, 19–22.12.1972). Actes* (Brussels: Crédit Communal de Belgique, 1975), p. 61 (*Pro Civitate*, 39).

[7] F. Zelck, 'De Staten van Brabant op het einde van de achttiende eeuw. Hun invloed op de besluitvorming op sociaal-economisch gebied, 1772–1794', unpublished Master's thesis, Vrije Universiteit Brussel (1986), p. 51.

of debt. The estates were left with only 3.8 per cent for their own expenditures.

The data provide us with a picture of the old fiscal regime. The role of the estates was important, but purely political. No provincial budget of any significance existed. Larger towns, which had substantial tax revenues at their disposal, constituted the only fiscal player other than imperial government.

When the Austrian Netherlands were annexed to France in 1795, the French authorities estimated the total revenue from taxation. They drew on the (incomplete) figures for the year 1782 and aggregated these to 16,671,325 guilders. The missing local income tax for Luxembourg, Hainault and Namur was estimated at approximately 1 million guilders, which took the total for the Austrian Netherlands up to 17.7 million. In addition, the revenue from taxation in the Prince-Bishopric of Liege was assessed at 814,383 guilders, while the *arrondissement* of Maastricht had an ascribed revenue of 275,696 guilders.[8]

However, some qualification is called for here. If we look into the archives of the French administration to see how the tax figure of 16,671,325 guilders was reached, we conclude that this sum does not relate to fiscal income in any narrow sense, but to *all* government revenue from local and provincial authorities. This is apparent even from the title of the summary and it is confirmed by the content of a number of categories which include income from government property, official levies, interest from capital assets, etc.[9]

Bigwood reproduced in detail the fiscal income of most of the provinces.[10] For Hainault, Luxembourg and Namur the figures are to be found in the archives of the French authorities. As we have already mentioned, there is no record of local taxes for these provinces. Consequently, we spread the French estimate of 1 million guilders across these three regions in proportion to their provincial tax revenue (see Table 3.1).

---

[8] R. Darquenne, 'Essai sur le poids de l'impôt en Belgique sous le régime français. Le cas du Hainaut', in *Finances publiques d'Ancien Régime. Finances publiques contemporaines en Belgique de 1740 à 1860. Processus de mutation. Continuités et ruptures (Colloque international, 19–22 Décembre 1972)* (Brussels: Crédit Communal de Belgique, 1975), pp. 259–306; see also E. Pérés de Lagesse and L. F. René Portiez, *Avantages de la réunion à la France de la ci-devant Belgique et pays de Liège et de Maestricht* (Paris, 1796), p. 9; and P. Verhaegen, *La Belgique sous la domination française, 1792–1814* (Brussels: Culture et Civilisation, 1981), Vol. II, p. 484.

[9] 'État général du produit des contributions directes et indirectes, et autres revenus quelconques, des ci-devant provinces Belgiques', Papiers Bouteville, n° 394, Archives générales du Royaume, Brussels.

[10] Bigwood, *Les impôts généraux*, 'annexe C, D, E, F, G, H, I, J'.

Table 3.1. *An estimate of local taxes in Hainault, Luxembourg and Namur for 1782 (in guilders)*

	Provincial taxation*		Local taxes		Total
Hainault	1,042,762 (52.4%)	+	524,000	=	1,566,762
Luxembourg	769,076 (38.6%)	+	386,000	=	1,155,076
Namur	178,798 (9.0%)	+	90,000	=	268,798
	1,990,636 (100 %)	+	1,000,000	=	2,990,636

Note: * 'État général du produit des contributions', Papiers Bouteville, n° 394, Archives générales du Royaume, Brussels.

If we take these critical observations into consideration, then the total taxation in the Austrian Netherlands for the year 1782 can be calculated, after adding customs duty:

Total tax levy *c.* 1782 (in guilders)			
	local and provincial taxes[11]	customs duty	Total
Austrian Netherlands	15,958,617	3,054,000	19,012,617

This total of *c.* 19 million guilders corresponds more or less to a calculation made by the Antwerp city council in 1796. If the customs duty is included in these calculations, the royal share goes up and the local share is thus reduced to less than a quarter of the total taxes levied.

The composition of taxation

It is clear from the statistical survey of its taxation system reflected in Table 3.2 that the Austrian Netherlands maintained an agricultural economy. Industrial activities scarcely figure for taxation purposes (1.2 per cent of the total). The monetization of the economy is apparent from the taxes on trade. Yet the overall share from taxes levied on commercial transactions remained rather small (the import, transit and export duties together can be estimated at one-fifth of the total). The degree of urbanization can be deduced partially from the share of the

---

[11] Ibid.

Table 3.2. *The composition of taxation in the Austrian Netherlands*

INCOME TAXES	
– On income from real estate (land, houses) and money investments:	40.8%
– On wages, salaries and profits:	4.0%
– *Subtotal*:	*44.8%*
CONSUMPTION TAXES	
– Transport (customs duties):	20.3%
– Turnover (excise):	34.8%
– *Subtotal*:	*55.1%*
PROPERTY TAXES	
– Transfer taxes and death duties:	0.1%
– Registration fees:	0.0%
– *Subtotal*:	*0.1%*
TOTAL:	100 %

Source: G. Bigwood, *Les impôts généraux dans les Pays-Bas autrichiens* (Louvain: Librarie française et internationale, 1900), 'annexe C, D, E, F, G, H, I, J' (1782).

excises, which came to over one-third of all of the taxes. But even more striking is the predominance of agrarian products in these taxes on the consumption of beer, bread and meat.

The agrarian character of the fiscal regime is also apparent from the taxes on income from land and buildings, which emanated first and foremost from cultivated land and only to a lesser extent from buildings. The tax system of the Austrian Netherlands affected the agricultural sector twice: both agricultural production and agrarian consumption were taxed. All other productive activities and consumption largely escaped the tax authorities of the Old Regime.

Differences between traditional and modern tax systems cannot be emphasized enough. Apart from the levy of a capitation tax, individual incomes were never directly taxed. Taxes affected either immovables (like land), of which the presumed income was taxed, or consumables (particularly foodstuffs).

Public goods

In discussing government expenditure, most studies restrict themselves to either royal or urban outlays. This distorts our view, because spending on defence at local level is barely visible, while the expenditure by central government gives the reverse impression. Moreover, the debts are usually considered as an independent item of expenditure. Debt servicing represents past expenditures and if we are to arrive at a meaningful conclusion about the provision of public goods, the purposes for which debt was accumulated and serviced need to be exposed.

Royal expenditure in the Austrian Netherlands at the end of the eighteenth century is already sufficiently well documented. This expenditure displays two striking characteristics. First, ordinary expenditure is balanced with the net income from taxation. Second, maintenance of the standing army accounts for most of the expenditure.

These figures are not sufficient to evaluate the *returns* for the taxpayers from government expenditure. That involves taking local and provincial government expenditure into account as well. For this purpose, we borrow our data from the *Etat général du produit des contributions... ainsi que des charges acquittées sur ces mêmes produits* [General state of the product of contributions...as well as charges acquired on the same products]. This summary was compiled when the Belgian *départements* were incorporated into the French administration in 1795. It drew on the large-scale financial survey for the year 1782, carried out under the rule of Joseph II. The transfers to the royal coffers related to *aides* and *subsides*. The expenditure for the sovereign's use was very diverse in nature (payments to government institutions such as the court, the army and the royal domains).

The public debt of towns and provinces was heterogeneous. The regional debt related mainly to the financing of extraordinary taxes in war years by means of loans. Local debt accumulated to fund public works, but these projects could be military (strongholds), economic (canals) or administrative (buildings). All one can say is that the greater part of the total burden of debt stemmed from defence expenditure.

Only one-third of the total local and provincial revenue from taxation was used for the government's own ends. Apart from administrative expenditure (salaries and operating costs), only public works constituted a significant item of expenditure. The government's contribution to poor relief was limited. The Church played the dominant role here, as it did in education.

The above-mentioned figures provide an overall picture of the total government expenditure in the Austrian Netherlands. Contrary to what is usually assumed, there was a balance between administrative and defence expenditure.

Recorded under local and provincial expenditure were *aides* and *subsides* amounting to *c.* 3.6 million guilders, which had been transferred to the royal coffers, so this sum reappears in the form of royal expenditure. This transfer should not be counted twice. Thus the total government expenditure amounted to around 18.5 million guilders.

In the absence of numerical data it is not possible to break down debts accurately between defence and administrative expenditures. But there is no doubt that most of the debt was raised to finance military outlays. So the balance between defence and administrative expenditure is clear.

A further division of the expenditure according to the category of taxpayer is both impossible and unnecessary because the share of salaries and operating costs is unknown. Yet there is no doubt that government expenditure directly stimulated the building trade in particular. Its indirect effect must be weighed up against spending on government personnel.

All this means that government expenditure exercised a redistributive effect only through economic activity. There is almost no evidence for social redistribution except for poor relief. It is therefore unnecessary to break down government expenditures of benefit to various groups of taxpayers.

Provincial tax burdens

For the Duchy of Luxembourg we have the cadastral survey of 1766 that enables us to calculate roughly the provincial income and the size of the population. Average income per person can be put at 19.6 guilders, or 100 guilders per family. The total tax levy comes to 3.15 guilders per head or *c.* 16 guilders per family.[12]

The French administration gives higher figures for per capita taxation in Luxembourg. For Hainault and Namur, too, there are estimates. For the other provinces it is possible to estimate tax burdens at the end of the Old Regime. The similarity across the regions is quite surprising (see Table 3.3). Only Flanders and Namur show variance. Unfortunately these figures cannot be compared to the average income for each province, but the differences in tax burden, expressed as shares of regional family incomes, were probably considerable.

In Leuven, tax in the second half of the eighteenth century amounted to 12 guilders per inhabitant.[13] For a family of four, the head of which was a master bricklayer, this corresponded to the wage for forty working days. On an annual basis (250 working days) the burden of taxation can

---

[12] A. Sprunck, *Etudes sur la vie économique et sociale dans le Luxembourg au XVIIIe siècle: I. Les classes rurales* (Luxembourg: Editions du Centre, 1956), pp. 79–80.

[13] L. Van Buyten, 'Het XVIIIde-eeuws Leuvens stedelijk financiewezen', *De Brabantse folklore* 258 (1988), 74–97; and L. Van Buyten, *De Leuvense stadsfinanciën onder het Oostenrijks regiem, 1713–1794*, 2 vols. (Leuven: Vrienden van de Leuvense stedelijke musea, 1982–1985).

Table 3.3. *Estimated tax revenues from different provinces (c. 1766)*

	Total tax revenue (inc. customs duties)	Taxation per capita
County of Flanders	7,570,040 gld.	12.5 gld.
Brabant	5,533,802 gld.	7.7 gld.
Western Flanders	1,440,938 gld.	7.5 gld.
Tournais(is)	587,478 gld.	7.3 gld.
Hainaut, Luxembourg and Namur	3,503,136 gld.	6.6 gld.
Mechelen	239,432 gld.	6.4 gld.
Gueldre	137,791 gld.	5.4 gld.

Sources: 'Etat général du produit des contributions directes et indirectes, et autres revenus quelconques, des ci-devant provinces Belgiques' (1796), Papiers Bouteville, n° 394, Archives générales du Royaume, Brussels; P. Moureaux, 'Les finances centrales des Pays-Bas autrichiens', *Finances publiques d'Ancien Régime. Finances publiques contemporaines en Belgique de 1740 à 1860. Processus de mutation. Continuités et ruptures. Colloque international (Spa, 19–22.12.1972). Actes* (Brussels: Crédit Communal de Belgique, 1975), p. 60; 'Etat de la population des Pays Bas autrichiens en 1784', in L. P. Gachard (ed.), *Analectes Belgiques ou recueil de pièces inédites, mémoires, notices, faits et anecdotes concernant l'histoire des Pays-Bas* (Brussels: Van Kempen, 1830), Vol. I, pp. 417–28; C. Bruneel and L. Delporte, *Le dénombrement général de la population des Pays-Bas autrichiens en 1784* (Brussels: Editions Critique, 1996).

in this case be estimated at 15 per cent of income. However, since the average income of the people of Leuven was less than that of a master bricklayer, that percentage is higher. Furthermore, taxation in Leuven rose substantially during the course of the eighteenth century.

At the beginning of the eighteenth century the government appropriated an average of 25 per cent of family income in the 150 villages of the Land van Aalst. In the second half of the century the tax burden fell to 20 per cent of the income of the rural population.[14] The contrast between the regions – the Brabant city of Leuven and the Flemish

[14] H. Van Isterdael, 'De invloed van de fiscaliteit op het inkomen van de plattelandsbevolking van het Land van Aalst in de 17de en 18de eeuw', in L. Janssens (ed.), *Handelingen van het Congres van de Federatie van Nederlandstalige Verenigingen voor Oudheidkunde en Geschiedenis van België* (Mechelen: Federatie van Nederlandstalige Verenigingen voor Oudheidkunde en Geschiedenis van België, 1988), pp. 291–308; and H. Van Isterdael, 'Belasting en belastingdruk: het Land van Aalst (17de-18de eeuw)', unpublished PhD thesis, Vrije Universiteit Brussels (1983). For a recent general survey on the County of Flanders, see E. Thoen and T. Soens, 'The social and economic impact of central government taxation on the Flemish countryside (end 13th–18th centuries)', in S. Cavaciocchi (ed.), *La Fiscalità nell'economia europea. Secc. XIII–XVIII* [Fiscal systems in the European economy 13th–18th centuries] (Florence University Press, 2008), pp. 957–71.

viscountcy of Aalst – clearly shows that averages must be treated with caution. Yet it is still useful to make such calculations for the purposes of comparison. By the end of the Old Regime the average rate of taxation in the Austrian Netherlands amounted to over 8 guilders per inhabitant. This was far more than in the Prince-Bishopric of Liège, which was known to be something of a tax haven, where every inhabitant paid an average of fewer than 2 guilders.[15]

It is difficult to draw inferences from tax burdens per capita. After all we know neither the average income of the people of the Austrian Netherlands nor how unequal their incomes were. Here, international comparisons might be illuminating.

For example, the *Assemblée Constituante* [Constitutive Assembly] estimated total taxes levied in France at the end of the Old Regime at 480 million francs. This signified a per capita tax of 20 francs, more than in the Austrian Netherlands where the average was 15 francs (8 guilders).[16] Yet nothing points to a lower per capita income in the Austrian Netherlands. In fact, the population density, which is a good barometer of agricultural productivity, was significantly higher in the Belgian *départements*.[17] Furthermore, we know that taxation in France in the eighteenth century fluctuated at around 10 per cent of the national product (excluding the service sector), and amounted to only one-half the English burden of taxation. In its turn this was considerably lower than in the United Provinces.[18] The real burden of taxation in the Austrian Netherlands looks low by international standards.[19]

A priori, that finding is not so surprising. Moreover, it was in line with the political structures of the Old Regime. Rulers sought absolute power over the state, but fiscally the reality of these regimes was very different. Joseph II rightly described the government of the Austrian Netherlands as an aristocracy. The sovereign and the ruling elite challenged each other for sovereignty but at fiscal levels we clearly see how the balance was held. Royal taxes could not be levied without the endorsement and

---

[15] 'État approximatif des impositions de la ci-devant principauté de Liège' (1796), n° 394, Papiers Bouteville, Archives générales du Royaume, Brussels. See also J. C. Jansen, 'État détaillé des diverses impositions qui se percevaient ci-devant dans les différens pays qui composent le département de la Meuse inférieure', *Studies over de sociaal-economische geschiedenis van Limburg* 9 (1964), pp. 40–1.

[16] Darquenne, 'Essai sur le poids de l'impôt', p. 276.

[17] Ibid., p. 278; and Jan Craeybeckx, 'Les débuts de la révolution industrielle en Belgique et les statistiques de la fin de l'Empire', *Mélanges offerts à G. Jacquemyns* (Bruxelles: ULB, Éditions de l'Institut de Sociologie, 1968), pp. 115–44.

[18] P. Mathias and P. O'Brien, 'Taxation in Britain and France, 1715–1810. A comparison of the social and economic incidence of taxes collected for the central governments', *Journal of European Economic History* 5 (1976), 601–50.

[19] Coppens, *De financiën*, pp. 174–6.

cooperation of ruling elites. But at the same time neither could the local and provincial authorities collect taxes for their own ends without the express agreement of the sovereigns.

Travellers who compared the situation in the Austrian Netherlands with other countries were struck by the paradox. In countries like England and the United Provinces, where representation of the wealthy classes had been extended, tax burdens were high. Monarchical regimes on the other hand were characterized by lower taxation, albeit with much arbitrariness in the tax assessments. In the Austrian Netherlands the balance of power between the sovereign and the ruling elite avoided both evils.

An English writer formulated this aptly: 'Governed according to their own laws, assured their property and personal liberty, paying nothing but the moderate taxes that they impose upon themselves, the Belgians enjoy the most beautiful gifts of a free constitution and can only congratulate themselves when they turn their eyes upon the countries that surround them, which are inhabited by peoples either subject to the most dreadful despotism or free but, within their freedom, crushed by taxes from which these provinces have the good fortune of being exempt.'[20] The same observation was expressed even more succinctly by the French writer Dérival: 'The farmer of the Austrian Low countries neither suffers the yoke of arbitrary taxation as in France nor the burden of taxation as in England.'[21]

The low productivity of a still overwhelmingly agrarian economy determined the limits of taxation. Both the sovereign and the ruling elite had an interest in moderating the tax levies. Moreover, local government was in the hands of the wealthy. As land-owners they had every interest in keeping the tax levy as low as possible, for taxes flowed into the city or royal coffers, while the rents went into their own purses.

Van Isterdael has exposed the link between rent and taxes. A low tax burden allowed for higher rents. There was considerable inequality in taxation between the different municipalities in the 'Land van Aalst'. In some villages a farmer paid almost twice as much per hectare as his neighbours. The rentals, however, were adjusted accordingly. Once both taxes and rent are aggregated, the differences between those who managed the land are substantially reduced (see Table 3.4). These comparisons do not take seigniorial rights and church tithes into account,

[20] Th. Juste, *Histoire des États-Généraux des Pays-Bas, 1465–1790* (Brussels: Bruylant-Christophe, 1864), Vol. II, p. 122.
[21] Ch. Vandenbroeke, *Vlaamse koopkracht. Gisteren, vandaag en morgen* (Leuven: Kritak, 1984), p. 225.

Table 3.4. *Rental and tax level in the 'Land van Aalst' (late eighteenth century)*

	Taxation/ha	Taxation and rental/ha
St Maria-Horebeke	11.06 lb.	76.70 lb. (x 1.2)
Okegem	16.10 lb. (x 1.5)	68.63 lb.
Erpe	18.54 lb. (x 1.7)	79.08 lb. (x 1.2)
Berchem	20.17 lb. (x 1.8)	66.28 lb.

Source: H. Van Isterdael, 'De invloed van de fiscaliteit op het inkomen van de plattelandsbevolking van het Land van Aalst in de 17de en 18de eeuw', in L. Janssens (ed.), *Handelingen van het Congres van de Federatie van Nederlandstalige Verenigingen voor Oudheidkunde en Geschiedenis van België* (Mechelen: Federatie van Nederlandstalige verenigingen voor Oudheidkunde en Geschiedenis van België, 1988), p. 301.

which may perhaps have helped to further level off the inequalities that still existed.

Even now it is difficult to come up with total figures for the fiscal share taken by the government and the share of rent, seigniorial rights and tithes in agricultural production. Vandenbroeke estimated that in the eighteenth century fiscal charges were 10 per cent of a farmer's income in the County of Flanders. In his sample survey, tithes weighed more or less as heavily, while the seigniorial rights had become almost negligible (1 per cent). Rent weighed heaviest, up to two to three times more than taxation.[22]

Taken across the Austrian Netherlands as a whole, however, tithes and seigniorial rights were certainly not of the same order as taxation. The French revolutionaries, who were in no way inclined to underestimate them, were of the opinion that they amounted to less than half of the total revenue from taxation.[23] All these charges reduced farmers' incomes to almost half. The government's share of these revenues remained minimal, however. The lion's share – the rents, tithes and seigniorial rights – went to private individuals.

The small share claimed by the tax authorities when compared to other transfers to property owners (rent, tithes and seigniorial dues) may explain why fiscal revolts were rare in the Austrian Netherlands. This not to say that there is no evidence of protest when tax grievances were aired, but the expression of such grievances seems to have been a provocation rather than a real motive. The 'tax' revolts of the

[22] Ibid., p. 243.
[23] Darquenne, 'Essai sur le poids de l'impôt', p. 278.

eighteenth century were part of a political struggle by urban interest groups whose aim was to preserve as much autonomy as possible. They protested against the curtailment of local privileges by central government. Participants in these protests were first and foremost representatives of trade guilds, who represented the city councils, and not the populace at large. Their actions were planned, rather than spontaneous popular uprisings. The only eighteenth-century popular movement worthy of mention was levelled at a proposed increase in the import duty on salt. The Brussels government avoided confrontation and in 1764 suspended the new tariffs.[24] The absence of opposition to taxation is most noticeable during the revolution against Joseph II at the end of the eighteenth century. Neither the conservative Statists, nor the more reformist 'Vonckists' made the tax system the main issue of their struggle against the emperor or a major point of contention.

Taken on its own, the burden of taxation in the Austrian Netherlands was low, both according to eighteenth-century international standards and from a nineteenth-century historical perspective. Yet, because of the low average income in this pre-industrial society and the additional deductions from income in the form of rent, seigniorial rights and tithes, that burden of taxation hit the great majority of the population extremely hard.

This explains what at first sight appear to be the paradoxical comments of impartial contemporaries. The receivers of the Land van Aalst alleged that 'the taxpayers, in paying a year of taxes, exhaust their capacities and thereby find themselves unable to contribute more'. Other official witnesses leave us in no doubt as to the low standard of living of the smallholder, 'who is sweating blood for a crust of bread to eat and a drink of water'. Even a member of a Brussels government committee did not hold back from writing: 'Flanders has the reputation of a province within a brilliant state, yet four-fifths of the labourers are very unfortunate individuals ruined by work, who have nothing but rye bread and water to nourish them.'[25]

So it would be wrong to confuse the low taxation in the Austrian Netherlands with a light fiscal burden. In the eyes of the French, this tax system might have seemed less oppressive and arbitrary than what

---

[24] K. Van Honacker, *Lokaal verzet en oproer in de 17de en 18de eeuw: Collectieve acties tegen het centraal gezag in Brussel, Antwerpen en Leuven. Standen en Landen*, Vol. 98 (Kortrijk-Heule: UGA, 1994); and Karin Van Honacker, 'Résistance locale et émeutes dans les chefs-villes brabançonnes aux XVIIe et XVIIIe siècles', *Revue d'histoire moderne et contemporaine* 47 (2000), 37–68.

[25] Van Isterdael, 'De invloed van de fiscaliteit', pp. 302–3.

they were accustomed to in their own country, but for the majority of the people, this taxation, though low, weighed heavily upon their margins of subsistence.

An industrial and liberal nation (nineteenth century)[26]

Belgium adopted French revolutionary patterns of taxation after the invasion in 1795 and maintained them, largely intact, to 1919, when income tax was eventually adopted. From the mid nineteenth century to the First World War, the taxation of wealth fell. The proportion of revenue from direct taxes on income declined from 36.8 per cent in 1840 to 25.2 per cent in 1912. The Belgian fiscal system rested largely upon the expedient of assessing indirect measures of income based on expenditures representative of affluence in the case of the *contribution personnelle*.

There were no general taxes on consumption in the nineteenth and early twentieth centuries. Only in 1919 was a stamp duty imposed on all commercial transactions. Before the First World War, Belgium relied upon customs and excise duties levied on a limited range of goods. The share of both customs and excise duties increased as a proportion of central government revenue between 1840 and 1912, from 14.5 to 23.6 per cent in the case of customs duties and from 23.3 to 35.4 per cent in the case of excise duties. The share of duties on consumption rose from 37.8 to 59.0 per cent (see Table 3.5).

Revenue from state property and enterprises could be estimated in 1912 at 5 per cent. It included income from railways and, to a lesser extent, the postal services. It is difficult to be more precise, for the accounts of these enterprises were not drawn up in a rigorous manner.

Local taxation fell as a proportion of public revenues. Between 1848 and 1912, the total of taxes in the *communes* rose from 17.1 to 40.4 million francs, that is an increase of 236.2 per cent. During the same period, taxes for the central government experienced an increase of

[26] The study of E. H. Kossmann, *The Low Countries, 1780–1940* (Oxford University Press, 1978), offers an excellent introduction to the political history of Belgium in the nineteenth century. The fiscal history of this period is covered by S. Van de Perre, 'De lasten van de macht. Fiscaal beleid in België, 1830–1914', 2 vols., unpublished PhD thesis, Katholieke Universiteit Brussels (2003); see also P. Janssens (ed.), *Fiscaal recht geboekstaafd* (Brussels: Fiscale Hogeschool, 1995), which provides a critical inventory of the principal fiscal manuals; and P. Janssens and S. Van de Perre, 'De aangroei van de fiscale wetgeving in de 19de en 20ste eeuw. Een kwantitatieve benadering', in M. Adams and L. J. Wintgens (eds.), *Wetgeving in theorie en praktijk. Wetgevingstheorie – legisprudentie* (Antwerp: Maklu, 1994), pp. 39–54.

Table 3.5. *The structure of Belgian taxes, central government (in million francs)*

	1840	1912
WEALTH		
– registration fees and stamp duties		44.5 (**14.7%**)
– death duties		3.3 (**1.1%**)
– *subtotal*:	19.8 (**25.4%**)	47.8 (**15.8%**)
INCOME		
– real estate (land and houses)	17.2 (**22.2%**)	30.0 (**9.9%**)
– bonds and shares	—	—
– wages and entrepreneurial profits	2.9 (**3.7%**)	19.7 (**6.5%**)
– global income	8.4 (**10.9%**)	26.6 (**8.8%**)
– *subtotal*:	28.5 (**36.8%**)	76.3 (**25.2%**)
CONSUMPTION		
– customs duties	11.2 (**14.5%**)	71.5 (**23.6%**)
– excise	18.1 (**23.3%**)	107.3 (**35.4%**)
– *subtotal*:	29.3 (**37.8%**)	178.8 (**59.0%**)
TOTAL:	77.6 (**100.0 %**)	302.9 (**100.0 %**)

373.8 per cent. In the middle of the nineteenth century, communal taxes were close to one-fifth of central government taxes. This local taxation was in part made up of *centimes additionnels* that were added to direct taxes collected by the government, and partly of direct taxes introduced by the local authorities themselves. Besides, large and middling towns had obtained the right (*octroi*) to levy a duty on goods entering the town. In 1860, these obstacles to the free circulation of goods were suppressed, and in compensation the government created allowances to preserve the revenues of cities, by diverting death duties from central to local revenues.

It is difficult to estimate the level of taxation in relation to the economy. In 1848, Godin calculated that central government taxation amounted to 83 million francs or 19 francs per capita. He took income per capita to be 350 francs and estimated the tax burden to be 5.5 per cent.[27] By the First World War, the relative burden of central taxation increased to 13.9 per cent of NDP and became more dependent on regressive indirect taxes.

[27] A. Godin-David, *Avant-projet d'une réforme générale des impôts* (Liège: N. Redouté, 1848), pp. 21, 31.

Fiscal evolution

Wealth

In Belgium, an emphasis was placed on the taxation of transfers of title by various registration, transcription and stamp duties. Registration duties fell both on the transfer of moveable property (although in practice often avoided) and on real property. These duties amounted to a significant tax of 5.5 per cent on the value of property, which was doubled by the addition of taxes on transfers and stamps, and by payments to lawyers. These transfer taxes accounted for 14.7 per cent of the revenue of the central government in Belgium in 1912, when death duties were only 1.1 per cent of revenue.[28]

It was difficult to increase death duties in Belgium, where they were a very sensitive political issue. Although death duties were introduced by the Directory in the law of 22 frimaire year VII (1 December 1798), small inheritances were exempt and the imposition of the duty on direct heirs was highly controversial. After the defeat of Napoleon in 1815, the provisional government decided to exempt direct heirs, and Willem I did not feel it was politically expedient to abandon that concession. What Willem *did* introduce was an oath that appealed to religious conscience in an attempt (ineffective, as it transpired) to avoid fraudulent declarations and evasion by failure to pay taxes on moveable property or personality. The oath was subsequently abolished during the Belgian revolution by the decree of 17 October 1830 on the grounds that it was both an encouragement to immorality and ineffective in increasing yields: 'considering … the immorality in which such a system of legislation is found embedded, for it tends to place citizens' interests against their consciences.'[29] As a result, taxation of property at death was more likely to fall on real property than on moveable property, which was under-assessed to a great extent. When the Liberals came to power in 1847, death duties were restored on direct heirs at a modest rate of 1 per cent, levied on individual inheritances above 1,000 francs rather than on the total size of the estate. The emphasis in Belgium, therefore, was on a graduation of death duties by the degrees of relationship, and not by the size of the estate. No further changes were made in death duties before the First World War, and the contribution of wealth taxes in gen-

---

[28] R. Deblauwe and P. Janssens (eds.), *Tweehonderd jaar frimairewet. De registratie- en successierechten in Vlaanderen, België en Europa* (Brussels: Larcier, 1999).
[29] *Pasinomie ou collection des lois … en Belgique*, 3e série (Brussels: H. Tarlier & E. Bruylant, 1833), Vol. I, p. 40.

eral to government revenue fell from 25.4 per cent in 1840 to 15.8 per cent in 1912.

Income

The share of revenue from taxes on income fell from 36.8 per cent in 1840 to 25.2 per cent in 1912. The important point was the efficiency with which revenue was extracted from various sources of income, whether from land or business profits, salaries or securities. In the nineteenth century, the fiscal system rested largely upon the expedient of a bundle of distinct taxes on income by using indirect indicators, which may be divided into three main categories: the *contribution foncière*, which accounted for about 60 per cent of direct tax revenues in 1846; the *droits de patente* which provided about 10 per cent of direct tax revenue; and the *contribution personnelle* which accounted for the remaining third or so.[30]

Income from real property was taxed by the *contribution foncière*. This provided a declining share of revenue, in part because of the change in the economic structure of the country, and in part because it was underestimated and lagged behind market values. The cadastral survey conducted between 1800 and 1843/44 established the revenue for each parcel of land or building as a function of the average income calculated from a sample of rents; the *contribution foncière* was proportionate to the estimated income or *revenu cadastral*. Since the estimated income was not changed until 1868, and continued to be underestimated on subsequent revisions, the *contribution foncière* lagged behind real income. The real rate of tax fell from about 15 per cent in the early nineteenth century to about 7 per cent at the time of the agricultural depression at the end of the century. Of course, it was politically difficult to increase the tax rate, and the contribution of the land tax to government revenue fell from 22.2 per cent of central government revenue in 1840 to 9.9 per cent in 1912.

A second form of income – dividends from government stocks and shares – was not taxed in Belgium before the end of the nineteenth century. A third category of income – entrepreneurial profits from trade, industry and the professions – was taxed by the *droits de patente*. The tax was levied on the presumed profits of an enterprise rather than the actual net income, and excluded incomes that did not entail

---

[30] Direct taxes are considered in a detailed, critical manner by J. Ingenbleek, *Impôts directs et indirects sur le revenu. La contribution personnelle en Belgique. L'Einkommensteuer en Prusse. L'income-tax en Angleterre* (Brussels: Misch & Thron, 1908); and J. Ingenbleek, *La justice dans l'impôt* (Paris: Berger-Levrault, 1918).

entrepreneurial management such as the wages of employees or salaries of civil servants, the military and clergy. Neither did the tax fall on farmers who rented their land, although those who owned their farms paid the *contribution foncière*. More contentious, and more difficult to justify from criticism as blatant self-interest, was the exclusion of lawyers; their privileged fiscal status was nevertheless preserved throughout the period.

The presumed profits from enterprise were estimated by three criteria which together produced an indication of taxable capacity: the nature of the economic activity; the scale of business measured by the number of workers, output, raw material consumption and the rental value of plant; and the population of the area in which the firm was located. These criteria were used to calculate a lump sum to be paid by each concerned: the scale established in 1819, for example, ranged from 1.06 francs for a carpenter or shoemaker in the country who worked alone or with one assistant, to 423 francs for a banker in Brussels or a ship owner in Antwerp. The maximum rate of the *droits de patente* was estimated by Godin at about 2 per cent of profits, and it was heavier on smaller concerns than on larger prosperous businesses.[31] Small trades and industries and the professions were relatively more heavily taxed than large businesses and industries, but it was difficult for them to secure a redress of their grievance or for the government to increase the yield from the *droits de patente*. Clearly, the complex scale based upon various criteria made any adjustment of the tax exceedingly difficult, for a plethora of trade and regional interests would be implicated. The *droits de patente* were, therefore, likely to become stereotyped and to lag behind economic growth and increasing profits. There was, however, an exception: joint-stock companies did not pay a lump sum and were taxed on profits appearing in their accounts, at a rate which varied from 1.3 to 2 per cent during the nineteenth century. This taxation of joint-stock companies was less favourable than the treatment of other forms of entrepreneurial profits through the *droits de patente*, which provides one explanation for the slow development of joint-stock companies in nineteenth-century Belgium. The *droits de patente* made only a modest contribution to total central government revenue, amounting to about 3.7 per cent in 1840 and 6.5 per cent in 1912.

There remained a final form of tax on income: the *contribution personnelle*. The *contribution foncière* and the *droits de patente* were imposed on the profits of agricultural, commercial or industrial enterprise, rather

---

[31] A. Godin, *Revenu de deux millions pour l'État, par une répartition plus équitable de l'impôt patente* (Liège: N. Redouté, 1847).

than a tax on the personal income from real estate or business. Personal income was taxed by the *contribution personnelle*, levied on taxpayers according to the presumed income determined by conspicuous expenditure, above all on their residences. The rental value of residences was taken as the most reliable indication of income, and in theory the tax was proportional to rent and hence to presumed income. In fact, rental values were underestimated by a margin which varied according to the size of the house. The very smallest houses were exempt, and properties with high rents were underestimated by the widest margin. The effective rate of tax was therefore heaviest on middle-class families in modest houses, and the tax rate varied between 1 and 15 per cent of the actual rent. Despite these obvious inequities, there was little chance of any revision. The rental values were fixed only very approximately in 1822, and were not subsequently adjusted; consequently, they lagged behind the actual level of rents and it was in no one's interest to support a revaluation that would remove inequities but increase everyone's taxation.

Further indicators of taxable capacity were the number of windows and doors, and (until 1879) the number of fireplaces. Although a tax on household furniture seemed to provide a means of correcting the inaccuracy and inequity of taxation of rental values, it was merely calculated as a function of the rental value of the property without estimating the actual value of furniture. These taxes on residence accounted for about 90 per cent of the *contribution personnelle*, the remainder consisting of taxes on two other items of conspicuous expenditure which somewhat increased the *contribution personnelle* paid by the rich: a tax on servants and horses. Until 1822, there was also a poll tax equivalent to three days' wages which was charged on all except the smallest incomes.

The *contribution personnelle* provided a declining proportion of revenue between 1840 and 1912, falling from 10.9 per cent to 8.8 per cent. The various components of the *contribution personnelle* (doors, windows, hearths, rental value, furniture, servants and horses) remained unchanged throughout the nineteenth century. Only the tax on houses was increased in 1879, but this modification did not have any fiscal importance. Before and after 1879, it was essentially the value of the dwelling (windows, doors, furniture and rent) that determined the level of the *contribution personnelle*; only the richest families had their own servants and horses. The reform of 1879 was intended to eliminate fraudulent means of obtaining the right to vote by exaggerating the number of hearths, in order to reach the tax threshold laid down by the franchise.

What was the outcome of the Belgian system of direct taxation of income for different social classes and economic interests? The *contribution personnelle* fell especially on housing, and on the owner rather than the tenant. The *contribution foncière* fell on land, in principle on the owner but in practice also on the farmer. The *droits de patente* applied to employers and the self-employed in commerce and industry. Landowners were probably the worst affected, for they were taxed on their residences, servants and leisure horses in addition to the *contribution foncière* on their land. Traders and entrepreneurs were somewhat better off, for the *droits de patente* on their profits were less of a burden than the *contribution foncière*. On the other hand, they were usually liable to the *contribution personnelle*. Other social classes escaped direct taxation in one way or another: farmers, lawyers and public servants did not pay *droits de patente*, and only paid the *contribution personnelle* if they had a reasonably affluent standard of living. Workers and low-paid salaried employees escaped all direct taxes.

Consumption

Taxes on consumption are often criticized on the grounds that they are regressive, falling on consumers without distinction and without taking income levels into account. However, much depends on the precise mix of commodities that are taxed, and what rates are applied to luxuries compared with necessities. In Belgium, customs duties ignored luxuries, the largest contributions coming from coffee (17 per cent of the total) and textiles (24 per cent), which were consumed by all classes. A similar pattern applies to excise duties, where luxuries accounted for only a quarter of receipts: 31 per cent of the revenue came from beer and 22 per cent from spirits and alcohol in 1848, which were consumed by all classes. The duty on salt, a necessity for the preservation of food, was abolished in 1870, which somewhat reduced the regressive nature of the tax system, but the only excise duties on commodities which were predominately consumed by the well-to-do were sugar, which did not appear in working-class budgets in the nineteenth century (14 per cent of excise revenue), and wine (10 per cent). Overall, the tax system became more regressive between 1840 and 1912. If it is argued that taxes on wealth, servants, horses and *droits de patente* fell entirely on the well-to-do, and that property owners were responsible for half of the *contribution foncière* (as suggested by Denis[32]), then it could be claimed

[32] Hector Denis, *L'impôt. Leçons données au cours publics de la ville de Bruxelles. Première série* (Brussels, 1889).

that through taxation of wealth and income these social classes in 1840 accounted for 40 per cent of the tax revenue of the state. In 1912, their share hardly reached 25 per cent. It is not possible to estimate their contribution to consumption taxes.

The political issues

The campaign for the introduction of income tax in Belgium at the end of the nineteenth century was intended to re-establish the equilibrium between consumption and direct taxes which had been disrupted in the second half of the nineteenth century. What was at stake was not the level of taxation, for it was generally accepted that the tax burden was low and there was no pressure for significant additions to government revenue; the issue was rather one of equalizing the incidence of taxation between classes.

When a majority of the population is working in agriculture or in small workshops, it is extremely difficult to tax the actual income received. The family was likely to live at least in part from the proceeds of the farm or 'out of the till' in shops; records were likely to be inadequate, if they existed at all. It was therefore easier to tax imputed income. A 'modern' income tax based on the actual global income from all activities was only feasible with the emergence of an industrialized and bureaucratized society, in which economic activity was carried on within large concerns with detailed records, and the workforce was more likely to be employed in specific occupations with well-established incomes.

The pattern of distribution of wealth and income could also influence the fiscal system, affecting the coverage of the tax. In Belgium, land-ownership was not dominated by large aristocratic estates and the economy continued to be dominated by small units for a long period of time. The failure to tax bonds and shares in Belgium, and the effective exemption of moveable property from death duties can be explained by a more even distribution of wealth. In that case, the choice was between taxing *all* incomes from stocks and shares or exempting them all. In the case of stocks and shares, the decision was for exemption; in the case of land, which was a much more significant source of revenue, the choice went the other way. It was necessary for revenue reasons to extend the *contribution foncière* to small owners. Indeed, it could be argued that the greater the inequality in the distribution of income and wealth, the more effective the taxation of income and wealth: a large revenue could be obtained from a smaller number of taxpayers. The general taxation of consumption made sense in Belgium because the middle class was less prosperous and the rich less dominant: revenue had to be produced from a wider social base, which was better achieved through taxes on basic consumption goods.

Of course, the willingness of the rich to consent to taxation rests upon their assessment of fiscal politics: they ask whether the payment of taxation is rational as an insurance premium for the maintenance of the unequal distribution of wealth, and whether the fiscal system as a whole is balanced between classes and interests. The upper chamber in Belgium – the Senate – was not hereditary. Senators were elected for a limited period by the same body of electors as the lower chamber, and as a result they did not have real independence *vis-à-vis* the electorate. The crucial point becomes the franchise for the lower chamber which, until the reforms of 1893, was closely defined in terms of the tax system. The close connection between the franchise and payment of direct taxes created a barrier to maintaining, let alone increasing, their proportion compared with indirect taxes. Until the constitutional reform of 1893, the right to vote in Belgium depended on the amount of tax paid *on income*. The implication of such an electoral system was that direct taxation mainly affected the middle classes: they were not likely to vote for an increase in the rate of taxation of incomes, which would both increase their own burdens, and at the same time broaden the electorate. In 1870, there were about five million inhabitants in Belgium, or a million families. About 10 per cent of the heads of families paid direct taxes of 42 francs and above, which gave them the right to vote in parliamentary elections: in the elections of 1870, 107,099 men cast votes. About 20 per cent of heads of families paid 20 francs and above, which allowed them to vote in provincial elections; and about 30 per cent paid 10 francs or above, which allowed them to take part in local council elections. There was, therefore, a direct connection between voting and taxation, so that any increase in direct taxes would widen the franchise; there was a strong political motivation, quite apart from financial self-interest, for limiting the growth of direct taxation. The electoral system contributed, therefore, to the rigidity of the taxation of income.

In Belgium, the demand for the introduction of income tax had striking implications.[33] The labour movement was split in two. On the one hand, there was the socialist party, with a commitment to social revolution; in their view, reform of the tax system and the introduction of an income tax was a first step to the abolition of private property and

---

[33] J. Schoysman, 'L'évolution de l'idée de la progressivité dans l'impôt en Belgique et son reflet dans la politique belge, 1830–1919', *Recherches sur l'histoire des finances publiques en Belgique* 2 (1970), 329–98, with references to discussions in parliament. See also Ingenbleek, *La justice.*

the equalization of wealth and incomes. Not surprisingly, the bourgeoisie was terrified by the prospect. On the other hand, a large part of
the labour movement remained within the Catholic party, which held
power from 1884 to 1914. This reformist wing of the labour movement
proposed a similar change in the tax system, but without the ambition of a fundamental change in society. However, their advocacy of
an income tax was blocked because other members of the Catholic
party feared its possible revolutionary implications. Although the franchise was extended in 1893 to all adult men, and labour representatives entered parliament with Christian democrats subsequently joining
the Catholic government, the first serious discussion of the income tax
came only in 1916, in the government of national union formed during
the war. During this debate, the British income tax was taken as a sym-
bol of the alternative division of taxation between social classes, and
of the inequality of the distribution of taxation in Belgium. In 1916,
reform of the tax system was needed to reintroduce equilibrium into a
fiscal structure, which, threatened by political and social tensions, was
challenging the legitimacy of the state.

4   The rise of the fiscal state in France, 1500–1914

Richard Bonney

France offers a contrast to most of the other fiscal states of Eurasia. It was a large, relatively unified, dynastic state at an early date – yet, in spite of the expansionist ambitions of its rulers, never as large as the Polish–Lithuanian union or Muscovy, let alone the sprawling Ottoman and Mughal states. Until German unification under Prussian leadership,[1] France had the largest population of taxpayers of any West European country. This permitted it to have the largest European land army in the seventeenth and eighteenth centuries, and a significant navy as well. Yet the paradox underlying French power, which threatened to undermine the whole structure, was that the country with the largest number of taxpayers in western Europe also had, until 1790, the largest number and highest proportion of fiscal exemptions.

As the titles of a number of recent studies suggest,[2] it is impossible to view the French monarchy of the Old Regime without consideration of this paradox of power: a dynasty with absolutist pretensions had perforce to grant privileges that had the effect, over time, of limiting the exercise of power, especially with regard to the implementation of change in fiscal matters. For change inevitably meant reform, and in the longer term reform meant the erosion, limitation, restriction or removal of privilege. These privileges became so deeply entrenched because they were multi-dimensional, granted as they were to different levels of society – to institutions, to provinces and regions, and to social groups and individuals. This multi-layered regime of privilege created intolerable tensions within government itself and between government and the rest

---

[1] The French population in 1911 was 41 million; that of Germany in 1910 was 64.6 million.

[2] A by no means exhaustive list would include such works as H. L. Root, *The fountain of privilege: political foundations of markets in old regime France and England* (Berkeley: University of California Press, 1994); G. Bossenga, *The politics of privilege. Old regime and revolution in Lille* (Cambridge University Press, 1991); M. Kwass, *Privilege and the politics of taxation in eighteenth-century France: Liberté, Égalité, Fiscalité* (Cambridge University Press, 2000).

of society. In the end, the structure imploded at the Revolution. As Jean-Laurent Rosenthal has written:[3]

The French Revolution was a fiscal revolution. That it was so in its consequences is clear from the dramatic increase in taxation that occurred between 1789 and 1820. Michael Kwass wants to argue it was a fiscal revolution in its causes. The argument he presents is simple: the rise of direct taxation on the privileged elite under Louis XIV slowly but surely mobilized the pivotal political groups in opposition to the crown. Hence, a real increase in fiscal burden drove a change in political culture and in ideology that led a systematic and effective opposition to further taxation by the crown. When coupled with the increasing cost of war, this spelled disaster for the *ancien régime*.

The expansion of the sale of offices in the sixteenth century

It is a matter of debate as to whether the fiscal foundations of the Old Regime should be placed with the long-term adventure of the Italian wars after 1494, which committed French kings for over fifty years to tax increases as required by the fortunes of war; or with the establishment of venality of office as a fiscal instrument of the crown in the 1520s.[4] The two issues, war and venality, were clearly linked, for as Philippe Hamon has shown, most of the officials who managed the king's finances in time of war were office-holders or eventually became office-holders in the course of their careers. The estimated 1,550 financial office-holders in post in 1515 (out of about 4,000 for all types of office-holder) were supplemented by other types of officials, whose aim was to purchase offices and by this means facilitate their social, political and financial advancement at the earliest opportunity.[5] This ready market for offices in all but the most adverse of circumstances explains the distinctively French phenomenon of the widespread purchase of office in effect as private property and the intrusion of private ownership rights into public administration. Venality of office occurred elsewhere, but nowhere other than in France was the phenomenon entrenched so broadly and so deeply in society.

---

[3] Review of Kwass, *Privilege and the politics of taxation* by Jean-Laurent Rosenthal: *H-France Review* 2:81 (August 2002). The dramatic rise in taxes is evident only when the 'inflation tax' of the *assignat* experiment is included in the calculations.
[4] R. É. Mousnier, *La Vénalité des offices sous Henri IV et Louis XIII*, 2nd edn (Paris: Presses universitaires de France, 1971); W. Doyle, *Venality. The sale of offices in eighteenth-century France* (Oxford: Clarendon Press, 1997).
[5] Thus at least 22 of 100 clerks whose career is known became office-holders: P. Hamon, 'Messieurs des finances': *Les grands officiers de finance dans la France de la Renaissance* (Paris: Comité pour l'Histoire Économique et Financière de la France, 1999), p. 71. See pp. 75–6 for the size of the proto-bureaucracy.

The rapid expansion of venality, which brought profits to the crown chiefly from the initial sales of office, though also from subsequent mutation fees, explains what otherwise would seem to have been an impossible feat: how it was that the real burden of direct taxes, borne chiefly by peasant taxpayers, did not increase greatly in real terms[6] from the reigns of Louis XI (d. 1483) to Charles IX (d. 1574). The annual increase in the value of taxation under Francis I was 1.5 per cent per annum, though there was a sharp but brief rise under Henri II (1547–59) to 5.7 per cent per annum.[7] It was not until the reign of Henri III (1574–88) that indirect taxes virtually doubled, while direct taxes increased some two and half times.[8] The conclusion that might be drawn, that the period of the French Renaissance was a 'taxpayers' paradise', must be avoided.[9] The crown coped poorly, on the whole,

[6] Whether calculated in terms of purchasing power in grain or in silver, though the calculation in silver exaggerates the real decline in income available to the monarchy prior to 1636 and its real increase after that date because of the depreciation of the *livre tournois* in terms of silver. (Cf. the calculations in E. Le Roy Ladurie, *The royal French state, 1460–1610*, trans. Juliet Vale (Oxford: Blackwell, 1994), pp. 74, 130, 157, based on A. Guery, 'Les finances de la monarchie française sous l'ancien régime', *Annales ESC* 33 (1978), 218–39, at 227.) There was both a significant population increase and significant inflation in the first half of the sixteenth century, so theoretically there was an increased number of peasant taxpayers available to discharge their tax burden from the sale of grain, the price of which rose more rapidly and higher than that of other commodities. Matters are never quite so simple, however. Provincial discrepancies and anomalies within provinces abounded, apart from the unreliability of the harvest, which might have a devastating effect on the capacity of taxpayers to pay their taxes: D. Potter, *War and government in the French provinces. Picardy, 1470–1560* (Cambridge University Press, 1993), pp. 238, 241.

[7] P. Hamon, *L'argent du roi. Les finances sous Francois Ier* (Paris: Comité pour l'Histoire Économique et Financière de la France, 1994), p. 77. Hamon notes that the annual increase under Francis I (1.5 or 1.44% per annum, depending on the precise period) was actually lower than under Louis XII (2.38% per annum), although he it was who was known as *père du people* because of his alleged fiscal moderation.

[8] R. J. Bonney, 'France, 1494–1815', in Bonney (ed.), *The rise of the fiscal state in Europe, c. 1200–1815* (Oxford University Press, 1999), p. 140. Cf. Sir George Carew on the reputation of the different French kings with regard to taxation: p. 138.

[9] Le Roy Ladurie writes: 'royal taxation was stabilized around 900 tonnes of silver per year for the whole of France; there was nothing unbearable in this state of affairs for the rural world, since the last big rise in agricultural prices devalued metal money in relation to the product of the land, which was becoming ever more expensive and more sought after. This lull in state or royal demand made on the whole a pleasant contrast with the formidable fiscal extortions of the period of Louis XIII and Louis XIV that … triggered off peasant fury against taxation.' E. Le Roy Ladurie, *The French peasantry, 1450–1660*, trans. A. Sheridan (Aldershot: Scholar, 1987), pp. 411–12. The observation is made largely on the basis of the figures for the royal *taille* at Montpellier, where it was only after *c*. 1620 that there was a significant increase above the price of wheat (p. 357, fig. 25). Le Roy Ladurie comments: 'the fiscal revolution carried out by Richelieu around 1630 resulted in a doubling of the real value of the tax burden on the peasant (rising from 6% to 12% or 13% of the gross agricultural income in Languedoc) (pp. 357–8).

with the impact of inflation on its revenue base and stumbled from one financial crisis to another; but, especially after 1562, it is doubtful if the taxpayers benefited in tangible ways unless they were exceptionally fortunate. The breakdown of law and order during the wars of religion, military levies in general,[10] and the phenomenon of 'double taxation' levied by rival military captains, in particular, were virtually certain to have ensured a miserable fate for many communities of taxpayers.

War finance and monetary devaluation under Louis XIII and Louis XIV

The restoration of internal peace after 1598, and the relatively pacific foreign policy of Henri IV, provided an opportunity for financial reorganization at the centre, under a strong finance minister (the duc de Sully);[11] for a significant default which imposed costs on nobles, officeholders and the privileged bourgeoisie who held government debt in *rentes*; and for a modest restructuring of taxation. Tax increases would have left these social groups unscathed because of their tax exemptions, and would have pushed 'the burden of fiscal adjustment onto the less prosperous groups who actually paid taxes'.[12] Instead, Sully's fiscal restructuring amounted to a reduced reliance on direct taxes, which facilitated a return to agrarian prosperity;[13] an increased reliance on newly established taxes (*affaires extraordinaires*) levied by the method of contracts (*traités*) with financiers; a consistent policy of farming indirect

[10] For military levies: J. B. Collins, *Fiscal limits of absolutism. Direct taxation in early seventeenth-century France* (Berkeley: University of California Press, 1988), p. 52. See pp. 147, 159–60 for *non-valeurs* and remissions at the end of the wars of religion.
[11] M. Antoine, *Le cœur de l'État. Surintendance, contrôle général et intendances des finances, 1551–1791* (Paris: Fayard, 2003), pp. 139–61 ; B. Barbiche and S. de Dainville-Barbiche, *Sully* (Paris: Fayard, 1997). The group biography of the finance ministers by F. Bayard, J. Felix and P. Hamon, *Dictionnaire des surintendants et contrôleurs généraux des finances* (Paris: Comité pour l'histoire économique et financière de la France, 2000), is available online at www.comite-histoire.minefi.gouv.fr/sections/comite_pour_lhistoi/-recherches_finances/les_hommes/liste_des_surintenda/view?igpde_lang_redirect=1.
[12] P. T. Hoffman, G. Postel-Vinay and J.-L. Rosenthal, *Priceless markets. The political economy of credit in Paris, 1660–1870* (University of Chicago Press, 2000), p. 91.
[13] Malet's figures for the yield from taxation suggest that reliance on the *taille* from the pays *d'élections* fell from 49.6% (1600–04) to 31.5% (1605–09) largely as a result of a rise in extraordinary income, that is to say from contracts for newly created taxes: R. J. Bonney, *The king's debts. Finance and politics in France, 1589–1661* (Oxford: Clarendon Press, 1981), p. 313. For the detailed figures: M. M. and R. J. Bonney, *Jean-Roland Malet: premier historien des finances de la monarchie française* (Paris: Comité pour l'Histoire Économique et Financière de la France, 1993).

taxes to consortia of financers;[14] and the regularization of income from venality through the controversial introduction of the *droit annuel* in 1604. This was in effect an insurance policy payable to the crown by office-holders to prevent the unexpected reversion of their offices to the crown on the death of the previous holder. The *droit annuel* was controversial in the eyes of conservatives such as Chancellor Bellièvre, who wished to reverse the tendency to make all judicial offices venal on the grounds that posts were secured by the rich rather than the well qualified. Advocates of Sully's approach, called anachronistic-ally by some historians the group who wished to 'instaurer l'État de finance',[15] argued that the *droit annuel* was a concession to office-hold-ers who had lost out in the reduction in the rate of interest payable on *rentes*. Their loyalty would be secured (as would the crown's financial interests) since, by providing greater stability, offices would become a more lucrative investment. The measure was a success, and the office-holders were prepared to pay significant sums for the renewal of the privilege of the *droit annuel* (5 per cent of the value of their offices in 1621, a further 20 per cent in 1630 and 12.5 per cent in 1639). It was only when the renewal of the privilege was at first denied in 1648 that the office-holders rebelled in the first Fronde.[16] The high point in the government's reliance on income from venality of office was reached in the years between 1620 and 1634, before France's formal entry into the Thirty Years War in 1635, but years that were marked by deepening internal and external military commitments.[17]

Sully's budgetary surplus proved to be the last before the ministry of Colbert,[18] as the military demands on a relatively weak and embry-onic French fiscal apparatus became increasingly severe. It is true that the introduction of provincial intendants, the control over direct taxes given them in 1642, and above all their powers of enforcement of pay-ment by the use of special brigades of troops, ensured that the central government was not completely starved of funds, which had become a serious possibility in the last two years of Richelieu's ministry.[19] But this

---

[14] It is from Sully's administration that the leases of the revenue farms can be enumer-ated: R. J. Bonney, 'The failure of the French revenue farms, 1600–60', *Economic History Review*, 2nd ser., 32 (1979), 11–32, at 26–8.

[15] Barbiche and de Dainville-Barbiche, *Sully*, p. 165.

[16] Collins, *Fiscal limits of absolutism*, pp. 84–5; R. J. Bonney, 'La Fronde des officiers: mouvement réformiste ou rébellion corporatiste', *XVIIᵉ Siecle* 145 (1984), 323–40.

[17] Bonney, *The king's debts*, p. 313; R. J. Bonney, 'Louis XIII, Richelieu and the royal finances', in J. A. Bergin and L. W. B. Brockliss (eds.), *Richelieu and his age* (Oxford University Press, 1992), pp. 99–133.

[18] Barbiche and de Dainville-Barbiche, *Sully*, pp. 248–53.

[19] R. J. Bonney, *Political change in France under Richelieu and Mazarin, 1624–1661* (Oxford University Press, 1978).

was not the whole story. The shortage of specie in the provinces necessitated a devaluation of the *livre tournois* in 1636, shortly after France entered the Thirty Years War.[20] This was to set a pattern that was to be replicated in the later wars of Louis XIV: in the century between 1602 and 1709, the *livre* lost 62 per cent of its value; it lost 40 per cent of its value between 1670 and 1726.[21] Shifts in the value of the currency offered the opportunity for substantial gains for those who correctly anticipated such changes,[22] which included the crown's own officials such as the *trésoriers de l'extraordinaire de la guerre*;[23] but the crown, at least in the short term, was the main beneficiary since the purpose of the devaluation was fiscal in nature. The cost of troops was reduced as expressed in its purchasing power in precious metal.[24] In the longer term, there can be no doubt that successive devaluations were counterproductive and worsened the fundamental problem, which was the limited amount of specie in circulation.[25]

The key issue was how to finance an army that grew rapidly in size because of the need to fight in several European theatres of war simultaneously, from a relatively modest force of some 10,000 men in 1610 to a gargantuan army, for the times, of some 340,000 to 400,000 men in the 1690s. Moreover, whereas under Richelieu there was a large discrepancy between the army size on paper and the actual reality, the abuses and false musters had been largely eliminated by the period of the Nine Years War.[26] Land contributions, as against resources from centrally imposed taxation, never contributed more than 12 per cent of the burgeoning military costs, and a campaign such as that of Villars in Germany in 1703, when over 40 per cent of his army's revenue came through contributions or the equivalent, was wholly exceptional. 'The

---

[20] Bonney, *The king's debts*, p. 170.

[21] Calculation of Guy Antonetti in F. Bluche (ed.), *Dictionnaire du grand siècle* (Paris: Fayard, 1990), p. 1050. Graph based on year 1726 = index 100 in Hoffman *et al.*, *Priceless markets*, p. 57. From p. 275: 'between 1670 and 1726, the crown sliced off some 40% of the *livre*'s silver content, and with each devaluation lenders watched their financial returns plunge.' Slight variation from p. 25 n. 34: 'between 1688 and 1726 the *livre* lost nearly half of its value in silver.'

[22] Hoffman *et al.*, *Priceless markets*, p. 23.

[23] G. Rowlands, *The dynastic state and the army under Louis XIV. Royal service and private interest, 1661–1701* (Cambridge University Press, 2002), p. 123.

[24] D. Parrott, *Richelieu's army: war, government and society in France, 1624–1642* (Cambridge University Press, 2001), p. 243.

[25] Rowlands, *The dynastic state and the army*, p. 127.

[26] Ibid., pp. 171, 263. Parrott, *Richelieu's army*, pp. 182–222. Both Rowlands and Parrott offer detailed criticisms of Lynn's interpretation, though Rowlands concedes that Lynn is correct in his assumption of 80–90% of theoretical strength for the actual strength of the army in the 1690s: J. A. Lynn, *Giant of the grand siècle. The French army, 1610–1715* (Cambridge University Press, 1997).

instruments of credit', Rowlands argues, 'were under-developed for the demands placed upon the state, while the amount of specie in circulation was insufficient and even shrank as a result of counter-productive government monetary policy.'[27]

In the second half of the seventeenth century, moreover, growing French competition with the Maritime Powers – the United Provinces and England – required the development of a fleet of the line simultaneously with this huge land army. By 1693, external defeat at La Hougue the previous year and subsistence crisis within the kingdom required a rethinking of strategy: financing the fleet of the line had to be curtailed in favour of a self-financing privateering war in order to keep the land campaign staggering on. Even so, a new direct tax, the *capitation*, had to be introduced in 1695. Withdrawn at the end of the war, it was reintroduced in 1701; a second new direct tax, the *dixième*, had to be established in 1710 to avert collapse at the end of the War of the Spanish Succession. Michael Kwass is correct in viewing these new devices as an attempt at taxing the privileged for the first time, even if they remained deeply unpopular with those affected as well as controversial in constitutional terms. (The first *dixième* was withdrawn in 1717 as a concession to those who opposed the continuance of a wartime measure.[28])

Reliance on extraordinary new taxes (*affaires extraordinaires*) reached an all-time high in the later wars of Louis XIV, while privileged corporations such as the *parlements* and provincial Estates also suffered from mounting fiscal pressure. Venal office-holders were poorly positioned to act as financial intermediaries for the crown because of pressures on their personal solvency. Pontchartrain exacted some 17 million *livres* from the *parlements* during the War of the League of Augsburg; Chamillart some 15 million in the early years of the War of the Spanish Succession. Desmaretz hoped to raise 24 million *livres* as a windfall to the crown in December 1709 as a result of the crown's abolition of the *droit annuel* in return for a one-off purchase or *rachat*. While the measure appeared to guarantee succession rights to office, it nevertheless posed a considerable financial challenge at the peak of the financial pressure of the War of the Spanish Succession and the money came in slowly. Venal office had come to have the taint of a bad investment, as Chancellor Pontchartrain had earlier acknowledged, because of the ruthless exploitation of this type of income by the crown in the last

[27] Rowlands, *The dynastic state and the army*, pp. 127, 365–6.
[28] R. J. Bonney, '*Le secret de leurs familles*: the fiscal and social limits of Louis XIV's *dixième*', *French History* 7 (1993), 383–416. Kwass, *Privilege and the politics of taxation in eighteenth-century France*.

two wars of Louis XIV.[29] Virtually every financial expedient had been exhausted: when the Regency government reversed policy by determining upon a visa of the floating debt, the abolition of offices created since 1689, the establishment of a *chambre de justice* against financiers who had profited in the last two wars, and the suppression of the *dixième*, it received full support from the *parlements* and other superior courts.[30] Compared to the outgoings on war, the cost of royal buildings, especially the construction of Versailles, though an extravagance that could scarcely be justified given the fiscal pressure on taxpayers, was nevertheless relatively low.[31]

The collapse of Law's System and its aftermath: relative monetary and fiscal stability

The story of the French role in the first European experiment in paper money has been told in detail elsewhere.[32] The issue of various forms of paper after 1701, *billets de monnaie*, treasury bills, bills of receivers-general and so on, left a considerable mass of devalued government assets at the end of the War of the Spanish Succession. Law's System was an attempt to extinguish the public debt, whilst also moving towards revenue unification and the transfer from a specie-based system to a system based on paper. At first, Law enjoyed the unconditional support of the Regent, but how long this could last in the face of a barrage of criticism

[29] Here the interpretation of Hurt, who argues that 'the financial pressures on the *Parlements* resembled those which precipitated the Fronde' is greatly to be preferred to that of Mark Potter, who argues that venality was 'further entrenched' in this period and the privileges of the office-holders confirmed: J. J. Hurt, *Louis XIV and the parlements. The assertion of royal authority* (Manchester University Press, 2002), pp. 105–7, 113. Had the *parlements* paid in full, and paid with alacrity, it would have been a different matter. Cf. M. Potter, *Corps and clienteles. Public finance and political change in France, 1688–1715* (Aldershot: Ashgate, 2004), pp. 39–40, 47: 'the crown's financial use of, or even dependence upon, certain offices protected the holders and preserved the patrimonial qualities of their offices.' Potter accepts Desmaretz's claim that the crown succeeded in raising the 24 million in full, which seems very doubtful. In any case, one-third of the payment was scheduled to be in *billets de monnaie*, which were rapidly depreciated. The decline in the value of offices by 1715 is convincing evidence that Louis XIV had exploited venality excessively: Hurt, *Louis XIV and the parlements*, p. 189. In 1722 the *droit annuel* was reintroduced with the exception only of the officers of the *parlements* and other superior courts (p. 197).
[30] Antoine, *Le cœur de l'État*, p. 397. The Regent had renamed the superior courts sovereign courts, a title not used since 1665, in 1715.
[31] R. J. Bonney, 'Vindication of the Fronde? The cost of Louis XIV's Versailles building programme', *French History* 21:2 (2007), 205–25.
[32] R. J. Bonney, 'France and the first European paper money experiment', *French History* 15:3 (2001), 254–72.

from the *Parlement* of Paris[33] and sectional interest groups such as the financiers and revenue farmers was open to question. The long period envisaged by Law to extinguish the debt required exceptional conditions of political stability which a Regency government was incapable of guaranteeing. The collapse of Law's System in July 1720 altered the nature of the debate on financial reform in France. Ideas of a national bank and a paper money solution to the crown's financial problems were not entirely discredited, but long delayed. England gained its national bank in 1694; as a result of Law's rushed attempt to turn his System into the French equivalent of the Bank of England after December 1718, France achieved its bank only in 1800. Hoffman, Postel-Vinay and Rosenthal contend that 'the financial schemes of the Regency had cost the state's creditors enormous sums. In nominal terms, they lost about half their claims on the state. In real terms they lost even more because the currency had depreciated.' The crown's default, the harshest before 1797, amounted in real terms to 1.5 billion *livres*. 'The Regency of 1715–23', they conclude, 'marked the climax to the government's attack on capital markets ... The short-run effect of this crisis was a crippling lack of confidence in financial assets – the levels of lending of the 1700s would not be matched again until the 1730s...'.[34]

There were two positive gains from the debacle of Law's System. The first was currency stability from 1726 to 1785, though this stability is only apparent in retrospect: no one knew for certain that Louis XV and Louis XVI would not manipulate the currency as their predecessors had done, so this period of stability did not, as in Britain, produce the dividend of lower interest rates.[35] The second was the decline, in real terms, of the state's total debt when measured in *livres* expressed in constant silver value. This fell by some 10 per cent between 1715 and 1789, although the structure of the debt itself was transformed: long-term debt rose at the expense of borrowing via short-term loans and the sale of offices.[36] The decline in real terms of the public debt was, for the monarchy, a profound disadvantage if it wished to preserve its autonomy in foreign policy, because it was only through new borrowing that an 'advanced war' (that is, a land war and naval war fought simultaneously) could be financed in the eighteenth century.

---

[33] Hurt, *Louis XIV and the parlements*, pp. 185–7. However, in terms of their personal finances, the system could be exploited by the office-holders to free themselves of their debts arising from *augmentations de gages* (p. 189).

[34] Hoffman *et al.*, *Priceless markets*, pp. 69, 85, 87, 275–6.

[35] Ibid., p. 109: 'how could a lender in, say, 1751, know the currency would remain stable?'

[36] Ibid., pp. 100, 105.

This gave Britain a significant, though not decisive, advantage over its Continental rival.[37]

Commentators are agreed that there was no *real* increase in French taxation between 1725 and 1785. Wartime tax increases did occur, but they were rarely sufficient to pay for the increased expenditure. Increased taxation paid for perhaps 72 per cent of the cost of the War of the Austrian Succession, but contributed much less towards the cost of the Seven Years War, a situation made worse because new tax measures did not come into place until 1760, the fifth year of the war. It would have been politically impossible to have increased direct taxes on the scale that was required to pay for the cost of the war (nearly 1,200 million *livres* over seven years). Even so, the war year 1761, when French revenues were equivalent to perhaps 12 or 13 per cent of national wealth, was the high point of taxation after 1715. This effort could not be sustained. As with Britain, 'tax smoothing' was required during the three great wars of Louis XV and Louis XVI: the percentage of supplementary expenses in each war covered by loan income rose in each war, from 28 per cent in the War of the Austrian Succession, to 74 per cent in the Seven Years War and 91 per cent in the American War. These figures were lower than in Britain, where 119 per cent of the supplementary expenses of the American War were covered by loan income. The three main wars under Louis XV and Louis XVI cost Britain more than France, while its population was only a third of its rival and its gross national product no more than a half.[38]

The fact that modern analysts are convinced that there was no *real* increase in French taxation between 1725 and 1785 masks a genuine historical difficulty: contemporaries thought otherwise. The common perception was that taxation had risen, and risen considerably in real terms.[39] Direct taxes, especially the *capitation* and the *vingtième*, were regarded as controversial by the privileged groups who were being brought increasingly into their net; but, as Kwass remarks, 'taxing the

[37] R. J. Bonney, 'Towards the comparative fiscal history of Britain and France during the "long" eighteenth century', in Leandro Prados de la Escosura (ed.), *British exceptionalism and industrialisation* (Cambridge University Press, 2004), pp. 191–215.

[38] Ibid., pp. 201, 209, a modified reading of F. Crouzet, *La grande inflation: la monnaie en France de Louis XIV à Napoléon* (Paris: Fayard, 1993), p. 66.

[39] Most of the growth in total GDP came from trade and urban production and services; Paris and western ports grew fat on the burgeoning Atlantic and colonial trade while agriculture stagnated. As a result, agricultural output undoubtedly fell as a percentage of GDP; thus taxes on agricultural output probably stayed flat or increased as a share of agricultural output. Even more important, direct taxes were such a maze of exemptions and privileges and regional variations that the burden of some taxes, particularly the *taille* would have fallen more heavily on the peasant villagers in those areas where a richer bourgeoisie was able to reduce its burden.

privileged did nothing to lighten the weight of taxation on the non-privileged. On the contrary, peasants and villagers were forced to pay new universal taxes in addition to the taxes they had always paid...'.[40] Direct tax revenue fell from 44 per cent of tax revenues in 1726 to 35 per cent in 1788 (and the new direct taxes fell from 30 per cent of the total tax yield to 22 per cent in the same period). In contrast, indirect tax revenues rose from 50 to 57 per cent of the total. Given that the imposition of indirect taxes posed fewer constitutional issues than direct taxes, as Malesherbes remarked, there should have been less, not more, agitation over taxation. The difference was that direct taxes were increasingly directed against the privileged, the most sensitive taxpayers in the kingdom, and those in the strongest position to voice their grievances.[41] On the eve of the Revolution, Kwass contends, 'universal taxes combined to raise far more revenue than the *taille* itself', some 58.2 per cent of direct taxes.[42] Land-owners denounced ministerial 'despotism' and the intendants for their attempts to reform direct taxes and the rolls of both *capitation* and *vingtième*, which led to increased fiscal pressure in the 1770s at a time that the fiscal exploitation of venality once more came to the fore. 'The use of verifications after 1771 and the tripling of the tax in the 1780s made sure that the crown captured a portion of land-owners' rising incomes', Kwass concludes.[43] The resistance of the office-holders, particularly the *Parlement* of Paris, to renewals of the *vingtième* demonstrate, in Julian Swann's words, that direct taxation 'was the principal cause of dissent in fiscal matters'; the 'vast majority' of the judges were hostile to increases in direct taxes and only in the decade after the Maupeou Revolution of 1771 were they temporarily quiescent.[44]

The French Revolution and state bankruptcy

The summoning of the Estates General, and the decision of the council of state on 27 December 1788 to double the representation of the third estate, demonstrated, as Kwass observes, that 'representation had become calculable and the weight of taxation was a key coefficient

---

[40] Kwass, *Privilege and the politics of taxation in eighteenth-century France*, p. 66.
[41] Ibid., pp. 67, 210–11. The poorer military nobility, who were also the most numerous part of the nobility, undoubtedly had to pay more *capitation* and *dixième* and *vingtième* without any increase, and perhaps a decrease, in their real incomes. It was this group that was the most vociferous in opposing the third estate's claims.
[42] Ibid., p. 68.
[43] Ibid., p. 93. Cf. pp. 85–6, 206–7.
[44] J. Swann, *Politics and the Parlement of Paris under Louis XV, 1754–1774* (Cambridge University Press, 1995), pp. 286–7, 290, 367.

in this new political arithmetic'.[45] Yet two surprising consequences emerged from this linkage of citizenship to the payment of direct taxation. The first was that, though there had been concern at the weight of direct taxes, they were at least considered legitimate and capable of being reformed, a conclusion based on observation of long-standing fiscal experimentation in certain provinces and the effort to make the new direct taxes truly universal.[46] In contrast, the indirect taxes 'provided no sound foundation for the construction of citizenship',[47] were loathed in terms of their regressive social impact and were considered incapable of being reformed.

The second consequence of linking citizenship to the payment of direct taxes was the expectation that elected representatives in the Estates General would insist on limiting the extent of tax increases and on the periodicity of tax grants. Indeed, the fiscal crisis gave them 'a powerful lever for prying a new constitution out of the monarchy's clutches'.[48] Direct taxes would therefore not rise, but would be pegged, notwithstanding the abolition of indirect taxes and the ecclesiastical tithe. The new regime of consent to taxation was a regime of lighter, rather than heavier, taxes as Necker had expected. Ramel contended that Frenchmen under the Revolution had paid only 300 million a year in taxes, when they should have paid 500 million, 'the rest being a net gain (*bénéfice*) for them'. Timothy Le Goff and Donald Sutherland conclude that 'it took the crisis of the Empire after 1810 to bring direct taxes up to the level legislators had hoped for in 1791', while indirect taxes also only made a reappearance under the First Empire.[49]

---

[45] Ibid., p. 305. J. Markoff, *The abolition of feudalism. Peasants, lords and legislators in the French Revolution* (Pennsylvania State University Press, 1996), p. 100. Cf. M. Touzery, *L'invention de l'impôt sur le revenu. La taille tarifée, 1715–1789* (Paris: Comité pour l'histoire économique et financière de la France, 1994).

[46] Kwass, *Privilege and the politics of taxation in eighteenth-century France*, p. 305: 'to peg citizenship to direct taxation would have been unthinkable without the *capitation* and the *vingtième*, taxes that guaranteed privileged property-owners a place in the new polity before the 1791 tax reforms were introduced.'

[47] Ibid.

[48] Hoffman *et al.*, *Priceless markets*, p. 175. From pp. 194–5: 'The members of the third estate and their allies knew that if they granted a permanent tax increase the king would no longer need the assembly. He might send the representatives home or use force against the assembly. Keeping the assembly alive would mean putting off a permanent solution to the government's fiscal policies ... By worsening the deficit, it made the crown dependent on the assembly ... The National Assembly was not trying to coax bondholders or taxpayers into footing the bill for the crown's debts. Rather, it was trying to force the king into accepting the assembly as a permanent representative body.'

[49] Bonney, 'The comparative fiscal history of Britain and France', pp. 211–12 for references and quotations.

With such an imposed restriction of traditional fiscal increases, the crown was faced with no alternative but to default on its obligations. There were only two ways in which this could be done. One was to follow the traditional techniques of default, which had been used as recently as 1770, and to impose a partial default which penalized those lenders least able to defend themselves. There were plenty of 'foreigners and politically weak provincials' who held a considerable amount of the government debt in 1789 and were an inviting target. As the representative of *la banque* rather than *la finance*, it was unthinkable that Necker should have presided over such a default. Yet the investments of the Genevans and Dutch between 1776 and 1788 amounted to between 24 and 41 per cent of the total value of new loans established by the crown and would have been vulnerable but for the concerted campaign of pamphleteers after 1787, such as Brissot who had equated a new default with ministerial 'despotism'.[50]

The second way was to follow John Law's precedent[51] and to issue fiat paper money. This was not the original purpose of the scheme of issuing paper against the collateral of church lands, but it is evident from the practice of individuals in the secrecy of the office of their notary that the public 'anticipated inflation – and ultimately the failure of the backed currency – and did so long before the *assignats* exceeded the value of the backing. They realized that the *assignats* needed fiscal discipline to succeed, and they must have suspected that the necessary discipline (a tax increase and lower expenses) was an unlikely outcome.'

[50] Hoffman *et al.*, *Priceless markets*, pp. 175, 197: 'a default of this magnitude – complete elimination of the foreign debt plus the reduction of interest payments on the domestic debt [to 6%] – was small by historical standards, and it would have brought the state's finances back into balance at the end of 1788.' From pp. 197, 198 n. 32: cancelling the debt altogether would have released about 220 million annually, 'enough to fight another small war'. R. Darnton, 'The Brissot dossier', *French Historical Studies* 17 (1991), 191–205; J.-P. Brissot, *Point de Banqueroute, ou lettres à un créancier de l'État sur l'impossibilité de la banqueroute rationale et sur les moyens de ramener le crédit et la paix* (London, 1787): 'no more private good faith, no more credit, and consequently no more commerce, no more industry and no more agriculture.' Visiting Paris in October, Arthur Young discovered that the question on everyone's lips was whether the king would default and, if so, whether the result would be civil war: A. Young, *Travels during the years 1787, 1788 and 1789*, 2 vols., (Dublin, 1793), Vol. I, pp. 129–30, 136–8 (13, 17 October 1787). Cited by T. M. Luckett, 'Hunting for spies and whores: a Parisian riot on the eve of the French Revolution', *Past and Present* 156 (1997), 116–143, at n. 21.

[51] The consequences of Law's System were still remembered, as is evidenced by references to Law in the parliamentary debates: Hoffman *et al.*, *Priceless markets*, p. 183 n. 8. A. E. Murphy, 'John Law and the *assignats*', in G. Faccarello and P. Steiner (eds.), *La pensée économique pendant la Révolution française* (Presses universitaires de Grenoble, 1990), pp. 431–48.

The legislators either fooled themselves or they attempted to fool the public, but by 1791 the deception had begun to unravel.[52]

Hoffman, Postel-Vinay and Rosenthal contend that the evidence from the Parisian private credit market 'completely changes our understanding of the revolutionary inflation and its consequences'. Divergent expectations of government fiscal and monetary policy during the French Revolution resulted from a 'decentralized credit market' which failed to 'aggregate information under rapid inflation'. In their judgement

the Revolution imposed three enormous losses on the Parisian economy: the government default of 1797, the inflation tax, and the damage done to private lenders when their loans were repaid in worthless *assignats*. Each loss totalled about two billion francs. The default was certainly not a consequence of the inflation; rather it was the financial conclusion of the political crisis of 1789. The reimbursement of private loans, though, was a direct result of the inflation, for it could never have occurred without the proliferation of the *assignats*... The inflation (and the government default too, for that matter) was hardly an efficient way to raise money. Indeed, for every *livre* the inflation tax raised, private investors suffered a one-*livre* loss.[53]

The 'long nineteenth century' (1801/15–1914)

Napoleon Bonaparte has been termed a man of the *ancien régime* in that he rejected the entire Revolutionary experience of paper money in favour of a strict monetarism.[54] In the long struggle against Britain, he confronted the 'paper pound' with traditionalist rectitude: the so-called *franc de germinal* of 1803 had the same value as the *livre tournois* of 1785. Calonne's 'fort judicieux' choice of a bimetallic ratio of 15.5 to 1 was thus re-established by the law of 7 Germinal An XI (27 March 1803), and this showed astonishing longevity, lasting for most of the nineteenth century, though France went over to the gold standard from 1876.[55] Though founded in January 1800, with rules of operation

[52] Hoffman *et al.*, *Priceless markets*, pp. 189–90.

[53] Ibid., pp. 206, 200 and table 8.2. The default on two-thirds of the debt caused a loss of 2.6 billion to the government's creditors. Revolutionary inflation cost 1.67 billion more.

[54] This section draws on R. J. Bonney, 'The eighteenth century. II. The struggle for great power status and the end of the old fiscal regime', in Bonney (ed.), *Economic systems and state finance* (Oxford: Clarendon Press, 1995), p. 355; Bonney, 'Revenues', p. 499; and Bonney, 'France, 1494–1815', pp. 151–2, 165–7.

[55] G. Thuillier, *La monnaie en France au début du xix⁽ᵉ⁾ siècle* (Geneva: Librairie Droz, 1983), p. 32; M. Flandreau, *The glitter of gold: France, bimetallism, and the emergence of the international gold standard, 1848–1873* (Oxford University Press, 2004). Chapter 8 analyses the end of bimetallism: 'It shows that the conventional view of an inescapable

specified by a law of 14 April 1803, the Bank of France had limited functions. The circulation of its banknotes did not exceed 112 million francs under the Empire, and therefore could not play a significant role in the mechanism of state payments. Instead, from 1806 onwards, the receivers-general were brought back in business as the government functionaries for the levy of direct taxes.

Indirect taxes, too, in the form of the *douanes* and *droits réunis* made a significant comeback under the First Empire. Unlike the direct taxes, indirect taxes provided Napoleon with a source of revenue that could be manipulated free from parliamentary control. By 1813 there was almost a balance between direct and indirect sources of revenue. The recent researches of Pierre Branda provide a detailed analysis of Napoleonic finance at the period of transition from an eighteenth-century to a nineteenth-century fiscal system.[56]

Any analysis of the 'long nineteenth century' (1801/15–1914) in terms of French state finance has to consider first the issue of political instability and 'regime change'. Three revolutions, two *coups d'état*, and three types of regime (monarchical, imperial and republican) made for critical disjunctures in fiscal policy. The most important development was growth in the size of the public debt, which rose from 1,272 million *livres* in 1815 to 4,627 million in 1830, virtually a quadrupling. The cost of war reparations to the Allies (1,863.5 million actually paid, or between 18 and 21 per cent of GDP), transformed into funded debt, had led to more than a trebling of the debt by 1821 to 4,173 million.[57] There seems much to commend the argument of Eugene N. White, advanced in 2001, that these were 'the largest reparations in terms of the burden on the economy that were [ever] actually paid, with a lasting negative impact upon growth'.[58]

The growth in national wealth was not spread evenly: the top strata of society, the landlords, the industrialists, the financiers and the *rentiers*,

---

collapse is not founded. France, endowed with a large share of the gold output of the 1850s and 1860s, had enough gold to weather the modestly rising silver output of the 1870s and 1880s. It had also enough gold to resist Germany's decision to adopt a gold standard in the early 1870s. Failure of international cooperation, it is argued, is what caused the emergence of the gold standard.'

[56] P. Branda, 'Les finances et le budget de la France napoléonienne', *Revue du Souvenir Napoléonien* (Dec. 2004–Jan. 2005 and Feb.–March 2005).

[57] E. N. White, 'Making the French pay: the costs and consequences of the Napoleonic reparations', *European Review of Economic History* 5 (2001), 337–65, at 341, 348. Note that White's data differs from that of L. Fontvieille, *Évolution et croissance de l'Etat français, 1815–1969* (Paris: ISMEA, 1976), p. 2043.

[58] White, 'Making the French pay', p. 355; also cited by F. Crouzet, 'The historiography of French economic growth in the nineteenth century', *Economic History Review* 56 (2003), pp. 215–42, at 235.

were the chief beneficiaries: it was in their interest that the various regimes – imperial, monarchist, republican – operated before 1914.[59] A well-managed portfolio of investments might grow by 1.8 per cent per annum between 1815 and 1850 and by 2.4 per cent per annum between 1851 and 1913. If the sums were reinvested, the growth rates of the portfolio would be respectively 7 per cent and 6.2 per cent, in an era when there was scarcely any taxation to pay on such investments.[60]

The July Monarchy witnessed a perceptible increase in expenditure: total expenses rose from 1,095 million *livres* in 1830 to 1,364 million in 1840, or 9.2 per cent of GNP.[61] At the same, the public debt remained stable or even declined somewhat. By 1847, expenditure had risen still further, to 1,630 million, considerably outstripping revenues. Under the Second Empire, government expenditure continued to rise in proportion to the ambitions of French foreign policy, first with regard to the Crimean War (1853–56), and later with adventures in Italy, in the colonies and in Mexico. Both revenues and expenditure peaked in 1855, but the public debt continued to grow every year until 1866. Expenditure reached 9.6 per cent of GDP by 1860, an increase of 1.1 per cent of GDP since 1850. The period between 1851 and 1873 was one of high prices, so increased levels of expenditure, revenues and public debt were an inevitable reaction if the state was to maintain its capacity in a period of inflation. In spite of these increases, France was found to be woefully unready to meet the Prussian threat in the war of 1870, the disaster of which swept aside the Second Empire. The 1871 war indemnity payable by France to Prussia amounted to 5,000 million, equivalent to one quarter of one year's GDP and more than two years of government revenue, or 1.6 times France's annual exports. France was

---

[59] R. E. Cameron, 'Economic growth and stagnation in France, 1815–1914', *Journal of Modern History* 30/1 (1958), 1–15; C. and M. Casson, *France and the economic development of Europe, 1815–1914. Conquests of peace and seeds of war* (Princeton University Press, 1961; repr. London: Routledge, 2000), pp. 36, 65.

[60] P.-C. Hautcœur, Z. Kang, C. Romey, T. Seck and A. Straus, *Le marché financier français au xixe siècle. I. Récit* (Paris: Publications de la Sorbonne, 2007), p. 12; Cf. P. Arbulu and G. Gallais-Hamonno, 'Valeurs extrêmes et changements d'appréciation du risque à la Bourse de Paris sur deux siècles, 1802–2000', *Finance* 23/12 (2002), pp. 145–76.

[61] These figures are drawn from the *Annuaire statistique rétrospectif* of 1929 published by the Statistique Générale de la France. This source was also used by François Bouvier in his analysis of the growth of French expenditure between 1815 and 1950: F. Bouvier, 'La croissance quantitative des finances publiques françaises et l'attitude des économistes (xixe–xxe siècles)', *Revue internationale d'histoire de la banque* 2 (1969), pp. 299–314. These figures are discussed in more detail in R. Bonney, 'The apogee and fall of the French *rentier* regime, 1801–1914', in J.-L. Cardoso and P. Lains (eds.), *Paying for the liberal state: The rise of public finance in nineteenth-century Europe* (Cambridge University Press, 2010), pp. 81–102.

rescued only by a sudden trade surplus in the years 1872–77; about half the increased burden of public debt was purchased domestically.[62]

Following the bloody suppression of the Commune, the Third Republic continued Napoleon III's policy of allowing the growth of the public debt, damping down the increase in expenditure and revenues at least until 1879. The growth of expenditure, which had been the norm for most years from 1815, was finally halted in 1883. As François Bouvier has observed, economic commentators were increasingly convinced that the state had 'grown too much'. Paul Leroy-Beaulieu in 1912 identified the causes for this growth in expenditure.[63] His contention was that the deputies elected to parliament wanted to see investments in their localities, and that collectively this was an important pressure towards increased expenditure. It seems unlikely, however, that this was as significant an overall factor as the increased costs of government in an era of inflation. The psychological impact on the deputies of the Third Republic of arguments such as those of Léon Say in 1886 against the continued growth of expenditure was nevertheless considerable. In principle, though the deputies wanted more expenditure in their localities, they also wanted to see a state that governed with a lighter rather than a more burdensome touch. For a relatively short period, between 1883 and 1891, this attitude prevailed and expenditure declined from 3,715 million to 3,258 million francs.

The effort could not be sustained, not least with the increase in prices after 1896 and with the need for rearmament as the militarist intentions of Germany became evident on the eve of the First World War. Yet as late as 1903, with expenditure at 3,597 million francs, it was still below that for 1883. A constant of French pre-First World War politics was that some day there would be another war with Germany, during which France would conquer and re-annex the provinces of Alsace and Lorraine that Germany had annexed. French military strategy depended on a large, active, allied Russian army in Poland threatening Berlin and forcing Germany to divide its armies while the French marched to the Rhine. The years 1894–1912 were ones of strict budgetary control. After 1895 the costs of national defence consistently exceeded those of debt servicing. A general income tax was not enacted in France until 1914, just a few weeks before the declaration of war. It was applied for the first time in 1915 (that is, the incomes of 1915 had to be declared by taxpayers at the beginning of 1916) and has

[62] White, 'Making the French pay', p. 353.
[63] Quoted by Bouvier, 'La croissance quantitative des finances publiques françaises', pp. 312–13.

been ever since. The exponential growth was between 1913 and 1914, with the outbreak of the First World War. With expenditure at 10,065 million francs, it may be estimated that the first year of the war saw expenditure at 22.1 per cent of GDP, while revenues amounted to only 10 per cent of GDP.

5   The politics of British taxation, from the Glorious Revolution to the Great War

Martin Daunton

> General rule: one can raise higher taxes, in proportion to the liberty of the subjects; and one is forced to moderate them to the degree that servitude increases. This has always been, and will always remain so. It is a rule drawn from nature, which does not vary at all; one finds it in all countries, in England, in Holland, and in all States in which liberty becomes degraded, right down to Turkey.
>
> Charles Montesquieu, *De l'esprit des lois, III*, 1748, chapter 7[1]

> It might be expected that in France a revenue of thirty millions might be levied for the support of the state with as little inconveniency as a revenue of ten millions is in Great Britain. In 1765 and 1766, the whole revenue paid into the treasury of France ... did not amount to fifteen millions sterling ... The people of France, however, it is generally acknowledged, are much more oppressed by taxes than the people of Great Britain.
>
> Adam Smith, *The Wealth of Nations*, 1776, book 1, 2, p. 47[2]

These two great representatives of the French and Scottish enlightenment realized that the finances of their two nations diverged.[3] Despite the larger population and great resources of France, it could raise less revenue than Britain – yet the French people believed that their burdens were greater. Apart from riots against the malt tax in Scotland in 1725, fuelled by Jacobite and nationalist hostility to a supposed breach of the terms of Union in 1707, and the 'excise crisis' of 1733–34, taxes

---

[1] Quoted in J. MacDonald, *A free nation deep in debt: the financial roots of democracy* (New York: Farrar, Straus and Giroux, 2003), p. 255.

[2] Quoted in MacDonald, *A free nation deep in debt*, p. 253

[3] This chapter draws on the text of two papers dealing with British taxation: 'The fiscal military state and the Napoleonic Wars', in D. Cannadine (ed.), *Trafalgar in history: a battle and its aftermath* (Basingtoke: Palgrave Macmillan, 2006), pp. 18–43; and 'Trusting Leviathan: the politics of taxation, 1815–1914', in D. Winch and P. K. O'Brien (eds.), *The political economy of British historical experience, 1688–1914* (Oxford University Press, 2002).

in Britain achieved a remarkably high level of consent and compliance.[4] In 1700–25, the English paid something over twice the French level of taxes per capita, and by the 1780s the discrepancy had widened to 2.7 times.[5] The contrast was still more obvious in the French financial and political crisis of 1788/89, when a much smaller financial burden than in Britain started the chain of events leading to the Revolution. The weakness of French finances contributed to the demise of the *ancien régime*, and the strength of British finances underpinned military and naval success.

Prior to 1688, taxes in England were usually in the range of 1.3 to 4.4 per cent of national income, a relatively low level compared with France. The accession of William III and wars with France between 1689 and 1697 took the level of taxation/spending to between 7.3 and 9.5 per cent of national income, and it remained at around 8 to 10 per cent until the outbreak of the French revolutionary wars. Between 1790 and 1810, total government expenditure in Britain rose from 12 per cent of GNP to 23 per cent. Britain became a 'fiscal state', the only such state in Europe by 1815. In a fiscal state, a steady and secure flow of tax revenues forms the basis for large-scale borrowing without the threat of default and hence the need for the state to pay high interest rates to obtain funds. Warfare needs both taxes *and* loans, as expenditure during a war far exceeds the annual flow of income from taxation. By the end of the war against Napoleon, about 55 per cent of the gross expenditure of the central government went in interest payments on loans.[6] The British government was able to sustain payments of interest on the national debt and to avoid defaulting on its loans. Clearly, two

[4] J. Brewer, *The sinews of power: war, money and the English state, 1688–1783* (New York: Knopf, 1989), p. 132; P. Langford, *The excise crisis: society and politics in the age of Walpole* (Oxford: Clarendon Press, 1975).

[5] Brewer, *Sinews of power*, p. 89; for a pioneering comparative account see P. Mathias and P. O'Brien, 'Taxation in Britain and France, 1715–1810: a comparison of the social and economic incidence of taxes collected for the central governments', *Journal of European Economic History* 5 (1976), 601–50, especially 610–11 and tables 7 and 8.

[6] The level of taxation is discussed in Mathias and O'Brien, 'Taxation in Britain and France', 603–11; P. O'Brien and P. A. Hunt, 'The rise of the fiscal state in England, 1485–1815', *Historical Research* 66 (1993), 158–60 and appendix 3, tables 3 and 4; O'Brien and Hunt, 'England, 1485–1815' in R. Bonney (ed.), *Rise of the fiscal state* (Oxford University Press, 1999), pp. 54–8; R. Middleton, *Government versus the market: the growth of the public sector, economic management and British economic performance, c. 1890–1979* (Cheltenham: Elgar, 1996), tables 3.1 and 3.2. On Britain as the first fiscal state, see R. Bonney, 'Introduction', in Bonney (ed.), *Rise of the fiscal state*, pp. 13–14; for the concept of the fiscal–military state, see Brewer, *Sinews of power*. On the emergence of government loans, see P. G. M. Dickson, *The financial revolution in England: a study in the development of public credit, 1688–1756* (London: Macmillan, 1967).

questions arise: first, why was Britain able to extract taxes at a higher level and with less resentment than in France?; second, why was it able to borrow on better terms than France, without default?

Taxation: legitimacy versus resentment

The British state was able to extract taxes much more easily than the French state in the course of the long eighteenth century partly as a result of timing. In the seventeenth century, the French were heavily involved in large-scale European land warfare and needed to find large sums of money in excess of the annual flow of tax revenues.[7] The solution was to sell offices and to 'farm' taxes. In both cases, the purchaser of the office or tax farm made a down payment in return for the future income from an office or the collection of taxes. Colbert consolidated the collection of most excise duties in one tax farm, the Farmers General – a drive for efficiency that gave the farmers more control over the fiscal system. In the 1780s, the Farmers General collected 150 million *livres* a year of which about 30 million were paid to officials, and 100 million were handed over to the Hotel de Ville in Paris for direct payment to debt holders; only 18 million *livres* went to the crown.[8]

The sale of offices offered another way of raising large sums of money. The crown sold offices in return for a capital sum, and also levied continuing payments to allow the right to sell or inherit the office; in return it paid a salary or *gage* to the office-holder to give a return on the investment. In the seventeenth and early eighteenth centuries, the crown received a large income from the sale of offices; the contribution of venality to revenues fell by the middle of the eighteenth century, and probably contributed only 5 per cent of the cost of the Seven Years War. The original justification of venality had been lost: as William Doyle remarks, 'What remained was the swollen bulk of the legacy, now largely there because it was there – too expensive, and extensive, even to dream of abolishing'.[9] By contrast, seventeenth-century England was much less involved in European land wars and so did not need to engage in tax farming or the sale of offices on anything like the scale of France. Indeed, tax farming was generally ended in the later

---

[7] Brewer, *Sinews of power*, pp. 7–14, 24.
[8] MacDonald, *A free nation deep in debt*, pp. 181, 196–8, 258–9; F. R. Velde and D. R. Weir, 'The financial market and government debt policy in France, 1746–1793', *Journal of Economic History* 52 (1992), 7–8.
[9] For a good account of the sale of offices, see W. Doyle, *Venality: the sale of offices in eighteenth-century France* (Oxford: Clarendon Press, 1996); the contribution in 1688–1715 is discussed on pp. 30–1, and later contributions on pp. 99–100.

seventeenth century: the farms of customs, excise and hearth tax were abolished in 1671, 1683 and 1684 respectively. The relatively low number of offices sold meant that the English state escaped from France's curse of 'a sprawling, tentacular state apparatus made up of venal office holders'.[10]

French reliance on the sale of offices and tax farming contributed to the lack of consent to taxation in the eighteenth century. The sale of offices meant that the bureaucracy was large, unaccountable and exempt from taxes. Office-holders took their fees and salaries, and left the work to paid deputies. Why would taxpayers wish to pay in order to support a venal system of administration? Why would they willingly hand over their taxes to a 'farmer' who retained the difference between the actual revenue and what he promised to pay the state? Tax exemptions extended to the Church and to the nobility, so that the payment of taxes was perceived as biased and partial. French taxes might be lower than in Britain, but they lacked consent and legitimacy.

The contrast was reinforced by the process of negotiating taxes with the subjects of the crown. In France, representative institutions were much weaker than in England and Britain, and there was no political forum for negotiating changes in the system of taxation. The Estates General – an assembly of the three estates of clergy, nobility and commoners – did not develop in the same way as the English parliament with control over finances, legislative authority and the ability to initiate policies. The Estates General was called by the king to provide advice, and had no legislative power, which rested entirely with the crown. By the second half of the seventeenth century, the monarch had established the right to impose taxes on his own authority and the Estates General were not called at any time between 1614/15 and 1789, when the decision marked a political crisis that soon escalated into revolution.[11]

Provincial Estates General with limited powers did survive in the *pays d'etats* such as Brittany, Burgundy and Provence. In Britain, separate Scottish and Irish parliaments were abolished at the time of the Union, so that there was one unified representative body which minimized (though it did not entirely remove) opposition to taxation. The survival of provincial Estates in France created fiscal complexities, for they had a variety of exemptions (such as Brittany's exemption from the salt tax), and each might challenge the power of the crown to levy taxes

---

[10] Brewer, *Sinews of power*, pp. 14–21, 23, 92–3.

[11] For a summary of the Estates General, see the on-line *Columbia Encyclopaedia* (6th edn, 2001–2005) at www.bartleby.com/65/st/StatesGe.html; W. Doyle, *The Oxford history of the French Revolution* (Oxford University Press, 1989), chapter 4.

without consent. The closest similarity is with the revolt of the Thirteen Colonies from British rule. The assembly in Massachusetts opposed the imposition of taxes by Britain to which it had not consented, leading to revolt and ultimate independence. In the case of France, similar tensions existed within the domestic sphere.[12]

In the absence of the Estates General, the only real counter to royal power came from the *Parlement* of Paris and the provincial *parlements* in a number of other cities around France. The Paris *Parlement* differed from the British parliament which passed legislation and took an active role in shaping policy. Its initial role was judicial rather than representative, with political influence as a result of registering royal edicts and hence providing a veneer of legitimacy. Although *parlement* had the right to remonstrate at any breach of tradition, the king could impose his will by summoning the *parlement* to his presence or by issuing an order that they obey. *Parlement* could resist change and defend privileges without making any positive proposals for reform, and Louis XV accordingly abolished the Paris *Parlement* in 1771 and replaced it with a new judicial court without the power of opposition. Not surprisingly, the result was highly unpopular and in 1774 Louis XVI restored *parlement*. Tensions soon reappeared. The ability to raise taxes required either wider political participation as in Britain or the adoption of a more absolutist policy as in 1770–74, but the French crown was not firmly committed to either approach.[13]

France lacked a political forum for negotiating changes in the system of taxation, unlike in England/Britain where acceptance of taxes was secured in parliament which met every year after 1688. In contrast with France, parliament controlled the taxing powers of the state. In 1697, parliament granted the crown a 'civil list' for its upkeep and for the salaries and pensions of judges, officials and courtiers. Parliament did not grant a permanent revenue to the king for additional expenditure, above all on war, which was voted for on an annual basis.[14]

Parliament was therefore a forum for negotiating an acceptable level of spending and the composition of taxes in Britain. Constraint

[12] Bonney, 'Revenues', in R. Bonney (ed.), *Economic systems and state finance* (Oxford: Clarendon Press, 1995), pp. 494–5; Brewer, *Sinews of power*, p. 132.

[13] J. H. Shennan, *The Parlement of Paris* (Ithaca: Cornell University Press, 1968), chapter 9 on *parlement* and taxes in the eighteenth century; W. Doyle, 'The parlements of France and the breakdown of the old regime, 1771–88', *French Historical Studies* 6 (1970) 415–58; Velde and Weir, 'The financial market and government debt policy', p. 7.

[14] E. A. Reitan, 'From revenue to civil list, 1688–1702: the Revolution settlement and the "mixed and balanced" constitution', *Historical Journal* 13 (1970), 571–88; Velde and Weir, 'Financial market and government debt policy', p. 6.

on the central executive resulted in a high level of consent, and resistance to taxation was limited. Of course, the distribution of seats in the Commons bore little relationship to the population, and large aristocratic land-owners had much influence. One outcome, as we shall see, was a fall in the contribution of land-owners to the revenues of the state. Nevertheless, commercial interests were represented by purchasing seats or by ensuring that local land-owners expressed their views through lobbying and bargaining at election time. Any changes in the structure of taxes or adjustment in duties were negotiated between different interests, whether north European merchants protesting against preference to timber from North America, woollen textile producers seeking to limit competition from Indian cotton cloth, or West Indian planters eager to secure markets for their sugar against the East India Company pressure for a free trade in sugar and a monopoly for their China tea.[15] The balance of custom and excise duties on different commodities was negotiated rather than imposed, and in the process economic interest groups were incorporated into the political system. Parliament was deeply jealous of its fiscal powers, as was apparent in the excise crisis of 1733–34. Robert Walpole's proposed extension of excise duties led to a fear that he intended to introduce a general excise on all commodities and hence to free the executive from parliamentary control. The county gentry, with their dread of a powerful central executive, united with commercial interests in opposition to the proposals.[16] Strict limits were set to the independence of the central executive from parliamentary control.

The ability of parliament to control the executive and monitor spending rested on the availability of reasonably accurate accounts supplied to parliament by the Treasury Commissioners. Britain was the first European state to compile a full statement of its financial position, which meant that its operations were visible. Representatives in parliament could challenge waste, so that taxpayers had some confidence that their payments were being used for the intended purpose. Similarly, the state's creditors had confidence that the state was solvent and honest. The same could not be said of France, where accounts simply did not exist – and when a financial statement was produced in 1781, the result was scepticism rather than confidence.[17]

---

[15] For one case study, see P. O'Brien, T. Griffiths and P. Hunt, 'Political components of the industrial revolution: parliament and the English cotton textile industry, 1660–1774', *Economic History Review* 44 (1991), 395–423; P. Langford, *Public life and the propertied Englishman, 1689–1798* (Oxford: Clarendon Press, 1991).
[16] Langford, *Excise crisis.*
[17] Brewer, *Sinews of power*, pp. 129, 131; J. E. D. Binney, *British public finance and administration, 1774–92* (Oxford: Clarendon Press, 1958); J. Hoppit, 'Checking the

Whereas the costs of the War of American Independence resulted in crisis in France, in Britain it led to 'economical reform' or a concern for administrative efficiency. Demands for an end to sinecures, a reduction in the costs of government and the court, and constraints on the excessive power of the executive, led politicians at Westminster to improve the efficiency of financial administration by controlling expenditure and preventing waste through the work of the Commission for Examining the Public Accounts of 1780 and parliamentary committees to examine expenditure and accounting methods in 1782, 1786 and 1792. The work was continued by William Pitt, who took steps to reduce the national debt and to adjust the level of duties in order to increase their yield, and to remove sinecures from the customs service. By taking action, ministers aimed to separate demands for economical reform from pressure for parliamentary reform and attacks on the crown. The government's desire for efficiency in order to protect the creditworthiness of the state coincided with the demands of the critics.[18]

Parliamentary scrutiny of spending meant that the British state was more public and accountable, and hence 'stronger rather than weaker, more effective rather than more impotent. Public scrutiny reduced speculation, parliamentary consent lent greater legitimacy to government action. Limited in scope, the state's powers were nevertheless exercised with telling effect.'[19] The seemingly absolutist French state was in reality weaker than the constitutional monarchy of Britain. Its revenues were 'owned' by others – the tax farmers and office-holders – with many exemptions and privileges. Although the need for reform was obvious to finance ministers, action was extremely difficult, for they lacked representative institutions to simplify and standardize taxation across the country. The power of the crown in France was severely limited in practice by bodies with the power to resist without responsibility; and the crown was not willing to adopt the British solution of a more formal constraint on its power in order to achieve greater effectiveness. The preferred solution was to turn to more direct and unfettered rule

leviathan', in D. Winch and P. K. O'Brien (eds.), *The political economy of British historical experience, 1688–1914* (Oxford University Press, 2002). On the French accounts, see Florin Aftalion, *The French Revolution, an economic interpretation* (Cambridge University Press, 1990), pp. 24–5.

[18] Brewer, *Sinews of power*, pp. 85–7; J. Torrance, 'Social class and bureaucratic innovation: The Commissioners for Examining the Public Accounts, 1780–87', *Past and Present* 78 (1978), 56–81; E. A. Reitan, 'Edmund Burke and economical reform, 1779–83', *Studies in Eighteenth Century Culture* 14 (1985), 129–58.

[19] Brewer, *Sinews of power*, p. xix.

without the ability to follow through its implications. By the time the Estates General was finally called in 1789, reform was too late.[20]

The method of collecting taxes was crucial to the relationship between subjects and the state. In France, collection was highly problematic as a result of tax farming, exemptions and regional variations, and the difficulties were intensified by reliance on internal customs barriers and the need for a paramilitary presence in internal trade. Many opportunities occurred for resistance and for hostility between taxpayer and tax collector. In Britain, tensions were reduced. There were no exemptions for nobles and clergy, no internal customs barriers and hence fewer tax officials to intervene in the trade of the country.[21] Consent to taxation was increased by using the taxpayers themselves to assess and collect some taxes. Not only did local elites validate taxes through parliament; they were also the local magistracy and commissioners for the land tax. The commissioners were not paid and were not officials of the crown; they were members of the land-owning or urban elites serving in the same way as they did as justices of the peace. The British system did have problems, for the land tax was granted by a parliament of land-owners in return for control over the finances of the crown, and was administered by them in the localities. Consent was achieved but adjustment to the land tax proved difficult. In theory, the land tax was levied at one of four rates, from 1 shilling to 4 shillings in the pound (from 5 to 20 per cent). In reality, the rates were standardised to produce a yield of £500,000 to £2 million, with no adjustment to take account of the rising value of land in the later eighteenth century or the differential growth of regions in the country. The agreement on the land tax of 1689 survived until 1799, when the pressures of the revolutionary war led William Pitt to introduce a new income tax. The land-owners' contribution to the finances of the state fell over the eighteenth century (see Table 5.1).[22]

The lack of buoyancy in the land tax meant that the government turned to other sources of revenue. Assessed taxes were imposed on conspicuous signs of wealth, such as male servants, hair powder and riding horses. They were designed to fall on the rich, and were administered by the same local commissioners as the land tax. The result was a degree of tax evasion and a fair degree of consent and legitimacy.

---

[20] Macdonald, *A free nation deep in debt*, pp. 258–9, 260–1.

[21] Brewer, *Sinews of power*, 128–9; Mathias and O'Brien, 'Taxation in Britain and France', pp. 636–9.

[22] W. R. Ward, *The English land tax in the eighteenth century* (London: Oxford University Press, 1963); G. J. Wilson, 'The land tax problem', *Economic History Review* 35 (1982), 422–26.

Table 5.1. *Direct and indirect taxes as a share (%) of total tax revenues in Britain*

Direct taxes on wealth and income		Indirect taxes on commodities			
(Land and assessed)		Customs	Excise	Total	Other
1711–15	31.1	26.4	35.9	62.3	11.1
1791–95	16.0	20.9	47.3	68.2	15.8
1811–15	29.2*	19.2	37.7	56.9	13.9
1831–35	10.0	36.6	34.7	71.3	18.7

Notes: * including income tax; source: B. R. Mitchell and P. Deane, *Abstract of British historical statistics* (Cambridge University Press, 1962), pp. 386–8, 392–3.

As we shall see, the commissioners administered the income tax between 1799 and 1816 with much the same trade-off between evasion and acceptance. By the early 1790s, the land and assessed taxes taken together had fallen to barely half their share of total taxation at the start of the eighteenth century. Land-owners and the wealthy controlled parliament and failed to maintain their proportion of the tax burden, yet without the serious problems of financial collapse experienced by France.

Customs duties were a major source of revenue at the start of the eighteenth century, but fell by the end of the century. Revenue from customs duties failed to keep pace with the growth in British trade in the eighteenth century. Tariffs were higher on manufactures than on food and raw materials, on goods from foreign countries than from the empire, and on luxuries than on necessities. In the eighteenth century, imports of food and raw materials grew more rapidly than manufactures, trade with the empire more rapidly than with foreigners, and necessities more than luxuries. Reforming the structure of duties was difficult, both for strategic reasons and because change would provoke outcry from vested interests. The customs service was an inefficient part of the state. Officials were appointed by the Treasury, often with more concern for political patronage than efficiency, and many had a life-long interest in the post. They were paid a modest salary and drew fees from the office, leaving the work to paid deputies who might supplement their income by offering advice to merchants on their payment of duties. The high level of duties on goods resulted in smuggling and evasion which was extremely difficult to police around the British coastline. Clearly, particular taxes in Britain provoked resistance, though usually at the level of smuggling brandy or tea past customs officials rather than tax revolts and a collapse of revenues. Unlike in France, there were no internal tariff barriers within Britain after the union with Scotland in 1707, so that tensions between the population and officers were mainly confined to the coastal areas and ports. Britain did not have a highly visible and deeply resented *milice financière* with a presence throughout the country.[23]

The major source of additional finance in the eighteenth century was the excise (see Table 5.1), where the mode of collection differed from both the local commissioners and the customs service in Britain, and from the fiscal system of France. Officials or Gaugers were appointed for their competence, which was ensured by a career ladder with promotion by merit and a pension on retirement. They were paid a salary rather than fees, so that they had an incentive to create efficient methods in order to reduce their workload, in contrast to customs officials who were paid fees and had an incentive to maintain existing procedures. The producers of excisable goods such as salt, glass and beer made monthly returns of their output to the Gaugers, who checked the figures for accuracy; the Gaugers were in turn monitored by Surveyors. In the case of large plants, such as in the glass industry, an officer was permanently assigned to monitor production. The excise duty on glass was high, at around twice the cost of production. The firms and excise officials were in constant negotiation over allowances for waste, which could on occasion result in a breakdown of relations. However, in most cases they worked together within acceptable bounds. Most producers preferred to work with officials to ensure that competitors were not taking an unfair advantage; and the task of administration was much easier if the excise officers could rely on the producers. The excise officials dealt with producers rather than the general public, and consequently tension did not permeate society.[24]

Borrowing: credible commitment versus default

The British state was able to borrow money on generous terms, at around a 2 per cent lower interest rate than in France between 1746 and 1793. In France, the state paid a 'default premium' throughout the eighteenth century and, in the words of Velde and Weir, 'the financial market was

[23] Brewer, *Sinews of power*, pp. 101–2, 130; P. K. O'Brien, 'The political economy of British taxation, 1660–1815', *Economic History Review* 41 (1988), 23–6.
[24] Brewer, *Sinews of power*, pp. 69–87, 101–14; O'Brien, 'Political economy', 26–8; T. C. Barker, *The glassmakers: Pilkington: the rise of an international company, 1826–1976* (London: Weidenfeld and Nicolson, 1977), pp. 34–5, 39, 41–3.

the economic conscience of the Old Regime'.[25] The British state never defaulted on its debts, so that the risks of lending were much lower than in France with its high risk of default. Neither did the British state attempt to escape from its debt through currency debasement and inflation – a temptation which many other countries did not resist. Creditors had justified suspicion of the security of loans to the French state, with partial defaults in 1720, 1759, 1770, 1788 and 1797. Although Louis XVI resolved not to default when he came to the throne in 1774, he had difficulties sustaining his policy given the lack of tax revenues to service the debt. His opposition to default provides the context for his calling of the Estates General, for in 1788 he suspended payments with the promise that they would be made good in the future, once the Estates General created new taxes to honour the debts. By rejecting default and calling the Estates General, he brought the *ancien régime* to its final crisis.[26] Borrowing rose to new levels, and between 1751 and 1787 debt service rose from 28 per cent of total expenditure to 49.3 per cent – still much lower than in Britain.[27] It was not that financial markets failed to develop in France, for the rate of interest on private loans was similar to the level in Britain.[28] The problem was that the French state did not have the confidence of creditors, or in the words of economists, it could not offer them a credible commitment to meet their claims. Risk was therefore discounted through higher interest rates. How is the difference in the security of loans and the credibility of the commitment of the two states to honour their obligations to be explained?

The answer is, in part, the different financial strategies of the two states. The French state resorted to a number of stratagems which merely intensified the problem and avoided the creation of a credible commitment. One was to borrow indirectly from the holders of venal offices. The crown could force office-holders to provide additional

---

[25] Velde and Weir, 'Financial market and government debt policy', pp. 15–19, 36; D. Stasavage, *Public debt and the birth of the democratic state: France and Great Britain, 1688–1789*, (Cambridge University Press, 2003), pp. 96–7; Brewer, *Sinews of power*, pp. 114–26. On the operation of the loan market in Britain, see Dickson, *Financial revolution*.

[26] See Velde and Weir, 'Financial market and government debt policy', pp. 9–10, 37; Macdonald, *A free nation deep in debt*, p. 252.

[27] Stasavage, *Public debt*, pp. 92, 95; R. Bonney, 'The eighteenth century II: the struggle for great power status and the end of the old fiscal regime', in R. Bonney (ed.), *Economic systems and state finance*, p. 347; Doyle, *Oxford history of the French Revolution*, pp. 78–85.

[28] Velde and Weir, 'The financial market and government debt policy', pp. 18–19; Macdonald, *A free nation deep in debt*, p. 250; see also P. Hoffman, G. Postel-Vinay and J.-L. Rosenthal, *Priceless markets: the political economy of credit in Paris, 1660–1879* (Chicago University Press, 2000), pp. 173–6.

capital by withholding *gages* to the officers, threatening to create more offices which would reduce the value of existing posts, or demanding lump-sum payments for the right to inherit or sell offices. The office-holders were obliged to repay their creditors on pain of surrendering their office; they had little recourse against the crown if their *gages* were suspended. Consequently, the lack of a credible commitment by the crown to honour its debts was passed from private lenders to the office-holders, a way of side-stepping rather than resolving the risk of default.[29] Much the same strategy was adopted with the provincial Estates, which could borrow money more cheaply than the crown. The crown might grant the right to collect duties in return for a capital sum which the Estates could secure on favourable terms. The value of duties increased over time, and in theory the crown could alter the terms of the grant to secure some of the additional revenue. However, the Estates were in a stronger position than office-holders in dealing with the crown, and were able to resist these attempts. The crown was therefore securing loans on more favourable terms at the expense of a loss of prospective revenue.[30] Again, the stratagem marked a lack of a credible commitment and did nothing positive to change market sentiment towards the crown.

Another strategy adopted in France was to turn to life annuities, which surpassed term loans from 1771. Men and women loaned money to the government in return for an income or annuity during their life – they were purchasing a pension for their retirement. The market for pensions was stable and relatively modest. The main concern of pensioners was to secure a decent income in old age; whether the return was good or bad depended on how long they lived. The gamble was worth taking: if they lived for many years, they had a good return; if they died in a few years, their rate of return was scarcely a major consideration. However, the bulk of annuities were issued on the lives of third parties, above all purchased by parents to provide for their children. An annuity on the life of a child was a risk at a time of high levels of mortality. An early

[29] Stasavage, *Public debt*, pp. 89–90; Doyle, *Venality*, pp. 14, 42–3, 95–6, 99, 122–6; D. Bien, 'Offices, corps and a system of state credit: the uses of privileges under the ancien regime', in K. M. Baker (ed.), *The French Revolution and the creation of modern political culture* (Oxford University Press, 1987); H. Root, 'Tying the king's hands: credible commitment and royal fiscal policy during the old regime', *Rationality and Society* 1 (1989), 240–58, at 247–9; M. Potter, 'Good offices: intermediation by corporate bodies in early modern French public finance', *Journal of Economic History* 60 (2000), 599–626, at 603.

[30] Potter, 'Good offices', 599–626; M. Potter and J. L. Rosenthal, 'Politics and public finance in France: the Estates of Burgundy, 1660–1790', *Journal of Interdisciplinary History* 27 (1997), 577–612; Stasavage, *Public debt*, p. 90.

death would result in a large loss of capital with little return, so that investors demanded a very high rate. Furthermore, annuities were even worse than term loans in creating an active market. The holder of an annuity might wish to convert the flow of income into a lump sum, but the return to any purchaser depended on the holder's life expectancy, which was difficult to predict and resulted in low valuations.[31]

British government loans took a very different form. Annuities were little used. Instead, loans were dominated in the second half of the eighteenth century by Consols – consolidated stock – introduced in 1754. The bonds were in a single issue, so that the credit of the British state was easily assessed and on public display through accounts presented to parliament. The Consols were long-term loans without a redemption date, paying interest indefinitely. A holder of a bond who wished to secure the capital sum needed an active market on which the bond could be sold and the right to interest transferred. Potential state creditors were more likely to accept a lower interest rate if the market for bonds was active and liquid, which was created by the London Stock Exchange. The British state relied on consolidated, long-term and traded loans.[32] In France, loans were short-term rather than perpetual; they were not traded; and they took many different forms with divergent terms and security. A tabulation of 1789 listed thirty-eight different loans, each with their own terms and collateral. A number of problems emerged in France. Potential investors were reluctant to accept long-term loans as a result of their justified concern about the credibility of the state's commitment to maintain interest payments in the future. Short-term loans reduced the creditors' risk but required the state to make capital repayments which placed additional strain on finances. The wide range of different short-term loans forced up the cost of borrowing, for assessing the risks of each issue was difficult, not least in the absence of government accounts.[33]

These differences between British and French borrowing strategies suggest to James Macdonald that 'the high cost of French borrowing was partly the result of the mistaken policies of its finance ministers'.[34] In reality, ministers had very little room for manoeuvre within the existing political system. More realistically, Velde and Weir argue that

[31] The differences are outlined in Macdonald, *A free nation deep in debt*, pp. 242–8, 251; on annuities, see Velde and Weir, 'Financial market and government debt policy', pp. 3–4, 28–36.
[32] Dickson, *Financial revolution*; Macdonald, *A free nation deep in debt*, p. 242.
[33] Velde and Weir, 'Financial market and government debt policy', p. 4; Macdonald, *A free nation deep in debt*, p. 243.
[34] Macdonald, *A free nation deep in debt*, p. 245.

the problems were structural, owing more to 'institutional, even constitutional flaws than to errors by individuals'. 'Persistent deficits were not the result of bad planning, court extravagance, economic weakness, or even an administration built on venal office-holders. Cleverer or more honest administrators could not have eliminated them. They arose from a political system that completely separated the privilege of spending from the obligation to pay taxes and at the same time left the public enough political power to resist taxation.'[35] The different strategies adopted to secure loans were a response to the underlying factors which gave the ministers little freedom for action.

A large part of the divergence was the result of Britain's possessing a more efficient fiscal system to provide security for the payment of interest. It was not the full explanation, for there was always the possibility that taxpayers (who were in the majority) could take advantage of creditors (who were in a minority) by defaulting. In the mid eighteenth century, there were around 50,000 to 60,000 creditors in an electorate of around 300,000, and the willingness of electors to maintain interest payments cannot be taken for granted.[36]

In the first half of the eighteenth century, some land-owners and old-fashioned merchants were fiercely hostile to loan contractors and financiers on the grounds that they were subverting 'republican virtue'. Land-owners had the leisure and liberty for the disinterested pursuit of public affairs and to bear arms in defence of the state, unlike the narrow, self-interested moneyed power.[37] Moneyed power was criticized as self-interested, and corrupting political life for their own ends – not least because many of the great loans contractors from Samson Gideon to Nathan Rothschild were foreigners and Jewish. Political economists shared the concern at the size of the debt and its effect on the economy and politics. David Hume feared that the size of the debt might lead to 'grievous despotism' through the dominance of financiers and the destruction of an 'independent magistracy'. He advocated a voluntary declaration of state bankruptcy to clear the debt. Although Adam Smith accepted the possibility of a more harmonious relationship between land and finance, he had similar reservations about the debt and proposed that the costs be shared by the colonies through the creation of Estates General for the British empire.[38] Why

---

[35] Velde and Weir, 'Financial market and government debt policy', pp. 3, 36.

[36] The estimate of Macdonald, *A free nation deep in debt*, p. 227.

[37] J. G. A. Pocock, *Virtue, commerce and history: essays on political thought and history, chiefly in the eighteenth century* (Cambridge University Press, 1985).

[38] The thinking of political economists on the debt is outlined in T. Dome, *The political economy of public finance in Britain, 1767–1873* (New York: Routledge, 2004);

was the promise of the state to service the debt sustained in the face of these concerns?

An obvious answer is that Britain had representative political institutions in contrast to France, and that a credible commitment was guaranteed by constitutional checks and balances which prevented taxpayers from taking advantage of lenders. David Stasavage is sceptical, arguing that checks and balances cannot prevent power falling into the hands of those favouring default. In his view, the answer is to be found in the nature of political divisions and the existence of parties. Where a society has 'multiple political cleavages', and the choice of party affiliations was determined by non-economic issues, the division between creditors and taxpayers was buried within a wider coalition of interests and opinions. In France, parties did not exist, so that any conflict between creditors and taxpayers was not contained within a wider coalition, and at times of financial crisis opinions could polarize around this one issue. In Stasavage's opinion, the greater likelihood of default in France reflected the absence of cross-cutting political alliances.[39]

Stasavage exaggerates the role of parties in preventing default, compared with representative institutions. Can parties be separated from the existence of the representative institutions they were seeking to control? Parties are not so likely in the world of court politics at Versailles as in the parliament of Westminster. Representative institutions were also important in underpinning consent to taxation, which provided the flow of income for servicing loans. The absence of any serious possibility of default, and the implausibility of a sharp divide between creditors and taxpayers, can be explained by factors other than the existence of parties.

Edmund Burke, in his *Reflections on the Revolution in France*, noted one major difference between the British and French systems of finance. The strength of British finance rested on a 'miscible' collaboration of landed and moneyed interests in a patriotic alliance.[40] In chemistry, two liquids are miscible if they dissolve completely in each other, whatever their proportions, and Burke believed that the same happened with financiers and land-owners. Stasavage is right to point to the lack of a clear political divide on the single fault line of creditors and taxpayers, but the explanation is not to be found only in the existence of

M. Daunton, *Trusting Leviathan: the politics of taxation in Britain, 1799–1914* (Cambridge University Press, 2001), pp. 39–40.
[39] Stasavage, *Public debt*, pp. 24, 39, 99, 129, 154, 156, 172.
[40] E. Burke, *Reflections on the Revolution in France* (London: Everyman's Library, 1910), p. 106.

parties. The complaint that moneyed power was subversive was submerged by a different view, that loans and the moneyed interest sustained British liberties and prosperity by defeating French Catholicism and winning new markets in the colonies. 'The *national Debt*', in the opinion of one supporter of loans, 'was contracted in Defence of our *Liberties* and *Properties*, and for the Preservation of our most excellent *Constitution* from *Popery* and *Slavery*.' Although financiers and the debt were potential threats to republican liberty, the solution was to contain them within a parliamentary system of close scrutiny of accounts and spending in order to defend British liberties and Protestantism against external threat.[41]

The commitment of the British state to pay its debts was linked with the credibility of any creditor in paying his debt – a serious consideration in such a highly commercialized society as Britain. Many taxpayers – merchants, industrialists and traders – were not likely to support default given their own reliance on credit. They had a general concern to maintain the sanctity of credit, and a very immediate fear that a loss of income might lead bond-holders to default on their own obligations and so threaten the entire, fragile, system of interlocking claims. Land-owners shared their concerns, for they were deeply involved in the financial world through their use of mortgages. They could borrow on the security of their estates in order to carry out improvements, to cover the costs of enclosure, to purchase the land of smaller neighbours, or to construct large country houses. Land and finance were 'miscible' as a result of the willingness of great land-owners to borrow to improve their economic position. At the same time, the composition of bond-holders shifted in the second half of the eighteenth century so that their ranks were no longer dominated to the same degree by foreigners and London moneyed interests. Most politicians and office-holders were bond-holders, so that default would harm their own interests. Bonds were held by insurance companies which dealt with a large number of policy-holders; charities purchased bonds as a secure investment, and so did widows. A concern for the stability of government loans was widespread.[42]

---

[41] J. Hoppit, 'Attitudes to credit in Britain, 1680–1790', *Historical Journal* 33 (1990), 305–22, 316–17; Brewer, *Sinews of power*, pp. 142–3, 161.
[42] On credit, see C. Muldrew, *The economy of obligation: the culture of credit and social relations in early modern England* (Basingstoke: Macmillan, 1998); on the changing composition of bond-holders, Dickson, *Financial revolution*; on the use of mortgages, Macdonald, *A free nation deep in debt*, p. 230.

War finance: acceptance versus exploitation

During the revolutionary and Napoleonic Wars, the British fiscal system continued to evolve to cope with the increasing demands for taxes and loans. Borrowing fell as a proportion of the costs of the war. In the War of American Independence, borrowing covered 82 per cent of the total costs, and the level was still higher in the revolutionary wars with France between 1793 and 1797, at 89 per cent. The proportion then fell in the Napoleonic Wars of 1798–1815, to 49 per cent. In the Seven Years War, government borrowing was 10.6 per cent of national income and in the War of American Independence, 10.0 per cent. During the first phase of the wars against revolutionary and Napoleonic France, the figure rose to 11.6 per cent, but fell back to 4.3 per cent in 1802–10 and 9.0 per cent in 1811–15.[43]

Taxes formed a larger share of the costs of the Napoleonic Wars than at any time in the eighteenth century. The additional taxation came in large part from increases to existing taxes (55 per cent of the additional tax revenue 1793–1815), with 36 per cent from new taxes, and above all the income tax introduced in 1799. The land tax and assessed taxes had fallen as a proportion of tax revenues, and Pitt introduced the income tax as a way of increasing the contribution from land-owners and wealthy members of society. He imposed a rate of 2 shillings in the pound (10 per cent) on incomes above £200, with abatements for incomes down to £60. The tax was seen as an exceptional wartime duty: it was abolished with the Treaty of Amiens in 1802, reinstated in 1803 on a somewhat different basis, and abandoned again in 1816. Initially, Pitt tried to collect the tax by aggregating an individual's income from all sources – an intrusive and complex process. After 1803, the tax was collected on each source or schedule in a way that minimized the intrusion of the state: tax was deducted automatically at source by the person paying rent or interest and dividends, and income from the profits of trade or business were assessed by local commissioners rather than by state officials. The commissioners were crucial to the legitimacy of the tax and, when they were suspended in the City of London in 1814, the outcry against the tax as a threat to liberties contributed to its post-war demise.[44] Of course, payment of the income tax was not universally popular, yet it did produce considerable revenue and did increase the

[43] Macdonald, *A free nation deep in debt*, p. 339; J. F. Wright, 'British government borrowing in wartime, 1750–1815', *Economic History Review* 52 (1999), 355–61, at 356.
[44] A. Hope-Jones, *Income tax in the Napoleonic Wars* (Cambridge University Press, 1939), pp. 2, 28–9, 68–9.

proportion from direct taxes (see Table 5.1). Britain was the most heavily taxed state in Europe: in terms of the amount of wheat purchased, the per capita taxation in Britain between 1803 and 1812 was almost three times that of France.[45]

Napoleon deeply distrusted debt, and applied the principles of prudent family finances to the state. He was, in the words of Louis Bergeron, 'more concerned with not falling into the mistakes of a recent past than with seeing solutions for the future'. He thought that Britain's reliance on loans would be its downfall, a 'gnawing worm' which would lead to disaster.[46] He was wrong, for France's failure to become a 'fiscal state' contributed to his downfall. In 1789, the National Assembly (the successor to the Estates General) resolved to continue collecting the existing taxes 'although illegally established and collected'. Not surprisingly, the result was resistance rather than legitimacy. Tax reform was confused with tax cuts, and the Assembly abolished indirect taxes. The worsening financial situation meant that new direct taxes were introduced in 1790: the *contribution foncière* (a tax on the revenue from land and buildings), *contributions* (a tax on external signs of affluence on moveable property) and the *patente* (a form of licence on trade and industry according to the type of trade, its size and location). These taxes amounted to a major reform of the fiscal system, and they continued to form the basis of French revenues in the nineteenth century. They were the equivalent of the land, assessed and income taxes in Britain. Indeed, the abandonment of the income tax in Britain in 1816 meant that France had a higher proportion of direct taxes and arguably a more equitable system of taxation. The reforms of 1790 marked a breakthrough in the longer term, but during the Napoleonic Wars difficulties of administration meant that the yield was disappointing and the deficit continued to mount under the massive burden of Napoleon's ambitions.[47]

---

[45] Bonney, 'Struggle for great power status', pp. 380–2, citing O'Brien, 'Political economy', pp. 13, 22; P. O'Brien, 'Public finance in the wars with France, 1793–1815', in H. T. Dickinson (ed.), *Britain and the French Revolution, 1789–1815* (Basingstoke: Macmillan, 1989), pp. 177, 182–3; Mathias and O'Brien, 'Taxation in Britain and France', pp. 610–11 and tables 7 and 8; F. Crouzet, *L'économie britannique et le blocus continental, 1806–1813*, 2nd edn (Paris: Economica, 1987), p. lxii; F. Crouzet, 'The impact of the French wars on the British economy', in Dickinson, *Britain and the French Revolution*, p. 208; E. A. Wrigley, 'Society and economy in the eighteenth century', in L. Stone (ed.), *An imperial state at war: Britain from 1689 to 1815* (New York: Routledge, 1994), pp. 74–5.

[46] Bonney, 'Struggle for great power status', p. 386; L. Bergeron, *France under Napoleon* (Princeton University Press, 1981), pp. 41–2, 44–51.

[47] Daunton, *Trusting Leviathan*, p. 54; Doyle, *Oxford history of the French Revolution*, p. 131; Aftalion, *French Revolution*, pp. 86–95; Bonney, 'Struggle for great power status',

The solution adopted in France had two, interconnected, elements: the introduction of *assignats* in 1790 and war. The *assignats* were paper money based on the expected proceeds of the sale of church land, but the government issued far more than the security offered by the sales of the land. The *assignats* were the main way of financing war after 1792, accounting for 82.4 per cent of the cost, compared with 5.4 per cent from taxes and 1.9 per cent from land sales. *Assignats* paid for war and war was a means of forcing occupied territories to accept *assignats*, so obliging them to provide money to sustain French armies. The demands on the occupied territories were massive, amounting to perhaps a quarter of the revenue of France by the late 1790s. The policy proved a disaster, for the value of the *assignats* fell to less than 1 per cent of their face value by 1796. The issue of large amounts of paper money resulted in inflation, which became the major form of 'taxation' by reducing the real level of debts and eroding the value of savings and incomes in a deeply disruptive way. Exploitation of the occupied territories led to resistance and revolt.[48]

The French fiscal system was put on a more secure basis from 1797 when the revenue from direct taxes increased, indirect taxes revived, and the cost of servicing the debt fell as a result of another partial default. But exploitation of the occupied territories remained crucial. When Napoleon came to power, he rejected the use of paper money and stabilized the currency – in contrast with the British, who abandoned the gold standard in 1797, introduced paper money and adopted inflationary finance. Britain was able to adopt more flexible policies as a result of its accumulated credibility; Napoleon had to adopt conservative monetary policies because of the lack of credibility. Furthermore, Napoleon had an aversion to loans and embarked on a reduction of the national debt. Financiers were, he remarked, 'the scourges, the lepers of the nation'. Of course, the default of 1797 meant that the credit of the French state was very poor and borrowing would have been difficult and expensive.[49] Napoleon's policy was to wage war to support war, and

pp. 347–8; R. Bonney, 'The state and its revenues in ancien régime France', *Historical Research* 65 (1992), 150–76, 175–6.
[48] Bonney, 'Struggle for great power status', pp. 349–52; S. E. Harris, *The assignats* (Cambridge, MA: Harvard University Press, 1930); Velde and Weir, 'Financial markets and government debt policy', pp. 17–18; Aftalion, *French Revolution*, chapter 4 and pp. 184–7; S. Woolf, *Napoleon's integration of Europe* (London: Routledge, 1991), p. 17.
[49] M. D. Bordo and E. N. White, 'A tale of two currencies: British and French finance during the Napoleonic war', *Journal of Economic History* 51 (1991), 303–16, at 314–15; Bergeron, *France under Napoleon*, pp. 37–51; Bonney, 'Struggle for great power status', pp. 353–7, citing Aftalion, *French Revolution*, p. 178; T. C. W. Blanning, *The origins of the French Revolutionary Wars* (New York: Longman, 1986), p. 196; S. Schama,

the largest source of revenue continued to be impositions on the occupied territories. Precise calculations are difficult, but on one estimate, half of the military expenses between 1804 and 1814 were paid by the occupied territories. Clearly, fiscal problems arose as the French armies were expelled from the conquered territories and tax had to increase at home.[50]

Losing and regaining legitimacy

Britain out-taxed, out-borrowed and out-gunned the French during the wars. The real problem for Britain came after the war. The failure to renew the income tax in 1816 and the continued rigidity in the land tax meant that the proportion of revenue from indirect taxes rose (see Table 5.1). The tax system was much more regressive as a result of dependence on customs and excise duties which fell on domestic producers and working-class consumers.[51] A high proportion of revenue went on the service of the national debt, so that it was easy to argue that the fiscal system was a device to take money from poor and industrious members of society and to transfer it to idle *rentiers* and the hangers-on at court. The external enemy was defeated and, in the view of many radicals, the main threat to liberty came from within, from the costs of servicing the debt and the *rentiers* it sustained; the menace of militarism and a luxurious court; the subversion of the social order by a class of rich financiers and mighty land-owners benefiting from pensions and sinecures.

The outcome was that the fiscal system lacked legitimacy, and the trust which characterized eighteenth-century taxation collapsed. There was a lack of trust both that fellow taxpayers were making a reasonable contribution to the expenses of the state and that the state was spending its revenues in a way which was equitable between classes and interests. The issue facing politicians was: How was trust in the state and the tax system to be re-established, and legitimacy restored? The process was remarkably successful, so that in the second half of the nineteenth

'The exigencies of war and the politics of taxation in the Netherlands', in J. Winter (ed.), *War and economic development* (Cambridge University Press, 1975), pp. 111–12, 117–18; S. Schama, *Patriots and liberators: revolution in the Netherlands, 1780–1813* (New York: Knopf, 1977), pp. 207, 238, 293–5, 305, 385, 446; Woolf, *Napoleon's integration of Europe*, p. 172.

50 Bergeron, *France under Napoleon*, p. 40; Woolf, *Napoleon's integration of Europe*, pp. 172–3; Aftalion, *French Revolution*, pp. 177–8; Bonney, 'Struggle for great power status', p. 355.

51 Hope-Jones, *Income tax in the Napoleonic Wars*, chapter 7; O'Brien, 'Political economy'.

century the British state, and the taxes which supported it, were widely seen as neutral between classes and interests.

A number of divergences between Britain and elsewhere in Europe provide pointers to the most significant factors. First, there were different trends in the level of taxation in relation to gross national product, so that the reduction in expenditure was longer and deeper than in other European countries. The British state was more successful than its counterparts in the rest of Europe in reducing the level of spending as a proportion of GNP after the Napoleonic Wars, and in keeping it down in the later nineteenth century.[52] The process of containment was a precondition for accepting the trustworthiness of the state, and was consciously undertaken by politicians and bureaucrats who were well aware of the temptations to themselves and the electorate of allowing government expenditure to rise. Second, the relative importance of direct and indirect taxes moved in opposite directions, with a marked fall in the share of indirect taxes in Britain and a marked rise in many European countries. Third, there were clear divergences in the nature of fiscal administration. The interaction of these three variables led to the creation and maintenance of an unusually high level of trust in the British state and hence of consent to taxation, which stands in striking contrast with the earlier widespread criticism of the 'tax-eater state' and 'old corruption'. The achievement of a high level of trust in the central state, and in fellow taxpayers, reduced the costs of collective action and created the opportunity for the British state to take on new functions in the early twentieth century.

The retrenchment of the Tory ministries between 1815 and 1830 and the export of some of the costs of the fiscal–military state to the empire marked a turning point in the fiscal–military state, reducing its claims on the economy below the levels of the eighteenth century.[53] But the shrinking state did not achieve legitimacy and trust as Tory ministers

[52] D. E. Schremmer, 'Taxation and public finance: Britain, France and Germany', in P. Mathias and S. Pollard (eds.), *Cambridge economic history of Europe, volume VIII, the industrial economies: the development of economic and social policies* (Cambridge University Press, 1989), p. 362; P. Harling and P. Mandler, 'From "fiscal-military" state to laissez-faire state, 1760–1850', *Journal of British Studies* (1993), 44–70; B. Baysinger and R. Tollison, 'Chaining Leviathan: the case of Gladstonian finance', *History of Political Economy* 12 (1981), 206–13; see also C. G. Leathers, 'Gladstonian finance and the Virginia School of Public Finance', *History of Political Economy* 18 (1986), 515–21.

[53] P. Harling, *The waning of 'old corruption': the politics of economical reform in Britain, 1779–1846* (Oxford University Press, 1996), pp. 165, 177–8; C. A. Bayly, 'The British military-fiscal state and indigenous resistance: India, 1750–1820', in L. Stone, ed., *An imperial state at war*, pp. 324–49.

hoped, in part because the strategy was designed to *prevent* a change in the franchise by showing that an unreformed constitution was effective, and in part because the taxes levied to pay for the reduced level of public expenditure were widely (and correctly) perceived to be inequitable.[54] The attempt to create a sense of trust in a patrician elite and state failed, and the constitutional reform so assiduously opposed by the Tories was introduced by the Whigs in the early 1830s. In 1832, the parliamentary franchise was extended and 'rotten' boroughs removed; in 1835, self-electing municipal corporations were replaced by elected councils; the judiciary was reformed; and the privileges of the Church reduced. Such institutional reform was portrayed as an onslaught on the structure of 'old corruption', and was linked with a further onslaught on expenditure. However, the legitimacy of the state was not reasserted, and public agitation mounted in the 1830s with protests against the new Poor Law, pressure for the removal of agricultural protection in the shape of the Corn Laws, and demands for universal adult male suffrage. The problem faced by the Whig government was that retrenchment left it open to charges of financial mismanagement, especially when a serious depression resulted in budget deficits. Although indirect taxes were reduced, the tax system was not reformed by introducing new taxes – and particularly the income tax which was anathema to radicals as the engine of warfare and a bloated state.[55] Despite the considerable reduction in the scale of spending by 1840, the British state was still far from achieving legitimacy and trust. Protection of landed interests suggested that policy was still biased; and the tax system was heavily dependent on indirect taxes which fell on working-class consumers and middle-class producers.

The successful creation of legitimacy and trust in the state rested upon the measures of the Tory ministry of Sir Robert Peel, whose policies were continued within the Liberal Party by William Gladstone. These politicians claimed that they – and the state – were disinterested. Their ambition was conservative, but in a different sense from the post-war Tory ministries which aimed to preserve the rule of a narrow political elite within an unreformed constitution. Rather, Peel concluded that the best strategy for preserving the rule of the political elite and protecting property was by adopting policies that were even-handed between all types of property, and between the propertied and the non-propertied. By constraining state expenditure, and as far as possible excluding the state from involvement with economic interests, it was

---

[54] O'Brien, 'Political economy'; B. Hilton, *Corn, cash and commerce: the economic policies of the Tory government, 1815–30* (Oxford University Press, 1977).

[55] Harling, *Waning of 'old corruption'*, pp. 197–227.

hoped to protect the political elite from challenge and to define the state as a neutral arbitrator between interests. Politicians must rise above personal greed and self-interest; they must also rise above any temptation to use the state to favour one interest against another, whether a trade group in search of protection or a social group seeking tax breaks.

In 1842, Peel reintroduced the income tax in an attempt to balance the budget, in two senses: first, by removing the deficit left by the Whigs and restoring order to government finances; and second by establishing a sense of equity between different types of wealth and income. In 1846, he took a further step by abolishing agricultural protection. His policy was continued by Gladstone, most notably in his budget of 1853. Peel and Gladstone established the principle that the state should not appear to favour any particular economic interest, and that taxes should be a carefully devised system of checks and balances. For example, any bias in the income tax against 'industrial' or earned income (which were liable to loss during ill-health or trade depression) compared with 'spontaneous' or unearned income (which was supported by capital assets producing income regardless of health or economic depression) should be balanced by taxation of property at death. Gladstone argued that a minimal state and retrenchment would remove the source of revenue sustaining parasitical hangers-on and warfare: retrenchment offered peace and liberty. Peel and Gladstone therefore articulated a language of public trust.[56] The creation of at least an *appearance* of neutrality was achieved more successfully in Britain than in other European countries, and particularly in Germany. The willingness of the elite to shoulder the burdens of the income tax, and to abandon agricultural protection, marked a triumph of 'disinterestedness'. The success of the policy was clear in 1848, when revolutions in the rest of Europe contrasted with the demise of Chartism. The radicals of mid-Victorian Britain were willing to trust elite politicians such as Peel and Gladstone and to accept the legitimacy of the state, rather than to castigate them as selfish and corrupt.[57]

---

[56] Harling, *Waning of 'old corruption'*, pp. 228–54; Harling and Mandler, 'From "fiscal-military" state to laissez-faire state'; Hilton, *Corn, cash and commerce*; H. C. G. Matthew, 'Disraeli, Gladstone and the politics of mid-Victorian budgets', *Historical Journal* 22 (1979), 615–43; Matthew, *Gladstone, 1809–1874* (Oxford University Press, 1986); E. F. Biagini, 'Popular Liberals, Gladstonian finance, and the debate on taxation, 1860–74', in E. F. Biagini and A. J. Reid (eds.) *Currents of radicalism: popular radicalism, organised labour and party politics in Britain, 1850–1914* (Cambridge University Press, 1991); E. F. Biagini, *Liberty, retrenchment and reform: popular liberalism in the age of Gladstone, 1860–1880* (Cambridge University Press, 1992).

[57] D. Read, *Peel and the Victorians* (Oxford University Press, 1987), pp. 288–9, 319; Biagini, *Liberty, retrenchment and reform*.

The ability to restrict the state, and to create widespread acceptance that it and the political elite were trustworthy, did not depend simply upon the assiduous cultivation of a sense of public duty by politicians and the creation of a class-neutral state. Both Gladstone and officials at the Treasury who were reared in Gladstonian financial orthodoxy were conscious of new dangers arising from the pursuit of votes by competing politicians and the ambitions of spending departments. They feared a replacement of retrenchment by expenditure, unless there were clearly established, rigid, conventions; it was easier to bring down spending from the heights of the Napoleonic Wars than to keep it at the new, lower level. Hence, the rhetoric of the neutrality of the state and of public duty, and the appeal to retrenchment and liberty, were sustained by detailed, technical accounting principles which were based on the practices of the late eighteenth century, but became a well-defined system in the middle of the nineteenth century. These principles were designed to constrain the state and to create trust and legitimacy.

The first principle was a rejection of the hypothecation of tax revenue, that is pledging particular revenues to particular purposes. Hypothecation would contribute to an increase in the role of the state, by treating it as a collection of services and functions, each of which was individually desirable with a protected source of revenue. In order to contain pressure for spending, revenue should be unified, and treated as a single pool of money which was separate from the purposes for which it was raised. No less important was a second principle: the rejection of the *virement* of funds. Although revenue was treated as a single sum without any ties to a specific purpose, expenditure was minutely subdivided by annual 'votes' of the Commons. This practice contributed to limits on government expenditure. A sum of, say, £1,000 might be voted for the construction of a new vessel for the Royal Navy and £500 for a Post Office in Aberdeen; a surplus of £150 on the first could not be used to cover a deficiency on the second, or diverted to some other purpose such as building a new prison in Manchester which would need its own 'vote'. The danger of *virement* was that spending would always rise to the available revenue, and would ratchet up expenditure.

A third principle followed: it was necessary to have annual votes by parliament, and spending plans should not be carried over from year to year. There was a very strong emphasis on the need for constant vigilance by parliament as a protection for the public against the spending plans of the executive. Radical reformers argued for an extension of the franchise less for its own sake in creating a more democratic political system, than as a means of changing the composition of members of parliament, in order to purge the Commons of 'interest' and to make parliamentary control more effective in eliminating militarism and waste.[58]

The ban on hypothecation and *virement*, and the insistence on annual votes, meant that there was the possibility of a surplus at the end of the year as a result of buoyant tax revenues, or underspending on any vote. A fourth financial convention was that any surplus should not be carried forward to the next year. Self-interested, ambitious politicians should be made to resist the temptation of carrying over surpluses in order to make a dramatic reduction in taxation before an election, which would turn the tax system into a 'gigantic system of jobbery'. Since 1829, the convention was that any surplus should be used to reduce the national debt, so releasing funds which could be more efficiently invested elsewhere. Repayment of the national debt would also create confidence that the state was trustworthy, so maintaining British credit and ensuring that the public would lend to the state in times of war when the revenue from annual tax revenues would need to be supplemented.[59]

By these means, barriers were constructed to the expansion of the state. These technical accounting procedures and the annual votes of the Commons were erected into matters of high constitutional principle, integral to English liberty and national identity. In the hands of Gladstone, the annual budget became a matter of high theatricality, or perhaps more accurately of religious ceremony. Instead of the Established Church providing the basis for a moral, organic state as he had initially hoped, 'fiscal probity became the new morality'.[60] The budget, and the consolidation of all sources of revenue into a single entity, made government finances transparent: it was clear to the public and taxpayers where money came from, and where it was going. Above all, spending was open to parliamentary scrutiny on an annual basis.

At the same time as public expenditure fell as a proportion of GNP, the structure of taxation shifted away from indirect taxes (in particular customs and excise) to direct taxes. Direct taxes on wealth and income rose from 25.2 per cent of central government revenue in 1831–35 to 52.3 per cent in 1911–14. British experience ran counter to the pattern in France, where the share of indirect taxes rose.[61] The comparative position of the two tax regimes was therefore reversed over the nineteenth century. The new direct taxes adopted in France in 1790 survived after

---

[58] M. Taylor, *The decline of British Radicalism, 1847–1860* (Oxford University Press, 1995), pp. 30–2, 45, 135; A. Hawkins, '"Parliamentary government" and Victorian political parties, c. 1830–1880', *English Historical Review* 104 (1989), 638–69.
[59] Daunton, *Trusting Leviathan*, pp. 74, 111–24.
[60] Matthew, *Gladstone*, chapter 3.
[61] Daunton, *Trusting Leviathan*, pp. 35, 54, 175–7.

the Napoleonic Wars, and provided a higher proportion of the revenue of the French state than direct taxes in Britain. However, they were not responsive to economic growth and difficult to reform. The *patentes*, for example, created a large number of categories according to location, trade and the size of the firm, and the payment was stereotyped by a scale of charges on the present profits. The yield did not rise in line with economic growth, unless the scale of charges was amended with serious political difficulties. In Britain, the yield of the income tax at any given rate in the pound of profit rose in line with economic growth. In other words, the French finance minister had to take explicit action to maintain revenue in line with economic growth; his British counterpart did not need to take action. Similarly, the *contribution personnelle* rested on personal tax and fell behind growth in the economy. The lack of flexibility in direct taxes meant that the French government found it easier to turn to indirect taxes. which were more likely to increase in line with economic growth.

How can the change in the structure of taxation be related to the constraints on the growth of the British state in the nineteenth century? At first sight, these two features might appear to be working in opposite directions: the introduction of the income tax might be used to raise more revenue for the state, so that containment of public expenditure occurred *despite* its existence. However, the reintroduction of income tax in 1842 was interpreted as a device to remove political tensions and so improve governability. Care had to be taken that it was not interpreted as a means of fuelling state spending. Free-traders attacked the protection of the landed interest and demanded the liberalization of the economy; they feared that the income tax offered an alternative to retrenchment and would be used to finance war.[62] Acceptance of the income tax therefore rested upon the assumption that it would help to constrain the state, rather than providing additional resources. Peel and Gladstone argued that the tax was temporary and would be abolished as soon as retrenchment had done its work: it was simply a socially equitable means of covering expenditure in the interim, before economic growth in a free market led to higher tax revenues.[63] Gladstone also argued that the tax would create a sense of political responsibility by bringing the public choice of electors into line with their private choice. There was a close correlation between paying income tax and possessing a vote in parliamentary elections under the terms of the Reform Act of 1832, so that electors had an incentive in voting for

[62] Hilton, *Corn, cash and commerce*; Taylor, *Decline of British radicalism*, p. 138.
[63] Biagini, 'Popular Liberals', p. 156.

cheap government: their public choices would have immediate private consequences in their tax bills.[64] The income tax was, therefore, linked to the process of retrenchment rather than to the provision of revenue for new functions.

Intention was one thing; outcome in the longer term was another. In the course of the nineteenth century, the high level of acceptance of the income tax meant that it could eventually provide the means of financing new government functions. The constraints imposed on the state in the mid-Victorian period, and the stress upon class neutrality, created a high degree of legitimacy and trust which removed the virulent attacks on the 'tax-eater' state of the early Victorian period. The success of Gladstonian financial reform created a high degree of acceptance of the central government's tax system in general, and of the income tax in particular, which increasingly became the crucial element in the finance of the British state, allowing the remission of indirect taxes and providing revenue in times of emergency.

The British income tax was remade between 1906 and 1914, by the introduction of a 'surtax' to provide higher, graduated taxes on large incomes, and of differentiation between earned and unearned income. The result was to increase the ability of the income tax to raise revenue without alienating a crucial electoral group of modest middle-class incomes. The strategy was to shift increases in income tax to large incomes, and especially to those with a large 'socially created' element, and to reduce taxation on modest middle-class incomes, and especially those of family men with dependent children. Such an approach provided a means for the Liberal Party to contain the growth of a separate Labour Party by offering increased social expenditure, and at the same time retain middle-class support by ensuring that the costs fell on the recipients of large 'unearned' incomes who could be separated from productive, morally superior, earned incomes. At the same time, Liberal fiscal policy offered a means of preserving free trade and limiting the appeal of tariff reform, which the Conservatives were proposing as a means both of providing revenue and of solving the problems of poverty through a stable, protected imperial market.[65] The British income tax had achieved acceptance and undergone reform before it

---

[64] Matthew, *Gladstone*, pp. 125–8; M. J. Daunton, 'The political economy of death duties: Harcourt's budget of 1894', in N. Harte and R. Quinault (eds.), *Land and society in Britain, 1700–1914: essays in honour of F. M. L. Thompson* (Manchester University Press, 1996), pp. 149–50.

[65] B. K. Murray, *People's budget 1909/10: Lloyd George and Liberal politics* (Oxford University Press, 1980); E. H. H. Green, 'Radical Conservatism: the electoral genesis of tariff reform', *Historical Journal* 22 (1985), 667–92.

was introduced in most outer European countries for central government revenue. In France, the income tax was only introduced in 1914 and it was not effective during the war; it was still a matter of contention and widely seen as a socialist threat. Similarly, Germany only introduced a Reich income tax in 1913, with serious problems for its relationship with the states, many with their own income taxes.

The income tax was introduced into Britain as a part of the strategy designed to dismantle the fiscal–military state and to constrain expenditure, but it also contained within itself the possibility of providing a buoyant source of revenue which was widely accepted as legitimate and fair. In Britain, direct taxes were more flexible and responsive to economic growth, allowing a remission of indirect taxes while keeping the income tax at a modest rate. However, the high reliance on income tax for central government revenue, a widening of the franchise to non-income tax payers, and the deliberate attempt to reduce the burden of direct taxation on modest middle-class family incomes, created the circumstances for a separation between public choices and private costs which might slacken the constraints on spending.

In the eighteenth century, the administration of the tax system incorporated taxpayers, and care was taken to remove sources of tension. When the income tax was reintroduced, both the assessment and collection of income tax were delegated to members of the tax-paying public. As with the land and assessed taxes, and the income tax before 1816, lay commissioners were chosen from the local business and professional community, with lay assessors to determine individuals' tax liability; the tax was collected on a commission basis by collectors drawn from the ranks of local businessmen. As a result, the number of government officials was small and they were mainly concerned with providing oversight and supplying information to the lay commissioners and assessors. Such an approach seemed curious to commentators from other countries, who preferred a more centralized and bureaucratic approach, but it contributed to creating trust in the state. The resistance to the income tax in 1816 arose from a perceived threat to local administration; and the income tax was not introduced into Ireland in 1842 as a result of the absence of local commissioners.[66]

The costs of collecting the income tax were minimized by avoiding the need to assess total income. As we noted earlier, the income tax in 1799 collected tax on global income from all sources, resulting in a low level of compliance; in 1803, the tax was collected on each schedule

---

[66] Daunton, *Trusting Leviathan.*

without seeking to establish the individual's entire income. The result was a significant increase in compliance and in yield. The new system rested upon the collection of as much tax as possible by deduction at source, so that a tenant farmer paid his rent to the land-owner net of tax, and handed the balance to the tax collector; similarly, tax was deducted from interest payments. The main difficulty came with profits from trade, industry and the professions, where it was impossible to collect at source on a flow of earnings; only at the end of the year would profits be established, and would it be known whether they were above the tax threshold. The way around this difficulty was to delegate tax collection and assessment to lay commissioners, assessors and collectors, so that the role of official bureaucrats was relatively modest. The commissioners in each district were also allowed to come to an agreement with organized trade associations on how to treat depreciation allowances, a matter of interpretation of the legislation which was delegated to the localities. Lay commissioners and assessors entrenched the income tax within civil society, so creating a high level of compliance, trust in the fairness of the tax, and widespread acceptance of the legitimacy of the state.

In practice, the power of officials – the surveyors or inspectors of taxes – increased over time, as the system became more complicated. However, the commissioners retained their function as the arbitrators between the state and its citizens. Increasingly, the smooth operation of the tax system and compliance came to rely on the relationship between the Inland Revenue and the taxpayers' professional advisers, rather than on the existence of the lay assessors and commissioners in the locality. The process of reaching agreements and precedents in the interpretation of tax codes was a matter of negotiation between autonomous professional bodies and tax officials rather than of formal administrative law. The relationship between these professional advisers and the tax authorities rested upon mutual support and respect, for the advisers needed a degree of confidence in the competence of the authorities in interpreting rules, and the authorities needed a degree of confidence in the integrity of the professionals. The nature of the relationship between professions and the state was another area of divergence between Britain and Continental Europe.[67]

---

[67] Daunton, *Trusting Leviathan*; R. Cocks, 'Victorian barristers, judges and taxation: a study in the expansion of legal work', in G. R. Rubin and D. Sugarman (eds.), *Law, economy and society, 1750–1914: essays in the history of English law* (Abingdon: Professional Books, 1984); C. Stebbings, 'The General Commissioners of income tax: assessors or adjudicators?', *British Tax Review* (1994), 52–64.

Tax advice was provided by solicitors and accountants, whose professional status and integrity rested upon the Law Society and the Institute of Chartered Accountants. The emergence of these bodies should be seen in the context of two features of the formation of the English state, which date from the seventeenth century. The first feature was the notion that the ideal form of law was precedent and immemorial custom, which guaranteed freedom and liberty.[68] Second, clubs, charities and trusts were given considerable powers and legal autonomy to provide services. The combination of these two elements meant that the state was careful not to interfere with the professions, which had a high degree of autonomy at a time when self-governing professions in France and Germany were being subjected to state control.[69] The result was important not only for the professions, but for constituting the British state. Raymond Cocks suggests that the involvement of lay commissioners and lawyers in the defining of tax law led to a confused, diffuse, ad hoc body of case law, which parliamentary draftsmen sought to control through ever more complex and technical Acts. A vicious circle emerged, of increasingly complicated law and methods of avoidance, with mounting costs of compliance.[70] The process could, however, be seen in a more positive light in the nineteenth century, contributing to the acceptance of the tax system as legitimate and trustworthy.

The counterpart of this partial delegation of administration and interpretation was the exclusion of interest groups from any bargaining over tax rates and exemptions included in legislation. The terms of finance acts were, as far as possible, general rather than particularistic, unlike the United States, where the tax system was written by Congress and was open to lobbying, which resulted in thousands of exemptions, deductions and credits for various activities, often in particular locations. Such a pattern applied in eighteenth-century Britain when the fiscal regime was so heavily dependent on indirect taxes and trade interests bargained in parliament. In the nineteenth and twentieth century, consent was created by different methods through the *exclusion* of interest-group negotiation and the propagation of an aura of independence. Unlike in the United States, tax measures emanated from the executive in circumstances of secrecy. The budget was written

[68] D. Sugarman, 'Bourgeois collectivism, professional power, and the boundaries of the state: the private and public life of the Law Society, 1825–1914', *International Journal of the Legal Profession* 3 (1996), 81–135.
[69] M. Burage, 'Revolution as a starting point for the comparative analysis of the French, American and English legal profession', in R. L. Abel and P. S. C. Lewis (eds.), *Lawyers in society, III* (Berkeley: University of California Press, 1989).
[70] Cocks, 'Victorian barristers'.

by the Chancellor, often with minimal discussion with his colleagues in Cabinet, following the advice of a small group of Treasury officials who had a strong commitment to general measures. The government rarely consulted even its own members, and the passage of the Finance Bill through the Commons was normally guaranteed as a result of the creation of party discipline from the 1870s.[71] Legislation might offer tax breaks to certain activities – for example, the purchase of life insurance – or might grant allowances for children or dependent relatives. However, these concessions were general and did not entail the exercise of any discretion by the tax authorities. The authorities did not wish to become involved in the use of the tax system to encourage particular types of activity, which would simply exacerbate the problems already existing in defining the general principles in the courts. Their aim was, as far as possible, to write the tax law in such a way that there was no discretion in its implementation; if the government wished to encourage particular activities, it should be in the form of explicit grants which were open to parliamentary scrutiny rather than through 'the jerrymandering of taxes'. As the Inland Revenue argued during the First World War: 'The object of taxation, as known in this country, is solely to provide money; taxes are of general application and, as equality of treatment between taxpayer and taxpayer is a cardinal principle, the scope and conditions of liability are closely defined by statute and discretionary powers are taboo.'[72]

Conclusion

The use of the income tax as a shackle on the state, and the process of delegation in administration combined with hostility to specific exemptions, created a very wide level of acceptance at an earlier date than in most other European countries. By creating the appearance of neutrality as part of the defence of property and the state, there was greater willingness to use central, direct taxation to fund new welfare services than in other countries. The process of establishing trust in the fiscal system was complicated and contingent. It cannot be simply read from the level of extraction, for there was mounting criticism of taxation in the early nineteenth century as expenditure fell as a proportion of the gross national product. The method of assessing and collecting taxes in

---

[71] S. Steinmo, 'Political institutions and tax policy in the United States, Sweden and Britain', *World Politics* 41 (1989), 500–35.

[72] Quoted in M. J. Daunton, 'How to pay for the war: state, society and taxation in Britain, 1917–24', *English Historical Review* 111 (1996), 882–919.

Britain worked with civil society, and limited hostility to bureaucratic intervention. By these means, the British state in the mid nineteenth century was able, with a remarkable degree of success, to move from deep suspicion to widespread acceptance. Collective action and taxation were given a new legitimacy.

Part II

Central and Eastern Europe

6   Finances and power in the German state system

Michael North

According to Bonney's (and Ormrod's) definition a fiscal state is characterized by the following features: it has a developed fiscal system and
can survive and overcome financial crises and experiences sustained
growth. Their definition matches only one European example: Britain
after the financial revolution. When its fiscal and financial system
acquired the 'sophisticated credit structures and a capacity for sustaining fiscal increases over time', Britain became a financial superpower
and overcame the Napoleonic bid for European hegemony.[1]

Germany remains in good company with other European countries
as it never became a model fiscal state before the nineteenth century.
Indeed, it never became a state before 1871! In the Middle Ages and
the early modern period, Germany was represented by the Holy Roman
Empire, a more or less stable union of secular and ecclesiastical territories, imperial and free cities and a number of de facto autonomous
towns, including the Hanseatic cities in the North. Although most of
them acknowledged the emperor as their supreme ruler, the political
connections remained weak. In the fifteenth century, a process of institutional cooperation (Moraw: *Verdichtung*) took place, in response to the
aggression of Hussites, Turks and wars against Burgundy and France.
In 1495, this institutionalization took the form of an imperial diet and
affected the fiscal system of the Empire. Apart from this process on the
imperial level, a second process of state formation took place within the
constituent parts of the Empire. Proto-states, described by historians
such as Gerhard Oestreich or Kersten Krüger, completed transitions
from domain to tax states.[2] Given that the fiscal system of the Empire

---

[1] R. Bonney, 'Introduction – the rise of the fiscal state in Europe. c. 1200–1815', in R.
Bonney (ed), *The rise of the fiscal state in Europe, c. 1200–1815* (Oxford University Press,
1999), pp. 1–17.

[2] G. Oestreich, 'Ständestaat und Staatsbildung in Deutschland', in G. Oestreich, *Geist
und Gestalt des frühmodernen Staates* (Berlin: Duncher and Humbolt, 1969), pp. 277–89;
K. Krüger, 'Gerhard Oestreich und der Finanzstaat. Entstehung und Deutung eines
Epochenbegriffs der frühneuzeitlichen Verfassungs- und Sozialgeschichte', *Hessisches
Jahrbuch für Landesgeschichte* 33 (1983), 333–46; K. Krüger, *Finanzstaat Hessen*

remained rudimentary, it is more illuminating to begin any overview with the cities and territories.

Municipal finances

The imperial cities and the Hanseatic cities in the North – some of them, such as Lübeck or Lüneburg, were imperial cities as well – were the most advanced with respect to administration, legal autonomy and fiscal and accounting structures. They collected property taxes and levied excises on commodities, first occasionally, but later annually. Besides these extraordinary taxes, a set of customs duties and tolls formed the major revenues of the cities. Among these river, road, port and city tolls were prominent. Market, burgher and jurisdiction fees and taxes on Jews formed another part of their revenues. Revenues from the mints may have been quite important, although the cities had to buy or procure large amounts of precious metals for the mint, which might have reduced profitability. Rents from the cities' estate also contributed to the budgets.

Evidence is available for the imperial city of Nuremberg (1431–40) in the form of accounts that display typical and major sources of municipal revenues and expenditures,[3] as reflected in Table 6.1.

The Nuremberg situation seems to be characteristic for an imperial city in Upper Germany. Quite astonishing is the large proportion of direct and indirect taxes that contributed regularly to the city's budget. One-third of expenditure could only be covered through loans and credit, especially by selling annuities. The expansion of public credit is exposed by the high proportion of interest payments in the expenditures that ranked above war and defence expenditures – a situation that seems to be characteristic of more than the modern tax state in the twentieth century.

The Hanseatic cities in the North of Germany were different. Hamburg, for instance, was able to finance its budget to a large extent by tolls and property taxes (*schoss*) that were raised from the fourteenth century and by the end of the sixteenth century stabilised at around 0.3 per cent. It was only in periods of excessive financial demands that Hamburg entered the capital market. Extraordinary demands

1500–1567. Staatsbildung im Übergang vom Domänenstaat zum Steuerstaat (Marburg: Elwert, 1980).

[3] P. Sander, *Die reichsstädtische Haushaltung Nürnbergs: dargestellt auf Grund ihres Zustandes von 1431 bis 1440* (Leipzig, 1902), pp. 417–18, 689–90, 701; E. Isenmann, *Die deutsche Stadt im Spätmittelalter 1250–1500. Stadtgestalt, Recht, Stadtregiment, Kirche, Gesellschaft, Wirtschaft* (Stuttgart: E. Ulmer, 1988), pp. 170–7.

Table 6.1. *Revenues and expenditures of the Imperial City of Nuremberg, 1431–1440*

Municipal revenues	Percentage
Direct taxes (property taxes)	20.27
Indirect taxes (excises on wine and beer)	21.21
Market duties (scales, toll) and mint	2.67
Jews and villages	3.17
Housing rents and sales, and public grain sale	6.04
Forests	0.99
Municipal enterprises	3.05
Sale of annuities	33.97
Others	8.63
Municipal expenditures	
Administration	7.52
War and defence	29.25
Jurisdiction	0.81
Poor relief	0.88
Building	17.96
Interest on loans and annuities	35.73
Purchases of seigniorial rights	7.77
Others	0.08

emanated, for example, from the purchase of neighbouring territories (1387), the acquisition of jurisdiction (1392), the war against Holland (1399–1403), the war against pirates (Ostfriesland, 1409), the wars against the Danish King Erik of Pomerania (1426–35), the war against Holland (1451–53), war against England and the building of the Alster-Trave-Channel (1472). For this last project 15,000 marks *lübisch* (Ml.) were raised by selling annuities. These financial engagements were reflected in the fluctuations in debt of Hamburg. For example, during the Schmalkaldic War when Hamburg supported the Protestant princes against the Catholic emperor, large loans had to be raised. Although tax revenues and tolls rose significantly, the city of Hamburg financed an increasing part of its budget from loans from the Schleswig-Holstein nobility – a new situation. In the fourteenth and fifteenth centuries, creditors (burghers/citizens of Hamburg and Lübeck) invested in Hamburg annuities, and by the sixteenth century Hamburg became financially dependent on the Schleswig-Holstein nobility. Families, including the Rantzau (145,000 Ml.), Alefeld (58,000 Ml.), Sehested (56,000 Ml.), Wisch (34,000 Ml.), Brockdorp (28,000 Ml.), Damme (27,000 Ml.), Pogwisch (26,000 Ml.), Reventlow (21,000 Ml.), Ratlow

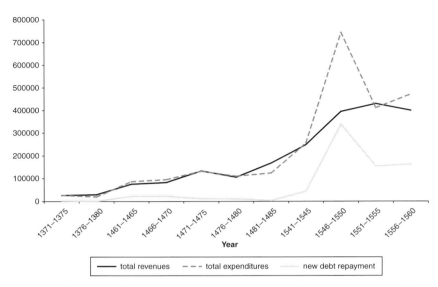

Figure 6.1 The central money household of Hamburg, 1371–1560[4]
Source: H. Reincke, 'Die alte Hamburger Stadtschuld der Hansezeit
(1300–1563)', in A. von Brandt and W. Koppe (eds.), *Städtewesen
und Bürgertum als geschichtliche Kräfte. Gedächtnisschrift für Fritz Rörig*
(Lübeck: M. Schmidt-Römhild 1953), pp. 270–1.

(17,000 Ml.), Buchwald (10,000 Ml.) and Rumor (4,000 Ml.) financed
extraordinary loans 'for the protection of the true religion' (see Figures
6.1 and 6.2). These noble families had made fortunes in the military, as
entrepreneurs and as large-scale grain producers for Western markets.
They also invested money in the provincial debts of the Southern Low
Countries.

Territorial finances

Compared to the advanced financial systems of imperial and Hanseatic
cities, the fiscal systems of secular and ecclesiastical territories seem
rather primitive. In these polities, the princes (dukes, counts or bishops)
exploited their own domains and the barons (*Herren*) collected feudal
rents from their tenants. In the Middle Ages, territorial states presented
no budgets and except for a few examples (such as the Teutonic Order)

[4] H. Reincke, 'Die alte Hamburger Stadtschuld der Hansezeit (1300–1563)', in A.
von Brand and W. Koppe (eds.), *Städtewesen und Bürgertum als geschichtliche Kräfte.
Gedächtnisschrift für Fritz Rörig* (Lübeck: M. Schmidt-Römhild 1953), pp. 270–1.

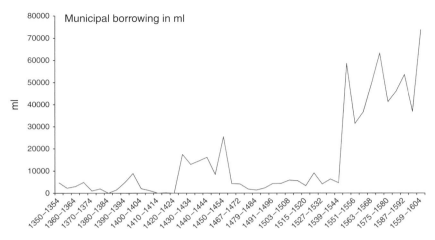

Figure 6.2 Municipal borrowing in Hamburg, 1350–1604

kept no written books. Princely domains were normally organized into administrative and fiscal units, the so-called *Ämter* at local levels. The itinerant court was maintained and supplied by local revenues from the *Ämter* in kind. Even when princely residences were established, apart from money rents, revenues in kind from the domain played an important role but were sometimes converted into money. Taxes were 'extraordinary' and could only be raised in cases of necessity. Sometimes excise taxes were extended from the towns to the whole of the territory, like the beer excise (*Tranksteuer*) in Saxonia. Market tolls, fees for military escorts (*Geleitgeld*), revenues from mines and mints as well as the taxation of Jews contributed to territorial revenues.

Extraordinary taxes were granted only by the estates under special circumstances and depended on their consent. For this purpose the representative assemblies of the territory or 'land' had to be called. The composition of the revenues varied greatly from territory to territory and over time. For example, the ecclesiastical electors of Rhine and the Palatinate appropriated revenues by levying custom tolls along the Rhine. The massive influx of gold from commerce enabled the electors to mint the famous Rhine guilder and thereby created a key currency for Western and Central Europe.[5] Since domains were small, rural rents played only a minor role. While an extraordinary levy on the Jews

[5] E. Isenmann, 'The Holy Roman Empire in the Middle Ages,' in Bonney, *The rise of the fiscal state in Europe*, pp. 243–80, especially pp. 247–9.

in the Electorate of Cologne in 1419 yielded 25,000 gilders, in Saxonia the situation was different. Domain revenues and income from mining dominated but they did not match Saxonia's expenditures. Engagement in the Hussite wars led Saxonia to become heavily indebted. Most domain revenues (from the *Ämter*) were pledged as security and the dukes depended on extra credits, supplied by such Jewish bankers as Abraham Esra. Fortunately, the silver mining boom from the 1470s enabled Saxonia to repay a part of its debt. Furthermore, the *Tranksteuer* (beer excise, 1470–76 onwards) increased ducal revenues. Saxonia's cities, especially Leipzig, guaranteed the debt. Apart from the towns, the majority of the creditors were local noblemen and burgers and were members of the Saxonian estates. Thus, the land's representatives at the diet were at the same time creditors and guarantors of Saxonia's state debt. After the Schmalkaldic War and at the Dresden diet of 1552, the elector allocated the revenues of the beer excise to the estates for the purposes of servicing debt.

They then collected the beer excise and took responsibility for the management of debt, and the electors became dependent on the consent of the estates to help them solve liquidity crises. This was indeed a decisive step for the formation of the early modern state. Only after the Thirty Years War, when the estates were no longer able to guarantee credit for the state did they lose power to the Jewish court factors and bankers who extended credit to electors.[6]

Oestreich sees the role of estates in tax administration as a crucial step in the development of a 'public fiscal and financial administration' for a particular stage of state formation in the sixteenth century. Krüger elaborated on Oestreich's concept with respect to Hesse, which was a well-organized 'domain state' with relatively efficient methods of collecting taxes from forest lands, salt production and trade at the *Ämter*. Revenues from the domain state, however, reached their limits when Hesse took part in military engagements against the emperor during the Schmalkaldic War. Military operations generated debts of a million guilders in the 1550s (*c.* ten times the income of the territory). And this financial crisis of the mid sixteenth century induced a shift towards a tax state. Repartition taxes on personal wealth were levies whereby noblemen were taxed together with non-nobles as a single

[6] U. Schirmer, 'Die Institutionalisierung fürstlicher Schulden in Sachsen im 15. und 16. Jahrhundert', in Gerhard Lingelbach (ed), *Staatsfinanzen – Staatsverschuldung – Staatsbankrotte in der europäischen Staaten- und Rechtsgeschichte* (Cologne: Böhlau, 2000), pp. 277–92. Schirmer, *Kursächsische Staatsfinanzen (1456–1656): Strukturen, Verfassung, Funktionseliten* (Stuttgart: In Kommission bei Franz Steiner, 2006).

Table 6.2. *Revenues and expenditures for central governance in Hesse, 1500–1568 (in guilders)*

	1500–09	1510–19	1520–29	1530–39	1540–49	1550–59	1560–68
Revenues							
Treasury	29,721	26,614	45,868	57,676	67,638	104,024	100,729
Taxes	2,838	1,500	6,000	27,701	48,285	51,504	62,459
Total revenues	32,559	28,114	51,868	85,377	115,923	155,528	163,188
Total expenditures	23,769	17,892	40,964	162,334	210,412	154,615	98,669
Surplus	8,790	10,222	10,904	—	—	913	64,519
Deficit	—	—	—	76,957	94,489	—	—
Refund	—	—	—	44,225	85,442	15,860	—
Loans				45,052	22,375		
Extraordinary expenditures	—	—	—	—	—	—	48,144
Surplus	**8,790**	**10,222**	**10,904**	**12,320**	**13,328**	**16,773**	**16,375**

Source: K. Krüger, *Finanzstaat Hessen 1500–1567. Staatsbildung im Übergang vom Domänenstaat zum Steuerstaat* (Marburg: Elwert, 1980), p. 297, table 133.

cohesive group of equitably taxed subjects.[7] A tax on wine and beer was also introduced on a regular basis and granted for numbers of years. The growing deficit, but also the growing importance of taxes in the revenues of Hesse, is clearly reflected in Table 6.2.

Compared with Hesse, Ducal Prussia (East Prussia) remained a domain state and taxes contributed to the territorial income sporadically. Since the estates refused requests for new taxes, expenditures could often only be funded by borrowing on the security of domain lands (*Ämter*) (see Table 6.3). Thus, members of the estates profited as the duke's creditors from the pawned *Ämter*. Furthermore, a collision of interests between the noble members and the representatives of the cities (Königsberg) prevailed with respect to taxes. When the duke asked for a tax grant, the nobility preferred a beer excise, whilst the cities pressed for a property tax. From the cities' point of view a beer tax was detrimental to the local brewing industries, since the cities of Königsberg already raised one-third of the country's total tax revenue from an excise on beer. They had to be persuaded to levy extra excises on beer for periods of one or two years.

---

[7] W. Schulze, 'The emergence and consolidation of the "tax state". I. The sixteenth century', in R. Bonney (ed.), *Economic systems and state finance* (Oxford: Clarendon Press, 1995), pp. 261–79, especially pp. 270–1.

Table 6.3. *Revenues and expenditures of Ducal Prussia, 1560–1619 (in Prussian marks)*

	1560–69	1570–79	1580–89	1590–99	1600–09	1610–19
Revenues						
Treasury	164,892	185,556	265,511	340,812	402,841	527,196
Taxes	36,194	14,976	—	—	—	17,478
Total revenues	201,086	500,532	265,511	340,812	402,841	544,674
Total expenditures	255,047	220,492	251,578	322,995	497,798	555,338
Surplus	—	—	13,933	17,817	—	—
Deficit	53,961	19,960	—	—	94,957	10,664
Pledges	29,721	18,420	—	—	12,000*	140,363*
Extraordinary expenditures	—	—	—	—	—	48,144
Surplus/Deficit	–24,240	–1,540	13,933	17,817	–82,957	129,699

Notes: * estimated averages; SOURCES: M. North, 'Finanzstaaten im Vergleich: Die Landgrafschaft Hessen und das Herzogtum Preußen im 16. Jahrhundert', in Werner Buchholz and Stefan Kroll (eds.), *Quantität und Struktur. Festschrift für Kersten Krüger zum 60. Geburtstag* (Rostock: Universität Rost, 1999), pp. 64–74, at pp. 65f; M. North, *Die Amtswirtschaften von Osterode und Soldau. Vergleichende Untersuchungen zur Wirtschaft im frühmodernen Staat am Beispiel des Herzogtums Preußen in der zweiten Hälfte des 16. und der ersten Hälfte des 17. Jahrhunderts* (Berlin: Duncker & Humblot, 1982), p. 329, table 77.

Imperial finances

The emperors also kept an itinerant court that had to be fed and supplied from the resources of the territories that they visited. The Roman emperor or German king also had his own hereditary domains at his disposal – the *Reichsgut*. They were, however, continuously dismembered by the creation of fiefs and donations but also by usurpation and pledges against loans in the fourteenth and fifteenth centuries. Meanwhile, the efforts of several kings to reclaim usurped parts from former imperial domains often failed. By the end, only the royal mints, the taxes paid by the imperial cities, the levies on the Jews and the fiscal exploitation of juridical services remained as imperial revenues. City taxes were further diminished by pledges to royal officers, princes, noblemen and to city corporations. Several cities also enjoyed tax exemptions for limited periods of time, and the emperors were then compelled to raise extraordinary taxes, which were sometimes successfully resisted.

To solve his deplorable financial situation the emperor invented new taxes, basically to fund warfare. For example, the first ordinary public tax, called 'golden penny' (*guldin pfennig*), paid per head by all Jews (over twelve years) with property worth more than 20 guilders, was levied by Emperor Louis of Bavaria in 1342. By the fifteenth century, the continuous threat by the heretical Hussites of Bohemia and the Osmanic Empire made the levy of imperial taxes inevitable.

The first tax, levied in 1422, arose from the financial demands of the Hussite war and was designed as a repartition tax (*Matrikularumlage*), whereby small military units of horsemen (*Gleven* = swords) were financed from the economic resources of ecclesiastical and secular princes, prelates, counts, barons and cities subject to the Empire. This tax became a model for later levies during the Empire's defence against the Turks in the sixteenth and seventeenth centuries. In 1427, a second tax for war against the Hussites was designed as a direct tax (*Quotitätssteuer*) on property. Although several territories collected the tax, only a small proportion of the revenue came into the imperial treasury. At the diets of Regensburg and Augsburg (1471 and 1474) the emperor asked again for an extraordinary tax to finance a national army and crusade against the Turks. These taxes, designed to tax profits and incomes, were not successful. Therefore the discussion at the diet of 1480 linked policy for a standing army to continuous annual taxes and referred to the examples of Hungary (that was regularly subject to Osmanic aggression), France and the Italian states. In 1486, Emperor Frederick III asked again for urgent assistance, the so-called 'hurrying help' (*eilende Hilfe*) of 163,000 guilders. The sum was partitioned among territorial rulers and cities (King Maximilian, six electors, the Arch-duke Sigismund of Tyrol and seventy imperial cities). A second demand for 500,000 guilders included six electors, twenty-one archbishops and bishops, eighteen abbots, eleven secular princes and fifty-eight cities. Continuous taxation seemed to be inevitable during the Empire's competition with other European powers. In 1495, the diet at Worms introduced permanent peace (*Ewiger Landfrieden*), an imperial jurisdiction and a general tax, the so-called common penny (*Gemeiner Pfennig*). An imperial representation, the imperial diet (*Reichstag*) took shape to make decisions about taxation. Meanwhile, the common penny was imposed on all inhabitants of the Empire over the age of forty (see Table 6.4), except princes, who assessed themselves.

Linked to war, the diet inaugurated state taxation for imperial warfare as well as the maintenance of the imperial jurisdiction and the maintenance of internal order. From an expected revenue of at least 300,000 guilders between 136,000 and 166,000 guilders were received

Table 6.4. *Per capita property taxes of the Gemeiner Pfennig*

Poor people	1/24 fl.
People with 500 fl.	0.5 fl.
People with 1,000 fl.	1 fl.

for military purposes, 10,000 guilders for the imperial jurisdiction (the *Reichskammergericht*) and 1,000 guilders for internal stability. Although imperial cities, the ecclesiastical princes and the prelates went along with the tax, several electors and secular princes were quite obstructive – several territorial estates declined to collect the common penny. It did not survive for long because territorial rulers and estates rejected imperial taxation as interference in their sovereignty.

New forms of taxation had to be introduced. Thus the model of a repartition tax (as in 1422) gained in popularity. The imperial estates fulfilled their obligations agreed at the Diet of Worms in 1521, which established a so-called 'Roman month' (*Römermonat*) for a fictive army of 4,000 horseman and 20,000 foot soldiers (*Fußsoldaten*), allocated to finance the coronation of emperors in Rome. This amounted to a notional 64,000 guilders a month. When the emperor asked for money the diet granted him a specified number of 'Roman months'; each allocated for the imperial subjects according to the repartition (*Matrikel*) of 1521. How many and how often Roman months were granted depended on the actual political situation and upon successful negotiations between emperors and the imperial estates. For example, in 1603, during the campaign against the Turks, the emperor received a maximum of eighty-six Roman months (550,400 guilders). During the thirty-seven-year reign of Charles V, the imperial diet granted only 73.5 Roman months. Even then, not every territory fulfilled its obligations. Nevertheless, imperial revenues rose from 2.5 to 3.5 million guilders in the first half of the sixteenth century to 30 million guilders from 1576–1606. Apart from the Roman months, in 1548 a second (annual) repartition tax for the maintenance of the *Reichskammergericht*, the so-called *Kammerzieler*, was introduced.[8] With continuous flows of

[8] Isenmann, 'The Holy Roman Empire', pp. 265–73; P. Schmid, *Der Gemeiner Pfennig von 1495* (Göttingen: Vandenhoeck & Ruprech, 1989). P. Moraw, 'Der "Gemeiner Pfennig": Neue Steuern und die Einheit des Reiches im 15. und 16. Jahrhundert', in Uwe Schultz (ed.), *Mit dem Zehnten fing es an. Eine Kulturgeschichte der Steuer*, 2nd edn, (Munich: Beck, 1986), pp. 130–42. W. Schulze, *Reich und Türkengefahr im späten 16. Jahrhundert. Studien zu den politischen und gesellschaftlichen Auswirkungen einer äußeren Bedrohung* (Munich: Beck, 1978).

imperial taxes, the financial administration of the Empire became more powerful. And the *Reichspfennigmeister*, the supreme head of the financial administration, Zacharias Geizkofler, increased the efficiency of imperial collection. During Geizkofler's period about 90 per cent of the grants were collected and contributed to a successful defence against the Turkish invasions. This situation changed after the Thirty Years War, when the desolate economic and financial situation reduced the ability of the territorial states and the Empire to match growing political needs.[9] Although the Empire still managed to finance its wars and defence efforts against France and the Turks, the gap between the Roman months granted and the Roman months collected increased. By the late eighteenth century, the situation had clearly deteriorated. Between 1793 and 1796, 230 Roman months with an amount of 15 million guilders were granted, but only 5 million guilders were actually collected.[10]

The growing political power of German territorial states after the Thirty Years War, coupled with their weak fiscal and financial systems, led their rulers to intensify their efforts to raise money in a variety of ways. One option was to employ the Jewish Court Factors (*Hoffaktoren*) or Court Jews (*Hofjude*) to raise loans at a time when the majority of merchant bankers in the *Reichsstädte* (like Nuremberg), who had suffered financial losses during the war, were no longer placed or willing to risk loans to the princes. In a hostile environment, Jewish moneylenders had no choice but to connect their fortunes to the finances of princes. For them, the fiscal demands of the German territorial states opened opportunities for economic and social advancement.

Furthermore, the rise of the *Hoffaktoren* was closely connected to the formation of the absolutist state and to struggles between the absolutist rulers and their estates over money and funding for the standing armies. The *Hoffaktoren* contributed to the autonomy of rulers and to their independence from the powerful estates in financial and, by implication, in political matters. The outcome was that *Hoffaktoren* became a target of accusations by the estates and were only protected by special personal relationships to the rulers. The *Hoffaktor* supplied courts with food, clothing and luxuries, and above all with credit and loans. They supplied local mints with silver and gold and often leased mints

---

[9] Schulze, *Reich und Türkengefahr*, pp. 362–3. N. Jörn, 'Beobachtungen zur Steuerzahlung der Territorien des südlichen Ostseeraumes in der Frühen Neuzeit', in N. Jörn and M. North (eds.), *Die Integration des südlichen Ostseeraumes in das Alte Reich* (Cologne: Böhlau, 2000), pp. 311–91.

[10] H.-P. Ullmann, *Der deutsche Steuerstaat. Geschichte der öffentlichen Finanzen* (Munich: Beck, 2005), p. 58.

for advances in cash. To raise capital, the *Hoffaktoren* made use of their manifold family networks, as well as Christian depositors.[11]

An important example of *Hoffaktoren* were Samuel Oppenheimer and his nephew Samson Wertheimer, who originated from the Jewish community in Worms and became financiers to the Habsburg Empire. Oppenheimer operated as a purveyor (*Kriegsfaktor*) to the imperial army in conflicts with France and the Turks, especially during the famous siege of Vienna in 1683. When he died in 1703, the *Hofkammer* owed him six mill fl. (German guilders) but defaulted on the debt. His nephew Samson Wertheimer avoided bankruptcy. His loans, extended during the War of the Spanish Succession, were redeemed, and he died in 1724 as one of the richest and most distinguished Jews of his time.[12]

Feidel David served the *Landgraf* of Hessen-Kassel in the mid eighteenth century and conducted negotiations for English subsidies during the Seven Years War. He was superseded by Meyer Amschel Rothschild, a Frankfurt moneychanger, who invested with profit Hessen-Kassel's gains from the 'trade in mercenaries' during the War of American Independence, and laid foundations for the rise of the Rothschilds in the following century. In Frankfurt, numerous Jewish merchants operated as *Hoffaktoren* for different princely or ducal courts. Among the most prominent was Joseph Süß Oppenheimer (1689–1738), a Frankfurt dealer in commodities and bills of exchange, who gained a leading position during the reign of Duke Karl Alexander of Württemberg. He managed finances for the household and Württemberg's standing army, helped to strengthen ducal absolutism and to eliminate the political participation of the Württemberg estates. After the duke's death, Oppenheimer was prosecuted, sentenced to death and executed.[13] At the end of the eighteenth century, the Dukes of Württemberg continued to employ the Kaullas of Hechingen as purveyors to the army. Together with the duke, they founded the *Württembergische Hofbank* in 1802 and prepared the path to nineteenth-century private banking.[14]

[11] H. Schnee, *Die Hoffinanz und der moderne Staat*, 5 vols. (Berlin: Duncker and Humbolt, 1953–1965); M. North, 'The great German banking houses and European merchants, 16th–19th centuries', in A. Teichova, G. Kurgan van Hentenryk and D. Ziegler (eds.), *Banking, trade and industry, Europe, America and Asia from the 13th to the 20th century* (Cambridge University Press, 1997), pp. 35–49, at pp. 39ff.

[12] M. Grundwald, *Samuel Oppenheimer und sein Kreis* (Vienna-Leipzig: Braumüller 1913); Selma Stern, *The court Jew: a contribution to the history of absolutism in Central Europe* (Philadelphia: Jewish Publication Society of America, 1950), pp. 86–8.

[13] Schnee, *Hoffinanz*, Vol. 4, pp. 109–48; Barbara Gerber, *Jud Süß. Aufstieg und Fall im frühen 18. Jahrhundert* (Hamburg: Christians, 1990).

[14] Schnee, *Hoffinanz*, Vol. 4, pp. 109–78.

Brandenburg-Prussian fiscal absolutism

Another option to circumvent the financial weakness or obduracy of the estates was to combine absolutism and permanent taxation. Thus, Brandenburg-Prussia limited the powers of estates and at the same time created the fiscal and financial basis for a standing army. These measures were introduced by the Great Elector, Frederick William, during the years 1641 and 1667 in order to rebuild Brandenburg-Prussia after the Thirty Years War. The elector introduced two permanent taxes, a direct tax (the contribution on landed property) and an indirect consumption tax (the excise in the towns). The excise consisted of a set of levies on most products in general use required by urban populations, in particular, beverages, brandy, cereals, meat, other foodstuffs such as spices, coffee, tobacco, textiles and building materials. In principle the policy combined extension to the maximum number of commodities with the lowest possible rates of tax.[15] Although the regional estates of most Brandenburg provinces approved the new taxes, in Prussia resistance, especially in the cities of Königsberg, was strong, and the Great Elector used military power to enforce the introduction of the excise. A direct tax on property was collected through land quotas by varying specifications in different provinces (tax on holdings, impost on gables or general tax on land). Assessments were sometimes based on yield, sometimes on the quantity of seed sown, the size of the holding or the number of hearths. Since feudal lords were allowed to shift the contribution to their tenants or peasants they had no problem in granting this tax. Noble manors in Brandenburg remained exempt from taxes, but in Prussia, Frederick William I (1713–40) introduced a land tax (*Generalhubenschoss*) that the Prussian nobility had to pay in order to acquire hereditary rights to property. Besides taxes, domestic tolls on roads, waterways and ports yielded quite a significant proportion of the revenue. In the early eighteenth century, the royal domain continued to be a major source of revenue (see Table 6.5) paid on leases to financially sound tenants. To raise the efficiency of the financial system, Frederick William I united the independent administrative chambers into a Supreme Finance, War and Domain authority (*General-Ober-Finanz-Kriegs- und Domänen-Direktorium*). This chamber administered both

---

[15] E. Schremmer, 'Taxation and public finance: Britain, France, and Germany', in Peter Mathias and Sidney Pollard (eds.), *The Cambridge economic history of Europe, volume VIII: the development of economic and social policies* (Cambridge University Press, 1989), p. 411.

Table 6.5. *Prussian state finance, 1688–1806*

	1688	1713	1740	1786	1806
Surface area in 1,000 km²	111	113	119	195	347
Population (millions)	1.5	1.6	2.2	5.4	10.7
Army (thousand men)	30	38	72	195	250
Total net revenue approx. (thousand *talers*)	3	4	7.4	19–20	27–31
Taxes, etc.	1.6	2.4	4	10–11	16–20
Income from state property	0.9	1.6	3.4	6–7	8
Military expenditure approx. (thousand *talers*)	2.5		6	12–13	16–17
Public treasure approx. (thousand *talers*)			8.7	55	17
Public debt approx. (thousand *talers*)				48.1	53.5
				(1794)	(1807)

Sources: D. E. Schremmer, 'Taxation and public finance: Britain, France and Germany', in P. Mathias and S. Pollard (eds.), *Cambridge economic history of Europe, Volume VIII, the industrial economies: the development of economic and social policies* (Cambridge University Press, 1989), p. 415; F.-W. Henning, 'Die preußische Thesaurierungspolitik im 18. Jahrhundert', in I. Bog, G. Franz, K.-H. Kaufhold, H. Kellenbenz and W. Zorn (eds.), *Wirtschaftliche und soziale Strukturen im saekularen Wandel. Festschrift für Wilhelm Abel zum 70. Geburtstag (Bd. 2: Die vorindustrielle Zeit: Außeragrarische Probleme)* (Hannover: M. & H. Schaper, 1974), pp. 95–110, pp. 399–416; A. O. von Loehr, 'Die Finanzierung des Siebenjährigen Krieges', *Numismatische Zeitschrift* 58 (1925), 95–110.

taxes and domain revenues and monitored expenditures for military purposes.

Prussia matched increasing expenditures for the army by increasing the revenues, while retaining a reserve of 8.7 million *talers* that was run down during the Austrian Succession (1756–63) and the Seven Years War. The latter war cost Prussia at least 125 million *talers* but a large amount of military outlays were financed by English subsidies (27 million) and by debasement and inflation (29 million). Moreover, the occupied territories of Saxony and Mecklenburg were compelled to pay a large *Kontribution* of 53 million. After the war, the currency was revalued to the cost of those holding coins. Prussia soon recovered financially and was able to rebuild its reserves which amounted to 55 million *talers* at Frederick II's death. But this again disappeared during the Revolutionary and Napoleonic Wars when Prussia sustained the dramatic territorial and financial losses that pushed it towards the financial revolution of 1806.[16]

[16] F.-W. Henning, 'Die preußische Thesaurierungspolitik im 18. Jahrhundert', in I. Bog, G. Franz, K.-H. Kaufhold, H. Kellenbenz and W. Zorn (eds.), *Wirtschaftliche*

Table 6.6. *Revenues of selected European countries*

	Total revenues in mil. *livres tournois*	Direct taxes in %	Indirect taxes in %	Total taxes in %	Other revenues in %
Hanover (1750/60)	7.23	26.4	25.3	51.7	48.3
Hamburg (1765/66)	4.25	30.3	25.9	56.2	43.8
Bavaria (18th century)	9.50–11.00	46.0	10.9	56.9	43.1
Saxonia (1770)	c. 18.00	48.5	12.8	61.3	38.7
Austria (1773)	91.68*	41.3	20.5	61.8	38.2
Kleve-Mark-Moers (1757/58)	3.03	43.4	20.8	64.2	35.8
Prussia (1765/66)	48.56	31.9	37.5	69.4	30.6
France (1773)	285.00**	46.4	42.9	89.3	10.7
Great Britain (1765)	223.90	20.8	68.9	89.7	10.3

Notes: * information about 1764/65 (Habsburg monarchy without the Netherlands and Lombardy); ** information about 1759; SOURCES: M. A. Denzel, 'Staatliche und kirchliche Steuersysteme im 18. Jahrhundert: Aspekte und Entwicklungslinien des Steuerwesens weltlicher und geistlicher Territorien im Heiligen Römischen Reich', in Simonetta Cavaciocchi (ed.), *Poteri economici e poteri politici secc. XIII–XVIII* (Firenze: Le Monnier, 1999), p. 674, according to P. C. Hartmann, *Das Steuersystem der europäischen Staaten am Ende des Ancien Regime. Eine offizielle französische Enquete (1763–1768). Dokumente, Analyse und Auswertung. England und die Staaten Nord- und Mitteleuropas* (Munich: Artemis, 1979).

Systems of state finance and per-capita tax burdens

Systems of state finance in Germany operating at the end of the *ancien régime* were diverse but can be compared, as in Tables 6.6 and 6.7.[17]

For several countries revenues from domains still played important roles. Even Hamburg had considerable revenues from tolls, municipal enterprises (mills, banks, lottery, crans), landed property and fees collected from the Jewish population and from those who wanted to become Hamburg citizens (so-called *Bürgergeld*).[18]

---

und soziale Strukturen im saekularen Wandel. Festschrift für Wilhelm Abel zum 70. Geburtstag (Bd. 2: Die vorindustrielle Zeit: Außeragrarische Probleme) (Hannover: M. & H. Schaper, 1974), pp. 95–110.

[17] O. Bachmayer, *Die Geschichte der österreichischen Währungspolitik* (Vienna: Manz, 1960), pp. 87–94; G. Probszt, *Österreichische Münz- und Geldgeschichte* (Vienna: Bohlau 1973), p. 526.

[18] P. C. Hartmann, *Das Steuersystem der europäischen Staaten am Ende des Ancien Regime. Eine offizielle französische Enquete (1763–1768). Dokumente, Analyse und Auswertung. England und die Staaten Nord- und Mitteleuropas* (Munich: Artemis, 1979), pp. 142–4.

Table 6.7. *Total tax burden per capita of selected countries in* livres tournois

	Total tax load	Direct taxes	Indirect taxes
Great Britain (1759)	23.3	6.3	17.0
(1788)	33.3	6.7	26.6
Hamburg (1765/66)	24.6	13.3	11.3
France (1788)	15.1	7.3	7.8
Saxonia (1770)	9.24	7.2	2.04
Prussia (1765/66)	7.5	3.44	4.06
Austria (1773)	7.48	3.78	3.7**
Kleve-Mark-Moers (1757/58)	6.7	5.5	1.2
Bavaria (1770)	6.0	3.75	2.25*
Hanover (1750/60er)	5.0	[2.5]	2.5

Notes: * inclusive monopoly of salt and beer; ** inclusive monopoly of salt and tobacco

Interesting variations in tax burdens are evident. In most countries the absolute burden was not high in relative terms. The citizens of Britain and Hamburg carried comparable burdens.[19]

Nineteenth-century German fiscal unification

The Revolutionary and Napoleonic Wars had severe consequences for most European countries and financial systems. Only Great Britain and to some extent Russia were able to resist French aggression and most parts of Europe had to reorganize and modernize their territories and financial systems to overcome the consequences of the French victories. After the dissolution of the Holy Roman Empire (1806) the Napoleonic Allies Bavaria, Württemberg and Baden tried to integrate recently acquired territories into their countries. Austrian resistance to Napoleon led to state bankruptcy in 1811 but financial reform did not succeed, due to opposition from the nobility. After a dramatic defeat in 1806, Prussia had no choice but to reform its bureaucracy and tried to enforce modernization 'from above' by introducing a personal income tax that challenged the tradition of exemptions for the nobility. The plan failed when the Prussian elites regained power after the final victory over France in 1815. Although a business tax (*Gewerbesteuer*) had been introduced together with the introduction of freedom of trade (*Gewerbefreiheit*) in 1811, noble resistance destroyed plans for income tax and the existing property tax – with thirty-three different principles

[19] Ibid., pp. 321–3.

.

Table 6.8. *The graduated tax system of 1821 (four [main] classes)*

1st class			2nd class			3rd class			4th class		
Especially affluent and rich inhabitants			Affluent residents			Lower bourgeoisie and peasants			Wage labourers, servants, day labourers		
1st	(sub)	class	2nd	(sub)	class	3rd	(sub)	class	4th	(sub)	class
144	96	48	24	18	12	8	6	4	3	2	1/2
		Tax liability in *talers* per annum									

Source: D. E. Schremmer, 'Taxation and public finance: Britain, France and Germany', in P. Mathias and S. Pollard (eds.), *Cambridge economic history of Europe, Volume VIII, the industrial economies: the development of economic and social policies* (Cambridge University Press, 1989), p. 431.

for assessment in the provinces (and *Regierungsbezirke*) – was retained. A compromise graduated tax (*Klassensteuer*) was, however, created, dividing the rural taxable population into four classes with respect to social status, whereby status indicated occupation and occupation indicated taxable wealth (see Table 6.8).[20]

In Prussian towns and cities, a substitute indirect tax (the so-called milling and slaughter tax, see Table 6.9) was introduced in relation to the consumption of bread and meat, alongside traditional excises on salt, tobacco and alcoholic beverages.

Former French allies Bavaria, Württemberg and Baden acted differently and introduced a new tax system based on French models on revenue from real property (land, buildings and business).[21] Over time, the mixed Prussian system in the North and the French system in the South prevailed. In the short run, the partial tax reforms resulted in growing revenues that did not match expenditures or reduce and consolidate the legacy of debt from warfare before 1815. New loans had to be negotiated. Prussia obtained credit from London (via the *Preussische Seehandlung*), while the southern German states attempted to increase creditworthiness by creating new parliamentary constitutions between 1818 and 1820. Diets controlled budgets and approved loans. In time, expenditures rose more slowly than the revenues, which stabilized the

[20] Schremmer, 'Taxation and public finance', pp. 430–1; B. Vogel, 'Staatsfinanzen und Gesellschaftsreform in Preußen', in Helmut Berding (ed.), *Privatkapital, Staatsfinanzen und Reformpolitik im Deutschland der napoleonischen Zeit* (Ostfildern: Scripta Mercaturae, 1981), pp. 37–57.

[21] Schremmer, 'Taxation and public finance', pp. 389–91.

Table 6.9. *Structure of Prussian tax revenue, 1816 and 1821*

Types of tax	1816 (thousand *talers*)	%	1821 (thousand *talers*)	%
I. Direct taxes				
1. Land tax	9,802	31.4%	9,326	26.6%
2. Business tax	1,362	4.3%	1,600	4.6%
3. Graduated tax	–	–	6,321	18.0%
4. Personal taxes in eastern provinces and Westphalia	1,387	4.4%	–	–
5. Furniture, door and window tax etc. in western provinces	868	2.8%	–	–
Total of I	13,419	42.9%	17,247	49.2%
II. Indirect taxes				
1. Customs duties	3,865	12.4%	3,600	10.3%
2. Consumption tax on foreign goods	–	–	4,300	12.3%
3. Consumption tax of consumables	–	–	5,000	14.2%
4. Milling and slaughter tax	–	–	2,000	5.7%
5. Urban excise in old provinces	8,681	27.8%	–	–
6. Rural consumption tax in old provinces	816	7.7%	–	–
7. Consumption dues	2,406	6.6%	2,910	8.3%
Unexplained difference	2,090			
Total of II	17,858	57.1%	17,810	50.8%
Totals of I and II	31,277	100%	35,057	100%

Source: E. Schremmer, 'Taxation and public finance: Britain, France and Germany', in P. Mathias and S. Pollard (eds.), *Cambridge economic history of Europe, Volume VIII, the industrial economies: the development of economic and social policies* (Cambridge University Press, 1989), p. 431.

finances of most German states. War and railway building in the middle of the nineteenth century again created debt both in the North and South; and after German unification in 1871 this process continued. Despite a financial reform in 1879, only the introduction of the new income tax (1891–93) in Prussia improved the situation fundamentally. Since the income tax was more effective than the systems operating in southern German states, they gradually switched to income tax systems during the following years. When Bavaria, as a latecomer, joined that tax system in 1912 the harmonization of the tax systems in the second German Empire had come to an end. Indirect taxes declined whilst direct income taxes became the major source of revenue for a unified German state.[22]

---

[22] Ullmann, *Der deutsche Steuerstaat*, pp. 22–47.

7   Financing an empire: the Austrian composite monarchy, 1650–1848

Renate Pieper

The construction of an empire is usually associated with a military policy of expansion based on a powerful army, a strong central government controlling a sound fiscal system, and a prosperous economy.[1] The image of the only European monarchy of the Old Regime whose lord, the Habsburg monarch, held an imperial title, does not fit easily into this framework. Instead perceptions of the performance of the Austrian monarchy from early modern times up to the nineteenth century are that it was characterized by military weakness, the impotence of the central government over the realm's territories, which were controlled by unruly landlords and estates, a fiscal regime that had to declare its bankruptcy more than once and economic backwardness.[2]

A priori, this rather gloomy picture stands in need of major corrections in order to explain the influence and the power of a realm that lacked ethnic, cultural, political and economic coherence but nevertheless survived the long-lasting attacks from another imperial power, the Ottomans, and constantly expanded its territories from the fourteenth century through the Napoleonic era. In 1787, Joseph II, son of the famous Maria Theresa, ruled over a territory of approximately 640,000 square kilometres and a population of more than 22 million people, almost as many as the Spanish or French kings. During the Napoleonic Wars the Austrian empire lost the Habsburg Netherlands

I would like to thank Prof. Dr. Thomas Winkelbauer for his valuable help and revision of the chapter. Likewise I would like to thank Dr. Bethany Aram for her revision of the English text.

[1] For the process of state and empire building in Europe, see W. Reinhard, *Geschichte der Staatsgewalt. Eine vergleichende Verfassungsgeschichte Europas. Von den Anfängen bis zur Gegenwart* (Munich: Beck, 1999); R. Bonney (ed.), *The rise of the fiscal state in Europe c. 1200–1815* (Oxford University Press, 1999).

[2] D. F. Good, *The economic rise of the Habsburg Empire, 1750–1914* (Berkeley/Los Angeles/London: University of California Press, 1984), pp. 7–10; P. G. M. Dickson, *Finance and government under Maria Theresia 1740–1780*, 2 vols. (Oxford: Clarendon Press, 1987), Vol. 2, p. 14; C. Capra, 'The eighteenth century. I. The finances of the Austrian monarchy and the Italian states', in R. Bonney (ed.), *Economic systems and state finance* (Oxford: Clarendon Press, 1995), pp. 295–314, at 296.

but finally acquired a former rival in the Mediterranean: the Republic of Venice. This policy of expansion was not only due to fortunate marriages, even if the Hungarian King Matthias Corvinus stated at the end of the fifteenth century, 'others make war, you, happy Austria, marry [*bella gerant alii, tu felix Austria nube*]', but also to large and expensive military enterprises. Territorial expansion really came to an end with the collapse of the era of restoration in 1848 and the subsequent loss of Lombardy (1859), Tuscany (1861) and Venice (1866), and by the marginalization of Austria within German affairs during the construction of a German empire by Prussia. Within a half-century Austria's former imperial composite monarchy disintegrated. This breakdown occurred as attempts to establish a modern centralized government and fiscal state in the Austrian Hereditary Lands finally succeeded.[3] Thus the transformation of the multi-ethnic Austrian empire from a composite monarchy of the Old Regime into a modern nation-state finally failed in 1914. In Austria, modern state-building and the development of a modern fiscal system were linked to fading imperial power, at least during the second half of the nineteenth century, whereas traditional forms of state finance with a rather limited central government had supported territorial expansion.

Long-term economic development in Austria was not seriously hampered by its decentralized pre-modern fiscal structure. While the monarchy maintained its position as a power within Central Europe up to 1914, the economy was often second in the ranking of continental European economies. Tyrolian silver and Hungarian copper mines boomed during the fifteenth and the early sixteenth centuries. On the

---

[3] In the eighteenth century the Austrian Hereditary Lands included: Austria above and below the Enns, Inner Austria (Carinthia, Carniola, Styria) and Vorderösterreich or Vorlande (Tyrol, Vorarlberg and the posessions in south-western Germany); R. Kann, *A history of the Habsburg Empire 1526–1918*, 2nd edn (Berkeley/Los Angeles/London: University of California Press, 1984), appendix 4, maps I–II; cf. G. Klingenstein, 'Was bedeuten "Österreich" und "österreichisch" im 18. Jahrhundert? Eine begriffsgeschichtliche Studie', in Richard Georg Plaschka, Gerald Stourzh and Jan Paul Niederkorn (eds.), *Was heißt Österreich? Inhalt und Umfang des Österreichbegriffs vom 10. Jahrhundert bis heute* (Vienna: Verlag der Österreichischen Akademie der Wissenschaften, 1995), pp. 149–220, at 179–83. In the sixteenth century the Habsburg monarchs had acquired the lands of the Bohemian crown (Bohemia, Moravia, Silesia, Upper and Lower Lusatia). Despite previous claims, rule over the territories of the Hungarian crown was effective only after 1699. During the eighteenth century Galicia, including the Bukovina and some Polish territories, were conquered. During the Napoleonic Wars Salzburg, Venice, Istria and Dalmatia were acquired. The Austrian Habsburg monarchs ruled also over the former Spanish Netherlands, Tuscany and Lombardy during the eighteenth century. Whereas the Spanish Netherlands were definitively lost during the Napoleonic Wars, Lombardy and Tuscany could be regained in 1815 for Habsburg rulers.

eve of the Thirty Years War Bohemian textiles and Styrian iron flourished. In 1767, Bohemia had a dynamic linen industry and pig-iron output in Styria was higher than in England.[4] On the eve of the First World War, when the empire had already lost part of its territory, pig-iron and steel production (now mostly from Bohemia) had reached the level of Belgium, whereas cotton production and the number of cotton spindles equalled or even exceeded that of France or Belgium.[5] Although the empire collapsed in 1918, its core, the Austrian Republic, still ranks among the richest countries of the world at the start of the twenty-first century. The extent to which the former experience of a decentralized fiscal regime contributed to continuous prosperity is the question addressed by this chapter.

Despite the fact that the historiography dealing with imperial finances has concentrated on the second half of the eighteenth century, especially on the reigns of Maria Theresa and her son Joseph II, for previous periods there are some general studies available as well. First, Rauscher has reconstructed expenditures for the second half of the sixteenth century.[6] Niederkorn and Ernst offered insight into Spanish subsidies on the eve of the Thirty Years War.[7] Winkelbauer studied the *contributionale* delivered by the estates for military purposes and the development of public borrowing during the seventeenth century. The second half of this period has received a thorough analysis by Bérenger.[8] Subsequent decades have been dealt with in articles and an overview by Mensi published as early as 1890, which still deserves reading.[9] The War of the Spanish Succession has received special attention.[10] Numerous fiscal

[4] Good, *Economic rise*, pp. 20–21.
[5] B. R. Mitchell, *European historical statistics, 1750–1970*, 2nd edn (New York, NY: Facts on File, 1980), pp. 217, 254, 258; cf. Good, *Economic rise*, pp. 241–52.
[6] P. Rauscher, *Zwischen Ständen und Gläubigern. Die kaiserlichen Finanzen unter Ferdinand I. und Maximilian II. (1556–1576)* (Munich: Oldenbourg, 2004); F. Edelmayer, M. Lanzinner and P. Rauscher (eds.), *Finanzen und Herrschaft. Materielle Grundlagen fürstlicher Politik in den habsburgischen Ländern und im Heiligen Römischen Reich im 16. Jahrhundert* (Munich: Oldenbourg, 2003).
[7] J. Niederkorn, *Die europäischen Mächte und der "Lange Türkenkrieg" Kaiser Rudolfs II. (1593–1606)* (Vienna: Verlag der Österreichischen Akademie der Wissenschaften, 1993); H. Ernst, *Madrid und Wien 1632–1637* (Münster: Aschendorff, 1991).
[8] T. Winkelbauer, *Ständefreiheit und Fürstenmacht. Länder und Untertanen des Hauses Habsburg im konfessionellen Zeitalter*, 2 vols. (Vienna: Ueberreuter, 2003), Vol. 1, 497–528; J. Bérenger, *Finances et absolutisme autrichien dans la seconde moitié du XVIIe siècle* (Lille: Atelier Reprod. des Theses, Université de Lille III, 1975).
[9] F. von Mensi, *Die Finanzen Österreichs von 1701–1740* (Vienna: Manz, 1890)
[10] J. Bérenger, 'A propos d'un ouvrage recent: les finances de l'Autriche à l'époque baroque (1650–1740)', *Historie, Economie et Societé* 3 (1984), 221–45; B. Holl, 'Gundaker Thomas Graf Starhemberg als Hofkammerpräsident (1703–1715). Eine Studie zur Finanzgeschichte Österreichs in der Barockzeit', unpublished PhD thesis, University of Vienna (1971); H. L. Mikoletzky, 'Die große Anleihe von 1706.

reforms were undertaken when the Austrian imperial power reached
its highest point among the European monarchies during the second
half of the eighteenth century, and this period is at the centre of historical interest. Besides the extensive work of Dickson one should mention
the recent dissertation of Hackl on crucial aspects of the reform programme.[11] In comparison to the reign of Maria Theresa and Joseph II,
the Napoleonic era and the postwar restoration of the absolutist state
have received less attention. The development of the imperial budget
during this period has been studied by Weiss and the almost contemporary description of Beer is useful for the end of Old Regime Austria
in 1848.[12]

All of these studies take the perspective of the central government
and seek to explain the shortcomings of the fiscal system within the
constraints of a composite monarchy. They consider state-building
and the development of a unified central budget as preconditions for
the prosperity of the empire. Yet other scholars dealing with economic

Ein Beitrag zur österreichischen Finanzgeschichte', *Mitteilungen des Österreichischen Staatsarchivs* 7 (1954), 268–93; A. Di Vittorio, 'Un caso di correlazione tra guerre, spese militari e cambiamenti economici: Le Guerre Asburgiche della prima meta del XVIII secolo e le loro ripercussioni sulla finanza, e l'economia dell'impero', *Nuova Rivista Storica* 66 (1982), 59–81.

[11] Capra, 'Eighteenth century'; Dickson, *Finance and government*; G. Otruba, 'Staatshaushalt und Staatsschuld unter Maria Theresia und Joseph II', in G. Otruba and M. Weiss, *Beiträge zur Finanzgeschichte Österreichs. Staatshaushalt und Steuern 1740–1840* (Linz: Trauner, 1986), pp. 3–55; B. Hackl, *Die Theresianische Dominikal- und Rustikalfassion in Niederösterreich 1748–1756. Ein fiskalischer Reformprozeß im Spannungsfeld zwischen Landständen und Zentralstaat* (Frankfurt: Lang, 1997); B. Hackl, *Die Theresianische Steuerrektifikation in Ober- und Innerösterreich 1747–1763. Die Neuordnung des ständischen Finanzwesens auf dem Sektor der direkten Steuern als ein fiskalischer Modernisierungsprozeß zwischen Reform und Stagnation* (Frankfurt: Lang, 1999); Kurt Janetschek, 'Die Finanzierung des Siebenjährigen Krieges. Ein Beitrag zur Finanzgeschichte des 18. Jahrhunderts', unpublished PhD thesis, University of Vienna (1959); J. Schasching, *Staatsbildung und Finanzentwicklung. Ein Beitrag zur Geschichte des österreichischen Staatskredits in der 2. Hälfte des 18. Jahrhunderts* (Innsbruck: Rauch, 1954); P. C. Hartmann, *Das Steuersystem der europäischen Staaten am Ende des Ancien Régime. Eine offizielle französische Enquete (1763–1768). Dokumente, Analyse und Auswertung. England und die Staaten Nord- und Mitteleuropas* (Munich: Artemis-Verlag, 1979); H. R. Hartmann, 'Finanzpolitik als Mittel der Bevölkerungspolitik im Kameralismus', unpublished dissertation, (1968); K. Unger, 'Wirtschafts- und Finanzpolitik Josef II.', unpublished PhD thesis, University of Vienna (1949); A. Beer, *Die Staatsschulden und die Ordnung des Staatshaushaltes unter Maria Theresia* (Vienna: Tempsky, 1895; reprint 1972).

[12] M. Weiss, 'Das Verhältnis von direkten und indirekten Steuern hinsichtlich ihrer Erträge und ihrer Bedeutung für den Staatshaushalt unter besonderer Berücksichtigung der Belastung der Steuerträger (1781–1847)', in Otruba and Weiss, *Beiträge*, pp. 57–246; A. Beer, *Die Finanzen Oesterreichs im XIX. Jahrhundert. Nach archivalischen Quellen* (Prague: Tempsky, 1877; reprint Vienna: Geyer, 1973); H.-H. Brandt, *Der österreichische Neoabsolutismus: Staatsfinanzen und Politik 1848–1860*, 2 vols (Göttingen: Vandenhoeck & Ruprecht, 1978).

performance largely ignore the effects of the central budget. Public finance is usually treated as a matter of fundraising for the operation of central institutions, and as part of the political struggle between the crown and the estates. Fiscal analysis deals with the Viennese authorities' demands for stronger positions in fiscal affairs with unruly territories. I suggest that this point of view should be reversed so that historians may consider the benefits of a decentralized fiscal structure for an empire composed of many nations, whose core could only be transformed into a nation-state when the empire had broken up.

Fiscal and political structures remained rather stable from the sixteenth to the early eighteenth century, and my account will focus on the reform period of the mid eighteenth century, which established the fiscal regime that survived until 1848. The historiography has accorded an overwhelming importance to administrative structures of the central institutions in Vienna, which I will describe first. Next, I will discuss the income structure of the monarchy with evidence from the central institutions in Vienna including ordinary and extraordinary taxes and levies as well as credit operations. Then, the regional and sectoral effects of state expenditures come under scrutiny. The analysis of the social incidence of taxation and expenditure requires a detailed investigation of the situation in each territory of the monarchy, therefore only general tendencies are addressed. Finally comparisons of income and expenditure offer insights into the successes and shortcomings of the multi-ethnic Austrian empire.

Administrative structures and general financial development

The first central administrative bodies of the composite Habsburg-Austrian monarchy were established by Ferdinand I, who had become acquainted with the benefits of central institutions during his youth in Spain. Ferdinand, the founder of the Austrian branch of the Habsburg dynasty, was the younger brother of the Emperor Charles V, who had divided his realms between himself and his brother in 1522. In 1526 Ferdinand inherited the Bohemian and Hungarian crowns from his brother-in-law and founded a court treasury (*Hofkammer*) the following year. This entity administered the ordinary revenues received by the crown (*cameralia*) from the Austrian Hereditary Lands and the kingdoms of Bohemia and Hungary. These *cameralia* included income from royal monopolies like salt, mining activities and several fees as well as customs and excise taxes levied principally on drink and meat.[13] Revenues received by the emperors from the Holy Roman Empire were also administered by the *Hofkammer*.[14] This treasury existed until the end of the Austrian monarchy but its jurisdiction was not extended to the territories acquired during the eighteenth and nineteenth centuries. In Hungary, public finances remained under the control of the Hungarian estates until the end of the empire. Indeed, after the revolution of 1848, Hungary became almost independent in fiscal affairs.[15]

The control over imperial income experienced by the *Hofkammer* remained severely restricted during the sixteenth and seventeenth centuries. An increasing part of revenues was farmed out to private entrepreneurs and to the estates, as was the case in the other European monarchies. Even if in theory consent from the estates was not required for the assessment of *cameralia* and crown officials should have collected them, during the seventeenth century the estates obtained rights to levy several *cameralia* and even approved the introduction of new ones as guarantees for the loans previously raised for the central government. Estates retained at least a part of the income from the *cameralia* to cover the administrative costs and to service loans. Thus, only a portion of the net income from the *cameralia* reached the court treasury in Vienna. During the sixteenth and seventeenth centuries, Habsburg monarchs sold off their territorial domains in order to redeem loans and thereby reduced the income of the court treasury even further. During the eighteenth century the crown recovered control over taxes, duties and monopolies previously farmed out, and introduced new taxes, like the monopoly on tobacco (1701) and the state lottery (1751). In 1775 and 1784, the custom duties were standardized, internal tolls reduced and, in 1829, a large number of excise taxes on consumption were also unified. All of these taxes (the *cameralia*) were designated for civil purposes

---

[13] The *cameralia* and the history of their administration are extensively described by Weiss, *Verhältnis*, pp. 93–123; see also Dickson, *Finance and government*, II, pp. 92f., 96f.; E. Klein, *Geschichte der öffentlichen Finanzen in Deutschland (1500–1870)* (Wiesbaden: Steiner, 1974), pp. 26–7; Mensi, *Die Finanzen Österreichs von 1701–1740*, pp. 9–12; Hartmann, *Steuersystem*, pp. 196–98; cf. Capra, 'Eighteenth century'.

[14] Winkelbauer, *Ständefreiheit*, I, pp. 509–15.

[15] J. Komlos, *The Habsburg monarchy as a customs union. Economic development in Austria–Hungary in the 19th century* (Princeton University Press, 1983); H. Matis, *Österreichs Wirtschaft 1848–1913. Konjunkturelle Dynamik und gesellschaftlicher Wandel im Zeitalter Franz Josephs I* (Berlin: Duncker & Humblot, 1972); R. Sandgruber, *Ökonomie und Politik. Österreichische Wirtschaftsgeschichte vom Mittelalter bis zur Gegenwart* (Vienna: Ueberreuter, 1995).

such as the payment of officers, pensions, the maintenance of the court and the repayment of loans.[16]

Military finance was not, however, controlled by the *Hofkammer*, but remained under the control of the chanceries of Austria, Bohemia and Hungary, dominated by noble families operating as agents of their estates. The administrative body that managed income and expenditures for military purposes was the war treasury (*Hofkriegszahlamt*). Before the end of the sixteenth century and the end of the wars with the Ottoman Empire, ordinary income from *cameralia*, loans and foreign subsidies remained insufficient to cover military expenses and emperors relied more and more on extraordinary taxes. In 1620, the estates finally recognized the emperor's right to ask for additional money to wage war, but they determined the totals, the period of payment, the form of the levies and controlled the collection of these taxes, called *contributionale*. Thus, the medieval *Bede*, a traditional aid occasionally paid by the estates, was gradually transformed into a more regular contribution to fund wars.[17] The name of the tax clearly indicates its military origins, because *contributionale* had been levied in money or kind by military entrepreneurs in command of mercenary troops during the Thirty Years War.[18] Initially *contributionale* was only voted by the estates for military necessities, but by the end of the seventeenth century, when almost all domains had been sold and many *cameralia* mortgaged, the emperors attempted to turn extraordinary contributions into an ordinary income. The estates of the Austrian Hereditary Lands and of the Bohemian crown were requested to grant the *contributionale* annually and, from the beginning of the eighteenth century, the emperor was even able to obtain consent for extraordinary taxation for periods of ten years (*Dezenalrezess*). In Hungary the estates refused to meet yearly and their extraordinary contributions levied since 1671 were only paid on a regular basis from 1721 onwards.[19]

---

[16] P. Berger, 'Finanzwesen und Staatswerdung. Zur Genese absolutistischer Herrschaftstechnik in Österreich', in Herbert Matis (ed.), *Von der Glückseligkeit des Staates. Staat, Wirtschaft und Gesellschaft in Österreich im Zeitalter des aufgeklärten Absolutismus* (Berlin: Duncker & Humblot, 1981), pp. 105–36, at p. 115; the boundaries between the competencies of the court chamber and the chanceries overlapped in some cases.

[17] Dickson, *Finance and government*, II, pp. 185f.; Hackl, *Steuerrektifikation*, pp. 27–38; Capra, 'Eighteenth century', pp. 296–98; Berger, *Finanzwesen*, pp. 115, 118–21.

[18] Winkelbauer, *Ständefreiheit*.

[19] Dickson, *Finance and government*, II, p. 255; Winkelbauer, *Ständefreiheit*, I, pp. 497–500, 506–9 studies taxation in Hungary and the levies on the *Dominicale* in Hungary and Bohemia for the late seventeenth century; Bérenger, *Finances*, p. 349; Dickson, *Finance and government*, II, pp. 397ff.; Winkelbauer and Bérenger mention yearly contributions from Hungary since 1671 with the exception of 1716–21.

Austrian and Bohemian estates distributed their contributions for the military expenses of the crown within their territories on the basis of landlords' declarations of their income from registered feudal rights. The military contribution developed into a direct tax on the land of the tenants (*Rusticale*), since feudal income was proportional to farm yields, while the property of landlords (*Dominicale*) initially remained tax free. In Bohemia, in addition to the land tax, consumption taxes were levied for the *contributionale*. During the War of the Austrian Succession, revenues from the military contributions had been insufficient, and immediately after the war (1748), Maria Theresa ordered a general revision of the registers of the feudal rights (*Gültbücher*). Her son, Joseph II, introduced an improved land register at the end of his reign (1789), which included the *Dominicale*. But fierce opposition from the nobility and clergy forced his successor, Leopold II, to revoke land taxes based on the new register in 1790. After the Napoleonic Wars Francis I tried once again to improve the land register (*Franziszeischer Kataster*) but in several territories the reform of land registration was delayed until 1880.[20] Although the Habsburg bureaucracy was unable to introduce a reformed land tax during the Old Regime, it did levy additional direct taxes. For example, during the reign of Maria Theresa the first attempt to introduce a personal income tax (*Klassensteuer*) was made in 1759 and applied to incomes that were not obtained from agriculture. In addition a poll tax and an inheritance tax were levied. For the Jewish population additional direct taxes were introduced at the same time (1776) and the clergy were made to contribute as well (*subsidium ecclesiasticum*, 1736). In spite of high expectations, the sums collected from these innovations were rather small. After the Napoleonic Wars direct personal taxes were either reformed or abolished. But a modern tax system based on a general income tax was not introduced until after the Revolution of 1848.[21]

In addition to ordinary and extraordinary taxes, in wartime loans had to be raised in order to cover deficits of expenditures over revenues. The administration of the extraordinary funds obtained through borrowing, as well as the servicing and repayment of debt, were undertaken by the *Hofkammer*. In the sixteenth century, most creditors were merchant bankers from Upper Germany, but Austrian creditors and the estates became important even before the Thirty Years War. The exorbitant costs of this long-lasting conflict were met at first by military

---

[20] Beer, *Finanzen*, pp. 164f. complains about the reluctance of the estates to revise the land registers.
[21] Berger, *Finanzwesen*, p. 121; Weiss, *Verhältnis*, pp. 89–98, 206.

entrepreneurs like Wallenstein and his financier Hans de Witte. But towards the end of the war, the crown reassumed control over its army and its finances and obtained credits from Jewish merchant bankers. Between 1672 and 1703 Samuel Oppenheimer financed a large part of imperial military activity. At his death in 1703, in the midst of the War of the Spanish Succession, the court chamber defaulted on its debt to Oppenheimer. For some time this arbitrary measure almost excluded the Austrian monarchy from access to the European credit market and the state had to declare its own bankruptcy. In 1706, the Austrian monarchy only obtained a loan on the London market with help from the English government.[22] In addition, following examples set by the Bank of England and the Hôtel de Ville of Paris, the Vienna City Bank was created as an independent institution for fundraising and the repayment of debts and debt management was entrusted to the *Bancodeputation*. The reputation of the Vienna City Bank was such that interest rates for government bonds dropped from 12–20 per cent to 6–8 per cent during the first half of the eighteenth century. As the Vienna City Bank was an autonomous institution, a new state bank (*Universal-Bancalität*) was created in 1714, but it nearly went bankrupt in 1721 and its debts were transferred to the Vienna City Bank.[23] In order to improve control of the *cameralia* and debt servicing in 1716, the *Finance-Conference* was established as a supreme advisory board controlling the *Hofkammer*, the *Bancodeputation* and the *Universal-Bancalität*.[24] This new administrative body tried to draw up comprehensive budgets to forecast revenues and expenditures. It survived the reign of Charles VI and his Italian wars but it was unable to increase state revenues on the eve of the War of the Austrian Succession. Therefore the *Finance-Conference* was abolished by Maria Theresa in the first year of her reign (1740). Eight years later (1748), when the war had come to an end, Maria Theresa and her advisor Count Friedrich Wilhelm Haugwitz, a Silesian refugee, attempted to curtail the influence of the estates in fiscal affairs. They

---

[22] Mikoletzky, 'Anleihe', pp. 268–93; this loan was only possible due to the intervention of the Duke of Marlborough and the English government. The estates of Silesia also made considerable allowances. The finances of the Spanish War of Succession are studied by Di Vittorio, 'Un caso'; Reforms during the reign of Maria Theresa are studied extensively by Dickson, *Finance and government*; a short version is given by Otruba, 'Staatshaushalt'.

[23] Holl, *Graf Starhemberg*, pp. 251–81; Winkelbauer, *Ständefreiheit*, I, pp. 515–28 offers a comprehensive overview; cf. Berger, *Finanzwesen*, pp. 128f.; F. Schönfellner, *Probleme der Staatsfinanzen und die Gründung der Wiener Stadtbank*, in Karl Gutkas (ed.), *Prinz Eugen und das barocke Österreich* (Salzburg/Vienna: Residenz-Verlag, 1985), pp. 215–20; Klein, *Geschichte*, pp. 33–41.

[24] Holl, *Graf Starhemberg*, pp. 446–83.

revised land registers to improve yields from the *contributionale*, and created a new central administrative entity, the *Directorium in publicis et cameralibus*. Its remit was no longer restricted to the *cameralia* and debt management, but extended to control the *contributionale*. In addition, the collection of taxes was withdrawn from the estates and entrusted to new collecting and supervising agencies established in the territories of the empire (*Repräsentationen und Kammern*), who reported directly to the Vienna *Directorium*. Even though these reforms excluded Hungary, the Austrian Netherlands and the Italian territories, they represented a decisive step towards centralization of the Austrian monarchy and towards the creation of an absolutist fiscal-cum-political regime.[25]

During the Seven Years War some of these reforms had to be revoked. Chancellor Wenzel Anton von Kaunitz-Rietberg abolished the *Directorium* in 1761, and the affairs of the court treasury, the Austrian-Bohemian chancery and the *Bancodeputation* were separated once again and thereby the estates regained control over the *contributionale*. But in the Austrian and Bohemian territories the *Repräsentationen und Kammern* remained, but were reorganized into *Gubernien*, and their functions limited to fiscal affairs. The Kaunitz reforms were strongly influenced by the physiocratic and utilitarian ideas of Joseph von Sonnenfels and the ideas of Ludovico Muratori from Naples and Pietro Verri and Cesare Beccaria from Milan.[26] However, the attempt to reform and re-decentralize favoured by the nobility of the estates was curtailed in 1762 by the creation of a new central institution charged with auditing, the *Hofrechenkammer*. This entity was, however, short-lived and had to be dissolved in 1773. After the death of Maria Theresa, her son, Joseph II, tried to continue with her enlightened political–administrative reforms. He not only ordered the revision of the old land registers, but the unification of the court treasury, the Austrian and Bohemian chancery and the *Bancodeputation* once again. But at his death in 1790, the strong opposition of the estates that had almost lost their fiscal autonomy except for local bookkeeping and auditing, put an end to the ambitious programme of enlightened reforms. Only the introduction of a single 'budget', that included all revenues and expenditures, survived from the reign of Joseph II.

---

[25] Berger, *Finanzwesen*, pp. 131–5.
[26] Capra, 'Eighteenth century', p. 305; G. Klingenstein, 'Between mercantilism and physiocracy. Stages, modes, and functions of economic theory in the Habsburg monarchy, 1748–63', in C. W. Ingrao (ed.), *State and society in early modern Austria* (West Lafayette, IN: Purdue University Press, 1994), pp. 181–214; cf. G. Klingenstein and H. Begusch (eds.), *Staatskanzler Wenzel Anton von Kaunitz-Rietberg, 1711–1794. Neue Perspektiven zu Politik und Kultur der europäischen Aufklärung* (Graz: Schnider, 1996).

Maria Theresa and Joseph II aimed to reform taxation and to alter the administrative system of checks and balances between the estates and the central government established during the sixteenth and seventeenth centuries. Even though there was some success in strengthening the position of Vienna, a considerable part of the tax reforms as well as administrative changes had to be revoked during and immediately after the Napoleonic Wars, when Leopold II and Francis II (I) faced internal opposition from the estates and external warfare at the same time. For example, the introduction of tax reform based on the new land register was dropped in 1790. The Austrian and Bohemian chancery regained independence in 1802. In 1829, a number of direct taxes were revoked. Despite these setbacks, Francis I reintroduced the *Hofrechenkammer* for central auditing and the *Gubernien* guaranteed the presence for the central administration at the territories level of the estates. Nevertheless, the old fiscal regime ended only with Revolution in 1848.[27]

Despite the rigidity built into the fiscal system, the monarchy was able to improve its position and to increase revenues and expenditures considerably over two centuries (1650–1847). This expansion occurred during a period characterized by moderate peacetime inflation. Banknotes and treasury bonds were issued to finance heightened military expenditure, but were usually pushed out of circulation when peace returned. After the Napoleonic Wars, the Austrian government reduced the circulation of banknotes considerably and the economy reverted to silver coinage.[28] The money of account used by the Vienna administration was fixed to the silver guilder. During the last decades of the sixteenth century (1570–90), the level of expenditures was about 2.5 million guilders (fl.).[29] Income in silver guilders doubled during the next fifty years. From 1650 to 1847, state revenues rose from 5 million fl. to 180 million fl. Thus in terms of silver the crown's budget increased during 200 years by 3,600 per cent (see Figure 7.1).[30]

---

[27] Otruba, 'Staatshaushalt', pp. 11–17; Berger, *Finanzwesen*, pp. 131–5; Weiss, *Verhältnis*, pp. 128–33. The number of chanceries varied during the eighteenth and nineteenth centuries.

[28] Dickson, *Finance and government*, II, pp. 369f. From 1692 to 1748 the silver content of the guilder was not altered at all. Between 1748 and 1750 its silver content was reduced by 7.14%. This monetary standard was adopted from 1753 on by most south German states and Saxony, and maintained until 1857. In the nineteenth century the Austrian guilders were referred to as *Conventionsmünzen*. Inflation was moderate except for the Napoleonic period: Alfred Francis Pribram (ed.), *Materialien zur Geschichte der Preise und Löhne in Österreich*, Vol. 1 (Vienna: Ueberreuter, 1938), pp. 661, 695.

[29] Winkelbauer, *Ständefreiheit*, I, pp. 509–15.

[30] From 1650 to 1850 the mean annual growth rate of imperial revenues was 1.7%.

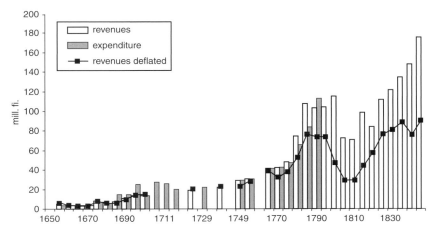

Figure 7.1 Revenues and expenditure of the Austrian monarchy
(1655–1845)
Sources: T. Winkelbauer, *Ständefreiheit und Fürstenmacht. Länder und Untertanen des Hauses Habsburg im konfessionellen Zeitalter*, 2 vols. (Vienna: Ueberreuter, 2003), Vol. I, pp. 509–15; J. Bérenger, *Finances et absolutisme autrichien dans la seconde moitié du XVIIe siècle* (Lille: Atelier Reprod. des Theses, Université de Lille III, 1975), pp. 349, 359; P. G. M. Dickson, *Finance and government under Maria Theresia 1740–1780*, 2 vols. (Oxford: Clarendon Press, 1987), Vol. II, pp. 380, 385f.; G. Otruba, 'Staatshaushalt und Staatsschuld unter Maria Theresia und Joseph II', in G. Otruba and M. Weiss, *Beiträge zur Finanzgeschichte Österreichs. Staatshaushalt und Steuern 1740–1840* (Linz: Trauner, 1986), p. 49; M. Weiss, *Das Verhältnis von direkten und indirekten Steuern hinsichtlich ihrer Erträge und ihrer Bedeutung für den Staatshaushalt unter besonderer Berücksichtigung der Belastung der Steuerträger (1781–1847)*, in Otruba and Weiss, *Beiträge*, pp. 224–7; silver price indices from Alfred Francis Pribram (ed.), *Materialien zur Geschichte der Preise und Löhne in Österreich*, Vol. 1 (Vienna: Ueberreuter, 1938), p. 695.

Growth rates varied considerably. During the second half of the seventeenth century, revenues and peacetime expenditures tripled, from 5 million fl. to 16 million fl. in fifty years.[31] After the War of the Spanish Succession, the reign of Charles VI was characterized by remarkable stability and annual income only increased by 37.5 per cent over forty years. Under the governments of Maria Theresa and Joseph II growth rates were at their highest. Peacetime revenues and

---

[31] From 1650 to 1850 the mean annual growth rate of revenues was 2.4%.

expenditures rose from 22 million fl. (1740) to roughly 90 million fl. (1790), i.e. they increased by 400 per cent in fifty years.[32] Due to the Napoleonic Wars income rose to 115 million fl., but by 1820 state revenues had dropped back to prewar levels. This short-lived decrease was caused in part by the postwar deflation of paper money. Income doubled over the following thirty years, and reached almost 180 million fl. in 1847.[33] Thus, despite all the constraints, the Austrian fiscal system was elastic. Before the Napoleonic Wars, state revenues and expenditures grew much more rapidly than the economy. After the Napoleonic Wars, taxes increased in line with industrial growth rates but faster than agricultural output, which employed the majority of the population.[34] During this second period, characterized by the first wave of industrialization and economic transformation, the limits of the Old Regime fiscal system were finally reached after almost thirty years of continuous and sharp increases.

Income structure

From 1650 to 1850, Austria's fiscal system of revenues displayed impressive flexibility. The *cameralia*, dominated by indirect taxes, and the *contributionale*, virtually equivalent to the direct taxation of agricultural incomes, provided the imperial state with revenues necessary for military and other purposes (see Figure 7.2). Between 1655 and 1673, before contributions were obtained from the kingdom of Hungary, income from *cameralia* accounted for more than half of all ordinary taxes. After the Third Dutch War and the defeat of the Hungarian

---

[32] From 1740 to 1890 the mean annual growth rate of revenues was 2.86%. Bookkeeping was reformed in the 1780s. Therefore the data offered by sources and publications differ a lot, even if only net revenues are taken into account. Data given by Dickson, *Finance and government*, are inferior to the diverging numbers offered by Otruba, 'Staatshaushalt', and those are lower than the data published by Weiss, *Verhältnis*. Therefore Dickson's data have been used until 1778 and from 1781 the reference is Weiss for income and Otruba for expenditure. Good, *Economic rise*, p. 37: the economic development was considerable during the mercantilist era and reached a peak in 1784. The depression of the Napoleonic period began in 1790. From the 1820s sustained economic growth set in.

[33] From 1820 to 1847 the mean annual growth rate of revenues was 2.6%.

[34] Good, *Economic rise*, p. 69: Austrian agricultural output (crops) increased from 1789 to 1841 at 1.0%/year; livestock 1818–1850 at 0.6%/year and agricultural population 0.6% /year, agricultural output/person at 0.4%/year; Bohemian agricultural output (crops and livestock) increased from 1756 to 1846 at 1.1%/year, annual population increase was 0.6%, and agricultural output/person rose 0.5%/year; Good, *Economic rise*, p. 46: the index of industrial production had annual growth rates from 1830 to 1845 around 2.5–3.3%; annual population increase for the same period was 0.7%, annual per capita industrial growth was thus 1.8–2.6%.

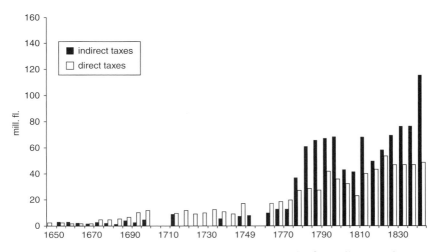

Figure 7.2 Revenues of the Austrian monarchy from direct and indirect taxes (1650–1845)
Sources: Winkelbauer, *Ständefreiheit*, Vol. I, pp. 509–15; Bérenger, *Finances*, pp. 317, 349; Dickson, *Finance and government*, Vol. II, pp. 380, 382f., 397ff.; Weiss, *Verhältnis*, p. 224f.; see Figure 7.1 for details.

nobility in 1671, a Hungarian contribution came into the Vienna treasury and funds received as military contributions now became higher than those from indirect taxes and other *cameralia*. In peacetime, *cameralia* accounted for approximately 40 per cent of the revenues administered by the imperial government. In times of war their significance was reduced to less than 20 per cent of all ordinary net revenues. This relationship between *cameralia* and *contributionale* that had prevailed since the last decades of the seventeenth century, changed during the reign of Joseph II. In the year of his death (1790), gross income received from *cameralia* amounted to double that of the *contributionale*. During the first decades of the nineteenth century, the *cameralia* funded at least 60 per cent of gross state revenues. From 1835, the relative importance of indirect taxes increased even further. On the eve of the 1848 Revolution, direct taxes accounted for only a quarter of gross income. From the seventeenth century to the 1780s, land taxes levied to pay for the *contributionale* became important and were responsive to demands from the Vienna treasury. By the end of the Old Regime the growth in income from direct taxes had fallen well below the growth from indirect taxes.

Under the administration of the estates, the net income of the Vienna treasury received from *cameralia* remained stationary (at 2–3 million fl.) during the second half of the seventeenth century. In the last years of the reign of Leopold I and after the War of the Spanish Succession, the treasury increased receipts from indirect taxes, and net yields from the *cameralia* were two-thirds higher (5–6 million fl.) than they had been a century earlier. Reform periods of Maria Theresa and of her son Joseph II witnessed steady increases in revenues from the *cameralia*. Due to the end of tax farming, the intervention of royal officials in the administrations in the territories, the introduction of new taxes and the elevation of tax rates, the net income from the *cameralia* rose from 5 million fl. in 1740 to 20 million fl. in 1778. After the death of his mother, Joseph II vigorously enforced the reform programme, and gross receipts from indirect taxes more than doubled during his short reign, a level that was maintained for the next decade. When monetary stability returned after the Napoleonic Wars, sums collected from the most important indirect taxes rose once again, and on the eve of the Revolution of 1848 almost 140 million fl. gross revenues from indirect taxes were obtained, equivalent to a 240 per cent increase within thirty years.[35] To sum up, one may distinguish two periods within these two centuries: during the first century, the Vienna treasury only obtained a moderate rise of income from *cameralia*; but during the years of enlightenment and the era of reform, revenues from indirect taxes increased very rapidly.

The major sources behind increased revenues from the *cameralia* included the salt monopoly, excises, customs and the tobacco monopoly (see Figure 7.3). During the whole period income from the royal salt monopoly was the most important. Second in importance were revenues from customs and excises. Earnings from the tobacco monopoly normally lagged behind. The growth in receipts from these four groups of taxes that had been similar varied after the reign of Joseph II. At first revenues from the salt monopoly increased and during the last decades of the eighteenth century the yields of the salt monopoly accounted for almost half the sums received from *cameralia*. The income from the salt tax dropped after the Napoleonic era, although it increased again

[35] Despite the exclusive circulation of paper money, the treasury used the silver guilder for its accounts and thus deflated the sums perceived in banknotes and treasury bonds. During the Napoleonic Era state bankruptcy was declared twice, in 1811 and in 1816. In 1810 the relation between banknotes (*Bancozettel*) and silver coins (*Conventionsmünze*) was 5:1. The bankruptcy of 1811 reduced the relationship to 2:1, but due to the renewed issuing of paper money (*Wiener Währung*) the rate deteriorated to 3.5:1 in 1815. The situation stabilized in 1819 at a ratio of 2.5:1: Weiss, *Verhältnis*, pp. 139f.

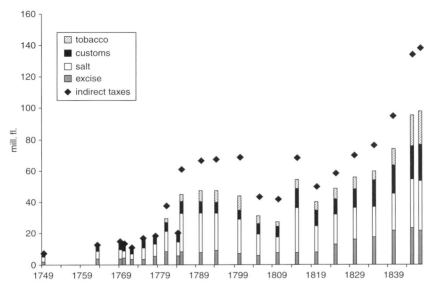

Figure 7.3 The structure of indirect taxation (*cameralia*)
(1749–1847)
Sources: Dickson, *Finance and government*, Vol. II, pp. 382f.;Weiss,
Verhältnis, pp. 225ff; see Figure 7.1 for details.

in the 1820s. Nonetheless, by the nineteenth century, the salt tax had
lost part of its outstanding position. Second in income were excise taxes
that doubled at the start of the reign of Joseph II but remained almost
constant thereafter. Only after 1829, when the assessment and administration of excise taxes were reformed, were further increases obtained.
A customs union of the Austrian and Bohemian territories – with the
exception of Vorderösterreich, Trieste and Fiume – was established in
1775 and, in 1784, Joseph II introduced a mercantilist system of tolls in
order to protect Austrian and Bohemian manufactures. Hungary was
not included in the customs union. The customs yields improved considerably between 1784 and the Napoleonic Wars. After the wars revenues recovered and experienced a steady growth from 1825 onwards.
The tobacco monopoly was the last of the important *cameralia* to be
thoroughly reformed. Income rose with the end of tax farming during the reign of Joseph II. By the end of the eighteenth century, yields
from the tobacco monopoly reached the level of customs duties. But
recovery from the Napoleonic Wars was slow. By 1847, the relative
structure of the *cameralia* that had prevailed during the reign of Maria

Theresa had been restored but the absolute level was far above the levels attained during her reign. Increased tax yields depended on several factors. Price increases in the case of salt and tobacco, higher rates for excises and customs, a growing population, the spread of consumption and economic development all contributed. The impressive position of the salt monopoly, in contrast to the tobacco monopoly, was due to the partially forced distribution of salt. This portion of the salt tax had the character of a per-capita system of taxation. Yields from the tobacco monopoly were also high when compared to revenues from customs and excises, which were levied not only on single goods, but on a broad range of articles.

The development of the *contributionale* (see Figure 7.2) differed from the *cameralia*. Levies for the military contribution fell at first on the Austrian and Bohemian hereditary lands as direct land taxes, and the contribution from Hungary only appeared in 1671 when net revenues jumped from 2–3 million fl. to 4–5 million fl. During the next decades income rose steadily to roughly 11 million fl. This level, which was obtained on the eve of the War of the Spanish Succession, was maintained during the epoch of Charles VI. But due to the loss of Silesia during the first years of the reign of Maria Theresa, net income from the contribution dropped by 20 per cent in the 1740s. Reforms introduced with a new land register in 1748 pushed revenues up to 17–18 million fl. In addition, new forms of direct taxes, like the *Klassensteuer*, were introduced after the Seven Years War, but their initial yields were low. The income from the contribution remained stable during the Napoleonic Wars, but after renewed efforts to reform the land registers by Francis I, revenues almost doubled to 37–38 million fl. between 1820 and 1847. Remarkably, this increase of the contribution was really a substitution for direct taxes introduced during, and abolished after, the Napoleonic Wars. The *Klassensteuer*, which had been transformed into a progressive income tax in 1799, the *Realitätensteuer* levied on urban real estates, and the *Personalsteuer*, a poll tax, yielded 50 per cent of the contribution in 1805 and 1815. After the war, only the poll tax was maintained, but at a reduced level.[36] At that time, the structure of direct taxation that had characterized the period of enlightened absolutism was restored. In the 1820s, *c.* 80 per cent of these taxes were land taxes levied on the incomes of the peasantry and only 20 per cent of the revenue was obtained by other personal taxes. Overall income from direct taxation

---

[36] Weiss, *Verhältnis*, p. 93 maintains that these three taxes were abolished only in 1829. But the tables published by him, p. 226, show that after 1816 only the *Personalsteuer*, i.e. the poll tax, survived, whereas income and real estate taxes were no longer levied.

increased slowly between 1794–1820 (36 million fl.) and 1846–47 (49 million fl.). During this period indirect taxation rose from a mean of 56 million fl. (1794–1820) to 136 million fl. in 1846–47.[37] Thus, the last decades of the Old Regime changed the balance between *contributionale* and *cameralia* that had been established at the end of the Thirty Years War. During the era of reform, indirect taxes that affected the urban populations of the empire prevailed over direct taxes on agricultural income.[38] Attempts at modernizing the system of revenues by introducing progressive personal income taxes, which had proved quite effective during the Napoleonic Wars, were dropped immediately when peace was restored.

Antipathy towards personal taxes by the landed nobility, the clergy and well-to-do financial elites reinforced the desire to maintain the regional distribution of taxation (see Figure 7.4). From the late seventeenth century until the mid eighteenth century, the Bohemian territories paid 40–50 per cent of the military contribution. During the same period, the share of Hungary rose from 17 to 30 per cent of the total. The amount of the contribution levied in the Austrian Hereditary Lands varied between 17 and 35 per cent of the whole sum. During the reign of Maria Theresa, Bohemia paid 40 per cent, Hungary 31 per cent and the Austrian territories 29 per cent of the contribution. These relationships, which might have been altered by maintaining the income taxes introduced during the Napoleonic Wars, were preserved by raising the contribution and repealing income taxes during the last decades of the *ancien régime*.[39]

The territorial distribution of the *contributionale* was quite different from that of the *cameralia*. Hungary paid only for the royal salt monopoly, but the complete range of all *cameralia* was levied in the Austrian and Bohemian hereditary lands. The relation between Austria, Bohemia and Hungary for indirect taxes was approximately 49:28:23 per cent in 1763–78 whereas in 1825–47 estimates suggest that it was 46:31:23 per

---

[37] The mean annual growth rate of all direct taxes was 1.15% from 1820 to 1847, whereas the mean annual growth rate of indirect taxes was 3.35% for the same period. This increase could be achieved in part by reducing administration costs considerably: Weiss, *Verhältnis*, p. 145.

[38] Excise tax rates varied according to the population of the cities. They were highest in Vienna: Weiss, *Verhältnis*, pp. 100–6, 146. Income from tobacco and lottery monopolies was mainly urban as well. Customs might have affected the urban population to a larger extent than rural people. Due to the mercantilist tariffs introduced by Joseph II, customs on Hungarian grain were quite important. This foodstuff was consumed by the increasing urban population. Salt was distributed to the consumers in rural and urban areas alike and used in agriculture and in industry.

[39] Bérenger, *Finances*, p. 349; Dickson, *Finance and government*, II, pp. 382ff., 397ff.; Weiss, *Verhältnis*, p. 224.

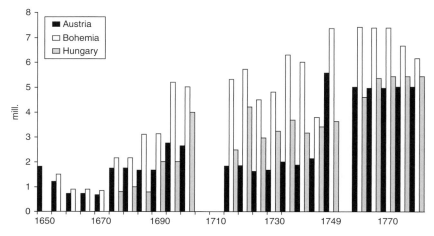

Figure 7.4 Regional distribution of the contribution (1650–1780)
Sources: Winkelbauer, *Ständefreiheit*, Vol. I, pp. 509–15; Bérenger, *Finances*, p. 349; Dickson, *Finance and government*, Vol. II, pp. 382f., 397ff.; Weiss, *Verhältnis*, pp. 224f; see Figure 7.1 for details.

cent. Despite a massive increase of indirect taxation, Austrian territories paid relatively less *cameralia* in the nineteenth century than they had paid in the eighteenth century. All taxes combined, Austrian territories paid 42 per cent, the kingdom of Bohemia 32 per cent and Hungary 26 per cent during the epoch of enlightened absolutism. These data are confirmed by estimates for the period of reform.[40] Stability in the territorial distribution of imperial revenues as reclaimed by the estates of the different kingdoms was achieved by changing the relation between the contribution and *cameralia* within the realms between the period of enlightened absolutism and the regime of reform.

By the end of the Old Regime, the distribution of imperial taxation between the Austrian Hereditary Lands, Bohemia and Hungary did not correspond to the distribution of population or to relative trends of industrial and agricultural production. In the 1820s, roughly 55 per cent of the population of the empire lived in Hungary, 24 per cent in

---

[40] For the nineteenth century see the data published by Weiss, *Verhältnis*, pp. 228–31; data for the eighteenth century have been calculated from Dickson, *Finance and government*, II, pp. 113, 380, 384. Revenues from Galicia, the Austrian Netherlands and the Italian territories are not taken into account. In 1775 and 1784 Galicia contributed *c.* 6%; the Austrian Netherlands delivered 11% of all net revenues in 1784. The Italian territories sent 8% of the imperial income in 1786.

the kingdom of Bohemia and 21 per cent in the Austrian territories.[41] Industrialization spread in Bohemia and Austria at this time. The share of the agricultural population in the whole empire including Hungary accounted for 72 per cent.[42] We may safely assume that between 1775 and 1847 taxes and income per capita were highest in Austria, second in the kingdom of Bohemia and lowest in Hungary.[43]

The distribution and development of tax income is not a good indicator of the social incidence of taxation. The landed nobility, the clergy and the cities received rents, taxes and all sorts of contributions, while royal taxes lowered the income that the local elites could obtain from their peasants and urban populations. The magnitude of the crowding out process of royal taxation was determined largely by the political power of the monarch *vis-à-vis* his realms. Therefore it is difficult to estimate the social effects of rising royal taxation, as only a part of it represented higher tax burdens on the peasantry and urban populations. The rest of the increasing taxation came from income transfers from the nobility, the clergy and the cities to the crown. Nonetheless it seems safe to assume that imperial taxation affected the lower strata of both rural and urban populations, as both paid poll taxes and indirect taxes as part of the salt monopoly. In addition, peasants contributed through land taxes levied on tenants' agricultural incomes, whereas the middle sectors of urban populations did not bear an equivalent direct tax burden. The revenues received directly from the nobility, the clergy and royal officers were insignificant. The system of imperial taxation favoured agriculture and capital since the majority of additional tax revenues were received from indirect taxes (excises, customs, tobacco) levied on consumer goods in the cities. Capital and industrial incomes, as well as services, remained quasi tax free for a long time. The monarch's political power was not sufficient to significantly increase land taxes and salt prices in Hungary and Bohemia.

The expansion of the Austrian empire depended not only on ordinary and extraordinary taxes but also on internal and external borrowing in times of warfare. These operations lowered the crown's net income

---

[41] Weiss, *Verhältnis*, p. 218: in 1828, Austria had 5.2 million inhabitants, Bohemia 5.9 million and Hungary 13.9; the relation between the three territories had been much the same in 1787: in Austria lived 3.6 million, in Bohemia 4.3 million, and in Hungary 9.1 million. In order to maintain comparable geographical units for the two centuries under consideration Galicia, the Bukowina, Lombardy and Venice are not taken into account.

[42] Good, *Economic rise*, pp. 47ff.

[43] For the eighteenth century, estimates given by Weiss, *Verhältnis*, p. 223, differ considerably from those of Dickson, *Finance and government*, p. 384. The data of Weiss for the regional distribution account only for less than 20% of gross revenues.

from taxes until the mid-eighteenth century, because taxes had to be farmed out in order to secure loans. Franchising was reversed during the reign of Charles VI and especially in the second half of the eighteenth century, when reforms ended tax farming. From then on, borrowing did not raise the costs of tax collection but rather increased expenditure on debt servicing. Total public debt stood at 70 million fl in the 1720s. Maria Theresa inherited a debt of 100 million fl in 1740. Thanks to the skilful management of Francis Stephen, the debt fell from 124 million fl. at the end of the War of the Austrian Succession to about 114 million fl. in 1756. But at the end of the Seven Years War, the debt had increased again to 284 million fl.[44]

Most loans were obtained during the seventeenth century on the international capital market by private bankers like Samuel Oppenheimer. At the end of the seventeenth century, the liquidity of the monarchy worsened but the emergence of domestic financiers at that time enabled the crown to obtain loans from the Austrian Hereditary Lands and from Bohemia. In addition to voluntary loans, forced loans were collected during wartime. The first attempt to issue paper money was made in 1762 with the issuing of *Banco-Zettel*. This measure was largely a failure, but necessity was so great during the following wars that banknotes were issued once again and drove silver out of circulation. During the Napoleonic Wars, paper money became the standard means of payment. After two state bankruptcies and monetary reform, silver coins began to circulate once again from the 1820s onwards.[45]

At times of crisis foreign subsidies became important. For example, extraordinary taxes from the Austrian and German estates (*Türkenhilfe* of approximately 60 million fl.) sustained the war against the Ottoman Empire (1593–1606). In addition, subsidies from Spain, the Vatican and Italian allies accounted for 7 million fl., almost 10 per cent of all extraordinary income. Remittances from Spain were helpful during the Thirty Years War, but the War of the Spanish Succession was financed in part with English and Dutch subsidies, which accounted for 18.8 per cent (9.4 million fl.) of the total additional costs of 50 million fl. During the War of the Austrian Succession, direct taxes paid for more than 50 per cent of the additional military expenses, credits covered almost 30 per cent, and foreign subsidies contributed 20 per cent (18 million fl.).

---

[44] Capra, 'Eighteenth century', pp. 298–306. Joseph II inherited 32 million fl. from his father in 1765, which he successfully used for debt service at first.

[45] Winkelbauer, *Ständefreiheit*, I, pp. 515–28; Schasching, *Staatsbildung*; Weiss, *Verhältnis*, pp. 139ff.; Peter Eigner and Erich Landsteiner, 'Finanzplatz Wien', in P. Csendes and F. Opll (eds.), *Wien. Geschichte einer Stadt*, 3 vols. (Vienna/Cologne/Graz: Böhlau, 2003), Vol. 2, pp. 215–26.

The Seven Years War was sustained with the help of French aid, which accounted for 8 per cent (21 million fl.) of the war expenditures of 260 million fl.; more than 60 per cent was financed by credit operations, and less than 30 per cent by ordinary and extraordinary contributions. Finally, during the Napoleonic Wars, 41 million fl. in English subsidies strengthened the position of the Austrian monarchy.[46] Part of the foreign aid was offered as credit facilities[47] another part was delivered in kind, usually troops. Even if the overall importance of these subsidies was not significant, foreign help could be crucial at times when the treasury was exhausted. War finances depended to a large extent on additional taxes at first, but after the mid eighteenth century, credit became more important than extra income from taxation. At the same time the relative importance of the European capital market decreased and, after the Seven Years War, Austrian imperial finances relied increasingly on the development of an internal capital market.

Expenditures

The impact of the debt on public finances characterized the structure of expenditures (see Figure 7.5). Debt servicing was not significant during the seventeenth century. Only 10 per cent of the expenditures were allocated to the payment of interests and redemption of capital before the War of the Spanish Succession. By 1729, more than a quarter of revenues was allocated to service debt. Due to continuous warfare and the end of tax farming, servicing the public debt accounted for more than a third of overall expenditures after the Seven Years War. That share decreased somewhat in the following decade, and during the reign of Joseph II roughly 20 per cent of the budget was needed to service public debt.

In addition to the increasing debt service, direct military expenditures accounted for the constant expansion of the imperial budget. During the seventeenth century in wartime more than 90 per cent of the expenditures were used for military campaigns; at the end of the eighteenth century, during the Turkish War of 1788–91, the share of the military budget was only about 60 per cent. This relative decrease of direct

---

[46] Winkelbauer, *Ständefreiheit*, I, pp. 515–28; Niederkorn, *Die europäischen Mächte*; Ernst, *Madrid und Wien*; Berger, *Finanzwesen*, p. 130; Dickson, *Finance and government*, II, p. 123; Janetschek, *Finanzierung*, pp. 119–21; Otruba, 'Staatshaushalt', pp. 52f.; Weiss, *Verhältnis*, p. 127; Beer, *Finanzen*, p. 171.

[47] K. Helleiner, 'Ein unbekanntes Kapitel aus der anglo-österreichischen Finanzgeschichte: Die Anleiheverhandlungen des Jahres 1794', *Mitteilungen des Instituts für Österreichische Geschichtsforschungen* 71 (1963), 395–407.

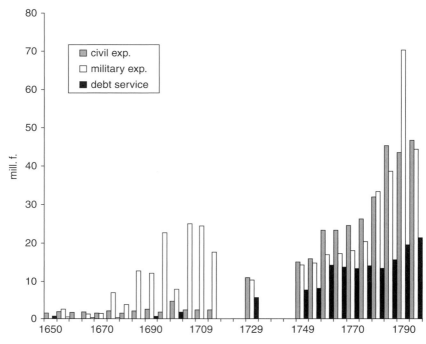

Figure 7.5 Expenditures of the Austrian monarchy (1650–1792)
Sources: Winkelbauer, *Ständefreiheit*, Vol. I, pp. 509–15; Bérenger,
Finances, pp. 238, 359; Dickson, *Finance and government*, Vol. II, pp.
385s; Otruba, *Staatshaushalt*, p. 49; see Figure 7.1 for details.

military expenditures was largely due to the rising weight of debt servicing. In peacetime, the absolute amount of military expenditures was
as high as civil expenditures during the seventeenth century. But the
situation changed during the Enlightenment. It is noteworthy that costs
for civil purposes increased not only in absolute terms but maintained
their relative position at roughly 50 per cent of the whole budget despite
the increased outlays for debt. Thus, the reforms of Maria Theresa and
Joseph II really strengthened the position of the civil administration.
This structure of expenditure was maintained during the first half of
the nineteenth century, when military costs accounted for roughly one-
third of all expenditure.[48]

[48] Beer, *Finanzen*.

The regional incidence of civil and military expenses differed considerably. Civil expenditures, such as administration costs and pensions were allocated in Austria, and especially in Vienna in the eighteenth century. Since the mid eighteenth century, royal treasury bonds and banknotes usually circulated in the major cities, particularly in Vienna. Military expenditures paid for the troops stationed on the borders of the Hungary and Bohemia. Another part was allocated to pay for weapons and textiles from Bohemia and Austria. In Hungary, state demand was concentrated on foodstuffs. Relative decreases in military expenditures in favour of civil and debt expenditures in peacetime led to net transfers of royal taxes to the Austrian territories at the end of the eighteenth century. Dickson estimated that in the 1780s the Austrian Hereditary Lands spent almost 25 per cent more than the sum collected within that part of the empire. While revenues collected in the kingdom of Bohemia exceeded the money spent in these territories by almost 10 per cent, in Hungary income from the contribution and the salt monopoly was 20 per cent higher than expenditures by the empire in that region.[49] Hence, the Hungarian and Bohemian estates were reluctant to increase direct taxation, although the allocation for weapons and clothing benefited industrialization in Bohemia.

During the post-Napoleonic era the Austrian Hereditary Lands improved their position within the empire even further. By then, Austrian territories had a more balanced income structure as indirect taxes rose less than elsewhere and the concentration of direct taxation on agriculture favoured capital formation in industry and services. Furthermore, this favourable situation was strengthened by the regional distribution of expenditures in the epoch of restoration. With civil expenditures concentrated largely in Vienna, the increasing importance of the public debt was an incentive for the development of a capital market in the capital of the empire, while military demands for industrial goods also favoured the Austrian territories.[50]

The kingdom of Bohemia contributed less to the royal treasury than the Austrian territories during the first half of the nineteenth century, but in comparison to Austria, the Bohemian tax structure was less balanced and the urban population bore an increasing share of indirect

[49] Dickson, *Finance and government*, II, pp. 111–13.
[50] P. Eigner, M. Wagner and A. Weigl, 'Finanzplatz: Wien als Geld- und Kapitalmarkt', in Günther Chaloupek, Peter Eigner and Michael Wagner, *Wien. Wirtschaftsgeschichte 1740–1938*, 2 vols. (Vienna: Jugend & Volk-Verlag, 1991), Vol. 2, *Dienstleistungen*, pp. 909–97; M. Wagner, 'Zwischen zwei Staatsbankrotten. Der Wiener Finanzmarkt im 18. Jahrhundert', *Wiener Geschichtsblätter* 32 (1977), 113–43; F. Baltzarek, 'Finanzplatz Wien – die innerstaatliche und internationale Stellung in historischer Perspektive', *Quartalshefte der Girozentrale* 15:4 (1980), 11–63.

taxation. In the post-Napoleonic period, a large part of the military budget still went to the kingdom of Bohemia, but as civil expenditures and debt service gained in importance, Bohemia benefited less from the empire than Austria. Notwithstanding the net transfer of income to Vienna, the Bohemian mining and textile industries received imperial support through the demands from the army and from the structure of taxation, which fell lighter upon non-agricultural incomes up to 1848.

The Hungarian contributions to the central budget remained low during the restoration, but imperial expenditures in Hungary were even lower in this period due to the increasing weight of civil expenditures. Furthermore royal income depended on a few taxes, especially on salt and land. Thus the most important sector of the Hungarian economy, agriculture, was taxed heavily. Military expenditures in Hungary concentrated on food and labour, so that the demands of the army had almost no 'modernizing' effects.

Economic impact of the imperial budget

Imperial revenues and expenditures enhanced already existing economic tendencies and the impact of the imperial budget on economic development increased from the mid seventeenth to the mid nineteenth century. In the second half of the seventeenth century the sectoral and regional structure of royal income and expenditure contributed to stabilize the realms after protracted periods of warfare (namely the Thirty Years War and the wars against the Ottoman Empire). Indirect and direct taxes were relatively balanced and net transfers to Vienna were rather moderate. During the first half of the eighteenth century economic expansion benefited from an almost constant level of taxation. Royal expenditures favoured Hungarian agriculture as well as Bohemian and Austrian industry. When economic expansion gained in importance and a basis for industrialization was established during the second half of the eighteenth century, the increased costs of debt servicing and enlightened reforms to the imperial finances strengthened the position of the Vienna government and of the Austrian Hereditary Lands within the empire at the expense of Hungary and Bohemia. In addition, the structure of imperial revenues and expenditures seems to have favoured capital formation and manufacturing. Thus the rapidly expanding revenues and expenditures of the empire enhanced emerging economic differences between agricultural and industrial regions. During the first half of the nineteenth century, the lack of a modern tax system, i.e. the overwhelming importance of indirect taxes and the reluctance of the estates to introduce income taxes for non-agricultural earnings, strengthened regional inequalities even further. Imperial expenditures, and especially the marked increase of civil administration and debt service, led to net transfers to the Austrian Hereditary Lands that favoured incomes from capital and urban real properties.

The imperial budget favoured social inequalities between the elites and the larger part of the population. For the elites, it was rather rewarding to enter the imperial service either as a military or as a civil servant. Initially they benefited from tax farming and then, from the eighteenth century, from imperial debt management, whereas their share of the tax burden was mainly restricted to indirect taxes and crowding out effects from the land taxes. The peasantry was taxed heavily by the land tax and indirect taxes but it did not benefit significantly from rising expenditures. The lower strata of the rural population, miners, urban artisans, local traders and shopkeepers, as well as the urban poor, paid rising rates of *cameralia*. This regressive incidence of taxation was counteracted somewhat by the effects of military expansion and by civil expenditures. Thus sectoral and social inequalities of an ever-increasing imperial budget initially favoured Austrian and Bohemian industrialization, while, after the 1820s, the progressive increases of indirect taxes contributed to the Revolution of 1848.

Comparing the Austrian empire to other European imperial powers it is noteworthy that administrative structures and bookkeeping in Austria and Spain were similar from the sixteenth to the mid nineteenth centuries.[51] Tax farming during the sixteenth and seventeenth centuries and the imperial administration of taxation from the eighteenth century were commonplace across Europe.[52] The land based elites' resistance to physiocratic and enlightened ideas that proposed increased land taxes, the introduction of an *impot unique* based on cadastres, and levying personal income taxes from non-agriculture incomes were common throughout Europe. In Austria, as well as in Spain and in Great Britain, imperial budgets had pro-cyclical effects on the economy and strengthened the uprising of industrialized regions. Vienna, Madrid and London had to face opposition from distant territories when they attempted to change their composite monarchies into centralized regimes and to distribute revenues on a fair basis with respect

---

[51] R. Pieper, *La Real Hacienda bajo Fernando VI y Carlos III (1753–1788). Repercusiones económicas y sociales* (Madrid: Insituto de Estudios Fiscales, 1992); R. Pieper, 'Contiendas imperiales y política fiscal: España y Gran Bretaña en el siglo XVIII', in E. Sánchez Santiró, L. Jáuregui and A. Ibarra (eds.), *Finanzas y política en el mundo iberoamericano. Del antiguo régimen a las naciones independientes 1754–1850* (Mexico: Instituto Mora/Universidad del Estado de Morelos/Facultad de Economía-UNAM, 2001), pp. 63–76.

[52] Bonney, *Rise of the fiscal state.*

to GDP and population. There were two major differences between the Austrian empire on the one hand, and Spain or Britain on the other. First, Austria had an elevated share of direct taxes (*contributionale*) from the eighteenth century. Thus, the very broad basis of Austrian imperial revenues lowered the regressive effects of taxation and enabled an expansionist budget and policies without any colonies overseas. Second, Austria had almost no navy, and military expenditures concentrated on the army. Therefore imperial endeavours focused on eastern and south-eastern Europe. Decentralization, stability in the regional distribution of revenues and expenditures, and a moderate net transfer of revenues to Vienna contributed to the long-lasting expansion of the empire and to its stability after the Napoleonic Wars.

8　The Russian fiscal state, 1600–1914

Peter Gatrell

Introduction

The Russian revolution of February 1917 brought to an end more than three centuries of rule by the Romanov dynasty. However, the abrupt and ignominious collapse of the imperial polity should not obscure the fact that successive tsars along with state officials and the military enlarged the Russian empire and simultaneously maintained a tight grip on its inhabitants for a prolonged period. How they did so is a question that has important implications for the student of fiscal states. At the same time, the tsarist economy developed only fitfully and fell behind its economically more developed rivals on the European continent. With some intermissions – notably the periods of rapid growth in the early eighteenth century and during the last two decades of the nineteenth century – Romanov Russia survived rather than thrived. Russia's rulers did not succeed in overcoming the fundamental elements of economic backwardness, and poverty in turn limited the fiscal capability of the tsarist state.

The formation and operation of the fiscal system can only be fully understood in the context of the prevailing institutional framework. The Russian empire was governed according to autocratic principles that remained in place for much of the period. Prior to the establishment of the Romanov dynasty in 1613, the Tsars of Muscovy (Ivan III, Vasilii III and Ivan IV, 'the Terrible') ruled with an iron fist, believing themselves accountable to no one except God. This absolutist tradition proved durable.[1] No form of parliamentary scrutiny of government, including its financial operations, emerged until after the revolution of 1905–06 and even then government ministers were accountable only to the tsar. Property rights remained limited. Elected local councils (*zemstvos*) and municipal authorities were established after 1860. They had the right to raise revenue, primarily in order to fund primary education

---

[1] M. Perrie (ed.), *The Cambridge history of Russia. Volume 1, from early Rus' to 1689* (Cambridge University Press, 2006).

and basic health services. But their relationship with central government remained frosty.[2]

Russia's entire social and political system was 'honeycombed with privilege'.[3] The subjects of the tsar belonged by birth to one of several estates or divisions (*sosloviia*), each of which owed obligations in return for the tsar's protection. The fundamental concept of ascription to an estate and to state service underpinned the entire political system from 1700 to 1917 and bound the different groups together. The premier estate was the nobility (*dvorianstvo*). Peter the Great (who ruled between 1682 and 1725) required male members of the nobility to serve the state. Catherine II (1762–96) revoked this formal obligation at the start of her reign. The nobility enjoyed important legal and economic privileges in return, notably the right to own serfs as well as land, and the decree of 1762 enabled many of them to devote more time to their landed estates. The other *sosloviia* were no less constrained by official regulation. Merchants, for example, were subdivided into different categories which determined the nature and extent of the business that they were entitled to conduct under licence from the government. Artisans constituted the lowest stratum of the urban tax-paying population.[4]

These arrangements affected the peasantry with particular intensity. For economic as well as administrative purposes, peasants were grouped into two main categories of service, state peasants and seigniorial peasants (serfs), with the remainder dependent upon either the Church or the royal household. State peasants worked primarily on forest land belonging to the state and discharged their obligations in cash and/or in kind. From the fourteenth century onwards peasants were gradually tied to the land and became the property of private nobles to whom they owed service that took the form of labour on the estate and/or a cash payment or quitrent (*obrok*). The Law Code (*Ulozhenie*) of 1649 formally removed from peasants the last vestiges of their right to move. Even after the emancipation of the seigniorial peasantry in 1861 most serfs did not escape a continued dependence on their erstwhile masters; at the same time the state purchased their freedom in return for levying annual redemption payments. All male peasants, including those working on Church and Crown lands, were liable to pay the poll

---

[2] T. Emmons and W. Vucinich (eds.), *The Zemstvo in Russia: an experiment in local self-government* (Cambridge University Press, 1982). On property rights, see O. Crisp and L. Edmondson (eds.), *Civil rights in imperial Russia* (Oxford: Clarendon Press, 1989).

[3] I take this apposite phrase from R. Brubaker, *Citizenship and nationhood in France and Germany* (Cambridge, MA: Harvard University Press, 1992), p. 35.

[4] D. Lieven (ed.), *The Cambridge history of Russia. Volume 2, Imperial Russia, 1689–1917* (Cambridge University Press, 2006).

tax, which was introduced in 1724 and not abolished until 1887; no other social estate faced this obligation.[5] I examine this issue in further detail later on. Furthermore, peasants were regularly expected to make extraordinary contributions in kind to help cover the costs of military expeditions or construction work. In return they might expect some assistance in times of dire need, as well as some state protection against the more extreme forms of exploitation. The social and political subordination of the serfs provoked intermittent peasant unrest, notably the Cossack revolt led by Stenka Razin in 1670 and the famous Pugachev revolt in 1773–74, inspired in part by the burden of taxation and more generally by the compelling vision of freedom. Nor did the abolition of serfdom bring protest to an end, as the events of 1905–06 demonstrated. The suppression of these disturbances imposed an additional cost upon the treasury.[6]

Russia's natural environment provided the context for the creation and extraction of resources by and for the state and the landlords. Much of the empire comprised inhospitable terrain that was not conducive to productive economic activity. Natural waterways were frozen for months at a time, and the course of the rivers made it difficult to move people and products from east to west. Furthermore, Russia was periodically afflicted by natural disasters, notably harvest failures, which required budgetary resources to deal with the consequences. Throughout the period under consideration Russia was a predominantly agrarian economy. This is not to dispute the establishment and durability of long-distance trade in furs, forest products, metalwares and some luxury items, nor is it to overlook the existence of handicraft activity and the growth of organized manufacturing, which brought great wealth to a handful of merchants and serf owners. All the same, the bedrock of economic activity was subsistence farming in the peasant household, clusters of which formed the land commune. The peasant household and the land commune developed under serfdom and persisted long after emancipation. Together they formed the centrepiece of the system whereby the tsarist state and Russian landlords extracted resources from the peasant population. The traditional three-field strip system

[5] N. I. Anan'ich, 'K istorii otmeny podushnoi podati v Rossii', *Istoricheskie zapiski* 94 (1974), 183–212.
[6] M. Perrie, 'Popular revolts', in Perrie (ed.) *Cambridge history of Russia*, pp. 600–17; D. Moon, *The Russian peasantry 1600–1930: the world the peasants made* (London: Longman, 1999), pp. 94–7. In practice it is difficult to distinguish the costs of suppressing the revolution from the costs of the war against Japan in 1904–05. Both fell into the category of 'extraordinary expenditures'. See P. Gatrell, *The last argument of tsarism: government, rearmament and industry in Russia 1900–1914* (Cambridge University Press, 1994), p. 92.

predominated. Cereal monoculture remained the norm. Peasant farmers struggled with primitive farm tools, and modest numbers of draft animals meant a relative dearth of animate power and a shortage of fertilizer. The problems of low-productivity agriculture were regularly addressed by contemporary economists and government officials without being resolved to anyone's satisfaction.[7]

Imperial rule, territorial aggrandisement and financial administration

We can break this topic down into various components. One is the extension of imperial rule and the consequences for the fiscal system and for resource extraction. Another is the relative paucity of officials who could exercise administrative control over the tax-paying population; this created a vicious circle, in so far as a lack of revenue hindered the expansion of the bureaucracy. A related issue is the political dynamic that emerged in the form of rivalry between the central state and the land-owning (serf-owning) nobility and between central and local government, particularly following the great reforms of the 1860s.

Following its prolonged and costly territorial consolidation under the rule of the Muscovite Tsars, whose authority was variously challenged by foreign powers such as the Polish-Lithuanian Commonwealth and Sweden, the Russian empire expanded to Ukraine in the south and Siberia and Central Asia in the east. (This had the incidental but important consequence that serfs found it progressively more difficult to escape the jurisdiction of serf-owning nobility.) The impact of this aggrandizement on the size of the population under tsarist jurisdiction is outlined in Table 8.1.

How imperial expansion affected the financial condition of the empire – its access to new resources but also new responsibilities – is something that cannot be passed over. During the eighteenth and early nineteenth centuries the story of Romanov Russia was largely one of uninterrupted expansion and growing military prowess. Although Peter the Great suffered defeat at the hands of Turkey in 1711, his strategic brilliance led to victory over the Swedish King Charles XII at the battle of Poltava in 1709 and secured Russian supremacy in the

[7] A. V. Dulov, *Geograficheskaia sreda i istoriia Rossii konets XV – seredina XIXv* (Moscow: Nauka, 1983); A. Kahan, *Russian economic history: the nineteenth century* (Chicago University Press, 1989), pp. 108–43; E. Kingston-Mann, *In search of the true west: culture, economics, and problems of development* (Princeton University Press, 1998).

Table 8.1. *Population of the Russian empire (millions)*

Census ('revision') date	Original territory	Annexed territory	Total population
1722	13	—	13
1762	19	—	19
1815	30.5	14.5	45
1859	45	29	74
1897	65	64	129

Source: P. I. Lyashchenko, *History of the national economy of Russia to the 1917 Revolution* (New York: Macmillan, 1949), p. 273.

Baltic.[8] For more than a century afterwards, Russia's rulers enjoyed the fruits of his success, the only sour note being Russia's failure to defeat Napoleon during the War of the Third Coalition (1805–07). Catherine the Great mounted a successful campaign against Turkey in 1768–74 and participated in the dismemberment of Poland. However, the story of diplomatic and military triumph came to an end with the disastrous Crimean War of 1853–56, which dramatically exposed Russia's military shortcomings in the contest with Britain and France. This defeat contributed to the decision by Tsar Alexander II to embark on a major programme of political, administrative, educational, financial and military reforms. Worse was to follow when Russia embarked on a costly adventure in the Far East, when the Russo–Japanese war culminated in defeat and humiliation. Russia's Great Power status was further dented by the experience of the First World War, which finally brought the curtain down on three hundred years of tsarist rule.

It is against the background of more or less continuous territorial aggrandizement and search for influence in Continental Europe, Central Asia and the Far East that we must locate the attempt to secure the human, material and financial resources to underpin geopolitical ambitions. These were expressed in an increasing commitment to military strength, in particular to the land forces. The size of the regular army increased from 200,000 in 1720 to 240,000 in 1740, and from 345,000 in 1756 to 450,000 at the end of the century.[9] Supplying the army as well as the navy with sufficient weaponry, uniforms, horses and foodstuffs posed relatively few problems until the mid nineteenth

[8] W. C. Fuller, *Strategy and power in Russia, 1600–1914* (New York: The Free Press, 1992), pp. 71–84.
[9] W. M. Pintner, 'The burden of defense in imperial Russia, 1725–1914', *Russian Review* 43 (1984), 231–59, at pp. 246–7.

century. This was partly thanks to Russia's metallurgical enterprises in the Urals and growing woollen textiles industry, and partly the result of devolving responsibility for the manufacture of basic goods such as boots and uniforms to the rank and file. The main costs to the treasury were those of providing a large army with food, uniforms and fodder, although in practice Russian soldiers often had to fend for themselves. The advent of new weapons technology towards the end of the nineteenth century did not fundamentally modify this picture, although of course the size of the total military budget did increase dramatically. By the beginning of the twentieth century, the proportion of total military expenditure devoted to naval armament began to increase. But the basic element remained the size of the standing army, which grew to 1.12 million in 1850 and stayed at that level until 1900, a function primarily of poor transportation, which required troops to be stationed along Russia's extensive land frontiers instead of being concentrated in the heartland and despatched to the frontier as and when necessary. Indeed, the poor quality of Russian communications created insurmountable problems in supplying troops. Military failings in the 1630s and again during the 1680s indicate that this was nothing new.[10]

Popular impressions notwithstanding, Romanov Russia was not a densely governed polity. During the eighteenth century the Russian state deployed no more than 5,000 full-time officials, whose qualities often left a lot to be desired. At the end of the nineteenth century the civil service had grown to around 150,000 officials, two-thirds of whom were employed in central government, but the ratio of officials to population (1.1 per thousand) was approximately the same in 1900 as it had been in 1850.[11] The results of under-government were that the tsarist regime came to rely instead upon military personnel to act as policemen whose authority was supplemented by the powers that the nobility exercised over their serfs.[12] One further implication of weak administration was that the state compensated by adopting a habit of clumsy periodic intervention in the affairs of the tsar's subjects. Arbitrary intervention (*proizvol*), which had been a characteristic feature of late medieval Russian finance, tended to become the norm rather than the exception thereafter. We should note also that officials were on the whole poorly

---

[10] Fuller, *Strategy and power*, pp. 31–4.
[11] S. Frederick Starr, *Decentralisation and self-government in Russia, 1830–1870* (Princeton University Press, 1972), p. 48; P. A. Zaionchkovskii, *Pravitel'stvennyi apparat samoderzhavnoi Rossii v XIXv* (Moscow: Nauka, 1978), p. 221.
[12] A. Kahan, *The plow, the hammer, and the knout: an economic history of eighteenth-century Russia* (University of Chicago Press, 1985), pp. 362–3; Fuller, *Strategy and power*, p. 97.

remunerated, which encouraged bribery and dishonesty. This blend of coercion and corruption did not give way to more modern forms of rule until the very end of the tsarist regime. Meanwhile peasants ended up policing themselves for much of the time. Self-administration manifested itself in collective obligation or *krugovaia poruka*, which included mutual responsibility for tax payments. This customary practice of reciprocity seems to have had firm roots in Russian peasant society, but it was underpinned by the state's readiness to devolve some of the costs of administration onto the peasant community.[13]

To sum up so far, the protracted growth of the Russian empire entailed the mobilization of human and material resources, which in turn subordinated the population to the state in myriad ways. In the words of the great pre-revolutionary historian, V. I. Kliuchevskii, 'the state swelled up, the people languished'.[14] Quite how far they languished is, as we shall see, a contested issue. Nonetheless it is safe to say that the mechanisms of state authority helped curb the accumulation of resources in the hands of the population. This implied that overcoming economic backwardness would also necessitate state intervention.

The state budget and fiscal reform

The concept of a state budget did not exist in pre-reform Russia. Russia's seventeenth-century rulers established a department of accounts to introduce some system into state finances, without making its operations transparent.[15] Thereafter the management of state finances continued to be shrouded in mystery. As a result the state did not provide any overall account of its income and expenditure until the end of the eighteenth century.[16] This murky state of affairs began to change following the Great Reforms, after which a clearer indication

[13] P. Gatrell, 'Economic culture, economic policy and economic growth in Russia, 1861–1914', *Cahiers du monde russe* 36 (1995), 37–52; Gatrell, 'Poor Russia: environment and politics in the long-run economic history of Russia', in G. Hosking and R. Service (eds.), *Reinterpreting Russia* (London: Edward Arnold, 1999), pp. 89–106. On the quality of government officials, see W. Pintner, *Russian economic policy under Nicholas I* (Ithaca: Cornell University Press, 1967), pp. 180–1.

[14] Quoted in G. Hosking, *Russia: people and empire, 1552–1917* (London: Harper Collins, 1997), p. xxiv.

[15] S. M. Kashtanov, *Finansy srednevekovoi Rossii* (Moscow: Nauka, 1988), remains the most authoritative guide to pre-1600 financial affairs. Non-Russian readers may consult G. Vernadsky, *Kievan Russia* (New Haven: Yale University Press, 1948), pp. 189–92 and Vernadsky, *Russia at the dawn of the modern age* (New Haven: Yale University Press, 1959), pp. 183–4.

[16] Kahan, *Plow, hammer, knout*, p. 319; R. D. Hellie, 'Russia, 1200–1815', in R. Bonney (ed.), *The rise of the fiscal state in Europe, 1200–1815* (Oxford University Press, 1999), pp. 481–505, at p. 496.

emerged of the size of the state budget and its different components. According to convention, the expenditure budget was divided into ordinary and extraordinary items, the latter including spending on war, railway construction, natural disasters and the redemption of government debt. Any annual surplus of ordinary income over expenditure was transferred to the so-called 'free balance' of the state treasury. The published budget recorded expenditure by government departments. However, it is difficult to ascertain spending on particular purposes because, for example, the budget for education might be spread across the ministries of education, internal affairs, defence and agriculture. With the establishment of the State Duma in 1906, tsarist officials were obliged to explain the breakdown of expenditure by category. But at the same time they succeeded in circumventing parliamentary attempts to restrict the government's freedom of manoeuvre.[17]

Arcadius Kahan argued that 'all the available evidence points to the leading role of government expenditures in budgetary formation'.[18] Certainly the Russian budget reflected the impact of frequent wars and civil conflicts. At the very outset the state's coffers had been emptied by the prolonged time of troubles that eventually brought Mikhail Romanov to the throne in 1613. Wars with Poland in 1633 and against the Crimean Khanate in the 1680s strained the budget further; increases in money issue led to the debasement of the currency. Peter the Great's campaign against Sweden at the turn of the century required provincial governors to collect a series of grain taxes, receipts of which were notoriously unreliable. Peter's successors attempted to reduce government spending on war, but the wars during the 1740s led to further budget deficits, fresh attempts to extract taxes and a renewed increase in the money supply. Nor, as we saw earlier, did Catherine the Great avoid military adventures. However, she did attempt to reduce state spending on the army and to devote resources to internal central and provincial administration, although this contributed to a worsening of the material condition of her troops as well as the quality of the navy.[19] Other significant outlays during her reign included construction projects, notably the foundation of St Petersburg and (in the 1750s) the spectacular Winter Palace on the banks of the Neva. Under Catherine the percentage of the total

[17] Details of spending in 1903 and 1913 are reported in A. Raffalovich (ed.), *Russia: its trade and commerce* (London: P. S. King, 1918), p. 331.
[18] Kahan, *Plow, hammer, knout*, p. 341.
[19] Fuller, *Strategy and power*, pp. 52, 100–2.

government budget spent on administration, including the court, rose from around 4 to 11 per cent.[20]

In considering the entirety of Romanov rule, however, we should not assume that the state budget was dominated by military expenditure. As a proportion of total budgetary outlays, military spending probably reached a peak of around 55 per cent at the time of the Napoleonic Wars before falling steadily to around 40 per cent in the 1820s to 1840s. It hovered around the 25–30 per cent mark in the later nineteenth century.[21] By the late nineteenth century an increased proportion of the ordinary state budget was being devoted to the operation of the railway system, a task that absorbed 20 per cent of the total on the eve of the First World War, compared to less than 3 per cent in 1885. Other items included maintaining the state monopoly on spirits, notably vodka. Payments on the state debt also accounted for a significant share of total state expenditure.[22]

At the beginning of the seventeenth century most government revenue derived from import duties and a tax on the sale of alcohol. Peter the Great imposed a number of arbitrary taxes, the most famous of which was a tax on the wearing of beards by leading noblemen. (Peasants paid the tax too, if they entered a town on business.) Other taxes were levied on glass, doors, bathhouses and beehives. Peter garnered additional revenue on a variety of indirect items and imposed high protective tariffs in 1724. Finally a number of extraordinary impositions were levied on peasants in order to meet the costs of building his new capital in St Petersburg and funding the construction of an imperial navy.[23] Thereafter Peter the Great sought to levy direct taxes more systematically. One measure included the creation of merchant guilds, which enabled the state to levy taxes on prosperous urban residents.

Much the most significant aspect of fiscal reform in pre-reform Russia was the introduction of the poll or soul tax (*podushnaia podat'*). This replaced the hearth or household tax introduced in 1679, whose limitations – including peasants' propensity to combine households in order to reduce their liability to pay – were exposed by its failure to cover the costs of the Great Northern War in 1700–21. Peter prepared the ground by conducting a census or 'revision' of the tax-paying population in

[20] S. M. Troitskii, *Finansovaia politika russkogo absoliutizma v XVIII veke* (Moscow: Nauka, 1966), p. 243.

[21] Pintner, 'Burden of defense', p. 248.

[22] P. A. Khromov, *Ekonomicheskoe razvitie Rossii v XIX–XX vekakh* (Moscow: Gosudarstvennoe izdatel'stvo politicheskoi literatury, 1950), pp. 524–9.

[23] E. V. Anisimov, *Podatnaia reforma Petra I: vvedenie podushnoi podati v Rossii, 1719–1728 gg.* (Leningrad: Nauka, 1982), pp. 21–35; Fuller, *Strategy and power*, p. 4.

Table 8.2. *Government revenue during the reign of Peter the Great*

	1680		1701		1724	
Taxes	000 roubles	%	000 roubles	%	000 roubles	%
Direct	601	38	1190	33	4672	54
Indirect	970	62	2442	67	4041	46
Total revenue	1571	100	3632	100	8713	100

Source: E. V. Anisimov, *Podatnaia reforma Petra I: vvedenie podushnoi podati v Rossii, 1719–1728 gg.* (Leningrad: Nauka, 1982), p. 278.

1719. This took two years to complete.[24] Peasant attempts to conceal the number of 'souls' from the census enumerators were liable to be severely punished, but this did not prevent peasants' mass flight (not for the first or last time) to outlying regions where tsarist writ did not run. The close link between the new tax and military requirements is revealed by the decision to create troop regiments to collect the tax, part of which they retained for their own maintenance. This measure did nothing to deter peasants from seeking to escape their new obligations. Subsequently the responsibility for tax collection passed to serf-owners or, in the case of state and Church peasants, to the appropriate authority.[25]

Notwithstanding these difficulties, the Petrine fiscal revolution (see Table 8.2) brought about a more than fivefold increase in nominal tax receipts and resulted in an increase in the contribution of direct taxes from 38 to 54 per cent. Taking into account the depreciation of the rouble, total tax receipts probably increased by a factor of 2.7. In per-capita terms (given an estimated taxable population of 4.07 million souls) the poll tax amounted to around 0.15 roubles in 1680; by 1724 this figure climbed to 0.82 roubles. In real terms this probably represented a threefold increase.

Scholars generally agree that the collection of tax revenue remained broadly stable during the second quarter of the eighteenth century, with some increase as a result of population growth. However, this stability disguised the extent of under-collection. A government commission in

[24] The classic source is P. Miliukov, *Gosudarstvennoe khoziaistvo Rossii v pervoi chetverti XVIII stoletiia i reforma Petra Velikogo*, 2nd edn (St Petersburg: Stasiulevich, 1905). Further revisions took place until 1857, on the eve of peasant emancipation.
[25] Anisimov, *Podatnaia reforma*, pp. 45–79, 233–58; Moon, *Russian peasantry*, pp. 254–6.

1747 suggested that the state normally collected between 70 and 80 per cent of the revenue it was due. The poll tax was reduced during times of particular hardship.[26]

In the course of the eighteenth century the poll tax was extended to outlying regions, such as the western borderlands, that had hitherto been exempt. One solution to pressing government needs was to increase the rate of taxation in the hope of generating additional receipts from the poll tax as well as from government monopolies on the sale of salt and particularly alcohol. Tariff duties were raised in 1757 (internal tolls were abolished in 1753). Indirect taxes increased as a share of total revenue towards the end of the eighteenth century. In 1762–64 Catherine the Great took over Church lands in order to lay claim to the revenue it had hitherto extracted from Church peasants. None of these observations should be allowed to obscure the fact that Russia's eighteenth-century rulers operated a sustained budget deficit.[27]

Between 1815 and 1853 the tsarist state enjoyed a period of virtually uninterrupted peace. Although there were no major strains on the government budget, minister of finances Egor Kankrin wrestled with recurrent deficits by curbing expenditure. He was less successful in seeking to raise additional revenue. During the first half of the nineteenth century Russian officials bemoaned the government's dependence on the peasantry as the chief source of state revenue, not least because the uncertain harvest rendered collection problematic. But the government did not take any significant measures to reduce its reliance on the rural population, hoping rather to tax the income of peasants who engaged in petty trade. For their part, urban merchants seem to have succeeded in concealing their capital from tax officials in order to minimize their liabilities. The most persistent critics of government policy, such as Admiral Nikolai Mordvinov, proposed a more liberal economic regime, including the abolition of restrictions on private enterprise as a prerequisite for economic growth. But their voices went largely unheard.[28]

Significant structural changes to the budget also took place in the final phase of tsarist rule.[29] The most important reform was the cancellation of the poll tax between 1883 and 1887, a decision that dispensed

[26] Kahan, *Plow, hammer, knout*, pp. 320–1. An up-to-date study is V. N. Zakharov, I. A. Petrov and M. K. Shatsillo, *Istoriia nalogov v Rossii, IX – nachalo XX v* (Moscow: ROSSPEN, 2006).
[27] Kahan, *Plow, hammer, knout*, pp. 322–8, 343; J. P. LeDonne, *Ruling Russia: politics and administration in the age of absolutism, 1762–1796* (Princeton University Press, 1984), p. 256; Moon, *Russian peasantry*, p. 100.
[28] Pintner, *Russian economic policy*, pp. 30–5, 55–6.
[29] Budget revenues increased from 960 million roubles to 3,000 million roubles between 1890 and 1914. Khromov, *Ekonomicheskoe razvitie*, pp. 504–13; Iu. N. Shebaldin,

with the last remaining tax levied exclusively on one social estate or *soslovie*.[30] Russia's rapid economic development was reflected in the growing importance of taxes on industrial activity, although they contributed only a small fraction of total revenue. Business taxes were introduced in 1885 during N. Kh. Bunge's tenure of the ministry of finances, but they did not replace existing charges made for a licence to trade. New property taxes also came into being, with the emphasis upon the person who was liable rather than his or her membership of a specific *soslovie*. Bunge took the view that commercial and industrial activity was 'relatively lightly burdened considering the existing arrangements for the taxation of land and other immovable property'.[31] Yet it proved difficult to replace the long-standing 'apportionment' of taxes (*rasklad*) with more modern arrangements that calculated profits or assessed the rateable value of property. One difficulty was finding sufficient tax personnel. As late as 1911 the entire empire employed no more than 1,500 inspectors, a further reminder of the modest reach of government that was mentioned earlier.[32]

The First World War brought about some innovation in fiscal practice. In May 1916 the government introduced a tax on corporate excess profits, at a basic rate of 20 per cent (kicking in at 'excess' profits of 8 per cent of nominal share capital) rising to a top rate of 40 per cent. Firms were allowed various deductions (such as generous depreciation charges) to offset their tax liability. However, the tax was not expected to raise more than 55 million roubles in its first year of operation. This did not prevent industrialists from complaining that the new tax would harm their attempts to replenish Russia's capital stock after the war.[33]

A personal income tax found favour with Russian reformers, such as the Decembrist F. P. Shakhovskii, who protested at the burden that

---

'Gosudarstvennyi biudzhet tsarskoi Rossii v nachale XXv.' *Istoricheskie zapiski* 65 (1959), 163–90.

[30] The poll tax survived in Siberia until 1899. Certain specific direct taxes reflected the peculiarities of imperial expansion, such as the hearth tax levied on towns and villages in Russian Poland and the tent tax (*kibitka*) in Central Asia.

[31] L. E. Shepelev, *Tsarizm i burzhuaziia vo vtoroi polovine XIX veka* (Leningrad: Nauka, 1981), p. 172. Given his radical views on *soslovie* and his coherent views about the appropriate role of government in economic affairs, Bunge is at least as interesting a public figure as the better-known Witte.

[32] Raffalovich, *Russia*, p. 335; A. Babkov, 'National finances and the economic evolution of Russia', *Russian Review* 3 (1912), 170–91; L. Bowman, 'Russia's first income taxes: the effects of modernised taxes on commerce and industry, 1885–1914', *Slavic Review* 52 (1993), 256–82; Y. Kotsonis, '"No place to go": taxation and state transformation in late imperial and early Soviet Russia', *Journal of Modern History* 76 (2004), 531–77, at p. 541.

[33] P. Gatrell, *Russia's First World War: a social and economic history* (London: Pearson, 2005), pp. 137–8, for references to contemporary literature.

the poll tax imposed on the Russian peasantry. However, the advocates of a tax on personal income did not achieve victory until the very end of the tsarist regime. The income tax introduced in 1916 represented a significant change in financial policy and political life, because traditional distinctions deriving from legal status no longer carried weight; that is, no one could claim exemption by virtue of belonging to a privileged estate. The individual taxpayer now dealt directly with the tax inspector (backed by new district assessment boards) and was required to disclose personal financial details. As one leading economist put it, 'the population ... should show greater willingness to reveal the true state of their incomes'. This amounted to an unprecedented emphasis upon civic duty.[34] To be sure, the principle was somewhat weakened by the realization that around half the population would not be liable, although many manual workers were expected to be caught in the net. In 1917, however, the depreciation of the currency made so many people liable 'that it became technically impossible to collect the tax'.[35]

The late tsarist budget was dominated by indirect taxes. In 1885, on the eve of the abolition of the poll tax, direct taxes comprised 33 per cent of total government revenue. But by 1913 the proportion had fallen to 17 per cent, much lower than Britain, Germany and Austria-Hungary and even lower than France.[36] Government revenue depended heavily on income from royalties or *regaliia* (primarily the monopoly on the sale of vodka) and income from government property including receipts from the operations of the railway network. The abolition of tax farming in 1863 enabled the state to secure revenue from new excise duties on the sale of spirits. Other taxes on personal consumption applied to tobacco, sugar, kerosene and matches. Bunge increased the rates on these commodities.[37] Revenue from customs duties increased as a result of general revisions to the tariff in 1891 and 1904 as well as partial changes before and after. Fiscal considerations were paramount, as suggested by the duties on imports of raw cotton (cotton only began to be cultivated

[34] A. M. Michelson, *Russian public finance during the* war (New Haven: Yale University Press, 1928), pp. 147, 161 (quoting Sobolev), 169–78. See also Y. Kotsonis, '"Face-to-face": the state, the citizen, and the individual in Russian taxation, 1863–1917', *Slavic Review* 63 (2004), pp. 221–46. In a departure from tsarist convention, employers and financial institutions were now obliged to report payments made to each individual.
[35] Michelson, *Russian public finance*, pp. 172, 196.
[36] Derived from A. L. Vainshtein, *Oblozhenie i platezhi krest'ianstva v dovoennoe i revoliutsionnoe vremia* (Moscow: Ekonomist, 1924), p. 128. See also Kahan, *Russian economic history*, p. 62.
[37] N. I. Anan'ich, 'K istorii podatnykh reform 1880-kh godov', *Istoriia SSSR* 1 (1979), 159–73; D. Christian, *Living water: vodka and Russian society on the eve of emancipation* (Oxford: Clarendon Press, 1990), pp. 353–81.

in Central Asia later in the nineteenth century) or the tariff on complex items of agricultural machinery that survived until 1898, much to the annoyance of textile merchants and land-owners respectively.

How can we explain the general reliance of the Russian state on indirect receipts which, after all, tend to be more volatile than direct taxes? The answer lies in a combination of political pressure and administrative capacity. The imposition of the famous poll tax posed political difficulties in the shape of peasant reluctance to pay. The business class and noble landlords successfully lobbied against attempts to levy significant taxes on corporate and personal incomes. The state lacked the means and personnel to conduct a serious investigation of personal income; the belated attempt to do so represented something akin to a cultural revolution. It was much more straightforward to collect revenue from Russian consumers at the point of sale. It is curious to note that, by contrast, local authorities as well as *volost* or district bodies were allowed to collect direct taxes in order to fund the services they provided. Thus the supposedly centralizing and autocratic Russian state allowed local bodies scope to do what it largely abstained from practising itself.

Many assertions have been made about the burden of taxation in Russian history. Miliukov famously argued that the total tax yield increased threefold as a result of the Petrine reforms, but his conclusions have been modified by later scholarship which suggests only a modest increase in taxation per head during Peter's reign.[38] At the other end of the century the picture is one of a declining per-capita tax burden in the 1770s and 1780s as a result of inflation. Government critics pointed to the accumulation of tax arrears as an indicator of the intolerable tax burden, but these seem more likely to be explained by intermittent calamities such as harvest failures rather than by systematic peasant impoverishment.[39]

In the later nineteenth century receipts from indirect taxes grew not just because of increased rates of taxation but as a result of the growth of consumption, which was in turn a function of increased migration to new urban centres. Lenin got it right in 1899 when he said that migration encouraged 'civilized habits and requirements' and exposed the growing urban population to new consumer tastes.[40] Thus the argument

---

[38] Miliukov, *Gosudarstvennoe khoziaistvo*; Anisimov, *Podatnaia reforma*, pp. 274–82; Moon, *Russian peasantry*, pp. 81–2.
[39] Kahan, *Plow, hammer, knout*, pp. 343–7.
[40] V. I. Lenin, *The development of capitalism in Russia* (Moscow: Progress Publishers, 1977), p. 582.

that government tax policies imposed significant hardship specifically on rural communities is in need of modification.[41]

One way of thinking about the rural tax burden is to relate taxation and other dues to peasants' income. Table 8.3 indicates that direct and indirect taxes represented around 22 per cent of peasants' cash income in 1901. By 1912 the proportion had fallen to around 19 per cent. But we should not lose sight of the significant additional cost to peasants of renting land from former serf-owners; many of the rural protests in 1905–06 and 1917 had their origin in rent strikes.

The basic data on ordinary revenue and national income are set out in Table 8.4. In per-capita terms tax revenue grew in real terms from around 9 to 20 roubles in the last half-century of tsarist rule. Growth in revenue per head was particularly marked in the quinquennium 1890–95, reflecting the introduction of new taxes and an upward revision in excise duties. Expressed in relation to national income per head of population, tax revenues increased from around 12 per cent in mid century to around 14 per cent at the start of the industrialization boom in the late 1880s, rising to 16 per cent before 1913. These were much smaller proportions than in Eastern Europe and comparable to Britain at an equivalent stage of industrialization.[42]

Budget deficits and the state debt

As the editors of this volume point out, debt accumulation and taxation are inextricably linked. The tsarist state, as we have seen, failed to meet its growing defence and other commitments out of ordinary revenue. In the course of the eighteenth century extraordinary expenditures were paid for by note issues and by currency debasement. Only later in the century did the government begin to look to external creditors. For most of the eighteenth century the tsarist state financed the budget deficit either by debasing the currency by reminting the coinage or by printing paper money (assignats). Peter the Great met part of the cost

[41] I. K. Ozerov, *Oborotnaia storona nashego biudzheta* (Moscow: Sytin, 1911), p. 156; Babkov, 'National finances', pp. 188–9; Walter Hoffding, 'Recent financial and trade policy of Russia', *Russian Review* 3 (1912), pp. 75–86. For more up-to-date discussion see O. Crisp, *Studies in the Russian economy before 1914* (London: Macmillan, 1976), p. 28; S. G. Wheatcroft, 'Crises and the condition of the peasantry in late imperial Russia', in E. Kingston-Mann, T. Mixter and J. Burds (eds.), *Peasant economy, culture and politics of European Russia, 1800–1921* (Princeton University Press, 1991), pp. 128–72; Kahan, *Russian economic history*, p. 94.
[42] J. R. Lampe and M. R. Jackson, *Balkan economic history: from imperial borderlands to developing nations* (Bloomington: Indiana University Press, 1982), pp. 233–5; P. Mathias, *The transformation of England* (London: Methuen, 1979), table 6.1.

Table 8.3. *Peasant tax and rental payments, European Russia (million roubles)*

	1901	1912
Direct taxes	182.7	221.4
Excises & customs duties	297.0	484.3
Rows 1 + 2	479.7	678.3
Rents etc.	279.0	375.9
Total of rows 1 + 2 + 3	758.7	1054.2
Peasants' cash income	2152.1	3581.3
Rows 1 + 2 as percentage of row 5	22.3%	18.9%
Rows 1 + 2 + 3 as percentage of row 5	35.3%	29.4%

Notes: Direct taxes include central and local government taxes and compulsory insurance levies. Indirect taxes include alcohol, sugar, kerosene, etc. Rents etc. includes interest paid to the Peasant Land Bank. Cash income is estimated by applying a coefficient of 21.67% (in accordance with Vainshtein's findings) to Paul Gregory's estimate of national income. Gregory's figures are adjusted in line with Malcolm Falkus's estimate of European Russia's share of total Russian national income, namely 87.2%; sources: data for 1901 from A. M. Anfimov, *Ekonomicheskoe polozhenie i klassovaia bor'ba krest'ian Evropeiskoi Rossii 1881–1904gg* (Moscow: Nauka, 1984), p. 110; data for 1912 from A. L. Vainshtein, *Oblozhenie i platezhi krest'ianstva v dovoennoe i revoliutsionnoe vremia* (Moscow: Ekonomist, 1924), pp. 147–8; P. Gregory, *Russian national income, 1885–1913* (Cambridge University Press, 1982), pp. 58–9; M. E. Falkus, 'Russia's national income in 1913: a re-evaluation', *Economica* 35 (1968), 52–73, at 55.

of the Northern War by minting coins with a smaller silver content. Another inflationary phase began during the Seven Years War, when the copper coinage was debased. During the reign of Catherine the Great the government looked, instead, first to note issue and then to foreign loans, as a source of financing its commitments.[43]

Russia's first major foreign loans were raised in Holland and among the Italian city-states. Later on the government made greater use of domestic loans, including secret borrowing from state savings banks. These transactions were subsequently converted into regular loans. Other debt arose from the decision to emancipate the serfs in 1861; loans made to peasants were incorporated into the state debt, the assumption being that peasants would repay the treasury.[44] Although peasants made annual repayments, much to their disgust, it should not

[43] Troitskii, *Finansovaia politika*, pp. 230–1.
[44] S. L. Hoch, 'The banking crisis, peasant reform and economic development in Russia, 1857–1861', *American Historical Review* 96 (1991), 795–820.

Table 8.4. *Taxation and national income in late tsarist Russia*

	Total ordinary revenue, million roubles	Revenue per capita, roubles, 1913 prices	Index, 1913 = 100	National income, roubles per capita, 1913 prices	Index, 1913 = 100	Tax per capita as percentage of national income per capita
1860	407.6	8.77	43.9	71.0	60.0	12.4
				(42.6)		(20.6)
				(39.1)		(22.4)
1885	762.3	8.82	44.1	72.5	61.2	12.2
				(45.0)		(19.6)
1890	943.7	10.10	50.5	72.6	61.2	13.9
1895	1255.8	14.12	70.6	86.8	73.2	16.3
1900	1704.1	15.60	78.0	100.2	84.5	15.6
				(67.1)		(23.3)
1905	2024.6	16.47	82.4	101.7	85.8	16.2
1910	2781.0	18.30	91.5	113.0	95.3	16.2
1913	3417.4	20.00	100.0	118.5	100.0	16.9
				(79.4)		(25.2)

Notes: Figures in brackets represent a crude attempt to compute monetized national income. I deducted the value of farm products consumed in kind from total national income estimated in P. Gregory, *Russian national income, 1885–1913* (Cambridge University Press, 1982), pp. 56–7, amounting to 38 % of the total in 1885, 33 % in 1900 and 33 % in 1913. I have assumed that the range in 1860 lay between 40 and 45%; both values are given in the table. Sources: P. A. Khromov, *Ekonomicheskoe razvitie Rossii v XIX–XX vekakh* (Moscow: Gosudarstvennoe izdatel'stvo politicheskoi literatury, 1950), pp. 452–4 (population), pp. 494–511 (ordinary revenue); national income estimates from Gregory, *Russian national income*, pp. 56–9.

be forgotten that the government ended up remitting much of their indebtedness.

Throughout most the nineteenth century the state budget was in deficit and as a consequence the government continued to seek foreign loans. Fresh debts were incurred as the tsarist state embarked on major development projects. Some of these were funded through the rapidly expanding domestic banking system, with state savings banks playing an important role.[45] The volume and distribution of issues are set out in Table 8.5.

[45] I. F. Gindin, *Russkie kommercheskie banki* (Moscow: Gosfinizdat, 1948); Crisp, *Studies in the Russian economy*, pp. 132, 154; B. V. Anan'ich, 'The Russian economy and banking system', in Lieven, *Cambridge history of Russia*, pp. 394–425.

Table 8.5. *Railway loans and other debt issues 1861–1914 (million roubles)*

	Public debt		Railway loans		Other debt	
	Domestic	Foreign	Domestic	Foreign	Domestic	Foreign
1861–1880	1317	2027	117	1777	1200	250
1881–1893	470	396	425	396	45	—
1894–1900	591	872	66	872	525	—
1901–1907	1409	1267	527	−42	882	1309
1908–1914	592	38	124	351	468	−313

Source: I. F. Gindin, *Russkie kommercheskie banki* (Moscow: Gosfinizdat, 1948), p. 394.

In the 1860s and 1870s, under the leadership of Mikhail Reutern, the ministry of finances promoted a massive programme of railway construction. Subsequently the government also acquired privately owned railway lines. Russia also incurred fresh obligations as a result of the catastrophic war against Japan in 1904–05. Government finance ministers devoted considerable amounts of time negotiating and renegotiating the terms under which Russian securities were placed on the European money markets. The difficult negotiations in 1905–06 are a case in point, but they culminated in a large loan that kept Russia on the gold standard and helped keep the tsarist state afloat for another decade.[46]

Taxation and industrialization

In what ways and to what extent did tsarist Russian fiscal policies either promote or hinder industrialization? Arcadius Kahan argued that tax policy hindered 'autonomous' industrial development, but he overstated the case, given what we know about flourishing activity across a wide range of industrial sectors. Olga Crisp established that the process of Russian industrialization embraced a mixture of state-led initiatives and private entrepreneurship in which small-scale businesses coexisted with large conglomerates.[47] What has often been missing from the discussion is detailed consideration of the impact of government tax policy on specific industries. The oil industry is an interesting case in point.

[46] P. Waldron, 'State finances', in Lieven, *Cambridge history of Russia*, pp. 470–3; B. V. Anan'ich, *Rossiia i mezhdunarodnyi capital: ocherki istorii finansovykh otnoshenii 1897–1914* (Leningrad: Nauka, 1970), pp. 170–6.
[47] Kahan, *Russian economic history*; Crisp, *Studies in the Russian economy*.

In the late tsarist period government officials contemplated a reduction in the overall tax burden on industry. In 1867 the influential Tiflis Commission recommended that crude oil production should be freed from all taxes, as in the United States, but that kerosene itself should be taxed at a rate of 65 kopecks per pud.[48] Despite the objections of the department of state economy, the ministry of finance insisted on the adoption of an excise tax on kerosene in 1872 to compensate for revenue lost by abolishing the tax farming arrangements (*otkup*) hitherto in force. The kerosene tax was modelled after the vodka tax. Refiners were required to pay tax levied according to the size and operating time of the stills. However, the refiners quickly found a way to reduce the rate, by learning to distil with such haste that, instead of paying the anticipated 25 to 40 kopecks per pud, they paid only 2 or 3 kopecks and sometimes even less. Furthermore, as well as raising relatively little revenue, the tax had a detrimental effect on the development of the refining industry. Short, fast-burning distillations resulted in kerosene of poor and unpredictable quality, far inferior to its rival American product. It also hindered attempts by refiners to manufacture a variety of petroleum products and make use of the potentially valuable by-products of kerosene distillation. In 1876 the government called upon the great chemist Dmitrii Mendeleev to examine at first hand the effects of taxation upon the petroleum industry. Returning from the United States in October 1876 he reported that if the Russian oil industry's potential were to be realized, the state had to free the industry from all taxes. It could not simply replace the excise on kerosene with some new form of taxation. Mendeleev noted that the US had taxed both kerosene and crude oil between 1862 and 1868 to help pay for the war effort, but that the tax on exported kerosene and then all kerosene had subsequently been dropped. At the same time, the US government provided additional support for its industry. According to Mendeleev, similar Russian aid was needed in the form of maintaining a tariff on imported kerosene. These recommendations were accepted by the ministry of finance, and the state council removed the excise duty on kerosene in 1877.[49] On his visit to Baku in 1883, one outside observer praised government policy for stimulating investment and growth:

No tax is levied on the industry, nor is there any restriction in the shape of official supervision or disabilities in regard to foreigners. It would be impossible

---

[48] One pud is equivalent to 16.38 kg.
[49] J. P. McKay, 'Entrepreneurship and the emergence of the Russian petroleum industry, 1813–1883', *Research in Economic History* 8 (1983), 47–91. I am grateful to Nat Moser for his advice on these issues.

for a business to be less meddled with. The Russian government has certainly made up for its past errors on this score. There is not an industry in Russia to-day where the *laissez-faire* doctrine is carried to such lengths as in the Baku petroleum trade, and in this respect it will stand comparison not only with that of Galicia, but with the freest portion of the United States' oil-fields.[50]

Burdened with budget deficits, the idea of a new tax reappeared on the agenda of the ministry of finance in the 1880s. Regarding new taxation as inevitable, Ludwig Nobel advocated a tax of 15 to 20 kopecks per pud on crude oil as the best means to raise prices, discourage waste, hinder crude oil exports and increase state revenues. Despite these efforts, in November 1887, Finance Minister Ivan Vyshnegradskii won the approval of the state council for a tax on domestic kerosene consumption of 40 kopecks per pud. The full impact of this tax requires further investigation, although one of its effects appears to have been an attempt by refiners to avoid the tax by reducing the proportion of kerosene that they extracted from crude oil.[51]

Concluding remarks

Certain conclusions may now be drawn about what the editors term the 'meta question' of success and failure in Russia's fiscal history. Russia invested in violence (the 'European pattern'), and this bought diplomatic and military supremacy for much of the period in question. At the same time Russia found it difficult to generate funds for sustained development. In this respect we need to bear in mind the recourse to direct government intervention and, towards the end of the period, tsarist Russia's reliance on foreign investment.

Russia was, in a famous phrase coined by the poet Nikolai Nekrasov, 'mighty but poor'.[52] The sprawling Russian empire stretched from the Baltic Sea in the north-west to the Black Sea in the south and to the Pacific Ocean in the Far East. Territorial acquisitions as well as natural expansion led to a significant increase in the size of the population under imperial control. In the early 1700s Peter the Great ruled a population of around 13 million. Nicholas II, the last Romanov, counted

---

[50] C. Marvin, *Region of the eternal fire: an account of a journey to the petroleum region of the Caspian in 1883* (Westport: Hyperion, 1976; first published 1888), p. 209.

[51] A. M. Alieva (ed.), *Monopolisticheskii kapital v neftianoi promyshlennosti Rossii, 1883–1914: dokumenty i materialy* (Moscow–Leningrad: Nauka, 1973), pp. 71–4, 112.

[52] Nekrasov's formulation gained currency when it appeared in Stalin's speech in February 1931 on Soviet industrialisation: J. V. Stalin, *Problems of Leninism* (Moscow: Progress, 1953), pp. 454–8.

around 126 million people as his subjects. The defence of territory and population established the chief imperatives for state expenditure.

How these imperial imperatives operated in practice is a question to which historians have recently begun to turn their attention. E. A. Pravilova has emphasized the perpetuation of traditional legal and financial arrangements in Finland, Poland, the Caucasus and Central Asia. The Finnish diet, for example, retained control of the budget and negotiated its own loans with foreign banks. Poland fared less well. During the first half of the nineteenth century, the tsarist administration entrusted Poland with responsibility for its own budget. This relative autonomy came to an end following the great revolt against tsarist rule in 1863 during which Polish patriots argued the case for 'freedom' from Russian rule. Meanwhile, in the Caucasus, the key oil-producing region of the Russian empire, tsarist officials had no intention of relinquishing any control of economic affairs. There is scope here for further research on the relationship between budgetary policy, economic development and imperial rule, as well as the implications these arrangements had for the evolution of the state following the Bolshevik revolution in 1917.[53]

Issues of fairness intruded with increasing frequency in the final decades of tsarist rule. Non-Russian spokesmen criticized the economic 'burden' imposed by tsarist administration, which required Poles, Ukrainians and Kazakhs to pay for the upkeep of their oppressors. Siberia too figured in some quarters as a 'colony' whose economic interests were subordinated to those of the Russian metropole.[54] Questions about fiscal policy also figured in political debate and in expressions of urban or rural discontent. Early nineteenth-century critics of autocracy, notably the Decembrists, urged the necessity of reducing the tax burden on the peasantry and eliminating tax abuses, but their defeat only served to encourage a prolonged period of silence on the part of nervous government officials. Curbs on freedom of the press and on political organizations provided little scope for criticism of the tsarist fiscal system, although some Russian economists openly attacked government policy and, as the working class grew in size, so too organized labour demonstrated greater assertiveness. The famous petition presented to the tsar by the Assembly of Russian Workers in January 1905 complained about government oppression and 'enslavement'. It

[53] E. A. Pravilova, *Finansy imperii: den'gi i vlast' v politike Rossii na natsional'nykh okrainakh, 1801–1917* (Moscow: Novoe izdatel'stvo, 2006). See also M. Batalina and A. Miller (eds.), *Rossiiskaia imperiia v sravnitel'noi perspektive* (Moscow: Novoe izdatel'stvo, 2004).
[54] N. M. Iadrintsev, *Sibir' kak koloniia* (St Petersburg: Stasiulevich, 1882).

included demands for the abolition of redemption payments and the introduction of a progressive income tax. The demonstrators demanded 'free, universal and compulsory education'. Their protest culminated in 'Bloody Sunday'. We should not exaggerate the political resonance of fiscal complaints to the exclusion of other considerations. The legitimacy of the state came into question for numerous reasons and harsh fiscal practice did not figure at the top of the list. However, it certainly reinforced the grievances articulated by workers, peasants, liberal writers and the non-Russian patriotic intelligentsia before and after the revolution of 1905.[55]

[55] The 1905 petition of the Assembly of Russian Workers is available online at http://artsci.shu.edu/reesp/documents/bloodysunday.htm.

Part III

South Atlantic Europe and the Mediterranean

9   From pioneer mercantile state to ordinary
     fiscal state: Portugal, 1498–1914

Eugenia Mata

Introduction

On 6 January 1501, King Manuel I of Portugal went to the village of
Restelo on the outskirts of Lisbon, from where Vasco da Gama's fleet
had famously departed three years before, and laid the first stone of
the Church of Saint Mary of Bethlehem, a memorial to the voyage.
The king was upset by the recent failure of his attempts to become
sovereign of a united Iberia (or at least to ensure such a role for one of
his descendants).[1] Pleased with the success of Vasco da Gama, Manuel
believed the voyage ensured a firm basis for the future prosperity of
the kingdom. This confidence was emphasized in the title of Lord of
Trade, Navigation and Conquest of Ethiopia, Arabia, Persia and India,
bestowed upon Vasco da Gama when his fleet returned.

The present chapter addresses how the small kingdom of Portugal
became a powerful maritime power that established a lasting link
between Europe and India. First, the fiscal basis of the early Portuguese
voyages of discovery is examined. Second, the King's plans to profit
from the monopoly of this trade link is discussed, along with a model of
the ideal mercantile state. Third, the collapse of Portugal's exceptional
commercial position between Europe and India and its gradual transition to an ordinary fiscal state are treated in the context of the Brazilian
empire and its collapse, and Portugal's first false start at modern economic growth.

A previous version of this chapter was published in the *Journal of Iberian and Latin
American Economic History* XXV:1 (Spring 2007), 123–45.
[1] In 1496, he married Isabel, daughter of King Fernando of Aragon and Queen Isabel of
Castile, as she was the heir apparent to both thrones. However, she died in 1498 and
two years later their son also died. Ultimately, the crowns of Castile and Aragon would
pass through Juana to her son Charles V.

The fiscal roots of world power

In 1400 (one century before King Manuel's inauguration of the church of the Jeronimite order in Lisbon), the kings of Portugal and Castile signed a truce that ended three decades of prolonged, intermittent warfare (1369–71, 1372–73, 1381–82, 1383–87, 1396–1400). Repeated and ineffectual attempts by both sides to interfere in each other's internal affairs had convinced both governments that the grounds for political gain lay elsewhere. Nonetheless, for Portugal, these wars had positive consequences from a fiscal point of view. In 1385, the *Cortes* – an assembly of representatives of the ecclesiastical, noble and popular orders – voted for the *sisas*, a tax on commercial transactions. Thereafter, this tax became the main source of fiscal revenue of the Portuguese crown. Curiously, the name of a similar Castilian tax – *alcavalas* – became a synonym for obstacles to trade in Portuguese. The extension of the fiscal rights of the crown beyond the traditional tariffs was unpopular due to increases and inflation. However, as the main Portuguese chronicler of these wars, Fernão Lopes, wrote, 'it is better for the kingdom to suffer, than to be lost'.[2]

The Portuguese kings chose to expand in Morocco for three main reasons. First, the infidel status of the country facilitated the portrayal of military endeavours there as a holy war. Second, Moroccan towns were points of arrival for trans-Saharan gold caravans and promised good business opportunities. Third, the country had been badly hurt, like the rest of the Mediterranean world, by the demographic crisis of the fourteenth century, so expansion seemed to present few problems. However, only the first proposition proved to be correct and the Portuguese found conquest to be more difficult than expected. Things began well in Ceuta (1415), but further advances were delayed until the third quarter of the century, and involved some bitter defeats. Moreover, Portuguese possessions remained isolated fortresses in a hostile country and so their economic value dwindled, as profitable trade looked for alternative outlets.[3]

Fortunately, Portugal had other cards to play. Not only were fishermen and traders ready to find fresh ground for maritime endeavours, but also, as would be expected in a feudal society, ecclesiastical and aristocratic lords were ready to give formal backing to these endeavours.

---

[2] F. Lopes, *Chronica de El-Rei D. João I* (Lisbon: Escriptorio, Bibliotheca Clássicos Portugueses, 1897–1898), Vol. I, p. 150: 'mais val terra padecer, que terra se perder'.
[3] V. Magalhães Godinho, *L'economie de l'empire Portugais, Os Descobrimentos e a Economia Mundial* (Lisbon: Editorial Presença, 1963–1971).

They traditionally provided judicial and defence services, collecting fiscal revenue in return. The feudal character of the Portuguese and Iberian societies in the medieval period has been the subject of much debate.[4] The tithe represented a general ecclesiastical tax paid by all Portuguese subjects. Local taxes called *foros* formed the basis of the feudal tax system that, according to geographical area, benefited local ecclesiastical or aristocratic lords, vassals to the king, or the king himself, if he happened to be the direct local lord.

Particularly active were the Knights of Christ, a religious military order established by the Portuguese branch of the Knights Templar when the order was suppressed. A member of the royal family named Henry the Navigator led the order. Although he hardly set foot on a ship himself, Henry promoted seaborne activities, and was rewarded with control of Madeira (late 1410s), the Azores (1430s) and trade with the western coast of Africa (1430s). This last eventually provided a direct link to the trans-Saharan gold trade, bypassing Muslim interlopers, as well as direct trade in ivory and slaves. Seafaring improvements were needed for these activities and important innovations facilitated regular high-seas voyages and the astronomical determination of latitude and longitude.

Slowly but surely, these maritime endeavours began to return profits and to provide a basis for further explorations. It is important to mention the economic organization of the colonization of Madeira and the Azores, because of their importance as experimental schemes in the colonization of the New World. Madeira was the first example of a plantation economy, set up when the Portuguese colonists discovered its suitability for the production of sugar. A slave workforce brought from the Canary Islands and the west coast of Africa became the backbone of this first epoch of Madeira's economy, which ended during the sixteenth century due to increased competition from American plantations (the second trump card of Madeira's economy would be the vineyard, developed during the seventeenth century). The Azores was the first example of a settlement economy, where European peasants tried to reproduce small-scale farming of typical European crops. At the same time, the gold, ivory and slave trade of the west coast of Africa also prospered.

During the 1460s, the eastward orientation of the northern coast of the Gulf of Guinea engendered hopes of a south-east route to the Indian Ocean. As these hopes were ended by the discovery of

---

[4] On the Portuguese side of the question see J. Mattoso, *A identificação de um país, ensaio sobre as origens de Portugal, 1096–1325*, 2 vols. (Lisbon: Editorial Estampa, 1985).

the southward turn of the African coast in the region of Cameroon, consolidation of the first Portuguese empire was framed on a concentration of all business in the hands of the crown. Credit for this concentration of power is usually given to King John II, who became the crucial figure in Portugal's centralization of royal power in the face of the traditional privileges of ecclesiastical and feudal lords, typical of late medieval and early modern Europe. (Of course, the centralization of royal power did not mean the suppression of the plurality of providers of public goods and fiscal systems, which survived until the early nineteenth century.) Expeditions followed that aimed to discover the south-east passage to the Indian Ocean, and succeeded in 1488 (Bartolomeu Dias's voyage). The fact that a further decade was needed to transform this discovery into a practical trade route by Vasco da Gama's voyage clearly illustrates the technological and financial difficulties of the project.

The first world system: a pioneer mercantile state

In the beginning of the sixteenth century the Portuguese mercantile empire comprised two elements. One was the splendid success of the 'Cape (sea) route' to India, monopolized by the Portuguese crown. This success was due to the potential for importing exotic Asian goods to European markets with low transportation costs.[5] Merchants were often authorized to engage in private business, but paid lump sums and custom duties for the privilege. Other European states were too busy building centralized administrations and for some time Portugal was alone in risking economic resources in uncertain enterprises. Thus, the premature Portuguese centralized state enjoyed a monopoly for a substantial period of time. Another element was Atlantic and Brazilian trade, under the divided control established by the Treaty of Tordesillas with Castile. The treaty was signed in 1494, roughly mid way between the two pioneering ocean voyages that opened the world: Columbus (1492) and da Gama (1498). Foreign competitors soon appeared and private business dominated, although the obligation to use Portuguese ports for the intermediation of colonial trade (the main rule of the Colonial Pact) was soon introduced.

The Cape route was particularly successful, as it accrued high profits on the goods brought from Asia into Lisbon, before they were re-exported to the rest of Europe. Foreign trade became an important source of fiscal revenues, particularly because of the monopolistic conditions

---

[5] Godinho, *L'economie de l'empire Portugais*.

in this trade for a long time. Revenues from duties on imports and exports multiplied seventeen-fold at the port of Lisbon from 1496 to 1593.[6] They may be considered as 'rent' provided by the exploitation of monopolistic conditions. While some core European countries were involved in warfare, the smallest of the Iberian countries ruled the waves of the first world system.[7] Charles V's empire mainly opposed France (1521–56) and Turkey (1569–80).[8]

It is important to consider if highly centralized state revenues helped to build a large trade empire, or if the large Portuguese trade empire of the sixteenth century helped to build the centralized state, as happened in England (according to Martin Daunton in Chapter 5). Although Portugal could not rule and administer vast territories in Asia, control over a network of strategic commercial centres through military fortresses and a superior naval power over local navies were enough to direct Asian trade. This system of ruling vast regions at minimum cost was invented by Afonso de Albuquerque and Francisco de Almeida.

In an abstract model, the ideal mercantile state monopolizes the connections between two important markets. From the foreign market (Asia) came the cargoes of an important commodity (at first chiefly pepper, later other 'drugs' such as cinnamon, cloves, nutmeg, coffee, etc., cotton and silk textiles, sophisticated pottery, etc.). As Camões put it:

> Leva a pimenta ardente que comprara;
> A seca flor de Banda não ficou;
> A noz e o negro cravo, que faz clara
> A nova ilha deMoluco, com a canela
> Com que Ceilão é rica, ilustre e bela
> (Camões, Lusíadas, IX, 14)

> [For he had some Malabaris, seized
> From those dispatched by Samorin
> When he returned the imprisoned factors;
> He had not peppers he had purchased;
> There was mace from the Banda Islands;
> Then nutmeg and black cloves, pride

---

[6] V. Magalhães Godinho, 'Finanças públicas e estrutura do estado', *Ensaios II* (Lisbon: Livraria Sá da Costa Editora, 1978), p. 56.

[7] G. Modelsky and W. Thompson, *Seapower in global politics 1494–1993* (Seattle: University of Washington Press, 1988).

[8] On the Portuguese efforts to preserve monopoly conditions for navigation and trade against piracy, see V. Magalhães Godinho, 'As incidências da pirataria e da concorrência na economia marítima portuguesa no século XVI', *Ensaios II* (Lisbon: Sá da Costa Editora, 1978).

> Of the new-found Moluccas, and cinnamon,
> The wealth, the fame, the beauty of Ceylon.][9]

The ideal mercantile state buys commodities and brings them to the home market (Europe) to be sold to eager and wealthy consumers. The profit of the operation is, of course, the product of the quantity bought, transported and sold, by the unit profit, which is the difference between the selling price and the sum of the buying price and the transport price.

Of course, what I call 'transport price' must include not only the transport price in the strict sense (which corresponds to the freight that would be paid to a provider of transportation services), but also the losses of cargo in shipwrecks (which corresponds to the premium that would be paid to a provider of insurance services) and the protection costs against predators of the business (mainly European and Maghrebin pirates in North Atlantic waters between the Azores and the Portuguese mainland). Of course, the ideal mercantile state provides transportation and protection and seldom makes insurance contracts.

The short-term strategic variable to be manipulated by the ideal mercantile state is, of course, the quantity of commodity to be bought, transported and sold. In practice, the ruler of the ideal mercantile state must find a middle ground between the absence of connections between two markets (which ensures a maximum difference between the selling and buying prices, but provides no profit, because there is no trade) and the full connection between the two markets (which reduces the difference between the selling and buying prices to the level of the transportation prices, and, therefore, also provides no profit).

The short-term problem is to find the best mid way to maximize total profit. The long-term problem is to preserve the monopoly of the connection, the familiar case of barriers to entrance. The main issue in the case of sixteenth-century Portugal is that the monopoly rested on the exclusivity of the technological and geographical knowledge needed to sail the Cape of Good Hope route, something that was impossible to preserve in the long run due to information leaks or because potential competitors could imitate the Portuguese by trial and error (and it was impossible for the Portuguese to ensure full control of the 'closed' sea they claimed in the South Atlantic and South Indian Oceans). 'In a century, between 1490–1496 and 1593, the revenue of the custom of Lisbon was multiplied by 17 – more than three times the coefficient of the increase in the kingdom. [...] The demonstration is peremptory: the

---

[9] L. Vaz de Camões, *Os Lusíadas*, trans. Landeg White, *The Lusiads* (Oxford University Press, 1997), p. 179.

institutions of monarchy and Portuguese state are rooted in the trade and the ocean navigation since the beginnings of the 1500s, and not in the land rent, or even domestic circulation."[10] By the late sixteenth century, the Portuguese monopoly of the Cape route collapsed, the result of competition from Dutch, English and French merchants. Portugal tried to resist throughout most of the seventeenth century, but by the 1660s it had only a minor share of the Cape route trade.

The second world system: the first step towards a fiscal state

Profitable activities attracted new partners. Before the 1560s, the main danger was piracy, as six large ships per year were enough to carry the annual cargoes. From the 1560s onwards, European countries attempted to manage sea voyages to Asia with new naval expertise, which put an end to the century-long Portuguese monopoly of the trade in Asian goods. Fluyts and other new ships were faster and more easily manoeuvred.[11] As European countries began trading in the Indian Ocean and conquering strategic seaports from 1620 to 1660, competition became the rule in the market with the actions of British and Dutch companies.[12] Due to the development of more efficient economic and financial institutions by those countries, Portugal lagged behind.[13]

Nevertheless, the number of rival European states engaging in geopolitical and mercantilist competition for trade and colonial empires was limited. Historical global conditions were much closer to the conditions of an oligopoly, with a succession of leading powers in the world market. In this second world system Portugal could no longer perform the leading role it had in the sixteenth century, and behaved as a follower. Modelsky and Thompson also refer to the 1580s as the turning point from the first to the second world system.[14] The trade in tropical commodities from the Americas was organized as an informal cartel – an oligopoly with separated production areas, monopolized selling areas in

[10] Godinho "Finanças Públicas e estrutura do estado", pp. 56–7.
[11] S. Monteiro, *Batalhas e combates da marinha portuguesa* (Lisbon: Sá da Costa Editora, 1990–93).
[12] Godinho refers to 1580 as a turning point. V. Magalhães Godinho, '1580 e a Restauração', *Ensaios II* (Lisbon: Livraria Sá da Costa Editora, 1978).
[13] This interpretation follows D. North, 'Institutions, transaction costs, and the rise of merchant empires', in *The political economy of merchant empires, 1350–1750* (Cambridge University Press, 1991).
[14] Modelsky and Thomson, *Seapower in global politics*. See also George Modelsky (ed.), *Documenting global leadership* (Seattle and London: University of Washington Press, 1988).

parts of Europe and competition in others. Wars between mercantilist states may be compared to redistribution processes within this cartel.[15]

For Portugal, the most favourable production area for trade in the second world system was Brazil. From the 1580s onwards, the origin of tropical goods that were traded in Lisbon shifted towards Brazilian coasts. Several tropical goods valued in European markets could be produced in this Portuguese colony, and provided high revenues. Brazilian sugar was cultivated by an African slave labour force and dominated Brazilian exports. However, dye-producing wood and tobacco were also attractive, providing large exports to Lisbon.[16] European countries managed to cultivate sugar in other South American possessions from 1650, and free business conditions were available for Portuguese merchants and private businesses. Decreasing prices in tropical goods (particularly sugar) in European markets were due to competition between Brazil and other producers (such as Dutch, French, English and Spanish colonies), as the provision of European markets by all these states reduced each one's share in the cargoes and lowered prices. According to Godinho's data for 1588, 1607 and 1619, the central state enjoyed stability in the main sources of revenues (which were about 1,110 *contos*, 1,439 *contos* and 1,556 *contos*, respectively) because 'a long trend for economic depression hurt the seventeenth century ..., which affects state revenues'.[17]

The eventual reduction of tax revenues from Brazilian trade and increases in expenditure due to war (against the United Provinces, England and France in order to preserve overseas possessions, and against the western Habsburg Empire to restore Portuguese autonomy) forced the Portuguese exchequer to introduce new taxes on consumption (*Real d'água*, a tax on the consumption of wine and meat, created in the 1630s) and income (royal tithe in the 1640s). Thus, the Portuguese state began to develop a more fiscal, and less mercantile, profile. As always, wartime periods obliged the creation of new taxes to support military expenditures. Defence was a first-rank priority and severe foreign tension gave way to an increasing tax burden.[18]

---

[15] On the movement of the core of the Portuguese colonial empire from Asia to Brazil, see V. Magalhães Godinho, 'Portugal, as frotas do açúcar e as frotas do ouro (1670–1770)', in *Ensaios II* (Lisbon: Livraria Sá da Costa Editora, 1978).

[16] J. Vicente Serrão, 'O quadro económico: Configurações estruturais e tendências de evolução', in J. Mattoso, *História de Portugal* (Lisbon: Círculo de Leitores, 1992–94).

[17] Godinho "Finanças Públicas e estrutura do estado", pp. 65–68 for data and p. 70 for the quotation.

[18] J. Braga Macedo, Á. Ferreira Silva and R. Martins Sousa, 'War, taxes and gold: the inheritance of the real', in M. Bordo and R. Cortes-Conde (eds.), *Transferring wealth*

When peace returned, the royal tithe was not abolished, and instead took a permanent place alongside excises and consumption taxes. These taxes were the principal basis for the future Portuguese fiscal system. Duties provided high revenues and the Portuguese central state could continue to feed its budget, as colonization in Brazil provided a mercantile revenue for the Portuguese exchequer. Heavy customs in overall taxation resulted not only from greater volumes of trade, but also from the easing of tax on imports. In Lisbon, a modest number of officers were enough to collect huge amounts of revenue. In 1641 and 1681 Lisbon customs represented 88 and 79 per cent of total customs revenue respectively.[19]

In the 1680s, gold mines were discovered in Minas Gerais in Brazil. A tax amounting to one-fifth of gold inflows from Brazil provided huge amounts of gold for coinage and supported public expenditure in the first half of the eighteenth century (from 1695 to 1754). Public revenues in 1716 already amounted to 3,792 *contos*, 'almost double those of thirty five years earlier', in real terms.[20] Because of the availability of large quantities of gold, this was the second significant role for Portugal in the world system and solidly supported its leading position in the world market. Brazilian-Portuguese gold fuelled trade with Great Britain and the Baltic region, and provided access to silver for trade in Asia. However, this new model was short-lived as Brazilian gold was almost exhausted by the middle of the eighteenth century.[21]

The Portuguese central state needed to satisfy permanent financial expenditures with domestic fiscal revenues, as did other European states. The Brazilian gold boom coincided with an elevated role for domestic taxes for two reasons. First, the eighteenth-century Portuguese kings inherited old domestic taxes (created in times of foreign threat, as explained above). Second, the Portuguese economy saw a period of short-term prosperity (rooted mainly in wine exports) that was not followed by long-term development. In this sense, the Portuguese case does not fit neatly into the European central state profile. As the country was much poorer, customs and rents from monopolies still provided much higher returns. Average data for the period 1762–76 (see Table 9.1) serves to illustrate this situation.

and power from the old to the new world: monetary and fiscal institutions in the 17th through the 19th centuries (Cambridge University Press, 2001).

[19] S. Sideri, *Comércio e poder : Colonialismo informal nas relações anglo-portuguesas* (Lisbon: Edições Cosmos, 1970).
[20] Godinho "Finanças Públicas e estrutura do estado", p. 71.
[21] J. Borges de Macedo, *A situação económica no tempo de Pombal – alguns aspectos* (Lisbon: Morais, 1982).

Table 9.1. *Portuguese public revenues*

Customs (domestic and foreign)	24.15%
Tobacco	17.00%
1/5 on gold	11.75%
Diamonds	4.95%
Royal tithe	10.35%
Sundry revenues	6.7%
Excise	6.25%
Overseas revenues	5.35%
Brazil wood	2.35%
TOTAL	100% (= 5,253 *contos*)

Source: F. Tomaz, 'As finanças do estado Pombalino, 1762–1776', in *Estudos e ensaios em homenagem a Vitorino Magalhães Godinho* (Lisbon: Sá da Costa Editora, 1988), pp. 362–3.

Moreover, the Old Regime allowed great discrepancies in taxation according to social status, birth conditions and local traditions. Only three taxes applied to everybody: two of them had been created in the past under threat of war while a local consumer tax, particularly on meat and wine, was absorbed by the central state in the seventeenth century and applied to all subjects and territories. As in other European countries, the late eighteenth century brought political centralization to Portugal and broader activities for the central state. Under pressure to move towards more secure collection, the government created a tax on wine, the staple agricultural export. The tax was created to support the University of Coimbra, and because of this association with higher education, it received the special name of 'literary subsidy' (*subsidio literario*).

In 1761, in order to increase efficient assessments and collections of revenue, Pombal's enlightened government introduced centralized accounting in the Royal Exchequer (*Erario Regio*). Functions included defence, justice, administration over the national territory, and education. In such an illiterate country, literacy became a concern and university teaching even demanded the creation of the *subsidio literario*, as explained above. However, this was only a first step towards a fiscal profile.

The second step towards a fiscal state

Wars against revolutionary and imperial France (1793–95, 1801) called for a new stamp tax and consumption tax. Furthermore, French occupations (1807–08, 1809, 1810–12) forced the royal family to take refuge in Brazil and to open ports to direct foreign trade. Brazilian independence soon followed (1822) and put an end to all remnants of the old mercantile state. As the Indian and Brazilian colonial empires were gone, and a new African colonial empire would not be created until after the Berlin conference in the late nineteenth century, a clear fiscal profile was imposed on the Portuguese state. The new African colonial empire was too poor in comparison with the previous empires and did not enjoy huge mercantile success.[22]

These changes present similarities with European liberal states.[23] Romantic ideas of freedom, equality and fraternity were widespread in the late eighteenth century and brought new ideals of justice and equity. The concept of the citizen aided the fiscal development of centralized states. The progress of fiscal systems in Portugal, as in other countries, was aided by the use of liberal ideas to frame new institutional arrangements, to abolish Church and feudal taxes, and to expand fiscal revenues in order to absorb traditional taxes. This was a slow and painful process. In Portugal, the imposition of a constitutional monarchy (1828–34) created a civil war and further decades of civil unrest (1830s and 1840s). Foreign borrowing supported the military expenditure needed to restore peaceful conditions. Liberal victory resulted in the legitimization of the central state as the only institution with the authority to collect taxes. Centralized states' monopolies on taxation allowed for the expansion of state revenues all over Europe. By expanding public tax collection, states aimed to fill the gap left by the abolition of other fiscal systems and to profit from the citizens' ability to pay. Despite the fact that many could afford the new tax burdens, resistance was common. Fiscal pressure often incited mob uprisings and social unrest, even though there was a general acceptance of new systems of public finance that were constitutionally established. The 'Maria-da-Fonte revolt' in the 1840s and the *Janeirinha* in Lisbon and Oporto in 1868 were the most visible episodes of resistance, and were sparked by two attempts to increase taxation.[24] These episodes may be interpreted as markers of a level of unease with the new taxes. Moreover, tax evasion was common, particularly in a small, poor country, where

[22] W. G. Clarence-Smith, *The third Portuguese colonial empire – a study in economic imperialism* (Manchester University Press, 1985).
[23] F. Comín, *Historia de la hacienda pública de España, 1808–1995* (Barcelona: Editorial Crítica, 1996), pp. 169–236.
[24] M. E. Mata, 'A actividade revolucionária no Portugal contemporâneo, uma perspectiva de longa duração', *Análise Social* 26:112–13 (1991), 755–69.

Table 9.2. *Ratio of customs revenues to fiscal revenue (%)*

Year	UK	Italy	France	Germany	Spain	Portugal
1850	23	—	9	22	13	41 [1852]
1860	37	16	7	16	11	44
1870	35	10	6	56	11	33
1880	29	12	9	56	15	39
1890	28	19	14	56	17	43
1900	23	19	12	53	18	33
1910	28	21	15	44	15	31

Sources: F. Comín, *Historia de la hacienda pública de España, 1808–1995* (Barcelona: Editorial Crítica, 1996), p. 219; M. E. Mata, *As Finanças Públicas Da Regeneração À Primeira Guerra Mundial* (Lisbon: Banco de Portugal, 1993), pp. 129, 136.

extraordinary customs duties had in earlier times relieved taxpayers of burdens by providing colonial revenues for the exchequer.

In nineteenth-century Portugal, government attempts to expand fiscal exaction led to the division of the traditional royal tithe into different taxes according to various taxable revenues (land, industry, etc.), in order to increase the collection throughout the 1850s and 1860s. However, customs continued to provide the lion's share for the exchequer. Table 9.2 shows comparative European data.

With the exception of Germany, the importance of customs duties in Portugal was unequalled in the selected sample of European countries in Table 9.2. This fact may result from the small size and the openness of the Portuguese economy, but it is surely also linked to three centuries of imperial customs. Other explanations may reside in the lower exaction cost of customs revenues and the lower political cost if compared to indirect and (especially) direct taxation.

Increased efficiency in tax collection meant improved public administration and the extension of the state bureaucracy throughout the country. This was a priority for the centralized state from the 1840s onwards, in order to develop a national fiscal network. However, high transportation and communication costs presented real problems, which were exacerbated by the fact that private initiatives generally built transportation facilities in Europe, but this was not the case in Portugal. In this way, difficulties arose in the administration of the Atlantic islands of Azores and Madeira. Facilities and services such as roads, railways, telegraph and later telephones, were presented in Portugal as being key to economic growth and modernization, and their cost was a source of considerable concern, as the goal of an efficient, viable Portuguese state included the provision of these services.

In this way, Portuguese politicians in the second half of the nineteenth century equated progress with material infrastructures and the provision of public goods.[25] Such a framework meant state subsidies for private companies or public provision in the case of the failure of a private operator. The state required more revenue for these new functions, which included health and education facilities as well as those outlined above. However, several obstacles to the collection of revenues existed. Rampant smuggling and tax evasion dented state revenues. Furthermore, traditional upper-class groups seem to have been the most evasive of Portuguese nineteenth-century taxpayers. It is known that land-owners sought to hide land revenues and failed to include properties in the national land cadastre.[26] Newly created luxury taxes based on external indicators of consumption, such as domestic waiters, carriages, coats of arms and transportation horses produced low revenues. In 1880, a deputy commented on the low number of taxpayers:

In Portugal taxes are not paid according to individual property, but inversely to political influence ... I will recall, as a simple example among so many others, an article of the luxury tax: only 33 persons pay tax for using coats of arms on their carriages!

In Portugal, where aristocracy is so abundant, where the class decorated with honorific titles is so large, where aristocracy has grown in a fantastic way [...] in Portugal where there are so many aristocrats, that their number even surpasses the non-aristocrats, it is strange that only 33 taxpayers pay for the use of arms on their carriages.[27]

As Comín noted, tax evasion was commonplace in Latin countries.[28] Tax evasion coupled with enlarged expenditure meant high public deficits, which were supported by public debt. In an increasingly globalized world, borrowing was easy at large European stock exchanges and the government planned an indebtedness cycle for Portuguese public finances. According to government blueprints, the foreign debt would be paid in the future, but in the early 1890s the state became partially

---

[25] M. E. Mata, 'As três fases do Fontismo: Projectos e realizações' in V. Magalhães Godinho, *Estudos e ensaios em homenagem a Vitorino Magalhães Godinho* (Lisbon: Sá da Costa Editora, 1988).

[26] M. E. Mata, 'A contribuição predial, contribuição de repartição ou contribuição por quota', *Revista de História Económica e Social* 24 (1988), 115–31.

[27] Deputy José Rodrigues de Freitas, *'Diário das Sessões da Câmara dos Deputados'*, session of 14 May 1880, DSD114, Parliament Archive, p. 2087.

[28] Comín, *Historia de la hacienda pública*, pp. 227–32.

bankrupt. The inefficiency of the approach chosen by the government is difficult to disguise.

According to a general pattern, there are three main phases for public indebtedness (which were planned by the Portuguese government in the 1850s).[29] In a first phase, a central state may seek loans and borrow from the market in order to finance public expenditure for investment. Justifications for this may include the failures of the market, the need for providing satisfaction of needs to present generations, the role of public goods in stimulating economic growth and welfare, and the long-term character of consumption provided by material infrastructures, which lasts for several generations. As future generations would also use the service of public investment, it should only be fair that present and future generations would finance their building together. Public debt left from present generations to future generations represents their participation in this collective effort. This phase is characterized by net government borrowing.

In a second phase, the government stops borrowing, society benefits from the public goods, previous investment matures, and gross domestic product and exports improve. As economic growth improves the government services the public debt.

In a third phase, previous public investment generates multiplier effects and, not only does society benefit from increased welfare, but the government can collect higher taxes on expanded economic activities in order to service the debt.

What went wrong in Portugal? In the initial state public debt already afflicted Portugal, as government turned to extensive borrowing when establishing the liberal regime. Domestic and foreign borrowing increased from the 1850s to the end of the 1880s, when leading European stock exchanges provided sizable loans to the Portuguese government. However, the more Portuguese bonds were issued and offered in foreign financial markets, the lower were their quotations in those markets. According to the official intelligence of the London Stock Exchange, the first world financial centre, they were frequently below 50 per cent, meaning that the real interest rate was more than twice the nominal interest rate. In this way, the funding collected from loans was small, although the Portuguese Exchequer was becoming responsible for high nominal amounts of foreign public debt, and international payments for the service were increasing more and more.

---

[29] For a Brazilian analysis, see M. de Paiva Abreu, 'A dívida pública externa do Brasil 1824–1931', Working-paper nº 83, Department of Economics, PUC, Rio de Janeiro.

Table 9.3a. *Portuguese foreign indebtedness compared to GDP, collected taxes, the service of the public debt and exports*

Year	D	Y	T	S	X
1851	83	255	9	4.7	?
1861	136	366	11	8.1	14.3
1871	308	469	15	15.0	22.4
1881	417	634	23	19.9	25.5
1891	583	811	30	29.6	31.4

Notes: 'D' means net borrowing, 'Y' represents gross domestic product, 'T' is the amount of tax collection, 'S' means the service of foreign public debt, and 'X' represents exports; units: D, Y, S and T in thousands of *contos*; source: M. E. Mata, *As Finanças Públicas Da Regeneração À Primeira Guerra Mundial* (Lisbon: Banco de Portugal, 1993), p. 255.

Table 9.3b. *Portuguese foreign indebtedness compared to the growth of GDP, collected taxes, the service of the public debt and exports*

Year	ΔD/D	d	ΔY/Y	y	ΔT/T	t	ΔS/S	s	ΔX/X	x
1851–61	0.64	4.7%	0.44	3.7%	0.22	2.0%	0.72	5.6%	?	?
1861–71	3.24	8.5%	0.28	2.5%	0.36	3.2%	0.84	6.3%	0.56	4.6
1871–81	0.63	3.1%	0.35	3.1%	0.53	4.4%	0.33	2.9%	0.14	1.3
1881–91	1.523	3.4%	0.28	2.5%	0.30	2.7%	0.49	4.1%	0.23	2.1

Notes: legend: 'ΔD/D' is the variation of net borrowing, 'ΔY/Y' is the variation of gross domestic product, 'ΔT/T' is the variation of tax collection, 'ΔS/S' is the variation of foreign public debt service, and 'ΔX/X' the variation of exports, while 'd' is the average annual accumulated growth rate of net borrowing, 'y' is the average annual accumulated growth rate of gross domestic product, 't' is the average annual accumulated growth rate of the amount of collected taxes, 's' is the average annual accumulated growth rate of the foreign public debt service, and 'x' is the average annual accumulated growth rate of exports; unit: D, Y, S and T in thousands of *contos*; source: calculations on Table 9.3a.).

Tables 9.3a and b provide the data. Borrowing outstripped economic growth. Borrowing also grew faster than tax revenues. The second and third phases outlined above were never reached.

The 1850s and 1860s correspond to the first phase of the indebtedness model. Borrowing did not stop in the following two decades. According to the public accounts, the product of public loans was larger than the total public investment pursued throughout these decades.[30] Borrowed revenues were used not only for public investment but also for expenditure:

Loans not always impoverish; they may even contribute to wealth if consumed in useful applications. If the loans the Portuguese government issued [...] would have been exclusively applied to the material and moral development of the country, we would be today the most flourishing and prosperous people of the world. Unfortunately, we have borrowed for ordinary expenditure, for the quotidian bread. Those who will come after us receive an immense debt as an inheritance, two railroads, half a dozen roads, and some, very few, schools. They buy these benefits expensively.[31]

Investment did not increase the GDP enough for sufficient taxes to be collected to service the entire public debt. Most of the public investment was devoted to building road and rail networks, to improving seaports and urban infrastructures. Not only did this effort require the importation of instruments and technology (which translated into problems for the trade balance), it also failed to stimulate industrial production and exports, because it is very well known today that public investment in transportation facilities and infrastructure has a long-run maturation character.[32] Another endeavour for public investment was the establishment of national networks for primary education in rural areas, and technical and high-school education in the large urban centres. The effects of educational improvements on industrialization were also far from immediate, as it is also well known today that these, too, produce benefits more in the very long run. Factories produced for cash-strapped consumers in a small domestic market, and there were several more difficulties in foreign markets where other industrialized countries dominated. With the exception of the 1870s, the public debt grew faster than taxes. Exports grew at a slower rate than foreign public debt service. Tables 9.3a and b show the poor performance of Portuguese exports and fiscal collection, when compared with the service of the public debt. This means that large-scale inefficiency in fundraising was coupled with a policy of excessively delayed reward effects for the resource allocation. In short, the ideal model did not work. Before the

[30] M. E. Mata, 'Order and progress or order versus progress? The Portuguese social dilemma of the mid 19th century', *Estudos de Economia* XIII:2 (1993), 115–28.
[31] F. Lobo, *As Confissões dos Ministros de Portugal 1832 a 1871* (Lisbon: Typographia Lisbonense, 1871), p. 90.
[32] M. E. Mata and N. Valério, 'Monetary stability, fiscal discipline and economic performance: the experience of Portugal since 1854', in B. Eichengreen, J. Reis and J. B. Macedo (eds.), *Currency convertibility. The gold standard and beyond* (London and New York: Routledge, 1996), pp. 204–27.

third phase was attained, state bankruptcy was unavoidable.[33] The principal reason for this was state inefficiency.

As Comín has noted: 'when the government is unable to fulfil the payment of public debt interest, bankruptcy shall be declared, openly or disguisedly.'[34] In 1892, Portugal's partial bankruptcy brought on a forced decrease of interest to 1 per cent and a suspension of amortization, evident in the government decree of June 1892, in the wake of the Baring crisis. The bank had traditionally been a lender to the Portuguese government. Short-run loans that were usually received as floating debt were no longer obtainable because of the South American crisis. The payment of interest and amortization could not be realized. From a geopolitical perspective, by the end of the nineteenth century, the sixteenth-century pioneer of overseas exploration had become an underdeveloped, indebted country. Political, literary and philosophical discussions on themes of decadency became widespread.

The bankruptcy of 1892 may be considered as an attempt to decrease $\Delta D/D$ through a decrease in the interest rate in order to reduce it to values close to the rate of GDP growth. The outflow of capital for debt service, coupled with a trade deficit, had brought on a shortage of metal in Portuguese banks the year before. A run on the banks led to a suspension of convertibility that could not be overcome. As convertibility was a pillar of the gold-standard regime, which had been in place since 1854, the abandonment of the gold standard in 1891 weakened Portugal's ability to obtain international loans. The following year, foreign lenders considered the bankruptcy default as something intolerable, as the Portuguese government failed to meet its obligations with lenders at international stock markets. From then on, foreign credit evaporated. Difficult negotiations with lenders for a conversion of the foreign debt would last until 1902. This financial disaster was laid at the feet of the political regime and especially the monarchy, leading to the victorious Republican revolution, which cast off the royal family and the monarchist regime in 1910.

Deprived of borrowing opportunities, the central state obtained budget equilibrium for ordinary revenues and expenditures in 1894–95, for total revenues and expenditures in 1904–05, and for effective revenues and expenditures in 1912–13, following the first effects of a new fiscal reform in 1911, which reinforced tax collection. This was a

---

[33] Mata, 'As três fases do Fontismo: Projectos e realizações'.
[34] Quoting T. Hoffman and K. Norberg (eds.), *Fiscal Crises, Liberty and Representative Government, 1450–1789* (Stanford University Press, 1994); Comín, *Historia de la hacienda pública*, p. 23.

posthumous exit for the pursued policy of public indebtedness and a final victory for the fiscal state in Portugal.

...

(It would not be for long, however. The exceptional historical events of 1914 would bring the First World War's budget problems, but this is another issue.)

10 Spain: from composite monarchy to nation-state, 1492–1914. An exceptional case?

Francisco Comín Comín and
Bartolomé Yun-Casalilla

Introduction

The history of Spain continues to be explained largely in fiscal terms. High taxation and uncontested Castilian absolutism, it is often claimed, were not only responsible for the economic backwardness of the country in the sixteenth and seventeenth centuries, but also impeded the efficient mobilization of resources during wartime. In the eighteenth century, timid Bourbon fiscal reforms led to incompetence. Thus the Spanish crown was not able to increase fiscal revenues in parallel with other European nations and at the rhythm of international necessity. From this viewpoint, the nineteenth century fiscal state has been considered an archaic system bereft of substantial reforms. Debts provoked by the late-eighteenth-century wars and the loss of colonies absorbed the country's capital, thus preventing economic change. Studied from an exclusively endogenous perspective, the emerging image of the liberal fiscal system is one of radical and absolute failure with economic backwardness as the outcome.

There is no doubt that some of these assertions are still tenable. Yet it is also possible to nuance this image or to provide more sophisticated explanations in the light of recent research in both fiscal and institutional history. The aim of this chapter is to revise some of these arguments or, alternatively, to offer more accurate views by bringing recent advances in political and institutional history as well as some new macroeconomic data into the debate. An asymmetric and occasionally comparative approach with England and France will be also proposed.

Castile and the Habsburg composite monarchy in the sixteenth and seventeenth centuries

In the early modern period, the territory that we today call Spain was a set of independent political units with their own institutional peculiarities:

Castile (with its American dominions), Aragon, Catalonia, Valencia, Majorca and Navarre. All of these political entities were under the rule of the Habsburgs, who were also kings of Sicily, Naples, Sardinia, Portugal and its empire (from 1580 till 1640), as well as Dukes of Milan, Savoy and Burgundy (the Franche-Comté, Flanders, the Low Countries, Luxemburg and the counties of Artois). The Habsburgs' interests were also projected towards areas such as the republic of Genoa, and other European dominions from which they were able to get resources and where their political presence was deep. These dynastic entities comprised an ensemble of political units with their own laws and customs, their own parliaments and fiscal systems and with a high degree of jurisdictional diversity. Nothing that one can call a *Spanish* fiscal system really existed and the fiscal *systems* operating in the space that we today call Spain depended on complex, dynastic games of interests.

Possibilities for raising taxes and financial and military resources, therefore, varied considerably from one dominion to the other, depending on different variables: the political constitution and the norms that regulated relations between king and parliaments, the particularities of the different fiscal systems themselves (type of taxes, the organization of credit, etc.), the demographic and economic characteristics of each area, the position of each dominion in a wider geopolitical and economic context, etc. The result was a high degree of diversity and two clashing logics: a dynastic one aimed at strengthening its 'international' character and a regional one that sought to maintain a strong local character. All of these 'states' were governed by principles of self-sufficiency very common in the epoch: (a) each kingdom's resources could only be used for the defence and good of the same kingdom; and (b) the monarch himself had to be self-sufficient. Only very exceptionally – in particular for the defence of Christendom – was the transference of resources to the king or to other political units under his rule constitutionally correct. In a world of increasing international tensions and wars, these contradictory principles would become the main problem for the Spanish Habsburg composite monarchy.

From the very beginning there were deep differences among the territories in macroeconomic terms. Though our figures should be taken as approximate, Table 10.1 shows that already at the beginning of the period under study Castile represented more than the 90 per cent of the theoretical *regular* income of the 'Spanish' Habsburgs on the Iberian Peninsula and more than the 60 per cent in all the western territories.[1]

---

[1] One should consider that these are very general estimates of crown income, which only give us an order of magnitude. Besides, and this concerns other estimates that

Table 10.1. *Crown income in different territories of the Spanish composite monarchy (data in grams of silver)*

	c. 1530	% of the total
Iberian estates		
Castile	50,394,883	69.1
Catalunya	1,948,750	2.7
Aragon	397,236	0.5
Valencia	658,480	0.9
Navarra	672,819	0.9
TOTAL	54,072,168	74.2
Italian estates		
Naples	10,103,783	13.9
Sicily	1,747,266	2.4
Milan	6,994,121	9.6
TOTAL	18,845,170	25.8
Low Countries	7,234,405	9.9
TOTAL	72,917,338	100.0

Sources: M. Artola, *La Hacienda del Antiguo Régimen* (Madrid: Alianza, 1982), pp. 144–6; B. Hernandez, *Fiscalidad de reinos y deuda pública en la monarquia hispánica del siglo XVI* (Universidad de Cordoba, 2002); M. Rodríguez-Salgado, *Un imperio en transición. Carlos V, Felipe II y su mundo* (Barcelona: Critica, 1992); F. Chabod, *Storia di Milano nell'epoca di Carlo V* (Turin: Einaudi, 1971); F. Calabria, *The cost of the empire. The finances of the Kingdom of Naples in the time of Spanish rule* (Cambridge University Press, 1991), p. 42; M. García Zúñiga, *Hacienda, Población y Precios (siglos XV –XVIII)* (Pamplona: Gobierno de Navarra, 1996); D. Ligresti, 'I bilanci secenteschi del regno di Sicilia', *Rivista Storica Italiana* CIX (1997), 894–937.

we will give in this chapter, the crown's resources were not limited to money, particularly in wartime, when forced billeting and local exactions, which do not appear in these figures, were very common. It was also frequent that cities and local nobilities mobilized men and resources which do not figure in the estimates of central revenues. It is also to be noted that these are theoretical figures (composed by parliament's services, foreseen taxes, etc.) that were not always collected in full and of which a part were used 'in situ' to compensate local elites and to enhance the king's clienteles in the country. These figures refer to regular income and are estimates from the different actors. In no case do they represent anything like a modern budget and they do not even include extraordinary resources coming from special agreements with different sources of money (towns, financial bodies, etc.). We have to admit in any case that more basic research is needed in this sense to produce a clear and precise idea of the big numbers of the Spanish composite monarchy's finances. We consider, however, that these orders of magnitude are already valuable for our purposes here. For the sake of unity with numbers for the period after 1554, we do not include here estimates of the Habsburgs' revenues from Central Europe and their Austrian territories. The sources are registered in Figure 10.1. It is to be noted that for the period before the eighteenth century, they are almost always estimates by civil servants or – in the worst and fewest cases – by observers such as ambassadors and others. They all have an

This meant that, without considering the use of extraordinary resources, by the 1550s the Habsburgs were able to get almost 1,200,000 British pounds from Castile (and America), more or less the equivalent of what the king of France took from his kingdom (see Table 10.2). A territory of five million inhabitants, without considering America, was able to provide as much revenue as another of almost twenty million.[2] It is quite understandable, therefore, that concentrating his efforts in Castile was the immediate and logical aim of Charles V.

The dynamism of the Castilian fiscal state is also evident. Again, Figure 10.1 should be taken cautiously, since before the nineteenth century the figures do not register proper budgets.[3] Yet the tendency in both nominal and real terms is very meaningful. Even in real terms, the Habsburg's theoretical income in Castile multiplied four times during the sixteenth century and maintained that level during the seventeenth century, in spite of the economic crisis of the kingdom and a reduction in the flow of American silver. A comparison with other European states is also revealing. If we consider Table 10.2, where England, France, Holland and Castile are represented, the conclusion is similar. Habsburg income in Castile grew faster than Tudor and Stuart income in England for the whole period, and particularly until the 1620s. Even though French data for 1511–20 can be problematic, it is difficult to imagine a better performance than the Castilian one. The comparison is also positive for the latter if we consider the period 1560–1610, for which the figures are more trustworthy. A comparison between England and Castile in the sixteenth and seventeenth centuries by using income in adjusted values with their respective price indexes shows a

approximate character and that is why we prefer to make general comments on them and to exercise great caution in the comparisons. For the eighteenth and nineteenth century there are more precise estimates produced by the very same fiscal administration of the Bourbons.

[2] We use round figures from J. Nadal, *La poblacion española: Siglos XVI a XX* (Barcelona: Ariel 1984), p. 72; F. Braudel and E. Labrousse (eds.), *Histoire economique et sociale de la France, Vol. I, 1450–1660* (Paris: Presses Universitaires de France, 1993), p. 904. These numbers are even more approximate, since the fact that they are given in constant English pounds at a moment when the price revolution in Spain was very intensive, might provoke some advantages for Castile. We should also say that in fiscal terms – that is deducting the income from American treasures – the Castilian estimates might be reduced by approximately 20 per cent. The difference, however, is big enough to maintain our argument regarding the great fiscal capacity of the Crown of Castile.

[3] It is also to be noted that these figures do not register the whole income of the crown nor do they refer to the whole fiscal burden, since cities, seigniorial landlords and ecclesiastic institutions also collected taxes – sometimes on behalf of the king – which are never included in these estimations. Their quantities, of course, varied over time in proportions impossible to calculate at the moment.

Table 10.2. *Crown revenues in England, France, Holland and Castile, 1500–1700*

	England	Index	France	Index	Holland	Index	Castile	Index
			Current English pounds (x1000)					
1501–10							296	80
1511–20	126	100	1800	100			375	100
1521–30								
1531–40							539	144
1541–50							980	261
1551–60							1193	318
1561–70	251	199	1280	71			1870	499
1571–80	224	178	2620	146			2701	720
1581–90	293	232	3040	169	302	100	2701	720
1591–1600	494	392	2130	118	473	157	4173	1113
1601–10	594	471	2430	135	867	287	4723	1259
1611–20			3070	171	788			
1621–30	605	480	4310	239	1516		3644	971
1631–40			8400	467	1958			
1641–50			9580	532	1799		3071	819
1651–60	1582	1256	10570	587				
1661–70	1634	1297	7640	424				
1671–80	2067	1641	9080	504	5000			
1681–90			9940	552			1256	335

Sources: Our own elaboration with data from R. Lachmann, *Capitalists in spite of themselves* (Oxford University Press, 2000), p. 170; and Figure 10.1, by using the same system to convert ducats into pounds; E. J. Hamilton, *Guerra y precios en España, 1651–1800* (Madrid: Alianza, 1988), p. 63.

similar situation (see Figure 10.2). Castilian resources grew faster than English ones until the first decades of the seventeenth century. From then onwards both demonstrated parallel tendencies until *c.* 1650. During the second half of the seventeenth century and the first decades of the eighteenth, the English crown's regular revenues overtook those of Castile and the pace of growth was faster in England, which can be at least in part attributed to the financial revolution that took place there in the late 1680s.[4] The case is similar when compared to France (see

[4] Our data from the mid seventeenth century may be the weakest of our series. That is why we prefer not to risk much analysis of this period. It is more or less obvious, however, that it was during the second half of the seventeenth century and the first decades of the eighteenth century – that is, during the English financial revolution – when England caught up with Castile.

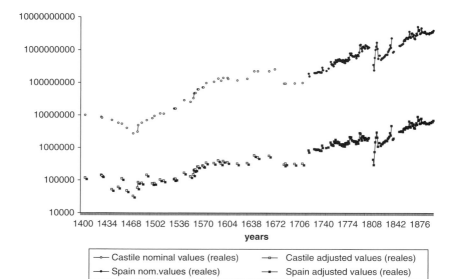

Figure 10.1 Crown revenues in Castile (1400–1715) and Spain (1722–1898)

Sources: Figure 10.1 is based on a variety of very disperse data. Particularly important for the fifteenth century has been M. A. Ladero Quesada, *La Hacienda Real de Castilla en el siglo XV* (Universidad de la Laguna, 1973). Most figures regarding the sixteenth and seventeenth centuries come from I. A. A. Thompson, *War and government in Habsburg Spain* and 'Castile: polity, fiscality and fiscal crisis', in T. Hoffman and K. Norberg (eds.), *Fiscal crises, liberty and representative government, 1450–1789* (Stanford University Press, 1994). We have also used for this period R. Carande, *Carlos V y sus Banqueros*, 2nd edn (Barcelona: Crítica, 1987) and M. Ulloa, *La Hacienda Real de Castilla en el reinado de Felipe II* (Madrid: Fundación Universitaria Española, Seminario Cisneros, 1977); A. Domínguez Ortíz, *Política y Hacienda de Felipe IV*, 6th edn (Madrid: Ediciones Pegaso, 1960); H. Kamen, *La España de Carlos II* (Barcelona: Crítica, 1981); M. Artola, *La Hacienda del Antiguo Régimen* (Madrid: Alianza, 1982). Some figures come from primary sources, such as the writings of Guicciardini in García Mercadal, *Viajes de extranjeros por España y Portugal: Desde los tiempos más remotos hasta comienzos del siglo XX* (Valladolid: Junta de Castilla y León, 1999), or *Estado*, leg. 4 and *Consejo y Juntas de Hacienda*, both in the Archivo General de Simancas. When this text was already finished a new work with figures for the seventeenth century appeared, which does not significantly change the main trends described here. See J. I. Andrés Ucendo and R. Lanza García, 'Estructura y evolución de los ingresos de la Real Hacienda de Castilla en el siglo XVII', *Studia Storica* 30 (2008), 147–90.

Table 10.2). The French fiscal state was clearly more efficient in macro-economic terms by 1621–30 and the rhythm of growth was faster in the second half of the century.

As the historical literature has frequently stressed, this relative fiscal efficiency was grounded in the use of depredatory methods like the capture of private silver cargoes coming from America or the floating of public debt in difficult times.[5] It is obvious that a financial revolution did not occur in Castile. The *Cortes* never controlled state expenditure and

Figure 10.1 (*cont.*)

For the eighteenth century we have used data from R. Pieper, *La Real Hacienda bajo Fernando VI y Carlos III (1753–1788). Repercusiones economicas y sociales* (Madrid: Instituto de Estudios Fiscales, 1992), where data for other periods and authors can also be found. Among them we have also used J. García-Lombardero, 'Algunos problemas de la administración y cobranza de las rentas provinciales en la primera mitad del siglo XVIII', in A. Otazu (ed.), *Dinero y Crédito (siglos XVI al XIX)* (Madrid: Banco Urquijo, 1978). For the second half of the eighteenth century we used figures from P. Merino, 'La Hacienda de Carlos IV', *Hacienda Pública Española* 69 (1981), pp. 139–82 and *Las cuentas de la administración central española, 1750–1820* (Madrid: Servicio de Publicaciones del Ministerio de Economía y Hacienda, 1987).

Our nineteenth-century figures all come from different works by F. Comín, particularly, *Hacienda y economía en la España contemporánea (1800–1936)*, 2 vols (Madrid: Instituto de Estudios Fiscales, 1988).

Price series to deflate nominal values have been taken from G. Feliu, *Precios y salarios en la Cataluña Moderna* (Madrid: Servicio de Estudios del Banco de España, 1991) and D. Reher and E. Ballesteros, 'Precios y salarios en Castilla la Nueva: La construcción de un índice de salarios reales, 1501–1991', *Revista de Historia Económica* 1 (1993), 101–51. Adjusted values for the fifteenth century have been calculated by using the wheat prices index of H. Casado, *Señores, mercaderes y campesinos: la comarca de Burgos a finales de la Edad Media* (Valladolid: Junta de Castilla y León, 1987). Prices and monetary values in silver have been taken also from E. J. Hamilton, *The American treasure and the price revolution in Spain, 1501–1650* (Cambridge, MA: Harvard University Press, 1934) and *War and prices in Spain, 1651–1800* (Cambridge, MA: Harvard University Press, 1947). We wish to thank Leandro Prados de la Escosura for his generosity in giving us his database of Catalan prices covering also the nineteenth century.

---

[5] See, for example, F. Ruiz Martín, 'La banca en España hasta 1782', in *El Banco de España. Una historia económica* (Madrid: Banco de España, 1970), pp. 5–196. The concept of bankruptcy to apply to these events is discussed by E. Lovet, *Philip II and Mateo Vázquez de Leca* (Geneva: Droz, 1977).

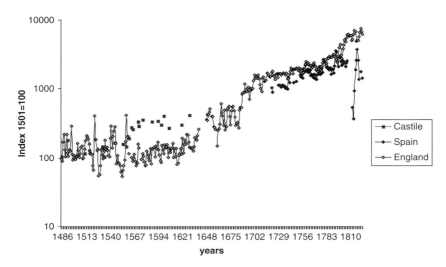

Figure 10.2 Crown revenues in Castile-Spain and England, 1486–1824

Sources: For Castile and Spain, see Figure 10.1. For England, data from P. O'Brien in *The European state finance database project* (Department of History, University of Leicester) directed by R. Bonney; see www.le.ac.uk/hi/bon/ESFDB/frameset.html. Specific price indexes of both countries were used to adjust revenues.

debt. Castile was thus a long way from the system of the post-rebellion Netherlands or that of the more mature financial revolution taking place in England in 1688.[6] Yet one should not think that this absolutist fiscal system was an uncontested iron structure out of control and beyond negotiation, as is commonly understood by economists and historians.[7]

Recent research in institutional and political history shows that the fiscal system pivoted on a set of conflictive pacts and very tense transactions between the monarchy and parliament, representing urban oligarchies as well as other social groups such as the Church, the aristocracy and bankers.

[6] See J. Tracy, *A financial revolution in the Habsburg Netherlands. Renten and rentiers in the County of Holland, 1515–1565* (Berkeley and Los Angeles: University of California Press, 1985); and J. Brewer, *The sinews of power. War, money and the English state, 1688–1783* (Cambridge University Press, 1990).

[7] Though part of their reasoning is addressed in a more complex direction that has to do with the creation of modern parliaments and institutions, these views remain very present in studies such as those of Acemoglou, Robinson and Johnson. See, for example, D. Acemoglou, J. A. Robinson and S. Johnson, 'The rise of Europe: Atlantic trade, institutional change and economic growth', *American Economic Review* 95 (2005), 546–79.

Tellingly, the biggest increases in our figures are explained by moments of the existence of intense negotiations, which refute the idea of a totally unbalanced absolutism. The *servicio ordinario*, a financial 'service' paid by the different towns usually through municipal taxes on consumption, increased during the sixteenth century only after periodic negotiations between king and the *Cortes*. The same might be said of the *servicio de millones*, beginning in the 1590s and the main source of income during the seventeenth century. Approved after very tense discussions between the king and the *Cortes* and then administered by a mixed *Comisión de Millones*, which represented the interests of the kingdom, the *servicio de millones* would end by creating the space for what some have called the kingdom's finances. Even taxes such as the *alcabalas* (originally 10 per cent of all commercial transactions), which was in theory strictly controlled by the king, was a crucial point of bargaining between crown and kingdom. In 1538, as a result of a pact between the two, the crown renounced renting these taxes at a general level in exchange for fixed and renewed payments, which gave the towns the possibility to collect the *alcabalas* within their own walls and territories and under their fiscal control. Peaks in crown revenue during the sixteenth century – in 1561 and 1575 – respond precisely to the negotiated renewal of these taxes. The fact that payments were agreed for long periods, usually more than ten years, proved to be beneficial for the country given the strong devaluation provoked by inflation. This was also a way to give stability and predictability to the king's income, which would be crucial for consolidating debt during the following two decades.

Crown bankruptcy and the capture of American treasure also entailed negotiations. Though these measures were taken by invoking the king's *absoluta potestas*, they also allowed negotiations with bankers, mainly the important Genoese families, on how to transform credits and silver cargoes into consolidated debt. During the sixteenth and seventeenth centuries the crown succeeded in making the Church approve a series of special fiscal services, which compounded one of the more flexible and potentially profitable lines of income. These services resulted from difficult bargaining, on one occasion ending in the local excommunication of Charles V. The same could be said about the services that individual nobles provided for the king, a type of income that obviously is not registered in our figures and whose negotiation was even more complex and diffuse.[8]

---

[8] The extremely rich literature on these matters is summarized in B. Yun-Casalilla, *Marte contra Minerva. El precio del imperio español, c. 1450–1600* (Barcelona: Critica, 2004), chapter 5.

It is also commonplace to explain the Habsburg's fiscal power in Castile by referring almost exclusively to the enormous riches collected in America. Yet some nuances have to be introduced here too. It should be emphasized that growth in the crown's income started much earlier than the 1530s, when American wealth became really important. Figure 10.1 shows that already during the 1480s the fiscal reforms introduced by the monarchs Ferdinand and Isabel had a positive effect. Furthermore, the proportion of precious American metals within total income was lower than one would have expected. Considering our sample, one could say that gold and silver provided only 4 per cent of crown revenue during the period 1501–25; 10 per cent between 1526–50; and 15.4 per cent between 1551–75. In the period 1576–1600, the percentage of precious metals over total revenue reached 20 per cent, and then remained high between 1601–25 at 16.5 per cent. Between 1626–50 it dropped to 11.4 per cent, and then to 11 per cent between 1651–75. A look at Castilian fiscal revenue during the sixteenth century shows that tax revenues, without the Indies, also grew both in nominal and real terms, at least until the last decades of the century.[9] American silver may have made a difference to other European powers, but only during the period 1575–1600 was it a really crucial part of the Habsburg's income. One should keep in mind that these revenues were unpredictable and volatile, which complicated their use as a means of advancing future expenditures by endorsing credit on them.

What was the key to the notorious *relative* efficiency of the Castilian fiscal system between 1500 and 1650 *in purely macroeconomic terms*? The explanation lies in a combination of different factors. The system's base was found in the character of the Castilian economy. As we have demonstrated in other works, by the sixteenth century Castile had the highest urbanization ratio in all Europe, after Italy and the Low Countries. By 1500 the proportion of people living in centres with more than 5,000 inhabitants was higher than in France and England, and this was still the case by 1600. During this period, the relatively fast urbanization process is evident in the fact that Castile's urban population also increased faster than in France or England. Only in the seventeenth and eighteenth centuries were the urbanization ratios in Castile surpassed by England, though never by France.[10] This circumstance highlights a

---

[9] See L. M. Bilbao, 'Ensayo de reconstrucción histórica de la presión fiscal castellana durante el siglo XVI', in E. Fernández de Pinedo (ed.), *Haciendas forales y hacienda real. Homenaje a D. Miguel Artola y D. Felipe Ruiz Martín* (Bilbao: Servicio Editorial, Universidad del País Vasco, 1990), pp. 37–61.

[10] More on this in B. Yun-Casalilla, 'City and countryside in Spain: changing structures, changing relationships, 1450–1800. Some proposals from economics', in J. A.

dynamic economy and an agrarian sector of increasing productivity.[11] In this context American bullion had a negative effect in the long run, as is well known, but it also created a constant flow of cash irrigating the country, which enhanced the potential of the fiscal system and gave Castile one of the main features of the early modern state, being a country where cash circulation was relatively abundant and fluid.[12]

The combination of bargained absolutism with American bullion was crucial and pacts between the crown and the *Cortes* gave political stability. The *encabezamiento de alcabalas* endowed the system with a high degree of security and predictability, thus enhancing the development of consolidated debt in the form of *juros* (debt endorsed by the kingdom's rents), whose origin was in the *asientos*, normally very high-rate and short-term credits given by big financiers. The negotiated character of the fiscal scheme complemented the high monetary fluidity generated by American metals to pave the way for a system that allowed for the conversion of high-rate short-term loans into low-rate long-term *juros*. This process was not restricted to the revenues of the *encabezamiento de alcabalas;* on the contrary, it was also applied to other sources of revenue, whose quantity might be uncertain but whose payment was guaranteed by the political stability and by the security of the crown.

The outcome was a consolidated debt system of unprecedented size in Europe, but which in no way could be considered a financial revolution or a response to political change. The abundance of money was also the key for relatively low rates of public debt. The *juros* – more precisely the *juros al quitar* – ran at 7 per cent interest for most of the century, reaching 5 per cent during the closing decades. This was one of the lowest interest rates in Europe.[13] In spite of the many short-term problems, these relatively low interest rates were enough to mobilize public finances in order to allow the military machinery to function effectively.

All of this was intrinsically linked to another process which is usually neglected in the literature. The conversion of short-term debt,

Marino (ed.), *Early modern history and the social sciences: testing the limits of Braudel's Mediterranean* (Kirksville: Truman State University Press, 2002), pp. 35–70.

[11] For a characterization of the Castilian and Spanish model of economic growth that goes against commonplaces and gives a more positive image, see Yun-Casalilla, *Marte contra Minerva*, pp. 175–244.

[12] C. Tilly, *Coerción, capital y los estados europeos, 990–1990* (Madrid: Alianza, 1990).

[13] See the figures that he gives for private credits in S. Epstein, *Freedom and growth. The rise of states and markets in Europe, 1300–1750* (London: Routledge, 2000), pp. 19–23. The author developed an interesting argument, with which we agree, demonstrating that political institutions are not necessarily the main cause of low risk and transaction costs.

often used by the king for European military campaigns, into a long-term debt endorsed by the kingdom's taxes, implicitly meant that the resources of Castile were used to defend the Habsburgs' interests and other kingdoms. It goes without saying that protests were voiced, particularly within the *Cortes*, but it is also evident that the dynastic and 'international' rationale was prevailing over localism. The Habsburgs were not self-sufficient and obviously used the resources of Castile for their own dynastic purposes. Many *procuradores* of the *Cortes* complained about this to both Charles and Philip, but (and this was the other effect of the pact) the cities, the nobility, the Church, the bankers and other political bodies reluctantly supported the policy as it was often to their advantage.[14]

Curiously enough, this fiscal state cannot be considered to be distinct from a judicial state, to use Schumpeter's terminology, since the fiscal system was ruled by institutions and political bodies with strong juridical components, such as the *Consejo de Hacienda*, of which one of the main functions was not to collect taxes, but to enforce the laws and traditional customs of the kingdom.

The negative side of the Castilian fiscal state

Recent historiography has contended that if we consider the Castilian fiscal system in macroeconomic terms alone, it was not as economically oppressive as previously thought. The crown's income represented approximately 10 per cent of GDP.[15] In addition, some studies have rightly emphasized the importance of public expenditure as a way to compensate for the negative effect of taxes on the domestic economy.[16] It is also obvious today that the so-called crisis of the seventeenth century, probably more dramatic in Castile than in many other areas of Europe, was not caused by the fiscal system alone, but by a set of forces of which this was only a part.[17] All of these considerations help to

---

[14] For more details see Yun-Casalilla, *Marte contra Minerva*, pp. 376–92.

[15] These are assumptions based on the figures of B. Yun-Casalilla, 'The American empire and the Spanish economy: an institutional and regional perspective', in P. O'Brien and L. Prados de la Escosura (eds.), *The costs and benefits of European imperialism from the conquest of Ceuta, 1415, to the treaty of Lusaka, 1974*, Proceedings of the Twelfth International Economic History Congress, *Revista de Historia Económica* XVI, 123–56, here pp. 126 and 128, tables 1 and 2.

[16] I. A. A. Thompson, 'Taxation, military expending and the domestic economy in Castile in the later sixteenth century', in *War and society in Hapsburg Spain* (London: Variorium, 1992).

[17] This is the thesis maintained by Yun-Casalilla in *Marte contra Minerva*, pp. 455–78.

balance, therefore, the traditional negative view. This does not mean, however, that the fiscal system was innocuous in economic terms.

The Castilian fiscal state was based upon a growing diversity of taxes, assessed and collected at local levels, which had crucial consequences for the economy and even for the functioning of the fiscal apparatus. On the one hand, a good part of the king's revenue never reached the Royal Treasury, which of course throws shadows on the over-optimistic interpretation of what we have called the efficiency of the fiscal system in *macroeconomic* terms.[18] On the other hand, the variety of taxes created a fiscal map that was highly fragmented and operated to increase the risks and the degrees of uncertainty in commercial activity, thus obstructing market integration. With the taxes in the hands of local authorities and patricians, the lion's share of the tax burden was borne by artisans and small workshops, mainly in the form of a direct excise on the consumption and trade of basic goods. Thus, despite the overall irrelevance in macroeconomic terms, the way in which taxes were paid could not but generate negative effects on commercial and industrial development. The crucial responsibility was not, therefore, only in the crown's side, but in the way local authorities handled the fiscal burden within towns and villages.

The system had deleterious effects on the financial structure and on business in vital areas of the economy. The international character of the 'composite monarchy' and the empire led to wars in distant regions, whose financing only could be met by the international German and Genoese banking houses. The political alliance between the Habsburgs and the republic of Genoa further enhanced the role of the latter within Castilian public finances. Yet one of the potential positive effects of the Castilian fiscal system – the strengthening of domestic banking – did not become a reality within the country, but in other regions of the Habsburg system, with Genoa in particular benefiting in many different ways.[19]

---

[18] This point, of course, does not nuance at all our assertions in comparative terms, since this problem was always present in all European states of the epoch. See, for example, for the case of France, R. Bonney, *The king's debts: Finance and politics in France, 1589–1661* (Oxford University Press, 1981); and J. B. Collins, *Fiscal limits of absolutism. Direct taxation in early seventeenth-century France* (Berkeley: University of California Press, 1988).

[19] See the different works by F. Ruiz Martín, e.g. 'Las finanzas españolas en tiempos de Felipe II', *Cuadernos de Historia. Anexos de la Revista Hispania* 2 (1968), 109–73; and 'Los hombres de negocios genoveses de España durante el siglo XVI', in H. Kellenbenz (ed.), *Fremde Kaufleute auf der iberischen Halbinsel* (Köln-Vienna: Böhlau, 1970), pp. 84–99.

Despite the attraction of the *juros*, the empire's financial management became extremely expensive. Many *asientos* were obtained at rates of interest between 20 and 30 per cent. This was in part a consequence of the growing Genoese monopoly of the international financial system and also of the fiscal 'violence' that the crown practised in moments of crisis, which elevated risk for this type of credit. It was also the consequence of the lack of a financial revolution.

Furthermore, it is to be noted that the mechanism of consolidating floating debt was not a modern one. As can be deduced from what we have already said, the *juros* circulated in a real market that extended even beyond the Castilian economy. They were sometimes acquired directly from the crown or big bankers. However, a considerable portion of them were the result of 'absolutist actions', which of course did not help to reduce risk and maintained high interest rates. Dramatic increases in debt until the mid seventeenth century demonstrated the weak side of this fiscal system, whose relative efficiency as a machinery for extracting resources we have underlined, but which, at least from today's perspective, had a negative impact on both economy and state in the long run.

The military revolution increased the costs of warfare and with the progressive depreciation of Spain's silver currency in relation to gold – the unit of account in the war zones of northern Europe – the cost of war went up and up. Meanwhile, the issue of debt absorbed a good part of mercantile savings, which contributed to transforming the social structure of the country. The war with Holland, which led to a high proportion of crown expenditure being distributed outside the kingdom, exacerbated the whole situation. The potentially positive effect on the domestic economy via public expenditure, therefore, was lower than one would expect. Instead, other areas of the composite monarchy, such as Lombardy and the Southern Low Countries benefited.

Difficulties in tax collection, the high costs of financial management and the increases in expenditure led to defaults and triggered extraordinary actions like the seizure of cargoes from the Indies, or the sale of public land, jurisdictions and even offices by the crown during the second half of the sixteenth century. The outcome was commercial instability and greater fragmentation of the jurisdictional and fiscal map, with consequent negative effects upon the development of the Spanish economy. Another repercussion was the increasing importance of direct taxes on the domestic consumption of basic products and the lesser relevance of duties on customs, which very much fits with the characteristics of a composite 'international' monarchy whose merchant communities had strong interests in trading among the different kingdoms.

Although the economic recession experienced in Castile from the end of the sixteenth century had an important agrarian component, it is true that the 'fiscal state' model was also a decisive factor. Since the late sixteenth century, the combination of high taxes on artisans and consumers with agrarian stagnation and industrial rigidity resulted in an economic recession that came to be visible by the first decades of the seventeenth century. The spatial compartmentalization of the economy, enhanced by fiscal 'localism' within the cities, gave rise to entry barriers that for several decades limited the possibilities for market integration and industrial specialization.[20] From 1610 onwards, the resort to debasement augmented uncertainty and transaction costs. Despite the reduction of interest rates on state debt – by the end of the seventeenth century many *censos*, a sort of mortgage credit, ran as low as 3 per cent in spite of legal regulations – investment in industry continued to be very low.

Decline flowed in large part from the failure to implement mercantilist policies. This resulted from the agreement between the crown and both the colonial elite and merchant community of Seville, and was linked to the interests of traders from Italy, the Low Countries and other European countries.[21] The Spanish colonial networks were the means of introducing and redistributing products from other countries in the Americas. Political corruption within the Empire – partially associated with absolutist bargaining – increased the protection costs of the composite monarchy without generating the impulse for economic change.[22] Rather than serving as a basis for the reduction of risk and transaction costs at home and abroad, the process of building up (or dismantling?) the state was bringing about the opposite situation.

The seventeenth century was a period in which extraordinary expedients were increasingly implemented: occasional and general *donativos*

---

[20] See B. Yun-Casalilla, 'Manufacturas, mercado interior y redes urbanas: recesión, reajustes y rigideces', in J. Alcalá-Zamora y E. Belenguer (coords.), *Calderón de la Barca y la España del Barroco* (Madrid: Centro de Estudios Políticos y Constitucionales, 2001), Vol. I, pp. 111–28.

[21] On this subject see the different works by J. M. Oliva Melgar, 'La metrópoli sin territorio. ¿Crisis del comercio de Indias en el siglo XVII o pérdida del control del monopolio?', in C. Martínez Shaw and J. M. Oliva Melgar (eds.), *El sistema atlántico español (siglos XVII–XIX)* (Madrid: Marcial Pons Historia, 2005), pp. 19–74; J. M. Oliva Melgar, *El Monopolio de Indias en el siglo XVII y la economía andaluza. La oportunidad que nunca existió* (Huelva: Universidad de Huelva, 2004); and 'La Carrera de Indias del siglo XVII al XVIII: del monopolio centralizado al comercio libre', in B. Yun-Casalilla (ed.), *Del Barroco a la Ilustración, cambio y continuidad. Vol. VII de Historia de Andalucía* (Barcelona: Planeta, 2006), pp. 198–211.

[22] We have developed this idea in greater detail in Yun-Casalilla, 'The American empire'.

(a sort of compulsory credit in exchange for political or economic privileges) from towns and corporations became common and debasement was repeated. Where Castile was concerned, with the 'crisis' in the Atlantic economy, which dramatically affected the crown's revenue in silver, and the demographic, agrarian and urban recession inside the country, it is obvious that this period weighed heavy on the kingdom's shoulders.

In the end, these problems would affect fiscal income too, as can be seen in Figure 10.1, where the decreasing figures of the 1680s reflect the crisis of a fiscal state that had been surpassed by other monarchies in the efficient mobilization of resources. From the beginning of the sixteenth century, pressure was felt in other parts of the composite monarchy, particularly in Naples, where a series of rebellions and independence wars occurred, but also in Sicily, Catalonia, Portugal and even in Castile. The complex fiscal equilibrium within the composite monarchy was broken, which led to political upheaval underlining the failure of the fiscal model.

The fiscal system of a Spanish absolutist proto-nation-state in the eighteenth century

In the light of the overall economic situation, it is not surprising that reform projects already emerged in the first half of the seventeenth century. Castile was not an exception, as the Count-Duke of Olivares's attempts clearly prove. Yet similar projects became more frequent in many other areas of Europe after the Peace of the Pyrenees (1659). In France, Colbert initiated reforms, which ended in the project of John Law at the beginning of the eighteenth century. It is significant that Law's central idea was to create a bank, which issued fiat money to control supply and reduce deficit, and was underpinned by a colonial trade company. The reform was thus strictly oriented to the financial side without any attempt at political change. A different model was the English one, where political changes paved the way for parliamentary control of the budget and debt as a basis for the financial revolution. After the Glorious Revolution of 1688, a positive economic conjuncture and the creation of the Bank of England stabilized monetary circulation and reduced risk and rates of interest for buyers of public debt.[23]

---

[23] A clear and parallel description of the two cases can be found in the excellent text of H. Van der Wee, 'Las Banque européene au Moyen Âge et pendant les temps modernes (1476–1789)', in H. Van der Wee (ed.), *La Banque en Occident* (Antwerp: Mercatorfonds, 1991), pp. 229–64. The English case is in Brewer, *The sinews of power*, passim.

In Castile, Charles II's ministers tried to centralize and rationalize the administration of taxes. They fought fraud, tried to stabilize the monetary system and reduced interest rates paid by the crown and the municipalities to 3 per cent; all of which was aimed at easing expenditures and fiscal pressure.[24] The solution came, however, not from fiscal reforms or the rise of a solid parliamentary system, but from the decomposition of the Habsburg composite monarchy. The turning point was the War of the Spanish Succession (1700–14), which ended with the loss of all non-peninsular European territories and the ascension of the Bourbon dynasty to the throne of Madrid.

With the *Decreto de Nueva Planta*, the French administrative system was introduced, which became the basis for extensive reforms aimed at centralizing tax organization and which were closely linked to warfare. The reforms also abolished most regional particularities, by extending the Castilian model to the rest of Spain, and introduced monetary stability.[25] During the eighteenth century different projects failed, such as the project of *Única Contribución*, which, after the elaboration of a very precise cadastre, aimed at rationalizing the tax system by substituting the huge variety of levies with a single and more general tax on personal income. But some other changes were successful, as was the liberalization of American trade from the Seville–Cadiz monopoly from 1766–67 onwards, which freed commerce from the negative control of the merchants controlling the Consulate. Also in 1782, the *Banco de San Carlos*, an embryo of the national bank, was created with the intention of reducing debt and issuing *vales reales* (royal vouchers) to attract private savings. Thus, though Law's experiment in France had slowed the financial revolution in Spain, in the long run progress of sorts was taking place, similar to France: financial modernization within an absolutist regime.

The effects of the reforms and the general economic expansion of the eighteenth century were soon evident. The increase in tax revenues in both nominal and adjusted prices and in English pounds sterling is clear in Figures 10.1 and 10.2 and in Table 10.3. The crown's nominal revenues went up from approximately 180 million *reales* a year in 1721–30 to more than 1,000 million in 1791–1800, an increase of 250 per cent in real terms. A comparison with other countries also gives a very positive image. As we said, the Spanish fiscal system had lost

[24] J. A. Sánchez Belén, *La política fiscal en Castilla durante el reinado de Carlos II* (Madrid: Siglo XXI de España Editores, 1996), pp. 321–6.
[25] R. Pieper, *La Real Hacienda bajo Fernando VI y Carlos III (1753–1788)* (Madrid: Instituto de Estudios Fiscales, 1992), pp. 66–96.

Table 10.3. *Crown revenues in England, France, the Netherlands and Spain, 1700–1800*

	England	Index	France	Index	The Netherlands	Index	Spain	Index
					English current pounds (x1000)			
1701–10	5900	107	7870	76				
1711–20								
1721–30	5500	100	10380	100	3600	100	2459	100
1731–40							2787	113
1741–50	8900	162	13150	127			3490	142
1751–60	7100	129	12430	120	4860	135	5310	216
1761–70							6429	262
1771–80	10400	189	16450	159			6920	281
1781–90	17000	309	19160	185			8993	366
1791–1800	39000	709			3690	103	14580	593

Sources: Our own elaboration with data from R. Lachmann, *Capitalists in spite of themselves* (Oxford University Press, 2000), p. 170; and Figure 10.1 by using the same system to convert ducats into pounds.

its relative predominance in comparison with France and England. By 1720, those differences were still very relevant. Measured in pounds sterling, the Spanish Bourbons' income was still a quarter of the French and a half of the English sovereigns'. Furthermore, as Table 10.3 shows, Spain was unable to surpass these countries during this period in the amount of resources mobilized. Though these figures should still be considered approximate, they convincingly demonstrate that Spanish governmental revenue grew faster at least until 1790. This image is corroborated by Figure 10.2, where the incomes of Spain and England are represented in adjusted values by using their respective price indexes. Only at the end of the century and during the first decades of the nineteenth century is the comparison of economic growth rhythms positive for England.

This positive trend had different causes. It is commonly accepted that administrative reforms in the Americas gave public servants more responsibility, aimed at reducing corruption, and implemented mercantilist policies between Spain and its colonies.[26] One is tempted to

---

[26] M. Burkholder and D. Chandler, *De la impotencia a la autoridad* (Mexico: Fondo de Cultura Económica, 1984).

say – and it has been said in the past – that the taxing capabilities of the metropolis over the colonies increased and, consequently, so did the silver coming from the Atlantic. An analysis of the available figures clearly supports this view. From the period 1726–40 to 1776–1800 the amount of silver coming from America passed from an average of about 40 to 88 million *reales* a year.[27] This trend is even more positive if we consider that during the second half of the century an increasing proportion of the American fiscal income was spent in the colonies both for administrative and military purposes.[28] But this image should also be nuanced. Spanish absolutism in America continued to be very weak and a good deal of the colonies' taxes did not reach the king's hands, as Grafe and Irigoin have convincingly shown. From that perspective one could even speak of failed colonial reform.[29] This is very much in tune with our estimates, which show that part of the flow of American silver to the crown in Spain clearly decreased from 19 per cent in 1725–50 to 11 per cent in 1776–1800.[30] Therefore, though American *direct* income grew, it is to be noted that this was not the key for increasing income on the peninsula.

This positive trend was due to the growing importance of customs duties on colonial products, some of them linked to the American trade, of which the most important was tobacco.[31] Tobacco, which constituted a royal monopoly, produced a high income at least until 1780, when it began to fluctuate. By 1751–75 tobacco income reached similar levels to that of silver coming from America, or the so-called *Rentas Generales*.[32] Expansion during the last few decades of the century was also due to the growth of the *Rentas Generales*, part of which was based principally on customs duties. This contrasts with the much slower growth of Provincial Revenues (*Rentas Provinciales*), dependent largely upon

[27] See Yun-Casalilla, 'The American empire', table 1, p. 126.

[28] Pieper, *La Real Hacienda*, pp. 150–7.

[29] R. Grafe and A. Irigoin, 'Nuevos enfoques sobre la economía política española en sus colonias americanas durante el siglo XVII' in F. Ramos and B. Yun (eds.), *Economía Política*.

[30] See Yun-Casalilla, 'The American empire', and tables 10.1 and 10.2 in the present chapter. The same phenomenon is stressed by Pieper, *La Real Hacienda*, p. 156. It should be said that the figures for the period 1726–50 are weaker than for the rest of the century, since they are based on only four observations. In any case, it is obvious that the so-called American treasure had a decreasing tendency, in comparison with both the highest values of the sixteenth century and those of the second half of the eighteenth century.

[31] A portion of the 'Spanish' tobacco came from Brazil and Virginia. But another part was of Cuban origin.

[32] Yun-Casalilla, 'The American empire'. Most of our figures for this come from Pieper, *La Real Hacienda*, pp. 113–16.

traditional taxes levied on the consumption of basic items by artisans or peasants. It also represents a measure of relaxation of the tax burden experienced by the more backward inland regional economies of Spain and a shift towards duties on foreign commerce. In fact, the *Rentas Generales* passed from around 35 million *reales* in 1753–56 to approximately 150 by 1787–88, whereas the *Rentas Provinciales* (the old *alcabalas, millones*, etc.) rose from around 45 to 75 million.[33]

It is difficult to measure the real effect of these changes. Nevertheless, in the Spanish case the evolution of revenues allowed clear increases in the level of military and naval expenditures, which reached 60 per cent of the current budget, a considerable proportion compared to the peak of 28 per cent reached in the sixteenth century.[34] This link between warfare and the tax system is even clearer if we consider the close connections between the tobacco monopoly and the army or if we think that some of the *Rentas Provinciales* were directly collected by *Tesorerías militares* (military treasuries).[35]

Compared with previous periods, these trends were probably more positive for the domestic economy. The dissolution of the composite monarchy meant that most state expenses, mainly military spending, were paid out within the peninsula, which was a stimulus for economic development, particularly for the industrial sector. Contrary to the Habsburg period, the Bourbon era witnessed a clearer connection between dynastic and national welfare. Besides, the mercantile component of foreign policy warranted a closer association between war and commercial interests. Finally, the transition from a composite monarchy to a Bourbon style of absolutism with a strong proto-national character reduced the costs of the state and the cost of protecting dynastic interests abroad.

Nevertheless, increases in revenue and expenditure continued to be inextricably linked to networks of interests that would only change with the crisis of the *ancien régime* and the bourgeois liberal revolution; they cannot be explained as part of a 'modernization' of the fiscal system. In contrast to England, where taxes were national and universal (i.e. 'paid by all subjects, regardless of rank'), Bourbon fiscal 'reforms', though surely positive in one sense, do not seem to have decisively eliminated high levels of localism in payment practices or social hierarchies where privilege and exception limited the extension of the state's fiscal base. Spanish fiscal reforms were tangled up in a traditional society where

[33] A precise and rigorous analysis in Pieper, *La Real Hacienda*, chapter 3.
[34] Our estimates from Pieper, *La Real Hacienda*, table 26, p. 161. We include army, navy and expenses for military equipment.
[35] Pieper, *La Real Hacienda*, passim.

privileges and exemptions from taxes were still important and where urban growth, and therefore fiscal capability, took place at a slower rate than in England.

Economic growth had a low starting point and was too slow and regionally differentiated to support any rapid extension to the tax base. A country with slow urban development found it difficult to mobilize the resources required to cope with the high levels of international tension and mercantilism in the eighteenth century. The relative weakness of local industry if one compares Spain to England or France, together with the high costs of protecting its empire in the Americas, implied, moreover, that the gains from empire and mercantilism accrued to the re-exportation trades rather than the domestic economy.

By the end of the eighteenth century, the Spanish model of economic and fiscal growth seemed to have failed. There then followed nearly a quarter of a century of revolutionary and Napoleonic Wars, which placed the fiscal system under unbearable pressure. In contrast to what had occurred in the seventeenth century, collapse coincided with political and social revolution that resulted in the crisis of the Old Regime.

The long and difficult transition to the liberal fiscal system, 1808–1845

The first decades of the nineteenth century witnessed a sequence of wars (the conflict against Napoleon, the American independence wars and the Carlist civil wars) and political discontinuity, which, in spite of different attempts, delayed any real tax reforms until 1845. Only after this date can we properly speak of a parliamentary and liberal fiscal system. Five periods can be distinguished: (1) wartime (1808–14), during which a liberal system was established by the *Cortes de Cadiz*; (2) the restoration of the absolutist system between 1814 and 1820; (3) the Triennium, a new liberal period (1820–23); (4) the so-called 'ominous decade' (1823–33), during which Fernando VII returned to power; and (5) Isabel II's ascension to the throne in 1833, and the beginning of a new period of liberalism which facilitated the reforms of 1845.

(1)   During the war of independence against France, 1808–14, the parliamentary regime was established for the first time. The *Cortes de Cádiz* (1812) enacted a Constitution and an economic programme that introduced liberal financial principles, linking budget policy and public debt management to annual approval by parliament. According to the Constitution, parliament had to approve the budget and control the treasury '*a posteriori*'. Taxes were to be

distributed among all citizens 'without any privilege' and in proportion to their wealth. Moreover, fiscal monopolies, customs and
the *Rentas Provinciales* (mainly *alcabalas*) were abolished, since they
were incompatible with 'national freedom' and 'public prosperity',
and replaced by a 'tax proportional to individual wealth'. Following
these principles, an extraordinary financial committee drafted a
project abolishing the *Rentas Provincials Estancadas* and establishing the 'direct contribution'. This tax consisted of a revised version
of the eighteenth-century *Única Contribución*, and proclaimed the
equality of tax laws. But it failed since there was no time for its
application.

(2) Reform projects were anathema to the reactionaries who took power
after Fernando VII's 1814 coup d'état and restored the taxes of the
Old Regime. From 1814, tax revenue tended to fall, due mainly to
the loss of the American colonies, the decrease in the volume of
foreign trade, and to the general disorder and administrative chaos
that prevented the collection of old duties (see Figures 10.1 and
10.2). The termination of coin and bullion remittances from the
Americas represented a serious reduction in revenue.[36] Although
foreign trade fell, revenues raised from customs duties did not fall
as much as ordinary revenues. After the war against Napoleon,
the treasury found that returns from the four traditional sources
of income (the Indies, customs duties, provincial taxes and monopolies) declined from 76 to 46 per cent. Given also the failure of
plans to keep the American colonies, absolutist finance ministers
were obliged to reform the traditional fiscal system, as was the case
with Martín de Garay in 1817 and López Ballesteros in 1826.[37]
Before 1814, the traditional dependence on resources from America
led successive finance ministers to the convenient view that fiscal
and financial problems would be solved in some way or another
without the need to enact tax reforms that might offend powerful
elites. They also anticipated that any increase in public expenditure would be temporary and could be financed with 'extraordinary resources', such as temporary taxes, voluntary loans, forced
loans, public bonds (*vales reales*) and land sales (disentailment or

[36] In the closing years of the empire, metal remittances from America, although smaller
than in previous decades, remained a substantial source of revenue that provided
security for raising loans. In the medium term, the remittances from the colonies that
had still not been entirely lost – mainly Cuba and the Philippines – were recovered.
[37] Historically, the ability of the Spanish state to draw upon colonial revenues delayed
tax reform, planned since the middle of the eighteenth century but repeatedly
postponed.

desamortización).[38] In an effort to compensate for the fall in permanent sources of revenue, extraordinary taxes were levied during the 1813–19 period and new taxes were tried by Martín de Garay, the financial wizard of Fernando VII. Garay's new taxes did not raise sufficient income, however, and recourse was made to extraordinary expedients. [39]

(3) After this absolutist interim of 1814–20, liberal principles were applied again during the so-called *Trienio Liberal* of 1820–23. The liberal constitution of 1812 was again put into place and new tax reforms were enacted. The national budgets of 1821–23, drawn up by finance minister Canga Argüelles and other liberals of the Triennium,[40] established a tax scheme similar to the French model that foreshadowed the 1845 system. During these three years the liberals softened the radical programme of the *doceañistas* (the men of the *Cortes de Cádiz*, so-called because their Constitution was proclaimed in 1812), but even these watered-down reforms proved unacceptable to Fernando VII after he was restored to absolute rule in 1823.

(4) Again, between 1823 and 1833, the arch-enemy of liberalism Fernando VII ruled as a despot and previous taxes and laws were restored. This attempt to return to the 1808 taxes did not work, however, and plummeting revenues led minister López Ballesteros to take some small steps to modernize the treasury in the 1820s.[41]

---

[38] F. Comín, 'Martín de Garay: una reforma tributaria posibilista', *Actas de las II Jornadas de Historia del Pensamiento Económico Español* (Zaragoza: Prensas Universitarias de Zaragoza, 2001); Comín, 'La metamorfosis de la Hacienda (1808–1874)', in *Josep Fontana. Historia y proyecto social* (Barcelona: Crítica, 2004), pp. 31–101; Comín, 'Contrebande et fraude fiscal dans l'Espagne du XIXe siècle', in G. Béaur, H. Bonin and C. Lemercier (eds.), *Fraude, contrefaçon et contrebande de l'Antiquité à nos jours* (Paris: Droz, 2006), pp. 45–163; G. Tortella and F. Comín, 'Fiscal and monetary institutions in Spain (1600–1900)', in M. D. Bordo and R. Cortés Conde (eds.), *Transferring wealth and power from the Old to the New World. Monetary and fiscal institutions in the 17th through the 19th Centuries* (Cambridge University Press, 2001), pp. 140–86.

[39] Comín, 'Martín de Garay: una reforma tributaria posibilista'.

[40] F. Comín, 'Canga Argüelles: un planteamiento realista de la Hacienda liberal', in E. Fuentes Quintana (ed.), *Economía y economistas españoles* (Barcelona: Galaxia Gutenburg, 2000), pp. 413–39.

[41] J. Fontana and R. Garrabou, *Guerra y Hacienda: la Hacienda del Gobierno central en los años de la Guerra de la Independencia* (Alicante: Instituto Juan Gil-Albert, 1986), pp. 65–70; F. López Castellano, *Liberalismo económico y reforma fiscal. La contribución directa de 1813* (Universidad de Granada, 1995); F. López Castellano, *El pensamiento hacendístico liberal en las Cortes de Cádiz* (Madrid: Instituto de Estudios Fiscales, 1999); F. Comín, *Las cuentas de la Hacienda preliberal en España (1801–1855)* (Madrid: Banco de España, 1990); J. Fontana, *Hacienda y Estado en la crisis final del Antiguo Régimen español, 1823–1833* (Madrid: Instituto de Estudios Fiscales, 1973), pp. 34, 86–9, 373; M. Artola, *La Hacienda del siglo XIX. Progresistas y moderados* (Madrid: Alianza, 1986), pp. 61–2, 64–5, 70.

López Ballesteros amalgamated various types of direct taxes and introduced novel customs and excise duties. Some of these fiscal innovations were direct taxes: the *contribución de paja y utensilios* and a refurbished version of the *frutos civiles* taxed land, real estate and incomes from property in crude and cumbersome ways, while the *subsidio de comercio* taxed commercial and industrial profits, again ineffectively because the necessary statistical information was missing. Other taxes were indirect, such as the *contribución de puertas*, paid on commodities sold in city markets, and excises on dried cod and liquor. But, the subsequent increase in revenues (see Figure 10.1) during the second period of absolutist rule under Fernando VII (1823–33) was due as much to an improvement in the overall economic situation as to López Ballesteros's reforms.[42]

(5) It was after Fernando's death that Spain's liberal revolution really occurred. During the Carlist Wars between liberals and absolutists (1833–40) a 'liberal revolution' took place, during which a series of modernizing economic measures were instituted and a parliamentary regime was established. Beginning in 1833, a series of medieval institutions (guilds, tithes, the *Mesta*, feudal land-ownership and internal customs) were abolished and a commercial code, disentailment of ecclesiastical properties, free trade and a liberal tax system were put into place. With these measures, private property rights were established and state intervention in the marketplace was reduced. Royal industrial factories were sold and a range of import restrictions reduced custom revenues. Traditional sources of revenue recovered partially, but only remittances from the colonies increased between 1834 and 1842.[43] Thus even liberals, faced with a fall in revenues, fell back on taxing colonies, disentailment and loans from the *Banco de San Fernando* (which in 1829 had replaced the old *Banco de San Carlos* as a source of public loans) and advances (*anticipos*) from Spanish creditors at high rates and warranties.

To summarize, the main characteristics of the transitional fiscal system of 1815–45 were as follows: (i) a persistent recourse to loans; (ii) provincial taxes (mainly the *alcabala*) and fiscal monopolies continued to provide a major portion of revenue, roughly 40 per cent of the total revenue in the period between the end of the eighteenth century

---

[42] Comín, 'Martín de Garay: una reforma tributaria posibilista'; J. Zafra, 'Algunas vertientes del fraude fiscal en la primera mitad del siglo XIX', *Hacienda Pública Española* 1 (1994), 145–53.

[43] Tax burdens on Cuba and the Philippines increased considerably.

and the early 1840s; (iii) the decline in trade and smuggling led to a fall in customs receipts from 18 to 10 per cent of total revenue in the same period; (iv) revenues from the Church fell from 13 to 7 per cent; (v) remittances from the colonies fell from 14 to 8 per cent; and (vi) new taxes brought in almost one-fifth of state revenue. At the same time, taxes were universalized for all citizens and for all of the different territories within the jurisdiction of the state, with the exceptions of the Canary Islands and the Basque country. Dwindling receipts and rigid expenditures produced chronic deficits, which oscillated between 20 per cent of total spending in 1801–7 and 33 per cent during the Carlist Wars (1833–40). Although budget deficits had been a constant in Spanish history, the situation grew markedly worse with the crisis of the Old Regime, the crisis of the American system and, finally, the loss of the colonies, for which Fernando VII fought wars while obstinately refusing to reform taxation, extorting financial assistance from bankers who had little assurance that they would be repaid. This situation was inherited by the liberals in 1833, along with the Carlist War. No wonder *desamortización* appeared as the only solution.[44]

The consolidation of the liberal regime and the nation-state fiscal system, 1845–1898

During the second half of the nineteenth century, the end of the Carlist civil wars brought a period of political stability, which allowed the Narváez government to definitively set up a liberal fiscal system. The 'Mon–Santillán reform' of 1845 was so-called because it was drafted by finance minister Alejandro Mon, with the close advice of Ramón de Santillán. Nevertheless, earlier improvements had already paved the way for their approach. As we have seen, between 1808 and 1845 the bases for a liberal system of public finance had already been established. Just prior to the 1845 reforms, progressive measures were in place when compared to the beginning of the century: modern taxes had been introduced by Martín de Garay (1817) and Luis López Ballesteros (1826) under absolutism, and also by the liberals during the Triennium and the Carlist War.[45]

---

[44] J. Fontana, *La quiebra de la monarquía absoluta* (Barcelona: Ariel, 1971, 2002), pp. 314; Comín, *Las cuentas de la Hacienda preliberal en España*, pp. 35–9.

[45] Comín, 'Martín de Garay: una reforma tributaria posibilista'; Tortella and Comín, 'Fiscal and monetary institutions in Spain (1600–1900)'; F. Comín and R. Vallejo, *Alejandro Mon y Menéndez (1801–1882). Pensamiento y reforma de la Hacienda* (Madrid: Instituto de Estudios Fiscales, 2002).

From a legal point of view, the French-style tax system introduced in 1845 brought many advances. It consolidated the liberal tax system and parliamentary management of the budget that had been incipient during the *Cortes de Cadiz* and the Triennium. The application of new reforms was imperfect, however, due to resistance from industrial magnates and land-owners to Mon's Law. As a matter of fact, this law was only enacted after important amendments were introduced and a commitment to the maintenance of old methods for estimating tributary bases and collecting taxes was reached. This agreement allowed these social groups both to elude tax payments and to shift a good deal of the tax burden onto peasants and urban consumers. Thus the old tax-collection scheme was preserved and had a negative impact on the system's efficiency.

The 1845 reforms augmented public income (see Figure 10.1) and reduced budgetary debt, but did not erase it altogether. The Mon–Santillán system never really solved the fiscal and financial problems inherited from the *ancien régime*. The budget was in deficit for all but four years (1876, 1882, 1893 and 1899) during the period 1845–1900. The major tax was the *contribución territorial*, which supplied about 20 per cent of ordinary income, and was collected in ways that undertaxed big land-owners and overtaxed small farmers. The political clout of the land-owning class and their opposition to official surveys of property values prevented the formation of a *Catastro*. Land tax assessments were essentially based on estimates by land-owners themselves. Furthermore, they were collected on the basis of local quotas (*cupos* or *repartimientos*). Quotas were assigned to each county and apportioned among taxpayers by local officials. Those with political power evaded taxes, and the burden was correspondingly shifted onto smaller farmers. Although actual fiscal pressure was not high, the clamour that was heard from many farmers about excessive taxation was not without justification.[46] The *contribución industrial y de comercio*, a tax that fell upon industrial and commercial activities and that was also levied by a quota system, yielded about 5 per cent of government revenue. The difficulty of determining a realistic basis for the taxation of commercial and industrial activity (where so many firms were small and informal) was much greater than for the yields of land and buildings. Combined,

---

[46] F. Comín, 'Public finance in Spain during the 19th and 20th centuries', in P. Martín Aceña and J. Simpson (eds.), *The economic development of Spain since 1870* (Aldershot: Edward Elgar, 1995), pp. 521–60; R. Vallejo, *Reforma tributaria y fiscalidad sobre la agricultura en la España liberal, 1845–1900* (Prensas Universitarias de Zaragoza, 2001).

these two 'direct' taxes raised about 25 per cent of total tax revenue. Other 'direct' taxes (on salaries, inheritances and stamp duties) produced an additional 10.2 per cent. The main indirect taxes were the hated *consumos* (excises on food and other consumer taxes) and customs duties. All these, combined with tobacco, salt and transport taxes, yielded 40 per cent. Of the remainder, lotteries yielded 8.3 per cent, more than disentailment at 5.6 per cent. Other incomes worth mentioning came from state properties and franchises, from payments in lieu of military service and from seigniorage. The tax burden, even after the Mon–Santillán reforms, looked heavily regressive.[47]

As to expenditures, about one-third of the budget went to meet debt payments and pensions for civil servants. Elevated expenses because of public debt payments continued to burden the liberal budget and limited possibilities to promote economic growth. Another third paid for the military, the police and the clergy. The maintenance of the Catholic Church constituted a peculiarity in Spanish finances, and absorbed funds needed for other purposes, such as defence, justice or the police, which were more in tune with the liberal state. Incidentally, the cost of maintaining the Church over four decades (1836–76), when incomes from disentailment were at their maximum, was actually larger than the amount earned from the sale of Church lands. The ministries of finances and public works received another 27 per cent of the budget. Three-quarters of the public works budget was devoted to public works proper and 14 per cent went to education. More than half of the finance budget was spent on the administration of lotteries and the manufacture of tobacco. However, to reduce the cost of managing a tobacco monopoly, it was leased out in 1887. Among the remaining expenditures, 1.5 per cent went to support the royal household, a considerable climb-down from Fernando VII's days, but a substantially higher proportion than today.[48]

Towards the end of the century, the Mon–Santillán reforms succeeded in reducing the deficit, but not completely. Between 1850 and 1890, the average deficit was around 12.4 per cent of total expenditure. The single most serious problem of budget administration during the second half of the nineteenth century was the structural deficit, which accumulated to around 3,185 million pesetas between 1850 and 1890, which implies an average yearly shortfall of 65 million pesetas – equivalent to

[47] F. Comín, *Hacienda y Economía en la España contemporánea (1800–1936)* (Madrid: Instituto de Estudios Fiscales, 1988); Comín, *Las cuentas de la Hacienda preliberal en España*; Comín and Vallejo, *Alejandro Mon y Menéndez (1801–1882)*.
[48] Comín, *Hacienda y Economía en la España*; F. Comín, *Historia de la Hacienda pública, II. España (1808–1995)* (Barcelona: Crítica, 1996).

12.4 per cent of total expenditure. Debt servicing imposed sacrifices on the country, and as the values of public bonds went down rates of interest went up. The long-term cause of Spain's structural deficit is to be found in the breakdown of the balance established during the *ancien régime*, whereby the excess of expenditures over domestic income was offset by American remittances. It took the Spanish state almost a century to cope with the reality of the drastic fall in the colonial tax surplus. Mid century, the liberals hoped that disentailment would replace American remittances, but this hope was in vain. Paradoxically, it was only after the definitive liquidation of the empire in 1898 that a series of ten successive budget surpluses was achieved for the first time in Spanish history.

Public debt: the chronic problem of the liberal state

Problems associated with servicing debt, already crucial in the eighteenth century, became critical in the first half of the nineteenth century with the costs of war, delays in the payment of budgetary obligations and the fact that the government was frequently in default of debt until the 1840s. Different governments resorted to disentailment, but this was clearly insufficient. Only after Mon's and Bravo Murillo's reforms in 1844 and 1851 did the debt problem start being resolved. From the 1840s, tax reforms and economic growth, partially due to institutional and social change, paved the way for the expansion of state income and expenditure at a faster pace than before (see Figure 10.1), but still slower than in countries such as France. Faced with a budgetary deficit and unable to issue more debt, the Ministry of Finance had to restructure the *Banco de San Carlos* in 1829. The new bank, the *Banco de San Fernando*, would later become the *Banco de España* in 1856, the loadbearer of state debt. Yet, being dependent on the needs of executive power, the *Banco de España* was an instrument for the monetization of debt, particularly after 1874, when it won the monopoly for issuing money. This dependence on the executive government and the almost systematic monetization of public debt would be a crucial obstacle to monetary policies aimed at improving the national economy.[49]

All in all, the financial irresponsibility of the state and insufficient tax revenues prevented a true financial revolution in nineteenth-century Spain. The market for sovereign bonds was scarcely developed among small savers because of the high risk that the state would not fulfil its financial commitments. After the bad experience of the *vales reales* at the

[49] Comín and Vallejo, *Alejandro Mon y Menéndez (1801–1882)*.

end of the previous century, from the beginning of the nineteenth it was very difficult to sell sovereign bonds in the domestic market, which was not only due to financial backwardness, but also due to the state's lack of prestige as a debt payer. Debt interest stopped being paid during the absolutist periods and foreign investors brought back in the subscription of Spanish bonds, particularly after absolutist governments ceased to recognize foreign loans (1823) and after the manipulation of the debt in Spain. Though Bravo Murillo carried out a public debt reform in 1851, its volume was such that debt management produced serious problems. Budgetary deficits kept feeding debt, and pushed mounting portions of public expenses to the payment of rates. When debt reached high levels, the finance ministers had no choice but to 'arrange' the debit in a way that was often considered as hidden debt in default, since they in fact meant reductions of the nominal and interest rates. Occasionally, as in 1851, these arrangements were not acceptable to foreign financiers, and led to the closure of foreign stock markets to Spain, forcing the government to resort to big international bankers, as had been the case in the sixteenth century. Irresponsible debt management had a severe impact on nineteenth-century policies of economic growth,[50] since these international creditors asked for high rates of interest as well as general compensations that privileged foreign financiers from France, Belgium and England. The biggest deficits occurred during the revolutionary periods (1855–56 and 1868–73). During these periods the state conceded 'general compensations' to creditors, which consisted of more favourable legislation for some foreign and national companies, mainly railway, banking and mining firms. The railway laws of 1855–56 expanded the sector while the banking system progressed thanks to the favour given to international firms. New laws and the privatization of public mines during the *Sexenio* enhanced the development of the extractive industry thanks to foreign capital. Debt servicing also played a role in the setting up of the central bank and the financial system. The *Banco de San Fernando* and the *Caja General de Depósitos* (1853) were created to directly fund the state treasury, which was unable to stand alone. A monopoly on mortgages was given to the *Banco Hipotecario* in 1872, and the monopoly on the emission of banknotes was conceded by

---

[50] J. Nadal, *El fracaso de la Revolución industrial en España, 1814–1913* (Barcelona: Ariel, 1975); G. Tortella, *El desarrollo económico de la España contemporánea. Historia económica de los siglos XIX y XX* (Madrid: Alianza, 1994); E. Llopis, 'La crisis del Antiguo Régimen y la Revolución liberal (1790–1840)', in F. Comín, M. Hernández and E. Llopis (eds.), *Historia Económica de España, siglos X–XX* (Barcelona: Crítica, 2002), pp. 165–202; P. Pascual and C. Sudrià, 'El difícil arranque de la industrialización, 1840–1880', in Comín *et al.*, *Historia Económica de España*, pp. 203–41.

some liberal ministers to the *Banco de España* in 1874, in exchange for cheap credits to the public finances. Private and public banks, therefore, became the lifebelt of a public finance system exhausted by critical financial problems in the short term. Thanks to the *Banco de España*, public debt started to be monetized from 1874 onwards, which became key in 1883, when gold coinage was suspended. It was then that the system became a fiat system where inflation tax could be implemented, what was called seigniorage during the Old Regime.[51]

Therefore, in spite of the legal and formal changes introduced in the constitutional and budgetary procedures from 1845 onwards, the mechanisms for servicing public debt were the same as during the Old Regime. The negative effects of debt and bad management lasted until 1899, when the reforms of Fernández Villaverde led to a budget surplus that brought an end to the inflationist policies of the *Banco de España*. Fernández Villaverde's final aim was to establish the gold standard in Spain, but his project failed in the parliament in 1903. Removal from the gold standard in the nineteenth century proved to be crucial in the Spanish case. Though Spain tried to join the Latin American Monetary Union with the setting up of the peseta, it did so too late, since the LAMU broke down in 1872. Spain's absence from international monetary systems, compounded by the policy of isolation from other countries in that century, was the price that the Spanish economy paid to finance the state treasury.[52]

General reflections on the long term: the mirror of France and England

The formation of the fiscal state first in Castile and then in Spain has often been seen from the perspective of exceptionalism and archaism. A detailed, comparative examination of the fiscal state's trajectory during these four centuries, however, offers a more complex image.

[51] P. Tedde, *El Banco de San Carlos* (Madrid: Alianza y Banco de España, 1988); P. Tedde, *El Banco de San Fernando (1829–1856)* (Madrid: Alianza and Banco de España, 1999); Comín and Vallejo *Alejandro Mon y Menéndez (1801–1882)*, pp. 185–95; Comín, *Hacienda y Economía en la España contemporánea*; Comín, *Historia de la Hacienda pública, II. España (1808–1995)*, pp. 158–65.

[52] F. Comín, 'Raimundo Fernández Villaverde: Un ministro de Hacienda ejemplar', *Anales de la Real Academia de Ciencias Morales y Políticas* 79 (2002), 637–75; Tortella and Comín, 'Fiscal and monetary institutions in Spain (1600–1900)'; F. Comín and M. Martorell, 'Laureano Figuerola y el nacimiento de la peseta como unidad monetaria', *Papeles y Memorias de la Real Academia de Ciencias Morales y Políticas* 1 (2003), 32–59; F. Comín, 'Les relations entre la Banque d'Espagne et le Ministère des Finances', in F. Bourillon, P. Boutry, A. Encrevé and B. Touchelay (eds.), *Des économies et des hommes. Mélanges offerts à Albert Broder* (Paris: Institut Jean-Baptiste Say/Éditions Bière, 2006).

The efficiency of the Castilian fiscal system as a machinery for mobilizing and sending resources beyond the kingdom is evident. This efficiency was not the outcome of an uncontested and unbalanced absolutism, but rather the consequence of a series of conflictive pacts, similar to other composite monarchies of the time. None of them experienced a financial revolution as in the Netherlands. On the contrary, a sort of 'negotiated absolutism' prevailed in these monarchical systems that was distant from the traditional idea of absolutism. Castile was no exception.

Even without a republican parliament, this difficult equilibrium paved the way for a consolidation of crown debt that was grounded on a more regular and secure perception of taxes as well as an increasing faith in the king, political stability and financial agents. Needless to say, the differences among the diverse absolutist fiscal systems were enormous. Nevertheless, the specificity of the Castilian case lies mainly in its silver American imports and the projection of a good deal of resources to the European battlefields. The availability of American silver was crucial because it constituted a source of liquidity beyond the kingdom's control, which gave the king a high margin of manoeuvre for the consolidation of debt. Occasionally this involved forced loans, thus increasing the inefficiency of the financial system and generating confusion between the king's and the kingdom's finances. This proved to be critical to justify the financing of the military resources of other states within the composite monarchy. Without a real financial revolution, some of its characteristics were, however, present.

Immersed in an international credit system, the Habsburgs could use Genoese bankers, with whom they were politically linked and who played the role of a sort of king's bank. To what extent this prevented the creation of a true national bank – which some desired – is difficult to say. In any case, the relationship between state and financial system differed from the one between the Bank of Amsterdam and later on the Bank of England and their respective political systems, which allowed for a massive transference of resources out of these countries. The consequences of the banking system were crucial in Castile. The transfer of public expenditure out of the kingdom and the subordination of the Castilian banking system to the Genoese 'cosmopolitan' system could only be negative for the domestic economy.

As in many other areas of Europe – the territories of the monarchy included – the burden of war in the seventeenth century led to mounting fiscal pressure that progressively shifted to services and forced loans. This provoked conflict and political tension as well as attempts at reform that, as in France, consisted of changes that did not affect the basic structure of the system. While a financial revolution in England led to parliamentary control of the budget and the creation of a national bank, France and Spain took the path – mainly after the failure of Law's project – of strong political centralism and the strengthening of the crown's power as the basis for investors' trust. The eighteenth century witnessed a shift from direct taxes on consumption to levies on imports or to state monopolies. Accompanying the expanded economy both in the peninsula and in the colonies, these changes were essential for the relative success of the new fiscal model. The break-up of the composite monarchy and the abolition of barriers between the different kingdoms on the peninsula concluded the establishment of a proto-national fiscal system, which embraced all of the territories that we today call Spain.

As in France, the eighteenth-century fiscal state was founded on a society of social orders and estates, where fiscal privilege, collision of jurisdictions and slow economic growth were the rule. Thus the efficiency of the system was more limited than in England, the main enemy of the Bourbon Madrid–Paris axis. Again, as in the French case, some advances were made, such as the creation of the *Banco de San Carlos*, which aimed at substituting for the lack of political changes. But overall the fiscal state engendered instability, and a crisis occurred that ended in revolution and the breakdown of the whole social system that underpinned it.

It cannot be said that the Spanish case was exceptional in the nineteenth century, though it did present several particularities with regard to other European countries. The Spanish nineteenth century was more economically positive than has been traditionally thought, but still the millstones of the fiscal system were present: (i) the persistence of an inefficient tax system until 1845; (ii) the rise of a liberal fiscal system which was denied the resources necessary to balance the budget; and (iii) the erroneous management of the public debt. Let us explain these three points.

First, Spain followed the French model in fiscal policy and many other aspects of economic policy. Yet there were considerable delays in adapting it to specific national circumstances and the results were not always positive. After the Napoleonic Wars, political realignment delayed the setting up of a parliamentary system, thus impeding the rise of liberal taxation and a financial revolution. After the ephemeral precedents of the *Cortes de Cadiz* and the Triennium, only from 1833 onwards can one say that a liberal parliament controlled the budget and debt. Even then, this was done within the scenario of civil war (the first Carlist war of the 1830s), which diminished trust in the political system. Creditors did not trust the political stability of the regime of

Isabel II, who fought against the Carlists. The delay of reform until 1845 – when the Narváez regime was able to guarantee a stable parliamentary regime – also prevented increases in tax income during a period when other states, particularly France, had already established the system that Spain had been trying to implement since the Canga Argüelles plan in 1821. Only after 1845 can one say that parliament controlled the state budget, and from 1851 onwards – with the so-called *Ley de Contabilidad Pública* – liberal principles of parliamentary control were in place.

Since all this coincided with a reduction in the efficiency of tax collection and the loss of American revenues, a reduction in military power occurred. Financial weakness thus prevented the continued possession of colonies (or their recovery after 1824). Even if the loss of the colonies implied directing public expenditure towards the domestic economy, the transition from empire to nation-state was a traumatic one in fiscal terms.

Second, though Spain imitated the French model, negotiations with the elites led to the retention of traditional tax-collection procedures. For the *contribución territorial*, for example, a new cadastre was not elaborated and the responsibility for collection was left to local elites who retained power due to political clientelism. The *contribución industrial* was in the hands of the guilds, restored in 1847 for this purpose. The *consumos* tax was collected by the villages and towns according to the previous system of *encabezamiento*. The maintenance of these mechanisms prevented the growth of tax incomes in parallel with economic progress, which would have been logical given that taxes were lineal. Since expenses grew faster than fiscal income, public debt was still high in spite of reductions after 1845. Furthermore, traditional procedures of collection prevented fiscal practices from being equitable – which was against the fiscal equality recognized by the Constitution – thus undermining the liberal regime's legitimacy.

The third particularity of the Spanish case is the absence of a financial revolution during the nineteenth century. Inadequate monetary policy was a huge obstacle to economic growth. The debt problem inherited from the absolutist state remained and thus conditioned economic policy and growth. Consecutive wars and political instability also increased debt. Until 1833, the different governments held little or no responsibility regarding public debt and Ferdinand VII repudiated it twice, refusing to pay the rates. Later, the liberals tried to honour their commitments but the high volume of debt and the permanent deficit brought about contentious measures, thus discouraging investors' trust and reinforcing government dependence on international creditors and the *Banco de España*. Though this situation improved thanks to the mid-century reforms, tax-collection practices, budget deficits and debt management left much to be desired. Combined, these factors prevented a real financial revolution and the rise of a national bank with a developed and autonomous monetary policy: the main task of the *Banco de España* was to finance the different governments.

11   Republics and principalities in Italy

Luciano Pezzolo

The nature of the Italian peninsula allows the comparison of institutions within different contexts, where traditions, historical events, geographical and political structures combine to influence institutional processes and vice versa. The complex and diversified institutional landscape of Renaissance and baroque Italy offers a rich laboratory to test hypotheses. Republics and principalities were not mere constitutional containers, but showed marked differences which were decisive for the formation of states and peoples. This chapter treats relations between fiscal systems and institutions, and particularly between republics (Venice, Genoa and fifteenth-century Florence) and principalities (the state of Milan, the Duchy of Savoy, the Duchy of Tuscany and the Kingdom of Naples).

The fiscal geography

The fiscal geography of most Italian states was the outcome of the late Middle Ages. Marked differences existed between the taxpayers of the capital, those of the subject towns and rural inhabitants. Direct and personal taxes fell mainly on the countryside while the citizens of major cities were usually exempt from such levies and paid taxes on consumption and commercial exchanges. The inhabitants of the capital city enjoyed special tariff conditions. Urban land-holders, moreover, paid fewer taxes on their properties in the hinterland than rural land-owners. These differences were also present in the southern territories, although the political weight of urban centres was less pronounced. Naples was exempt from ordinary direct taxation, feudal lords paid a specific tax and city dwellers were less burdened than rural taxpayers.[1]

---

[1] For a general view, G. Vitolo (ed.), *Città e contado nel Mezzogiorno tra Medioevo ed Età moderna* (Salerno: Laveglia, 2005); P. Jones, 'Economia e società nell'Italia medievale: la leggenda della borghesia', in R. Romano and C. Vivanti (eds.), *Storia d'Italia Annali* (Torino: Einaudi, 1978), Vol. I, pp. 185–372. More quantitative data and details will

This picture, however, changed during the early modern period. Under the pressure of political and military needs, the internal fiscal equilibrium was questioned and new systems emerged.

The economies of late Renaissance and early modern Italy experienced structural changes that widened and deepened their fiscal bases. For example, the budgets of the Republics and principalities heavily involved in maritime commercial activities – such as Genoa and Venice – included high percentages of ordinary revenues drawn from duties on international trade. Until the end of the sixteenth century, Venice, as one of the most important hubs of the interchange between East and West, depended on customs duties. Revenues from trade began to decline during the seventeenth century, when the Venetian government increased taxation on domestic consumption and on the wealth of its citizens. Staple foodstuffs and land bore the brunt of fiscal pressure, and exemplified the intensified competition that Venice came under in international trade. Before that time and until the first half of the sixteenth century part of the Republic's tax burden had been transferred to foreign merchants and consumers through heavy taxation on goods in transit. When its entrepôt trade declined the tax burden shifted onto local taxpayers. Thus, the revenue structures of both the Venetian and Genoese republics underwent significant changes between the fifteenth and the eighteenth centuries.[2] For Genoa, the ratio between trade and consumption revenues was four to one in 1450. In the mid eighteenth century, it was about even (1:1.1).[3]

Although the Milanese economy was 'commercialized', data from Renaissance budgets show that the ducal government experienced difficulties in collecting taxes on commercial transactions. In 1463, taxation on trade accounted for about 30 per cent of total revenues and taxation on urban consumption slightly exceeded 10 per cent.[4] Thus, the weight of direct taxation looked heavier in Milan than elsewhere. That burden was not, however, based on taxes levied on income and wealth but rather on the proceeds of levies gathered from rural families compelled to buy monopolized salt; through poll taxes on 'heads';

be presented in my forthcoming book, tentatively entitled *Mars and Pluto. War and finance in Italy, 1350–1700.*

[2] L. Pezzolo, *Una finanza d'ancien régime. La Repubblica veneta tra XV e XVIII secolo* (Napoli: ESI, 2006), p. 47; R. T. Rapp, *Industry and economic decline in seventeenth-century Venice* (Cambridge, MA: Harvard University Press, 1976), p. 141.

[3] G. Felloni, 'Stato genovese, finanza pubblica e ricchezza privata: un profilo storico', in G. Felloni, *Scritti di storia economica* (Genova: Società Ligure di Storia Patria, 1999), p. 398.

[4] C. M. Cipolla, 'I precedenti economici', in *Storia di Milano* (Milano: Fondazione Treccani Degli Alfieri, 1953–54), Vol. VIII, pp. 369–73.

and, via goods and services requisitioned for armies. Similar taxes prevailed in other states, particularly fifteenth-century Lombardy, and their burdens intensified under Spanish rule. Throughout the sixteenth and seventeenth centuries, direct taxation constituted a large share of Milanese revenues. Taxation in the Duchy of Savoy resembled that of the neighbouring Lombardy. Direct taxes accounted for at least half of the total income, and their role grew during the seventeenth and eighteenth centuries. Likewise, direct taxation constituted an overwhelming share of the budget of the Kingdom of Naples until the seventeenth century. Thereafter indirect taxation increased so as to equal the revenue from direct taxes.[5]

Central and local powers

The first obstacle met by governments when issuing a new tax was the problem of its legitimacy. Even if the principle that the sovereign had to 'live on his own' was not as strongly evinced in Italy as it was in France, nonetheless protests arose which aimed to limit government actions in the fiscal sphere. Resistance did not question the rights of government to levy taxes but rather demanded a legitimated process, consistent with the real needs and aims of the state.[6] Emergencies, the need to defend frontiers, the prince's honour, or the Christian faith provided valid reasons for taxation. One of the most pervasive reasons underlying requests for money to subjects was the defence of the Catholic faith. In that way, the ideological apparatus of religion provided effective support for early modern states. In short, the Church helped to legitimize a secular fiscal system, and the duties of subjects to pay taxes.

Nevertheless, though not always evident, political constraints exerted strong influences on governmental choices in the field of fiscal policy. They are evident in the terms used to name new taxes (*subsidy, aid, grant,*) which underline how taxation was a negotiated process. A tax was regarded as more of a 'gift' than an expropriation. Taxation implied reciprocal relations between princes and taxpayers; a relationship entailed an exchange of money for something else, which acknowledged rights and duties.

---

[5] For a long-term overview of direct taxation in Italy, see L. Pezzolo and E. Stumpo, 'L'imposta diretta in Italia dal medioevo alla fine dell'ancien régime', in S. Cavaciocchi (ed.), *La fiscalità nell'economia europea (secoli XIII–XIX)* (Firenze University Press, 2008), pp. 75–98.

[6] M. Bianchini., 'La tassazione nella seconda scolastica', in A. De Maddalena and H. Kellenbez (eds.), *Fisco, religione e stato nell'età confessionale* (Bologna: Il Mulino 1989), pp. 48–9.

In Italy, centralized states pursued variations of two key strategies. The first involved an attack on local power structures, designed to limit the prerogatives of urban oligarchies in fiscal and other spheres. For example, Florence emerged thanks to determined exertions against towns in its hinterland. Volterra rebelled in 1429 against proposals for a *catasto*. Arezzo revolted in 1409, 1431, 1502 and 1529. Pisa fought a war between the late fifteenth and the early sixteenth centuries, which forced the Florentine state to return functions previously exercised by city councils.[7] The Dukes of Savoy followed the same policy. From the late sixteenth century, they took political actions aimed at restricting urban autonomy and in favour of enhancing the political and social role of the aristocracies. States sometimes opposed resistance (often violent) by taking strong military action. The Dukes of Savoy built up a strong repressive apparatus in Piedmont in contrast to the more ameliorative strategy pursued by the Tuscan state. Although the duke's will was not boundless, the growth of fiscal pressure was linked with the coercive capability of central power. In practice, exemptions continued to be enjoyed even in Piedmont. Nobilities retained their fiscal prerogatives and exemptions well into the century of the great reforms.[8]

An alternative strategy, adopted by Venice and Milan, differed significantly. A strong tradition of growth with autonomy marked the urban centres of the Po Valley. Both the Dukes of Milan and the Venetian aristocracy had to negotiate deals and allow 'liberties' to subject towns. In fiscal terms that meant a mosaic of immunities, privileges and exceptions with respect to the fiscal demands of the prince or of the *dominante*. During the sixteenth century, the Venetian power elite began, however, to interfere with the political and institutional equilibrium on the mainland (the so-called *dominio da terra*). Humouring the *contadi*'s aspirations to set themselves free from the close control

---

[7] C. Vivoli, 'Tra autonomia e controllo centrale: il territorio pistoiese nell'ambito della Toscana medicea', in L. Mannori (ed.), *Comunità e poteri centrali negli antichi stati italiani* (Napoli: CUEN, 1997), pp. 146–7; P. Benigni, 'Oligarchia cittadina e pressione fiscale: il caso di Arezzo nei secoli XVI e XVII', in *La fiscalité et ses implications sociales en Italie et en France aux XVIIe et XVIIIe siècles* (Rome: Ecole Française de Rome, 1980), p. 55; M. Luzzatti., *Una guerra di popolo* (Pisa: Pacini, 1974); G. Petralia, 'Imposizione diretta e dominio territoriale nella repubblica fiorentina del Quattrocento', in *Società, istituzioni, spiritualità. Studi in onore di Cinzio Violante* (Spoleto: Centro italiano di studi sull'alto Medioevo, 1994), pp. 639–52; G. Petralia, 'Fiscality, politics and dominion in Florentine Tuscany at the end of the Middle Ages', in W. J. Connell and A. Zorzi (eds.), *Florentine Tuscany. Structures and practices of power* (Cambridge University Press, 2000), pp. 65–89.

[8] G. Symcox, 'L'età di Vittorio Amedeo II', in P. Merlin, C. Rosso, G. Symcox and G. Ricuperati, *Il Piemonte sabaudo. Stato e territori in età moderna* (Torino: UTET, 1994), pp. 406–10.

of urban centres, Venice actually slowly dismantled the fiscal preroga-tives of urban taxpayers. Relations between centre and mainland were mediated by the growing financial needs of the state; the loss of over-seas territories; and the expansion of the economic interests of the Venetian patriciate in land and capital located on the mainland; not to mention the emergence of a new economic and social elite in the countryside. When fiscal advantages granted to citizens were severely reduced between the sixteenth and the seventeenth centuries, the grow-ing fiscal burden was not, however, more equitably distributed among the different local towns, *contadi* and valleys. During the seventeenth century, some attempts to exploit income sources that had previously succeeded in eluding the tax net took place. If in Venice more attention was devoted to taxing financial transactions, on the mainland, com-mercial capital became the specified object of taxation. Land-owners also faced heavier fiscal pressure, particularly during wars against the Turks, which gave the state reasons to progressively cancel a whole ser-ies of traditional immunities and exemptions. By the end of the eight-eenth century, the Venetian taxation system looked quite different from that of the Renaissance. Privileges had been reduced; universal taxes burdening all subjects, regardless of their legal and social status, were in place; the key role played by urban elites was a distant memory; and government controls over communal finance had become a constant concern.[9]

For the Savoyard duchy, evolution towards fiscal centralization seems to result from coercive actions. In the Venetian republic and the state of Milan revenues that flowed into central government coffers depended to a large extent on the consent of local bodies. The Tuscan case looked similar to the Piedmontese model during the Renaissance but later it shifted towards the Lombard–Venetian model of negotiation with lead-ing local elites. Neapolitan financial history could also be considered similar to this model. Undoubtedly the Habsburg government man-aged to raise enormous amounts of money from Neapolitan taxpayers, but it had to rely on the feudatories' consent.[10]

In the eighteenth century, Italian governments met difficulties in levying taxes which fell uniformly on all subjects. Along with assessment

---

[9] For a profile of Venetian financial history in the early modern age, see Pezzolo, *Una finanza*.

[10] A. Calabria, *The cost of empire. The finances of the kingdom of Naples in the time of Spanish rule* (Cambridge University Press, 1991); G. Galasso, 'Economia e finanze nel Mezzogiorno tra XVI e XVII secolo', in A. De Maddalena and H. Kellenbenz (eds.), *Finanze e ragion di Stato in Italia e in Germania nella prima età moderna* (Bologna: Il Mulino, 1984), pp. 45–88.

difficulties, the main problems were the immunities and privileges that hindered the setting of a universal tax (though to a lesser extent than in the past). It is, however, worth asking if similar ideas about universal taxes were shared by ruling groups. Privileges have too often been considered as a sign of weakness in old regime states; as remnants of a medieval past and a brake on the development of the 'modern' state willing to subdue all taxpayers to its will. The persistence of immunities has been readily criticized by historians, who have pointed to privileges as the main restraint on the development of fiscal systems. We should, first of all, evaluate in quantitative terms the income fraction that eluded taxation by way of exemption. If in Spain and France large patrimonies were merely brushed by taxes, in northern and central Italy privileged areas were quite small, and did not represent a great concern for governments. After the great assessment of 1731, the Piedmontese nobility enjoyed exemptions as low as 8 per cent of their total ascertained wealth, and a similar percentage was estimated for ecclesiastical estates.[11] In the Republic of Venice, privileged lands accounted for a negligible portion of the whole assessed properties.[12] The Neapolitan case is quite different. The noble and feudal land-owners enjoyed large privileges and Naples was exempt from direct taxation. Nevertheless, the growing fiscal demands of the Spanish government reduced, de facto, the importance of these immunities. In fact, the principle of extraordinary taxation allowed the government to circumvent the privileges of subjects, and thus the capital's inhabitants were subject to the same burden as common taxpayers.[13] It was quite unusual to find estates completely free from taxes in the eighteenth century.

The great Enlightenment reforms aimed mainly at eliminating abuses that were too often attached to specific exemptions. Recognized immunities were not questioned, but entrustments that had spread illegally were. It has been correctly stated that for governments of the time 'the primary objective was to reduce the cost to the state of noble privilege and to make it seem less arbitrary'.[14] Different concerns, more focused on preserving fiscal interests, were directed towards Church properties. Developments during the Enlightenment led to limiting traditional ecclesiastical immunities, though they were not completely

---

[11] Symcox, 'L'età di Vittorio Amedeo II', p. 408.
[12] See, for example, Padova, Archivio di Stato, Archivio Civico Antico, Territorio, 268, fasc. 1079, cc. 24r ff.
[13] G. Galasso, *Storia del Regno di Napoli*, 5 vols. (Turin: UTET, 2006), Vol. III, pp. 127–8.
[14] S. Clark, *State and status. The rise of the state and aristocratic power in Western Europe* (Montreal: McGill-Queen's University Press, 1995), p. 161.

abolished.[15] The ordinary taxation of the Church entailed, on the one hand, the beginning an unwelcome conflict with Rome and, on the other, tapping income sources that would affect powerful elites. Venetian and Florentine nobilities enjoyed considerable revenues from ecclesiastical offices and benefices, and the maintenance of exemptions safeguarded a part of the family income. The delicate role of controlling souls played by the clergy, moreover, suggested that governments should be respectful.

One might wonder whether the ruling elites of the old regime were willing to eliminate any form of fiscal privilege. Granting tax exemptions was a useful power mechanism for the prince. The privilege stressed a particular relationship between the beneficiary (a noble, a community, a family, a social order ...) and the grantor; a subtle mutual relationship bound them to one another. Exemptions were often the government's main means of weaving patronage networks. Arguably, the diminution of fiscal privileges during the early modern age reflected changes in the forms of patronage adopted by the leading groups of the political centre. In other words, not the fiscal system but other sectors, such as administrative and military structures, became the main areas for the development of clientelism.

A further element underlying distinctions among taxpayers concerned the very notion of social hierarchy. *Ancien régime* society was constituted of bodies, estates, orders, each of them precisely defined and acknowledged. Accordingly, the tax burden reflected not only power relations among groups, but also the different positions of taxpayers within society. Although in principle the government's intention was to tax all subjects in proportion to their economic capabilities, in practice the distribution of the fiscal burden conformed to social rankings. Even in early eighteenth-century Piedmont it was stated that different fiscal duties fell on properties according to the taxpayers' social status. Also the 1731 *perequazione* ('equalization') implied distinctions among noblemen, the bourgeoisie and peasants.[16] This fact was not, however, considered an attack on the equity principle that had to underlie a 'just' fiscal policy.

---

[15] See, for Tuscany, R. Bizzocchi, 'Politica fiscale e immunità ecclesiastica nella Toscana medicea fra Repubblica e Granducato (secoli XV–XVIII)', in H. Kellenbenz and P. Prodi (eds.), *Fisco religione Stato nell'età confessionale* (Bologna: Il Mulino, 1989), pp. 355–85; E. Brambilla, 'Per una storia materiale delle istituzioni ecclesiastiche', *Società e storia* 7 (1984), 395–450; E. Stumpo, 'Un mito da sfatare? Immunità ed esenzioni fiscali della proprietà ecclesiastica negli stati italiani fra '500 e '600', in *Studi in onore di Gino Barbieri*, 3 vols. (Pisa: IPEM, 1983), Vol. III, pp. 1419–66.

[16] G. Quazza, *Le riforme in Piemonte nella prima metà del Settecento*, 2 vols. (Modena: Soc. Tip. Ed. Modenese, 1957), Vol. I, pp. 66n., 145.

The emergence of direct taxation

Late medieval Italian city-states provided outstanding examples of connections between private interests and fiscal policies. Direct taxation was not very popular. These states were able to tax trade, staple foodstuffs and subjects resident in their hinterlands and dominions. Regular direct taxation on a poll basis (and sometimes on wealth) fell on peasants. The burden of billeting troops also fell mostly on the countryside. One alternative to taxing the citizens of republican cities consisted of the system of forced loans. This mechanism of taxing citizens by means of borrowing at interest (generally about 5 per cent) worked quite well as long as the financial conditions remained favourable. Taxpayers were required to contribute amounts calculated according to their assessed wealth as recorded in an *estimo*. They obtained government bonds that could be freely traded. Between the fourteenth and the fifteenth centuries, the constant pressures on state finances from warfare placed the system in difficulties. Interest rates were cut and the market prices of government securities dropped. By the fifteenth century, forced loans were more like a form of direct taxation rather than loans to the state.

Along with this crisis, the need to tax land on a regular basis emerged almost everywhere. From the middle of the sixteenth century, therefore, ordinary direct taxation appeared in all Italian states, but contributing very different shares of total state revenues. In the Venetian republic and in Tuscany, net receipts from direct taxation were quite small, while in the Milanese state and in Piedmont, the *mensuale* and the *tasso* dominated the state budget. At that time, taxation was neither as clear nor as direct as it is today. Back then, governments decided on the total required for a given assessment but left local authorities to apportion and collect the money. Thus, the Piedmontese *tasso*, which in principle fell on land rents, could actually be paid by the community through poll taxes on excises or on foodstuffs. Nevertheless, the growing importance of direct taxation exposes the needs and plans of late Renaissance governments for wider fiscal bases free from exemptions and immunities that constrained regular flows of revenue into central coffers.

While the sixteenth century witnessed the emergence of regularized direct taxation almost everywhere, the following centuries were characterized by a broadening of the taxable basis for forms of direct taxation. Pressure to collect and burdens on taxpayers were by no means constant. For instance, in the late sixteenth century, the Venetian budget showed a decline in yields from direct taxation. A similar policy prevailed in Piedmont from 1660–90.[17] Direct taxation carried political problems on its train and whenever possible, governments gave priority to reducing the burdens of direct tax before other forms of taxation. Furthermore, during the sixteenth century, the objects of direct taxation were not yet clearly specified and included land, rents, wages, polls, and profits and interest. In the seventeenth century, in the context of a marked reallocation of capital from trade to land and financial intermediation, some governments tried to tap income sources previously overlooked. For example, from the early seventeenth century, some governments attempted to tax the financial returns from *censi* (long-term loans secured on land). In the Venetian republic, Piedmont, Piacenza and Lombardy, subjects lending money were required to pay taxes.[18] However, the difficulties involved in measuring returns from financial operations and the reluctance of lenders to comply with the law led to failure. Nevertheless, the attempt does point to the attention paid by Italian states to movements of resources between sectors of their fiscal bases. But *censi* involved taxing the very rich and for this reason officials could not rigorously enforce the law. The attempt also reveals governments' concern with debt and the burdens on communities in servicing debt that eroded the capacities of citizens to pay taxes.

Over the seventeenth and eighteenth centuries, direct taxation changed. Progressively, corvées related to billeting, personal obligations to support the army, supplies and services exacted from peasants were first extended to urban taxpayers and then modified from payments in kind into cash payments. These steps reduced tensions between soldiers and civilians when the need to support growing numbers of soldiers led states to seek a more balanced distribution of the burden between town and country. Furthermore, the monetization of this obligation prompted peasants to enter the market economy. Obviously, warfare intensified the burdens of supporting troops, however levied.

Over the period, important changes occurred in the methods of tax assessment and collection that were less significant for customs and excises than for taxes on real estate and people. The intractable problem of obtaining information forced governments to transform direct

[17] L. Pezzolo, *L'oro dello Stato* (Venezia: Il Cardo, 1990); E. Stumpo, *Finanza e stato moderno nel Piemonte del Seicento* (Roma: Istituto Storico Italiano per l'età moderna e contemporanea, 1979), p. 264.
[18] G. Corazzol, *Livelli a Venezia nel 1591* (Pisa: Pacini, 1989); C. Rosso, 'Il Seicento', in *Il Piemonte sabaudo*, p. 211n.; P. Subacchi, *La ruota della fortuna* (Milano: Angeli, 1996), p. 20; S. Pugliese, *Condizioni economiche e finanziarie della Lombardia nella prima metà del secolo XVIII* (Torino: Miscellanea di storia italiana, 3rd ser., 21, 1924), pp. 243–5.

into poll taxes during the seventeenth and eighteenth centuries. For example, taxes first conceived and levied as duties on flour were later levied as poll taxes. Sometimes tax yields improved and medieval poll taxes often proved less burdensome for the lower classes.[19] States introduced distinctions between taxpayers through classifying them by age, status and, however roughly, into income classes. Slowly, the concept of progressive taxation was emerging.

At the same time, plans were implemented to measure and value landed property in Piedmont, Lombardy and the Veneto. The eighteenth-century cadastres, even if not always reliable, constituted a fundamental stage in fiscal history.[20] Their initial importance was to restrict immunities and exemptions rather than to jack up receipts from taxes on land.

Turning to the efficiency of Renaissance fiscal systems, the data suggest that net yields placed in short compass at the disposal of the central treasury amounted to about 70–80 per cent of predicted obtainable totals. The data also show that times taken to complete collections were usually long for direct taxes. Customs and excise duties tended to flow in at faster rates and franchised collection allowed treasuries to receive part of the negotiated leases in advance. In this period, governments favoured tax farming (franchising) because that system generated larger yields, usually collected directly by government agencies. Tax farmers could acquire better data and information about commercial flows and consumption than servants of the state.

Of course fluctuations in the economy affected levels of revenue received year after year. Data from sixteenth-century budgets are read by historians as a reflection of economic expansion. But we should be cautious because the following century (characterized by phases of depression and stagnation) witnessed several cases of persistent increase in the revenues of states. Although Florentine revenues seem to reflect a long period of economic stagnation between the late sixteenth century and the early eighteenth century, when the budget settled at around a million *scudi*. Meanwhile, the revenues of the Venetian republic and the Savoyard duchy grew to impressive levels. These upswings emanated, however, from involvement in international conflicts and

---

[19] A. Contini, 'La riforma della tassa delle farine, 1670–1680', in F. Angiolini, V. Becagli and M. Verga (eds.), *La Toscana nell'età di Cosimo III* (Firenze: Edifir, 1993), pp. 241–74; L. Pezzolo, 'Dal contado alla comunità: finanze e prelievo fiscale nel Vicentino (secoli XVI–XVIII)', in C. Povolo (ed.), *Dueville. Storia e identificazione di una comunità del passato* (Vicenza: Neri Pozza, 1985), pp. 381–428.

[20] R. Zangheri, *Catasti e storia della proprietà terriera* (Turin: Einaudi, 1980), pp. 71–130.

wartime pressures for funds. In general, fiscal flows followed exogenous shocks due to war or plague, rather than those induced by economic fluctuations.

Republican and princely debts

During the fifteenth century, debt crises led to reforms to the financial system. Some governments issued bonds that competed with other assets sold on open markets. But a real public debt detached from forced loans, and characterized by the full marketability of state bonds on primary markets, really came on stream in the sixteenth century. Alongside long-term debt, short-term indebtedness persisted. Recourse to short-term credit was widespread, especially in principalities, and it continued to be the fastest and easiest way to cope with state demands for liquidity. Bankers, occasional financiers, courtesans, officers, wealthy people and foreign capitalists made up a world of court finance revolving around princes, always in urgent need of money and often compelled to accept loans and credits on very onerous terms.

Two different models of state indebtedness emerged in Italy: on the one hand, a long-term debt typical of republican states, and on the other hand, a short-term debt, as a feature of princely states. This distinction was never clear-cut, but seems to be a useful way to analyse financial policy for these centuries.

Let us take three examples. Between the 1520s and the 1530s the Venetian government issued a series of annuities to be sold on the domestic financial market. These loans – the so-called *Depositi in Zecca* ('deposits in mint') – became the backbone of state debt right down to the end of the republic in 1797. The main characteristics of Venetian bonds were: attractive interest rates (between 6 and 8 per cent); simple rules for the redemption of capital; exemptions from taxes; protection from expropriation; and the marketability of bonds. Venice soon abandoned the system of forced loans and relied on the markets protected by the state and where creditors' interests were secured by regular levies of taxes. The value of the debt was sustained and strengthened by the commitments of the state to its creditors.

The system in Milan was similar but somewhat different. Until the early sixteenth century the state of Milan did not have a consolidated debt. The main tools of indebtedness were forced loans and/or short-term loans, through bills of exchange issued by bankers and local financiers. When needed, moreover, fiscal receipts were sold to lenders. From the mid sixteenth century, a remarkable expansion of loans assigned on tax revenues occurred, while state expenditure and fiscal resources simultaneously widened. The rulers' endless demands for cash to fund armies provoked a persistent state of emergency, both in Castile and the European provinces of the Habsburg Empire. The spiral of war–taxation–indebtedness led to resorting to short-term loans (*partiti* and bills of exchange at high interest rates) on a massive scale. The Habsburg debt was managed by private international financiers, who provided liquidity for the state through their commercial networks using and monetizing bills of exchange. The system operated at a high cost to taxpayers. Funded debt, by contrast, depended on tax and the share of tax revenues available to service the accumulation of long-term debt.[21]

The Neapolitan case is very close to the Milanese one. In Naples the government also resorted to both short-term loans at high interest and to long-term loans assigned to fiscal revenues. But, unlike the Milanese example, the Neapolitan economy proved to be unable to meet the gigantic effort called for from the Habsburgs. By the middle of the seventeenth century, after the great revolt of 1648, the whole fiscal and financial system collapsed. The government limited itself to collecting a small amount of revenues, while the great majority of receipts was pocketed directly from state creditors.[22]

In conclusion, the princely model accords with a resort to a large floating debt along with growing consolidated and funded debt. The prince obtained money above all from financiers within and surrounding his court. He pledged fiscal revenues as interest and gave creditors rights to levy their returns and rents directly either from taxpayers or from tax officials. Some elements mark a difference between the princely model and the republican one. The latter seemed to rely on the market, where every investor enjoyed the same rights. The former, on the other hand, showed some features of cronyism. Different interest rates were paid by the Milanese government according to the importance of lenders. It was likely that a great noble earned from his investment in state debt more

---

[21] G. Luca, 'L'alienazione delle entrate dello Stato di Milano durante l'età spagnola: debito pubblico, sistema fiscale ed economia reale', in M. Rizzo, J. J. Ruiz Ibañez and G. Sabatini (eds.), *'Le forze del Principe'. Recursos, instrumentos y limites en la práctica del poder soberano en los territorios de la Monarquìa Hispanica* (Universidad de Murcia, 2003), Vol. I, pp. 181–210.

[22] A. Calabria, 'Finanzieri genovesi nel Regno di Napoli nel Cinquecento', *Rivista storica italiana* 101 (1989); L. De Rosa, *Il Mezzogiorno spagnolo tra crescita e decadenza* (Milano: Il saggiatore, 1987); G. Muto, *Saggi sul governo dell'economia nel Mezzogiorno spagnolo* (Naples: ESI, 1992); A. Bulgarelli Lukacs, *L'imposta diretta nel Regno di Napoli* (Milan: FrancoAngeli, 1993); Galasso, 'Economia e finanze'; R. Mantelli, *L'alienazione della rendita pubblica e i suoi acquirenti dal 1556 al 1583 nel Regno di Napoli* (Bari: Cacucci, 1997); I. Zilli, *Lo Stato e i suoi creditori. Il debito pubblico del Regno di Napoli tra '600 e '700* (Naples: Edizioni Scientifiche Italiane, 1997).

than a small merchant or an artisan. The famous financier Antonio D'Aquino, who in the 1630s and 1640s controlled the financial market in Naples, managed to purchase state credits at a low price from common investors, who were unable to get the interest rate, because he was paid by the Treasury.[23] In addition, bond-holders of the Monte di San Carlo in Milan, an institution that managed the Milanese debt, were never sure of being paid regularly and at the standard interest rate.[24]

Douglass North has put forward the testable hypothesis that the interest rate provides 'the most evident quantitative dimension of the efficiency of the institutional framework'.[25] Italian data (see Table 11.1) show a tendency for interest rates to converge: the spread (about seven points) that marked the costs of borrowing for renaissance governments fell to around one point by the end of the eighteenth century. Meanwhile, costs for loans declined from 9–10 per cent in the mid sixteenth century to 4–5 per cent in the early eighteenth century. It is also clear that some states paid less than others for loans, and reasons for variance can be offered.

First, military strains influenced the cost of borrowing. Genoa, for example, fought few wars, while the Italian dominions of the Habsburgs were requested to fund long and expensive conflicts. Furthermore, cities such as Genoa and Venice could count on large potential supplies of investible funds even after their commercial success had faded away. Apart from the relative scope and scale of local financial markets the interest rates also mirrored the trust investors retained in states as debtors. From the end of the Italian wars onwards, the Venetian and Genoese governments avoided defaults and reassured their creditors by paying interest regularly and redeeming or converting bonds efficiently.[26] In addition, rulers and oligarchies held large portions of debt and that reduced risk. Urban patricians were unlikely to default on loans that would endanger one of their most important sources of income. The identification of interests between creditors and ruling

[23] R. Villari, *La rivolta antispagnola a Napoli. Le origini 1585–1647* (Bari: Laterza, 1967), p. 148.
[24] For political influence on the management of the Monte see C. Marsilio, 'Debito pubblico milanese e operatori finanziari genovesi (1644–1656)', *Mediterranea. Ricerche storiche* 5 (2008), 149–72.
[25] D. C. North, *Institutions, institutional change and economic performance* (Cambridge University Press, 1990), p. 69.
[26] L. Pezzolo, 'The Venetian government debt 1350–1650', in M. Boone, K. Davids and P. Janssens (eds.), *Urban public debts. Urban government and the market for annuities in western Europe (14th – 18th centuries)* (Leuven: Brepols, 2003), pp. 61–74; L. Pezzolo, 'Bonds and government debt in Italian city states, 1250–1650', in W. Goetzman and G. Rouwenhorst (eds.), *The origins of value. Financial innovations that created the modern capital market* (Oxford University Press, 2005), pp. 145–63.

Table 11.1. *Interest rates on government loans in Italy, 1450–1799*

	Florence	Genoa	Venice	Milan	Bologna	Naples	Piedmont
1450–59		4	4				
1460–69		3.6	4				
1470–79	3.25	3	4				
1480–89	3	2.8	5				
1490–99	2.25	2.5	5				
1500–09		2.8	5		8		
1510–19		3.2	5		8		
1520–29		2.8	6.5		8	9.5	
1530–39		2.2	7		8.2	10.1	
1540–49		2.4	5	8.3	8	9.1	
1550–59	12	2.4	3.5	11	8	9	
1560–69	7	2.6	6	12.3	7.6	9	10.5
1570–79		3	8	9.7	6.6	8.7	
1580–89		3.2	5	8.8	6	8.5	
1590–99	5	3.5		7.9	6.5	7.4	
1600–09		3.8	4	7.9	6	7	
1610–19	5	3.5	5	6.6	6		
1620–29	5	3.4	5	6.8	5		
1630–39	5	3	5	7.5	5		3.75
1640–49	4.5	3.1	6	5	4.7		3.75
1650–59		3	6	5.8	4.5		5.5
1660–69		2.5	5.8	5.7	4	5.8	5.5
1670–79		2.6	2.5	5	4	6.1	3.75
1680–89		2.3		4.8	4	4.2	4.5
1690–99		2.5		6.2	3.5	3.7	5
1700–09		2.4	4.5			4.9	5
1710–19	4.5		5.8			5.5	5
1720–29	4		4.2			5.3	
1730–39	3	2.5	3.8			4.2	
1740–49	3.5	2	3.6			5	
1750–59	3.25	2.5	3.5			5.3	4
1760–69			3			4.8	3.5
1770–79			2.1			4.8	
1780–89			2.3			5.1	
1790–99			3.3			5.4	

Source: L. Pezzolo, *Mars and Pluto. War and finance in Italy, 1350–1700* (forthcoming).

elites provided a secure basis for the accumulation of public debt. This identity was surely stronger in republican states than in principalities. In the former, the interests of the wealthy elites resident in capital cities strengthened the credibility of the states' financial commitments. Princes were not considered to be nearly as reliable. Money cost more in the Italian dominions of the Habsburg monarchy because a series of financial crises marked the relations between bankers and the crown. During these crises, the monarchy retained more freedom of action than its weaker creditors. Republics were not identified with a mortal person or dynasty; they were seen as immortal polities.

Of course trust also depended on the fiscal health of states. It is likely that, during the sixteenth century, general economic conditions, including the growth of trade, consumption and tax receipts, facilitated borrowing. Raising tax revenues assigned for the payment of interest reassured lenders; and the security of creditors grew gradually along with the strengthening of state sovereignty. Revenues flowed in from well-defined and regular taxes, no longer subjected to local negotiation. Republican debt, based on the affluence of towns, enjoyed other advantages. Creditors could monitor commercial flows and thereby evaluate the health of public finances. Compliance towards taxation and the lack of major tax revolts also strengthened the creditworthiness of states. Naples demonstrated how the Habsburg government reached the economic limit of taxation. Fiscal pressures in the 1630s and 1640s ignited a revolt, which forced the government to considerably lower fiscal requests. The economic system of the kingdom proved unable to meet the growing demand of the state, which eventually defaulted.

Efficient debt management must also be stressed, and a financial system, based upon open markets (the republican model) reduced information costs for both government and subscribers to loans. Even if they were theoretically a state secret, information on republican finances was available to many patricians – that is to creditors. While access to information at court was probably difficult, narrow credit markets implied that relations between prince and lenders were not at all transparent. In republics, the issue of bonds was available to all potential investors. In principalities, differences among creditors prevailed. As already stated, investors with power and status stood a better chance of repayment than smaller investors did. Patronage embodied in the princes also spilled over into debt management and raised the costs of servicing loans and credit. The princely model did, however, offer other opportunities for profit through social mobility, superior to those available in republics. The financial history of Piedmont, for example, exposes several cases of commoners who managed to reach the higher levels of the social hierarchy by lending to princes in exchange for titles and feudal privileges rather than straightforward monetary returns.[27]

---

[27] See Stumpo, *Finanza e stato moderno*; S. Cerutti, *Mestieri e privilegi* (Turin: Einaudi, 1992), pp. 97–8.

All governments paid a risk premium on their debts. Compared with rents secured on land, the premium risk of state bonds was usually about two percentage points and it was, moreover, more commonplace in principalities than republics. Indeed, in the mid sixteenth century, 'public' interest rates stood below 'private' counterpart rates.

Distinctions between princely and republican models should not, however, be drawn too sharply. Throughout the seventeenth and eighteenth centuries, princely states also established institutions that improved the collection of revenues and widened markets for debt beyond restricted court or narrow urban circles to regional levels. Financial innovations that can be compared to the so-called financial revolutions that occurred later in Holland and England appeared to attract creditors. Italian innovations in the financial sector helped rulers to raise large amounts of money at modest costs. Except in Piedmont, not all of the money was raised for military purposes.

As early as the Renaissance, some Italian states (Venice, Milan and Florence) displayed those close and familiar correlations between economic prosperity, financial capacity, fiscal efficiency and political power. Geopolitical and economic competition on the peninsula forced the states to look for more rational means of financing ordinary as well as extraordinary deficits. The huge availability of capital allowed for the exploitation and transformation of money into military strength. After the end of the Italian wars, when most Italian city-states fell under the control of great European powers, the picture changed and fiscal and financial policies were designed to meet the needs of imperial monarchies, first the Spanish and later the Austrian empires. The Piedmontese duchy somehow maintained independence and utilized domestic resources together with loans from allies to engage in European warfare. Wars for expansion, an effective fiscal system, favourable economic and social conjunctures, and chance laid the basis for Piedmontese geopolitical success.

Another independent state, the Republic of Venice, again after the favourable Renaissance phase, had to cope with defensive wars in order to limit Ottoman expansion. Despite the republic's remarkable capacity for mobilizing financial resources, its geopolitical destiny was decided by the potential scope and scale of small states that could not follow the paths taken by larger powers such as Britain, France, Austria and Russia.

Of course, fiscal capacities and efficiencies must be assessed in relation to fiscal bases or fiscal potential. For example, in mid-seventeenth-century Genoa, for every 100 lire of personal income almost 22 lire was taken annually by tax collectors, undoubtedly a high percentage for the

Table 11.2. *Central revenues and per capita 'burden' in Italy, 1420–1789 (working days of a labourer in the building trade)*

	Milan	Venice	Florence	Genoa	Naples
1420–29			9		
1450–59		6			
1550–59		6	6	8	4
1560–69			6		7
1590–99					4
1600–09		5		12	5
1620–29			7		
1640–49	7		6		15
1650–59	8			9	
1700–09		8			
1750–59					5
1760–69	15	8			
1770–79	19				
1780–89	22				

Source: L. Pezzolo, *Mars and Pluto. War and finance in Italy, 1350–1700* (forthcoming).

times.[28] Data for Piedmont and Lombardy in the eighteenth century show that these states appropriated taxes at British ratios and tax burdens were less unequally distributed than in France. Furthermore, their subjects transferred most taxes to central governments. For example, a small Piedmontese farmer paid 12.8 per cent of his own income in state taxes, and only 1.4 per cent in ecclesiastical and feudal dues.[29] The Kingdom of Naples in the seventeenth century, on the contrary, accumulated enormous tax arrears that hindered the fiscal health of the state. This was the result of diminishing tax returns due to a dramatic gap between the financial needs of the government and the economic circumstances of society. As little as 800,000 ducats were collected from a grant of 1.5 million ducats offered by Naples in 1638.[30]

Table 11.2 shows a comparison among Italian states considering the amount of taxes at the disposal of the central treasuries and the per-capita 'burden' expressed in the number of working days of a labourer.

[28] G. Felloni, 'Distribuzione territoriale della ricchezza e dei carichi fiscali nella repubblica di Genova, e Stato genovese, finanza pubblica e ricchezza privata: un profilo storico', in Felloni, *Scritti di storia economica*, I (Genoa: Societa Ligure, 1999), p. 230.
[29] G. Prato, *La vita economica in Piemonte a mezzo il secolo XVIII* (Torino: Società Tip. Ed. Nazionale, 1908), p. 468.
[30] Galasso, *Storia del Regno*, pp. 166, 178, 189.

Data tell different stories. By the end of the *ancien régime*, some Italian states had achieved high levels, relatively speaking, of fiscal efficiency. Limits had been reached because their revenues funded wars rather than capital formation. It is not easy to connect fiscal efficiency to the construction of institutions for economic growth. During the Renaissance, states that managed to reconcile the interests of local elites and fiscal needs were small republics. Towards the end of the *ancien régime*, these republics could no longer compete with the great powers and their Italian dominions and satellites. Despite significant differences among several states, it does not seem that taxation in central and northern Italy provoked permanent and bloody tensions between states and subjects. In the south, on the other hand, the great revolt of 1647–48 marked a significant turning point. It was the peak of an increasing fiscal burden that, after the Spanish restoration, was lowered considerably. Thus, in the eighteenth century, Neapolitan taxpayers enjoyed more favourable conditions than previously. Napoleon's arrival on the peninsula changed the situation drastically. Italian taxpayers had to bear a heavy fiscal burden imposed to support his futile attempt to conquer Europe.

12 The formation of fiscal states in Italy: the Papal States

Fausto Piola Caselli

Since Clemens Bauer's 1928 article there has been a great deal of litera-ture on the Papal States.[1] Bauer focused on the unique path of religious, economic and institutional developments in a very 'long' sixteenth cen-tury, from the end of the fifteenth to the beginning of the seventeenth century.[2] The period of papal finances, which had begun in 1417 with the return from Avignon, concluded with the Tridentine Council. The Reformation had upset not only the consciences of the believers, but also the traditional spiritual income, which in the end was regularly guaran-teed only by the Italian clergy.[3] In late sixteenth century the spiritual yield still represented a good 20 per cent of all pontifical earnings, but the percentage was on a steep descent.[4] The Apostolic Chamber was obliged to find alternative sources of financial support, more so because the city of Rome, as the shop window of Catholicism, had to demon-strate to the Protestant world its monuments, its welfare and its financial solidity. Internal and external wars, as always, soaked up government coffers, though military costs were not as high for the Church as they were in other Italian regional states.[5] However, on the international stage, the maintenance of alliances was very expensive, as seen in 1598, when a contingency sent into Hungary to aid against the Turks had cost 1,500,000 *scudi*, almost a whole year's worth of income.[6] With the con-quest of Ferrara, at the end of the century, the extent of the Pontifical

---

[1] C. Bauer, 'Die Epochen der Päpstfinanz', *Historische Zeitschrift* 138 (1928), 457–503.
[2] The literature is surveyed in A. Gardi, 'La fiscalità pontificia tra medioevo ed età moderna', *Società e storia* 33 (1986), 509–57.
[3] P. Partner, 'Papal financial policy in the Renaissance and Counter-Reformation', *Past and Present* 88 (1980), 47.
[4] I. Grisar, 'Päpstliche Finanzen, Nepotismus und Kirchenrecht unter Urban VIII', *Miscellanea Historiae Pontificiae* 7 (1943), 221–2; M. Rosa, 'La "Scarsella di Nostro Signore": aspetti della fiscalità spirituale pontificia nell'età moderna', *Società e storia* 38 (1987), 830–4.
[5] C. Capra, 'The Italian states in the early modern period', in R. Bonney (ed.), *The rise of the fiscal state in Europe c. 1200–1815* (Oxford University Press, 1999), p. 438.
[6] J. Delumeau, *Vita economica e sociale di Roma nel Cinquecento* (Firenze: Sansoni, 1979), p. 204.

State in Italy was second only to the Kingdom of Naples. The annexation of Urbino in 1631 and a few years later that of the much more economically important dukedom of Castro, consolidated a territory that
would remain unchanged until the Treaty of Tolentino (1797). Showing
considerable foresight, the Apostolic Chamber entrusted the management of the provincial treasury to major Florentine and Genovese bankers, in this way weakening the power of the local feudal aristocracy and
extending the area of tax collection.[7] In Rome, the College of Cardinals
lost its traditional political role and state affairs were presented to the
Consistory only when the Pope and his inner circle had already made
decisions.[8] If state absolutism could rely upon trouble-free relations with
the provinces, it required the full possession of the capital city.

Control of Rome

Starting in the late 1500s, the city government was completely deprived
of power by the central Curia, which fully expropriated the city's
remaining autonomy. As Delumeau proved, integral control of Rome
by the central government did not represent a simple conquest of territory; rather it entailed an inevitable political measure, without which
the rise of the fiscal state could not occur.[9]

Full control of the city was reached little by little, after a restless
period marked by episodes of violent struggle with local noblemen, and
then ratified by a *pax romana* in 1511, which did not ensure stability for
many years. During the great food crisis from 1533 to 1534, there was
almost an open revolt.[10] However, by the end of the 1500s, the city's
glorious autonomy was only a memory.[11] The constitutions of 1580,
which decreed the overturn of the power system, were considered so
important to the pontiffs that they were confirmed many times, even
as late as 1847.[12] City authorities were left with duties of minor responsibility, such as protecting the religious and artistic heritage, keeping

[7] M. Caravale, *La finanza pontificia nel Cinquecento. Le province del Lazio* (Napoli: Novene, 1974), p. 121.
[8] P. Prodi, *Il sovrano pontefice. Un corpo e due anime: la monarchia papale nella prima età moderna* (Bologna: Il Mulino, 1982), p. 179.
[9] J. Delumeau, 'Les progrès de la centralisation dans l'Etat pontifical au XVIe siècle', *Revue Historique* 85 :226 (1961), 405.
[10] M. M. Bullard, 'Grain supply and urban unrest in Renaissance Rome: the crisis of 1533–34', in P. A. Ramsley (ed.), *Rome in the Renaissance. The city and the myth* (Binghamton, NY: Centre for Medieval and early Renaissance Studies, 1982), p. 284.
[11] M. Monaco, *Lo Stato della Chiesa* (Lecce: Milella, 1978), p. 188.
[12] P. Pavan, 'I fondamenti del potere: la legislazione statutaria del Comune di Roma dal XV secolo alla restaurazione', *Roma moderna e contemporanea* 4:2 (1996), 327–31.

the streets clean and controlling the system of weights and measures. Nothing better describes the city's humiliation than the few words spoken by Pope Sixtus V to the three Capitoline *conservatori* in 1586. The Pope scornfully informed the town administrators that, given their absolute incompetence, he was forced to exclude them from the Roman *annona*, the important and strategic food supply department. They would be left only with the role of executing the pontiff's decisions and little more.[13] From then onwards, the Roman food supply policy was headed by the Chamber with good results, maintaining a remarkable surplus until the crisis of 1763.[14]

Dependence on the Apostolic Chamber emerged speculatively in the city's finances. The city was left with only a few taxes to cover the expenses of La Sapienza University, and with small grants for the major capitolini officers. In 1674, when earnings on meat were definitively diverted to the Apostolic Chamber, the city's income came to the miserable total of 50,000 *scudi* per year, a sum that would later remain unchanged for almost two centuries.[15] In contrast, the city's contribution to the state balance sheets was extremely important. It provided about a quarter of the annual revenue at the end of sixteenth century,[16] and more in the following two centuries, as seen in Figure 12.1.[17]

The Apostolic Chamber had excellent reasons to keep the city under its control. Roman taxes, gifts and various duties could secure the state a good 40 per cent of its yearly income, even during the last period of economic decline.

Administrative networks

The network of administrative and accounting relationships with the small towns of the states was established in the same period. In 1588, Sixtus V, within a larger reorganization of the Curia, created a Congregation *pro gravaminibus sublevandis* that dealt with solving

[13] C. De Cupis, *Le vicende dell'agricoltura e della pastorizia nell'agro romano. L'annona di Roma giusta memorie, consuetudini e leggi desunte da documenti anche inediti. Sommario storico* (Roma: Tipografia Nazionale di G. Bertero, 1911), p. 199.

[14] H. Gross, *Rome in the Age of Enlightenment: the post Tridentine syndrome and the ancient regime* (Cambridge University Press, 1990), p. 186.

[15] F. Colzi, *Il debito pubblico del Campidoglio. Finanza comunale e circolazione dei titoli a Roma fra Cinque e Seicento* (Napoli: Edizioni Scientifiche Italiane, 1999), p. 122.

[16] P. Partner, 'The Papacy and the Papal States', in Bonney, *The rise of the fiscal state*, p. 366.

[17] Sources: F. Piola Caselli, 'Evoluzione e finanziamento del debito pubblico pontificio tra XVII e XVIII secolo', in G. De Luca and A. Moioli (eds.), *Debito pubblico e mercati finanziari in Italia. Secolo XIII–XX* (Milano: FrancoAngeli, 2007), pp. 218–20 and notes 6–7, p. 218.

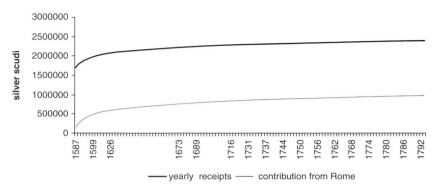

Figure 12.1 Rome's contribution to the state balance sheets

controversies in fiscal matters with the communities of the provinces. The pontiff's primary purpose was to involve the organs of the local governments, and five senior officers of the Chamber immediately visited the provinces.[18] Following this experience, the Congregation of the *Buon Governo* was established in 1592, which laid down the foundations for a disciplined and unitary administration of the whole pontifical territory. The Congregation made decisions concerning the division of taxes among the various communities and approved the annual budgets that all communities were obligated to send to Rome. This was only one among many obligations foreseen in the thirty-one articles governing the procedures to be followed in financial relations between the centre and the periphery of the states. The communities were required to keep a series of accounts which were inspected periodically. The communities' profits had to be used primarily for servicing any past debts, then for financing local food supplies, and subsequently for public works; nonetheless they were to be deposited in the *Monti di Pietà* in Rome.[19] Although facing continual hostility from the baronial regions, from the end of the sixteenth century, the Pontifical States grew gradually and tenaciously, closely following the model of development of many other European states.[20]

[18] C. Penuti, 'Aspetti della politica economica nello Stato Pontifico sul finire del 500: le visite economiche di Sisto V', *Annali dell'Istituto storico italo-germanico in Trento* 2 (1976), 184.

[19] E. Lodolini, *L'Archivio della S. Congregazione del buon governo (1592–1847). Inventario* (Roma: Istituto Poligrafico dello Stato, 1956), p. 17.

[20] A. Caracciolo, 'Lo Stato pontificio tra Seicento e Settecento: problemi della formazione dello Stato moderno' in R. Paci (ed.), *Scritti storici in memoria di Enzo Piscitelli* (Padova: Antenore, 1982), p. 202.

A long-term perspective

Until the mid 1600s the steady increase of fiscal revenues was absolutely necessary to guarantee the new needs of a state managing temporal affairs. Papal finances developed under the influence of political and military emergencies.[21] Besides wars, other emergencies consumed financial resources, such as sudden periods of famine that held the potential to weaken papal power.

Once the era of great change was over, from the mid 1600s onwards, papal policy became less dynamic as the treasury was burdened by public debt and taxation reached its highest levels ever, factors that symbolized the onset of economic decline. The Chamber budgets and accounts registered very similar, if not identical, figures each year, mirroring the general stability. The frequent elections of new popes, followed by a high turnover in the curial ranks,[22] prevented the Chamber from developing a coherent political economy in the long run. In 1708 the *tassa del milione* was established and yielded only modest earnings, but it was nonetheless the most innovative aspect of fiscal policy during the period. It was not until the election of Pius VI Braschi, who had acquired administrative experience as General Treasurer from 1766 to 1773, that some changes were introduced. A land taxation act provoked heated reactions, and ultimately remained substantially unused. By contrast, the new customs system introduced at state borders in 1786 was more effective. It aimed to modify the thin fiscal balance between the centre and the provinces, which had been in place for many years.[23] The Napoleonic invasion was, however, at the door, and the fiscal novelties did not produce significant structural results.

Fiscal policy in the Papal States between the late 1600s and the 1700s has received scant attention from scholars. However, the process of formation of the fiscal state seems to have been much more coherent and efficient during that period than it had previously been, when it is analysed over the long term using the abundant registers and ledgers that have survived from the era.[24]

---

[21] Partner, 'The Papacy and the Papal States', p. 371.
[22] R. Ago, *Carriere e clientele nella Roma barocca* (Bari: Laterza, 1990), p. 23.
[23] C. Capra, 'Le finanze degli stati italiani nel secolo XVIII', in *L'Italia alla vigilia della rivoluzione francese* (Roma: Istituto per la storia del risorgimento italiano, 1990), p. 151.
[24] A. Caracciolo, 'I Bilanci dello Stato ecclesiastico fra XVI e XVIII secolo: una fonte e alcune considerazioni', in *Mèthodologie de l'Histoire et des sciences humaines: mélanges en l'honneur de Fernand Braudel* (Toulouse: Privat, 1973), pp. 99–103 was the first to stress the importance of yearly balance sheets from the late sixteenth to late eighteenth

Budgets

The Papal Curia operated with an ancient accounting tradition. Already at the beginning of the fourteenth century it had set up an advanced school of public accounting in the papal palace at Avignon, and for almost the entire century it regularly kept accounts of income and expenditures. With the return of the Pope to Rome, bookkeeping became rather less professional and was entrusted to representatives of great Florentine or Genoese banks. Balance sheets were drawn up only intermittently, mostly at the election of a new pope or when the Curia needed an overview of available resources.

The accounts, however, represented only grand totals of all possible forms of income from the various treasuries and from the duties levied in Rome and the provinces. No overall controls existed over income from the numerous departments or from independent banks, or over shortfalls between the amounts paid to the Curia or franchises for the collection of duties and actual amounts levied by the contractors.

From the mid seventeenth century, accounts became more regular, until they were drafted yearly. The bookkeeping system was improved thanks to the directions of the Chamber's chief accountant Nunziato Baldocci.[25] Later on, the Chamber's entire accounting system was reformed in 1746, when fourteen different ledgers were established.[26] Among these, a separate sector was reserved for the general customs of Rome, the earnings of which continued to be vital to papal finances. As for balance sheets, surpluses and deficits usually compensated for each other from year to year. The financial situation was stable and the Chamber achieved some good results during the pontificate of Benedict XIV (1740–58). Losses became uninterrupted only in the last decade of the century, as Figure 12.2 indicates.[27]

The documentation available confirms the considerable efforts made to keep public finances under control throughout the 1700s, through calculations, reports and comparisons. In 1712 the income and expenses of Rome's customs were analysed for almost eighteen years between 1689 and 1707, during the delicate period in which the Chamber began to privately run the capital's customs, abandoning the traditional nine-year concessions to private bankers. In 1731 an outline was drawn up,

centuries. Documentation is kept in 'Camerale II – Conti di entrata e di uscita della Camera', Archivio di Stato di Roma (ASR from here on).
[25] Details and accounting criteria are in G. V. Parigino (ed.), *Il bilancio pontificio del 1657* (Napoli: Edizioni Scientifiche Italiane, 1999), pp. 16–19.
[26] Capra, 'Le finanze degli stati italiani', 153.
[27] Sources as indicated for Figure 12.1 in note 17.

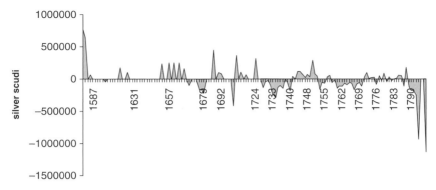

Figure 12.2 Chamber accounts yearly balance

in order to make a long-term comparison with the 1631 balance sheet, focusing particularly on income from the provinces and the global amount of public debt with interest paid. Later on, when the financial situation became critical, the Chamber drew up an exhaustive table confronting all sources of income and all varieties of expenses for a ten-year period from 1780 to 1790.[28] The servicing of debt always produced abundant documentation.

The debt

The history of papal debt is one of efficient management by the Apostolic Chamber. It started in 1526 and accumulated over the second half of the sixteenth century. Following Florentine practice, each issue for a loan was called *monte*, and each *monte* was made of *luoghi* ('bonds'), nominally worth 100 Roman *scudi* each. Life annuities raised a yearly interest of 12 per cent, whilst long-term issues paid only 10 per cent, although interest rates were soon lowered, down to 10 and 5 per cent at the end of the sixteenth century.[29] The debt accumulated until 1684–87, when the various loans still outstanding were converted in two operations, into the consolidated debts named *Monte* of Saint Peter, at an interest rate of 3 per cent.[30] In slightly over a century and a half, the Curia had

[28] 'Camerale II – Conti di entrata e di uscita della Camera', Vols. 5, 7, 14, ASR.
[29] F. Piola Caselli, 'La diffusione dei luoghi di monte della Camera Apostolica alla fine del XVI secolo. Capitali investiti e rendimenti', in *Credito e sviluppo economico in Italia dal Medio Evo all'Età Contemporanea* (Verona: Gafiche Fiorini, 19), pp. 198, 200, tables I and II.
[30] R. Masini, *Il debito pubblico pontificio a fine Seicento. I monti camerali* (Città di Castello: Edimont, 2005), pp. 136–7.

authorized the issue of 187 *monti*. The proceeds from 71 financed central government finances, 55 extinguished debts of the Roman nobility, 23 were for the city of Rome and 38 for other cities.[31]

From then on, the new issues simply replaced old ones. The last pontifical loan was the *Monte Nuovo* for a total of 600,000 *scudi* at a 3 per cent interest rate, issued in 1793 to both fund the army and strengthen the coastline. The 6,000 *luoghi* found subscribers within two years, which shows that papal bonds were still in demand. One-third of the capital was deposited by Genovese and Florentine families and the market price of each bond was always above its nominal value.[32]

Overall, the amount of the papal debt went from the initial 200,000 to 5.6 million *scudi* in 1592, to 28 million in 1657, finally stabilizing at 40 million *scudi* towards the end of the century. In the eighteenth century the total amount of loans, both papal and of the city of Rome – excluding the debts of the nobility and of the small cities – remained between 40 and 50 million *scudi*, with an increase registered only in the last decade of the century.[33] Notwithstanding its debt, the papacy never went bankrupt and interests were always regularly paid. As a matter of fact, the Chamber's bonds business could produce additional earnings. New issues were always sold below par to major bankers and subscribers, who earned a good spread on the secondary markets. Moreover, bankers could apply to provide further services such as the very profitable tax farming in Rome.

Market prices remained higher than the bonds' face value. As late as 1782, 3,937 bonds, at a 3 per cent interest rate, were bought at a price of 127 *scudi* for every 100 of the face value.[34] Per-capita interest payments paid by the Chamber, from 22 Roman *baiocchi* in 1576 reached a peak of 73 in 1657, and declined slowly down to 56 *baiocchi* at the end of the following century.[35]

---

[31] 'Camerale II – Archivio della Camera', Vol. 10, ASR.

[32] D. Strangio, 'Debito pubblico e deficit di bilancio dello Stato della Chiesa. Il Monte Nuovo della difesa (1793–1814)', *Studi romani* 48 (2000), 98.

[33] D. Strangio, *Il debito pubblico pontificio. Cambiamento e continuità nella finanza pontificia dal periodo francese alla restaurazione romana* (Padova: Cedam, 2001), table 1, pp. 59–65.

[34] D. Strangio, 'Debito pubblico e riorganizzazione del mercato finanziario nello Stato ecclesiastico nel '700', *Roma moderna e contemporanea* 2 (1994), 83–103, 188.

[35] F. Piola Caselli, 'Public debt, state revenue and town consumption in Rome (sixteenth–eighteenth centuries)', in M. Boone, K. Davids and P. Janssens (eds.), *Urban public debt. Urban government and the market for annuities in Western Europe (14th–18th centuries)* (Turnhout: Brepols, 2003), p. 96, table II.

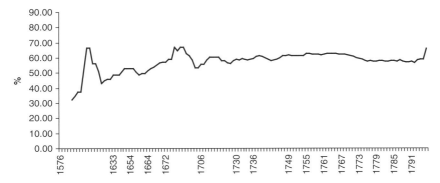

Figure 12.3 Debt interests

All in all, the papal debt was always kept under control. Interest paid out increased quickly in the first half of the seventeenth century, and afterwards remained steady at around 60 per cent of total yearly revenue, as seen in Figure 12.3.[36]

The great success in the management of public debt was substantially due to two reasons. First of all, each of the Chamber's issues was guaranteed by fiscal or property sources that were considered absolutely reliable, so much so that there were no doubts regarding the regular payment of interest. Second, the interest rates were in any case remunerative compared to the alternative investments possible, which only pertained to immovable property. The Apostolic Chamber also knew how to earn the trust of depositors by elaborating extremely efficient administrative mechanisms, without risks and – strangely enough for the period – quite transparent. This is demonstrated by the publication in 1615 of a debt code pertaining to the circulation of *monti*. In 1686, when the Chamber decided to transfer all the funds that were in circulation, which at that time benefited from many different interest rates, into new bonds at the rate of 3 per cent, reimbursement of the old investments was offered at a market price, which in that period was about 130 *scudi* each. Bonds were exempt from all taxes, except for a small purchase tax, which was used to cover administrative costs, in addition to any mediation costs by brokers.[37] It is therefore not surprising that

[36] Sources as indicated in note 17 for Figure 12.1.
[37] For the efficiency of papal debt see also F. Piola Caselli, 'Public debt in the Papal States: financial market and government strategies in the long run', in F. Piola Caselli (ed.), *Government debts and financial markets in Europe* (London: Pickering & Chatto, 2008), pp. 107–8.

private savers and local institutions immediately purchased new *luoghi di monte* issues when they were released. Among the subscribers there were craftsmen, office workers and specialized labourers, and 27 per cent of the bonds were registered to women.[38]

The fiscal system

The development of the papal fiscal system took place in the aftermath of the Reformation, with the establishment of the *monti* and a number of direct taxes, the latter yielding minimal revenues.[39] Taxation peaked between 1630 and 1650 with the introduction of a series of heavy taxes on consumption. Thereafter, reductions in taxes occurred with the institution of a single tariff at state borders, and the abolition of internal tolls during a brief season of Church enlightenment.

The first sign of the state presence in the periphery arrived with the exceptional taxation of one ducat per hearth in 1531 and in 1536. Two new dime-taxes on the clergy, and a one-twentieth tax on Jews, were then introduced, followed by an increase in the levy on salt, a measure that triggered rebellions in Perugia, Rimini and other minor towns. In 1543, a *sussidio triennale* on lands was introduced to raise 300,000 *scudi* per year and it soon became annual. Rates of taxation were uncertain and often negotiated with local elites. A tax on meat followed in 1553, on wine in 1585 and a further tax to finance the papal fleet was introduced in 1588.[40]

In the seventeenth century, taxes fell mainly upon consumption and included monopolies on tobacco and spirits. Increases in the prices of salt, meat and wine followed, together with the new institution, in 1630, of the mill tax for Rome. In 1662, a programme for tax relief began and the costs of salt, flour and meat fell.[41] In 1681, tax exemptions for office-holders in the Curia and for ecclesiastical land-owners were abolished. In 1702, all tax immunities for the nobility came to an end. In 1708, a new 'Million Tax' was levied, that raised 1 million *scudi* per year for the army for war against Austria. This taxation was assessed on income

---

[38] Masini, *Il debito pubblico pontificio*, p. 177.

[39] For the connections between taxes and debt, mainly in the eighteenth century, see D. Strangio, 'Debito pubblico e sistema fiscale a Roma e nello Stato pontificio tra '600 e '700', in S. Cavaciocchi (ed.), *Fiscal systems in the European economy from the 13th to the 18th centuries: atti della 'Trentanovesima settimana di studi'*, 2 vols. (Firenze University Press, 2008), Vol. 1, pp. 500–3.

[40] An outline of sixteenth-century tax system is in E. Stumpo, *Il capitale finanziario a Roma fra Cinque e Seicento. Contributo alla storia della fiscalità pontificia in età moderna (1570–1660)* (Milano: Cedam, 1985), pp. 102–19.

[41] Colzi, *Il debito pubblico del Campidoglio*, p. 130.

estimated for every state locality, and was expected to yield somewhere between 59 to 157 *baiocchi* per head.[42] In 1746, at a time of fiscal crisis, a Committee was created to propose changes that might free entrepreneurs from taxation, abolish restrictions on the domestic market and improve financial information in order to calculate the real economic situation of municipalities outside Rome.[43]

Direct versus indirect taxation

In many cases, distinctions between direct and indirect taxation are rather theoretical and refer only to the official documents that established them, frequently having no connection with the real situation of local taxation. Until the end of the seventeenth century, the papal state had no fiscal bureaucracy of its own. Tax collection was franchised out to treasurers, bankers and contractors, who were given police powers over the taxpayers. Contractors then exacted payment from the local authorities who were almost always left free to collect *pesi camerali* in whatever ways they saw fit.[44] These taxes nominally levied by the Curia on income or property could then be transformed into an excise, or even paid as part of the returns from communal property.

Among entries appearing in the papal balance sheets, indirect taxes classified as tolls, excises and customs duties are clearly indicated, but it is impossible to divide their revenues as money raised from direct or indirect forms of taxation. That could only be done by studying local taxation. In general, where some semblance of a tradition of local autonomy survived, on taxes levied on land or supplementary excises or tolls where the nobilities ruled, only consumer goods were subjected to taxation. Major cities were usually subject only to duties and excises and were exempted from direct taxation. In 1708 the powerful towns of Ferrara and Bologna were totally exempted from the heavy Million Tax, levied on the patrimonies of all towns and local communities to finance the army.

Local budgets for the cities of Imola, Assisi and Corneto are suggestive. In Imola, the revenues collected went up by 545 per cent between 1520 and 1605. Taxes on lands represented 25 per cent of this total and the rest consisted of excises (*gabella grossa*, mill tax, wine and meat).[45]

---

[42] L. Nina, *Le finanze pontificie sotto Clemente XI (Tassa del milione)* (Milano: Treves, 1928), p. 321; and Strangio, 'Debito pubblico e deficit di bilancio', pp. 91–2.
[43] Records, reports and projects published from 1748 onwards are kept in 'Camerale II – Dogane', Vol. 2, ASR.
[44] Gardi, 'La fiscalità pontificia', 534.
[45] C. Rotelli, 'La finanza locale pontificia nel Cinquecento: il caso di Imola', *Studi Storici* 9 (1968), 141–2.

The taxes for the Curia represented 60 per cent of expenditures by the city in 1520, and reached 80 per cent towards the end of the century.

In Assisi, direct and indirect taxes were roughly equal until 1680. Thereafter taxes on consumption declined.[46] Curia taxes formed 75 per cent of all revenues in 1460 but fell to 65 per cent forty years later. The total delivered in 1660 came to about 7,000 *scudi*, falling to 5,000 *scudi* forty years later.[47] Corneto was a prosperous place and 45 per cent of taxes collected there were for the Curia, and levies on consumption of meat and flour more than covered that obligation. The town's income came from taxes on property.[48]

The data cited above suggests that for places beyond the reach of city governance, taxes could only be collected in the form of an imposition on consumer goods. Furthermore, up to two-thirds or more of taxes levied locally were assessed for the Curia. In the papal state, which lacked land registers, it was not possible for central government to calculate the real value of land for the purposes of taxation. The land register, drawn up in 1681, was based on sworn tax declarations and it was never actually used. The second register *Piano*, prepared under Pius VI in 1777 and 1783, was also never utilized. As for the countryside around Rome, laws published in 1743 and 1764 included provisions for levying taxes on incomes from property and land, but these were not implemented. Another attempt to tax the income from land rents, urban real estate and seigniorial dues was made in 1793.[49] Again the yields were meagre.

Town customs

By contrast, the customs system was very well organized, and provided the papal treasury with a safe and easily calculated income. As was usual in many European countries, customs were farmed or franchised. State administrations were not up to managing the complex operations, and handed them over to merchant bankers for a predetermined lease and price. Big contractors could, in turn, run the collection or lease the 'farm' to other entrepreneurs, and share in the profits. In the papal state, the Curia did not expect down payments and was satisfied if the

[46] A. M. Girelli, *La finanza comunale nello Stato Pontificio. Il caso di Assisi* (Padova: Cedam, 1992), p. 58.

[47] Ibid., pp. 40–9, 58 and 62–3.

[48] A. M. Girelli and S. Masi, 'In tema di finanza locale. Un progetto di ricerca per la storia dello Stato Pontificio. Il caso di Corneto', in *Annali del Dipartimento di Studi Geoeconomici Statistici Storici per l'Analisi Regionale* (Bologna: Pàtron, 2000), p. 154.

[49] Strangio, 'Debito pubblico e deficit di bilancio', pp. 93–4.

amounts due were paid directly to bankers who managed its loans and paid interest on the papal debt every two months.

Despite their complexity, customs were administered impeccably and, with the salt tax, accounted for a growing share of the Curia's revenues. The Curia normally offered contracts and leases for nine years on the basis of competitive tenders.[50] Contractors required guarantees from bankers as well as technical expertise. They contracted to pay fixed amounts but could count on higher returns based on an approximate estimate of the goods subject to assessment. The operations were very speculative and the detailed tenders prepared by the Curia contained provisions to pay the fixed rent conditions of the lease if and when fortuitous events changed the tax yields. Around 1575, the difference between the tender and the net income from customs in Rome could be between 10 and 20 per cent a year.[51] At the beginning of the next century the difference between retail fixed prices for meat and those used by the Curia to calculate the lease was close to 15 per cent, but the collection costs were borne by the contractors. When their profits declined, the organization of Roman customs was removed from private bankers and taken over by the Curia administration in 1698.[52]

From at least the early 1600s, the customs system was managed with administrative firmness and precision, as is demonstrated in the rich documentation that exists for Rome. Contracts for customs offices were written up according to detailed specifications, which included all possible clauses. They included cases of war, natural disasters (as in fact happened during the outbreak of the plague in 1630 and 1656) or depreciable events, which could force the Papal Court to reside more than sixty miles away from Rome. In all these cases, which altered regular commerce, the annual fee could undergo a congruous reduction. However, there were also other causes such as the one occurring in 1653 when the customs officer Francesco Ravenna asked for and obtained a *diffalco* or a deduction of annual fees, because the production by the craftsmen's shops in Rome had significantly increased, thus consequently reducing the incoming flow of goods. The customs office's accounts had to be kept according to meticulously detailed norms and

[50] First contracts were drawn up for five or seven years only: F. Guidi Bruscoli, 'Banchieri appaltatori e aumento della pressione fiscale nello Stato pontificio tra Quattro e Cinquecento', in Cavaciocchi, *Fiscal systems in the European economy*, Vol. 1, p. 870.

[51] J. Delumeau, *Vie économique et sociale de Rome dans la seconde moitié du XVIe siècle*, 2 vols. (Paris: De Boccard, 1957–59), Vol. 1, p. 128.

[52] F. Piola Caselli, 'Merci per dogana e consumi alimentari a Roma nel Seicento', in *La popolazione italiana nel Seicento* (Bologna: Cooperativa Libraria Universitaria Editrice, 1999), pp. 394–6.

included a daybook with a ledger, along with other minor registers. Despite the increase of the Roman population, which in the 1600s grew only 25 per cent, the cost of customs contracts tripled in less than one century, going from 180,000 *scudi* in 1593 to 380,000 in 1654, and closing at 542,000 in 1689 – the last contract let out to private individuals. The Chamber developed its own system of bureaucracy. Tax exemptions for influential members of the Curia and other important people totalled 15 per cent of total revenues, and by 1681 these exemptions had been dramatically reduced, to the point where they were quite insignificant. On the whole, the Roman customs offices give the impression of shrewd and prudent management. From the mid seventeenth century onwards, the Chamber's accounting registered a balance between the income and expenditures of the private contractors, and profits were most likely made both by the privilege of being inside the Curia and by the possibility of managing large cash flows, quite valuable in periods of money shortage.

The new customs system at the borders

Throughout the eighteenth century, customs at the town gates represented the main element of the fiscal structure, in spite of the debate that emphasized the urgent need for free trade which was then developing in economic and political circles.[53] By the end of the 1760s, the future Pope Braschi and the Roman banker Girolamo Belloni began to elaborate a project for the collection of customs that aimed at eliminating the local customs barriers that obstructed internal commerce, and well-known scholars and economists cooperated with them. In 1775 a high-ranking officer, after travelling for six months, marked out the exact perimeter of the state over a total of 404 miles. Finally, in 1786, reforms were passed, in line with those already followed for years by many great European nations.[54] Taxes were to be collected on all goods divided by market categories, measure and value, considering both cases of importation into the territory and those continuing towards the capital, while exportation was taxed only in a few particular cases. The taxation varied from about 9 to 12 per cent of the value of the goods, sometimes peaking for luxury products.

The following year the Chamber wrote an accurate description of the new customs situation, with a map of all the cities and active customs

---

[53] A. Caracciolo and M. Caravale, *Lo Stato pontificio da Martino V a Pio IX* (Torino: Utet, 1978), p. 502.

[54] E. Lo Sardo, *Le gabelle e le dogane dei papi in età moderna* (Roma: Archivio di Stato, 1994), pp. 32–4.

offices, which totalled 90, including Rome. There were 504 regular workers among military officers and civilians, costing an annual 21,000 *scudi* for salaries and an additional 1,000 *scudi* for office rent, with the total cost of the system being about 22,000 *scudi* per year, excluding the customs administration of the city of Rome. All considered, it was a modest cost, equalling about 5 per cent of all the taxes yielded. Provincial treasurers continued to act as collectors in their territories, in the new system as well. As for Rome, the goods that had already been taxed at the state borders were subject to another tax of 3 to 6 per cent.[55] This was clearly incongruous but was sustained by the city's high consumption flow, which produced, as always, a large amount of income.

Soon after constructing the system of customs at the borders, the Chamber sought to establish whether or not the new system worked – or at least as far as Rome was concerned – given that its running costs had increased about 20 per cent. The calculation made by Chamber accountant Franco Sterlini compared the average annual profits of the decade before the tax reform (1775–84) to those of the three-year period after reform (1786–89). From a general view, the results confirmed that after the tax reform there was a satisfactory income from the new system and that, on the whole, it was able to earn a net 10 per cent increase, due to the prevailing taxation of foodstuffs.[56] Roman consumption was still the backbone of taxation. As for the other large cities of the Papal States, it was not possible to defeat the resistance of Bologna, Ferrara and their territories, who were soon exempted from the system and allowed free commerce throughout papal lands. On the whole, the new customs structure was not considered particularly positive. Although the revenue of the state did not decrease, there were many misunderstandings and logistical difficulties at the local level. The new system was strongly criticized, and in 1794 the treasurer, Ruffo, was dismissed. Nevertheless, taxation at borders did not modify the fiscal dynamics between Rome and the provinces. In the long run both fiscal sources remained almost unvaried, suffering only a temporary loss in 1787, immediately after the new law, and felt mainly in the provinces. Even if balance sheet documentation for 1794 and 1795 is lost, Table 12.1 clearly demonstrates how the Chamber's financial situation changed only on the eve of the Napoleonic invasion.

[55] 'Camerale II – Dogane', Vol. 4, int. 1 and 4, ASR.
[56] 'Camerale II – Dogane', Vol. 6, int. 4, ASR.

Table 12.1. *The origins of tax revenues (Roman scudi)*

	Yearly total receipts	Taxation from Rome	%	Taxes from provinces	%	Various income	%
1592	1,601,195	282,999	18	823,360	51	494,836	31
1619	1,790,521	259,004	14	896,257	50	636,260	36
1633	1,934,616	326,622	17	988,029	51	619,965	32
1657	2,684,515	552,486	21	1,429,789	53	702,240	26
1689	2,511,883	547,137	22	1,119,682	44	845,064	34
1706	2,469,005	595,296	24	1,135,460	46	738,249	30
1716	2,390,488	582,880	24	1,148,920	48	659,732	28
1724	2,716,650	669,413	25	1,246,116	46	801,121	29
1736	2,395,459	626,230	26	1,263,292	53	505,937	21
1746	2,220,128	661,510	30	1,040,604	47	518,014	23
1756	2,150,477	647,156	30	1,007,596	47	495,725	23
1766	2,121,499	611,657	29	1,008,404	48	501,438	23
1776	2,343,254	656,084	28	1,134,618	48	552,552	24
1784	2,341,769	610,686	26	1,168,788	50	562,295	24
1785	2,378,166	588,265	25	1,149,741	48	640,160	27
1786	2,420,326	628,633	26	1,149,017	47	642,676	27
1787	2,247,996	614,920	27	980,696	44	652,380	29
1788	2,598,161	632,746	24	1,086,538	42	878,877	34
1790	2,331,097	623,193	27	1,046,067	45	661,837	28
1791	2,351,744	610,168	26	1,128,052	48	613,524	26
1792	2,485,646	596,825	24	1,220,600	49	668,221	27
1793	2,330,425	567,442	25	1,148,395	49	614,588	26
1796	1,824,362	442,820	24	865,907	48	515,635	28

Sources: 1592 and 1619: W. Reinhard, *Papstfinanz und Nepotismus unter Paul V. (1605–1621). Studien und Quellen zur Struktur und zu quantitativen Aspekten des päpstliche Herrschaftssystems*, 2 vols. (Stuttgart: Anton Hiersemann, 1974), Vol. 2, pp. 246–8 and 335–7; 1633: 'Miscellanea Armadio XI', Vol. 85a, Archivio Segreto Vaticano; 1657: Parigino, *Il bilancio pontificio del 1657*, pp. 42–55; 1789–96: 'Camerale II – Conti di'entrata e di uscita della Camera', Vols. 3–15, ASR.

Fiscal burdens

From Sixtus V's pontificate onwards, taxes amounted to two-thirds and later to three-quarters of the Chamber's income. The significance of the city of Rome grew markedly in relation to the role of the periphery and provided one-third of all tax income. Taxes classified as indirect in the accounting records of the Curia remained in the 50 per cent range, rising towards 60 per cent by the end of the seventeenth century. The remaining 40 per cent consisted of indirect and direct taxes whose provenance is difficult to classify without further research into local finance. The division between indirect and direct taxes probably shifted over time from 70/30 to 80/20 per cent.

Fiscal pressures seem to have remained constant for an initial period. This occurred when the state was mainly financed by way of recourse to loans and credit. The papal debt turned out to be a form of delayed taxation. Indeed, the real leap in fiscal pressure took place during the reigns of the Barberini and Pamphili popes, and more clearly in Rome than in other areas. After the mid seventeenth century, that pressure became steady, with a trend of decline from the mid eighteenth century onwards.

It is also clear that differences existed in the level of taxation imposed in Rome and the provinces. Using population data,[57] it is possible to calculate the fiscal burdens per capita borne by citizens of Rome and the provinces as recorded by the Chambers' accountancy and seen in Table 12.2.

By the beginning of the sixteenth century, taxation in Rome was substantial because it was the only assured income for the treasury. By the end of the century, when full control over the territory had been established, Romans paid at least six times more than other citizens of the state. The first possible explanation for this clear difference points towards indirect taxation and the very high consumption of goods in Rome.[58] In all probability, expenditure on consumption outside the capital failed to appear in treasury records, whilst in Rome not a single *baiocco* would escape the attention of the Curia officers.

The principal cause of variation between Rome and the other areas was linked to the levels of taxation imposed. Taxes on consumer goods in Rome were higher than anywhere else in the state. During the reign of Urban VIII, at least ten increases occurred in taxation that were particular to Rome. If the mill tax was six *scudi* in the city, it was only half that in the territories. During the reign of Innocent XI, meat was taxed by 5.4 *quattrini* to the pound in Rome, whereas in Bologna it remained at 3, and at 2 elsewhere.[59] In 1689, this duty was abolished everywhere but Rome, as it provided a regular and straightforward yield. By the end of the seventeenth century, consumer taxes in Rome amounted to 10 per cent of the declared value. The *tariffa tassativa* ('duty tariffs') of 1788 indirectly confirmed the divide between the Roman duty system and that in the other parts of the Papal States. It proposed a series of tax

---

[57] The increase of the town population was slightly higher than that of the state: Piola Caselli, 'Evoluzione e finanziamento', pp. 222–3.

[58] J. Revel, 'Les privilèges d'une capitale: l'approvisionnement de Rome à l'époque moderne', *Annales E.S.C.* 30 (1975), 567.

[59] Colzi, *Il debito pubblico del Campidoglio*, p. 130.

Table 12.2. *Per capita fiscal burdens, 1592–1796 (Roman silver giulii)*

	Rome	Provinces
1592	28.3	4.3
1619	23.5	4.7
1633	29.7	5.2
1657	52.6	8.4
1689	43.8	6.3
1706	44.1	6.1
1716	43.2	6.2
1724	49.6	6.7
1736	46.4	6.8
1746	49.0	5.6
1756	41.5	5.1
1766	39.2	5.1
1776	42.1	5.7
1786	38.6	5.1
1793	34.0	4.9
1796	26.5	3.7

Sources: as for Table 12.1.

rates according to value; however, the rates on merchandise entering Rome were increased by one-half.[60] Through applying different taxation rates to consumption, the Curia implemented a primitive form of fiscal pressure that distinguished between those considered rich or poor. The Curia's system of taxation was not based on fiscal equity but aimed to return the highest income possible. This model of different rates for different levels of income was not unknown in Italy; indeed, it had been previously introduced in the Florentine and Sienese land registers in the fourteenth century.[61] By the end of the seventeenth century, a number of European countries were laying the foundations for progressive systems of direct taxation, evident in the English land tax. The papal tax system had already been doing this, in its own way.

Finally, if we conjecture and add 30 per cent for increases in local taxation for the non-metropolitan areas, taxation for the entire population of the Papal States (including the capital) can be calculated as having increased from 0.25–0.3 to 1–1.2 *scudi* between the beginning of the sixteenth century and the end of the eighteenth century, doubling

---

[60] Piola Caselli, 'Merci per dogana e consumi alimentari', p. 398.
[61] E. Fiumi, 'L'imposta diretta nei comuni medioevali della Toscana', in *Studi in onore di Armando Sapori* (Milano: Istituto editoriale cisalpino, 1957), p. 348.

in the first century years and doubling again in the following fifty years, but remaining more or less stable thereafter.[62] Considering the silver coin debasement in the long run, the per-capita amounts paid for taxes were therefore equivalent to 9–10 grams of sterling silver in 1525 and to 21 grams in 1592. They reached a peak of 42 grams in 1657, lowering then to 36 grams in 1724 and to 21–27 grams only in the second half of the eighteenth century.[63] According to Carboni's figures, the fiscal burden in other European countries was probably much higher: in 1750 it was 40.4 silver grams per capita in Venice, 62.5 in France, 136.1 in Great Britain, 285 in the Netherlands and only 26.5 in the Church States.[64]

As a matter of fact, the second half of the 1600s was a true turning point in the history of Rome. This has been discussed very little. The whole financial system was made progressively more rational and modern. At the end of the century, the introduction of the Chamber's bureaucracy in substitution for the antique system of private banking had overturned many traditional administrative concepts in the Roman Curia. As a consequence, the sale of offices was forbidden. The battle against nepotism, baronial privileges and fiscal exemptions achieved positive results. The Roman *annona* produced a cash surplus, thanks to a fortunate spell of high crop yields. The debt service was reorganized at a reduced rate of interest, but not even a single investor abandoned the fabulous *luoghi di monte*. When taxation yields became feeble, the state lottery could easily compensate for any fiscal loss.[65] In spite of Italian economic decadence, the papal financial and fiscal system remained stable for long periods, supported by high levels of consumption and by its own efficiency.

[62] According to figures in Partner, 'Papal Financial policy', p. 41, taxation to the state in 1525 could be nearly two *giulii* per capita.

[63] The *scudo* was equal to ten silver *giulii*. The silver *giulio* coin decreased from 3.6 sterling silver grammes in 1502, to 2.94 grammes in 1566, to 2.91 in 1684 and to 2.45 in 1754: G. Londei, 'La monetazione pontificia e la zecca di Roma in età moderna (secc. XVI–XVIII)', *Studi romani* 38 (1990), 3–4.

[64] M. Carboni, *Stato e finanza pubblica in Europa dal medioevo ad oggi. Un profilo storico* (Torino: Giappichelli, 2008), table 2.3 p. 62.

[65] In 1784, Roman lottery net income was about 160,000 *scudi*: F. Colzi, *La fortuna dei Papi. Il gioco del lotto nello Stato pontificio tra Sette e Ottocento* (Napoli: Editoriale Scientifica, 2004), p. 97.

13 The evolution of fiscal institutions in the Ottoman Empire, 1500–1914

Şevket Pamuk

Introduction

The Ottoman Empire stood at the crossroads of intercontinental trade, stretching from the Balkans and the Black Sea region through Anatolia, Syria, Mesopotamia and the Gulf to Egypt and most of the North African coast for six centuries until the First World War. For most of the seventeenth and eighteenth centuries, its population exceeded 30 million (of which the European provinces accounted for half or more; Anatolia and Istanbul for 7 to 8 million, other Asian and North African provinces for another 7 to 8 million) but declined thereafter due to territorial losses.

One might have expected that the economic institutions that sustained this large, multi-ethnic entity for so long would be of interest to economic historians. Unfortunately, recent studies by E. L. Jones, Rondo Cameron and David Landes that provide surveys of non-European empires as well as explanations for the rise of the West, like many of their mainstream predecessors, have shown little interest in understanding the Ottoman land regime, manufactures, state economic policies or the daily existence of ordinary men and women. The Empire is depicted in these accounts as a centralized, monolithic entity lacking in internal dynamism and differentiation.[1] In the most recent account by Landes, the Ottoman Empire is reduced to a caricature of nomads and raiders, despotism, military conquest, corruption and looting: 'The Ottoman Empire was a typical despotism, only more warlike.'[2] With this perspective, however, the longevity of the Ottoman Empire

---

[1] E. L. Jones, *The European miracle. Environments, economies and geopolitics in the history of Europe and Asia*, 2nd edn (Cambridge University Press, 1987), pp. 175–91; Rondo Cameron, *A concise economic history of the world, from Paleolithic times to the present*, 2nd edn (Oxford University Press, 1993), pp. 81–3; David Landes, *The wealth and poverty of nations: why some are so rich and some so poor* (New York: W. W. Norton and Co., 1998).

[2] Landes, *The wealth and poverty of nations*, p. 398.

becomes an anomaly and even a mystery: 'The empire of the Ottoman Turks proved more durable (than the Moghul Empire of India). That in itself is a *mystery*, because after some two hundred and fifty years of expansion (1300–1550), its downhill course should have brought about fragmentation and liquidation in a matter of decades.'[3]

Kenneth Pomeranz has recently argued that core regions of China and western Europe were not very different from each other during the eighteenth century, not only in terms of technology and the levels and trends of development in their everyday economies but also in terms of the functioning of their economic institutions, land and labour markets, degree of commercialization and even the legal and social regimes governing large accumulations of commercial and financial capital. Were it not for the large amounts of energy and land resources provided by the New World, he emphasizes, western Europe may not have experienced the industrial breakthrough that began in the second half of the eighteenth century.[4] Whether parts of China and western Europe were so close to each other in terms of institutions or not, it is difficult to argue that Ottoman institutions, technology, property rights, land markets and the legal and social regimes governing capital accumulation were similar to those in western Europe during the eighteenth century.

For most of its six-century existence, the Ottoman Empire is best characterized as a bureaucratic, agrarian empire. The economic institutions and policies of this entity were shaped to a large degree by the priorities and interests of a central bureaucracy. The Ottoman state and society showed considerable ability to reorganize as a way of adapting to changing circumstances in Eurasia from the seventeenth to the nineteenth centuries. The central bureaucracy managed to contain the many challenges it faced with its pragmatism, flexibility and habit of negotiation to co-opt and incorporate into the state the social groups that rebelled against it. The Ottoman state also showed considerable flexibility at adapting not only its military technology but also its fiscal, financial and monetary institutions in response to the changing circumstances.

A comparison with the other two Muslim empires of Eurasia, the Safavids and the Mughals brings the Ottoman trajectory into sharper focus. The political economy of these three empires showed similar patterns of evolution during the sixteenth and seventeenth centuries. They all enjoyed a long period of stability, agricultural expansion and

---

[3] Ibid., p. 396. Emphasis my own.
[4] K. Pomeranz, *The great divergence, China, Europe and the making of the modern world economy* (Princeton University Press, 2000).

growing prosperity during the sixteenth century followed by severe fiscal and military difficulties and rising internal conflicts during the seventeenth century. The decline of central political institutions in all three of the empires was accompanied by the rise of provincial elites which had a greater say on the evolution of regional economies. During the eighteenth century, both the Mughals and Safavids disintegrated under the pressure of tribal invasions. While the Mughals were taken over by the British, the Safavids were replaced by a regional Persian kingdom (the Qajars).[5] In contrast, the eighteenth century until the 1770s was a period of recovery, stability and economic expansion for the Ottoman Empire. Despite wars and internal conflict from the 1770s to the 1830s, the Ottomans managed to regroup and survive into the modern era with a strong central state and many of their central institutions intact.

On its own terms, then, the Ottoman regime may be viewed as successful. Pragmatism, flexibility, willingness to negotiate, and an ability to adapt their institutions to changing circumstances were traits that enabled the Ottomans to retain power until the modern era while many of their contemporaries in both Europe and Asia were unable to do so. Ultimately, however, pragmatism and flexibility were utilized and change was allowed only as far as necessary for the defence of the traditional order. Many of the key institutions of the traditional order, such as the state ownership of land, urban guilds and restrictions on private capital accumulation, remained intact until the nineteenth century.

This chapter provides an overview of the long-term changes in the Ottoman fiscal institutions from the sixteenth century until the First World War from this perspective of pragmatism and flexibility. It examines the changing Ottoman strategies and institutions in dealing with tax collection, debasements, and internal and external borrowing. State finances were in good shape and there was little need for borrowing until the last quarter of the sixteenth century. Ottoman institutions of private and public finance retained their Islamic lineage and remained mostly uninfluenced by developments in Europe until the end of the seventeenth century. The Ottoman government continued to rely on tax farming for both tax collection and short-term borrowing purposes, as had been the practice of most Islamic states. State finances came under increasing pressure in the seventeenth century and again from the 1770s onwards. European institutions of both private and public finance began to grow in influence during the eighteenth century.

---

[5] C. A. Bayly, *Imperial meridian, The British empire and the world, 1780–1830* (Harlow: Addison Wesley Longman, 1989).

Ottoman state borrowing in the European financial markets during the nineteenth century led to a default in the 1870s and the partial control of state finances by European creditors until the First World War. This chapter begins with an overview of the use of money and credit in the Ottoman economy.

Money and credit

For a long time it has been assumed that the use of money in the Balkans and Anatolia was limited to long-distance trade and parts of the urban sector.[6] Recent research has shown, however, that the urban population and some segments of the countryside were already part of the monetary economy by the end of the fifteenth century. Even more significantly, there occurred a substantial increase in the use of money during the sixteenth century, both because of the increased availability of specie and the increasing commercialization of the rural economy. The evidence for this important development comes from a number of sources. First, recent research has pointed out that population growth and urbanization during the sixteenth century were accompanied by the growth of economic linkages between the urban and rural areas. As a result, there emerged in the Balkans and Anatolia an intensive pattern of periodic markets and market fairs where peasants and larger land-holders sold parts of their produce to urban residents. These markets also provided an important opportunity for the nomads to come into contact with both peasants and the urban population. Large sectors of the rural population came to use coinage, especially the small denomi-nations of silver *akçe* and the copper *mangır*, through their participation in these markets.[7]

The growing density of population during the sixteenth century thus increased the density of exchange not only in the urban areas but also incorporated large segments of the rural population into this process. The Balkans and Anatolia were certainly not unique in this respect. As Braudel has pointed out, the same trend towards more frequent use of markets and money by large segments of the population also prevailed

---

[6] F. Braudel, *Civilization and capitalism, 15th–18th century, Vol. III: the perspective of the world* (New York: Harper and Row, 1984), pp. 471–3.

[7] S. Faroqhi, 'The early history of Balkan fairs', *Südost-Forshungen* 37 (1978), 50–68; S. Faroqhi, 'Sixteenth-century periodic markets in various Anatolian sancaks', *Journal of the Economic and Social History of the Orient* 22 (1979), 32–80; S. Faroqhi, 'Rural society in Anatolia and the Balkans during the sixteenth century', *Turcica* 9 (1977), 161–96, and 11 (1979), 103–53; and H. Inalcık, 'Osmanlı Idare, Sosyal, ve Ekonomik Tarihiyle ilgili Belgeler: Bursa Kadi Sicillerinden Seçmeler', *Belgeler* X (1981), 1–91.

in the western Mediterranean region.[8] While the developments in the western Mediterranean have drawn considerable attention from historians, the social and cultural as well as economic implications of this trend are yet to be adequately studied in the case of the eastern Mediterranean.

It has often been assumed that the prohibition of interest in Islam prevented the development of credit, or at best, imposed rigid obstacles in its way. Similarly, the apparent absence of deposit banking and lending by banks has led many observers to conclude that financial institutions and instruments were, by and large, absent in Islamic societies. It is true that a religiously inspired prohibition against usurious transactions was a powerful feature shared around the Mediterranean during the Middle Ages, by both the Islamic world and Christian West.[9] While the practice of *riba*, the Arabic term for usury and interest, is sharply denounced in a number of passages in the Qur'an and in all subsequent Islamic religious writings, already in the classical era, Islamic law had provided several means by which the anti-usury prohibition could be circumvented, just as the same prohibitions were circumvented in Europe in the late medieval period. Various legal fictions, based primarily on the model of the 'double-sale' were, if not enthusiastically endorsed by jurists, at least not declared invalid. Thus, there did not exist an insurmountable barrier against the use of interest-bearing loans for commercial credit.

Neither Islamic prohibitions against interest and usury nor the absence of formal banking institutions prevented the expansion of credit in Ottoman society. Utilizing the Islamic court records, the late Ronald Jennings has shown that dense networks of lenders and borrowers flourished in and around the Anatolian cities of Kayseri, Karaman, Amasya and Trabzon during the sixteenth century. Over the twenty-year period which his study covered, he found literally thousands of court cases involving debts. Many members of each family and many women are registered in these records as borrowing and lending to other members of the family as well as to outsiders. These records leave no doubt that the use of credit was widespread among all segments of the urban and even rural society. Most lending and borrowing was on a small scale and interest was regularly charged on credit, in accordance with both Islamic and Ottoman law, with the consent and approval of the court

---

[8] F. Braudel, *The Mediterranean and the Mediterranean world in the age of Philip II*, 2nd edn, 2 vols. (London : Collins, 1972) Vol. I, pp. 355–461.

[9] For a recent discussion of the classical Islamic views on interest, see N. A. Saleh, *Unlawful gain and legitimate profit in Islamic law: Riba, Gharar and Islamic banking* (Cambridge University Press, 1988), pp. 9–32.

and the ulema. In their dealings with the court the participants felt no need to conceal interest or resort to tricks in order to clear legal hurdles. Annual rates of interest ranged from 10 to 20 per cent.[10]

One important provider of loans in Istanbul, the Balkans and the Anatolian urban centres were the cash *vakif*s, pious foundations established with the explicit purpose of lending their cash assets and using the interest income to fulfil their goals. These endowments began to be approved by the Ottoman courts in the early part of the fifteenth century and had become popular all over Anatolia and the Balkan provinces by the end of the sixteenth century. An interesting development that became more pronounced during the eighteenth century was the increasing allocation of the funds to the trustees of these endowments. The trustees then used the borrowed funds to lend at higher rates of interest to large-scale moneylenders (*sarraf*) at Istanbul who pooled these funds to finance larger ventures: most importantly, long-distance trade and tax farming.[11]

Not surprisingly, a lively debate developed during the sixteenth century within the Ottoman ulema regarding whether the cash *vakif* should be considered illegitimate. The cash *vakif*s were opposed by those who believed that only goods with permanent value, such as real estate, should constitute the assets of a pious foundation and that the cash *vakif*s contravened the Islamic prohibition of interest. The majority of the ulema, however, remained eminently pragmatic and the view that anything useful for the community is useful for Islam ultimately prevailed. During the heated debate, Ebusuud Efendi, the prominent, state-appointed religious leader (*Seyhulislam*) of the period, defended the practice from a purely practical point of view, arguing that abolition of interest taking would lead to the collapse of many pious foundations, a situation that would harm the Muslim community.[12]

Rise of a centralized state, 1450–1580

During his thirty-year reign, Mehmed II (1445 and 1451–81) successfully built from an emerging state dependent upon the goodwill and manpower of the rural aristocracy an expanding empire with a large army and bureaucracy. As a result, the central government began to

[10] R. C. Jennings, 'Loans and credit in early 17th century Ottoman judicial records', *Journal of the Economic and Social History of the Orient* 16 (1973), 168–216.

[11] M. Çizakça, *A comparative evolution of business partnerships, the Islamic world and Europe with specific reference to the Ottoman Archives* (Leiden: E. J. Brill, 1996), pp. 131–4.

[12] J. E. Mandaville, 'Usurious piety: the cash waqf controversy in the Ottoman Empire', *International Journal of Middle East Studies* 10 (1979), 289–308.

control a larger share of the resources and revenues at the expense of the provinces. A number of harsh measures were used during this process. In addition to higher taxes, state monopolies were established in basic commodities such as salt, soap and candle wax, and in their sale to private merchants. Land and other properties in the hands of private owners or pious foundations were confiscated. A policy of forced colonization and tax concessions was used to bring skilled artisans and other immigrants from Anatolia and the Balkans to reconstruct and repopulate the capital city of Istanbul. Finally, very detailed laws were issued to control and regulate the daily economic life in the leading cities of the empire: Bursa, Edirne and Istanbul. The interventionism exhibited by the central government in fiscal, economic and monetary affairs during this period was unmatched in later periods.

The revenues of the central treasury increased considerably as a result of these measures. The treasury also benefited from the territorial conquests of the period and the extraction of one-time or annual tributes from vassal states, often paid in gold ducats. Not all of the new revenues were immediately spent, however. In the absolutist logic of Mehmed II, a strong treasury was also a means of power and independence for the ruler. The central government thus followed a policy of accumulating large reserves in the treasury. Budget surpluses and the accumulation of reserves contributed further to the fiscal strains and shortages of specie being experienced by the economy and society at large.[13]

The reign of Mehmed II was also unique in Ottoman history in terms of government attitudes towards debasements. The silver content of the *akçe* had changed very little from the 1320s until the 1440s. During the three decades of his rule, however, debasements were used as regular policy to finance costly military campaigns and to expand the role of the central government. Between 1444 and 1481, the silver content of the Ottoman unit was reduced by a total of 30 per cent through debasements undertaken every ten years. The basic reason for the periodic use of debasements by Mehmed II was to raise revenue for the central treasury. The debasements thus complemented increased taxation and other fiscal measures adopted by Mehmed II to concentrate a greater share of the resources at the centre, to support the growing needs of

[13] H. İnalcık, 'The Ottoman economic mind and aspects of the Ottoman economy', in M. Cook (ed.), *Studies in the economic history of the Middle East* (Oxford University Press, 1970), pp. 207–18; B. A. Cvetkova, 'Sur certain reformes du regime foncier du temps de Mehmed II', *Journal of the Social and Economic History of the Orient* 6 (1963), 104–20. N. Beldiceanu, 'Recherches sur la Reforme Fonciere de Mehmed II', *Acta Historica* 4 (1965), 27–39.

an expanding bureaucracy and a central army as well as to finance the military campaigns.[14]

Mehmed's harsh fiscal measures and strong interventionism met with strong discontent if not opposition. One important source of the discontent was the ulema, who lost control of larges sources of revenue with the expropriation of the pious foundations by the state. The owners of the privately held lands (*mülk*) which were expropriated by the state joined them. Similarly, the nomads, warriors and aristocrats of the frontier areas, who had regularly joined the military campaigns and contributed to their success, were also opposed to increased centralization and taxation. Nonetheless, Mehmed II was able to continue with these policies until the end of his reign through a combination of increased power at the centre and the success of his military campaigns, which resulted in considerable territorial expansion and booty for many of the groups involved. In the longer term, the opposition of the janissaries and other groups to the policy of periodic debasements contributed to the stability of the *akçe*. After the death of Mehmed II, his son Bayezid II was forced to reconcile with and seek the support of precisely those groups that his father alienated during his long and forceful reign. In addition to returning the assets of some of the pious foundations and lands expropriated by his father, he promised to end the policy of debasements. During the following century, *akçe* returned to the stability it had enjoyed before the reign of Mehmed II. The weight and silver content of the *akçe* changed very little from 1481 until 1585.

State economic policies

To understand Ottoman economic policies or practices, it is necessary to examine the nature of the Ottoman state and its relations with different social groups. After the successful centralization drive of Mehmed II in the second half of the fifteenth century, the policies of the government in Istanbul began to reflect much more strongly the priorities of this bureaucracy. The influence of various social groups, not only of land-owners but also of merchants and moneychangers, over the policies of the central government remained limited.

The central bureaucracy tried, above all, to create and reproduce a traditional order with the bureaucracy at the top. The provisioning of the urban areas, long-distance trade and imports were all necessary for the stability of that social order. The state tolerated and even

---

[14] S. Pamuk, *A monetary history of the Ottoman Empire* (Cambridge University Press, 2000), pp. 47–58.

encouraged the activities of merchants, domestic manufacturers more
or less independent of the guilds, and moneychangers as long as they
helped reproduce that traditional order.[15] Despite the general trend
towards the decentralization of the Empire during the seventeenth and
eighteenth centuries, merchants and domestic producers, who were
the leading proponents and actual developers of mercantilist policies
in Europe, never became powerful enough to exert sufficient pressure
on the Ottoman government to change or even modify these traditional
policies. Only in the provinces were locally powerful groups able to exert
increasing degrees of influence over the provincial administrators.

In a recent article, Mehmet Genç examined the economic functions
and priorities of the central bureaucracy, based on years of research
on the archives of the central government.[16] After cautioning that
these never appeared in purely economic form but always together
with political, religious, military, administrative or fiscal concerns and
pronouncements, he argues that it is, nonetheless, possible to reduce
the Ottoman priorities in economic matters to three basic principles.
The first priority was the provisioning of the urban economy including
the army, the palace and the state officials. The government wanted
to assure a steady supply of goods for the urban economy and especially for the capital city. The bureaucracy was very much aware of the
critical role played by merchants in this respect. With the territorial
expansion of the Empire and the incorporation of Syria and Egypt
during the sixteenth century, long-distance trade and control of the
intercontinental trade routes became increasingly important and even
critical for these needs.[17] Foreign merchants were especially welcome

[15] Carlo Cipolla has argued that there was a virtual identity between the merchants
and the state in the trading towns of medieval Italy: 'More than once the action of
the guild of merchants seemed to imply the affirmation, *l'etat c'est moi.*' Ottoman
merchants during the early modern era could not possibly make a similar claim.
Instead, as Udovitch has concluded, for the merchants of eleventh-century Egypt,
Ottoman merchants could at best proclaim *'l'etat n'est pas contre moi'.* C. M. Cipolla,
'The economic policies of governments, the Italian and Iberian Peninsulas', in M.
M. Postan, E. E. Rich and E. Miller (eds.), *The Cambridge economic history of Europe,*
3 vols (Cambridge University Press, 1963), Vol. III, pp. 397–429; A. L. Udovitch,
'Merchants and *Amirs*: government and trade in eleventh-century Egypt', *Asian and
African Studies* 22 (1988), 53–72.
[16] Mehmet Genç, 'Osmanli Iktisadi Dünya Görüsünün Ilkeleri', *Istanbul Üniversitesi
Edebiyat Fakültesi Sosyoloji Dergisi* 3 (1989), 175–85; for a similar argument, see Halil
Inalcik, 'The Ottoman economic mind', pp. 207–18; Halil İnalcık, 'The Ottoman
state: economy and society, 1300–1600', in Halil Inalcık and Donald Quataert (eds.),
An economic and social history of the Ottoman Empire, 1300–1914 (Cambridge University
Press, 1994), pp. 44–54.
[17] H. Inalcık, 'The Ottoman state: economy and society, 1300–1600', pp. 48–52, 179–
379; also P. Brummett, *Ottoman seapower and Levantine diplomacy in the age of discovery* (Albany: State University of New York Press, 1994), pp. 131–74.

because they brought goods not available in Ottoman lands. Ottoman encouragement of European merchants and the granting of various privileges, concessions and capitulations as early as the sixteenth century can be best understood in this context. Occasionally, however, foreign merchants also contributed to domestic shortages by exporting scarce goods and the Ottomans had to impose temporary prohibitions on exports.[18]

The emphasis on provisioning necessitated an important distinction between imports and exports. Imports were encouraged as they added to the availability of goods in the urban markets. In contrast, exports were tolerated only after the requirements of the domestic economy were met. As soon as the possibility of shortages emerged, however, the government did not hesitate to prohibit the exportation of basic necessities, especially foodstuffs and raw materials.[19]

The contrasts between these policies and the practices of mercantilism in Europe are obvious. It would be a mistake, however, to identify concern with the provisioning of urban areas solely with Ottoman or Islamic states. Frequent occurrences of crop failures, famine and epidemics, combined with the primitive nature of the available means of transport, led most if not all medieval governments to focus on the urban food supply and more generally on provisioning as the key concerns of economic policy. These Ottoman priorities and practices had strong parallels in the policies of the governments in western and southern Europe during the late Middle Ages, from the twelfth to the fifteenth centuries.[20] The contrasts between Ottoman and European economic policies emerged during the era of mercantilism in Europe.[21] One important reason why mercantilist ideas never took root in Ottoman lands was that merchants and domestic producers whose ideas and perspectives were so influential in the development of

---

[18] H. Inalcık, 'İmtiyazat', *Encyclopedia of Islam*, 2nd edn (Leiden and New York: E. J. Brill, 1971); and İnalcık, 'The Ottoman economic mind'.

[19] Inalcık, 'The Ottoman economic mind'; B. Masters, *The origins of Western economic dominance in the Middle East: mercantilism and the Islamic economy in Aleppo, 1600–1750* (New York University Press, 1988), chapter 6.

[20] E. Miller, 'France and England' and C. M. Cipolla, 'The economic policies of governments – the Italian and Iberian Peninsulas', in M. M. Postan, E. E. Rich, and E. Miller (eds.), *The Cambridge economic history of Europe*, Vol. 3, pp. 290–340, 397–429.

[21] The Ottomans were not unaware of mercantilist thought and practice. Early eighteenth-century historian Naima, for example, defended mercantilist ideas and practices and argued that if the Islamic population purchased local products instead of the imports, coinage would stay in Ottoman lands; see Naima, *Tarih-i Naima*, ed. by Zuhuri Danışman (Istanbul: Danışman Yayınevi, 1968), Vol. 4, pp. 1826–7 and Vol. 6, pp. 2520–5; also Inalcık, 'The Ottoman economic mind', p. 215.

these ideas in Europe did not play a significant role in Ottoman economic thought.[22]

Genç points out that a second priority of the centre was fiscal revenue. The government intervened frequently to collect taxes from a broad range of economic activities and came to recognize, in the process, that, at least in the longer term, economic prosperity was essential for the fiscal strength of the state. In the shorter term, and especially during periods of crisis, however, it did not hesitate to increase tax collections at the expense of producers.

A third priority, which was closely tied to the other two, was the preservation of the traditional order. For the Ottomans, there existed an ideal social order and balance between social groups such as the peasantry, the guilds and the merchants. The sultan and the bureaucracy were placed at the top of this social order. There was some flexibility in this view. The ideal of what constituted this traditional order and the social balances may have changed over time with changes in the economy and society. The government took care to preserve as much as possible the prevailing order and the social balances, including the structure of employment and production. From this perspective, for example, rapid accumulation of capital by merchants, guild members or any other group was not considered favourably since it would lead to the rapid disintegration of the existing order.[23]

As a result, the government's attitude towards merchants was profoundly ambiguous. On the one hand, merchants, large and small, were considered indispensable for the functioning of the urban economy. Yet, at the same time, their profiteering often led to shortages of basic goods, bringing pressure on the guild system and the urban economy more generally. Thus the central administration often considered as its main task the control of merchants, not their protection. At the same time, however, the control of merchants was much more difficult than the control of guilds. While the guilds were fixed in location, the merchants were mobile. Needless to say, the official attitude towards financiers and moneychangers was similarly ambiguous.[24]

In pursuit of these priorities, the Ottoman government did not hesitate to intervene in local and long-distance trade to regulate the markets

[22] For mercantilism in Europe, compare F. Eli Heckscher, *Mercantilism*, rev. 2nd edn (London: George Allen and Unwin, 1955); D. C. Coleman, *Revisions in mercantilism* (London: Methuen and Co., 1969); and R. B. Ekelund Jr. and R. F. Hebert, *A history of economic theory and method* (New York: McGraw Hill, 1990), pp. 42–72.
[23] S. F. Ülgener, *İktisadi İnhitat Tarihimizin Ahlak ve Zihniyet Meseleleri* (Istanbul Üniversitesi İktisat Fakültesi Yayinlari, 1951), pp. 92–189.
[24] H. İslamoğlu and Ç. Keyder, 'Agenda for Ottoman history', *Review, Fernand Braudel Center* 1 (1977), 31–55.

and ensure the availability of goods for the military, the palace and, more generally, the urban economy. In comparison to both Islamic law and the general practice in medieval Islamic states, the early Ottomans were definitely more interventionist in their approach. In economic and fiscal affairs, as well as in many administrative practices, they often issued their own state laws (*kanun*) even if those came into conflict with the shariat. The practices they used, such as the enforcement of regulations (*hisba*) in urban markets and price ceilings (*narh*), had their origins in Islamic tradition but the Ottomans relied more frequently on them. In addition, in the provisioning of the army and the urban economy, deliveries at fixed prices were required from merchants for some of the more important goods.[25]

Genç's scheme is very useful in analysing the priorities and intentions of the Ottoman bureaucracy. As Genç himself emphasizes, however, priorities and intentions need to be distinguished from the actual policies. Whether the governments succeeded in bringing about the desired outcomes through their interventions depended on their capabilities. It has already been argued that there existed serious limitations on the administrative resources, organization and capacity of states in the late medieval and early modern periods. They did not have the capacity to intervene in markets comprehensively and effectively. The mixed success of government actions inevitably led the Ottoman authorities to recognize the limitations of their power. As a result, Ottoman governments moved away from a position of comprehensive interventionism as practised during the reign of Mehmed II towards more selective interventionism in the later periods.

Unfortunately, this evolution and the more selective nature of government interventionism after the fifteenth and sixteenth centuries has not been adequately recognized. The laws issued by Mehmed II and his immediate successors continue to be referred to as examples of government interventionism in the economy. The inability of many historians to make a more realistic assessment about interventionism is primarily due to a state-centred perspective. In addition, there are a number of practical reasons why archival evidence has misled historians to

[25] S. F. Ülgener, 'Islam Hukuk ve Ahlak Kaynaklarinda Iktisat Siyaseti Meseleleri', in *Ebülula Mardin'e Armagan* (Istanbul: Kenan Matbaasi, 1944), pp. 1151–89; M. S. Kütükoğlu, *Osmanlılarda Narh Müessesesi ve 1640 Tarihli Narh Defteri* (İstanbul: Enderun Kitabevi, 1983), pp. 3–38. For the texts of late fifteenth- and early sixteenth-century laws regulating the markets in large Ottoman cities, see Ö. Lütfi Barkan, 'Bazı Büyük Şehirlerde Eşya ve Yiyecek Fiyatlarının Tesbit ve Teftişi Hususlarını Tanzim Eden Kanunlar', *Tarih Vesikaları* 1/5 (1942–43), 326–40; 2/7, 15–40; and 2/9, 168–77.

exaggerate both the frequency and the extent of state intervention in the economy. One basic source of error has been the unrepresentative nature of the available material. Each government intervention is typically recorded by a document in the form of an order to the local judge (*kadi*) or some other authority. In contrast, there are no records for the countless numbers of occasions when the government let the markets function on their own. Faced with this one-sided evidence, many historians have concluded that state intervention and regulation was a permanent fixture of most markets at most locations across the Empire.

Another bias is related to the fact that a large number of the available documents provide evidence of state intervention directly related to the economy of the capital city.[26] This evidence has led many historians to assume that the same pattern applied to the rest of the Empire. In fact, Istanbul was unique in terms of both size and political importance. With its population approaching half a million, it was the largest city in Europe and west Asia during the sixteenth century. As was the case with monster cities elsewhere, government economic policy often revolved around it. In contrast, the central government was much less concerned about the provisioning of other urban centres; the state organization was not as strong there and the local authorities, who were appointed by the centre, were more willing to cooperate with the locally powerful groups, the guild hierarchy, merchants, tax collectors and moneychangers.[27]

A more realistic assessment of the nature of Ottoman state interventionism in the economy is long overdue. When the biases of archival evidence and the limitations of the power and capabilities of the state are taken into account, Ottoman policy towards trade and the markets is best characterized not as permanent and comprehensive interventionism, but as selective interventionism. In the later periods, interventions were used primarily for the provisioning of selected goods for the capital city and the army and during extraordinary periods when shortages reached crisis conditions.

Second, interventions in the economy did not necessarily mean that the government succeeded in bringing about the desired outcomes.

---

[26] Istanbul was a giant, consuming city dependent on its vast hinterland. The classic work on the economy of the capital city and the nature of state intervention in that economy remains R. Mantran, *Istanbul dans la seconde Moitie du XVIIe Siecle* (Paris, dépositaire: A. Maisonneuve, 1962), pp. 233–86. Also Inalcık and Quataert, *An economic and social history of the Ottoman Empire*, pp. 179–87.

[27] See, for example, H. Inalcık, 'Bursa and the commerce of the Levant', *Journal of the Economic and Social History of the Levant* 3 (1960), 131–47; Masters, *The origins of Western economic dominance*; and D. Goffman, *Izmir and the Levantine world, 1550–1650* (Seattle: University of Washington Press, 1990).

Pre-modern states did not have the capability to intervene in markets comprehensively and effectively. These limitations were even more apparent in the case of the money markets. In comparison to the goods markets and long-distance trade, it was more difficult for governments to control physical supplies of specie or coinage and regulate prices, that is, exchange and interest rates.[28] Ottoman administrators were well aware that participants in the money markets, merchants, moneychangers and financiers were able to evade state rules and regulations more easily than those in the commodity markets. Observing the mixed success of government actions, they learned that interventionism in money markets did not always produce the desired results.

Tax collection and internal borrowing during decentralization, 1580–1780

The evolution of Ottoman fiscal institutions during the seventeenth and eighteenth centuries provides a good example of the ability of the Ottoman state to contain the challenges it faced with pragmatism, flexibility and its habit of negotiation to co-opt and incorporate into a broad alliance, if necessary, the social groups that challenged its authority.

While loans to kings, princes and governments were part of the regular business of European banking houses in the late medieval and early modern periods, in the Islamic world advances of cash to the rulers and the public treasury were handled differently. They took the form of tax-farming arrangements in which individuals possessing liquid capital assets advanced cash to the government in return for the right to farm the taxes of a given region or fiscal unit for a fixed period. Tax farming thus dominated the Islamic world from the Mediterranean to the Indian Ocean, from the earliest days to the early modern period.

From the very beginning the Ottomans relied on tax farming for the collection of urban taxes. Until late in the sixteenth century, however, the agricultural taxes which constituted the largest part of the tax revenues were collected locally and mostly in kind within the *timar* system. *Sipahis*, state employees who resided in the rural areas, were expected to spend these revenues to equip and prepare a given number of soldiers for the military campaigns. Until the second half of the sixteenth century, state finances were relatively strong thanks to the revenues obtained through the rapid territorial expansion of the Empire and the

---

[28] P. Spufford, *Money and its use in medieval Europe* (Cambridge University Press, 1988), passim; S. D. Goitein, *A Mediterranean society, the Jewish communities of the Arab World as portrayed in the documents of the Cairo Geniza, Vol. I: economic foundations* (Berkeley and Los Angeles: University of California Press, 1967), pp. 209–72.

state did not feel the need to increase the revenues collected at the centre. There are examples of short-term borrowing by the state during the sixteenth century. These services earned the financiers, mostly Jews and Greeks, the inside track on some of the most lucrative tax-farming contracts.[29]

However, with the changes in military technology during the sixteenth century and the need to maintain larger, permanent armies at the centre, pressures increased to collect a larger part of the rural surplus at the centre. As a result, the *timar* system began to be abandoned in favour of tax farming and the tax units were auctioned off at Istanbul.[30] The shift away from the *timar* system had been designed to increase the cash receipts at the centre, but the decline of state power vis-à-vis the provinces reduced the expected benefits from this change. Bureaucrats in the capital and provincial groups began to share tax-farming revenues with the central government during the seventeenth century.

In the longer term, further deterioration of the state finances increased the pressures on the central government to take greater advantage of the tax-farming system for the purposes of domestic borrowing. The central government thus began to increase the length of the tax-farming contracts from one to three years to three to five years and even longer. It also demanded an increasingly higher fraction of the auction price of the contract in advance. Tax farming was thus converted to a form of domestic borrowing, with the actual tax revenues being used as collateral by the central government.

Further steps were taken in the same direction with the introduction, in 1695, of the *malikane* system in which the revenue source began to be farmed out on a life-time basis in return for a large initial payment to be followed by annual payments.[31] One rationale often offered for this system was that by extending the term of the contract, the state hoped that the tax contractor would take better care of the tax source, most importantly the peasant producers, and try to achieve long-term increases in production. In fact, the *malikane* allowed the state to use tax revenues as collateral and borrow on a longer-term basis. In comparison to the

[29] Inalcık and Quataert, *An economic and social history of the Ottoman Empire*, pp. 212–14.
[30] H. İnalcık, 'Military and fiscal transformation in the Ottoman Empire, 1600–1700', *Archivum Ottomanicum* 6 (1980), 283–337.
[31] M. Genç, 'A study of the feasibility of using eighteenth-century Ottoman financial records as an indicator of economic activity', in Huri İslamoğlu-İnan (ed.), *The Ottoman Empire and the world economy* (Cambridge University Press, 1987), pp. 345–73.

straightforward tax-farming system, it represented an important shift towards longer-term borrowing by the state.

With the extension of their term and the introduction of larger advance payments, the long-term financing of these contracts assumed an even greater importance. The private financiers thus began to play an increasingly important role in the tax-collection process. Behind the individual who joined the bidding in the tax-farming auctions, there often existed a partnership that included financiers as well as the agents who intended to organize the tax collection process itself, by dividing the large initial contract into smaller pieces and finding sub-contractors. Non-Muslims were prohibited from holding most *malikane* contracts, but Greeks, Armenians and Jews were very much part of this elite as financiers, brokers and accountants. These arrangements were mostly in the form of an Islamic business partnership involving both Muslims and non-Muslims.[32] Over the course of the eighteenth century, some 1,000 to 2,000 Istanbul-based individuals, together with some 5,000 to 10,000 individuals based in the provinces, as well as innumerable contractors, agents, financiers, accountants and managers, controlled an important share of the state's revenues. This grand coalition of Istanbul-based elites and the rising elites in the provinces constituted a semi-privatized but interdependent component of the regime.[33] Many provincials were able to acquire and pass from one generation to the next small and medium-sized *malikane* shares on villages as long as they remained in favour with the local administrators or their Istanbul sponsors. For both the well-connected individuals in the capital city and those in the provinces, getting a piece of government tax revenues became an activity more lucrative than investing in agriculture, trade or manufacturing.

It is significant that these changes in the tax-collection and revenue-sharing system did not alter the legal basis of land-ownership until the nineteenth century. Despite the rise of provincial elites, most agricultural lands remained *miri* or state land with the peasant households holding the usufruct while the *sipahis* gave way to tax farmers who were then replaced by *malikane* owners. State ownership on land combined with usufruct by the peasant household, a key institution of the classical Ottoman order, thus remained intact until the modern era.

In the longer term, however, the *malikane* system did not fulfil the expectations of central government. It actually led to a decline in state

---

[32] Çizakça, *A comparative evolution of business partnerships.*
[33] A. Salzman, 'An ancien regime revisited: "privatization" and political economy in the eighteenth-century Ottoman Empire', *Politics and Society* 21 (1993), 393–423.

revenues because of the inability of the state to regain control of the revenue sources after the death of the individuals who had purchased them.[34] The central government thus began to experiment with other methods for tax collection and domestic borrowing as state finances came under increasing pressure from the 1770s onwards. After the end of the war of 1768–74, which had dramatically exposed the military as well as financial weaknesses of the Ottoman system, the financial bureaucracy started a new and related system of long-term domestic borrowing called *esham*. In this system, the annual net revenues of a tax source were specified in nominal terms. This amount was divided into a large number of shares which were then sold to the public for the life-time of the buyers. The annual revenues of the source continued to be collected by the tax farmers. The *esham* generally sold for six to seven times the annual net payments, which remained fixed.[35] As the linkage between the annual government payments to *esham* holders and the underlying revenues of the tax source weakened, the *esham* increasingly resembled a life term annuity quite popular in many European countries of the period.

One motivation for the new system was to broaden the base of state borrowing and reach beyond the limited numbers of large financiers who tended to dominate the *malikane* auctions towards a larger pool of small and medium-sized lenders. However, the inability of the state to control or limit the sales of the *esham* between individuals and the difficulties in preventing the heirs of the deceased from continuing to receive payments seriously limited the fiscal benefits of this system. During the next half-century, the state vacillated between abolishing the *esham* during periods of fiscal stability and expanding it when fiscal pressures mounted and additional funds had to be secured with little regard for their long-term cost.[36]

In a recent study we examined the long-term trends in the cash receipts of the Ottoman central administration, expressed in both tons of silver and also per-capita terms making use of all the available Ottoman budget documents.[37] This study makes clear that despite all efforts, per-capita and total Ottoman revenues during the eighteenth century were not any higher than those in the sixteenth century.

[34] Genç, 'A study of the feasibility'.
[35] Y. Cezar, *Osmanlı Maliyesinde Bunalım ve Değişim Dönemi: XVIII. yy.dan Tanzimat'a Mali Tarih*, (Istanbul: Alan Yayıncılık, 1986), pp. 81–3; M. Genç, 'Esham', *İslam Ansiklopedisi* 11 (1995), 376–80.
[36] Cezar, *Osmanlı Maliyesinde Bunalım*, pp. 128–34, 198–200.
[37] K. Kivanc Karaman and Şevket Pamuk, 'Ottoman state finances in European perspective, 1500–1914', *Journal of Economic History* 70:3 (2010), 593–629.

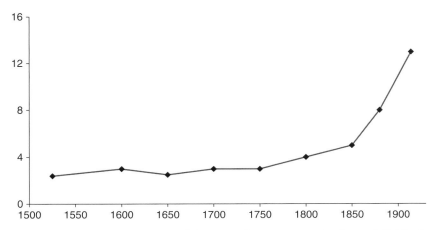

Figure 13.1 Revenues of the central government / estimated GDP of
the Ottoman Empire (%)

Admittedly crude estimates also suggest that in the core areas of the
Empire, direct cash receipts of the Ottoman government remained
below 4 per cent of GDP during the early modern era. While estimates
of GDP are subject to relatively high margins of error, data for the
daily wages of construction workers in the urban centres, especially in
the leading urban centres, are much more abundant and much more
reliable. Our calculations indicate that the annual per-capita cash revenues of the Ottoman central administration did not exceed three days'
wages for an unskilled construction worker in Istanbul and remained
below two days' wages for most of the early modern era. Even when we
include indirect revenues such as the contributions of *timar* and other
soldiers in military campaigns, the per-capita revenues of the central
administration rarely exceeded four days' wages in any given year (see
Figure 13.1).

The study also compares the revenues of the Ottoman central administration in the early modern era with those of the leading European
states. Total Ottoman revenues were greater than those of all European
states except France and Spain during the sixteenth century. This
pattern is consistent with Ottoman military power vis-à-vis the leading European states, as the Ottomans did quite well militarily during
the sixteenth century. Per-capita tax revenues of the Ottoman central
administration were also comparable to those of larger European states
but was below those of city-states like Venice and Holland in the sixteenth century.

Revenues of most European states increased sharply during the seventeenth and especially the eighteenth centuries. Most striking in this respect were England and Holland but others including Austria and Russia also experienced significant increases in tax revenues. At a time when the Ottoman central administration was struggling with the adverse effects of political and fiscal decentralization, these large increases in revenues across Europe led to the emergence of large differences in state revenues between the Ottomans and most European states. These differences reached their peak, in most cases, during the second half of the eighteenth century when the revenues not only of the more successful and more powerful states in western Europe but also those in central and eastern Europe such as the Austrian monarchy and Russia, with which the Ottomans engaged militarily, increased sharply. The Ottomans were able to hold their own militarily against Austria, Venice and Russia during the first half of the eighteenth century. As the fiscal gap widened further during the second half of the eighteenth century, however, Ottoman military performance began to falter.

One important cause was the significant differences in population trends. The population of the Ottoman Empire changed very little from the middle of the sixteenth century until the end of the eighteenth century. In contrast, population in most European countries that are included in our comparisons increased sharply during the early modern centuries, doubling or more than doubling in many cases. Another potential cause of the growing differences in revenues was the differences in GDP per capita. However, differences in terms of GDP per capita between European countries and the Ottoman Empire remained relatively limited until the nineteenth century. The two important exceptions are the Netherlands and Great Britain where GDP per capita was significantly higher during the early modern era. Another cause of the emerging differences in revenues was the rapidly growing differences in tax revenues of the central administrations as a percentage of GDP or total income. While this ratio remained mostly unchanged in the Ottoman Empire, it increased significantly in most European countries during the early modern era, especially during the eighteenth century. Part of this difference was due to basic factors that made tax collection easier, such as geography, rate of urbanization and monetization. It was also due to politics and the relations between the central administration and the elites. The Ottoman administration and provincial notables often cooperated in tax collection and military service during the seventeenth and eighteenth centuries. However, a long-term, credible and stable political deal with well-defined obligations and privileges did not emerge. In the absence of such a deal, the central administration had severe difficulties in ensuring a steady supply of tax revenues.

The evolution of Ottoman tax-collection institutions during the seventeenth and eighteenth centuries illustrates the state's ability and willingness to reorganize as a way of adapting to changing circumstances, albeit slowly and often with considerable time lags. This pragmatism and flexibility also provide important clues for understanding the longevity of the Empire as well as the key position of the central bureaucracy until the end. In order to remain at the top, the central bureaucracy was thus willing to share the tax revenues with the provincial groups during the seventeenth and eighteenth centuries until it was able to reassert itself in the nineteenth century.

It also appears that the Ottomans were willing to borrow or adapt European fiscal institutions well before the nineteenth century. Despite recent research on the evolution of the Ottoman forms, the causal connections between the evolution of the Ottoman institutions of public finance as outlined here and the evolution of the European institutions of public finance during the seventeenth and eighteenth centuries have not yet been investigated. The parallels between the two are quite striking, however. It is likely that increasing economic and financial integration with Europe after the sixteenth century brought about rapid changes not only in the institutions of private finance but also in those of public finance.[38]

During the war of 1787–92, the government also considered the possibility of borrowing from abroad, from France, Spain or the Netherlands, which would have been a first for the Ottoman state. The Dutch government indicated in 1789 that it was not in a position to lend and referred the Ottoman government to the private sector. However, due to the difficulties in Europe arising from the French Revolution, and the reluctance on the Ottoman side, this possibility was not pursued any further. Another proposal was to borrow from Morocco because it was a friendly Muslim country, but it soon became clear that the resources of that country were quite limited. From the late eighteenth century until the 1840s, extraordinary wartime taxes and the expropriation of

---

[38] G. Parker, 'The emergence of modern finance in Europe, 1500–1730', in C. Cipolla (ed.), *The Fontana economic history of Europe*, 6 vols (London: Collins/Fontana, 1972–1978), Vol. 2, pp. 560–82. For the case of France, the country most likely to have influenced the changes in Ottoman institutions of public finance, see D. R. Weir, 'Tontines, public finance and revolution in France and England, 1688–1789', *Journal of Economic History* 49 (1989), 95–124; and F. R. Velde and D. R. Weir, 'The financial market and government debt policy in France, 1746–1793', *Journal of Economic History* 52 (1992), 1–39.

the wealth of prominent individuals, especially of those who had accumulated their wealth in the service of the sultan, continued to serve as additional means of raising fiscal revenue.[39]

Second wave of fiscal centralization at the dawn of the modern era, 1780–1850

The reign of sultan Mahmud II (1808–39) was a very difficult period for the Empire and the central government. During these three decades the government was forced to deal with a series of uprisings, nationalist revolutions and wars abroad. While it was able to suppress the various uprisings of notables in both the Balkans and Anatolia, the Serbian and Greek revolutions led to the secessions of these territories from the Empire. Much more costly to the state finances than any of these was a series of wars against Russia (1806–12 and 1828–29), Iran (1820–28) and Egypt (1831–33 and 1838–39).

This was also a critical period for Western-style, centralizing reform. Attempts at military reform had begun earlier, during the reign of Selim III (1789–1807), but progress had been limited due to the opposition of the janissaries. These efforts gained momentum after the abolition of the janissaries in 1826. As the size of the new army (*Nizam-i Cedid*) rose from a mere 2,000 around the turn of the century to 120,000 in the late 1830s, pressures on state finances increased.[40] Roughly speaking, about half of the budget expenditures were allocated for military spending from the late eighteenth century until the 1840s; this share was considerably higher during periods of war.[41]

Another important and difficult task was the reorganization and modernization of the bureaucracy. The strategy of the reformist and centralizing sultan Mahmud II was to eliminate the intermediate authorities in both the capital and the provinces. However, as the reform movement began to spread beyond the military arena in the 1820s, to administration, justice and education, the demands for resources increased as well. Precise budget figures do not exist, but recent estimates suggest that the expenditures of the central government increased by 250 to 300 per cent after adjusting for debasements and inflation, from about 18 million current *kurush* or 2 million *ducats* at the end of the eighteenth century to about 400 million current *kurush* or 7 million *ducats* at the

[39] Cezar, *Osmanlı Maliyesinde Bunalım*, pp. 89–92, 137–8.
[40] S. J. Shaw and E. Kuran Shaw, *History of the Ottoman Empire and modern Turkey, Vol. II, 1808–1975* (Cambridge University Press, 1977), pp. 1–54.
[41] Cezar, *Osmanlı Maliyesinde Bunalım*, pp. 244–80.

end of the 1830s. To deal with changes of such magnitude constituted a financial task of enormous proportions for the central government. As a result, one of the key goals of the reform process was the reorganization of state finances and greater centralization of the revenues. As part of these efforts the multiple treasuries and budgets of the earlier era were gradually dissolved for a single budget system.[42]

The political and administrative capacities of the central government often determined the limits on fiscal revenue. Without an administrative network for tax collection, the government had been forced to share tax revenues with the powerful groups in the provinces. In the 1820s, however, the central government began to undermine the powerful alliance between the high-level bureaucrats and financiers in the capital and the notables in the provinces. As a result, it was able to exert greater control over tax-collection process. Ottoman budgets for the nineteenth century show very clearly that the centralizing reforms that began at the end of the eighteenth century and continued until the First World War led to large increases in the revenues of the central administration. We estimate that the revenues of the central administration rose from about 3 per cent of GDP in the second half of the eighteenth century to 5 to 6 per cent of GDP by the middle of the nineteenth century and to more than 10 per cent of GDP in the decades before the First World War.[43] This sharp rise in many ways reflected an attempt at catching up, or the results of delayed political and fiscal centralization for the Ottomans. This rise in revenues undoubtedly helped the Ottoman government to improve its military capabilities and keep the Empire together until the First World War. Nonetheless, due to the costs of military and administrative reform, expenditures continued to rise at a faster pace. For this reason, the government was forced to devote a large part of its energies, from the late eighteenth century onwards, towards developing new methods of long-term internal borrowing.

From the 1770s until the 1840s the Ottoman state finances frequently experienced large budget deficits. These deficits reached their peak during the 1820s and 1830s. In response, the state attempted to increase its control over revenue sources, made use of various forms of internal borrowing and, when the short-term fiscal pressures mounted, resorted to debasements. The highest rates of debasement in Ottoman history took place during the reign of sultan Mahmud II. The timing and magnitude

---

[42] Ibid., pp. 235–301.
[43] K. Karaman and Ş. Pamuk, 'Ottoman state finances in comparative European perspective, 1500–1914', *Journal of Economic History* 70 (2010), 593–629. See also Figure 13.1.

of these debasements suggest that the government was quite sensitive to the costs of debasements, especially the political opposition they generated amongst the janissaries and other urban groups.

Debasements had an impact on virtually all groups in Ottoman society and, in turn, each group took a position. Most men and women, both urban and rural, were clear about the consequences of different ways of dealing with the coinage, and who gained and who lost. The groups that stood to lose the most from debasements were those who were paid fixed amounts in terms of the unit of account. The most important groups in this category were the employees of the state, the bureaucracy, the ulema and especially the janissaries. There existed a large overlap between the guild members and the janissaries after the latter began to moonlight as artisans and shopkeepers in the seventeenth century.

Mahmud II was well aware of the limitations imposed by the janissaries and related urban groups. From the very beginning of his reign he wanted to replace the janissaries with a Western-style army. During the early years of his long reign, however, he did not have the political support to make this critical move. After the janissaries were finally defeated and the order was abolished in 1826, a major constraint in the way of debasements was lifted. Only two years later, the government began the largest debasement ever in Ottoman history, reducing the specie content of the *kurush* by 79 per cent within a period of four years.[44]

External borrowing, 1850–1914

For the Ottoman Empire the nineteenth century was a period of greater integration into the world economy, brought about by rapid expansion in foreign trade and European investment. It was also characterized by major efforts at Western-style reform aimed at the centralization of the Empire, in administration, education, law and justice as well as economic, fiscal and monetary affairs. The Ottoman economy was increasingly transformed into an exporter of primary products and an importer of manufactures. The foreign trade of the areas within the 1911 borders of the Empire, Macedonia, Anatolia and Syria, increased by about fifteen-fold between the 1820s and the First World War.[45] This process was facilitated by the construction of ports and railways and

[44] Pamuk, *A monetary history*, pp. 193–200.
[45] C. Issawi, *The economic history of Turkey, 1800–1914* (University of Chicago Press, 1980), chapter 3; and Ş. Pamuk, *The Ottoman Empire and European capitalism, 1820–1913: trade, investment and production* (Cambridge University Press, 1987), chapter 1.

the establishment of modern banking institutions, mostly by European capital. As a result, the commercialization of agriculture proceeded rapidly in Macedonia, western, north-eastern and central Anatolia and along the Syrian coast. The rural population was drawn to markets not only as producers of cash crops but also as purchasers of imported goods, especially of cotton textiles. These developments substantially increased the demand for and the use of money, especially in these more commercialized regions.

For European governments, and especially the British who were concerned about Russian expansionism to the south, the success of Ottoman reforms was considered essential for the territorial integrity of the Empire. European governments also believed that the rapid expansion of commercial ties with Europe based on the principle of comparative advantage and European direct investment was essential for the development of the Ottoman economy. The European governments linked Ottoman access to European financial markets to fiscal reform and monetary stability.

In the 1840s, under domestic and international pressure, the Ottoman government abandoned debasements and embraced bimetallism and stable coinage. It was hoped that this move would achieve greater price stability and help expand both trade and capital flows between Europe and the Ottoman Empire. The adoption of bimetallism did not mean the end of Ottoman monetary difficulties, however. The expansion of the Empire's internal tax base by the commercialization of peasant agriculture, the extension of cultivation onto unused lands and the development of other forms of primary production such as mining proceeded only slowly. Moreover, a large fraction of the revenues collected from peasant producers continued to remain in the hands of tax collectors. At the same time, military expenditures continued to mount. Ottoman governments had difficulties balancing the budget and resorted to a variety of methods, both short and long term, to deal with the fiscal problems.

One method of raising fiscal revenue which began to be used in 1840 was the printing and circulation in the Istanbul area of interest-bearing paper money called *kaime*. Since their volume remained limited, the *kaimes* performed reasonably well until 1852. A new phase in the history of the *kaime* began in 1852 when paper money that did not bear any interest was put into circulation for the first time. During the Crimean War large amounts of *kaime* were printed and the market price expressed in gold liras declined to less than half the nominal value. One gold lira began to be exchanged for 200–220 *kurushes* in *kaimes*. In 1861 a record volume of *kaimes* flooded the markets and the exchange rate against the gold lira plummeted to 400 paper *kurushes*. The first experiment in paper money thus resulted, more than a decade after its initiation, in a major wave of inflation. With popular protests and general discontent, the government finally agreed to retire the *kaimes* in 1862 with the help of short-term loans obtained from the Imperial Ottoman Bank.[46]

There was one other occasion before the First World War in which the government resorted to non-convertible paper money. After the Ottoman government declared a moratorium on external debt payments in 1876, it became impossible to borrow from the European financial markets or the Imperial Ottoman Bank. With the Serbian uprising and the outbreak of the war of 1877–78 with Russia, the need for fiscal revenue became even more urgent. *Kaimes* were issued in both small and large denominations and were proclaimed legal tender in all parts of the Empire. Because of the large volume, however, the exchange rate of the *kaime* declined within two years, to 450 *kurus* for the gold lira. They remained in circulation for close to three years and were retired at the end of the decade.[47]

In 1854, during the Crimean War, the Ottoman government began to sell long-term bonds in the European financial markets and this soon became the most important means of dealing with the recurring budget-ary difficulties. In the early stages of this process, the Ottoman govern-ment was supported by its British counterpart and wartime ally, which guaranteed the first bond issue against the Ottoman annual receipts from the Egyptian tribute. In the following two decades, the Ottoman government borrowed large sums in London, Paris, Vienna and else-where under increasingly unfavourable terms. The net proceeds of these issues were directed almost entirely towards current expenditures, how-ever. Only a small fraction was spent on infrastructure investment and on increasing the capacity to pay back. By the second half of the 1860s, Ottoman finances had deteriorated to the point where new bond issues had become necessary to maintain the debt payments. A moratorium was in sight but the financial markets kept the process going, lured by the unusually high rates of return.[48]

---

[46] A. Akyildiz, *Osmanli Finans Sisteminde Dönüm Noktasi: Kagit Para ve Sosyo-Ekonomik Etkileri* (Istanbul: Eren Yayincilik, 1995) pp. 50–90; R. Davison, 'The first Ottoman experiment with paper money', in O. Okyar and H. Inalcık (eds.), *Social and economic history of Turkey (1071–1920)* (Ankara: 1980), pp. 243–51 at 245; M. Erol, *Osmanlı İmparatorluğu'nda Kağıt Para (Kaime)* (Ankara: Türk Tarih Kurumu Basımevi, 1970), pp. 5–7.

[47] Akyıldız, *Kağıt Para*, pp. 91–174; Erol, *Osmanlı İmparatorluğu'nda*, pp. 15–27.

[48] C. Clay, *Gold for the sultan, Western bankers and Ottoman finance, 1856–1881* (London: I. B. Tauris Publishers, 2000); for an earlier treatment, see D. C. Blaisdell, *European financial control in the Ottoman Empire* (New York: Columbia University Press, 1929).

After the financial crises of 1873 led to the cessation of overseas lending by the European financial markets, the government was forced to declare in 1875–76 a moratorium on its outstanding debt which stood at more than 200 million pounds sterling. After protracted negotiations, the Ottoman Public Debt Administration (OPDA) was established in 1881 to exercise European control over parts of the Ottoman finances and ensure orderly payments on the outstanding debt, whose nominal value was reduced approximately by half during the negotiations. For the following three decades until the outbreak of the First World War, a sizable share of government revenues were controlled by the OPDA and applied to debt payments. This control and the regular payments on the debt were quite reassuring for the European financial markets. As a result, the Ottoman government was able to resume borrowing towards the end of the century. With the rise in military spending, both external borrowing and the annual payments on the outstanding debt gained momentum after the turn of the century. The almost permanent search for new loans led, in turn, to new dependencies and complications in Ottoman foreign policy. On the eve of the First World War, the volume of annual borrowing as well as the outstanding external debt had once again reached the unusually high proportions witnessed in the 1870s.

It may be useful to consider the long-term balance sheet for the mid-nineteenth-century regime change from debasements to stable currency and external borrowing. Relative monetary stability, the rapid expansion of foreign trade and European direct investment should appear on the positive side. The annual rate of growth of Ottoman foreign trade averaged close to 5 per cent in real terms during the nineteenth century. There is also some evidence for economic growth in the period before the First World War which can be linked to the growing commercialization of the Ottoman economy.[49] Monetary stability undoubtedly contributed to economic growth. At the same time, however, the default of 1875–76, the establishment of the Ottoman Public Debt Administration and the surrender of some of the leading sources of revenue to the European creditors in 1881 also suggest that the Ottomans paid a heavy price for borrowing large amounts from abroad before putting their fiscal house in order.

---

[49] V. Eldem, *Osmanlı Imparatorluğu'nun İktisadi Şartları Hakkinda Bir Tetkik*, (Istanbul: İş Bankası Yayinları, 1970), pp. 302–9; O. Okyar, 'A new look at the problem of economic growth in the Ottoman Empire, 1800–1914', *Journal of European Economic History* 16 (1987), 7–49.

Conclusion

This chapter has examined the long-term changes in the Ottoman fiscal institutions from the fifteenth century until the First World War. It focused on the changing Ottoman strategies and institutions in dealing with tax collection, debasements, and internal and external borrowing. For most of its 600-year existence, the Ottoman Empire is best characterized as a bureaucratic, agrarian empire. The economic institutions and policies of this large entity were shaped to a large degree by the priorities and interests of a central bureaucracy. The influence of various social groups, not only of land-owners but also of merchants and moneychangers, over the policies of the central government remained limited. Despite the general trend towards the decentralization of the Empire during the seventeenth and eighteenth centuries, merchants and domestic producers, who were the leading proponents and actual developers of mercantilist policies in Europe, never became powerful enough to exert sufficient pressure on the Ottoman government to change or even modify these traditional policies. Nonetheless, the Ottoman state and society showed considerable ability in reorganizing as a way of adapting to changing circumstances in Eurasia from the seventeenth to the nineteenth centuries. With its pragmatism, flexibility and habit of negotiation, the bureaucracy managed to contain many challenges, both internal and external, and succeeded in maintaining a traditional order. Even the reforms of the nineteenth century are best understood as attempts to maintain the privileged position of the centre as well as the territorial integrity of the Empire.

State finances were in good shape and there was little need for borrowing until the last quarter of the sixteenth century. Ottoman institutions of private and public finance retained their Islamic lineage and remained mostly uninfluenced by the developments in Europe until the end of the seventeenth century. The Ottoman government continued to rely on tax farming for both tax collection and short-term borrowing purposes, as had been the practice of most Islamic states. State finances came under increasing pressure in the seventeenth century and again from the 1770s onwards, however. European institutions of both private and public finance began to grow in influence during the eighteenth century. Ottoman state borrowing in the European financial markets during the nineteenth century led to a default in the 1870s and the partial control of state finances by European creditors until the First World War.

Before the Industrial Revolution and the European expansion of the nineteenth century, the central bureaucracy faced its most serious challenge from the notables of the provinces. Despite a protracted struggle lasting almost two centuries, however, the *ayan* did not establish alternative institutions and channels of capital accumulation. Despite their interests in trade, agriculture and manufacturing, tax farming remained the most lucrative enterprise for them. Key economic institutions of the traditional Ottoman order such as the state ownership of land, urban guilds, provisionism and selective interventionism remained mostly intact during this period. In the early part of the nineteenth century, the centre, supported by the new technologies, was able to reassert its power over the provinces. On the whole, this environment did not prove conducive to the emergence of new forms of economic organization and technological change was limited. Ottoman institutions undoubtedly changed during these centuries but not exactly in the direction of capitalist economic development.

Nonetheless, on its own terms, the Ottoman regime can be viewed as successful. Pragmatism, flexibility, a willingness to negotiate and an ability to adapt their institutions to changing circumstances were traits that enabled the Ottomans to retain power while managing a transition to modern centralism, while many of their contemporaries in both Europe and Asia, including the Mughals and the Safavids, were unable to do so. Ultimately, however, pragmatism and flexibility were utilized and change was allowed only as far as necessary for the defence of the traditional order.

Part IV

Asia

14   The continuation and efficiency of the Chinese fiscal state, 700 BC – AD 1911

Kent G. Deng

In the Old World, China was among the first to establish a fiscal state. It was also one of the first societies that undertook the task of empire-building. What is most remarkable, however, is that a fiscal state in conjunction with an empire lasted for so long on the East Asian mainland – from the third century BC to 1911. The findings of this chapter show that the need for a fiscal state (and an empire) came predominantly from the Chinese response to external threats. Likewise, changes associated with the Song economic revolution and the Qing 'opening up' were also rooted in ways to handle those threats. The threats, nevertheless, came from very different sources.

Factual background: how a fiscal state emerged

A fiscal state took shape in China very early on: at the latest during the late Zhou period (770–221 BC), better known as the Spring and Autumn (770–476 BC) and Warring States (476–221 BC) periods. During these five centuries, the Zhou territory was fragmented and political, economic and military competition among rival units was the norm. This half millennium was thus a critical period for state-formation and state-building in Chinese history when a new relationship between the state, the elite and ordinary citizens and a non-clan-based social organization evolved. The late Zhou multiple political systems also served as the main catalyst for a fiscal state to develop for the purposes of defence and/or offence. However, this process witnessed extremely bloody rivalries between political units. Table 14.1 displays the numbers of military offences launched by various states during the entire Warring State period. As a result, the number of units declined steadily. A turning point occurred after 236 BC when the Qin overpowered all remaining kingdoms and unified China. Notice that the Qin had launched almost three times as many offences as the Zhao, the next power in the pecking order.

Table 14.1. *Major military offences launched in China, 475 BC – 221 BC*

Period	Yue	Zheng	Shu	Jin	Lu	Wei	Song	Qi	Yan	Han	Zhao	Wei'	Chu	Qin	Total
475–56 B.C.	1	—	—	5	1	—	—	—	—	—	—	—	—	2	9
455–436	—	—	—	1	—	—	—	—	—	—	—	—	2	2	5
435–416	—	—	—	—	—	—	—	—	—	1	—	1	1	1	4
415–396	—	1	—	1	1	—	—	—	—	1	2	6	2	1	15
395–376	—	—	1	2	1	—	—	3	—	4	6	4	2	5	28
375–356	—	—	—	—	1	1	1	1	1	2	7	—	10	5	29
355–336	—	—	—	—	—	1	1	3	—	1	—	—	—	5	11
335–316	—	—	—	—	—	—	1	5	—	1	2	3	1	12	25
315–296	—	—	—	—	—	—	—	5	—	3	5	4	1	11	29
295–276	—	—	—	—	—	—	—	1	1	1	4	1	3	18	29
275–256	—	—	—	—	—	—	—	—	—	1	3	1	2	18	25
255–236	—	—	—	—	—	—	—	—	—	2	6	3	2	12	25
235–221	—	—	—	—	—	—	—	—	—	—	—	—	—	10	10
Total	1	1	1	9	4	2	3	18	2	17	35	23	26	102	244
% in total	0.4	0.4	0.4	3.7	1.6	0.8	1.2	7.4	0.8	7.0	14.4	9.4	10.7	41.8	100

Source: F. Zhongxia, Z. Xing, T. Zhaolin and Y. Boshi, *Zhongguo Junshishi Fujuan Shang* [A military history of China, supplement I] (Beijing: PLA Press, 1985), pp. 127–92.

Table 14.2. *Early spread of de facto private land ownership*

Year	Kingdom	Location	Fiscal policy
685 BC	Qi	lower Yellow River valley	differential taxes on the output capacities of land
594	Lu	lower Yellow River valley	taxes on land under cultivation
548	Chu	middle Yangtze valley	taxes on agrarian output
540	Zheng	middle Yellow River valley	taxes on land area under cultivation
356	Qin	middle Yellow River valley	taxes on land with outright property rights

Sources: Based on Z. Ming, *Zuo Zhuan* [Master Zuo's chronicle] (*c.* 454 BC, Beijing: Zhonghua Books, reprint, 1981), Entry 'Twenty-fifth Year under Duke Zhao of Lu'; B. Gu, *Han Shu* [The history of the Han Dynasty] (AD 82, Beijing, Zhonghua Books, reprint, 1982), pt. 1, ch. 'Economy'; Li Ruilan, 'Li Kui Bianfazhongde Jin Dili Zhijiao' [The policy of Maximizing agricultural production in Li Kui's socio-economic reform], *Lishi Jiaoxue* (*History in Education*) 6 (1986), 33–5.

Behind this long struggle for hegemony, which led to the unification of China, was severe competition for military, political and economic strength. With the rise of agricultural productivity came agricultural surpluses; and the rural sector began to attract the attention of state-builders both as an important source of revenue and for young soldiers, and also as a source of legitimacy. Negotiations between rulers and farmers led to the recognition for the first time in Chinese history of private land-holding rights including private land-ownership. Such a trend was present in all the powerful political kingdoms from the second half of the Spring and Autumn period (see Table 14.2). Given that the Qin Kingdom was known for its outright private land-ownership, high-yield agriculture and well-disciplined peasant soldiers, its final victory was not a surprise.

In the Qin Kingdom, a reform which had a profound impact on the course of Chinese history was carried out, known as Shang Yang's reform (*shangyang bianfa*, Shang Yang: *c.* 390–338 BC). The focus of the reform was on 'a foundational law, involving farming and weaving, and preparing for wars' (*neili fadu, wu gezhixiu, shouzhan zhibei*).[1] Direct taxes in the form of land taxes and labour corvée services were imposed, and its weight in total revenue increased to surpass that from the indirect taxes. Fiscal priorities consequently pushed the status of

---

[1] S. Qian, *Shi Ji* [The book of history] (Beijing: Zhonghua Books, 91 BC, reprint, 1982), Vol. 6 'Biography of Qin Shihuang'.

the peasantry to the top of the social ladder and relegated merchants to the bottom. By the time of the Qin campaigns for unification, the policy had been thoroughly tested.

After Shang Yang's reform, the Qin succeeded in maximizing both revenue and the numbers of fighting men. And the Qin, a once poor agrarian kingdom located on marginal land of the north-western plateau,[2] captured more and more territory in the wealthy North China Plain through warfare. The militia–peasantry was rewarded promptly under a nation-wide scheme launched in 216 BC, which allowed 'commoner-farmers to claim and own land' (*shi qianshou zishitian*).[3] In contrast, the Qin's main rivals separated their professional armies from unarmed farmers. The Qin system of military-backed private land-ownership was replicated across all territories captured in the process of empire-building. From the Qin period onwards, measures to ensure a supply of soldiers and food surpluses made China's fiscal state insep-arable from empire-building. China's fiscal state became an imperial fiscal state.

The imperial nature of this fiscal state led to unintended con-sequences that eventually transformed the nature of the Chinese economy and the relationship between state and society. First, pri-vate ownership became the mainstream, and the rural sector became the dominant sector. Second, the state became a fiscal state with a centralized bureaucracy and a standing army. Third, organizing and coordinating defence along the border became the inescapable respon-sibility of the bureaucracy, with a permanent defence budget. Fourth, the majority of the population became legally free, land-holding, tax-paying citizens. Rural males were obliged to serve in the army. Such a combination of institutions made the Qin's ambition to unify China possible. The relationship between the state and the peasantry bene-fited both parties and endured for some two millennia. The legacy went on in the 1940s–50s, with the minimum of modern inputs, armies of Chinese peasants fought two modern war machines. They destroyed the ferocious Japanese and forced the United States to give up North Korea.

In hindsight, land-holding property rights directly enhanced economic and military power among rival kingdoms during and fol-lowing the Warring States period in Chinese history. During that era, the number of competing political units fell dramatically from 140

---

[2] The Qin was so unimportant that Confucius ignored its existence in his lobby tour in West China (known as 'xixing budao qin').
[3] Qian, *Shi Ji*, chapter 'Emperor Qin Shihuang'.

to just 7, and their average size increased steadily. In 255 BC, when the hegemonic Zhou collapsed, a new round of political and military struggles lasted for decades among the remaining rival kingdoms: the Han, Wei, Chu, Zhao, Yan, Qi and Qin, accompanied by huge loss of life and destruction of capital. Were the conflicts necessary and beneficial? Counterfactually, would China have been better off if the multiple state system had had remained in operation after 255 BC? After all, interstate competition during the Spring and Autumn period (770–476 BC) and Warring States period (476–221 BC) gave Sinitic civilization an impetus to progress without parallel in Chinese history. The costs of replacing multiple kingdoms with a single empire must have been enormous.

Nevertheless, the basic question is why the Chinese (or proto-Chinese) felt the need to unify vast territories and populations of the East Asian mainland with such enormous costs in human lives and capital assets? Was there a need for a fiscal state to form and maintain the imperial polity we call China?

The answer lies in the threat from China's neighbouring nomads from the north and west instead of squabbles from within. Even during the bloody internecine wars, kingdoms built their defence lines, as many as ten of them, facing the north and/or the west.[4] Clearly, there was a threat from that direction which overruled dangers from internal confrontations. The irony of history decreed that the Chinese had to kill each other in civil wars in order to unify the land and cooperate with each other in order to fend off the nomads. Soon after China was unified, one of the greatest public projects in pre-modern world history, known as the Great Wall, was pushed ahead by the Qin authorities to link together all of the existing walls and integrate them into a single line for external defence. Since then, China has been the only 'walled empire' in world history.

Even after the construction of the Great Wall, the nomadic threat did not go away. In effect, as the data in Table 14.3 reveal, invasions and confrontations continued for centuries.

---

[4] Based on information from Y. Jin (ed.), *The Great Wall*, 4th edn (Beijing: Cultural Relics Press, 1986), p. 97; ZDC [Zhongguo Ditu Chubanshe, Compilatory Board of the Maps of China] (ed.), *Zhonghua Renmin Gongheguo Fensheng Dituji* [Collected Provincial Maps of the People's Republic of China] (Beijing: China's Atlas Press, 1990); Z. Xiukun, T. Zhaolin, K. Ning, T. Wenhuan, S. Shibi, C. Yangping, Z. Ansheng, X. Fei, Z. Chunyi and Z. Shufang, *Zhongguo Junshishi* [A Military History of China], Vol. 6 (Beijing: PLA Press, 1991), pp. 69–84, 111–13; H. Wailu (ed.), *Zhongguo Dabaike Quanshu Zhongguo Lishi* [Encyclopaedia of Chinese History] (Beijing and Shanghai: China's Encyclopaedia Publisher, 1992), pp. 784, 1332–3.

Table 14.3. *Major nomadic invasions across the Great Wall and into China*

Year	Area attacked
176 BC	Chang-an*
200 BC	Middle reaches of the Yellow River†
AD 44	Chang-an*
714	Chang-an*
761–3	Chang-an*
762	Middle reaches of the Yellow River†
780–7	Chang-an* and middle reaches of the Yellow River†
1125–6	Beijing, Kaifeng* and middle reaches of the Yellow River†
1211	Middle reaches of the Yellow River†
1212–3	Beijing†
1215	Beijing† and Kaifeng†
1218	Middle reaches of the Yellow River†
1222	Chang-an†
1229	Kaifeng and middle reaches of the Yellow River†
1629	Beijing*
1635–5	Beijing* and middle reaches of the Yellow River†
1644	Beijing*

Notes: * China's capital of the time; † China's strategic region; sources: based on information from Y. Jin (ed.), *The Great Wall*, 4th edn (Beijing: Cultural Relics Press, 1986), p. 98; ZDC [Zhongguo Ditu Chubanshe, Compilatory Board of the Maps of China] (ed.), *Zhonghua Renmin Gongheguo Fensheng Dituji* [Collected Provincial Maps of the People's Republic of China] (Beijing: China's Atlas Press, 1990); F. Zhongxia, Z. Xing, T. Zhaolin and Y. Boshi, *Zhongguo Junshishi Fujuan Shang* [A military history of China, supplement I] (Beijing: PLA Press, 1985), pp. 111–18, 244–8; H. Wailu (ed.), *Zhongguo Dabaike Quanshu Zhongguo Lishi* [Encyclopaedia of Chinese History] (Beijing and Shanghai: China's Encyclopaedia Publisher, 1992), pp. 312, 452–5, 580, 805–6, 1120–2, 1332–3.

Clearly the Great Wall made China safer but not completely invasion-free, and the external threat was the main factor holding China together as an empire for most of its imperial history. Over time, nomadic threats and pressures became endogenized in the Chinese political and socio-economic system. They played the most important role in the formation of a fiscal state and the consolidation of the Chinese empire.

The nature of the Chinese imperial fiscal state (until 1840)

The success of China's imperial fiscal state depended upon three factors: a salaried administrative elite, universal taxation and 'internal colonization'.

The origins of a centralized bureaucracy to run an empire can be traced back to the rise of the *shi* stratum in the Spring and Autumn period (770–476 BC). *Shi* were a group of well-educated meritocrats who specialised in statecraft.[5] Without the *shi* China lapsed into feudalism as it did during the Western Zhou period (*c*. 1030–771 BC).

Second, the Chinese state collected a huge aggregate sum of revenue from a large population but in small amounts per capita. This low-cost fiscal option mobilized economies of scale for the paramount task of sustaining the defence of China's sedentary agrarian population against nomads from the north. In this context, the size of the political unit needed to be big enough to encompass those economies. Total taxable revenue was in turn determined by the physical limits with which surpluses could be produced and by the moral or political limits for how much of the surpluses were allowed to be extracted. Thus a low tax rate may mean either low levels of surplus capacity (and thus low productivity) or a benevolent state, or both. In pre-modern China, the moral limitations on extraction certainly left room for population growth and domestic and foreign trade.[6]

Third, and related to the first two points, there was a persistent need to expand the empire in all directions. 'Internal colonization' accommodated an enlarged agrarian population and increased state revenue. Given that the cost of maintaining the Great Wall defence line was more or less fixed, an enlarged territory meant more revenue for the Imperial Treasury, as well as new administrative posts for the elites who ruled newly captured territories and civilian settlements.

Thus, both the legitimacy of the fiscal state and the rationale for the Chinese empire were determined by demands for external security. This applies to the Manchu Qing Dynasty (1368–1644), a period when China's defence lines shifted beyond the Great Wall to places like Siberia and Turkistan (*xinjiang*).

In combination, the three factors outlined above underpinned the extensive growth bias in the Chinese economy. These three factors also embodied several important linkages to policy: (i) they institutionalized a low taxation regime (known as 'light corvée and gentle taxes' (*qingyao bofu*); (ii) they institutionalized a bias towards balanced budgets; (iii) they endorsed a small-scale government (bureaucrats were usually about 5 per cent of the total population) but favoured a large standing army (which always employed more men than the bureaucracy); and

---

[5] G. Deng, *The premodern Chinese economy – structural equilibrium and capitalist sterility* (London and New York: Routledge, 1999), pp. 18–22.
[6] Ibid., chapters 2–4.

(iv) they promoted the development of the agricultural sector as the main source of revenue and army recruits.

In absolute terms, state revenues were impressive. From 1784 to 1820, China's total revenue from land taxes and tolls was 29.6 to 30.2 million *taels* of silver per annum (1,104.1–1,126.5 metric tons). That remained stable and predictable. From 1841 to 1890, despite a lot of changes in society the Qing government still collected 29.4 to 33.7 million *taels* of silver a year.[7]

But, behind the extravagant appearance of the imperial court, the state only controlled a fraction of China's GDP, amounting to some 8 per cent under the Qing.[8] The lion's share of the tax revenue was used to feed the army that was made up of young men recruited from rural China. The rest funded basic public works (roads and canals) and embryo social security (in the form of public granaries for food price stability and famine relief). The bureaucrats' salaries were tiny compared with the budgets for military and public works. China thus had an unusually cheap government for its total GDP.

Taxes were often collected in kind (typically grain and cloth) instead of in cash. This was simply because food and clothes were needed by the army and bureaucracy more so than cash. Taxes in kind removed the state from market dependency and uncertainty, although payments in kind may not have been the most efficient way to extract revenue from the economy. However, fiscal strategy was consistent with the logistics of the army. Indeed, given the low tax rate (hardly ever more than 10 per cent of the total agricultural output), such inefficiency was tolerated by the state and its taxpayers.

Occasionally the Chinese state deviated from the norm and became hungry for revenue on the one hand and incompetent in protecting the empire's territory and agriculture on the other. When this happened, more often than not, internal rebellions and external invasions, or a combination of the two, occurred and a regime change would restore China's traditional fiscal regime.[9] Fully aware of the problem of rebellions, the Qing state went so far as to freeze not only the tax rate but also total revenue from 1712 until 1840, which enabled the population to benefit from declining taxes during an era of economic growth.

---

[7] L. Fangzhong, *Zhongguo Lidai Huko Tiandi Tianfu Tongji* [Dynastic data of China's households, cultivated land and land taxation] (Shanghai: Shanghai People's Press, 1980), pp. 387, 397–8, 401, 415–16.

[8] A. Feuerwerker, 'The state and the economy in Late Imperial China', *Theory and Society*, 13 (1984), 300; see also Deng, *Premodern Chinese economy*, app. G.

[9] Deng, *Premodern Chinese economy*, chapters 4–5.

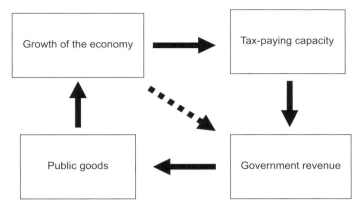

Figure 14.1 The fiscal cycle in the Chinese economy
Note: Solid arrows indicate the normal loop. The broken arrow represents a 'rent-seeking short-cut', attempted under the Qin.

Generally speaking, the Chinese state cannot, it seems, be represented as a rent-seeking despot.

Readjustments of the system (until 1840)

There were four components of the Chinese fiscal system: (i) the economy as the tax base; (ii) the tax-paying capacities of the general public (including both economic and psychological tolerance towards tax burdens); (iii) government revenue-cum-budget; and (iv) public goods including national defence and basic social security. These components formed a loop of mutually reinforcing connections so that the system was able to continue indefinitely, subject to shocks (see Figure 14.1).

At the very beginning under the Qin, when the system was under trial, the state had a rather limited influence on the economy. At that stage, there was a great temptation for state to engage in excessive rent-seeking because there were no clearly defined ceilings for taxation. Indeed, the Qin regime (221–207 BC) short-circuited the loop, completely ignoring the physical and moral tax-paying limits. The Qin ruler did not fully comprehend the actual power of his taxpayers, consisting of owner-farmers with moral sensibilities. The Qin attempt to short-circuit this cycle stimulated a nation-wide rebellion that proved fatal to the ruler.

This bitter lesson was well taken. The Early Han (206 BC– AD 24) established a tradition of a light tax burden (extracted either in produce or labour). The official adoption of Confucianism as the state philosophy helped greatly in 'acclimatizing' and regulating the fiscal behaviour of the state by referring to pitfalls of the rent-seeking behaviour exemplified under the Qin and under recommending a 'fair' level of taxation in relation to the state of the economy.[10] The central concept of Confucian 'good statecraft and statesmanship' (*ren*) began to play a central role in Chinese politics and set the fiscal code of conduct for rulers in post-Han China. The new principle was a separation between the availability of tax revenue (as measured by the prosperity of the economy) and the acceptability of tax revenue (judged by the willingness of people to pay more taxes). Clearly, Confucianism recognized taxpayers' rights and operated to curb the rent-seeking tendencies of the state. Most dynasties operated under these constraints. If not, political disasters and tax revolts occurred in response to rent-seeking.

A marked step towards a low-tax regime was taken under the Qing (1644–1911), when government revenue from the Land-Poll Tax (*ding-yin*) was permanently frozen by an imperial edict in 1712 at a ceiling of 33.5 million *taels* of silver per year,[11] a fiscal policy that remained in place until the very end of the Qing (see column I of Table 14.4).

It is clear that the imperial state of the Qing took its public accountability very seriously. Its strategy can be seen as the culmination of China's political and moral economy.

Mutation of the fiscal approach

The peculiarities of Chinese state- and empire-building led to a persistent long-term fiscal dependence upon the rural economy, mainly agricultural production. This is clearly demonstrated by the Qing tax structure (see Table 14.4). Although commercial taxes increased both in relative and absolute terms from time to time, the weight of the rural/agricultural taxes was overwhelming before the eighteenth century.

However, there were two short periods when commercial taxes surpassed the agricultural ones in fiscal importance: the first appeared under the Song (960–1279) – an era of China's medieval

---

[10] W. Genyou (ed.), *Sishu Wujing* [The annotated four books and five classics of Confucianism] (Beijing: China's Friendship Press, 1993), passim.

[11] See Z. Erxun (ed.), *Qingshi Gao* [Draft of the history of the Qing Dynasty] (Beijing: Zhonghua Books, 1927, reprint, 1977), Vol. 121 'Economy'.

Table 14.4. *Trends in tax revenues and tax structure of the Qing regime (in tael), 1652–1820*

Year	Grain equivalents (I_1)*	Land-poll (I_2)	Salt (II_1)	Customs duties (II_2)	Other (II_3)	I:II
1652	8,767,200 (5,620,000 piculs)	21,260,000	2,120,000	1,000,000	—	9.6:1
1682	9,890,400 (6,340,000 piculs)	26,340,000	2,760,000	2,000,000	—	7.6:1
1766	12,975,768 (8,317,800 piculs)	32,910,000	5,740,000	5,400,000	4,490,000	4.1:1
1820	—	30,206,144	—	2,932,796†	—	10.3:1
1861	—	32,813,304†	—	5,036,371	—	6.6:1
1885	9,334,080	23,022,687	—	14,178,227	—	2.3:1
1903	3,097,000	32,732,000	—	30,423,243	—	1.2:1

Notes: * Conversion based on the mean price of 1.56 *taels* per *picul* derived from the price range of 0.94–2.18 *taels* per *picul* in rich farming regions of Yangzi and Pearl deltas of the seventeenth and eighteenth centuries; see R. B. Marks, 'Rice prices, food supply, and market structure in eighteenth-century South China', *Late Imperial China* 2 (1991), 64–116; W. Yie-chien, 'Secular trends of rice prices in the Yangzi Delta, 1638–1935', in T. G. Rawski and L. M. Li (eds.), *Chinese history in economic perspective* (Berkeley: University of California Press, 1992), pp. 35–68. † The 1812–50 quota, used as a proxy; SOURCES: based on Z. Boudi, *Zhongguo Caizheng Shi* [A history of state finance in China] (Shanghai: Shanghai People's Press, 1981), pp. 419–21, 426; L. Fangzhong, *Zhongguo Lidai Huko Tiandi Tianfu Tongji* [Dynastic data for China's households, cultivated land and land taxation] (Shanghai: Shanghai People's Press, 1980), pp. 10, 253–7, 264–7, 380, 400, 401, 414–18, 426; T. Xianglong, *Zhongguo Jindai Haiguan Shuishou He Fenpei Tongji* [Statistics of customs revenue and its distribution in modern China] (Beijing: Zhonghua Books, 1992), pp. 63, 66, 126–8.

economic revolution – and the second in the post-Opium War period (1840–1911).

For two reasons the Song state moved away from China's age-old physiocratic doctrine to create new sources of revenue for its coffers (see Table 14.5). First, Song bureaucrats and military personnel received big pay raises for their loyalty towards the founder of the new dynasty, Zhao Kuangyin (r. 960–76), leader of a coup d'état that was clearly short of legitimacy. Second, a profound change occurred in the strategy for external security, from military deterrent against invaders to monetary bribery to achieve peace. State expenditures thus suddenly rose, which led to deficit finance, a very rare occurrence in China's fiscal history (see Table 14.6). To maintain fiscal strength, the Song government resorted to mercantilism and instituted a cluster of measures

Table 14.5. *Changes in government non-agricultural revenues* * *(annual, in min)*

Year	Salt	Tea	Wine	Other
995–7	—	—	2,779,000	—
1017–21	—	—	7,796,000	—
1034–37	—	590,000	—	—
1049–53	—	—	14,986,196	4,000,760
1054–63	—	1,672,000	—	—
1064–67	—	1,012,776	12,862,466	5,992,735
1068	36,400	—	—	—
1074	183,100	—	—	—
1084	337,900	—	—	—
1102–6	—	3,200,000	—	—
1116	—	10,000,000	—	—
1165–73[†]	41,585	—	3,000,000	—

Note: * Song taxes included three components (1) indirect taxes on consumers, (2) licence fees from producers, and (3) profits from government sales and re-sales; source: T. Tuo (ed.), *Song Shi* [History of the Song Dynasty] (1345, Beijing: Zhonghua Books, reprint, 1985), vols. 184–5. [†] Southern Song.

Table 14.6. *Deficit finance under the Song* *

Year	Revenue (in 10^6 coins)	Expenditure (in 10^6 coins)	Balance
997	70,893	86,950	−16,057
1007	47,211	49,749	−2,538
1021	140,298	168,044	−27,746
1048	122,592	111,785	10,807
1049	126,252	±126,252	±0
1064	101,906	100,399	1,507
1065	116,138	120,343	−4,205
1086	82,491	91,910	−9,419
1190*	68,001	±68,001	±0
1253*	120,000	250,000	−130,000

Notes: * Southern Song; source: W. Shengduo, *Liangsong Caizhengshi* [A history of government finance of the Northern and Southern Song periods] (Beijing: Zhonghua Books, 1995), pp. 678–86.

to encourage trade and handicrafts. This led to an extended economic revolution marked by achievements in metal and porcelain production, maritime trade and the circulation of paper currency.[12]

But the Song fiscal and economic revolution did not last, basically because the state did not pay enough attention to defence. The Song army was defeated and China was conquered by the Tartars and Mongols. In the process, the regime lost its legitimacy to rule and large numbers of Chinese farmers actually returned to territories controlled by nomads. They thus turned their backs on the commercial frenzy of the Song domain. This action of the Chinese farmers exemplifies the rationality behind the construction and maintenance of China's fiscal state and empire.[13] Paradoxically, it was under the Yuan Mongols (1271–1368) that traditional physiocratic norms and tax structures were restored. That strategy was further strengthened under the Ming, when the Han Chinese resumed their control over the empire in 1368.

A second period of structural change occurred after the Opium War (1839–40), when China was forcibly opened to foreign trade (see Table 14.7). Although, from then on, China faced severe competition on world markets and, as a result, suffered from mounting trade deficits on a regular basis (see Table 14.8), the vigorous growth in foreign trade did create an alternative tax base for the Chinese state outside agriculture. It was politically safe to tax the increased trade.

Meanwhile, war reparations following China's military defeats by foreign powers and military expenditures in the prolonged struggle with the Taiping rebels promoted fiscal crises for the Qing state. China's war reparations from 1842 to 1900 accounted for 713 million *taels* for silver (26,595 metric tons), over twenty times the annual state revenue of the Qing Land-Poll Tax during the same period.[14] Furthermore, while Taiping rebels controlled the lower reaches of the Yangzi River (the Jiangnan area) they cut off the wealthiest region of the Chinese economy from the state's fiscal base. For the Qing state, the only way out

---

[12] See, for example, R. M. Hartwell, *Iron and early industrialism in eleventh-century China* (University of Chicago Library, 1963); R. M. Hartwell, 'Markets, technology, and the structure of enterprise in the development of the eleventh-century Chinese iron and steel industry', *Journal of Economic History* 1 (1966), 29–58; Y. Shiba, *Commerce and society in Sung China*, trans. M. Elvin (Ann Arbor: Center for Chinese Studies of the University of Michigan, 1969); M. Elvin, *The pattern of the Chinese past* (Stanford University Press, 1973); G. Deng, *Chinese maritime activities and socioeconomic consequences, c. 2100 B.C –1900 A.D.* (New York, London and West Port: Greenwood Publishing Group, 1997), chapter 2; and Deng, *Premodern Chinese economy*, chapter 6.

[13] Deng, *Premodern Chinese economy*, pp. 301–20.

[14] See Z. Doqing, *Zhongguo Jingjishi Cidian* [Encyclopaedia of Chinese economic history] (Wuhan: Hubei Books, 1990), pp. 874–80; Tang, *Statistics of customs*, p. 33.

Table 14.7. *Establishment of new customs for foreign trade, 1860–1908*

Year	SEC	SI	NEC	NI	Aggregate
1860	3	—	—	—	3
1861	4	—	2	—	9
1862	1	—	—	—	10
1863	—	2	1	—	13
1864	1	—	—	—	14
1876	1	—	—	—	15
1877	2	2	—	—	19
1887	2	—	—	—	21
1889	1	1	—	—	23
1891	—	1	—	—	24
1896	2	1	—	—	27
1897	4	1	—	—	32
1899	2	1	1	—	36
1902	—	1	1	—	38
1904	—	1	—	—	39
1907	1	—	2	—	42
1908	—	—	—	2	44
Total	24	11	7	2	44
% of total	54.5	25.0	15.9	4.6	100.0

Notes: 'SEC' = Southeast Coast including Taiwan; 'SI' = South Inland; 'NEC' = Northeast Coast; 'NI' = North Inland; source: based on T. Xianglong, *Zhongguo Jindai Haiguan Shuishou He Fenpei Tongji* [Statistics of customs revenue and its distribution in modern China] (Beijing: Zhonghua Books, 1992), pp. 54–60.

was to accumulate foreign debts. China's outstanding debt soared along with revenues from trade (see Tables 14.9 and 14.10). Overall, indirect taxes, especially customs duties, played an important role in serving China's mounting foreign debts to keep the empire going. Undoubtedly, some tax efficiency was achieved in this context even if it was done for the wrong reason.

The data show clearly that during the late Qing period, China's tax structure once again tipped towards commerce. From 1820 to 1910, revenues from customs duties increased over tenfold but were extracted from roughly the same number of taxpayers (see Table 14.10). The impact was profound: the traditional revenue base in agriculture lost its position in the state finances. Compared to Song, the main difference was that in the late Qing, no force like the Mongols existed to restore China to its timeless doctrine of agricultural fundamentalism. This marks the beginning of modern China.

Table 14.8. *China's trade balances with India and Britain,* 1834–1870*

Period	V (I)	Idxa	Tea†	Idxb	V (II)	Idxc	Opium§	Idxd	V (I–II)	Idxe
1834–37	45.0	100	91.0	100	53.3 (20.2)	100	54.1	100	−8.3	100.0
1837–40	42.7	95	88.2	97	40.3 (22.6)	77	40.1	74	+2.4	−28.9
1840–43	31.1	69	94.1	103	39.3 (19.8)	74	49.7	92	−8.2	99.8
1843–46	53.4	119	90.8	100	79.8 (25.7)	150	57.8	107	−26.4	318.1
1846–49	63.9	142	82.0	90	69.1 (22.9)	130	63.2	117	−5.2	62.7
1849–52	66.6	148	85.9	94	88.5 (19.9)	166	63.4	117	−21.9	263.9
1852–55	83.6	186	75.6	83	86.7 (20.2)	163	70.0	129	−3.1	37.3
1855–58	98.7	219	50.1	55	98.2 (20.2)	184	68.8	127	−0.5	6.0
1858–61	84.6	188	67.9	75	153.6 (27.5)	288	61.6	114	−69.0	831.3
1861–64	118.0	262	71.6	79	150.3 (26.3)	282	68.6	127	−32.3	389.2
1864–67	127.5	283	76.7	84	170.4 (33.9)	320	56.5	104	−42.9	516.9
1867–70	104.5	232	94.9	104	210.5 (39.5)	395	51.2	95	−106.0	1,277.1
Average	76.6		80.7		109.9 (24.9)		58.8		−26.8	

Notes: 'V (I)' = total value of China's export to Britain in 10^5 pounds sterling; 'V (II)' = total value of China's import from India plus Britain in 10^5 pounds sterling, values in parentheses being the shares of Britain's direct exports to China; 'V (I–II)' = China's trade balance 10^5 pounds sterling; 'Idx$a$–e' = indices for changes; * a three-year average, based on the financial year, calculated from April to the following March, the overlap being thus only nominal; † percentage of the total value of China's exports to Britain; § percentage of the total value of imports to China from India plus Britain; source: based on Chen Ciyu, 'Yi Zhong Yin Ying Sanjiao Maoyi Wei Jizhou Tantao Shijiu Shiji Zhongguode Duiwai Maoyi' [Study of nineteenth-century Sino-foreign trade based on the trade triangle of China, India, and Britain], in Zhongguo Haiyang Fazhanshi Lunwenji Bianji Weiyuanhui [Editing Committee for *Maritime history of China*] (ed.), *Zhongguo Haiyang Fazhanshi Lunwenji* [Selected essays on the maritime history of China], Vol. 1 (Taipei: Academia Sinica, 1984), pp. 144–5.

Final remarks

The *raison d'être* for a fiscal state to take shape in China was to establish external security against the nomads on its northern and western borders. The long evolution and survival of that fiscal state indicate that the Chinese managed to reach an equilibrium between the elite and the peasantry, between national defence and political legitimacy, between rent-seeking and Confucian self-discipline.

China's fiscal state remained small and relatively cheap. It was designed to fulfil specific political, military and socio-economic tasks. China's imperial fiscal state was thus suited to and worked well for the long-run growth and stability of an economy dominated by agriculture.

Table 14.9. *Government foreign debts, 1861–1898*

Year	Purpose	Sum (in silver *tael*)	Debtor	Annual interest (%)
1861–66	Counter-Taipings	1,609,925*†	Foreign merchants in JS, FJ and GD	?
1867–68	Counter-Muslim Rebellion	2,200,000*	Foreign merchants in SH	18.0
1874	Taiwan defence	2,000,000§	British bank	8.0
1875	Counter-Muslim Rebellion	3,000,000†	British banks	10.5
1877–78	Counter-Muslim Rebellion	6,750,000§	British bank	15.0
1883–85	Coastal defence	13,602,300§	British bank	9.0
1886	Naval upgrading#	980,000§	German bank	5.5
1887–88	Flood control	1,968,800*†	British bank	7.0
1893–95	Coastal defence (1)	42,090,000§¶	British and German banks	6.0–7.0
1895–96	War reparation to Japan	200,000,000¶	French and Russian banks	4.0–5.0
Total		274,201,025		

Notes: * loans for 2 years; † loans for 2–5 years; § loans for 6–19 years; ¶ loans for 20 years and over; # fund abused for the construction of the Summer Palace; 'JS' = Jiangsu; 'FJ' = Fujian; 'GD' = Guangdong; 'SH' = Shanghai; source: based on T. Xianglong, *Zhongguo Jindai Haiguan Shuishou He Fenpei Tongji* [Statistics of customs revenue and its distribution in modern China] (Beijing: Zhonghua Books, 1992), pp. 34–41.

Whenever the imperial fiscal state moved away from its agrarian base, either voluntarily (under the Song) or involuntarily (at the end of the Qing), the empire ran into instability, even if deviations did create favourable conditions in the short run for commercial growth.

This outcome implies that although China's imperial state in its original form operated in harmony with its fiscal base and the economy, it proved to be incapable of transforming the economy to achieve modern growth and development.

Table 14.10. *Changes in China's tax structure (in silver tael), 1820–1910*

Year	I		II		I:II	Taxpayers	Index	Farmland†	Index
	Agricultural taxes*	Index	Customs duties	Index					
1820	30,206,144	100	2,932,796§	100	10.3	353,377,694	100	779,321,984	100
1825	—	—	—	—	—	379,885,340	108	—	—
1830	—	—	—	—	—	394,784,681	112	—	—
1835	—	—	—	—	—	401,767,053	114	—	—
1840	—	—	—	—	—	12,814,828	117	—	—
1845	30,213,800	100	—	—	—	421,342,730	119	—	—
1850	—	—	—	—	—	429,913,134	122	—	—
(1851	—	—	—	—	—	—	—	756,386,244	97)
1855	—	—	—	—	—	318,845,752	90	—	—
1860	—	—	—	—	—	—	—	—	—
1865	—	—	8,245,394	281	—	260,697,717	74	—	—
1870	—	—	10,041,826	342	—	271,793,461	77	—	—
(1873	—	—	11,257,824	384	—	—	—	756,631,857	97)
1875	—	—	12,893,471	440	—	305,014,000¶	86	—	—
						368,063,232	*104*		
1880	—	—	14,692,208	501	—	288,559,000#	82	—	—
						368,153,866	*104*		
1885	32,356,768	107	14,056,914	479	2.3	295,881,000★★	84	—	—
						358,036,060	*101*		
(1887	32,792,627	109	16,411,544	560	2.0	377,636,000	107	911,976,606	117)
1890	33,736,023	112	19,100,657	651	—	333,242,000††	94	—	—
						380,717,468	*108*		
1895	—	—	20,694,712	706	—	332,336,000§§	94	—	—
						379,682,395	*107*		

Table 14.10. (cont.)

Year	I Agricultural taxes*	Index	II Customs duties	Index	I:II	Taxpayers	Index	Farmland†	Index
(1898	—	—	22,976,817	783	—	319,719,000¶	90	—	⌒
						367,324,219	*104*		
1900	—	—	24,456,571	834	—	—	—	—	—
(1903	28,086,771	93	27,659,313	943	1.0	—	—	—	⌒
(1904	—	—	28,132,456	959	—	—	—	—	⌒
1905	—	—	30,965,612	1056	—	—	—	—	—
1910	—	—	35,340,714	1205	—	—	—	—	—
(1912	—	—	—	—	—	368,146,520	104	—	⌒

Notes: Entries in parentheses are supplementary to show continuation of the data. Italicized numbers are estimates weighted to include the missing provinces. Mean values are applicable to Anhui (6.30%), Shaanxi (4.66%), Gansu (4.40%), Guangxi (1.32%), Yunnan (2.04%) and Guizhou (0.49%). Jilin (0.09%) and Xinjiang (0.10) are based on the limited statistics from one year. Taiwan is excluded due to the absence of data; the formula is: $p'_i = \dfrac{P_i}{(1-n)}$. Where P'_i is the estimate for the period i; P_i, the incomplete aggregate for population of the period i; n, the combined share of the missing provinces in China's total; * including the Land–Poll Combined Tax, Grain–to–Cash Conversion (*liangzhe*) and Silver Loss Discount (*haoxian*); † in *mu*; § estimated figure based on the highest share of the customs duty revenue (8.85%) during 1652–1766; ¶ no data for seven provinces (Anhui, Shaanxi, Gansu, Xinjiang, Taiwan, Guangxi and Yunnan); # no data for nine provinces (Jilin, Anhui, Shaanxi, Gansu, Xinjiang, Fujian, Taiwan, Guangxi and Yunnan); ** no data for eight provinces (Anhui, Gansu, Xinjiang, Fujian, Taiwan, Guangxi, Yunnan and Guizhou); †† no data for six provinces (Anhui, Gansu, Xinjiang, Taiwan, Guangxi and Yunnan); §§ no data for six provinces (Anhui, Gansu, Xinjiang, Taiwan, Guangxi and Yunnan); ¶¶ no data for eight provinces (Jilin, Anhui, Gansu, Xinjiang, Fujian, Taiwan, Guangxi and Yunnan); source: based on L. Fangzhong, *Zhongguo Lidai Huko Tiandi Tianfu Tongji* [Dynastic data for China's households, cultivated land and land taxation] (Shanghai: Shanghai People's Press, 1980), pp. 10, 253–4, 256–7, 264–7, 380, 400–1, 414–18, 426; T. Xianglong, *Zhongguo Jindai Haiguan Shuishou He Fenpei Tongji* [Statistics of customs revenue and its distribution in modern China] (Beijing: Zhonghua Books, 1992), pp. 126–8.

15   Taxation and good governance in China, 1500–1914

R. Bin Wong

This chapter presents key features of the Chinese fiscal system between the sixteenth and early twentieth centuries. It builds primarily on a combination of Chinese and Japanese scholarship, as well as the author's own research. Earlier studies relied on printed sources which stated both a large number of rules and procedures as well as discussions of the many problems and challenges confronted by officials collecting taxes; more recent work on the eighteenth and nineteenth centuries draws as well upon archival sources, especially from the central government archives. Some scholarship stresses the tensions between centre and locale and the particular difficulties of relying on corvée labour for local government services.[1] Other work has shown dramatically different fiscal situations across Chinese provinces in the nineteenth century, with the central government seeking to gain accounting control over diverse expenditure needs.[2] Because the government did not have a modern notion of budgets there is little aggregate data of the sort available for the fiscal operations of many modern states. The demographic and territorial scale of empire makes such data collection and processing virtually impossible to imagine during the period under study. While a sense of changing magnitudes of revenue and expenditure can be suggested, institutional topics are the most feasible to examine.

This chapter considers how Chinese notions of good governance, based on light taxation and the provision of social goods, pursued between 1500 and the mid nineteenth century, came to be undermined by an expanding set of demands and difficulties confronting the Chinese state. More specifically it shows: (i) the sixteenth-century

Thanks to K. Pomeranz, J.-L. Rosenthal and an anonymous reviewer for comments on earlier drafts of this chapter.

[1] See I. Shigeki, *Chūgoku kinsei zaiseishi no kenkyū* [A study of the fiscal system in Late Imperial China] (Kyoto University Press, 2004).
[2] See S. Yamamoto, *Shindai zaisei seishi kenkyū* [Studies of Qing dynasty fiscal history], (Tokyo: Kyūko, 2002); X. Shen, *Wan Qing caizheng zhichu zhengce yanjiu* [Studies of late Qing fiscal expenditures] (Beijing: Zhongguo renmin daxue chubanshe, 2006).

state's abilities to mobilize and move revenues around the agrarian empire despite having a very limited bureaucracy; (ii) the vertically integrated eighteenth-century bureaucracy's strategies for collecting most of its taxes without encouraging rent-seeking activities or giving local-level officials much opportunity to create autonomous bases of power and authority; (iii) Chinese success at good governance, which depended on an alliance between officials and local literati, large land-owners and merchants who together formed the local elite; (iv) the varied consequences of government efforts to raise extraordinary revenues in the early seventeenth and eighteenth centuries; and (v) the changing expenditure demands of the late nineteenth and early twentieth centuries that undermined long-standing ideas about good governance and transformed the institutions of the state. The pre-1850 state was able to supply order and security over a space equivalent to much of Europe, excepting the few decades on either side of the 1640s when the Ming dynasty fell and the Qing dynasty established itself. Within this empire there were few monopolies, low tariffs, and a well-developed separation of economic and political powers, which allowed for broadly parallel processes of commercial growth in China and Europe.[3] The unravelling of those successes shifts China from being a territory within which Smithian dynamics of economic expansion were well supported by state policies to becoming a fiscally fragmented empire that fell under increasing political pressures from within and from without, ultimately collapsing into a collection of competing regimes with territorial reunification not achieved again until 1949 with the establishment of the People's Republic.

In contrast to most other governments in the world around 1500, the Chinese state had more than fifteen hundred years of past fiscal principles and policies upon which to draw in order to decide upon those measures deemed most appropriate. The Ming dynasty, which began its rule in 1368, drew upon some earlier practices, but also made a sharp shift from practices under the previous Yuan dynasty and especially the Song dynasty (960–1279), whose rulers had relied on a mix of commerce and agriculture for their taxes. Viewing China in the second half of the fourteenth century, the founding Ming emperor, in contrast, envisioned a simple agrarian society settled on the land, living peacefully with little connection to larger networks beyond nearby villages.

---

[3] R. B. Wong, *China transformed: historical change and the limits of European experience* (Ithaca: Cornell University Press, 1997); K. Pomeranz, *The great divergence: China, Europe and the making of the modern world economy* (Princeton University Press, 2000).

He thus made agriculture the overwhelming source of tax revenues. By 1500, the realities of increasing amounts of commerce in different parts of the empire offered his successors ample opportunities to shift or expand tax collection to commerce, but they did not seize these opportunities in any of the ways in which many rulers elsewhere in Europe and Asia did. Tapping commercial revenues would not become permanently important in China until the second half of the nineteenth century. The repeated choice to stress agricultural taxation reflected broader ideas about good governance.

Understanding the relationship between taxation and good governance allows us to reconsider the ways in which the late imperial Chinese state is portrayed. Generally speaking, the Chinese state is presented in one of two ways, whether in the specialist or the comparative literature. The despotic state generates fear and uncertainty because its acts are the product of a malevolent, autocratic emperor who interferes in the lives of common people. In contrast, the lumbering and ineffective bureaucratic state fails to do much of anything, let alone anything good, because it is too small and far removed from the daily lives of common people to make much difference. These views share an assumption that the state could do nothing positive. They routinely fail to make any effort to establish concrete criteria for successful or unsuccessful government. The capacities and limitations of fiscal operations suggest that the late imperial state is best understood neither as a despotic and arbitrary government nor as an ineffective and subsequently irrelevant state. In particular, it made positive contributions to the possibilities for economic growth – rent-seeking was limited, the provision of social goods was substantial, and predation as an alternative to exchange for gaining wealth was rare.

Sixteenth-century patterns of resource mobilization and movement

In 1500 the central government levied taxes on peasants in two main forms, grain and labour service. Over the next couple of centuries these were both converted into monetary payments which made the movement and spending of revenues far easier and more flexible. Taxes were collected in each of the Ming empire's roughly 1,100 counties by magistrates who sought with uneven success to keep up with land-ownership changes and the opening of new lands. Agricultural taxes were divided into two main categories: those that remained in the county to meet local administrative expenses and those that were forwarded to the capital or diverted to another part of the empire. Taxes sent to the capital paid for central administrative costs; they were joined by additional levies in grain from the rice-rich provinces along the Yangzi River, sent up the Grand Canal to help feed the capital. For expenses within the provinces, the central government earmarked agricultural taxes in the southern half of the empire to support soldiers, while those in northern counties went to support the resident princes of the imperial family.[4] Much uncertainty attends estimations of levels of taxation. The most comprehensive effort to estimate the multiple levies on the land suggests that total tax was less than 10 per cent of the value of the harvest in most cases, sometimes far less. Only in the rich Yangzi delta did rates approach 20 per cent of the harvest.[5] Since many rural households, especially in the Yangzi delta area also engaged in handicraft production, the percentage of total household income taxed was typically much lower and closer to the range of taxation rates observed in other parts of the empire.

The Ming state did not have any comprehensive accounting system for tracking its revenues and expenditures. This should hardly surprise us since the creation of such a system for an agrarian empire would be an organizationally remarkable accomplishment. The Song dynasty kept separate accounts for a far larger and more diverse set of taxes that spanned both agricultural and commercial sources.[6] Pressured by military threats that first removed the northern half of the empire from its control and ultimately led to their defeat by the Mongols, Song bureaucrats had considerable financial expertise; they tapped the expanding economy of what some scholars have called the Song commercial revolution, and organized economic exchange in frontier areas where private merchants were less active. The Ming state reduced the fiscal complexity of its operations by relying heavily on agricultural taxes. Despite its lack of a comprehensive accounting system, officials were able to keep track of most of the revenues sent to the capital and those left at local levels. Moreover, Ministry of Revenue officials were able to move revenues around the empire among locales in order to meet extraordinary needs, thereby reducing the need to tax at higher levels within locales to provide resources.

---

[4] R. Huang, *Taxation and governmental finance in sixteenth-century Ming China* (Cambridge University Press, 1974), p. 182.

[5] Ibid, p. 174.

[6] See W. Bao, *Songdai difang caizhengshi yanjiu* [Studies on local fiscal history during the Song dynasty] (Shanghai: Shanghai guji chubanshe, 2001); C. Lamouroux, *Fiscalité, comptes publics et politiques financiers dan la Chine des Song* (Paris: Collège de France Institut des Hautes Etudes Chinoises, 2003).

The political ideal of light taxation preached by Ming officials had a venerable intellectual pedigree. From classical times forward political thinkers argued that light taxation reduces burdens on the people; with wealth stored among the people they are better able to prepare for the uncertainties of harvests and avoid hardships. When the people are well fed and free of subsistence anxieties there will be social stability and as a result political security for those who rule. The principles of modest taxation were thus joined to a broader set of principles intended to promote food supply security. At different points of the Ming dynasty efforts were made to establish granaries within each county to provide grain in bad harvest years. Projects like these were a bit different from other extraordinary projects, especially major water control efforts, which were spatially specific and to which resources could be directed from other parts of the empire. Granary institutions therefore required additional resources that were raised specifically for this purpose.[7]

The sixteenth-century state supplied public order as well as social goods such as water control and granaries. Long-distance commerce flourished in this period as networks of merchants spread across different parts of the empire. Commercial taxes were light and levied at rates set by the central government, which meant that gross differences in tax incidence across the empire were far less likely than they would have been under a political system of divided sovereignties, like that existing in Europe. There was in addition a general division between economic and political powers. The wealthiest groups in society, merchants and landlords, were not organized self-consciously to pursue their particular interests. There were no institutionalized mechanisms for their voices to influence government policies in ways that would preferentially favour them over others. Such practices were basic to the organization of European societies and the relationships of elites to their states. The Chinese state bureaucracy was largely composed of individuals selected for office after passing civil service examinations, the more important positions going to individuals who had passed all three levels of the examinations. Their power and authority derived from their governmental position rather than from their autonomous sources of wealth and status. This structure of political and economic relations was stable in key respects from the late fourteenth to the sixteenth centuries. It facilitated the Smithian growth dynamics that accounted for the economy's prosperity during this period.

---

[7] P.-E. Will and R. B. Wong, *Nourish the people: the state civilian granary system in China, 1650–1850* (Ann Arbor: University of Michigan Center for Chinese Studies, 1991), pp. 10–14.

By the early seventeenth century, fiscal needs began to grow due to the military expenses required to meet increasing threats to domestic order from rebel groups and border security problems posed by some of the empire's northern neighbours. Heavy and arbitrary taxes were imposed in some of the richer urban centres, causing protests by merchants and craftsmen that made raising extraordinary revenues difficult.[8] The appeal to commercial revenues proved short-lived and inadequate. The Ming dynasty was brought down by domestic unrest and then conquered by the Manchus entering the empire from the north-east, who proceeded to craft a fiscal system modelled largely on Ming dynasty practices.

The bureaucratic structure, the collection of taxes and their use in the eighteenth century

The Manchus, who established their Qing dynasty in 1644, adopted many of the basic governmental institutions used in the preceding Ming dynasty. The Board of Revenue (*hu bu*), one of six functionally distinct ministries that comprised the basic central government structure, handled most revenue collection. A separate imperial household administration (*neiwufu*) took care of the imperial family's finances. To promote an effective vertically integrated bureaucracy, the Manchus followed some procedures begun in earlier dynasties as well as elaborating additional mechanisms for promoting desired behaviour. Strict laws of avoidance prohibited officials from serving in their natal provinces or with officials to whom they were related either by kinship or examination experiences. The emperor's goal was to inhibit the formation of networks of interest at lower levels that could be mobilized to oppose policies that he and his central government officials advocated. This goal was part of a larger agenda pursued by eighteenth-century emperors. Frequent rotation of officials kept them from developing close ties with local elites that might become a serious threat to central government control. The Manchus strengthened territorial administration by establishing routine provincial-level administration centred on the governor and the governor-general, the latter usually having administrative oversight of two provinces, while the former directly administered a particular province; the previous dynasty did not have these

---

[8] S. Fuma, 'Late Ming urban reform and the popular uprising in Hangzhou', in L-Cooke Johnson (ed.), *Cities of Jiangnan in Late Imperial China* (Albany: State University of New York Press, 1993), pp. 47–80; R. von Glahn, 'Municipal reform and urban social conflict in Late Ming Jiangnan', *Journal of Asian Studies* 50 (1991), 280–307.

positions as routine posts but instead sent out officials with these titles to address specific and extraordinary tasks. Qing governors, who initially numbered fifteen and grew to twenty-three later in the dynasty, were expected to play a leading role in the fiscal, military, legal, educational and welfare activities initiated by officials in their jurisdictions. Another important official at the provincial level was the provincial administration commissioner or provincial treasurer who was a Board of Revenue official; he shared responsibilities for provincial finances with the governor and governor-general.[9] The key level of government beneath the province was the county, where routine administration took place; more than 1,300 of these units existed across the empire. The county, together with the provincial level of government, formed the two most important bureaucratic strata outside the centre. County magistrates were responsible for initial land-tax collections and provincial officials for managing the use of revenues within the province, forwarding taxes to the capital, and diverting some resources to other destinations. With a more closely coordinated and vertically integrated bureaucratic chain of authority over fiscal resources, the Qing state could move its resources flexibly to respond to needs as they arose.

As under the Ming dynasty, land taxation supplied the majority of routine revenues used by the Qing state. Completing a process of commutation from grain to silver begun in the sixteenth century, the early eighteenth-century state continued to divide annual tax collections into two basic categories: funds statutorily kept within the province and those sent to the capital. Officials at the centre and the provinces shared authority over fiscal resources. Provincial officials could request funds from elsewhere at the same time as they could be ordered to send resources elsewhere. In the Ming dynasty roughly 40 per cent of the revenue collections were kept locally but in the Qing dynasty the figure was only 20 per cent.[10] Not only did the eighteenth-century government move more of the revenues it controlled to the centre and between provinces than the sixteenth-century government had done, but its officials serving at and below the provincial level possessed no fiscal authority of their own to make new levies, an ability that local officials in the previous dynasty had enjoyed. A system of checks and balances in which

---

[9] The governor's authority over the provincial treasurer increased in the second half of the eighteenth century. Z. Li, *Tang Song Yuan Ming Qing zhongyang yu difang guanxi yanjiu* [Studies of the relationship between central and local government in the Tang, Song, Yuan, Ming and Qing dynasties] (Tianjin: Nankai daxue chubanshe, 1996), p. 355.

[10] Y. Zhou, *Wan Qing caizheng yu shehui bianqian* [Late Qing fiscal policies and social changes] (Shanghai: Shanghai renmin chubanshe, 2000), p. 26.

responsibility for revenue collection and disbursal was shared among different officials further kept officials from acting on their own.[11]

The Qing fiscal system made it difficult for officials in any province to build up resource bases that could be kept independent of coordinated use by officials beyond their jurisdictions. This was one reason that local and regional officials were far less likely in this empire than in other agrarian empires to capture power and authority at the expense of the political centre. As a result of deliberate policies, the county level of government was chronically underfunded. County magistrates were expected to hire much of their own staff and pay them out of their own funds. These funds included fees they charged for adjudicating court cases and gifts offered by local elites seeking to win official favour. Concerned with the amount of informal revenue collection that some magistrates were engaged in, the Yongzheng emperor sought to supplement official salaries with a stipend to 'nourish virtue' during the 1720s.[12] But by the late 1730s, officials under the Qianlong emperor had decided to place those monies in the provincial treasury for ad hoc use as needs arose. Again the complementary principles of limiting resource concentration at local levels and encouraging resource flows coordinated within and between provinces to meet extraordinary needs meant that higher levels of government could manage taxation flows and expenditure demands without delegating to local officials so much responsibility that they might become separated from the vertically integrated bureaucracy. Higher-level officials also made inspections of the fiscal accounts of county officials on both routine and unannounced bases, thorough reviews being conducted when officials were reassigned. They could be held responsible for financial irregularities that were uncovered even after they left a particular office. The pressures on many officials, not only those at the county level, instilled in them what one scholar has called a 'probationary ethic'.[13]

The central government derived relatively little of its income from trade. Domestic commerce was lightly taxed and generally faced few restrictions from officials. Grain was a bit of an exception since officials were either anxious to protect local supplies from export to other parts of the empire areas or anticipating much-needed imports to feed their populations pursuing handicrafts and cash crops. Salt was the major

[11] Z. Zhou, *Wan Qing caizheng jingji* [Late Qing fiscal economy] (Jinan: Jilu shuzhuang, 2002), p. 3.

[12] M. Zelin, *The magistrate's tael: rationalizing fiscal reform in eighteenth-century Ch'ing China* (Berkeley: University of California Press, 1984).

[13] T. Metzger, *The internal organization of the Ch'ing bureaucracy: legal, normative, and communication aspects* (Cambridge, MA: Harvard University Press, 1973).

exception to unfettered domestic trade; for revenue purposes the state maintained control over production and distribution, registering salt-producing households and licensing merchants who enjoyed stipulated areas from which to buy and within which to sell. Annual revenues from licensing the salt trade reached some six to seven million *taels* annually during the second half of the eighteenth century.[14] The Ming state had depended on these merchants to help ship grain out to soldiers along the northern frontier, while the earlier Song state had taken an even more active hand in organizing lucrative trade ventures, but by the eighteenth century these types of state use of merchants or direct control over commercial activities were no longer important.[15] Foreign trade was also regulated with security issues more than revenue needs inspiring eighteenth-century state policies. Limiting commercial taxation generally and avoiding government restrictions on trade other than salt and foreigners seeking to trade at Chinese ports meant that most forms of trade developed without any official interference. There were relatively few opportunities for rent-seeking and other forms of economic distortion that reduced the efficient allocation of resources and products.

For 1766, land taxes collected in monetary form accounted for some 68 per cent of routine revenues, salt revenues about 12 per cent, commercial taxes 11 per cent and miscellaneous sources the remaining 9 per cent. If taxes collected in grain are expressed in terms of the monetary value and added to these totals, land taxes account for 73 per cent, salt 10 per cent, commercial taxes 9 per cent and miscellaneous 8 per cent of total revenues.[16] Land taxation rates were higher in the richer provinces and portions of the revenue raised in these provinces were sent not to the centre but to other poorer provinces. The two provinces of Jiangsu and Zhejiang, within which lay the Jiangnan delta, the empire's wealthiest region, accounted for roughly a quarter of the total agricultural tax of the empire but had probably less than 20 per cent of the empire's population.[17]

---

[14] B. Zhou, *Zhongguo caizheng shi* [A history of Chinese fiscal policies] (Shanghai: Shanghai renmin chubanshe, 1981), p. 434.

[15] T. Terada, *Sansei shonin no kenkyu* [An analysis of Shanxi merchants] (Kyoto: Dohosha, 1972); P. J. Smith, *Taxing heaven's storehouse: horses, bureaucrats, and the destruction of the Sichuan tea industry, 1024–1224* (Cambridge, MA: Harvard University Council on East Asian Studies, 1991); R. Bin Wong, 'Dimensions of state expansion and contraction in Imperial China', *Journal of Economic and Social History of the Orient* 37 (1994), 54–66.

[16] Zhou, *Wan Qing caizheng jingji*, p. 29.

[17] Y-Wang, *Land taxation in Imperial China, 1750–1911* (Cambridge, MA: Harvard University Press, 1973), pp. 89–90.

Officials serving in more-developed provinces recognized their roles as members of a larger vertically integrated bureaucracy to coordinate decision-making with officials in other provinces and at the centre to create both routine and extraordinary flows of resources to poorer areas. Without these resource transfers it is difficult to imagine how the Qing state could have succeeded in consolidating its frontiers. As a result, officials at least implicitly divided the agrarian empire into three kinds of zones. The most economically prosperous were commercially developed and produced fiscal surpluses to be used in the landlocked frontier regions that formed a second kind of zone. A third and intermediate zone of regions that utilized resources and techniques to replicate many of the practices first developed in the first kind of zone filled in the spaces between economic cores and the empire's frontiers.[18]

Some analysts might interpret the state's movement of resources to the frontiers as a diversion of revenues from locations where they would achieve higher returns on the assumption that if higher returns were to be gained in frontier settings, market institutions would have appropriately channelled them in that direction. There are at least two reasons that such assumptions are inappropriate and inadequate. An assumption of market allocation of capital and labour is inappropriate because factor markets integrating core and periphery were not available in the eighteenth century. The assumption is inadequate because the government's goals for moving resources included enhancing the political security of border regions by buttressing their social stability on a more secure economic foundation. The political viability of the empire was conceived by officials to depend, at least partially, on creating broadly comparable levels of material prosperity across all provinces. Even if such a goal was impossible to reach, it inspired deliberate efforts to improve production and distribution in ecologically poor and economically less-developed regions as basic components of good government.

The Qing dynasty was able to coordinate fiscal flows through a vertically integrated bureaucracy, using communications methods not yet developed under the Ming dynasty. But to be successful at penetrating widely and deeply below the county level beyond what was possible with the often meagre county-level staff, officials depended upon forming alliances with local elites. The challenge for the central government was to see that the local official–elite relations largely served the broader interests of central government and empire. A vertically integrated

[18] R. B. Wong, 'Relationships between the political economies of maritime and agrarian China, 1750–1850', in G. Wang and C.-K. Ng (eds.), *Maritime China and the overseas Chinese communities* (Wiesbaden: Harrassowitz Verlag, 2004), pp. 19–31.

bureaucratic structure was feasible in part because it reached below the county level in only some cases. The limited penetration of the late imperial state at the local level supports the image of an ineffective state. But this view ignores the trade-offs between deeper bureaucratic penetration of local society and the maintenance of a vertically integrated bureaucracy. It also downplays the significance of the lowest level of officials depending on elites to help them achieve good government.

The social and economic implications of official–elite relations

The Neo-Confucian agenda for local social order depended on local elites helping to repair roads, bridges and temples, to fund granaries and schools, and in some areas an even broader spectrum of benevolent activities, including orphanages and the care of widows. At the core of this local elite were individuals who had studied for the civil service examinations and consequently learned the same principles for promoting social order as officials understood. Taxes could be collected in smaller amounts and only a fraction kept at local levels and yet considerable services provided when elites met their Confucian duties to fund and manage various local institutions.[19] On occasion it seems that elites preferred to manage local welfare efforts without official participation, but the more common norm appears to be a mix of official and elite efforts with both finding the joint shouldering of these expenditures reasonable.[20] In some cases, officials attempted to monitor activities in a routine fashion, for example, community granaries, but in other cases there was little direct oversight.[21] Beyond issues of welfare, elites also were expected to exhort through moral example and mediate disputes to avoid recourse to official courts and law.

Officials and elites were subject to the same moral appeals. Officials and elites both knew there was only so much the one could expect from or demand of the other; there was little in the way of coercion and interest-based exchange was not made formal and explicit through the use of contracts and agreements in the way typical of European government–elite relations in the early modern era. Officials and elites in early modern Europe had more reasons to develop clear contractual understandings as this was a period in which successful rulers and their

---

[19] Wong, *China transformed*, pp. 105–26.
[20] M. Mori, 'Juroku-juhachi seiki ni okeru kosei to jinushi denko kankei' [Famine relief and landlord–tenant relations from the sixteenth to eighteenth centuries], *Toyoshi kenkyu* 27 (1969), 69–111.
[21] Will and Wong, *Nourish the people*, pp. 63–9.

centralizing bureaucracies were extending and deepening their control over local societies. In fiscal terms, ever-increasing state needs for funds to build armies and bureaucracies meant that some kinds of negotiation and exchange were increasingly necessary to garner the desired monies; European states with parliamentary forms of government ended up raising more taxes than those without.[22]

The eighteenth-century Chinese state had long had a large and complex bureaucratic structure and had long solved the challenges of competing with well-organized elites like European nobilities, urban elites and clerics. Well before European states would promote common cultural activities in the nineteenth century, Chinese governments had been engaged in a cultural project of creating an empire of Confucian believing and acting subjects. Good governance in a Chinese vein depended on all these features. Success in the eighteenth century depended on the emperor and central government officials aggressively pushing policies intended to implement a Neo-Confucian agenda of social order. This agenda included land clearance, the dissemination of agricultural and craft knowledge, water control and grain storage as methods to improve the population's material security.

Local elites joined officials by contributing some of the funds necessary to implement Neo-Confucian policies of social order. Both officials and elites pursued these activities. Because these were conducted at the local level and information on expenditures did not reach higher levels of government consistently, it is impossible to estimate the aggregate scale of these expenditures. We know, for instance, that a mix of official and elite financial and organizational efforts was responsible for the additional storage of tens of thousands of tons of grain, between the mid-1730s and early 1780s.[23] The political significance of the relationship between officials and elites has been debated by specialists due in part to the absence of a clear division of labour between officials and elites and their joint interest in maintaining social order. Some believe elites support officials, while others claim that officials support the social order of local elites. Another uncertainty concerns the inclusion or exclusion of local elites within what we think of as the government. Both ambiguities become less important if we accept the mutual benefits accruing to both local officials and elites with their joint efforts to supply local social goods and services. The state relied upon local elites to meet a portion of the material and organizational demands of

[22] P. T. Hoffman and K. Norbert, *Fiscal crises, liberty, and representative government, 1450–1789* (Stanford University Press, 1994).
[23] Will and Wong, *Nourish the people*, pp. 63–72.

local order, in addition to relying on bureaucratic capacities to move resources across areas in a flexible manner, an ability that reduced the need of any particular area to build up fiscal reserves. Despite the frequent successes of these efforts, there were times when the state needed to mobilize and spend larger sums of tax monies.

Extraordinary fiscal operations in the eighteenth and nineteenth centuries

The formation of European states after 1500 makes us very familiar with rulers aggressively seeking to expand their resource bases. The development of financial markets and banking institutions was intimately related to the efforts that European rulers made to secure loans. In contrast, before 1850 Chinese state officials did not borrow against future revenue streams; instead, they moved resources around the empire to meet some of their extraordinary needs. This spatial flexibility over a territory as large as Europe's many countries considered together allowed the Chinese state to substitute spatial transfers for temporal ones. In addition to seeking loans, European rulers relied increasingly on non-routine taxation. The Chinese state also made extraordinary efforts to raise revenues, but unlike European states, did not chronically make such efforts until after 1850. Also unlike European states, the Chinese reasons for resource mobilizations before the mid nineteenth century were not so exclusively military. The episodic nature of extraordinary Chinese revenue demands and their use for civilian as well as military purposes are both significant. First, the Ming and Qing states did not chronically press upon their subjects demands for new and additional revenues – a practice that would have been fundamentally inconsistent with Chinese norms of good governance. Second, because the purposes of extraordinary fiscal operations in fact yielded direct benefits to many people, the kinds of friction and difficulties encountered by European rulers could be less problematic in the Chinese case.

While we comfortably employ the term 'campaign' to refer to military operations, scholars rarely refer to civilian government activities in the same terms. Yet the use of 'campaign' to refer to a recurring feature of Qing administration is useful. These governmental efforts varied in their intentions, processes of development and institutional outcomes, but they all required intensive bureaucratic labour and often entailed additional resources beyond what was easily available within the government. Consider below two kinds of examples.

Irrigation projects specifically and water control works more generally, for example, often required state-led campaigns. The degree of official monitoring and regulation after the project's completion varied considerably. All water control projects were intimately enmeshed within particular ecologies.[24] Amidst spatial variations, some temporal trends can be discerned. In general, the early Qing state made efforts to organize water control projects in different parts of the empire. Typically, officials would mobilize resources and manpower to make major repairs and seek to establish a framework within which the maintenance of water works could be managed by local officials and elites working together. This logic of relying on campaign-like bursts of activity to order water control efforts followed by modest routine activity by officials was progressively undermined by the competing interests of parties to water control efforts. Those people whose land reclamation efforts narrowed river channels and diminished lake surfaces promoted the dangers of flooding and brought them into conflict with officials seeking to avoid natural disasters. Even without these problems, the technical challenges of water works wearing out and rivers shifting their course alone would have made desirable repeated large-scale mobilizations of manpower and resources. Water control efforts were typified by bursts of bureaucratic energy and resources devoted to creating stable situations that became increasingly difficult to maintain without subsequent campaign efforts. Zhou Zhichu estimates routine river conservancy and water control projects to cost more than two million *taels* annually in the eighteenth century. Special projects of extraordinary repairs amounted to another 1.5 million *taels* annually. Finally, he estimates the combination of routine and extraordinary repairs needed for the sea coast water works in Jiangnan to be another half million *taels* annually for a total of some four million *taels* annually, nearly half of which entailed non-routine expenditures.[25]

A second example comes from food supply management issues. The granary system depended for its expansion on periodic campaign-like efforts to mobilize and store additional amounts of grain. These succeeded between the late seventeenth and late eighteenth centuries in amassing hundreds upon hundreds of tons of grain. Unlike water control issues, there weren't ecological dangers created by the granary system's expansion, though some officials pondered the possibilities of

---

[24] A. Morita, *Shindai suiri shakaishi no kenkyu* (Tokyo: Kokusho Kankokai, 1990); P. Perdue, 'Water control in the Dongting Lake Region during the Ming and Qing periods', *Journal of Asian Studies* 41 (1982), 747–65; P.-E. Will, 'State intervention in the administration of a hydraulic infrastructure: the example of Hubei Province in late imperial times', in S. Schram (ed.), *The scope of state power in China* (Hong Kong: Chinese University Press, 1985), pp. 295–347.

[25] Zhou, *Wan Qing caizheng jingji*, p. 27.

official operations interfering with market principles. Like water control processes, the challenge of creating routine maintenance and supervision proved in some ways more difficult than mobilizing men and resources for a campaign-like effort to establish granaries and subsequent campaigns to augment their reserves. One important mechanism to raise funds to expand granary reserves was to sell the status of low-level degree holders to wealthy people seeking to increase their symbolic and social capital. The cost was typically over one hundred *taels* for a degree. Through such programmes, initiated and managed at the provincial level, several million *taels* were collected, as well as contributions in kind, between the 1720s and the 1740s. Later efforts in the 1760s to use this technique for grain mobilizations were less successful.[26]

In contrast to successful early modern European states that were seeking to expand their bureaucratic capacities and fiscal resources, the Qing officials preferred to mount extraordinary campaigns with uneven efforts at routinizing the products of these initiatives. The Qing state preferred to maintain a low statutory rate of land taxation and add to this various land surtaxes and other taxes on an as-needed basis. A second contrast with European state-building concerns – the relationships between officials and elites – has been sketched in the previous section. Central governments in Europe expanded their capacities and claims at the same time as the limits to their expansion were increasingly clearly drawn; those boundaries would be repeatedly renegotiated, in the process affirming the importance in many cases of a divide between 'state' and 'civil society'. In China, elites were mobilized by officials to help implement campaign-like initiatives in the case of granary construction; elites worked in more uneasy collaboration and at times competition with officials with respect to water control and land clearance. While distinctions similar to 'private' and 'public' were drawn in some instances, these did not become part of larger negotiations demarcating well-bounded spheres of autonomy and activity for elites.

The campaign-like nature of state activism in Qing China resulted in varying degrees of institutionalization. Some government campaigns created results that officials were expected to add to their monitoring activities. Sometimes these could be operations over which only a cursory inspection was maintained, as was often the case with water control activities. For other activities, however, there could be new procedures created. The mid-eighteenth-century push to expand granary reserves outside the county seats meant creating accounting procedures for the annual reporting of changes in stocks by individual granaries to the

---

[26] Will and Wong, *Nourish the people*, pp. 49–53.

county government, by county officials to the province and by provincial officials to the central government. In both the water control
and granary cases, official campaigns were intended to put in place
operations for which elites would often take immediate responsibility.
Both water control activities and food supply management also include
examples of competing interests among officials and elites. Officials
worried about private land reclamation schemes that increased flooding
possibilities, while elites could prefer managing food supply crises without official supervision of their activities.[27] These differences did not,
however, promote a fixed and formal division of official and elite activities into separate spheres of activity. The shifting boundary between
government and private activities was less often a barrier than a fluid
marker of the state's intermittent intervention into activities to promote social order, as data on both granaries and local schools suggest.[28]
Granary administration became part of the eighteenth-century county
magistrate's regular duties; he was expected to keep accounts for both
the ever-normal granary in the county seat as well as the community
and charity granaries often dispersed throughout the county. The limitations to the routine taxation and monitoring of granaries underscore
the fragility of government institutions.

Many specific institutions of local order, including granaries, schools
and the *baojia* system of household registration for mutual surveillance
were created through intensive efforts but were unlikely to be sustained
at a high level of effectiveness for more than a few decades without infu-
sions of resources or organizational energy. The combination of civilian
campaigns and fragile institutions allows us to reconcile superficially
contradictory images of the state as aggressive and interventionist or
as weak and ineffective. Both images have their foundation in realities
that vary both spatially and temporally across the empire. In general,
the eighteenth-century state was more activist toward local social order
than its nineteenth-century successor; state efforts were more salient
in the peripheries of provinces, regions and the empire than in economic and political cores. But even when eighteenth-century officials
embarked on major campaigns to promote domestic social order they
recognized a tension between increased official efforts and a reliance
upon local elites and communities to be more self-regulating and self-

---

[27] See Morita, *Shindai suiri shakaishi no kenkyu;* Perdue, 'Water control in the Dongting
Lake Region during the Ming and Qing periods'.
[28] R. B. Wong, 'Confucian agendas for material and ideological control in Modern
China', in T. Huters, R. B. Wong and P. Yu, (eds.), *Culture and state in Chinese history: conventions, accommodations, and critiques* (Stanford University Press, 1997), pp.
303–25.

sustaining. The Yongzheng emperor's expansion of official interventions led to some routinization of expanded official responsibilities in the early Qianlong reign, but by the 1760s and the 1770s officials were more likely to rely upon elites and communities to manage local institutions on their own. The pattern of civilian granary activities in the eighteenth century exemplifies these spatial and temporal dimensions of state activism. From per-capita granary reserves, officials generally stored more grain in provinces that were less economically developed and politically more peripheral, while periodic bursts of effort to expand granary reserves in the first half of the eighteenth century were followed by increasing efforts to routinize supervision and accounting, culminating in the late nineteenth century with decisions to reduce official supervision of some operations and an overall decline in granary operations.[29]

The bursts of government energy that made sharply visible the presence of official activities to large numbers of people were often prompted by imperial decisions. The ability of eighteenth-century emperors to invoke large-scale bureaucratic responses to their directives evokes for outside observers images of autocracy and despotism. But we should note as well the limited duration of these intensive government-led campaigns and the uneven institutionalized results they produced – uneven by design as much as by default. Neither the emperor nor his officials generally favoured expanding the government's tax base beyond what was deemed minimally necessary. A central ideological commitment to light taxes oriented officials towards seeking resource-efficient means to keep routine government activities inexpensive if not few. The limited temporal duration of political campaigns and of much of the financing associated with them means that the abilities and intentions for what some observers have conceived as despotic behaviour were less present than we might expect. At the same time, the repeated mounting of political campaigns for a wide variety of purposes means that images of a lumbering and ineffective state distant from the people and largely irrelevant to them also fail to focus on the range of activities undertaken by the government. Early and mid Qing dynasty political campaigns undermine the beliefs in either a despotic state or an irrelevant state. Neither half of this binary choice proves particularly persuasive in accounting for what the eighteenth-century state became able to do.

The crucial importance of political campaigns to Qing dynasty strategies of government undermines two additional binary contrasts. First, there is a contrast between 'arbitrary' power and 'infrastructural'

---

[29] Will and Wong, *Nourish the people*, pp. 23–92, 296–300.

power as alternative forms of political power.[30] We tend to think of the capacity of rulers to exercise their personal whims to be the opposite of bureaucratically organized power generating rule-governed operations. But what the example of the Qing state suggests is a far more complementary relationship between the two. The eighteenth-century government bureaucracy responds to a range of initiatives, those prompted by the emperor being among the most important. For their parts, the Qing emperors increased and improved the structures through which they could amass information from officials and deliberate on appropriate policy choices across a wide range of subjects. Imperial capacities for effective intervention depended crucially on expanding bureaucratic infrastructures. Such interventions were arbitrary in the sense that they were not simple outcomes of law-like rules, but they were often not arbitrary in the sense of being taken on a whim and without careful reasoning. A second binary contrast between 'extraordinary' and 'routine' operations is also undermined by Qing state activities. Chinese bureaucratic infrastructures expanded in the eighteenth century, but these capacities were not utilized in the same manner from year to year. Many activities, including some of those associated with water control and food supply management, were too infrequent to be labelled 'annual' or 'routine' and yet they took place more commonly than seem to fit the conventional meaning of 'extraordinary'. The repeated use of political campaigns and their different institutional outcomes fall along a continuum with 'routine' and 'extraordinary' as simply the two distant endpoints.

I use the term 'campaign' for these Chinese practices because it allows me to relate these practices to twentieth-century political developments in China. In the present comparative context it may help more to highlight the features of Chinese campaigns that parallel fiscal practices of more recent times in a wider variety of settings. These Chinese campaigns are akin to much later public works or school projects in the United States funded by special tax or bond initiatives. Both raise resources for specific purposes quite separate from routine operations.

The expansion of the Qing state allowed for both spatial and temporal variations in the character of bureaucratic activities, some in principle, and others simply in practice. We've seen various indications that the importance of local conditions was generally recognized: the mixes of official and elite efforts varied according to local conditions; government directives frequently acknowledged the importance of local conditions, while official deliberations often included consideration

---

[30] M. Mann, *Sources of social power* (Cambridge University Press, 1986).

of local and provincial variations. The intermittent nature of political campaigns is only the most salient feature of temporal fluctuations in the intensity of official efforts. More generally, officials were expected to respond to potential problems before they became large and unwieldy. This meant sustaining surveillance strategies to pick out annoyances before they became significant. This vigilant anxiety about local order did not mean reporting every minor problem to higher levels since, unless such problems became serious, the locale was in fact well ordered as far as higher-level officials were concerned. Once, however, difficulties came to the attention of higher-level officials it was easy to cast blame on lower-level bureaucrats for their failure to anticipate the now more serious problems.

In searching for difficulties, activities that otherwise were tolerated became unacceptable because of the outcomes they putatively caused. The likelihood of such situations arising increased during the late eighteenth century owing to three sets of factors. First, the more activities officials engaged in, the more likely they were to make mistakes, to do something that caused a problem. Second, the more that official activities required coordination among officials making their own decisions, the more likely that disagreements and failures to discharge responsibilities would take place. Third, difficulties could increase because of changes in the larger social and natural environments within which government activities took place. The increase in government activities from the mid seventeenth to the late eighteenth centuries did create problems that were noted by officials but in large measure these were kept under reasonable control. Sometimes it meant scaling back government activities; at the end of the eighteenth century it often meant reducing the degree and complexity of inter-governmental coordination, in particular among provincial-level officials.[31] But the intrinsic challenges of sustaining the kind of intermittent political campaigns of a state with a complicated vertical hierarchy at the top of which sat activist emperors were in large measure met as the state was transformed over a century and a half of increasing direct and indirect intervention.

Not until the final years of the eighteenth century did it become clear that there were both internal bureaucratic and external changes in environment that made the likelihood of sustaining the trajectory of expanded state activism both less likely and yet more necessary for social stability and political security. During the first half of the nineteenth century, provincial treasuries were depleted, in part because of

---

[31] The reduced coordination among granary operations across provinces is a particularly clear example. Will and Wong, *Nourish the people*, pp. 75–98.

the costs of suppressing a large rebellion at the end of the eighteenth century. Fiscal poverty led officials to collect additional surtaxes and face additional protests from people unwilling to pay higher taxes. But these difficulties pale before the fiscal challenges that would emerge at mid century and, perhaps surprisingly, be met by the state. Gone for good were eighteenth-century social stability and political success which depended on the techniques of good governance and relationships among officials and elites presented above. In the second half of the nineteenth century, the state could no longer limit itself to low levels of taxation or supply the goods and services it previously had.

Fiscal expansion and state transformations, 1850–1914

Beginning in the 1850s, the central government faced a number of very large rebellions as well as several smaller-scale challenges to its authority in other areas. A combination of bad harvests, exhausted ecologies and growing populations in poorer areas created many locales that were difficult to govern. These were not areas where simply keeping taxes at a low level would make them thrive. They were instead economically peripheral areas that were ecologically fragile. Efforts to impose official order when the dangers of unrest surfaced often incited further opposition to the government. Through several distinct sequences of mobilization and protest, rebellions emerged in different parts of the empire. It would have been easy to predict the fall of the Qing dynasty in the 1850s as it faced widespread unrest with no certain ways of expanding its fiscal and military powers necessary for continued control. The state, however, did mobilize the monies and manpower needed to quell the disturbances. Fiscal expansion was a fundamental component of the state's transformation. These changes entailed the destruction of a previously successful logic of low taxation and good governance.

The late nineteenth-century failure to sustain the logic of good governance typical of the eighteenth century was simultaneously an indicator of the state's success at rapidly expanding its revenues when new demands arose.[32] In 1849 the government raised some 42.5 million *taels* of revenue, with 77 per cent of this coming from agriculture and the balance from commerce. Thirty-six years later revenues had climbed to more than 77 million *taels*, the increase largely due to a quadrupling of the commercial revenues. Expenditure levels had remained in the range

---

[32] This and the following paragraph are based on Wong, *China transformed*, pp. 155–6.

of 30–40 million *taels* annually between the 1720s and the early 1840s. They then doubled to 70–80 million *taels* annually between the 1860s and the early 1890s.[33] The capacity to increase revenues and expenditures in this manner is hardly the sign of a weak state, as the Chinese state of this period is often portrayed. But it is an indicator of a significant transformation.

Much of the increased revenue was raised through the Maritime Customs collections. In addition to being used as security on foreign loans which were used to help pay for the 1867 Muslim rebellion suppression in north-west China, customs revenues were used in the 1880s to build railways.[34] The development of Chinese central government control over customs revenues is a clear indication of the state's ability to create new infrastructural capacities. When the late-nineteenth-century central government is not judged by its failure to survive beyond 1911 but is instead compared with the eighteenth-century central government, its fiscal capacities were clearly augmented, in part because it adapted certain foreign methods of raising funds.[35] But these Chinese increases were nothing compared to the nearly 302 million *taels* of revenue gathered in 1911, the final year of the dynasty – agricultural taxes had grown from roughly 30 to roughly 50 million *taels* with another 45 due to miscellaneous sources; more than 207 million came from commercial taxes – whatever the late Qing state's weaknesses, raising money was not among them.[36] Unfortunately, the Japanese indemnity equalled a full year's receipts and the Boxer indemnity was one-and-a-half times as large. These are the charges that made China's fiscal situation so precarious and ultimately untenable.

The expansion of new revenues and new expenditures threatened older ideas about good governance. Officials and elites were

---

[33] T. Hamashita, *Chugoku kindai keizaishi kenkyu* (University of Tokyo Institute of Oriental Culture, 1989), p. 66.

[34] Ibid., pp. 68, 72.

[35] Hamashita (1989) and Peng (1983) both discuss the expansion of state revenues and expenditures after the 1860s. Like Wei (1986), they generally see a weakening of central government control over finances. Li (1990), however, reminds us that even if provinces developed considerable autonomy in the collection of new taxes, they used them in the 1860s and 1870s to fulfil central government financial needs. By the closing decades of the nineteenth century, the central government asserted more control over revenue mobilization and disbursal. S. Li, *Ming Qing caijing shi xintan* [A new study of Ming and Qing period economic and fiscal history], (Taiyuan: Shanxi jingji chubanshe, 1990), p. 334; Z. Peng, *Shijiu shiji houban qi de Zhongguo caizheng yu jingji* [Chinese fiscal administration and economy in the second half of the nineteenth century], (Beijing: Renmin, 1983); G. Wei, 'Qingdai houqi zhongyang jiquan caizheng tizhi di wajie' [The collapse of the fiscal system of central authority in the late Qing], *Jindaishi yanjiu* 1 (1986), 207–30.

[36] Wei, 'Qingdai houqi zhongyang jiquan caizheng tizhi di wajie', p. 227.

increasingly unable to meet these older expectations for several reasons. Fundamental to the difficulties was the increasing taxation that undermined earlier political logics. First, extraordinary mobilizations of resources and manpower were no longer campaigns of limited duration that occurred in any one area infrequently. During the second half of the nineteenth century fiscal and bureaucratic expansion became chronic. Second, local elites were increasingly brought into more formal government positions, including tax collection. Their broadening responsibilities made close monitoring of their activities more difficult and allowed the possibilities for abusive behaviour to grow. Third, the success at expanding late-nineteenth-century revenues came at the cost of creating new bureaucratic structures that became difficult to organize and coordinate through a vertically integrated bureaucracy. Some new operations, like the Imperial Maritime Customs Administration, were simply separate; others, like the transit tax (*likin*) collections, were gradually incorporated into the regular bureaucracy, but their presence complicated fiscal coordination among levels of the government greatly. Fourth and finally, by the first decade of the twentieth century, central government officials were so anxious for revenues that they cared little how provinces came up with funds as long as governors forwarded the amounts the centre made them responsible for collecting.

Not only did the thirst for additional revenues become almost a chronic condition after 1850, but the institutional mechanisms the eighteenth-century state might have used to move resources between provinces to meet pressing needs no longer functioned. Provincial treasuries had been depleted in the first half of the nineteenth century and the land tax, the principal source of resources before, was simply inadequate. The turn to domestic transit taxes and to maritime customs was meant initially to fund military responses to domestic rebellion and subsequently to finance the government's responses to foreign challenges. As provincial-level officials took the initiative to raise new funds and form armies to defeat rebels in the 1850s and then to develop new industries and arsenals in the 1860s and 1870s, they gained powers they previously had not enjoyed. But it would be too simplistic to view these changes as a simple devolution of power to the provinces for three reasons. First, provincial officials continued to identify with the political centre; they were not aiming to establish autonomy and ultimately to compete with the centre in order to become independent. Second, the central government subsequently developed increased supervision over both transit taxes and maritime customs through new forms of accounting designed explicitly to keep track of these revenues that previously had not existed.[37] Third, the centre was able to develop new principles of assigning to provinces many resource responsibilities at the very end of the dynasty; provinces may have been left to their own devices for meeting the centre's demands, but they accepted the needs expressed by higher levels of government.[38]

The central government made efforts to consolidate its control over new sources of revenue like transit taxes and maritime customs and over older sources that were being rapidly expanded, such as the salt administration. The Imperial Maritime Customs Administration was a joint Sino–Western bureaucracy led by a British bureaucrat formally serving the Qing state. The import and export taxes collected by this administration provided a crucial source of new revenue and future collections were used as the guarantee on loans made by foreign banks. Indeed, the connection between foreign banks and the Maritime Customs Administration grew even closer by the early twentieth century when these tax collections were deposited in Shanghai's foreign banks, which then transmitted funds to Qing officials.[39] The Maritime Customs Administration came to handle domestic transit tax collections as well. After the fall of the dynasty in 1911, the Salt Administration also took on foreign leadership and, like the Maritime Customs Administration, became an effective central bureaucracy.[40] At the same time, these bureaucracies were not integrated either with other central government bureaucracies or as part of a larger vertically integrated bureaucracy typical of the eighteenth century. In the late nineteenth century the central government also made quite separate efforts to increase its control over its agrarian tax base for two reasons. First, officials recognized that problems with local governance attended the expansion of tax collections at the local level, and the inability to meet the older norms of good government meant a greater need for efforts at monitoring and regulation. Competing with this concern was a second matter that became increasingly pressing after 1900, namely, the need to insist that all locales meet ever-larger demands for taxes needed to pay off the massive indemnities imposed by foreign governments after troops from eight countries marched into Beijing to demand that the government punish the Boxer rebels who

[37] K.-C. Liu, 'Wan Qing dufu quanli wenti shangquan' [A discussion of the problem of late Qing provincial governor power], in Liu, *Jingshi sixiang and xinxing qiye* [Statecraft thought and new industries] (Taibei Shi: Lianjing, 1990), pp. 247–93.

[38] Li, *Ming Qing caijing shi xintan*, p. 334.

[39] Hamashita, *Chugoku kindai keizaishi kenkyu*, p. 85.

[40] J. C. Strauss, *Strong institutions in weak polities: state building in republican China, 1927–1940* (Oxford University Press, 1998).

were threatening foreign (and Chinese) Christians with death and the destruction of property.

The massive indemnities imposed in 1895 by the Japanese after defeating the Qing in a war concerning their competing power and influence over Korea, and in 1900 by the consortium of countries responding to the Boxers, defined the fiscal demands on the last imperial state in China. It becomes impossible to think meaningfully about the state's use of fiscal policies to support economic growth specifically or economic activities more generally since its over-riding purpose had become meeting the foreign-imposed demands for huge sums of money. The Qing state had made a long and unhappy journey from its eighteenth-century situation when it had been able to maintain low rates of taxation, promote and coordinate services and goods provided by lower levels of government, and avoid preying heavily upon commercial wealth for its own purposes. The principles of good governance worked in an eighteenth-century world in which the foreign pressures on the Qing empire were largely limited to groups coming off the steppe. By deliberately limiting the capacities of county officials to amass and disburse revenues the central state was simultaneously better able to keep control over its bureaucracy and to insulate its subject population from major rent-seeking extraction by its officials. This approach, however, also forced local officials to create their own financial opportunities and mechanisms to pay for their bureaucratic costs and, as the demands on local officials grew in the nineteenth century, the institutional logic of the eighteenth-century state was no longer as effective.

The collapse of the Qing dynasty in 1911 spelled the end of an imperial system of rule, marked for several centuries by the elaboration of a vertically integrated bureaucratic structure. Provinces declared their 'independence' of the centre to bring down the last dynasty and some reasserted their 'independence' in 1913 and again in 1916. One of the important ways their defiance of the central government was expressed came from refusals to forward land taxes. Until the mid century, when the Communists came to power, no government could claim to rule the entire country through a vertically integrated bureaucracy that they controlled down to the county level. Not surprisingly, there wasn't any coherent fiscal system either. Difficulties came from two directions. On the one hand, the eighteenth-century bureaucratic system for collecting revenues no longer functioned; the nineteenth-century development of the *likin* and the maritime customs both occurred outside the previous structures and the latter especially promoted the development of functionally specific bureaucracies, complicating intra-bureaucratic relations. On the other hand, local needs for revenues began increasing in the first decade of the twentieth century as counties were told to begin new schools, fund police forces and pursue other projects intended to improve administration; in later decades increased exactions continued to be made for a combination of military and civilian purposes.

Increasing demands for tax revenues by competing levels of political authority created a complex and chaotic fiscal situation. The proportion of revenues going to services that people could recognize as beneficial declined as domestic war-making between rival military figures grew after 1916 and the costs of doing government business in the style of Western governments rose. Similarities between twentieth-century China's fiscal situation and those of European states in an earlier era are qualified by two important sets of differences. First, Chinese elites did not develop institutionalized forms of representation that allowed them a voice in negotiating the taxation needs of the government. Related to this are far larger differences in the construction of political authority and relations between rulers and their subjects. Second, however intense the competition among Chinese political leaders became, the ideal of a central government asserting authority over a territory the scale of Europe was never seriously challenged. The Chinese Communist revolution, for all its dramatic changes, restored a unitary state in which fiscal issues were once again decided at the centre and the definitions of good governance stressed the goal of material security for urban and rural masses.

16   The rise of a Japanese fiscal state

Masaki Nakabayashi

Introduction and context

Tokugawa Japan bequeathed a relatively stable tax basis to the New Imperial Government after the Meiji Restoration in 1868. After constructing a framework for marketing bonds in Japan, the new state then went to the London market for foreign loans. The rise of a Japanese fiscal state can be traced along three tracks. The first includes the centralization and stabilization of tax revenues initiated under Hideyoshi Toyotomi from the 1580s to the 1590s. This reform allowed central and local government to collect up to 40 per cent of gross agricultural output as taxes were taken over and provided fiscal stability for the Tokugawa regime. After the Meiji Restoration removed the fiscal autonomy of feudal estates, all tax revenues came under the control of the central government. In 1890, Japan became a constitutional state and taxation and expenditure had to be approved by the diet, which sought to curtail military expenditures. By the late 1890s, the diet agreed to tax increases and provided the administration with raised expenditures for capital formation.

Although some feudal estates issued bonds and notes, the Tokugawa Shogunate (the central government) did not, which meant that neither the capital Edo (later Tokyo) nor Osaka developed markets for government loans. The New Imperial Government began to issue bonds right after the Meiji Restoration, which led to the creation of a modern capital market in Japan. However, the Meiji government was anxious about the risk of being colonized by Western powers and it had hesitated to sell its securities on international markets until the late 1890s. Japan joined the gold standard in 1897, which increased the state's access to international capital markets. The turning point came, however, in 1904–05. When Japan was at war with Russia the state issued large

This study has been supported by the JSPS Grant-in-Aid for Scientific Research, No. 18203024.

numbers of bonds on the London capital market, which were endorsed by British merchant banks. After victory over Russia, connections to the international capital market became an important instrument for both fiscal and macroeconomic stability. Bonds issued on the international market decreased 'crowding out' effects on the domestic capital market, while imports of capital enabled the central bank to follow flexible monetary policies. In the early 1900s, when Japanese private companies had not yet established reputations in the international financial market, government bonds dominated capital imports. Thus fiscal policy provided macroeconomic stability for the Japanese economy.

During the first phase of development into a modern 'fiscal state', the international financial market played a critical role. However, the government managed its foreign debt in ways that circumvented the risks of colonization. Once a well-armed state was established, the Japanese government entered the London financial market without coming under political threats to its sovereignty.

The early modern fiscal state, 1192–1867

From ancient empire to feudal state

Since the late sixth century, Japan's imperial rulers attempted to borrow sophisticated political institutions and technologies from the Chinese empire. In 710, the Taiho Imperial Legal Codes – a copy of the legal codes of the Chinese empire, written in classical Chinese – were introduced. The codes provided a framework for a tightly centralized political system, but the government lacked the required resources to enforce it. Therefore, in the provinces, powers were delegated to members of the imperial family, nobles and large temples, which granted them the authority to collect some rents and taxes. This was the origin of Japan's manorial system.

In many manors, real executive power passed into the hands of professional warriors called Samurai, which originally meant 'servants'. Samurai kept order in local communities, and collected taxes on behalf of lords, but retained a portion for themselves. By the eleventh century, especially in some regions distant from the imperial capital (Kyoto), the Samurai banded into groups led by nobles who established the power necessary to rule the provinces.

In 1192 a group of Samurai in eastern Japan finally established their own government, the Kamakura shogunate, which followed common law rather than the Imperial Legal Codes. In fiscal terms, the Kamakura shogunate remained part of the manorial system until the twelfth century. Its revenue came from manors held by the shogunate, and the income of all Samurai continually depended on rents guaranteed by the nominal owners of manors. The key feature of the manorial system was that the rights to rule and to collect taxes from people were not distinguished from ownership of land, allowing owners to claim a residual return. Thus, the sovereignty over ownership of land was fragmented. For example, the sovereignty over any piece of land officially belonged to the emperor, who delegated powers to collect rents to members of the imperial family or to higher-class nobles such as the Fujiwara family. Duties, along with privileges to collect rents, were then delegated to middle-class metropolitan nobles or local nobles, but the maintenance of order and the collection of land taxes from peasants passed down the line to local Samurai, who took a cut for their services. Thus, the ownership and control over land was fragmented.[1]

Land and tax reforms from the 1590s to the 1600s

In the fourteenth and fifteenth centuries, Japan entered a period of internecine warfare which almost destroyed the manorial system. An expanded period of warfare and disorder was brought to an end by Nobunaga Oda and his successor, Hideyoshi Toyotomi, who introduced radical land and tax reforms in the 1590s. The essential features of the reforms were: (i) Toyotomi claimed that all Japanese land was ruled by him, and he delegated authority to one (and only one) feudal lord he recognized as subordinate and ruler over a specific domain, and allowed him to collect taxes; (ii) Toyotomi fixed the standard rule of taxation to be levied by his feudal lord on peasants; and (iii) the authority guaranteed each peasant family the right to cultivate one and only one piece of registered land.

After the reform, a plot of land had only one lord who held powers of taxation and only one holder with rights to cultivation. Feudal lords were committed to the enforcement of a tax policy declared *ex ante*, and peasants gained the claim to the residual of their crop after net taxes. Toyotomi's reforms sought to maximize land tax revenues over the long term by protecting the peasants' rights.[2]

When Ieyasu Tokugawa took over the state from the Toyotomi family and established the Tokugawa Shogunate in 1603, he continued the ongoing tax reform and guaranteed property rights for the peasantry.

[1] K. Nagahara, *Nihon chusei shakai kozo no kenkyu* [Research on the social structure of medieval Japan] (Tokyo: Iwanami shoten, 1973), pp. 28–53.
[2] M. Araki, *Bakuhan taisei shakai no seiritsu to kozo* [Formation of the Shogunate feudalist society and its structure], 4th edn (Tokyo: Yuhikaku, 1986), pp. 3–178.

The Tokugawa Shogunate itself was a feudal lord as well as the central government. The shogunate's taxation policy on its own domain was followed by other feudal lords as a model. Three categories of taxes were levied: the 'primary tax' (*hon nengu*), 'small crops' (*ko mono nari*) and 'charter fees' (*myoga kin*), along with other kinds of indirect taxes. The primary tax was a land tax officially denominated by the amount of rice, and a considerable portion was in practice paid in kind. Outputs and taxes were measured in *koku*. One *koku* was 180.39 litres. Small crops were levied on crops other than rice. Charter fees were imposed on privileged merchants residing mainly in big cities such as Osaka, Edo and Kyoto.

The primary tax became the main source of revenue in Tokugawa Japan. The shogunate and feudal lords conducted inspections of rice production in their domains from the 1590s to the 1600s. These reported figures formed the tax base for the primary tax. By the early eighteenth century, taxation policy was basically sharecropping. The shogunate and feudal lords levied taxes of 40 or 50 per cent on crop outputs with remissions for years of poor harvests. There existed only one land-holding farmer and only one feudal lord on each piece of land, hence this tax included the portion equivalent to 'rent' in western European manors, whose ownership belonged to feudal lords.

In the early eighteenth century, the Tokugawa Shogunate changed its taxation policy by fixing the amount assessed. The shogunate reviewed outputs for each peasant for several years, and then determined the tax assessed on each farm. This fixed amount of tax was effective for the next several years. Thus, while peasants bore the risks of fluctuation in output, their claim to all of the residual encouraged them to increase production, which meant that registered peasants were fully recognized as land-owners.[3]

Tokugawa Japan was fragmented into small states and domains governed by feudal lords, and each lord held taxation autonomy. Although it is difficult to aggregate revenues for all feudal lords, the revenue of the shogunate domain from the primary tax is available from 1716 to 1841. After the reform of taxation in the 1710s, tax revenue increased moderately, which indicated that the new taxation policy gave peasants stronger incentives towards efficiency. This shows that the tax revenue of the Tokugawa Shogunate was fairly stable, as reflected in

---

[3] M. Iwahashi, 'The institutional framework of the Tokugawa economy', in A. Hayami, O. Saitô and R. P. Toby (eds.), *The economic history of Japan:1600–1990. Volume 1: emergence of economic society in Japan, 1600–1859* (Oxford University Press, 1999), pp. 98–104.

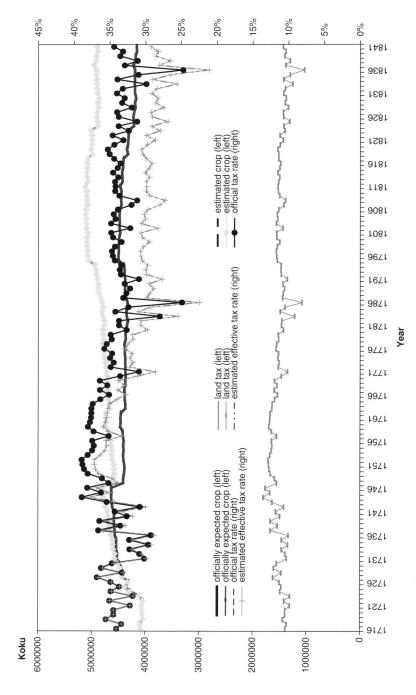

Figure 16.1 Land tax collection of the Tokugawa Shogunate Domain, 1716–1841

Koku

Legend:
- officially expected crop (left)
- officially expected crop (left)
- official tax rate (right)
- estimated effective tax rate (right)
- land tax (left)
- land tax (left)
- estimated effective tax rate (right)
- estimated crop (left)
- estimated crop (left)
- official tax rate (right)

Year

Table 16.1. *Population and rice production in the Tokugawa period*

Year	Population thousands	Cultivated acreage thousands of cho	Rice production thousands of koku	Labor productivity koku per capita	Land productivity koku per cho
	a	b	c	c/a	c/b
1600	1,200	2,065	19,731	16.44	9.55
1650	1,718	2,345	23,133	13.47	9.86
1700	2,769	2,841	30,630	11.06	10.78
1720	3,128	2,927	32,034	10.24	10.94
1730	3,208	2,971	32,736	10.20	11.02
1750	3,110	2,991	34,140	10.98	11.41
1800	3,065	3,032	37,650	12.28	12.42
1850	3,228	3,170	41,160	12.75	12.98
1872	3,311	3,234	46,812	14.14	14.47

Source: Miyamoto, 'Quantative aspects of Tokugawa economy', p. 38.

Figure 16.1. Although the official rate of taxation was nearly 35 per cent in this period, that rate was based on official estimates of crop outputs. These estimates hardly changed over time. However, Miyamoto estimated that country-wide crop production increased from 31 million *kokus* in 1700 to 41 million *kokus* in 1850, and land productivity (crop per cho) also rose.[4]

Tax rates for the Tokugawa domains were generally lower than those of other feudal lords, and the autonomy of the villages was stronger. The shogun peasants had stronger incentives to increase productivity and the increase in output may have been considerable. To construct a conservative estimate, I applied the country-wide increase in the rate of land productivity to the shogunate domains, and estimated crop outputs for the eighteenth and nineteenth centuries and effective tax rates (see Table 16.1).[5] On this estimation, effective tax rates drop below 30

[4] M. Miyamoto, 'Quantative aspects of Tokugawa economy,' in Hayami et al., *The economic history of Japan*, pp. 36–84; M. Miyamoto, *Kinsei Nihon no shijo keizai: Osaka Kome Shijo bunseki* [Market economy of early modern Japan: analysis on the Osaka Rice Market] (Tokyo: Yuhikaku, 1988); 1 cho = 1,093 square metres.

[5] Put y_t and y_{t+n} as crop in the tth year and $(t + n)$th year. Then average growth rate r between tth year and $(t + n)$th year is shown by $r = (y_{t+n}/y_t)^{4/n} - 1$. From Table 16.1, we have average growth rate r in 1720–1730, 1730–1750, 1750–1800 and 1800–1850. 'Officially expected crop in the domain' (a) in Appendix 16.1 can be interpreted as a proxy of acreage rather than real crop. Thus we can estimate crop in the tth year b_t by

per cent in the early nineteenth century. The shogunate provided strong incentives for peasants to increase productivity.

This occurred because the shogunate employed few officials in rural areas and delegated the process of assessment to villages. Tax rates imposed on villages were a kind of contract between the shogunate and the village. As long as the village paid the prescribed tax, the village kept its autonomy. This was an efficient way of collecting taxes, and economized on the costs of ruling rural society. But the lack of monitoring meant that asymmetric information existed between the village and the shogunate. When harvests failed, the villagers called for tax cuts. Because the shogunate wanted to stabilize tax revenue in the long term, tax cuts were accepted if really bad harvests were evident. However, incremental increases in productivity were hard to observe, and any renegotiation for tax increases involved huge costs for the shogunate, since it depended on autonomous villages as instruments of governance. While the shogunate could maintain stable land tax revenues, marginal increases in agricultural productivity were not taxed. As a result, as seen in Tables 16.2 and 16.3, the shogunate relied more on indirect taxes from merchants in the big cities in order to raise expenditure for salaries and civil services.[6]

Public finance in Tokugawa Japan

Imported Chinese coins were the currency in Japan until the shogunate developed its own currency system. The shogunate began to mint gold coins denominated by 'ryo' in 1603, and copper coins in 1636.[7] The shogunate copper coins replaced Chinese coins and Japan finally held its own independent currency system for the first time in its history. While this provided favourable conditions for note and bond issuing, the shogunate did not issue either bonds or notes, although it acquired some extra revenue accompanied with recoinage as seigniorage profit accruing from the debasement of the value of gold coins (Table 16.2). On the other hand, the shogunate allowed other feudal lords to issue bonds in Osaka, a shogunate city and the financial centre then, and to issue notes that were to circulate only within their own domains.

$b_t = (1 + r) \times (a_t/a_{t-1}) \times b_{t-1}$. For 1721–1730, 1731–1750, 1751–1800 and 1801–1841, we used r calculated by the procedure above. Before 1720, we assume that the 'Officially expected crop a' was fairly close to real crop, thus we inserted a_{1716} to a_{1720} as b_{1716} to b_{1720}.

[6] Y. Oguchi, 'The finances of the Tokugawa Shogunate,' in A. Hayami *et al.*, *The economic history of Japan:1600–1990*, pp. 198–201.
[7] Miyamoto, 'Quantative aspects of Tokugawa economy,' pp. 58–9.

Table 16.2. *Revenue structure of the Tokugawa Shogunate*

		thousands of Ryo		
		1730	1843	1844
General Account	Land tax (Nengu, paid officially in kind of rice)	a	509.0	603.7	646.8
	Direct tax for state public works (Kuniyaku, paid in cash)		24.9	20.2	7.2
	Direct tax for small public works (Kobushin, paid in cash)		26.9	22.4	23.3
	Direct tax for special civil service (Shoyakusho no, paid in cash)		55.0	45.9	71.3
	Indirect tax (Goyokin, paid by cash)		29.0	158.0	706.4
	Subtotal	b	644.8	850.2	1,455.0
		a/b	79%	71%	44%
Special Accounts	Surplus from selling tax rice (Kome uri harai dai)		112.9	45.7	32.1
	Repayment of loans (Sho kashitsuke hen no, paid in money)		20.8	208.8	165.7
	Surplus from recoinage		10.4	394.4	856.4
	Other revenues		9.8	43.8	66.3
	Subtotal	c	153.9	692.7	1,120.5
Total		b+c	798.7	1,542.9	2,575.5

Source: Y. Oguchi, 'Tmpoki no seikaku (Specific features of Tempo period),' in N. Asao, S. Ishii, K. Inoue, K. Oishi, M. Kanoh, T. Kuroda, J. Sasaki, Y. Toda, K. Naoki, K. Nagahara, M. Bitoh, A. Fujiwara and T. Matsuo, eds., *Iwanami koza Nihon rekish 12: Kinsei 4 [Iwanami series on Japanese history 12: Early modern 4]*, Iwanami Shoten Tokyo 1976, pp. 325–362.

Table 16.3. *Expenditure structure of the Tokugawa Shogunate*

			thousands of Ryo		
			1730	1843	1844
General Account	Salaries of public servants (Kirimai, Yakuryo)		297.3	405.0	428.3
	Expenses of Shogunate house (Okumuki)		60.4	91.9	89.0
	Civil services (Yakusho)		149.5	337.0	288.8
	Public works		68.5	73.0	68.0
	Subsidies		12.1	146.5	183.7
	Expenses for Nikko visit		0.0	101.0	2.0
	Restoration of the Edo castle		0.0	0.0	836.1
	Other expenditures		5.2	66.5	57.5
	Subtotal	a	593.0	1,220.9	1,953.4
Special Accounts	Government purchase of rice		103.5	96.8	95.0
	Government lending		34.9	127.7	80.8
	Subtotal	b	138.4	224.5	175.8
Total		$a+b$	731.4	1,445.4	2,129.2

Source: Ohguchi, 'The finances of the Tokugawa Shogunate', pp. 195, 210.

Feudal lords delivered tax rice from their home to Osaka and Edo, and sold it there. They sold bills denominated by rice before harvest by way of auction. In Osaka, merchants who won an auction sold rice bills at the Dojima Rice Market (*Dojima Kome Kaisho*), officially authorized by the shogunate in 1730. At Dojima, rice bills were traded both on the spot and in futures markets, which made the Dojima the world's oldest futures market. The prices of rice bills were very efficiently determined based on expectations for the harvest and the creditworthiness of the issuing feudal lord.[8] As long as he kept a good credit history, the feudal lord could issue more rice bills than the real expected harvest for the year. The rice bill market served as short-term local government bonds. The shogunate court strictly protected the claims of rice bill holders and promoted the growth of the rice bill market.[9]

[8] Miyamoto *Kinsei Nihon no shijo keizai*, pp. 163–232; Y. Takatsuki, 'The formation of an efficient market in Tokugawa Japan', Institute of Social Science, The University of Tokyo, Discussion Paper Series, F-143, November 2008.

[9] Y. Takatsuki 'Kinsei Nihon kome shijo ni okeru zaisanken no hogo' [The protection of property rights in Tokugawa Japan: the case of Osaka rice exchange market], *Rekishi to keizai* [The journal of political economy and economic history] 205 (October, 2009), 42–3.

Feudal lords were also financed by big financiers in Osaka and Edo, such as Mitsui, Konoike and others, some of whom founded modern banks after the Meiji Restoration. Because each domain preserved sovereignty in domestic affairs, jurisdiction over bilateral trades between feudal lords and financiers who were shogunate subjects was not clear. Hence big financiers curbed the moral hazard by building long-term relationships with feudal lords. If a feudal lord failed to credibly fulfil his obligations, he would lose the long-term benefit of a prime interest rate much lower than the market rate. The threat of losing a long-term favourable rate prevented feudal lords from cheating financiers.[10]

Therefore large feudal lords could be financed through rice bill issuance and relational financing in Osaka. For small feudal lords without a good credit history the shogunate sometimes arranged cooperative financing by financiers in Osaka and Edo, by offering judicial intervention when they defaulted.[11]

The Meiji Restoration: 1868–1889

Abolition of the feudal system and fiscal centralization

The shogunate retained sovereignty over diplomacy and national security. However, when Commodore Perry of the US Navy arrived with four battleships at Uraga off Edo bay, the shogunate could not interdict them. Furthermore, when Perry came back the following year with seven battleships, the shogunate concluded a treaty of peace and amity under which Japan was obliged to open the Shimoda port in Shizuoka and the Hakodate port in Hokkaido; to treat the United States as a most-favoured nation; to accept a consul at Shimoda Port; and to give the US consular jurisdiction. In turn, the US was obliged to give Japan neither most-favoured-nation treatment nor consular jurisdiction. Under the Tokugawa, peasants paid taxes while the Samurai held responsibility for national security. Thus, this shameful treaty with a foreign country made both feudal lords and the people sceptical about the Tokugawa Shogunate's defence of Japan.

In 1858, the shogunate concluded a treaty of friendship and commerce with the United States, under which Japan was obliged to open Yokohama, Nagasaki, Niigata and Hyogo as treaty ports, and to give up

---

[10] Y. Mori, *Daimyo kin'yu shi ron* [A history of feudal lord finance] (Tokyo: Ohara Shinseisha, 1970), pp. 137–83.

[11] T. Kagawa, *Edo Bakufu goyokin no kenkyu* [Research on policy finance of the Tokugawa Shogunate] (Tokyo: Hosei University Press, 2002), pp. 3–6, 85–136.

tariff autonomy. Sudden integration into the international markets generated drastic changes in relative prices. Huge losses fell upon relatively disadvantaged industries such as cotton growing while correspondingly large benefits went to relatively advantaged industries such as silk reeling. This opening-up destroyed the existing commercial networks of the large privileged merchants. The shogunate then lost the Boshn Civil War with the domains of Choshu and Satsuma.

In 1871, the New Imperial Government abolished the autonomy of 260 feudal estates and domains, and declared sovereignty over all of Japan. Feudal lords received government bonds to compensate for the loss of financial benefits from their domains, but they also lost authority over those domains. Henceforth, the tax revenues of Japan belonged to its central government.

Land tax reform in the 1870s

In Tokugawa Japan, a registered farmer held exclusive rights to cultivate his farm and to its output net of tax. When he sold or collateralized his farm, the trade was legally governed by the village office only if the other party was another resident of the village in which he was registered as a resident. Otherwise trade was not legally governed and had to be completely self-enforced.[12] In 1872, the New Imperial Government officially allowed peasants to sell and buy their farms. In 1873, a Land Tax Act was promulgated which guaranteed modern property rights to farmers who had been registered by the shogunate or a feudal lord as a taxpayer and prescribed that the land tax be paid in money, not kind. The basis for taxation was determined as follows. First the prefectural government inspected the productivity of farms, calculated average returns and derived their market values. Three per cent of the 'land price' was designated as the land tax from each farm. For the purposes of taxation, this 'price' became an officially fixed price. The imperial government had announced the land tax would be cut before it defeated the shogunate, but the 3 per cent was higher than expected and it caused some peasants to rise in revolt. Although the revolt was suppressed by the army, the government conceded to a tax rate of 2.5 per cent. Land tax revenues then increased rapidly and regained Tokugawa levels by the mid-1870s, as shown in Figure 16.2. But the New Imperial

---

[12] Different from trades of farmland, a holder of non-farmland in a city was not required to be a resident of the local society, and contracts of trade of the property right of land in a Shogunate city were enforced by the Shogunate's court. Hence the land market in a Shogunate city such as Edo was quite active without any restriction of trades and with third-party enforcement of trades.

millions of yen

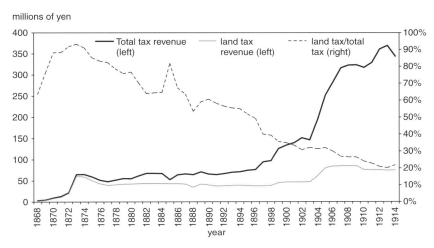

Figure 16.2 Land tax revenue in total tax revenue of the central government, 1868–1914

Government faced continuously occurring civil wars until the largest one ended in 1877, and was compelled to issue considerable amounts of notes that led to rapid inflation and tax cuts in real terms that stimulated investments in agriculture.

In 1882, Matsukata Masayoshi became minister of finance and instituted a deflationary policy whereby the government repaid its debts from the budget surplus (see Appendix 16.3). An important effect of the policy was real increases in land tax, which damaged the rural economy (especially in eastern Japan), because it coincided with a downturn in the European economy in 1882. Silk reeling (the export industry of eastern Japan), was hit both by the international business cycle and by fiscal policy at the same time.[13] During the 1880s, government revenues continued to depend on the land tax (see Figure 16.2) and that dependence remained as strong as it had been in the mid Tokugawa period (see Table 16.2).

Government bonds in the domestic capital market

In order to modernize the financial system, the government promulgated a national bank act in 1872, which copied the American system.

[13] M. Nakabayashi, 'The rise of a factory industry: silk reeling in Suwa District', in M. Tanimoto (ed.), *The role of tradition in Japan's industrialization: another path to industrialization* (Oxford University Press, 2006), pp. 184–7.

millions of yen

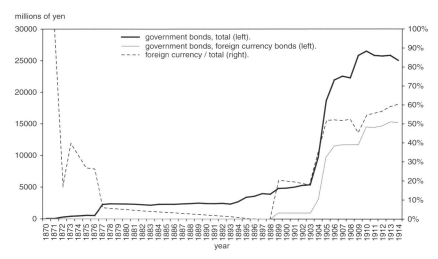

Figure 16.3 Amount of central government-issued bonds, 1870–1914

Nationa: banks were joint-stock companies with privileges to issue banknotes as currency. One hundred and fifty-three national banks were established and correspondence networks among them operated to integrate fragmented financial markets. Given the ongoing integration, the New Imperial Government issued government notes and bonds and these operations, together with the transformation of feudal lords' revenues into consul bonds, increased the circulation of bonds and represented the emergence of a capital market in Japan.

Matsukata set out to modernize the financial system by establishing the Yokohama Specie Bank (a state-backed foreign exchange bank) in 1880. Furthermore, following the British model, he established the Bank of Japan in 1882 as the central bank with a monopoly over the right to issue notes. The Bank of Japan provided for the convertibility of banknotes to silver coins, and remained on the silver standard until October 1897, when it moved to the gold standard.[14] With a stable currency and modern financial market, the government acquired a well-functioning market for its debts. From the late 1870s, the volume of domestic bonds gradually increased (see Figure 16.3).[15]

---

[14] In this period the Mexican dollar was the key currency in treaty ports of East Asia, so 1 Japanese yen coin contained the same amount of silver as 1 Mexican dollar did.

[15] T. Kamiyama, *Meiji keizai seisakushi no kenkyu* [Research on the economic policy of Meiji Japan] (Tokyo: Hanawa shobo, 1995), pp. 9–77.

Japan's fiscal state under the new constitution: 1890–1914

Battles in the diet

After being promulgated in 1889, the new constitution for the Empire of Japan became effective in 1890 and, like the Prussian constitution, basically gave strong powers to the lower house. If the government failed to persuade the diet to sanction an annual budget, it had to live with the budget of the previous year. Japan's constitution did not explicitly assume a cabinet system, rather the prime minister and other ministers were appointed independently by the emperor. But opposition parties retained a majority in the lower house.

The government sought to build a strong military to stand up to Western powers, but the opposition parties, led by a Liberal Party supported by rich land-owners, cared more for economic development than military power. Thus they supported large cuts in taxation. However, Clause 67 of the constitution prescribed that items falling under the sovereignty of the emperor in the budget could not be cut by the diet. Unless the cabinet agreed, the diet could not reduce military expenditures.[16] However, the Sino–Japanese war over the 'independence' of Korea attenuated the conflict between government and the diet. Facing a national emergency, the diet immediately gave approval to a large increase in military expenditure.

Rising taxation with increasing capital formation

Prices began to rise again in the late 1880s. Japan remained on the silver standard while European countries and the US decided to take the gold standard from the 1870s to the 1890s, which led to the decline of the international price of silver and the depreciation of the Japanese yen. This fuelled the inflation of domestic prices and led to the decrease of governmental revenues. The cabinet needed to raise more revenue from the taxation of land.

Meanwhile, after the Sino–Japanese war, the Liberal Party (the leading opposition party) changed its policy. The party wished to increase expenditure for public welfare and to that end approved tax increases in exchange for the government's commitment to considerably increase expenditures for public welfare, especially for infrastructure. This

---

[16] J. Banno, J. A. Ainscow, trans., *The establishment of the Japanese constitutional system* (London: Routledge, 1995).

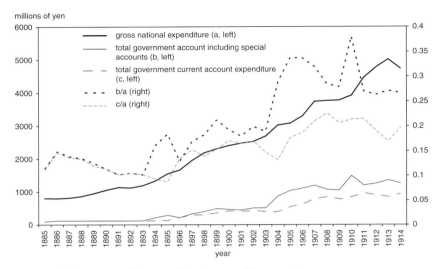

Figure 16.4 Gross national expenditure and government
expenditure, 1885–1914

strategic change by the Liberal Party resulted in the establishment of
the de facto parliamentary cabinet system, whereby ministers secured
majority support from the lower house. Thereafter the ratio of government expenditure to gross national expenditure steadily increased
(see Figure 16.4). Military spending and governmental expenditures
on capital formation surged in the late 1890s. As reflected in Figures
16.4 and 16.5, the cabinet became seriously committed to investment in
social infrastructure, especially from the late 1890s to the early 1900s,
a high period of Japanese industrialization.[17]

Government borrowing on the international capital market

In its early years the imperial government hesitated to issue government bonds on the international market because it recognized that
debt defaults led to a loss of fiscal sovereignty to foreign powers.
Nevertheless, Japan's victory in the Sino–Japanese war weakened this
anxiety. In October 1897, Japan switched from the silver standard to

---

[17] T. Mitani, 'The establishment of party cabinets, 1898–1932,' Peter Duus, trans.
and ed., *The Cambridge history of Japan. Volume 6: the twentieth century* (Cambridge
University Press, 1988), pp. 59–76; Banno, *The establishment of the Japanese constitutional system.*

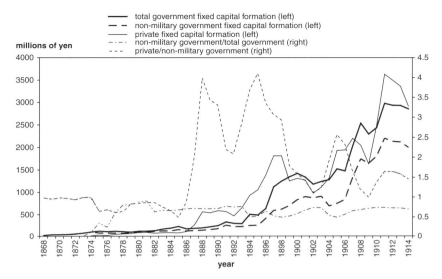

Figure 16.5 Fixed capital formation by government and private
sectors, 1868–1914

the gold standard under which the exchange rate of the Japanese yen
was pegged to the pound sterling in order to gain better access to international financial markets.[18] As long as the Japanese yen was pegged to
silver, the issue of bonds on the London market would require a premium to compensate for the risk of falls in the price of silver. In 1898,
the government resumed borrowing on the London market (see Figure
16.3). Bond issuance shot up during the Russo–Japanese war from 1904
to 1905. After the war, the London market retained a critical role in
Japanese fiscal policy. To avoid high interest rates and crowding-out
effects, the government sold bonds on the London market even after
the end of the Russo–Japanese war.[19]

The transition to the gold standard and operations on international
financial markets had important implications for budgetary policy and
for sustaining macroeconomic stability. In business cycles, the economy inevitably experienced short-term account deficits on the balance

[18] T. Suzuki, *Japanese government loan issuers on the London capital market: 1870–1913*
(London: The Athlone Press, 1994), pp. 65–6. The government's goal was reached
as the country's premium significantly decreased. N. Sussman and Y. Yafeh,
'Institutions, reforms, and country risk: lessons from Japanese government debt in
the Meiji Era', *Journal of Economic History* 60:2 (June, 2000), pp. 457–8.
[19] Kamiyama, *Meiji keizai seisakushi no kenkyu*, pp. 205–86.

of payments in up-phases. After the Japanese capital market had been integrated into the international market, this short-term deficit was not a serious problem any more. Inflows of foreign capital offset a short-term current account deficit and the Bank of Japan did not need to trigger a financial crisis and recession by sudden increases in interest rates.[20]

By defeating Russia, the government established a good reputation for the purposes of borrowing on international financial markets. Government contracts to sell bonds were given to the Yokohama Specie Bank. The London branch office of this bank persuaded British merchant banks to endorse and then sell Japanese government bonds. The gold standard before the First World War was basically a sterling exchange standard. The balance at the London branch of the Yokohama Specie Bank was in fact included in reserves of the Bank of Japan, which determined official discount rates.[21] The Japanese government and the Japanese economy obtained foreign capital by the yield decided by the London market according to the path of growth that the market expected for the Japanese economy. After the Russo–Japanese war, the international financial market came to provide a sustainable channel for capital imports through the issue of government bonds, given the fiscal behaviour of the Japanese government.

Conclusions

The Tokugawa Shogunate had guaranteed property rights to peasants as long as they paid taxes. It also respected the autonomy of local communities as long as those communities took responsibility for taxation. This institution provided the shogunate with a stable tax base. Land tax was the main source of revenue not only for the Tokugawa Shogunate, but also for the New Imperial Government after the Meiji Restoration.

After 1890, the constitution devolved the authority to approve budgets to the lower house of the diet, at a time when the government was eager to increase tax revenue in order to expand military capacities. The leading opposition party eventually approved of high levels of military expenditure provided that the government remained committed to investment in social infrastructure. This political deal produced a fiscal policy that enhanced productivity and increased tax revenues.

[20] Net export ([Exports] – [Imports]) must equal Net capital outflow. Thus net capital inflow offsets net import.
[21] Kamiyama, *Meiji keizai seisakushi no kenkyu.*

The New Imperial Government issued bonds on the domestic market from the 1870s. Japan then moved from the silver to the gold standard in 1897, in order to gain greater access to international financial markets. The government began to issue bonds on the London market in the late 1890s, and the amounts surged during the Russo–Japanese war from 1904–05, which provided the government with a stable way to fund expenditures. Access to the London market had another implication. In the early twentieth century, when no Japanese firm had established access to international capital markets, government bonds were the way to import capital. This channel enabled the government and the Bank of Japan to promote growth-oriented fiscal and monetary policies, despite short-term current account deficits. While Japan's central government had built a stable tax base in the seventeenth century, it lacked a sustainable financing mechanism until it entered the London market in the late 1890s. By this decade, Japan possessed all the attributes of an effective fiscal and financial state.

Appendix 16.1. *Rice production and land tax revenues of the Tokugawa Shogunate's Domain, 1716–1841*

			Land Tax				
	Officially expected crop in the domain	Estimated crop	Officially calculated amount	Paid in kind	Paid in money	Official tax rate	Estimated effective tax rate
	(Koku)	(Koku)	(Koku)	(Koku)	(Ryo)		
Year	a	b	c			c/a	b/a
1716	4,088,530	4,088,530	1,389,570	1,074,035	115,176	34%	34%
1717	4,098,371	4,098,371	1,365,060	1,080,090	102,494	33%	33%
1718	4,044,570	4,044,570	1,435,542	1,127,181	111,765	35%	35%
1719	4,050,850	4,050,850	1,393,529	1,092,581	109,236	34%	34%
1720	4,057,180	4,057,180	1,395,682	1,098,490	107,949	34%	34%
1721	4,066,500	4,069,249	1,305,650	1,027,061	100,722	32%	32%
1722	4,043,320	4,048,788	1,414,290	1,115,508	108,478	35%	35%
1723	4,112,390	4,120,735	1,303,930	1,050,289	91,534	32%	32%
1724	4,278,370	4,289,949	1,488,360	1,190,997	107,910	35%	35%
1725	4,360,670	4,375,427	1,466,215	1,166,544	108,849	34%	34%
1726	4,310,100	4,327,609	1,500,691	1,204,965	107,182	35%	35%
1727	4,414,850	4,435,781	1,621,980	1,374,545	110,750	37%	37%
1728	4,409,753	4,433,655	1,465,486	1,181,659	101,501	33%	33%
1729	4,446,688	4,473,812	1,608,354	1,292,703	114,346	36%	36%
1730	4,481,056	4,511,437	1,551,345	1,233,428	115,654	35%	34%

Appendix 16.1. (*cont.*)

Year	Officially expected crop in the domain	Estimated crop	Officially calculated amount	Paid in kind	Paid in money	Official tax rate	Estimated effective tax rate
	(Koku)	(Koku)	(Koku)	(Koku)	(Ryo)		
	a	b	c			c/a	b/a
1731	4,530,908	4,569,682	1,365,049	1,080,557	100,769	30%	30%
1732	4,521,401	4,568,146	1,392,391	1,062,635	119,558	31%	30%
1733	4,541,744	4,596,802	1,461,986	1,153,187	113,489	32%	32%
1734	4,541,816	4,604,992	1,343,519	1,061,441	101,655	30%	29%
1735	4,539,331	4,610,600	1,462,706	1,137,432	119,238	32%	32%
1736	4,565,359	4,645,224	1,334,481	1,018,661	115,445	29%	29%
1737	4,567,151	4,655,253	1,670,819	1,314,779	128,643	37%	36%
1738	4,580,554	4,677,159	1,533,133	1,181,529	127,282	33%	33%
1739	4,583,446	4,688,377	1,668,584	1,313,907	127,838	36%	36%
1740	4,581,523	4,694,685	1,492,492	1,153,881	122,431	33%	32%
1741	4,586,472	4,708,055	1,570,388	1,228,550	123,445	34%	33%
1742	4,614,502	4,745,193	1,419,558	1,140,592	98,989	31%	30%
1743	4,624,664	4,764,040	1,636,409	1,298,149	122,666	35%	34%
1744	4,634,076	4,782,165	1,801,855	1,462,749	123,262	39%	38%
1745	4,628,935	4,785,295	1,676,322	1,335,114	124,001	36%	35%
1746	4,634,065	4,799,057	1,766,214	1,422,876	124,602	38%	37%
1747	4,415,820	4,581,117	1,551,214	1,237,156	117,334	35%	34%
1748	4,411,241	4,584,448	1,590,491	1,270,661	117,702	36%	35%
1749	4,397,089	4,577,809	1,673,573	1,354,984	117,411	38%	37%
1750	4,390,109	4,578,613	1,693,726	1,380,425	115,691	39%	37%
1751	4,394,525	4,590,948	1,704,664	1,389,211	115,471	39%	37%
1752	4,409,637	4,614,504	1,715,630	1,398,975	115,947	39%	37%
1753	4,413,541	4,626,378	1,680,002	1,365,578	115,165	38%	36%
1754	4,407,515	4,627,853	1,650,387	1,336,747	114,783	37%	36%
1755	4,412,347	4,640,739	1,642,551	1,336,213	113,371	37%	35%
1756	4,406,064	4,641,946	1,649,384	1,331,264	116,328	37%	36%
1757	4,420,503	4,665,012	1,552,846	1,262,896	105,630	35%	33%
1758	4,426,889	4,679,630	1,649,532	1,332,456	116,202	37%	35%
1759	4,471,712	4,734,983	1,701,560	1,383,755	116,464	38%	36%
1760	4,461,631	4,732,276	1,685,345	1,369,539	115,982	38%	36%
1761	4,465,654	4,744,530	1,680,127	1,359,958	117,523	38%	35%
1762	4,458,083	4,744,474	1,674,699	1,354,852	117,320	38%	35%
1763	4,375,836	4,664,797	1,643,963	1,334,204	113,262	38%	35%
1764	4,376,432	4,673,300	1,636,386	1,324,862	113,954	37%	35%
1765	4,387,292	4,692,797	1,594,040	1,284,248	113,332	36%	34%
1766	4,387,045	4,700,447	1,538,971	1,241,941	108,724	35%	33%
1767	4,394,756	4,716,649	1,598,767	1,287,527	114,163	36%	34%
1768	4,378,684	4,707,325	1,547,248	1,229,794	116,619	35%	33%
1769	4,378,574	4,715,145	1,594,461	1,275,740	117,153	36%	34%

Appendix 16.1. (*cont.*)

	Officially expected crop in the domain	Estimated crop	Land Tax			Official tax rate	Estimated effective tax rate
			Officially calculated amount	Paid in kind	Paid in money		
	(Koku)	(Koku)	(Koku)	(Koku)	(Ryo)		
Year	*a*	*b*	*c*			*c/a*	*b/a*
1770	4,371,923	4,715,922	1,467,010	1,131,973	123,549	34%	31%
1771	4,375,647	4,727,899	1,353,282	1,021,543	123,363	31%	29%
1772	4,375,961	4,736,212	1,525,624	1,193,539	123,281	35%	32%
1773	4,378,819	4,747,297	1,508,026	1,175,311	123,413	34%	32%
1774	4,379,699	4,756,259	1,530,615	1,208,170	119,349	35%	32%
1775	4,387,091	4,772,321	1,520,866	1,199,900	117,750	35%	32%
1776	4,387,201	4,780,489	1,569,988	1,250,265	117,405	36%	33%
1777	4,392,791	4,794,652	1,556,681	1,237,369	116,793	35%	32%
1778	4,372,435	4,780,482	1,517,858	1,190,441	118,462	35%	32%
1779	4,373,996	4,790,253	1,525,452	1,194,575	119,859	35%	32%
1780	4,371,639	4,795,746	1,427,789	1,124,839	108,691	33%	30%
1781	4,348,278	4,778,163	1,465,836	1,147,934	114,663	34%	31%
1782	4,332,441	4,768,789	1,460,933	1,138,370	116,529	34%	31%
1783	4,350,709	4,796,972	1,219,484	968,418	95,865	28%	25%
1784	4,360,521	4,815,899	1,492,139	1,172,935	116,465	34%	31%
1785	4,330,634	4,790,956	1,403,708	1,093,200	114,412	32%	29%
1786	4,341,213	4,810,759	1,081,485	851,493	83,945	25%	22%
1787	4,361,544	4,841,440	1,444,933	1,164,205	112,291	33%	30%
1788	4,384,334	4,874,945	1,433,377	1,162,389	108,395	33%	29%
1789	4,384,279	4,883,104	1,410,414	1,118,088	107,612	32%	29%
1790	4,380,524	4,887,150	1,442,995	1,159,230	105,731	33%	30%
1791	4,382,813	4,897,950	1,356,289	1,088,669	99,550	31%	28%
1792	4,393,572	4,918,253	1,470,399	1,187,978	105,196	33%	30%
1793	4,393,000	4,925,906	1,476,278	1,199,720	103,481	34%	30%
1794	4,403,622	4,946,144	1,471,301	1,190,091	105,320	33%	30%
1795	4,504,516	5,068,000	1,545,767	1,257,316	107,963	34%	31%
1796	4,507,226	5,079,601	1,559,023	1,269,573	108,164	35%	31%
1797	4,501,193	5,081,356	1,561,828	1,274,532	107,273	35%	31%
1798	4,504,565	5,093,739	1,544,821	1,256,977	107,609	34%	30%
1799	4,499,020	5,096,048	1,501,108	1,121,107	107,801	33%	29%
1800	4,493,395	5,098,259	1,552,740	1,265,727	107,103	35%	30%
1801	4,474,977	5,081,896	1,558,351	1,273,466	106,658	35%	31%
1802	4,488,636	5,101,959	1,443,666	1,170,456	102,311	32%	28%
1803	4,485,711	5,103,187	1,562,872	1,272,120	107,627	35%	31%
1804	4,487,780	5,110,099	1,536,203	1,266,228	107,990	34%	30%
1805	4,487,885	5,114,782	1,546,915	1,277,485	107,771	34%	30%
1806	4,482,740	5,113,480	1,519,075	1,250,456	107,447	34%	30%
1807	4,453,870	5,085,084	1,425,102	1,163,522	107,211	32%	28%
1808	4,459,079	5,095,577	1,391,881	1,151,226	96,261	31%	27%

Appendix 16.1. (*cont.*)

	Officially expected crop in the domain	Estimated crop	Land Tax				Estimated effective tax rate
			Officially calculated amount	Paid in kind	Paid in money	Official tax rate	
	(Koku)	(Koku)	(Koku)	(Koku)	(Ryo)		
Year	a	b	c			c/a	b/a
1809	4,457,080	5,097,840	1,501,989	1,230,897	108,436	34%	29%
1810	4,455,394	5,100,462	1,527,031	1,256,777	99,994	34%	30%
1811	4,478,873	5,131,919	1,532,910	1,241,483	108,476	34%	30%
1812	4,434,556	5,085,677	1,520,969	1,240,486	102,732	34%	30%
1813	4,437,458	5,093,549	1,501,877	1,221,763	103,459	34%	29%
1814	4,442,669	5,104,084	1,535,799	1,249,917	105,053	35%	30%
1815	4,423,929	5,087,092	1,501,023	1,214,791	105,240	34%	30%
1816	4,423,274	5,090,880	1,483,067	1,196,505	105,212	34%	29%
1817	4,412,452	5,082,959	1,518,991	1,231,283	105,629	34%	30%
1818	4,334,570	4,997,701	1,519,374	1,233,374	104,982	35%	30%
1819	4,352,548	5,022,910	1,537,207	1,250,568	105,133	35%	31%
1820	4,333,634	5,005,549	1,490,752	1,205,297	104,672	34%	30%
1821	4,326,489	5,001,758	1,433,694	1,148,678	104,968	33%	29%
1822	4,320,482	4,999,273	1,496,240	1,208,342	105,244	35%	30%
1823	4,333,886	5,019,261	1,403,384	1,117,660	105,592	32%	28%
1824	4,223,923	4,896,276	1,427,619	1,158,677	98,889	34%	29%
1825	4,223,068	4,899,656	1,317,840	1,065,745	94,194	31%	27%
1826	4,229,389	4,911,371	1,428,537	1,163,502	97,406	34%	29%
1827	4,218,089	4,902,622	1,434,498	1,166,669	98,523	34%	29%
1828	4,194,554	4,879,621	1,339,578	1,077,787	96,223	32%	27%
1829	4,201,033	4,891,522	1,399,289	1,133,201	97,797	33%	29%
1830	4,182,691	4,874,514	1,378,578	1,113,204	97,715	33%	28%
1831	4,201,301	4,900,574	1,429,328	1,162,448	97,980	34%	29%
1832	4,204,038	4,908,145	1,396,390	1,120,504	101,292	33%	28%
1833	4,205,910	4,914,715	1,258,230	1,005,367	96,022	30%	26%
1834	4,202,806	4,915,473	1,427,193	1,150,709	101,648	34%	29%
1835	4,205,570	4,923,097	1,304,313	1,036,653	98,054	31%	26%
1836	4,202,493	4,923,888	1,039,970	807,068	93,161	25%	21%
1837	4,229,581	4,960,051	1,392,915	1,122,234	100,023	33%	28%
1838	4,194,210	4,922,963	1,305,746	1,046,104	97,412	31%	27%
1839	4,192,637	4,925,510	1,407,218	1,140,499	99,311	34%	29%
1840	4,166,475	4,899,146	1,382,698	1,138,359	97,735	33%	28%
1841	4,167,613	4,904,860	1,434,342	1,168,412	97,737	34%	29%

Source: Official expected crop and land tax: S. Mukouyama, 'On tori ka tsuji kakitsuke [Record of tax collection],' in S. Mukouyama, *M. S. Zakki* (Memorandum by Seisai Mukouyama), Tempo-Koka Hen, Vol. 3, Tokyo: Yumani Shobo, 2003. Estimated crop: See the text.
Note: 1 koku = 180.39 litters = 5.12 US bushels.

Appendix 16.2. *Gross national expenditure: Current prices, 1885–1914*

millions of Yen

Year	Personal Consumption Expenditure	General Government Consumption Expenditure	Gross Domestic Fixed Capital Formation	Government Sector	Exports of Goods and Sevices and Factor Income Received from Abroad	Imports of Goods and Services and Factor Income Paid Abroad	Surplus on Current Account	Gross National Expenditure at Market Prices	Government Consumption and Fixed Capital Formation in GNE
	a	b	c	d	e	f	$g=e-f$	$a+b+c+g$	$(b+d)/g$
1885	652	60	97	23	42	45	−3	806	10%
1886	630	63	101	18	55	49	6	800	10%
1887	664	62	100	18	59	67	−8	818	10%
1888	677	62	133	20	74	80	−6	866	9%
1889	755	59	141	22	78	78	0	955	8%
1890	869	66	153	25	65	97	−32	1,056	9%
1891	903	63	160	34	89	76	13	1,139	9%
1892	888	70	153	30	102	88	14	1,125	9%
1893	970	66	165	29	100	104	−4	1,197	8%
1894	1,009	124	220	51	125	140	−15	1,338	13%
1895	1,160	148	251	49	150	157	−7	1,552	13%
1896	1,308	118	308	62	135	203	−68	1,666	11%
1897	1,545	111	402	112	191	292	−101	1,957	11%
1898	1,808	131	426	125	200	371	−171	2,194	12%
1899	1,776	150	376	134	257	245	12	2,314	12%
1900	1,914	183	391	143	259	333	−74	2,414	14%

Appendix 16.2. (cont.)

millions of Yen

Year	Personal Consumption Expenditure	General Government Consumption Expenditure	Gross Domestic Fixed Capital Formation	Government Sector	Exports of Goods and Sevices and Factor Income Received from Abroad	Imports of Goods and Services and Factor Income Paid Abroad	Surplus on Current Account	Gross National Expenditure at Market Prices	Government Consumption and Fixed Capital Formation in GNE
	a	b	c	d	e	f	$g=e-f$	$a+b+c+g$	$(b+d)/g$
1901	1,898	201	379	134	310	304	6	2,484	13%
1902	1,984	202	335	118	332	316	16	2,537	13%
1903	2,103	241	366	124	370	384	−14	2,696	14%
1904	2,259	546	364	128	383	524	−141	3,028	22%
1905	2,278	626	517	152	401	738	−337	3,084	25%
1906	2,312	485	540	147	540	575	−35	3,302	19%
1907	2,787	338	634	204	617	633	−16	3,743	14%
1908	2,884	307	663	254	506	594	−88	3,766	15%
1909	2,880	320	597	229	539	556	−17	3,780	15%
1910	2,967	338	689	244	587	656	−69	3,925	15%
1911	3,295	407	860	298	619	718	−99	4,463	16%
1912	3,657	370	857	294	727	837	−110	4,774	14%
1913	3,920	339	861	293	844	951	−107	5,013	13%
1914	3,595	354	806	285	799	816	−17	4,738	13%

Source: K. Ohkawa, N. Takamatsu and Y. Yamamoto, *Estimates of long term statistics of Japan since 1868: 1 National Income* (Tokyo: Toyo Keizai Shimposha, 1974), pp. 178, 184–85.

Appendix 16.3. *Tax revenues of central government: Current prices, 1885–1914*

								millions of yen
Year	Tax Total	Land Tax	Income Tax	Corporation Tax	Liquor Tax	Customs Duty	b/a	Consumer price index in rural area
	a	b	c	d	e	f		
1868	3.157	2.009				0.720	64%	
1869	4.399	3.355				0.502	76%	
1870	9.323	8.218				0.648	88%	
1871	12.852	11.340				1.071	88%	
1872	21.845	20.051				1.331	92%	
1873	65.014	60.604			0.016	1.685	93%	
1874	65.303	59.412			0.961	1.498	91%	
1875	59.194	50.345			1.683	1.718	85%	
1876	51.730	43.023			2.555	1.988	83%	
1877	47.923	39.450			1.911	2.358	82%	
1878	51.485	40.454			3.050	2.351	79%	
1879	55.579	42.112			5.100	2.691	76%	100
1880	55.262	42.346			6.463	2.624	77%	114
1881	61.675	43.274			5.511	2.569	70%	126
1882	67.738	43.342			10.646	2.613	64%	118
1883	67.659	43.537			16.329	2.681	64%	99
1884	67.203	43.425			13.490	2.750	65%	95
1885	52.581	43.033			14.068	2.085	82%	95
1886	64.371	43.282			1.053	2.989	67%	87
1887	66.255	42.152	0.527		13.069	4.135	64%	86
1888	64.727	34.650	1.066		17.063	4.615	54%	83
1889	71.294	42.161	1.052		16.439	4.728	59%	87
1890	66.114	40.084	1.092		13.912	4.392	61%	94
1891	64.423	37.457	1.110		14.686	4.539	58%	89
1892	67.167	37.925	1.132		15.812	4.991	56%	91

Appendix 16.3. (cont.)

| | | | | | | | | millions of yen |
Year	Tax Total	Land Tax	Income Tax	Corporation Tax	Liquor Tax	Customs Duty	b/a	Consumer price index in rural area
	a	b	c	d	e	f		
1893	70.004	38.808	1.238		16.637	5.125	55%	93
1894	71.286	39.291	1.353		16.130	5.755	55%	96
1895	74.697	38.692	1.497		17.748	6.785	52%	105
1896	76.387	37.640	1.810		19.476	6.728	49%	113
1897	94.912	37.964	2.095		31.105	8.020	40%	129
1898	97.629	38.440	2.350		32.959	9.092	39%	139
1899	126.034	44.861	4.837	1.520	48.918	15.936	36%	132
1900	133.926	46.717	6.368	2.244	50.293	17.009	35%	147
1901	139.574	46.666	6.836	2.176	58.017	13.630	33%	144
1902	151.084	46.505	7.460	2.267	63.738	15.501	31%	150
1903	146.163	46.873	8.247	2.355	52.821	17.378	32%	158
1904	194.362	60.939	14.369	3.753	58.286	23.159	31%	161
1905	251.275	80.473	23.278	7.945	59.099	36.757	32%	168
1906	283.468	84.637	26.348	9.435	71.100	41.853	30%	172
1907	315.983	84.973	27.291	8.345	78.406	50.027	27%	189
1908	322.636	85.418	32.144	8.918	83.590	40.067	26%	182
1909	323.407	85.693	32.800	8.254	91.480	36.423	26%	175
1910	317.285	76.291	31.722	7.527	86.701	39.949	24%	176
1911	329.071	74.936	34.755	9.713	86.032	48.518	23%	189
1912	360.969	75.365	38.933	11.474	93.861	68.496	21%	199
1913	369.479	74.635	35.591	13.068	93.223	73.722	20%	205
1914	343.708	74.925	37.157	13.222	95.781	44.228	22%	190

Source: Tax revenue: K. Ohsato, Hundred-year statistics of the Japanese economy (Tokyo: Statistics Department, The Bank of Japan, 1966), p.136. Price index: K. Ohkawa, M. Shinohara and M. Umemura, Estimates of long term statistics of Japan since 1868: 8 Prices (Tokyo: Toyo Keizai Shimposha, 1967), p. 135.

Appendix 16.4. *Total government expenditures (current prices), 1868–1914, in millions of Yen*

Year	General Account					Total Government Expenditure	
	Central Government	Local Government	Transfer	Net Total	Special Account		Military and war-related expenditure
	a	c	d	e=a+c−d	f	g=e+f	h
1868	30.5			30.5	0.0	30.5	5.6
1869	20.7			20.7	0.0	20.7	4.0
1870	20.1			20.1	0.0	20.1	2.7
1871	19.2			19.2	0.0	19.2	3.8
1872	57.7			57.7	0.0	57.7	10.5
1873	62.6			62.6	0.0	62.6	11.6
1874	82.2			82.2	0.0	82.2	15.9
1875	69.2			69.2	0.0	69.2	12.2
1876	59.3			59.3	22.4	81.7	35.6
1877	48.4			48.4	18.8	67.2	42.4
1878	60.9			60.9	0.4	61.3	25.0
1879	60.3	24.2	2.6	81.9	2.6	84.5	26.4
1880	63.1	27.7	3.6	87.2	3.6	90.8	27.3
1881	71.4	34.5	1.4	104.5	1.4	105.9	26.8
1882	73.4	38.1	1.3	110.2	1.3	111.5	27.0
1883	81.0	36.8	1.7	116.1	1.7	117.8	33.3
1884	76.6	36.0	1.5	111.1	1.5	112.6	34.9
1885	61.1	30.3	1.9	89.5	1.9	91.4	32.4
1886	83.2	35.7	2.2	116.7	2.2	118.9	34.9
1887	79.4	33.7	1.7	111.4	1.7	113.1	36.4
1888	81.5	35.0	1.8	114.7	1.8	116.5	36.5
1889	79.7	38.3	4.3	113.7	5.2	118.9	37.5
1890	82.1	40.7	3.6	119.2	0.0	119.2	34.1
1891	83.5	42.8	10.5	115.8	0.0	115.8	37.0

Appendix 16.4. (cont.)

Year	General Account Central Government	Local Government	Transfer	Net Total	Special Account	Total Government Expenditure $g=e+f$	Military and war-related expenditure
	a	c	d	$e=a+c-d$	f		h
1892	76.7	46.1	5.1	117.7	0.0	117.7	36.8
1893	84.5	48.6	11.7	121.4	0.0	121.4	37.3
1894	78.1	50.8	4.6	124.3	91.4	215.7	140.5
1895	85.3	55.5	4.4	136.4	149.4	285.8	133.8
1896	168.8	67.4	11.5	224.7	-9.8	214.9	93.4
1897	223.6	84.4	10.5	297.5	33.3	330.8	132.4
1898	219.7	92.7	7.8	304.6	96.3	400.9	134.6
1899	254.1	110.0	10.7	353.4	137.8	491.2	139.9
1900	292.7	128.6	9.2	412.1	52.6	464.7	159.9
1901	266.8	150.7	9.1	408.4	38.3	446.7	133.7
1902	289.2	153.9	10.8	432.3	72.9	505.2	114.8
1903	249.5	158.9	11.0	397.4	111.7	509.1	180.9
1904	277.0	128.4	7.8	397.6	474.8	872.4	726.7
1905	420.7	131.0	8.5	543.2	497.2	1,040.4	843.2
1906	464.2	167.8	12.0	620.0	491.7	1,111.7	514.4
1907	602.4	201.0	17.5	785.9	409.1	1,195.0	358.7
1908	636.3	230.2	16.9	849.6	222.5	1,072.1	344.1
1909	532.8	263.1	16.9	779.0	274.9	1,053.9	319.0
1910	569.1	280.6	12.4	837.3	653.5	1,490.8	332.8
1911	585.3	389.2	14.7	959.8	245.4	1,205.2	350.1
1912	593.5	328.6	11.4	910.7	345.6	1,256.3	342.3
1913	573.6	292.7	12.6	853.7	506.6	1,360.3	335.1
1914	648.4	299.3	14.5	933.2	330.9	1,264.1	345.5

Source: K. Emi and Y. Shinoya, Estimates of long term statistics of Japan since 1868: 7 Government Expenditure (Tokyo: Toyo Keizai Shimposha, 1966), pp. 168–69, 186–87.

Appendix 16.5. *Gross domestic fixed capital formation, 1868–1914*

millions of Yen

Year	Government				Private			Total
	a	Non-military b	Construction c	Equipment d	e	Construction f	Equipment g	h=a+e
1868	19.320	19.020	14.120	4.900				19.320
1869	34.170	32.510	29.280	3.230				34.170
1870	36.560	35.990	32.410	3.580				36.560
1871	39.440	38.300	33.180	5.120				39.440
1872	54.140	50.730	41.310	9.420				54.140
1873	72.370	71.810	58.720	13.090				72.370
1874	99.660	99.400	80.920	18.530	11.140		11.140	110.800
1875	118.530	76.570	61.990	9.690	26.520		26.520	145.050
1876	107.910	73.830	66.090	12.630	17.890		17.890	125.800
1877	117.500	72.620	57.420	15.200	43.960	0.370	43.590	161.460
1878	107.310	68.870	54.030	14.840	55.400	0.500	54.900	162.710
1879	96.800	80.490	64.240	16.250	65.230	0.530	64.700	162.030
1880	117.920	99.270	74.790	24.480	87.230	0.400	86.830	205.150
1881	118.310	101.920	74.030	27.890	92.040	0.300	91.740	210.350
1882	130.290	113.230	87.280	25.950	71.660	0.270	71.390	201.950
1883	167.260	125.750	98.530	27.220	84.190	7.930	76.260	251.450
1884	189.510	124.630	95.920	28.710	83.210	9.940	73.270	272.720
1885	229.900	156.380	121.680	34.700	76.940	8.960	67.980	306.840
1886	174.400	123.660	99.820	23.860	109.630	20.190	89.440	284.030

Appendix 16.5. (*cont.*)

millions of Yen

| Year | Government | | | | Private | | | Total |
| | Non-military | | Construction | Equipment | | Construction | Equipment | |
	a	b	c	d	e	f	g	h=a+e
1887	185.070	132.490	109.050	23.440	264.490	112.480	152.010	449.560
1888	197.250	140.370	116.400	23.970	560.950	251.290	309.660	758.200
1889	222.010	157.390	133.420	23.970	541.120	300.630	240.490	763.130
1890	248.780	177.850	147.730	30.120	586.370	291.890	294.480	835.150
1891	334.660	259.480	217.820	41.660	568.170	217.430	350.740	902.830
1892	301.170	226.480	183.260	43.220	470.340	183.710	286.630	771.510
1893	295.460	227.210	187.630	39.580	650.910	236.910	414.000	946.370
1894	503.890	252.630	211.490	41.140	932.360	321.390	610.970	1,436.250
1895	489.520	256.590	205.820	50.770	1,053.530	392.210	661.320	1,543.050
1896	632.030	411.370	342.960	68.410	1,382.090	482.750	899.340	2,014.120
1897	1,119.810	590.390	476.430	113.960	1,809.670	804.000	1,005.670	2,929.480
1898	1,247.230	618.460	477.840	140.620	1,810.560	848.060	962.500	3,057.790
1899	1,343.210	700.700	547.020	153.680	1,252.430	736.140	516.290	2,595.640
1900	1,422.320	829.930	638.410	191.520	1,310.830	666.490	644.340	2,733.150
1901	1,338.030	899.710	670.420	229.290	1,271.030	757.950	513.080	2,609.060
1902	1,179.520	871.060	642.010	229.050	976.450	663.590	312.860	2,155.970
1903	1,238.880	908.740	661.540	247.200	1,112.070	748.880	363.190	2,350.950
1904	1,281.140	688.600	458.590	230.010	1,316.560	568.580	747.980	2,597.700
1905	1,520.500	747.370	525.220	222.150	1,930.930	672.080	1,258.850	3,451.430
1906	1,476.020	837.200	580.960	256.240	1,940.440	877.890	1,062.550	3,416.460

1907	2,037.140	1,337.930	995.210	342.720	2,199.950	922.120	1,277.830	4,237.090
1908	2,535.940	1,741.420	1,314.050	427.370	2,045.780	944.430	1,101.350	4,581.720
1909	2,295.090	1,642.490	1,211.220	431.270	1,627.760	867.100	760.660	3,922.850
1910	2,436.280	1,800.450	1,337.900	462.550	2,478.750	1,439.050	1,039.700	4,915.030
1911	2,976.390	2,202.700	1,670.900	531.800	3,629.180	2,172.040	1,457.140	6,605.570
1912	2,934.130	2,132.420	1,498.430	633.990	3,500.540	1,451.660	2,048.880	6,434.670
1913	2,928.860	2,119.830	1,482.190	637.650	3,360.240	1,396.180	1,964.050	6,289.100
1914	2,853.300	1,997.140	1,359.530	637.610	2,912.230	1,376.550	1,535.680	5,765.530

Source: K. Emi, *Estimates of long term statistics of Japan since 1868: 4 Capital Formation* (Tokyo: Toyo Keizai Shimposha, 1971), pp. 224–27.

Appendix 16.6. *Central government debts in current prices, 1868–1914, in millions of Yen*

| Year | Long-term Government Securities | | | Short-term Government Securities | Borrowings | Total |
| | Total | Domestic Bonds | Foreign Currency Bonds | | | |
	a			b	c	$d=a+b+c$
1870	48.800		48.800			48.800
1871	48.800		48.800			48.800
1872	280.560	231.760	48.800			280.560
1873	406.400	245.360	161.040			406.400
1874	469.190	313.030	156.160			469.190
1875	558.100	409.160	148.940			558.100
1876	539.270	397.720	141.550			539.270
1877	2,268.540	2,134.550	133.990		113.360	2,381.900
1878	2,373.640	2,247.400	126.240		150.000	2,523.640
1879	2,351.980	2,233.690	118.290		150.000	2,501.980
1880	2,343.380	2,233.250	110.130		150.000	2,493.380
1881	2,311.270	2,209.540	101.730		150.000	2,461.270
1882	2,255.110	2,162.020	93.090		150.000	2,405.110
1883	2,176.620	2,087.560	89.060		100.000	2,276.620
1884	2,298.610	2,213.850	84.760		120.000	2,418.610
1885	2,312.550	2,232.400	80.150		153.960	2,466.510
1886	2,299.940	2,224.720	75.220		198.180	2,498.120
1887	2,379.810	2,309.870	69.940		179.750	2,559.560
1888	2,425.470	2,361.170	64.300		145.230	2,570.700
1889	2,500.530	2,442.270	58.260		100.000	2,600.530
1890	2,432.360	2,380.560	51.800		320.000	2,752.360
1891	2,426.260	2,381.370	44.890		320.000	2,746.260

1892	2,458.940	2,421.450	37.490		320.000	2,778.940
1893	2,358.140	2,328.570	29.570		320.000	2,678.140
1894	2,736.280	2,715.180	21.100		525.000	3,261.280
1895	3,417.590	3,405.560	12.030		679.000	4,096.590
1896	3,573.350	3,571.010	2.340		530.000	4,103.350
1897	3,992.450	3,992.450	0.000		220.000	4,212.450
1898	3,912.530	3,912.530	0.000		220.000	4,132.530
1899	4,809.670	3,883.370	976.300		252.000	5,061.670
1900	4,864.640	3,888.340	976.300		323.000	5,187.640
1901	5,022.260	4,045.960	976.300	100.000	563.000	5,685.260
1902	5,301.800	4,325.500	976.300	100.000	444.400	5,846.200
1903	5,389.620	4,413.320	976.300	0.000	783.490	6,173.110
1904	9,736.470	6,612.310	3,124.160	350.000	701.490	10,787.960
1905	18,703.860	8,999.760	9,704.100	990.000	1,442.000	21,135.860
1906	21,957.070	10,495.460	11,461.610	962.000	351.560	23,270.630
1907	22,543.460	10,886.450	11,657.010	227.000	279.940	23,050.400
1908	22,283.060	10,626.050	11,657.010	370.000	275.050	22,928.110
1909	25,828.040	14,171.290	11,656.750	190.000	494.350	26,512.390
1910	26,503.550	12,031.400	14,472.150	100.000	1,199.860	27,803.410
1911	25,836.650	11,462.160	14,374.490	500.000	1,084.750	27,421.400
1912	25,732.190	11,162.470	14,569.720	350.000	1,424.490	27,506.680
1913	25,841.220	10,546.340	15,294.880	0.000	1,023.920	26,865.140
1914	25,063.710	9,915.310	15,148.400	0.000	1,433.480	26,497.190

Source: K. Ohsato, *Hundred-year statistics of the Japanese economy* (Tokyo: Statistics Department, The Bank of Japan, 1966), p.158.

17   Fiscal states in Mughal and British India

John F. Richards[†]

The aim of this chapter is to compare the public finances of the Mughal empire and the finances of its imperial successor, the British East India Company. To a considerable degree, one may argue that there was direct continuity between these systems. The British adopted the essential features of the Mughal fiscal system, including its currency, in Bengal and South India, the regions of their earliest large territorial conquests. Changes occurred over time, but the Mughal origins of the British fiscal system remained noticeable throughout the entire period of the East India Company and later imperial British rule in India.[1]

[†] John Richards sadly passed away as this volume was being developed. We rescued this essay from the paper he presented at the Buenos Aires conference, but are only presenting some of the tables and figures for editorial reasons. We have not edited the text, which is why a note on the data follows. This note refers to the annual data on which tables and figures are based and which are not included in this volume due to editorial constraints. The reader can find them in J. Richards, 'The finances of the East India Company in India, c. 1766–1859', *London School of Economics Working Papers* 153:11 (August, 2011), pp. 1–29. The editors thank Tirthankar Roy for welcoming the idea of publishing them.

[1] NB: on Tables and Figures: the tables are based on data found in the House of Commons, Sessional Papers for various years. Between 1757 and 1781 East India Company financial information is printed in various parliamentary committee reports and papers concerning India, collected and edited by Sheila Lambert and published under the title *House of Commons Sessional Papers of the Eighteenth Century* (Wilmington, DE: Scholarly Resources, 1975). From 1782 onwards, the East India Company submitted its financial data to parliament in an annual series titled 'East India Company's Accounts and Papers'. These yearly reports supply most of the data entered into the tables. Other sources also found in the Sessional Papers are cited for specific tables. These include successive nineteenth-century parliamentary review committee reports on the East India Company from 1812–14, 1831–32 and the early 1850s. The Irish University Press publishes the latter in a separate series, or they may be consulted in either the printed volumes or the microfiche edition of the nineteenth-century House of Commons Sessional Papers. Until the 1830s the East India Accounts and Papers show returns separately for Bengal, Madras and Bombay as well as the dependencies like St. Helena, Bencoolen or Prince of Wales Island. Total figures for East India Company accounts do not appear until the 1830s. All figures have to be added together for each year. These accounts were not converted to pounds sterling until very late. Bengal reported its data in the money of account called the 'current rupee'; Madras in the gold pagoda; and Bombay in Bombay rupees. Each had a different value. Conversions

There were other important similarities between the two regimes. Both were war states. Both the Mughals and the British were aggressive, expansive, states that invested heavily in their armies and in conquest. The Mughal empire steadily added territories until it encompassed nearly the entire subcontinent and Afghanistan by the 1690s. The British empire added territories in nearly continuous wars of conquest throughout the century of East India Company rule (1757 to 1859) until it too, ruled the subcontinent and beyond, to include Burma.

Both were centralized autocratic states ruled by a single figure – the Mughal emperor and the British governor general, later viceroy – who issued edicts, laws and regulations to be obeyed throughout the subcontinent. Both deployed bodies of military and civil administrators who were subject to posting anywhere in the empire at the command of their superiors and who had either attenuated or non-existent local bases of power. Many of the Mughal elite were foreign born; nearly all of the British were aliens. Both imperial systems imposed a common non-Indian language for administration and high culture: Persian for the Mughals; English for the British. Both empires had strong ties to two minority religions in India: Islam for the Mughals and Christianity for the British.

Both Mughal emperors and British governors general presided over vibrant, growing economies with steadily rising populations. At its fullest extent in the early eighteenth century the Mughal population was probably about 150 million. By 1859 the subcontinent's population had risen to approximately 193 million. Each regime relied upon the impressive productivity of India's agriculture and industry to generate a continuing export surplus and a corresponding inflow of monetary payments for Indian goods. Each regime benefited from a continuing process of clearing, settlement and cultivation of new lands in the subcontinent. India fed its growing population and produced a surplus until it hit Malthusian constraints in the late nineteenth century.

Mughal finance

The Mughal empire was an agrarian empire.[2] The Timurid dynasty based its wealth and power upon the state's ability to tap directly into

to sterling are made according to the official rate: 10 current rupees to the pound; 2.5 Madras pagodas to the pound; and 8.8888 Bombay rupees to the pound. The figures given in the tables are still in draft form and require further correction and adjustment. There are likely to be errors in data entry, calculation, budget categories or currency conversion. However, it is unlikely that the overall trends shown in the charts will be substantially altered by these corrections.

[2] J. F. Richards, *The Mughal Empire* (Cambridge University Press, 1993). Unless otherwise noted, this section draws upon material from my book.

the enormous agrarian productivity of a greater and greater share of the lands of the Indian subcontinent. The ultimate goal of the Mughals was to impose a uniform or regulation tax, rather than a tribute, system throughout the empire. They aimed at fixing a tax demand based on an evaluation of the relative productivity of each cultivator and his fields. They wished to shunt aside and neutralize the position of rural aristocrats, to scrape aside the hard resistant shell of local warlord power in the countryside in order to deal directly with peasant communities. They did not want to collect produce, but cash in imperial coin. Successive emperors made steady progress towards this objective from the mid sixteenth to the early eighteenth century.

The Mughal empire was highly monetized. Rather than collect foodgrains in kind to store and use as salary payments, as did the rulers of Tokugawa Japan, the Mughal emperors insisted on payments of taxes made in imperial coin. The regime relied on the operation of powerful, flexible market systems and a high-volume, high-quality coinage to make this policy work.

The Mughal emperors imposed a uniform trimetallic coinage system throughout the empire. Only imperial coin could be used to pay taxes and the regime only used its own coin to pay its officials and soldiers. Minting was open and accessible to anyone possessing either bullion, or foreign or anachronistic coins on payment of a mint fee. Imperial mints turned out tens of millions of coins in gold, silver and copper. All coins issued were of high metallic purity and noteworthy design and manufacture. During the sixteenth century the basic coin was the heavy copper *dam* used in great quantities for taxes, wages, commodity purchases and other routine exchanges. By the early seventeenth century, as the value of copper climbed relative to silver, the silver rupee became a commonly used coin. Supplies of New World gold and silver and Japanese silver flowed copiously into Mughal mints for coining. Throughout the period of the centralized empire, until the 1720s, no debasement occurred in Mughal coin. Gold issues remained nearly pure and silver rupees never dropped below 96 per cent purity.

The Mughals employed what is usually called a land revenue system to extract a large share of the total harvests produced by peasant cultivators under its control. Land revenue demands constituted about nine-tenths of regularly imposed Mughal taxes. The land tax acted like a giant pump that pulled foodgrains and other crops into the market system and made the surplus available for the state and for urban populations. Coin paid by grain dealers and traders for agricultural produce flowed into the countryside temporarily. Cash obtained by rural society rapidly flowed out, partly in the form of market purchases of salt, iron and other commodities and as tax payments to imperial treasuries. State cash disbursements to several million persons drawing their salary and support from imperial and noble households and from military service sent a flow of payments for goods and services back into the economy.

The remaining one-tenth of revenues came from customs duties of between 2.5 and 5 per cent of value imposed at major markets, sea ports and land frontier posts; from licences and fees charged to groups of urban merchants and craftsmen, and from profits made by the prolific imperial mints, among other miscellaneous sources. Not so regular, but certainly of great importance, was a continuing flow of plunder and tribute into the imperial coffers. Ongoing territorial expansion meant that plundered royal hoards augmented the emperor's finances. Tribute payments imposed on subordinate principalities not yet conquered were another source of imperial income.

Under the regulation (*zabt*) land revenue system devised during Akbar's long reign (1556–1605), imperial officers carried out cadastral surveys to determine on a field-by-field basis the area under plough cultivation. Simultaneously, they gathered data on the crops grown, the average yields by quality of soil and market prices paid for these for both the autumn and spring harvests. They measured lands irrigated by wells or water diverted from rivers. With area, yield and price data in hand officials established tabular data from which to calculate a standard assessment for each field that could be summed to arrive at an annual revenue demand for the lands of each village community. The regime demanded about one-third of the harvest of foodgrains such as rice, wheat and millet and about one-fifth of the value of more valuable saleable crops such as tobacco, vegetables, poppy, sugar or indigo. Imperial officers assessed fruit trees at so much per tree and domestic livestock at so much per animal. The state encouraged expansion by offering tax-free periods for those who brought new land into cultivation.

As contemporaries knew very well, the Mughal emperors had immense revenues and accumulated enormous resources. Unfortunately, fiscal data for the empire are so scanty and unsystematic that compiling detailed long-term data on revenues and expenditures is simply not possible. In the present state of our documentation, the best that we can do is compare revenues and general fiscal health at three points: in the late sixteenth century, the mid seventeenth century and the early eighteenth century.

Table 17.1. *Plausible budget for the Mughal empire, 1595–1596*

	Million rupees
Total annual income	99.01
(Effective *jama* 1995–96)	
Annual expenditures	
Salary bill of mansabdars	
Personal (*Zat*) salaries	20.69
Allowance for war elephants etc.	9.29
Trooper payment (*Suwar*)	50.97
Total	80.95
Central military establishment	
Cavalry and foot	3.57
Animals/stables	4.85
Arsenal and armour	0.55
Total	8.97
Imperial household (including harem and building construction)	4.69
Total expenditures	94.60
Balance	4.41
Grand total	99.01

Shireen Moosvi has worked up a plausible budget for the empire for 1595–96, toward the end of Akbar's fifty-year reign, as displayed in Table 17.1.[3]

There are several noticeable aspects to this statement. Of the total 94.6 million rupees actually spent, 81 million never reached the central treasury, but was diverted to the *mansabdars*. Those men holding imperial rank were only 1,671 persons who disposed of 82 per cent of total Mughal revenues. From this huge sum they were obliged to spend 51 million rupees on their military contingents. *Mansabdars* were also required to support a set number of warhorses, war elephants, transport animals and carts as well, for which they received an additional 9.3 million rupees. Their personal salary payments totalled 20.7 million rupees. In 1595, the men who held imperial *mansabs* brought to the muster a minimum of 141,053 and perhaps as many as 188,070 armed and mounted heavy cavalrymen.

Revenues and expenditures made by the emperor directly were relatively small. The entire imperial household with its great conspicuous consumption took only 5 per cent of the total expenditures. The

[3] S. Moosvi, *The economy of the Mughal Empire, c. 1595: a statistical study* (Aligarh, Delhi and New York: Aligarh Muslim University and Oxford University Press, 1987).

centrally commanded artillery, cavalry, infantry and arsenals required another 9.5 per cent of imperial expenditure. According to this estimate, the emperor could count on a surplus each year of 4.4 million rupees from ordinary operations.

Beyond this surplus, Akbar would have been enriched by war plunder, by tribute from dependent states and, to a certain extent, by gift exchanges between him and his officers at court. What is clear is that he did build a surplus to be stored in the imperial vaults. At Akbar's death in 1605, his treasuries contained gold, silver and copper coin and uncoined gold and silver bullion and worked objects worth between 139 and 166 million rupees. That is, state reserves were between 1.4 and 1.7 times the annual income of the empire. The great mass of set and unset precious stones, jewellery and decorated objects also in the repositories probably doubled the size of the reserve.

Mid way through Shah Jahan's reign (1627–56), in 1647, the considerably enlarged empire had assessed annual revenue of 220 million rupees – more than twice as great as that of Akbar. From this total 445 *mansabdars* holding personal ranks of 500 and above claimed 135.4 million rupees for themselves and their followers or 61.6 per cent of the assessed revenue demand. This figure is roughly similar to that in Akbar's reign where 487 *mansabdars* with ranks of 500 and above took 66.7 per cent of the total revenue.[4] At this point, the emperor had set the crown territories at 30 million rupees or 13.7 per cent of total revenues. The emperor maintained 40,000 infantry and troops as well as 7,000 cavalry at court and paid them in cash 16 million rupees per year. Despite spending 25 million rupees on the construction of grand palaces, forts, tombs, hunting retreats and gardens across North India, Shah Jahan had accumulated imperial reserves worth 95 million rupees: half in coin and half in jewellery and other valuables. This, of course, was a considerable decline to less than half annual revenues from Akbar's reserves. Shah Jahan was in fact rebuilding the reserves after what appears to have been profligate expenditure by his father Jahangir (1605–27).

By the 1680s various administrative manuals and other compendia record both the assessed revenue (*jama*) and the actual collections (*hasil*) for individual provinces and for the empire as a whole. Table 17.2 presents these data for the empire enlarged by the conquests of the Sultanates of Bijapur and Golconda in 1686–87.[5]

---

[4] Ibid., pp. 222–3.
[5] I. Habib, *The agrarian system of Mughal India, 1556–1707*, 2nd rev. edn (New Delhi and New York: Oxford University Press, 1999). Data calculated from Appendix D

Table 17.2. *Assessed revenue and actual collections in the Mughal empire*

Years	Assessed revenue (rupees)	Collections (rupees)	% collections to assessed revenues
1687–91	345,058,900	232,418,890	67.36
1701–02	328,316,407	272,428,855	82.98

These figures suggest that the usual or average total revenues actually collected in the late Mughal period were about 255 million rupees for the entire empire. This is the equivalent of 2,854 metric tons of silver if converted from silver rupees of 96 per cent fineness and 11.66 (179 grains) weight. Or, to put this another way, average imperial revenues were approximately 25.5 million pounds sterling at the eighteenth-century rate of exchange.

By the end of Aurangzeb's reign in 1707, despite that emperor's difficulties and expenditures in the wasting Deccan wars, his son Prince Muazzam, later Bahadur Shah (1707–12) used a substantial reserve to good advantage in the war of succession that ensued. The prince seized 6.6 million rupees from three provincial treasuries as he moved from Kabul to Agra. When he reached the capital, his officers counted coined and uncoined gold and silver worth 240 million rupees. The liquid reserves of the empire were greater than the average annual returns at that time.[6]

Within a remarkably short time after Aurangzeb's death, however, the centralized institutional fabric of the Mughal empire quickly unravelled. Between 1707 and 1719 there occurred four hard-fought wars of succession waged by princely brothers claiming the imperial throne. Each successive conflict further weakened the power and authority of the newly victorious emperor as over-mighty nobles dictated their terms to desperate contenders. By the 1720s, the empire was no longer a tightly centralized entity. The Mughal emperor was no longer a chief executive capable of mobilizing men, money and information and moving these resources at will across the entire subcontinent. Instead, the former structure had stretched and loosened. Mughal provinces were fast becoming nascent regional Indo–Muslim kingdoms.

'Revenue Statistics'. Assessed revenues were expressed in copper *dams*. I have converted these to rupees at the conventional 40 *dams* per rupee ratio.

[6] J. F. Richards, 'Mughal state finance and the premodern world economy', *Comparative Studies in Society and History* (1981), 285–308, at 293.

East India Company finance

On 23 June 1757, Robert Clive, commanding a small force of East India Company professional troops, defeated and killed Siraju-ud-daula, the ruling Nawab of Bengal, on the battlefield of Plassey.[7] The battle marked a significant turning point in world history, for it permitted the British East India Company to gain control over the rich resources of the Mughal successor state in north-eastern Bengal and Bihar. This was the starting point for a century-long process of British conquest and dominion over the entire Indian subcontinent and beyond. Between 1757 and 1859 there were few years in which soldiers of the East India Company and British armies did not march and fight in either internal pacification campaigns or in external wars. The latter resulted in annexation of new territory or the reduction of independent Indian rulers to the status of tightly controlled Indian puppet rulers as 'Indian Princes'. Officials of the East India Company, a trading company turned territorial state, tapped the productive people and resources of Bengal and the eastern Gangetic valley to fund the protracted military campaigns necessary to conquer India. Over the same century, these resources also supplied the wherewithal for a century-long transfer of wealth from India to Great Britain.

In 1765, after the Treaty of Allahabad, the British East India Company assumed full control of Bengal's finances. Since the reign of Aurangzeb, Bengal had generated large revenue surpluses that the Nawabs of Bengal remitted every year as tribute to Delhi. The company could now use the considerable powers of the centralized late Mughal state with its well-honed processes of revenue assessment and collection to its own ends. Apart from fixed allowances to the Nawab and his court, the entire revenues of this vast region were now at their disposal. In 1765 company officials in India and at home looked to Bengal's anticipated annual revenue surplus to pay for the yearly export of cloth, saltpetre, indigo and other commodities that sailed on East India Company vessels. No longer would the company have to pull together shipments of gold and silver coin and bullion to pay for its incoming cargoes. Bengal's taxes would defray the cost of purchase, leaving only the expenses of processing and shipping Bengal's cloth and other commodities sold in London. East India Company profits should soar to undreamed-of heights.

Important as it was, however, the regime in Bengal formed only one part of the fast-growing East India Company presence on the Indian

---

[7] P. J. Marshall, *Bengal: The British bridgehead: Eastern India, 1740–1828* (Cambridge University Press, 1988).

subcontinent. In 1757, Madras on the south-eastern coast and Bombay on the western coast were each fortified city-states with their own commercial and, increasingly, political activities and interests. Each city and its territories were under a separate East India Company administration that was not under the direct control of the governor in Bengal. The governors of Madras and Bombay each ruled over a mixed Indian and European population and controlled lands situated beyond the city walls. Both Madras and Bombay had long-established institutional cultures with distinct and distinctive fiscal systems. Each had a separate currency, with Bengal using the company or Sicca rupee, Madras the gold pagoda, and Bombay the Bombay rupee. Each conducted its own purchases of Indian goods and sale of imports. Perhaps most important, both Madras and Bombay were more and more embroiled in Indian diplomacy and politics beyond their borders.

The East India Company court of directors and the governor general of Bengal and his council slowly made headway in the ongoing struggle to impose a unified political and fiscal system upon all British possessions in India. They were aided in this effort by parliament's continuing efforts by means of legislation and investigative committees to hold the East India Company responsible and accountable for its Indian territories. Beginning with the Regulating Act of 1773 and followed by Pitt's India Act of 1784, the East India Company was transformed into what was essentially a responsible colonial ministry. A board of control, headed by a president appointed by the prime minister, determined policy and sent orders to its governor general at Calcutta. The latter in turn assumed greater powers over Madras and Bombay.

The company continued to exercise its monopoly over European trade with India, but there was an increasing separation between the commercial and political/administrative branches of the company. By 1833, parliamentary action ended all East India Company trade with India and left it solely a colonial regime.

Beginning in the 1781–82 fiscal year, the company submitted annual reports to parliament on its revenues, expenses, debt and trade. These East India Company accounts, published regularly in the Sessional Papers of the House of Commons, supply the data necessary to complete an annual time series of the finances of the East India Company until 1859. Similar data published in an early Parliamentary Committee report make it possible to do a compilation for the years 1766 to 1771. At this point, however, without archival research it is not possible to reconstruct a reliable, detailed data series for the period 1772 to 1781.

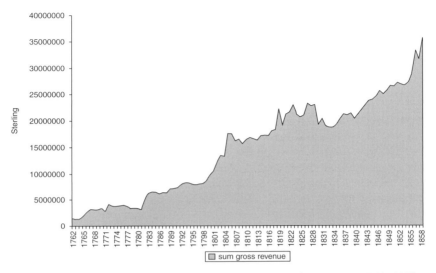

Figure 17.1 East India Company gross annual revenues, 1762–1859

Despite their accessibility and completeness, the annual East India Company fiscal reports present some difficulties. Bengal, Madras and Bombay, as well as outlying centres such as Canton, St Helena, Fort Marlborough and Bencoolen, all state their revenues and expenses separately. Each uses a different currency that is only occasionally converted into pounds sterling. Although there are uniform revenue and expense categories, each presidency or factory has its own peculiar categories and quirks. The East India Company accountants did not supply summed and totalled company-wide figures until the mid nineteenth century. These difficulties partly explain why no earlier scholar has assembled a uniform, systematic time series for the complete East India Company finances.

The complete data series for revenues is set out in Figure 17.1. Between 1762, five years after Plassey, and 1859, at the demise of the East India Company, gross annual revenues rose from 1.5 million pounds sterling to 36 million pounds sterling. Although these figures are not adjusted for relative value, nevertheless this very large increase results primarily from adding territories and revenues to the rule of the East India Company. The rise in revenues is an index of the prolonged, bloody British conquest of the Indian subcontinent. The initial victories at Plassey and Buxar placed an area of 378,000 square km and 30 million

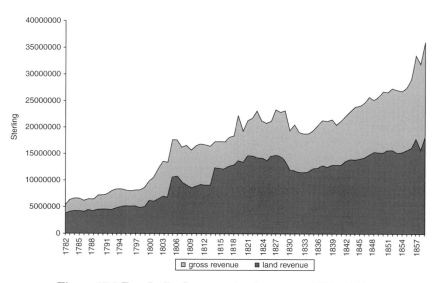

Figure 17.2 East India Company land revenue, 1782–1859

inhabitants under company rule. Successful war and aggressive diplomacy brought the total area under direct British administration to 2.5 million square km and 145 million persons by 1859. Several hundred protectorates ruled by dependent Indian rulers, the so-called 'princely states', comprised another 1.5 million square km with a population of 48 million. By the end of the company period, the protected states and territories were fiscally autonomous and contributed very little to the revenues of British India.

The East India Company was deeply influenced by the extant late-Mughal revenue system that its officials found in operation in Bengal, Bihar, the Andhra Coast and in Hindustan during the eighteenth century. Even thereafter, as the company conquered territories ruled by non-Mughal Indian rulers, its officers discovered that in Maratha, Rajput or even Sikh territories, the basic structure and terminology of the Mughal revenue system had survived in at least an attenuated fashion.

Land revenue continued to be the mainstay of the regime until the end of British rule in India, but its share of gross revenues was far less than under the Mughal emperors. From 70 per cent of the gross collections in 1782 the land revenue had dropped to 50 per cent by 1859 (see Figure 17.2). To some extent this trend was the result of the 1793 Permanent Settlement enacted in Bengal, parts of Bihar and Andhra

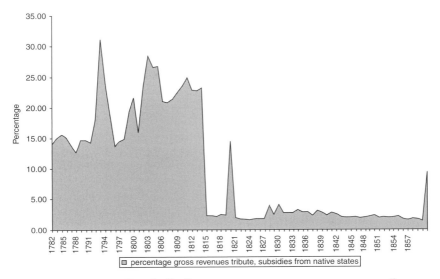

Figure 17.3 East India Company percentage gross revenues tribute, subsidies from native states

where the nominal revenue assessment could not be raised even when landlords and their tenants brought new lands under cultivation. To a larger degree, however, new taxes not imposed by the Mughals accounted for the land revenue's declining share. Company officials began early to diversify their tax base so that the new regime was not so overwhelmingly dependent upon agrarian production.

A significant source of revenue in the first half-century of company rule was treasure plundered in the company's wars and tribute paid in imposed war indemnities. In addition, Indian princes also made large, regular payments in return for the loan of company troops that were stationed within their territories. These rented forces helped to defend the regime against external attack and also discouraged internal coups. Between 1782 and 1814, tribute, military rentals and plunder averaged just less than one-fifth of all East India Company revenues (19.8 percent; see Figures 17.3 and 17.4). After the final Maratha campaigns ending in 1818 that produced British dominance over much of central and western India, plunder largely disappeared and tribute levelled off to a much lower level. Indian princes either lost territory that was converted to directly administered revenue-paying areas or, if they remained on the

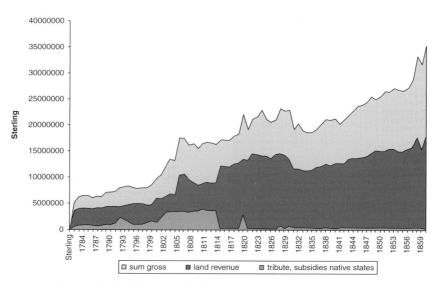

Figure 17.4 Tribute and subsidies

thrones of much-shrunken territories, they were relieved of the burden of tributary payments (see Figures 17.3 and 17.4).

One of the most onerous of these new taxes was the salt tax, which averaged 11.4 per cent of total company revenues (see Figure 17.5). The tax was actually an official monopoly imposed in 1772 over the production of salt in the coastal salt-boiling regions of coastal Bengal and, after its annexation in 1803, Orissa. The Nawabs of Bengal had awarded the right to collect an impost on salt to favoured officials, but production and trade in the commodity was open. In 1781, European officials, called 'salt agents', took over the task of supervising and controlling the work of the salt boilers (*malangis*) on the coast. The salt agents gave out advances, fixed production schedules, stipulated amounts to be produced and regulated quality. Layers of Indian salt wholesalers bought up the salt at a fixed official price and carried out transport and distribution for retail sale throughout the company territories.[8]

The company and the Indian salt merchants prospered; the salt boilers and the Indian consumer suffered under this monopoly. With the

[8] Ibid., pp. 111–12; S. Choudhury, *Economic history of colonialism: a study of British salt policy in Orissa* (Delhi: Inter-India Publications, 1979); B. Barui, *The salt industry of Bengal, 1757–1800: a study in the interaction of British monopoly control and indigenous enterprise* (Calcutta: K. P. Bagchi, 1985).

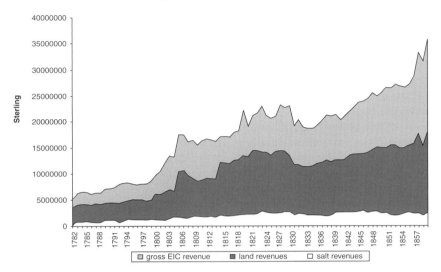

Figure 17.5 East India Company salt revenues, 1782–1859

added capacity from Orissa's salt producers, the monopoly generated an average 2.3 million pounds sterling each year between 1803 and 1859. According to the Select Commission of 1831–32, under the monopoly the price of salt rose steeply over the pre-British level in the Bengal of the Nawabs. Witnesses testified that the price of salt constituted a real hardship on ordinary persons in Bengal. One witness stated that whereas in 1760 the cost of sixty pounds of salt, the average yearly consumption for a family, would have been 4 per cent of an ordinary labourer's wages, by 1830 this figure had soared to an onerous 10 per cent. With high prices came adulteration and large illicit production and smuggling of salt.[9] Critics continued to question the salt tax and to point out its injurious and regressive nature throughout the colonial period.

Opium was the other profitable state monopoly begun by the company. During the 1770s the company asserted an official monopoly over the production, wholesale and retail sale and export of the narcotic drug.[10] By the late 1790s, the company appointed British officials as 'opium agents', to regulate and control poppy growing and to manage the processing of raw opium at two state-run factories at Ghazipur and

---

[9] Barui, *The salt industry of Bengal*, p. 142, citing material from *Report from the Select Committee on Salt, British India*, 1836.

[10] J. F. Richards, 'Indian empire and peasant production of opium in the nineteenth century', *Modern Asian Studies* 15:1 (1981), 59–82.

Benares. The company fixed the area to be sown with poppy, determined the price to be paid to growers and gave them an assured market for their product.

Some processed opium moved through private wholesalers to government-licensed excise shops to meet domestic demand. However, by far the greatest amount went to auction sales held regularly in Calcutta, at which Indian and British merchants bid for chests of export or provision opium to be sent to China or to Southeast Asia.[11] In addition to the profits of the official monopoly in India, British and Indian merchants also made lucrative profits and amassed great fortunes from the trade. Indian opium exports to China brought back vital shipments of silver as part of India's favourable balance of trade. These opium payments, in turn, balanced the monies the East India Company and its later private successor paid for tea in China as tribute from India flowed to Great Britain. So important was the trade that Britain fought the first Opium War with the Qing regime in 1839–42 over the latter's attempts to interdict the illegal import of opium into China.[12]

By 1830, when confronted with the possibility of opium exports from the princely states of western India, so-called 'Malwa opium', the British established an ingenious system of prohibiting the export of opium from any Indian ports on the west coast save Bombay. At Bombay, opium exporters paid a per-chest fee nicely calculated to be cheaper than the cost of smuggling through Sind before 1843 or the ports of Portuguese India. Under this pass system, the company government did manage to tap into the profits of the Malwa opium exports and to keep them from becoming so cheap that they undercut Bengal opium produced under the state monopoly.

Opium revenues rose absolutely and proportionately throughout the company period. During the last fifteen years of company rule opium returns averaged 15.5 per cent of total gross revenues (see Figure 17.6). Although opium returns tended to fluctuate, the long-term trend was generally upwards. Together, opium and salt produced on average 18.9 per cent of gross revenues. In the last fifteen years of company rule their share climbed to 25.1 per cent, as opium became one of the most valuable commodities sold in world commerce.

Customs imposts formed another initially small, but rising source of revenue. During the earlier decades of company rule customs fluctuated

[11] N. P. Singh, *The East India Company's monopoly industries in Bihar with particular reference to opium and saltpetre, 1773–1833* (Muzaffarpur, Bihar: Sarvodaya Vangmaya, 1980).

[12] J. F. Richards, 'The opium industry in British India', *Indian Economic and Social History Review* 39 (2002), 149–80.

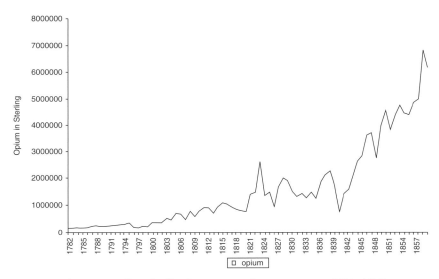

Figure 17.6 East India Company opium revenues, 1782–1859

between less than 2 to nearly 5 per cent of gross revenues per year. However, in 1815 collections rose to 6.7 per cent and averaged 7 per cent of gross returns until 1859. Customs duties came from maritime and inland trade duties. Maritime customs rose steadily as India's sea-borne trade grew. Growth in maritime revenues counterbalanced the trend in inland customs. The East India Company inherited from the Mughals and their successors a dense thicket of customary duties on inland trade. These were collected at checkpoints manned by armed guards placed along major land and riverine routes. Each major market town and city also imposed duties on goods sold within its boundaries either as direct market taxes levied on transactions or as import tariffs levied at the time of entry into the town or city.[13] Under earlier regimes these taxes were mixed together with a combination of trade, house or ground rent and trade taxes under the term *sair*. Generally local officials or *zamindars* collected these imposts under some form of farming arrangement. The East India Company by 1790 had begun abolishing most of the various *sair* taxes and prohibited local *zamindars* or notables from this form of tax collection. However, the company maintained its own internal customs posts and collected internal transit duties for

---

[13] P. Banerjea, *History of internal trade barriers in British India; a study of transit and town duties* (Calcutta: Asiatic Society, 1972).

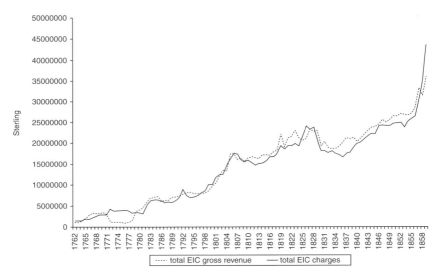

Figure 17.7 East India Company revenues and expenses, 1762–1859

most of its rule. In England and India, however, liberal and utilitarian opposition to the costs and constraints of the system continued to build. Finally, Governor-General Bentinck commissioned an investigation by Charles Trevelyan. Trevelyan's 1934 report denounced the system and its publication forced the company directors to end all internal transit duties in the Bengal Presidency.[14]

In its role ruling vast lands and peoples, the East India Company rapidly built up a massive standing army, a large civil bureaucracy and a systematic judicial and police establishment. Much to the consternation of the East India Company directors in London, successive governors general learned that large though total revenues might be, expenditures for even minimal levels of administration, internal order and external defence were equally great. In some years the regime ran at a deficit, but in most revenues covered expenses. Revenues compared with direct expenditures in India are shown in (Figure 17.7).

By far the greatest single expense category was military. The East India Company built one of the largest standing armies in the world, staffed by long-serving professional Indian sepoys and British officers. The company also paid the expenses of regiments and detachments

---

[14] Ibid., pp. 97–118; C. E. Trevelyan, *A report upon the inland customs and town duties of the Bengal presidency* (Calcutta, 1835).

from the British regular army that served in India. During the long-drawn-out wars with the French in South India, Madras and Bombay vigorously recruited and maintained large armies. As early as 1766, the company maintained an army of 32,379 professionals of whom 9,443, or 29 per cent, were Europeans of various nationalities. By 1781, the army had quadrupled in size to 124,000, of whom 23,000 were Europeans – many of the latter Royal Army British troops. By 1851, the pre-mutiny army totalled 289,529 men, of whom 17 percent, or 49,408, were British company or Royal troops.[15] By and large, salaries to Indian sepoys formed a channel for investment in circumscribed rural areas from where each Presidency army traditionally recruited its nearly hereditary forces. Part of the salaries of company officers flowed as remittances back to Britain.

Historians have blamed excessive military spending for East India Company deficits and rising public debt. However, it is not at all clear that the data support this argument. Douglas Peers has argued that, rather than military costs, it was the swiftly growing expense of the civil establishment that strained successive company budgets in the early twentieth century. He points out that the East India Company was able to manage even extraordinary wartime expenses, such as the 4.8 million pounds sterling cost of the First Burma War in 1824–26, by borrowing at rates of interest that reflected confidence in the government.[16]

From the 1760s to the 1850s, the share of military spending dropped steadily. In 1762, just over 900,000 pounds sterling in military costs was 80 per cent of total expenditures in that year. In 1857, for the fiscal year ending in April just prior to the May outbreak of the Revolt of 1857, military spending was over eleven times larger, at 11.5 million pounds sterling, but the army costs amounted to only 37 per cent of total Indian expenditures (see Figure 17.8). Of course, military spending rose sharply during and after the 1857 Revolt to end a declining trend.

---

[15] Banerjea, *History of internal trade barriers in British India*, pp. 342, 361.
[16] D. M. Peers, 'War and public finance in early nineteenth-century British India: the first Burma War', *International History Review* 11:4 (1989), 628–47. Historians have traditionally argued that the source of Britain's difficulties in India was the cost of the first Anglo-Burmese War (1824–26). However, by the 1820s the East India Company's financial system and posture was quite capable of bearing such costs, and British–Indian finances were sounder than has previously been thought. Examination of India's tax system, the government's non-military spending, and the financing of the first Anglo-Burmese War indicates that India's financial crisis stemmed more from instability in worldwide trade and unchecked expenditures on civil administration than from short-term increases in military spending. D. M. Peers, *Between Mars and Mammon: colonial armies and the garrison state in India, 1819–1835* (New York: Tauris Academic Studies, 1995).

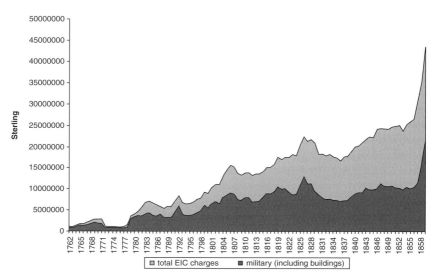

Figure 17.8 East India Company military expenses, 1762–1859

Over the long term, the civil establishment does not seem to have become disproportionately more costly. By design, the East India Company maintained an expensive colonial service. Under principles established by Cornwallis, high salaries were supposed to ensure probity and an end to the corrupt fortune-taking of the first two decades after Plassey. All commissioned military officers and all higher-ranking officials were Europeans bound by oath as covenanted servants of the East India Company. Nonetheless, charges for the civil service averaged only 8.4 per cent for the 1782 to 1859 period and rarely exceeded 10 per cent of total expenditures (see Figure 17.9). From about 400 million pounds sterling in 1782, the annual sums paid to British Company servants rose 6.5 times to 2.6 million pounds sterling in 1857 – a much more modest increase than that of the army. (After the Revolt, however, civil expenditures suddenly shot up to 4 million pounds sterling in 1858 and 1859.) The recipients of these high salaries saved much of their pay and brought back their accumulated savings to Britain when they retired. Of course, this category missed the salaries and expenses of British civil servants who managed the opium and salt monopolies or who served as customs officials, and whose expenses were recorded as charges under separate budgetary headings.

Expenses for courts and the police did increase noticeably in the nineteenth century. Despite their reluctance to spend, the London authorities were forced to expand the courts and improve police systems

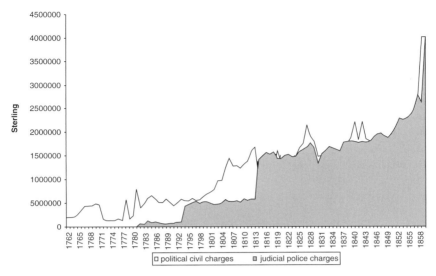

Figure 17.9 Political and judicial/police expenses, 1762–1859

throughout British India. By 1857, these costs were equivalent to those of the civil establishment at 2.8 million pounds sterling, or 9.1 per cent of company expenditures for that year (see Figure 17.9).

Another cost that became significant only in the last years of company rule was that of public works. Company accounts listed the expenses for non-military company buildings, fortifications and other durable structures. But this sort of expenditure was confined to projects of direct use for the state. The mind-set of the court of directors and the board of control did not lend itself to allocating funds for the public welfare – one of the most serious faults of early British rule in India. Between 1782 and 1859 expenditures on buildings, roads, irrigation and other projects averaged no more than 2 per cent of total outlays (see Figure 17.10). The company even failed to repair and maintain roads, river embankments and bounded storage tanks for irrigation that had been the responsibility of earlier regimes. When, in 1823, the governor general in council decided to devote a portion of anticipated surplus revenues to works of public improvement, the court of directors rejected this proposal. When the directors learned of heavy expenditures on buildings in the mid-1820s, they wrote to the governor general to condemn this extravagance.[17]

---

[17] Banerjea, *History of internal trade barriers in British India*, pp. 320–1.

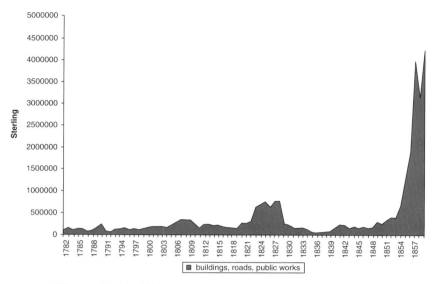

Figure 17.10 Buildings, roads, public works, 1782–1859

It was only after passage of the Charter Act of 1833 had closed East India Company trading operations that a shift occurred. After that date, the regime began a systematic policy of building and improving public works. For example, the regime invested 2.2 million pounds sterling in improving three grand trunk roads: Peshawar–Delhi–Calcutta; Calcutta to Bombay; and Bombay to Agra. In the 1850s the state began work for the first time on new irrigation projects. The Ganges Canal that tapped into the perennial water flow of the Himalayan river sources, finished in 1854, cost 1.4 million pounds sterling. The Kaveri, Godavari and Krishna river systems in the south were also completed.[18]

Finally, interest on the East India Company debt was a heavy, continuing charge on the company's revenues. Soon after Plassey, the company began issuing interest-bearing bonds in order to remedy continuing cash shortages in the treasuries. Between 1792 and 1859 interest payments constituted between 8 and 12 per cent of total annual expenditures (see Figure 17.11). In absolute terms the East India Company debt in India continued to climb with a steep rise after 1800 (see Figure 17.12). The bonded debt for 1762, just under 275,000 pounds sterling,

---

[18] Ibid. pp. 322–3; I. Stone, *Canal irrigation in British India: perspectives on technological change in a peasant economy* (Cambridge University Press, 1984).

Figure 17.11 Percentage of interest paid in India to total East India Company expenses, 1792–1859

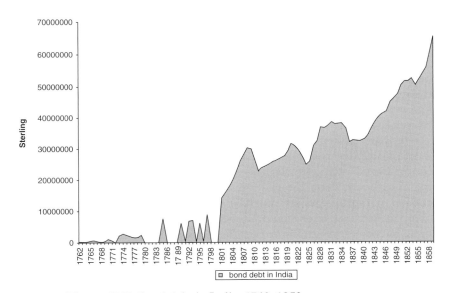

Figure 17.12 Bond debt in India, 1762–1859

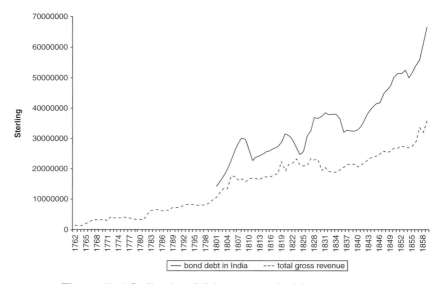

Figure 17.13 Indian bond debt compared with gross revenues, 1762–1859

had soared 241 times to reach 66.1 million pounds sterling by the end of the 1859 fiscal year. Annual interest payments moved similarly from a few thousands sterling per year to 2.8 million pounds sterling by 1859. The Indian bonded debt grew from 1.8 times annual revenues in 1762 to reach a high of 2 times annual revenues in 1833 before dropping back to 1.8 in 1859 (see Figure 17.13). Simultaneously, the company maintained a much smaller outstanding bonded debt in Britain that had reached 3.9 million pounds sterling in the 1850s before the frantic borrowing of the 1857 Revolt years.

Company officials publicly advertised each new bond issue when it went on sale and sold bonds to any and all-comers. Nearly all the early buyers were British. Slowly, however, a number of Indians began investing in company debt. Interest rates often had to be as high as 10–12 per cent to attract buyers for much of the period. However, by the 1830s company bonds had settled down to the 4–6 per cent range as the company never defaulted and it became obvious that the British were the paramount power in the subcontinent.

What drove this growing public debt? One possible answer is that the company borrowed to finance its wars and the conquest of the Indian subcontinent and beyond. P. Banerjea, writing in the 1920s, put the matter succinctly: 'The main cause of the growth of the public debt of India was war. In fact, the history of Indian debt may be described as the history of Indian warfare in its financial aspect.'[19] This is an argument that has considerable weight. The East India Company, like the Mughals, spent heavily on its army and on aggressive war – even extending to Afghanistan and Myanmar. However, as we have noticed earlier, rising revenues from new territories more or less kept pace with growing expenditures – especially in view of the directors' parsimony in regard to investment for public goods. Moreover, the proportion of revenues devoted to the military budget declined slowly, but significantly, in the first half of the nineteenth century. Military costs do not explain borrowing on such a scale; nor do the much-denounced excessive salaries of the company's British civil servants and judiciary.

Determining the causes of long-term deficit spending is both uncertain and complicated. For the first half-century of its rule, the East India Company made no serious effort to differentiate the finances of its commercial transactions from those of its ruling or territorial operations. Finally, when in 1812 the Select Committee on the Affairs of the East India Company recommended splitting the commercial from the governmental functions of the company, it becomes somewhat easier to untangle the threads of company finance.

Despite these difficulties, however, the root cause of company deficits and debt was clearly the annual tributary demands made upon a colonized India by Britain. The East India Company ran deficits, not because of its Indian expenditures, but because every year the company tapped into the territorial revenues of India to pay for money and goods to be shipped to Britain. Two of the largest elements in that annual transfer were first, the cost of Indian goods – cotton and silk textiles, raw silk, saltpetre and indigo – paid for by the company from territorial revenues that were shipped for sale at the East India Company auction sales in London, and second, the expenses arising from supporting East India House, the company headquarters in London, the preparatory schools for civil servants and military officers, Haileybury and Addiscombe, and other non-commercial costs associated with colonial rule.

Contemporary British critics of the East India Company and its Indian empire were in no doubt of the pernicious effects of the new economic relationship between Britain and India. For example, Edmund Burke, who knew more about India than any other man in British public life, was scathing in his denunciation of this exploitative relationship. Burke

---

[19] Banerjea, *History of internal trade barriers in British India*, p. 120.

was a driving force in the investigations of the Select Committee of parliament that sat in 1782 and 1783 to investigate how the new British possessions in India could be ruled both to further the interests of the metropolitan country and simultaneously to promote the 'Happiness of the Native Inhabitants'.[20] Burke described the Indian economic issue as follows:[21]

> But at, or very soon after, the Acquisition of the Territorial Revenues to the English Company [...] a very great Revolution took place in Commerce as well as in Dominion; [...] From that Time Bullion was no longer regularly exported by the English East India Company to Bengal, or any part of Hindustan; (...) A new Way of supplying the Market of Europe by means of the British Power and Influence, was invented; a Species of Trade (if such it may be called) by which it is absolutely impossible that India should not be radically and irretrievably ruined [...]
>
> A certain Portion of the Revenues of Bengal has been for many years set apart, to be employed in the Purchase of Good for Exportation to England, and this is called The *Investment*, The Greatness of this investment has been the standard by which the merit of the Company's Principal Servants has been generally estimated; and this main Cause of the Impoverishment of India has generally been taken as a Measure of its Wealth and Prosperity [...] This Export from India seemed to imply also a reciprocal Supply, which the Trading Capital employed in these Productions was continually strengthened and enlarged. But the Payment of a Tribute, and not a beneficial Commerce to that Country, wore this specious and delusive appearance.

Burke estimated that in the four years ending in 1780 the investment averaged no less than one million pounds sterling and 'commonly Nearer Twelve hundred thousand pounds'. This was the value of the goods sent to Europe 'for which no Satisfaction is made'.[22]

The transfer continued without interruption and with formal approval from parliament. In 1793, a parliamentary inquiry firmly established priorities for the net territorial revenues of India. These funds were first to be applied to the expenses of raising and maintaining the land and naval forces of India, both native and British, and the costs of forts, garrisons and 'Warlike and naval stores'; second, to pay the interest and debts owed by the company; and third, to pay for the civil and commercial establishments at each company settlement. After these

---

[20] E. Burke and P. J. Marshall, *India: Madras and Bengal 1774–1785* (Oxford: Clarendon Press, 1981), p. 18.

[21] Ibid., pp. 223–4.

[22] Ibid., p. 226. Burke in a note conceded that the sale of goods sent from Britain to India that averaged about one hundred thousand pounds annually should be deducted from the million pounds sterling figure.

obligations were met, the company was to allocate to Calcutta, Madras and Bombay, 'a Sum of not less than one Crore [ten million] of Current Rupees in every year to be applied in the Provision of the Company's Investment of Goods there'.[23] And, finally, that as the company paid off its debts either in India or Britain, the court of directors was authorized to increase the annual investment by the exact sum by which the interest on the debts were reduced. By this 1793 parliamentary directive, the company was enjoined to take ten million current rupees (1 million pounds sterling) each year for the investment from the territorial revenues of colonial India.

The fiscal difficulties created in Calcutta by the heavy costs of the annual investment were certainly recognized by the governors general and senior officials of this period. For example, on 12 June 1789, Lord Wellesley, newly appointed governor general of the East India Company, sent a detailed financial minute or letter to London shortly after his arrival at Fort William in Calcutta. In this cogent summary, he described to the court of directors the financial crisis that he faced. For the next fiscal year, 1798–99, Wellesley anticipated a shortfall of 2.1 million Sicca rupees (2.4 million pounds sterling at 2 shillings 3 pence per rupee) and he asked that the court send to India immediately on board HMS La Virginie 15 million Sicca rupees (1.7 million pounds sterling) in specie to help offset this deficit. The immediate cause of the deficit was the cost of the annual investment. Over the previous two fiscal years, 1797 and 1798, the cost of goods and commercial charges together had been 49.6 million current rupees. Over the same period bills of exchange drawn upon the court of directors by Indian purchasers had only put 11.3 million current rupees into the Calcutta treasury. And, in the same two years, surplus Indian territorial revenues and the sale of European goods available for purchase of the investment amounted to only 17.8 million current rupees. The shortfall in just two years was therefore 20.5 million rupees (approximately 2.3 million sterling). The proposed investment for the 1799 fiscal year, 'from all our Indian Possessions, including the supply promised to Canton' totalled 24.1 million current rupees. But the Indian revenues and sale of European goods could only offer 7.8 million current rupees for that purpose.

Wellesley observed: 'This annual demand for the purpose of investment, upon a scale so far exceeding the annual means of the three

---

[23] Great Britain, Parliament, House of Commons Sessional Papers, East Indies, 12 February 1793, in Sheila Lambert, (ed.), *House of Commons Sessional Papers of the eighteenth century*, v. 91, Clause XXIII, p. 205.

Presidencies, is the principal cause of our present deficiency.'[24] However, he did not ask to have this demand ended:[25]

However disproportioned this demand may be to our resources in India, I neither expect nor desire it to be reduced; and being convinced of the great advantages derived from an enlarged scale of investment to the affairs of the Company at home, to the most important interests of our Indian Possessions, and to the general prosperity of the British empire, I consider the present amount of the investment as a charge of which no diminution can or ought be made in any subsequent year.

The other causes of this financial embarrassment lay in recent increases in both the civil and military establishments in all the Presidencies as well as 'in the expenses incident to the acquisition and maintenance of our several conquests in India', the costs associated with a planned expedition against Manila, and the faltering of several ordinary revenues such as lower than expected opium sales and heavy arrears in land revenues. Another cause was the 'heavy addition to our debt under the accumulated pressure of a high rate of interest and of the obligations contracted for the annual discharge of large portions of the principal'.[26]

On the latter point, Wellesley noted that both public and private credit suffered great difficulties in India because of the scarcity of money and extraordinarily high rates of interest. Furthermore the public securities of the company were selling at a severe discount that ran as high as 13.5 per cent on the 8 per cent Bengal bonds and up to 20 per cent on the 8 per cent Madras bonds. He did not think it would be possible to offer bills on London to obtain cash given the state of the private money market. He estimated the total deficiency for all three Presidencies for 1797 to be 12.9 million rupees. Therefore, he recommended that he be permitted to offer a new open-ended bond series at 10 per cent annual interest with a ten-year loan period. The interest on the new bonds would be payable annually in cash at Calcutta or by fifteen-month bills of exchange on London at a favourable exchange rate of 8 Sicca rupees for a pound sterling (2 shillings 6 pence). Similar terms would apply upon expiration of the ten-year term. In closing his financial letter, Wellesley promised to ensure that all the Presidencies imposed the strictest economies in both civil and military expenditures.

[24] 'Minute of the Governor General Lord Wellesley, dated 12th June 1798: exhibiting The Financial State of India, on his arrival in that Country', House of Commons, Sessional Papers, East India Affairs, p. 22. See also Banerjea, *History of internal trade barriers in British India*, pp. 88–9.
[25] 'Minute of the Governor General Lord Wellesley, dated 12th June 1798', p. 22.
[26] Ibid., p. 24.

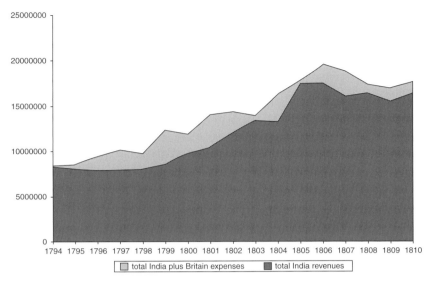

Figure 17.14 East India Company deficits based on total India–British expenses, 1794–1810

After 1793, the company zealously maintained its annual investments. Between 1794 and 1810, the average annual cost of the investment was 1.4 million pounds sterling. This heavy recurring expenditure plus the sums determined by the company to be 'political charges' in London, drained the Indian budget. It appears that the territorial Indian revenues did meet military and other expenses in the country in this period. During the seventeen fiscal years between 1794 and 1810 – a time of intense military activity in India – annual deficits were relatively modest. Seven out of the seventeen years showed a surplus, ten were in deficit. For the period the total deficits averaged 56,000 pounds sterling per year or a total of 960,000 pounds sterling. However, if we add in the cost of the investment (that is the purchase price of Indian goods to be shipped to London every year) and the sums determined by the company to be 'political' in nature, the financial situation changes dramatically. For the 1794–1810 period, deficits averaged 1.8 million pounds sterling per year for a total of 30.5 million pounds sterling (see Figure 17.14). The funds needed seem to have come from sustained borrowing. Between 1795 and 1810 company debt in India rose from 5.9 million to 25.9 million pounds sterling. Company debt in London rose from 2.0 million to 4.9 million pounds sterling over the same period – for a total increase of 22.9 million pounds sterling.

This calculation is only suggestive and far from definitive, but it does point to the role of India to Britain transfers. Only a global calculation of East India Company revenues and expenditures in Britain and Asia can be definitive. Such an exercise would have to account for European goods sent for sale to India and their profits; for the cost of stores and weapons sent to India; for Indian payments to the East India Company establishment at Canton; for overall company profits on trading; and for annual dividends paid to shareholders.

In a recent contribution, Javier Cuenca Esteban has renewed the question of Indian transfers to Britain. Esteban makes the intriguing argument that 'without the accumulated credits from Indian transfers since 1757, Britain's financing of land warfare during the French wars could have been compromised'.[27] He puts the 'arguably minimum transfers' from India to Britain between 1757 and 1815, Plassey and Waterloo, at 30.2 million pounds sterling. This figure is the estimate of exports from which there was no compensating import for India. Commodity exports totalled 38 million pounds sterling, but Esteban deducts 7.8 million pounds sterling in bullion sent from Britain to India over the same period. Without these transfers from India, 'Britain would have required mounting foreign borrowing in 1772–1820, to seemingly unsustainable levels after 1809'.[28] While this argument is directed at the effects on the metropolitan country, the effects of the transfer or drain were also important to India. The Indian public debt stood at 31.4 million pounds sterling in 1820.

After the separation of the company's commercial and political financial accounts, tracking charges to Indian territorial revenues became somewhat easier. Company accounts distinguished a class of territorial expenses incurred in Britain that were chargeable to the Indian revenues. After the 1833 charter renewal that abolished the company's commercial operations, calculating what were called 'home charges' become straightforward – anything spent by the company in Britain was an expense for the Indian treasury. Whether all these charges represented a transfer of wealth from India as a drain or tribute or whether some or all should be considered payments for services rendered is a difficult question and one that this chapter cannot really answer. However, the impact of the home charges upon Indian budgets between 1815 and 1859 is clear.

---

[27] J. C. Esteban, 'The British balance of payments, 1772–1820: India transfers and war finance', *Economic History Review* 54 (2001), 56–8.
[28] Ibid., p. 67.

There were few years in which the Indian budget was not in deficit. For the entire period, deficits reached a cumulative total of 76.9 million pounds sterling or an annual average of 1.7 million pounds sterling. The combined deficits of 21.5 million pounds sterling for 1858–59 in the immediate aftermath of the 1857 Revolt of course skew this result. Even if we end with 1857, however, deficits totalled 53.8 million on an annual average of 1.3 million pounds sterling. The Indian public debt in 1857 stood at 55.7 million pounds sterling with an additional bonded debt in Britain of 3.9 million.

These long-term East India Company fiscal data reveal several characteristic features of the company's fiscal approach: First, decision-makers at home and in India were bent on creating a usable revenue surplus each year suitable for commercial investment (until 1833) and paying dividends to the holders of East India Company stock. To do so, they raised their revenue demands in each territory acquired to levels equal to the highest assessments made by previous Indian regimes. Second, those surpluses produced were never adequate to meet the combined administrative, military and commercial expenses of the company. Third, the company resorted to borrowing on interest-bearing bonds in India and at home in steadily rising amounts to meet its obligations. Fourth, the escalating cost of the East India Company armies and of incessant warfare formed the greatest single fiscal burden for the new regime. Finally, the Company allocated negligible funds for public works, for cultural patronage, for charitable relief or for any form of education. The Company confined its generosity to paying extremely high salaries to its civil servants and military officers. Otherwise parsimony ruled. These characteristics marked the East India Company fiscal system from its inception to its demise in 1859.

Conclusion

The overall revenues of the Mughal empire and the East India Company seem to be roughly congruent. At its greatest extent in the late seventeenth century the Mughal empire collected revenues of about 255 million silver rupees or roughly 25.5 million pounds sterling from the perhaps 150 million persons inhabiting the subcontinent at that time. The Mughal emperors drew substantial tax or tribute throughout their domain whether dependent princes remained in power or not. In 1857, the East India Company collected 33.3 million pounds sterling in revenues. The East India Company levied taxes on 145 million persons inhabiting areas under direct British rule and took very little by way of tribute from the 48 million persons ruled by native princes in native states. However, to draw any conclusions beyond this as to the relative weight of Mughal or British revenue burdens upon society is not really possible.

As mentioned earlier, there were many continuities in revenue collection, most clearly in the state's dependence upon the land tax – although the proportion declined from a high of nine-tenths to seven-tenths under the British. The East India Company developed a number of new revenues such as those from stamp fees, the opium and salt monopolies, and from customs duties.

In expenditure, although some continuities persisted, there were important changes. Certainly military costs remained the largest single category for both regimes – although this was a declining proportion of total costs for the East India Company. Under the Mughal system, several hundred of the highest-ranking *mansabdars*, including the imperial princes, disposed of the greater portion of imperial revenues in a decentralized system. Their spending for their troops, for their servants, artisans and other members of their grand households, for artistic patronage, and for public works such as sarais, endowments, tanks, bridges and other good works flowed directly back into the economy. Under the East India Company, a substantial portion of government revenues drained out of India back to the United Kingdom as savings, remittances and direct state payments for services. And, as we have seen, only a miniscule amount of East India Company funds were invested in roads, irrigation, markets or any other public works until the 1850s.

Two radically new developments occurred in Indian public finance between 1720 and 1859. The first is the establishment and growth of a large public debt by the East India Company. No Mughal emperor found it necessary to borrow monies for either ordinary or extraordinary expenditures. Even in the worst of times, the emperors controlled liquid reserves in gold, silver and jewels far in excess of annual expenditures. Individual imperial officers often borrowed funds from large Indian banking firms when on campaign or when monsoon failures caused shortfalls in collections from their *jagirs*, but these generally were repaid promptly. Overall, the empire remained solvent and liquid. This was in sharp contrast to the East India Company, which from the earliest days of its seizure of Bengal could not have sustained its military and its commercial investment without borrowing funds. To obtain loans, the East India Company turned to the device of the public subscription of fixed-term bonds and notes with a specified interest rate. These instruments were available to Indians and British alike. The rates offered followed a long-term downward course as the financial public's confidence in the prospects and stability of the regime rose.

The rise in public debt accompanied new forms of detailed fiscal reporting to the public. The East India Company's double-entry fiscal system may have been technically superior to that of the Mughals (and that point has yet to be determined), but the real innovation was parliament's requirement for annual fiscal reports from the East India Company. These reports were then published in the annual printed volumes of the Sessional Papers of the House of Commons. From these reports, the investing public and, for that matter, anyone interested, could determine the fiscal status of the British Indian empire. Earlier the Mughal emperors, in common with most absolutist monarchs, remained tight-lipped about their finances. Occasionally Mughal historians or officials set out the revenues and expenditures of the empire, but this was never in response to official policy. The new publicly available fiscal data made possible frequent lively debates about policy and finance both in India and in Britain.

The Mughal empire, for all its sophistication, was an early modern state; the British-Indian empire, a modern state of steadily increasing complexity. The fiscal system of the Indian Raj that had evolved by the end of the colonial period was a far more articulated and precise instrument of rule than that of the Mughal empire.

18   Afterword: Reflections on fiscal
      foundations and contexts for the formation
      of economically effective Eurasian states
      from the rise of Venice to the Opium War

Patrick K. O'Brien

Historically, effective states evolved along particular path-dependent trajectories and eventually emerged to govern successful economies that provided high standards of living with security for the majority of their citizens. Over the centuries that succeeded the rise of Venice (widely regarded in its golden age as a paradigm fiscal state), their primary concerns were never economic. They did not routinely engage with Smithian programmes for the protection of property rights, the reduction of transaction costs, the coordination and extension of markets, the promotion of competition or the encouragement of innovation. Most devoted entirely limited resources directly or indirectly to investments for the creation of agricultural, industrial and social overhead and human capital. Instead they appeared in the historical record for this period to have been overwhelmingly preoccupied with their own survival and formation. Power almost always and everywhere prevailed over profit during several centuries of violence perpetrated to contain or initiate invasions across vulnerable frontiers; to suppress threats to sovereignty over populations and resources from aristocratic magnates, warlords, nomads, urban oligarchies, ecclesiastical prelates, rebellious under-classes and other contenders for authority located within the porous borders of empires, realms, republics and cities. Dynastic continuity, territorial security and aggrandizement, effective monopoly over internal coercion and the integration of provinces, cities, regions and hinterlands, as well as diverse ethnic, religious and elite social groups into national or imperial polities in order to make them subject to laws, promulgated, adjudicated and enforced by a sovereign source of authority were and (albeit in more attenuated forms) have continued to be the core objectives of states.

   Thus the mega point that close attention to the enormous and sophisticated literature in political and geopolitical history exposes for consideration by economists is this: only when pre-modern states became less preoccupied with external takeovers, safer from internal insurrections and efficient enough to construct or to hire the administrative capacities and information required to assess and collect taxes (and thereby to acquire credit or raise loans on the security of their revenues or assets) could they begin to devote more attention and resources to the establishment of institutions and to the formation of physical and human capital for the promotion of economic growth. When, how, where and why states ruling empires, realms and republics across Eurasia obtained the revenues to retain the kind and degree of centralized and effective power to implement policies for economic development that both satisfied the greed of their elites for wealth and privileged status and in modern times the demands of all their subjects for rising standards of living, along with the prerequisites for security, stability and revenue, is a key concern of all the authors who have written chapters for a book which is designed to encourage programmes of research into the comparative history of political economy in the east and west of Eurasia.

All of its authors assume, moreover, that historical investigations into multiple and diverse cases of state formation of well-funded fiscal states is a prerequisite for any grounded comprehension of why some economies and societies established and maintained institutions favourable to economic growth before others. They anticipated that an analysis of the very different strategies pursued by various Eurasian empires, monarchies and oligarchies as they endeavoured to construct effective fiscal and financial systems would expose something significant about the nature and significance of the political economy behind divergent trends in productivity and standards of living between different parts of the global economy as it evolved for roughly a half-millennium down to the twentieth century.

Since effective states were states that possessed sufficient fiscal and financial capacities for purposeful actions; without adequate command over resources central governments would be compelled to provide reduced provision for essential public goods such as external security and internal order. Furthermore, and by default, underfunded states could only relinquish responsibilities for the construction of legal and institutional frameworks for exchange, for the coordination of markets, for innovation and for physical and human capital formation to private enterprise and/or to lower-level and nominally subordinated governmental authorities, less likely to realize the economies of scale and scope associated with centralization. Modern liberal political economy maintains that delegation of responsibilities to private enterprise and to local authorities was invariably a cheaper and more efficient strategy to pursue. That view dates, however, from an age when political stability, good order and geopolitical conflict could be taken as contained at manageable levels. Prior, to say, 1815, little in the historical record suggests that laissez-faire involving limited and more devolved levels of central governance might have increased rates of economic growth.

In the prevailing medieval and early modern international order of geopolitical violence, conquest, imperialism and mercantilism, as well as weakly enforced laws and rules for the protection of production and exchange located within and beyond the frontiers of empires, realms and republics, marked by divided sovereignties, the formation of well and consistently funded centralized states remains (in the view of most historians who study these centuries) something approximating to prerequisites for securing greater gains from trade and from domestic and foreign investment in the accumulation of physical and human capital and for the production and diffusion of useful and reliable knowledge. With all their manifold imperfections, tendencies to aggression, proclivities for predation and indifference to the maintenance of privately sponsored institutions promoting long-term growth, the formation of centralized states with the fiscal and financial capacities required to provide minimal degrees of external security and internal stability, as well as protection for property rights, the integration and coordination of markets remained necessary for development to continue. In brief and general terms, this is the current and familiar claim for the elaboration and analysis of the geopolitical, political, geographical, economic, organizational, technological, cultural and other conditions behind the construction and maintenance of fiscal and financial systems by the sample of Eurasian states represented in this volume.

State formation was part and parcel of the process of long-run growth and could well be an important chapter in narratives designed to explain divergence between Eastern and Western economies, and possibly a key factor behind the observed sequence of leaders, followers and convergence in any global history of modern industrialization.

Since historians do not anticipate that there could be anything approximating to a general theory of state formation, it is unfortunate that they have not yet been able to construct the database required to tabulate, calibrate, graph and compare long-term trends and cycles in the amounts of revenue (domain income, taxes, credits and loans) available for expenditures by Eurasian states from, say, 1492 onwards – a period when their interconnections became stronger, more regular, increasingly competitive and often violent. Plausible statistics for some polities for particular periods of time are in print. They can be validated, deflated and calibrated to support statements about levels, cycles and trends in total revenues received as taxes, credits and loans by some European states and by Asian and European empires. Occasionally revenues appropriated by states as taxes or received as rents from their domains can be expressed as *shares* of national incomes but, alas, rarely as ratios for aggregated imperial outputs for China, the Mughal empire or the Habsburg or Ottoman dominions. Divided by populations they could also provide indicators of changes over time and across countries in the levels of funds available to states for the provision of public goods and/or for 'wasteful' expenditures by rulers upon goods and services that carried no benefits. Such data might also represent expenditures that might conceivably be regarded as positive for the long-term growth of the economies or social welfare of the populations over which they claimed dominion and sovereignty.

In short, comparisons across Eurasia's empires, monarchies, republics and other polities could be facilitated by converting their revenues into real equivalents, including quantities of grain, grams of silver or hours of labour time. This kind of 'mercantilist arithmetic' would be entirely heuristic to display and contemplate and would facilitate a more structured and grounded discussion of major contrasts in the evolution of fiscal regimes for the formation of states. Given that statistical evidence for a valid database is not, or unlikely to become, available, my afterword on the chapters published in this volume must fall back upon a second-best solution. I will implicitly refer to scattered data, but concentrate upon the histories as case studies of contrasts in developments towards the long-run formation of adequately funded Eurasian states. Ultimate limitations upon what any of these states could conceivably have extracted as revenue upon a regular basis were given by the total outputs produced by subject workforces, with the land, natural resources and capital stocks located within the frontiers of empires, realms and republics over which they claimed sovereign rights to appropriate taxes; plus, I will add potentially taxable commodities and liquid assets imported into their territories and net returns from their domains. Such revenues could be supplemented by funds they managed to borrow from their subjects or from the citizens and governments of other countries. Obviously the more extensive the overall size of the imperial, national or city economies over which states claimed sovereignty and property rights to taxation, the larger *ceteris paribus* the bases available for purposes of taxation and *mutatis mutandis* the potential security for servicing the loans and credits necessary to defend and run states.

As our 'Introduction' observed, before and until imports and re-exports became significant components of any economy, its potential fiscal base remained circumscribed initially by the size and productivity of the state's own domain and as that declined by the overall scale, structure and productivity of the domestic economy available for taxation. Furthermore, the levels of tax revenues appropriated by states could be seriously constrained by the powers of emperors, monarchs or oligarchies to secure compliance with their rising demands for taxes and by the administrative systems and instruments available to them for the regular and stable assessment and collection of taxes.

Limitations imposed by the size, structural characteristics and efficiency of a domestic economy could in theory be circumvented with difficulty by policies designed to augment production, to raise productivity and to increase taxable imports. Alternatively, states could invest in the conquest and expropriation of the territories and assets of rival states. Resort to warfare and conquest for purposes of taxation were, however, costly and risky strategies to pursue. The chapters published in this volume and other case studies reveal that the capacities available to pre-modern states to assess, collect and concentrate revenues under central control (and thereby support borrowing) were everywhere more or less severely constricted by balances of power within polities; by open resistance, by widespread evasion, by a lack of economic information, by resort to counter-productive and short-term gains from predation and perhaps, above all, by the small scale and low quality of the public bureaucracies, nominally subordinate political authorities, or from franchised firms employed for the assessment, collection and transfer of taxes into the coffers of central governments. All pre-modern fiscal systems were difficult to establish and expensive to use (see page 15).

Each state experienced unique difficulties in raising revenues that depended upon its own particular historical, geographical, geopolitical and political situation as well as evolving opportunities afforded by the scale and structure of economies underlying each and every fiscal base. Nevertheless, all Eurasian states confronted a set of comparable constraints which they accepted, evaded, solved or failed to transform as they moved in various ways and at different rates along their path-dependent and explicable trajectories towards the construction of more centralized and better-funded fiscal and financial systems for governance. It is these common fiscal and financial problems and records of experiments with successful and unsuccessful solutions that provide opportunities for comparative history and prospects for a grounded (but only a middle) range of generalizations for any set of case studies in fiscal history.

All such narratives in comparative history face (or avoid) the problem of initial conditions. For this collaborative academic enterprise authors determined the chronologies that they found relevant and interesting for a given polity. Nevertheless, their choices have produced a general and predictable clustering in the centuries after 1500 and a recognition that an 'Imperial Meridian 1783–1815' in European and Asian history marks not only an endpoint, but also a conjuncture in the history of state formation when geopolitical and internal pressures on states to reform and reconstruct their traditional (feudal), fiscal and financial systems intensified and persisted almost everywhere over the century down to the First World War (1914–18). Thus, attention has been directed in most chapters to the establishment, reform and reconstruction of fiscal and financial institutions as that ubiquitous process proceeded – or rather staggered – from war to war, crisis to crisis for some four centuries after 1492. Some authors preferred, however, to begin their analyses well before that date. Deng's chapter on China reminds us that the history of Eurasian taxation goes back for millennia. The chapters on Portugal, Habsburg Spain, the Italian states, the Ottoman dominions and Mughal India show why the fiscal and financial systems of empires, realms and republics had settled into stasis or sclerosis long before the seventeenth century (Mata, Chapter 9, Comín and Yun, Chapter 10, Pezzolo, Chapter 11, Pamuk, Chapter 13 and Richards, Chapter 17).

While the political and geopolitical conditions for other polities (Holland, England, Prussia, Russia) allowed for rising levels of taxes, credits and loans, they needed to fund public goods for survival, stability, territorial and overseas expansion and for the varying types and degrees of fiscal centralization required to support the institutional developments, formation of physical and human capital, innovation and cultural reordering behind the slow faltering and confined rates of long-run economic progress observed across Eurasia over the last five hundred years. Clearly the size of the polities included in this volume measured in terms of populations, taxable wealth and total products varied all the way from the vast Ming-Qing Empire in the east to the tiny kingdom of Portugal, located on the extremity of Eurasia in the far west (Mata, Chapter 9, Deng, Chapter 14). Over the centuries that succeeded the famous conjuncture in world history associated with the rediscovery of the Americas in 1492 and the extension and deepening of connections by seaborne transportation around Europe, across the Atlantic and between the West and Asia, the prospects for states seeking to appropriate tax revenues and raise loans increased or declined with the size of territories, natural resources, populations and international commerce over which they claimed fiscal rights. Thus extensive margins for taxation expanded and/or contracted with the conquest of lands, the subjugation of populations and with rising and

falling shares of international trade in goods and services falling into
the fiscal nets of states. For example, and after ignominious expulsion
from imperialism on the mainland of Europe in 1453, the fiscal potential of the English state collapsed, but then expanded along all three
vectors right down to 1914 (Daunton, Chapter 5). From the vantage
point of 1815 that trend, interrupted by the loss of thirteen colonies
in North America, looks singular. Two fiscal states virtually disappeared. One when most of the taxable capacity of the papal dominions was absorbed into the kingdom of Italy in the nineteenth century.
The second when the fiscal base of the Mughal empire in India was
expropriated by the English East India Company and passed under
the control of the government of the United Kingdom between 1756
and 1808. The province of the southern Netherlands only emerged as
an autonomous fiscal state (Belgium) in 1830. The other states in the
sample experienced cycles of expansion and decline in their potential to appropriate taxation – cycles that are closely correlated to their
geopolitical fortunes and misfortunes in warfare and in mercantilist
competition with other states. For example, Venice (arguably the most
effective fiscal and financial state in the world when Columbus redis-
covered the Americas) lost maritime bases to the Ottoman Empire
and its established position of dominance in East–West commerce to a
succession of maritime rivals: Portugal, the Netherlands and England
(Pezzolo, Chapter 11). In turn, Portugal and the Netherlands eventually ceded their short-lived positions of primacy in transcontinen-
tal commerce to England (Fritschy, 't Hart and Horlings, Chapter 2,
Mata, Chapter 9).

Without exception, but in completely different degrees and at different times in their history, all seventeen states extended the scope
and scale of the fiscal bases potentially exploitable for purposes of taxation. They did so by agreement and mergers and by way of coercion,
conquest, annexation and colonization. The ups and downs, gains and
losses and extinction of autonomous polities in this geopolitical process
of state formation as it proceeded over the centuries has been analysed
in detail in the political histories of republics, realms and empires, and
can be most readily comprehended with reference to historical atlases
constructed to cover Eurasia.

Agreements to merge previously separated states normally included
reservations, exceptions and exemptions from taxation as well as procedures for future changes as exemplified in the original fiscal constitutions for the European provinces of the Austrian and Spanish
empires (Pieper, Chapter 7 and Comín and Yun, Chapter 10) for the
United Provinces of the Netherlands (Fritschy, 't Hart and Horlings,

Chapter 2), for the *pays d'elections* under a centralizing French monarchy (Bonney, Chapter 4), for the cities and princely dominions that signed up to be included in a Holy Roman Empire for Germany (North, Chapter 6) and for those independent Italian towns incorporated into the Venetian republic or papal dominions (Pezzolo, Chapter 11, Piola Caselli, Chapter 12). In contrast to those fiscal regimes that emerged from dynastic marriages and/or diplomatic agreements, taxation imposed upon conquered territories and cities annexed in the aftermath of warfare, rebellion, plunder and tribute often left the societies and economies of conquered polities not only materially worse off than before, but reduced their 'colonized' populations to positions of second-class subjects, paying more than the original inhabitants for the privilege of being subjected to the rule of a new emperor, monarch, prince, grand duke or urban oligarchy. Inequality of treatment for purposes of taxation could solidify into rules and conventions whereby the shares demanded from provinces and cities for direct taxes to support states levied upon income and wealth depended upon their original status and modes of entry into an empire, realm or republic (Bonney, Chapter 4, North, Chapter 6, Pieper, Chapter 7, Gatrell, Chapter 8, Comín and Yun, Chapter 10, Pezzolo, Chapter 11).

Prolonged and persistent demands for taxation recognized as punitive in origin and intention were likely, however, to provoke resistance, raising the costs of coercion and the risks of internal instability. In time most states prudently attempted to move on to a fiscal regime of universal taxation in order to secure loyalty to a dynasty and to promote some sense of a common political identity. They endeavoured to obtain feasible levels of compliance with their demands for higher and regular flows of revenue. Once annexed, territories and societies gradually became established parts of a conglomerated empire, composite kingdom or federated republic. Thereafter, the fiscal policies designed to determine regional or provincially specified quotas of total revenues required to support central government for an empire, kingdom or republic were everywhere matters for political negotiation. States sought to minimize resistance to taxation and to maximize the net inflows of revenues under their control. Over time the sources of regional inequalities observed in the data and the historical evidence for persistent resistance to central demands for revenues had much more to do with balances of political power between the court and local power elites; to asymmetric information available to metropolitan rulers and the politically subordinate rulers in charge of local economies and their organizational capacities to appropriate taxes, rather than the increasingly remote origins and distant locations of the provinces, cities and estates that made up the confederated republics, realms and empires of Europe and Asia before 1914.

Although areas of territory, accessible natural resources, sizes of populations and values of foreign trade set limits to potential levels of revenue obtainable by states, those limits were not nearly as predetermined as many emperors, monarchs and their advisers supposed at the time, or modern economists might assume. States in charge of smaller polities clearly compensated for their restricted access to the extensive fiscal bases ostensibly accessible to empires by engaging more intensively in overseas trade, an economic activity often more easily taxed than domestic incomes and production (Fritschy, 't Hart and Horlings, Chapter 2, Daunton, Chapter 5, Mata, Chapter 9, Pezzolo, Chapter 11). Thus the extensive agrarian empires to the east of Europe and of West, South and East Asia, carried lower burdens of taxation per capita per square kilometre of territory than their smaller and more ostensibly vulnerable rivals. But the latter compensated for their economic and geopolitical disadvantages in mercantilist ways by promoting the agglomeration of domestic production in towns and concentrating production on exports and upon economic activities enjoying increasing returns to scale. Exports encouraged taxable imports and tariffs enabled firms to absorb taxes. Second, their monarchs and ruling elites could offset the disadvantages of scale by constructing fiscal regimes with complementary political constitutions that promoted greater degrees of compliance with the higher demands for taxation per capita by allocating revenues to expenditures on public goods such as defence, centralized administration, legal frameworks, institutions for the protection of property and the coordination of markets and other costly public goods recognized by taxpayers as necessary and useful for their security and the protection of their persons and above all, their property, status and privileges.

Thus, states ruling over smaller polities could enjoy relative advantages flowing from loyalty and national identity by governing similar geographies and cohesive societies, regions at comparable levels of economic development and populations less alienated by race, religion and culture from emperors, aristocracies and educated elites, attempting to manage and tax far-flung and heterogeneous empires. Although the areas of territory, access to natural resources, size of populations and values of foreign trade over which states claimed to exercise fiscal sovereignty set limits for potential levels for taxation, the meta question of how effectively different states mobilized and optimized that potential to fund public goods to support institutions for security with sustained economic growth is altogether more difficult to answer.

What might be gleaned from bilateral or multilateral reciprocal comparisons of the case studies of Eurasian fiscal systems published in this volume is how strongly conditioned their capacities for rule and revenue were by the scale geographies and geopolitical situations of the political units that states attempted to defend, maintain and expand. Of course, and in large measure, the scale of these units can also be strongly correlated to the dynastic ambitions of emperors, kings, patricians and oligarchies, and the extent to which the imperialistic tendencies embodied in the Eurasian state system could be held in check by the geopolitical and political realities of their locations and situations. For example, fortuitously, but fortunately, the predatory tendencies of English kings and aristocrats towards the mainland of Europe were halted decisively and permanently by French monarchs, knights and cannons as early as 1453. For its prosperous golden age the Venetian oligarchy retained a shrewd appreciation of the territorial and fiscal limits to their power. Apart from Charles V, Spain's monarchs lacked all sense of imperial overstretch. From small fiscal bases and beginnings the kings of Prussia and emperors of Muscovy and Austria conquered territories and populations that they confederated with makeshift fiscal systems into empires that somehow survived the vicissitudes and costs of interstate rivalry and conflicts down to 1914.

After centuries of expansion the Mughal empire afflicted by internecine strife was incorporated into a British empire that seized its revenues and diverted profits from intercontinental commerce with South Asia away from all the kingdom's former maritime rivals, including Portugal, Spain, the Netherlands and France. After failures to construct or hire franchised bureaucracies to assess, collect and despatch sufficient and sustainable levels of tax revenues to rule effectively and efficiently over their heterogeneous polities, rulers of the Habsburg dominions and Ottoman Empires (Spanish, Austrian and Turkish) lost taxable territory and wealth on the mainland of Europe. Napoleon's attempt to create a French empire with a viable fiscal regime hardly had time to move on from plunder to taxation in the west. Japan's empire in the east lasted for about fifty years without any significant fiscal gains for the metropolitan state. While the Qing empire's enormous territorial extension into Central Asia in the eighteenth century and the late imperialism (or the carving-up of Africa among European powers, 1882–1902) increased governmental expenditures far more than any revenues or taxable incomes derived from these atavistic episodes in geopolitics.

Emperors, monarchs, nobilities and urban oligarchies of early modern times attempted for centuries to enforce their claims to fiscal rights over the cultivable lands, natural resources, capital and labour time contained within the borders of territories that their predecessors and dynasties had agglomerated and confederated into Eurasian empires, kingdoms, dominions and city-states. Over time the borders of these pre-modern states were extended, conquered, lost and restored more often than not without regard to the potential of and prospects for sustaining fiscal regimes to fund defence against hostile takeovers, aggressive foreign policies, sufficient controls over the means of coercion to preclude domestic challenges to their sovereignty; to maintain internal order and to allocate modest surpluses to sustain institutions, form capital and encourage innovations for long-term economic development. Everywhere across Eurasia, regardless of the constitutional form of a polity or the underlying potential of its economy to supply stable average annual flows of tax revenues into the coffers of central states, expenditures on public goods were fiscally constrained and matters for political negotiations and concessions to the realities of power and the costs of coercion.

The form and constitutional arrangements for negotiations over taxation (coupled with credits and loans) varied over time and across polities. Some fiscal regimes operated embedded in constitutions providing for formal and regularized systems of consultation with aristocratic elites and assemblies of plutocracies. Others dealt with established and traditionally constituted provincial and local authorities (e.g. estates of noble families) upon whom politically arranged responsibilities for the assessment, collection and despatch of taxes demanded for proto-states had been devolved, often at a high cost for central government (Yun-Casalilla, Chapter 1).

Conventions, traditions and ideologies (e.g. Confucianism or Christianity) played into negotiations over 'acceptable' levels of demand for ordinary and for extraordinary understandings over taxation and the debts of rulers. They also influenced the range of commodities, services, personal incomes and wealth selected as eligible as a basis for the assessment of liabilities for taxation. In this age when the access of states to information about their fiscal bases remained entirely limited and their organizational capacities to monitor either local power elites, franchised firms (of tax farmers) or bureaucracies assessing, collecting and handling taxes appropriated, ostensibly on their behalf, also remained rudimentary, the costs incurred to obtain stable and increasing flows of taxation (with access to credit on the security of taxes) continued to be very high (Yun-Casalilla, Chapter 1).

Successful states can be recognized as those that somehow and usually after a state crisis, constructed fiscal regimes that optimized shares of the taxable surpluses available within the frontiers of metropolitan and colonized territories over which states claimed sovereignty.

Over several centuries in which the technologies and organizational forms for the exercise of power at a distance remained rudimentary, the foundational conditions for establishing, maintaining and extending fiscal regimes to support developmental (Weberian) states seem far too complex to be accounted for by underspecified or irrelevant theories, based on rational choices; references to unmeasurable connections to economic and social structures, or to a congenial tradition of liberal thought, going back to Montesquieu, of linking successful fiscal states to parliamentary forms of government.

What seems to have been neglected by economics, politics and other social sciences is the geopolitics of the long and violent histories involved in drawing and re-drawing frontiers and its legacies of large, decentralized, underfunded and weak imperial regimes impelled to take over smaller and vulnerable polities. Historians have long recognized that many European states became too small to survive. Equally, as this exercise in collaborative fiscal history suggests, early modern empires in the West as well as the East (agrarian and urban) became too large and heterogeneous to evolve into developmental or Weberian states. If this observation turns out to be valid, it may have been significant enough to be represented as a major source for the differentials in real wages currently being exposed in databases designed to measure convergence and divergence in Eurasian standards of living across space and time.

Index

absolutism 15, 20
  in Austria 166n8, 167n12, 170n16, 175,
    180, 182
  in Brandenburg-Prussia 156–9
  in Castile 15, 233, 240–57, 263
  in France 15, 25
  in German States 156, 157–9
  in the Papal States 286
  in Tsarist Russia 191–2, 210n27
Adorno, Botta and *persuader à la*
    flamande 69
affaires extraordinaires 96
  reliance on 99–100
agriculture
  abolition of protection in Britain 133
  Chinese fiscal dependence on 344, 349,
    355–6
    and grain levies 356, 360
    use of taxes 356
  and landholding rights in China 337
  and Netherlands economy 74–5
  Russian subsistence farming 193–4
  see also timar system
aide, the 44, 67–8
  approval of 69
  determination of amount 68
Akbar Shah, land revenue system 413
  direct revenue and expenditures 414
  and *mansabdars* 414
  war plunder and gifts 415
Albuquerque, Afonso de, system of rule
    in mercantile state 219–20
alcabalas, and bargaining between crown
    and kingdom 241, 243
  see also Rentas Provinciales
Almeida, Francisco de, system of rule in
    mercantile state 219–20
American silver, importance for
    worldwide fiscal systems 7–8,
    22, 242, 251
American trade, liberalization of 249
American War of Independence

borrowing costs 127
  effect on financial administration
    117
Apostolic Chamber
  bureaucratic system of 298
  and control of Rome 287
  and management of debt 291
    reasons for success 293–4
  see also border customs
  Canga Argüelles 255, 265
assignats 105
  and inflation 106
  and war finances 129
Aurangzeb, and Deccan wars 416
Austria
  direct taxes in 171, 180
  growth rates in 175–6
  long-term economic development of
    165–6
  peasants' tax contribution 183
  position within Empire in post-
    Napoleonic era 187
  progression to fiscal state 26–7
  royal taxation 183
  social incidence of taxation 183
  see also crown revenues; Habsburg
    Empire
Austrian Netherlands
  agricultural economy 74–5
    limits on taxes 80
  aristocratization of estates 70
    and costs of defence 70
  bookkeeping in 69
  debt servicing 75–6
  expenditure balance between defence
    and administration 76–7
  expenditure and social redistribution
    77
  living standards in 82
  and military conflicts in Central
    Europe 69–70
  political regime of 67, 79